THE *New*

GOLDEN BOUGH

A NEW ABRIDGMENT OF THE CLASSIC WORK

BY Sir James George Frazer

EDITED, AND WITH NOTES AND FOREWORD

BY Dr. Theodor H. Gaster

CRITERION BOOKS · NEW YORK

A NOTE
TO THE READER

First published in England in 1890, *The Golden Bough,* by Sir James George Frazer (1854–1941), a distinguished Scottish classicist and anthropologist, consisted originally of two volumes. Eventually expanded to twelve volumes in all, these were followed in turn by a supplement entitled *Aftermath.*

A pioneer study in magic and religion linking primitive concepts and modes of thought to the many institutions and folk customs they underlie, *The Golden Bough* was a milestone in the interpretation of man's cultural past. It represents a profoundly significant contribution to the history of ideas.

However, since the conception and first publication of *The Golden Bough,* man's knowledge of primitive thought and folklore, religion and society, has been systematized and vastly increased. Some of the elements in the original have been outmoded and superseded; the values of some of its arguments have shifted; the reliability of some of Frazer's sources—many of them the unscientific observations of missionaries and travelers—has been impeached; and some of his premises shaken by the findings of modern scholarship. The completely new, one-volume abridgment presented here, prepared by an outstanding authority, makes available a condensation of Frazer's twelve-volume monumental work (incorporating, also, appropriate selections from the supplementary thirteenth volume), faithful to the original in all basic respects, while eliminating secondary material now obsolete as a result of the vast anthropological and other scientific studies of the intervening years. Holding to the eight major divisions of the original, Dr. Theodor H. Gaster, editor of the new abridgment, has cut away excess verbiage, made a fresh division of subtopics, and numbered paragraphs for easy cross-reference to Frazer's own comprehensive notes (unavailable in earlier one-volume editions) and to his own new Additional Notes. In cases where modification of

Frazer's views is required in the light of newer discoveries and of research into primary sources, Dr. Gaster has provided in the Additional Notes suitable supplementary data, as well as detailed references to the newer literature. Notes, a complete index, and the text proper are all carefully co-ordinated, and a synopsis and substantial foreword analyzing Frazer's work and comparing it with this new abridgment are included. Dr. Gaster has prepared, also, a new analytical table of contents, whereby the reader is able to see at a glance the relation of every part of the book to the central theme.

The NEW Golden Bough gives the reader easy, logical access to one of the richest works of the human imagination, and restores it as a living, working classic and an indispensable reference work.

Dr. Gaster, author of many distinguished books and articles on religions and civilizations of the past, is a specialist in comparative religions, especially of the Near East, a folklorist of international reputation, and master of twenty-nine languages and dialects. His major work, Thespis, is a study of the ritual origins of the drama; he has also made a distinguished translation and appreciation of the Dead Sea Scrolls. Dr. Gaster has been Chief of the Hebraic Section in the Library of Congress, Curator of the Department of Semitic and Egyptian Antiquities in the Wellcome Museum, London, and Fulbright Professor in History of Religions at the University of Rome. He is also one of the contributors to The Standard Dictionary of Folklore, Mythology and Legend.

CONTENTS

PART II: TABOO AND THE PERILS OF THE
SOUL (143–188)

PART III: DEATH AND RESURRECTION: THE
RHYTHM OF NATURE (189–207)

PART IV : DYING AND REVIVING GODS (208–302)

Contents   xiii

primitive "magical" mentality—has now been shown to be a mere product of late nineteenth-century evolutionism, without adequate basis. It likewise eliminates Frazer's identification of the sacred tree at Nemi as an *oak*—a very doubtful theory indeed, and one about which he himself was later to express misgivings.

Furthermore, this abridgment attempts, by means of extensive additional notes, to put into the hands of the readers a fairly comprehensive (though, of course, not exhaustive) guide to more recent literature on the various topics with which the work deals, and thus at the same time to orientate him towards alternative views or material (e.g., from the civilizations of the ancient Near East) which were not available when Frazer wrote, but which possess a significant bearing on his thesis.

In the several cases where Frazer's views now require to be modified in the light of subsequent research, but where mere omission or radical alteration would destroy the whole sequence of his argument, short paragraphs have been inserted in the Additional Notes, alerting the reader to the principal difficulties or objections and sometimes suggesting a different construction of the data. It may be useful here to summarize the main points on which such modification would now appear to be necessary:

(1) Frazer's interpretation of the priesthood at Aricia and of the rites which governed succession to it has been almost unanimously rejected by classical scholars. The sanctuary at that place was probably no more than an asylum for runaway slaves; and the golden bough, far from being a vessel of divine power or identical with that carried by Aeneas on his journey to the nether world, was in all likelihood simply the branch characteristically borne in antiquity by suppliants at a shrine. Accordingly, Frazer's elaborate exposition of primitive customs and their modern survivals must now be read as a treatise in its own right, and not as an illustrative commentary on the ancient Latin institutions. (Since, however, it is impossible to eliminate all reference to the latter without destroying the whole structure of the book, it has seemed best to retain it with this express warning that it must now be regarded only as an artistic and fanciful *leitmotif,* not as a factual scaffolding, and that the title, *The Golden Bough,* is in truth a misnomer.)

(2) The basic contention that in primitive cultures the king is primarily the bringer of life overlooks the fact that he is just as much the representative and epitome of those who receive it. Accordingly, the things that he does and suffers in ritual procedures are not always, as Frazer supposes, acts performed vicariously on behalf of his people; as often as not they merely dramatize and typify what the people as a whole are doing at the same time. When, for instance, the king serves as the bridegroom in a ritual marriage, or when he undergoes periodic death and resurrection, he may really be

acting *with* his people rather than *for* them, i.e., concentrating in his own person and "passion" what they themselves are doing and symbolizing concurrently in rites of sexual license, lenten abstinences and mortifications, suspensions of normal activity, and the like.

(3) In postulating "homoeopathy"—that is, the principle that "like produces like"—as one of the primary bases of Magic, Frazer cites in proof the numerous rites in which something desired is simulated in advance, e.g., rainfall by pouring water, or sunlight by kindling fire. In this, however, he overlooks the crucial distinction between *dramatized petition* and *magical procedure*. In many of the cases cited all that is really involved is a *prayer in gesture;* the performers are merely showing the gods or spirits what they want done; and, far from believing (as Frazer supposes) that their acts will be automatically effective, they usually accompany them by express invocation of those superior beings! Hence, while the general contention may be sound enough, the particular evidence adduced in support of it must be received with caution.

(4) It is now no longer accepted that the "dying and reviving" gods of ancient religions, i.e., such figures as Tammuz, Adonis, Attis, and Osiris, merely personify vegetation. (Andrew Lang called this "the Covent Garden school of mythology," in allusion to London's well-known fruit market.) Rather are they to be considered as embodiments of "providence" in general —that is, of the divine force which permeates a community or region and gives it life and increase. The myths and rituals associated with them are thus no mere allegories of sowing and reaping, but are designed rather to account for the rhythm of nature by furnishing reasons (e.g., umbrage or discomfiture) why that providence is periodically withdrawn or absent.

Moreover, in the particular case of Osiris, it has been pointed out by Egyptologists that his character as a god of vegetation is not, in fact, original, but secondary, and that he was primarily a representation of the defunct pharaoh, his entire myth and ritual being concerned with the succession to the kingship rather than with the rhythm of vegetation.

(5) The concept of a single over-all Corn-spirit or Tree-spirit—a concept which Frazer adopted from Mannhardt and then developed into one of the cardinal elements of his thesis—has been seriously challenged by more recent investigators on the grounds that it fuses into an artificial and purely schematic unity what the primitive actually recognizes as any number of distinct and disparate spirits, each personifying a different aspect, impact, or association of grain or trees.

(6) In his discussion of the widespread institution of the Scapegoat, Frazer overlooks the salient distinction between rites in which an animal serves as a mere surrogate for a human culprit and those in which it serves to remove a collective miasma which the community confesses in a blanket formula but precise responsibility for which cannot, for one reason or an-

other, be pinned on any specific individual. The two things have different motivations and should not be confused through mere outward similarity.

(7) In the treatment of Fire-festivals, no adequate distinction is preserved between the custom of extinguishing and rekindling fires at harvest or at the death of the king as a symbol of the seasonal or occasional eclipse and regeneration of corporate life—"put out the light, and then put out the light" —and that of lighting them as a magical procedure for reluming the dying sun. Here again, outward similarity of procedure does not attest identity of motive or underlying concept, and many of the practices which Frazer explains as of solar significance are not really so.

Quite apart from these specific points, more recent inquiry, with its wider coverage, its first-hand observation, and its improved techniques, has also called into question several basic aspects of Frazer's general method. Thus it has been objected that throughout his work he pays far too little regard to the necessity of *cultural stratification,* tending to place *all* "savage" customs and beliefs on a single vague level of "the primitive." Consequently, much of the material which he adduces as evidence of primitive or rudimentary modes of thought is in fact the product of considerable mental evolution and involution, even though it may still be far removed from our own yet higher stage of development. Moreover, in certain particular cases, what Frazer and his contemporaries commonly accepted as instances of the most primitive civilizations extant have been recognized by subsequent research to be nothing of the kind. It has been shown, for example, by Willhelm Schmidt that the Australasian Arunta, whom Frazer cites as parade exhibits of the aboriginal primitive, really represent an intrusive higher culture. Nor, even within any one or other particular area, does Frazer take into sufficient account the factor of internal evolution—that is, that even among a group of men who to us are savages all institutions and beliefs do not necessarily remain at the original primitive level. In short, he fails persistently to distinguish between the *savage* and the *primitive,* so that on closer analysis many of his examples turn out to be irrelevant or even misleading.

Equally open to criticism is Frazer's attitude toward contemporary folk customs. Rarely does he investigate their documented history, usually adopting *a priori* the principle that an explanation along historical lines is necessarily a mere later veneer, an attempt to justify or validate an older and more primitive institution. That folklore is indeed studded with such transmuted survivals no one, of course, would wish to deny; but more recent studies have suggested that a decent respect must be paid also to the factor of genuine local reminiscence and commemoration, and likewise that similarities between modern and primitive usages may often be more outward than inward. A case in point is Frazer's identification of the King of the Bean, who presides over Whitsuntide "beanfeasts" in Europe, as a survival of the ancient and primitive custom of appointing sovereigns (*qua* vessels of the spirit of fertility) on a yearly basis. This turns a deaf ear to a very simple and obvious metaphor, and overlooks the fact that in ancient Greece, for example, "king" (*basileus*) was a common title for the chairman at *any* banquet.

Lastly, there is the question of sources. All too often, it is alleged, Frazer bases his arguments on naive and amateurish accounts of native customs and local ceremonies—accounts furnished by ill-equipped tourists or biased missionaries, but now long since superseded by more disciplined observation. Moreover, even when (as usually) he cites more than one authority, these are not infrequently "much of a muchness" in their unreliability, so that the plethora of documentation merely "compounds the felony." And all too many of them were—like Frazer himself—totally ignorant of native languages, so that they are apt perforce to squeeze distinctive concepts into the molds of their own mentality and forms of expression, or to abuse native terms (e.g., *taboo*) by employing them in too wide and indeterminate a sense.

A proper recognition of its ephemeral elements should not, however, obscure appreciation of the permanent values of *The Golden Bough,* nor create the impression that it is simply a useful repository of facts. It may be said without reasonable fear of contradiction that no other work in the field of anthropology has contributed so much to the mental and artistic climate of our times. Indeed, what Freud did for the individual, Frazer did for civilization as a whole. For as Freud deepened men's insight into the behavior of individuals by uncovering the ruder world of the subconscious, from which so much of it springs, so Frazer enlarged man's understanding of the behavior of societies by laying bare the primitive concepts and modes of thought which underlie and inform so many of their institutions and which persist, as a subliminal element of their culture, in their traditional folk customs.

To be sure, Frazer was not himself the discoverer of the "facts" on which his presentation was based. They were excerpted almost entirely—in a series of notebooks carefully transcribed and indexed—from earlier compilations (notably those of Richard Andree, Alfred Bastian, and Willhelm Mannhardt) and from the reports of countless travelers and missionaries in all parts of the globe. But, apart from the fact that no one before had covered the ground so thoroughly, it was Frazer more than anyone else who first sought to classify and co-ordinate this vast body of material and to construct out of it an over-all picture of how, at the primitive level, Man in general thinks and acts, and of how that primitive mentality persists sporadically even in the more advanced stages of his development. It is in this attempt to *construe* the data in universal terms, just as much as in its unparalleled coverage of them, that the distinctive significance of *The Golden Bough* really lies; and this it is that has earned for it the status of a classic. What, in effect, Frazer did was not only to enable us to see more clearly "the rock whence we were hewn," but also to provide a broad, psychological frame of reference within which the phenomena of particular cultures, ancient and modern alike, might be more adequately interpreted and understood. And if now this King of the Wood has had to yield to his successors, it must not be forgotten that, in terms of the ancient myth, it is his own essence that they are inheriting, and that their title to kingship—until they are themselves overthrown—derives, in the first place, from their having plucked a branch from the tree which, in his time, he so jealously guarded.

THEODOR H. GASTER

SYNOPSIS

I: The priest of the sacred grove of Diana at Aricia, on the shores of Lake Nemi, was called the King of the Wood. This title indicates that he was regarded originally as an incarnation of the spirit of the woodlands. His function, in that ruder period, was to control and regulate fertility and vegetation. Such royal and priestly stewards of nature (or of particular departments of nature) are found among primitive peoples everywhere.

They operate by means of *magic;* and an examination of magical practices all over the world reveals that magic is based on the two major principles of (*a*) homoeopathy, i.e., the idea that "like produces like"; and (*b*) contagion, i.e., the idea that things or persons which have once been in contact can for ever after influence each other.

In accordance with the first of these principles, the king serves also as the bridegroom of a female spirit (identified at Aricia with the nymph Egeria) and has to mate with her annually to produce fecundity for the people. Such "sacred marriages" are abundantly attested in both ancient and primitive usage. They are a formal expression of the idea that sexual intercourse can promote vegetation—an idea which likewise inspires the orgiastic practices characteristic of primitive seasonal festivals.

II: As the embodiment of the spirit of fertility, the priestly king is a human god, and special care has to be taken to prevent any impairment of his "soul" or vital essence. The "soul" of all human beings, it is believed, can quit the body temporarily in moments of sleep, sickness, or stress; grow enfeebled through old age; or be deliberately extracted by malevolent magicians. Accordingly, all human beings are subjected, among primitive peoples, to a more or less elaborate system of *taboos,* by which such calamity is supposedly prevented. These taboos affect, for instance, their intercourse with strangers, their diet and eating customs, their relations with near

AUTHOR'S INTRODUCTION

I offer my book as a contribution to that still youthful science which seeks to trace the growth of human thought and institutions in those dark ages which lie beyond the range of history. The progress of that science must needs be slow and painful, for the evidence, though clear and abundant on some sides, is lamentably obscure and scanty on others, so that the cautious enquirer is every now and then brought up sharp on the edge of some yawning chasm across which he may be quite unable to find a way. All he can do in such a case is to mark the pitfall plainly on his chart and to hope that others in time may be able to fill it up or bridge it over. Yet the very difficulty and novelty of the investigation, coupled with the extent of the intellectual prospect which suddenly opens up before us whenever the mist rises and unfolds the far horizon, constitute no small part of its charm. The position of the anthropologist of to-day resembles in some sort the position of classical scholars at the revival of learning. To these men the rediscovery of ancient literature came like a revelation, disclosing to their wondering eyes a splendid vision of the antique world, such as the cloistered student of the Middle Ages never dreamed of under the gloomy shadow of the minster and within the sound of its solemn bells. To us moderns a still wider vista is vouchsafed, a greater panorama is unrolled by the study which aims at bringing home to us the faith and the practice, the hopes and the ideals, not of two highly gifted races only, but of all mankind, and thus at enabling us to follow the long march, the slow and toilsome ascent, of humanity from savagery to civilisation. And as the scholar of the Renaissance found not merely fresh food for thought but a new field of labour in the dusty and faded manuscripts of Greece and Rome, so in the mass of materials that is steadily pouring in from many sides—from buried cities of remotest antiquity as well as from the rudest savages of the desert and the jungle—we of to-day must recognise a new province of knowledge which will task the energies of generations of students to master. The study is still in its rudiments, and what we do now will have to be done over again and done better, with fuller knowledge and deeper insight, by those who come after us. To recur to a metaphor which I have already made use of, we of this age are only pioneers hewing lanes and clearings in the forest where others will hereafter sow and reap.

But the comparative study of the beliefs and institutions of mankind is fitted to be much more than a means of satisfying an enlightened curiosity and of furnishing materials for the researches of the learned. Well handled, it may become a powerful instrument to expedite progress if it lays bare certain weak spots in the foundations on which modern society is built—if it shews that much which we are wont to regard as solid rests on the sands of superstition rather than on the rock of nature. It is indeed a melancholy and in some respects thankless task to strike at the foundations of beliefs in which, as in a strong tower, the hopes and aspirations of humanity through long ages have sought a refuge from the storm and stress of life. Yet sooner or later it is inevitable that the battery of the comparative method should breach these venerable walls, mantled over with the ivy and mosses and wild flowers of a thousand tender and sacred associations. At present we are only dragging the guns into position: they have hardly yet begun to speak. The task of building up into fairer and more enduring forms the old structures so rudely shattered is reserved for other hands, perhaps for other and happier ages. We cannot foresee, we can hardly even guess, the new forms into which thought and society will run in the future. Yet this uncertainty ought not to induce us, from any consideration of expediency or regard for antiquity, to spare the ancient moulds, however beautiful, when these are proved to be out-worn. Whatever comes of it, wherever it leads us, we must follow truth alone. It is our only guiding star: *hoc signo vinces.*

To a passage in my book it has been objected by a distinguished scholar that the church-bells of Rome cannot be heard, even in the stillest weather, on the shores of the Lake of Nemi. In acknowledging my blunder and leaving it uncorrected, may I plead in extenuation of my obduracy the example of an illustrious writer? In *Old Mortality* we read how a hunted Covenanter, fleeing before Claverhouse's dragoons, hears the sullen boom of the kettle-drums of the pursuing cavalry borne to him on the night wind. When Scott was taken to task for this description, because the drums are not beaten by cavalry at night, he replied in effect that he liked to hear the drums sounding there, and that he would let them sound on so long as his book might last. In the same spirit I make bold to say that by the Lake of Nemi I love to hear, if it be only in imagination, the distant chiming of the bells of Rome, and I would fain believe that their airy music may ring in the ears of my readers after it has ceased to vibrate in my own.

J. G. Frazer

Cambridge
18th September 1900

Easy the way
Down to Avernus; night and day the gates
Of Dis stand open. But to retrace thy steps
And reach the upper air—here lies the task,
The difficulty here. . . .
Midway thick woods
The passage bar, and, winding all about,
Cocytus' black and sinuous river glides.
But if such strong desire be thine to float
Twice o'er the Stygian lake; if the mad task
Delight thee, twice to see the gloomy realms
Of Tartarus, learn what must first be done.

Hid in the leafy darkness of a tree,
There is a *golden bough*, the leaves and stem
Also of gold, and sacred to the queen
Of the infernal realm. The grove around
Hides it from view; the shades of valleys dim
Close in and darken all the place. But none
The deep recesses of the underworld
Can venture down, till he has plucked the spray
With golden tresses. Fair Proserpina
Demands this gift as hers alone. When plucked,
Another shoot fails not, but buds again
With the same golden foliage and stalk.
Therefore look high among the leaves and seize
The branch, when found. 'Twill give itself to thee
With ready will, if fate shall favor thee.
If otherwise, no strength nor sharpened steel
Can sever it. . . .

THE KING

OF THE WOOD

1. No one who has seen the calm water of the Lake of Nemi, lapped in a green hollow of the Alban hills, can ever forget it. Diana herself might still be lingering by this lonely shore, haunting these woodlands wild. In antiquity this sylvan landscape was the scene of a strange and recurring tragedy. On the northern shore of the lake stood the sacred grove of Diana Nemorensis—that is, Diana of the Woodland Glade. The lake and the grove were sometimes known as the lake and grove of Aricia. In that grove grew a certain tree round which, at any hour of the day and probably far into the night, a grim figure might be seen to prowl. In his hand he carried a drawn sword, and he kept peering warily about him as if at every instant he expected to be set upon.[1] He was at once a priest and murderer; and the man for whom he was watching was sooner or later to murder him and hold the priesthood in his stead. For such was the rule of the sanctuary: a candidate for the priesthood could succeed to office only by slaying the incumbent priest in single combat, and could himself retain office only until he was in turn slain by a stronger or a craftier. Moreover—and this is especially significant—he could fling his challenge only if he had first succeeded in plucking a golden bough from the tree which the priest was guarding.

[1] [PUBLISHER'S NOTE: The reader will encounter three types of notes in this volume. Very occasionally, a special footnote will appear at the bottom of the same page as the material to which it refers; this will, of course, be self-evident. Normally, however, Frazer's notes and references to his sources will be indicated by small figures in the text (such as the [1] above); the note will then be found, grouped with all similar ones for the entire Part, in the pages following the regular text of the Part itself. Thus, the note corresponding to [1] in Paragraph **1** above appears on page 101, under the head "Notes," and may be there identified as Note 1 for Paragraph **1**.

[Gaster's "Additional Notes" are similarly grouped by Part, following the "Notes." These include his comments on specific numbered paragraphs and, under descriptive headings, on major topics developed by Frazer over several paragraphs. Thus, Gaster's comments on Paragraph **1** above may be found on page 125, together with a discussion of "The King in Primitive Society," the theme Frazer introduces in Paragraph **2**.]

The post which was held by this precarious tenure carried with it the title of King of the Wood; but surely no crowned head ever lay uneasier or was visited by more evil dreams. For year in year out, in summer and winter, he had to keep his lonely watch, and whenever he snatched a troubled slumber it was at the peril of his life. To gentle and pious pilgrims the sight of him might well have seemed to darken the landscape, as when a cloud suddenly blots out the sun on a bright day. The dreamy blue of Italian skies, the dappled shade of summer woods, and the sparkle of waves in the sun can have accorded but ill with that stern and sinister figure. Rather we picture to ourselves the scene as it might have been witnessed by a belated wayfarer on one of those wild autumn nights when the dead leaves are falling thick, and the winds seem to be singing the dirge of the dying year. It is a sombre picture, set to melancholy music the background of forest showing black and jagged against a lowering and stormy sky, the sighing of the wind in the branches, the rustle of withered leaves under foot, the lapping of cold water upon the shore, and in the foreground, pacing to and fro, now in twilight and now in gloom, a dark figure with a glitter of steel at the shoulder whenever the pale moon, riding clear of the cloud-rack, peers down at him through the matted boughs.

The strange rule of this priesthood has no parallel in Classical antiquity and cannot be elucidated from extant Classical sources. There is about it the unmistakable savour of a barbarous age, and, surviving into Imperial times, it stands out in striking isolation from the polished Italian culture of the day, like a primeval rock rising from a smooth-shaven lawn. Yet, it is just this rudeness and barbarity that allows us a hope of explaining it. For if we can show that a similar custom has existed elsewhere; if we can detect from those analogies the motives which led to its institution; if we can prove that those motives have operated widely, perhaps universally, in human society and if we can show that they were indeed at work, along with some of their derivative institutions, in Greece and Rome; then we may fairly infer that at some remoter age they likewise gave birth to the bizarre procedure at Nemi.

In default of direct evidence, such an inference can, of course, never amount to demonstration. But it will be more or less probable according to the degree of completeness with which it fulfils the conditions just indicated. The object of the present work, then, is, by meeting those conditions, to offer an explanation of the priesthood at Nemi.

[In the nature of the case, that particular institution will serve at the same time as a point of entry into the wider world of primitive belief and custom as a whole. The inquiry will be necessarily complex and intricate, and at several points we may well be in danger of not seeing the wood for the trees. It may therefore be useful at the outset to spell out the four main questions to which we shall seek answers. They are:–

1. What was the nature and function of the mysterious priest at Nemi?
2. Whence did he derive the power and authority necessary to discharge that function?
3. Why could he attain office only by slaying his predecessor? What, in fact, was betokened by these periodic assassinations?
4. What was the significance of the golden bough which the would-be assassin had first to pluck?]

2. The first point that commands our attention is that the priest at Nemi was known as a *king,* viz., as the King of the Wood.

From the purely formal point of view there is, to be sure, nothing very remarkable about this union of a royal title with a priestly office; it was, in fact, quite common in ancient Italy and Greece. At Rome and in other cities of Latium, for instance, there was a priest called the Sacrificial King or King of the Sacred Rites, and his wife bore the corresponding title of Queen.[1] In republican Athens the second annual magistrate of the state was likewise called the King, and his wife the Queen, and the functions of both were in the sphere of religion. The "king," for example, superintended the celebration of the Eleusinian mysteries, the Lenaean festival of Dionysus, and the torch-races which were held at several of the great Athenian festivals.[2] Similarly, many other Greek democracies had titular "kings," whose duties, so far as they are known, seem to have been essentially sacerdotal, revolving around the Common Hearth of the state.[3] Some of them, in fact, had several such kings holding office simultaneously.[4] Thus of the two contemporaneous kings in Sparta, one served as priest of Zeus Lacedaemon, the other of Heavenly Zeus.[5]

3. Nor need we confine our examples to Greece and Rome. In ancient times, such cities of Asia Minor as Zela and Pessinus were regarded as religious capitals, and they too were ruled by "kings" who combined religious with temporal authority.[1] Teutonic kings too seem, in the older heathen period, to have served at the same time as high priests;[2] while the offering of public sacrifices is duly prescribed in the traditional ritual lore of China as one of the duties of the Emperor.[3] Again, the king of Madagascar functioned also as high-priest of the realm and presided at the sacrifices that were offered at New Year in behalf of the communal welfare;[4] while in the Galla states of Eastern Africa, it was the native king who used to perform the public sacrifices on the hilltops and supervise the immolation of human victims;[5] and the dim light of tradition reveals a similar combination of royal and priestly duties in the kings of that delightful region of Central America whose ancient capital is marked by the stately and mysterious ruins of Palenque.[6]

4. But this is by no means the whole story; for the fact is that among primitive peoples the king is frequently a *magician* as well as a priest; indeed he appears to have often attained to power by virtue of such supposed proficiency in the black or white art. Hence in order to understand the evolution of kingship and the sacred character with which that office has commonly been invested by primitive or barbarous peoples, it is essential to have some acquaintance with the basic principles of magic in general and to form some conception of the extraordinary hold which it has had on the human mind in all ages and countries. It is to that subject, therefore, that we must first address ourselves.

THE ROOTS

OF MAGIC

5. Analysis shows that magic rests everywhere on two fundamental principles: first, that *like produces like,* effect resembling cause; second, that *things which have once been in contact continue ever afterwards to act on each other.* The former principle may be called the Law of Similarity; the latter, that of Contact or Contagion. From the one the magician infers that he can produce any effect he desires merely by imitating it in advance; from the other, that whatever he does to a material object will automatically affect the person with whom it was once in contact. Practices based on the Law of Similarity may be termed Homoeopathic Magic; those based on the Law of Contact or Contagion, Contagious Magic. Both derive, in the final analysis, from a false conception of natural law. The primitive magician, however, never analyzes the mental assumptions on which his performance is based, never reflects on the abstract principles involved. With him, as with the vast majority of men, logic is implicit, not explicit; he knows magic only as a practical thing, and to him it is always an art, never a science, the very idea of science being foreign to his thinking.

HOMOEOPATHY

6. Perhaps the most familiar application of the principle that like produces like is the attempt which has been made by many peoples in many ages to injure or destroy an enemy by injuring or destroying an image of him. For thousands of years this practise was known to the sorcerers of ancient India, Babylon and Egypt, Greece and Rome;[1] and it is still employed by cunning and malign savages in Australia, Africa, and America. When, for example, an Ojibway Indian desires to work evil on anyone, he makes a little wooden image of his enemy and runs a needle into its head or heart, or he shoots an arrow at it, believing that wherever the needle pierces or the arrow strikes the image, his foe will at the same instant be seized with sharp pain. If he intends

7

to kill the person outright, he burns or buries the puppet, uttering magic words as he does so.[2] So when a Cora Indian of Mexico wishes to kill a man, he makes a figure of him out of burnt clay, strips of cloth, and so forth, and then, muttering incantations, runs thorns through its head or stomach.[3] Similarly, the Peruvian Indians used to mould images of fat mixed with grain to imitate persons whom they disliked or feared, and then burn the effigy on the road where the intended victim was to pass.[4] Again, in the Torres Straits a mode of encompassing a man's death was to prick a wax model of him with the spine of a sting-ray; when he next went fishing, it was believed, a sting-ray would puncture him in the corresponding part of his body.[5]

If an Aino of Japan desires to destroy an enemy, he fashions a likeness of him out of mugwort or the guelder-rose and buries it upside down in a hole or under the trunk of a rotten tree, with a prayer to the demons to carry off the man's soul or make his body rot along with the tree. Sometimes, indeed, an Aino woman will try to get rid of her husband in this way by wrapping up his head-dress in the shape of a corpse and burying it deep in the ground, while she prays that he may rot and die with it.[6] The Chinese too profess the belief that you can harm a man by maltreating or cursing an image of him, especially if you have first taken care to write on it his name and horoscope.[7]

In Burma a rejected lover sometimes resorts to a sorcerer and engages him to make a small image of the scornful fair one, containing a piece of her clothes or something which she has been in the habit of wearing. Then, to the accompaniment of certain charms, the doll is cast into the water. As a consequence the girl is supposed to go mad.[8]

The ancient books of the Hindus attest the use of similar practices among their remote ancestors. To destroy his foe a man would fashion a figure of him in clay and transpierce it with an arrow which had been barbed with a thorn and winged with an owl's feathers. Or he would mould the figure of wax and melt it in a fire.[9]

Analogous devices are employed by the Moslems of North Africa. Thus an Arabic treatise on magic directs that if you wish to deprive a man of the use of his limbs you should make an image of him out of wax and engrave on it both his own and his mother's name, using for the purpose a knife the handle of which must be made of the same substance; then you must strike that limb of the image which answers to the one you wish to disable; straightway the latter will be paralyzed.[10]

Among the Ibo and Ijebu of Southern Nigeria, "a mud or wax image is modelled in the rough semblance of the man whom it is desired to injure and, while incantations are made, this is damaged by being pierced with a nail or spear, or it is decapitated."[10a] In Loango the magician fashions an image of his victim out of a root, pith, or wood, and with appropriate incantations throws it into a river or the sea or the wilderness, holds it in the fire, or hangs it in the smoke. As the image rots, shrivels up, or is reduced to ashes, the victim suffers a corresponding fate.[10b] The same practice is recorded also in a Greek inscription of the fourth century B.C. from Cyrene, in North Africa. Cyrene was founded by Greek colonists from the island of Thera in the Aegean, and in founding it the Therans passed a very stringent decree directed against all such recreants as either refused to sail with the colonists or having sailed with them might later desert and return to their native soil. Waxen images of all such traitors were to be made and burned, doubtless for the purpose of bringing down destruction on their heads.[10c]

7. Nowhere, perhaps, were the magic arts more carefully cultivated, nowhere did they enjoy greater esteem or exercise a deeper influence on the national life than in the land of the Pharaohs. Little wonder, therefore, that the practice of enchantment by means of images was familiar to the wizards of Egypt. A drop of a man's blood, some clippings of his hair or parings of his nails, a rag of the garment which he had worn, sufficed to give a sorcerer complete power over him. These relics of his person the magician kneaded into a lump of wax, which he moulded into the likeness and dressed after the fashion of his intended victim, who was then at the mercy of his tormentor. If the image was exposed to the fire, the person whom it represented straightway fell into a burning fever; if it were stabbed with a knife, he felt the pain of the wound.[1] Thus, for instance, a certain superintendent of the king's cattle was once prosecuted in an Egyptian court of law for having made figures of men and women in wax, thereby causing paralysis of their limbs and other grievous bodily harm. He had somehow obtained a book of magic which contained the spells and directions how to act in reciting them. Armed with this powerful instrument the rogue had shut himself up in a secret chamber, and there proceeded to cast spells over the people of his town.

The use of the wax figures was not disdained by the priests of Amen-Ra at Thebes in Egypt, for they regularly burnt a wax figure of the fiend Apep, who daily endeavoured to prevent the sun from rising. This figure was in the form of a serpent of many folds, on which the name Apep was written or cut. A case made of papyrus inscribed with spells containing curses was prepared, and, the wax figure having been placed inside it, both case and figure were cast into a fire made of a special kind of plant. Whilst they were burning the priest recited curses, and stamped upon them with his left foot until they were rendered shapeless and were finally destroyed. This magical ceremony was believed to be very helpful to Ra, the Sun-God, who uttered over the real Apep spells which paralysed him, and then killed him by the fiery darts of his rays, and consumed him.[1a]

In ancient Babylonia also it was a common practice to make an image of clay, pitch, honey, fat, or other soft material in the likeness of an enemy, and to injure or kill him by burning, burying, or otherwise ill-treating it. Thus in a hymn to the fire-god Nusku we read:

"Those who have made images of me, reproducing my features,
Who have taken away my breath, torn my hairs,
Who have rent my clothes, have hindered my feet from treading the dust,
May the fire-god, the strong one, break their charm."[2]

8. But both in Babylon and in Egypt this ancient tool of superstition, so baneful in the hands of the mischievous and malignant, who also pressed into the service of religion and turned to glorious account for the confusion and overthrow of demons. In a Babylonian incantation we meet with a long list of evil spirits whose effigies were burnt by the magician in the hope that, as their images melted in the fire, so the fiends themselves might melt away and disappear.[1] Every night when the Egyptian sun-god Ra sank down to his home in the glowing west he was assailed by hosts of demons under the leadership of the arch-fiend Apepi. All night long he fought them, and sometimes by day the powers of darkness sent up clouds even into the blue sky to obscure his light and weaken his power. To aid the sun-god in this daily struggle, a ceremony was daily performed in his temple at Thebes. A figure of his foe Apepi, represented as a crocodile with a hideous face or a serpent with many coils, was made of wax, and on it the demon's name was written in green ink. Wrapt in a papyrus case, on which another likeness of Apepi had been drawn in green ink, the figure was then tied up with black hair, spat upon, hacked with a stone knife, and cast on the ground. There the priest trod on it with his left foot again and again, and then burned it in a fire made of a certain plant or grass. When Apepi himself had thus been effectually disposed of, waxen effigies of each of his principal demons, and of their fathers, mothers, and children, were made and burnt in the same way. The service, accompanied by the recitation of certain prescribed spells, was repeated not merely morning, noon, and night, but whenever a storm was raging, or heavy rain had set in, or black clouds were stealing across the sky to hide the sun's bright disc. The fiends of darkness, clouds, and rain felt the injuries inflicted on their images as if they had been done to themselves; they passed away, at least for a time, and the beneficent sun-god shone out triumphant once more.[2]

9. If homoeopathic or imitative magic, working by means of images, has commonly been practised for the spiteful purpose of putting obnoxious people out of the world, it has also, though far more rarely, been employed with the benevolent intention of helping others into it. In other words, it has been used to facilitate childbirth and to procure offspring for barren women. Thus among the Esquimaux of Bering Strait a barren woman desirous of having a son will consult a shaman, who commonly makes, or causes her husband to make, a small doll-like image over which he performs certain secret rites, and the woman is directed to sleep with it under her pillow.[1] Amongst the many ceremonies which a Thompson Indian girl of British Columbia had formerly to perform at puberty was the following. She had to run four times in the morning, carrying two small stones which had been obtained from underneath the water. These were put in her bosom; and as she ran, they slipped down between her body and her clothes and fell to the ground. While she ran, she prayed to the Dawn that when she should be with child she might be delivered as easily as she had been delivered of these stones.[2] Similarly among the Haida Indians of the Queen Charlotte Islands a pregnant woman would let round stones, eels, chips, or other small objects slip down over her abdomen for the sake of facilitating her delivery.[3] Among the Nishinam Indians of California, when a woman is childless, her female friends sometimes make out of grass a rude image of a baby and tie it in a small basket after the Indian fashion. Some day, when the woman is away from home, they lay this grass baby in her hut. On finding it she holds it to her to nurse it, and sings it lullabies. This is done as a charm to make her conceive.[4] The Huichol Indians of Mexico believe in a certain Mother who is the goddess of conception and childbirth, and lives in a cave near Santa Catarina. A woman desirous of offspring deposits in this cave a doll made of cotton cloth to represent the baby on which her heart is set. After a while she goes back to the cave, puts the doll under her girdle, and soon afterwards is supposed to be pregnant.[5] With a like intent Indian women in Peru used to wrap up stones like babies and leave them at the foot of a large stone, which they revered for this purpose.[6] Among the Makatisses, a Caffre tribe of South Africa, a traveller observed a woman carefully tending a doll made out of a gourd, adorned with necklaces of glass beads, and heavily weighted with iron ore. On enquiry he learned that she had been directed by the medicine-man to do this as a means of obtaining a child.[7] Among the Basutos childless wives make rude effigies of clay, and give them the name of some tutelar deity. They treat these dolls as if they were real children, and beseech the divinity to whom they have dedicated them to grant them the power of conception.[8] In Anno, a district of West Africa, women may often be seen carrying wooden dolls strapped, like babies, on their backs as a cure for sterility.[9] In Japan, when a marriage is unfruitful, the old women of the neighbourhood come to the house and go through a pretence of delivering the wife of a child. The infant is represented by a doll.[10] The Maoris had a household god whose image was in the form of an infant. The image was very carefully made, generally life-size, and adorned with the family jewels. Barren women nursed it and addressed it in the most endearing terms in order to become mothers.[11]

10. Magical images have often been employed for the amiable purpose of winning love. Thus to shoot an arrow into the heart of a clay image was an ancient Hindu method of securing a woman's affection;[1] while the Chippeway Indians used to prick the hearts of images of those whose love they wished to win and insert magical powders into the punctures, meanwhile addressing the effigies by the names of the persons they represented and bidding them requite their affection.[2] Similarly too ancient witches and wizards used to melt wax in fire in order to make the hearts of their sweethearts melt of love.[3] Such customs, still commonly observed in some parts of Catholic Europe, are interesting because they shew how in later times magic comes to be incorporated with religion. The moulding of wax images of ailing members is in its origin purely magical: the prayer to the Virgin or to a saint is purely religious: the combination of the two is a crude, if pathetic, attempt to turn both magic and religion to account for the benefit of the sufferer.

11. The natives of New Caledonia make use of effigies to maintain or restore harmony between husband and wife. Two spindle-shaped bundles, one representing the man and the other the woman, are tied firmly together to symbolise and ensure the amity of the couple. They are made up of various plants, together with some threads from the woman's girdle and a piece of the man's apron; a bone needle forms the axis of each. The talisman is meant to render the union of the spouses indissoluble, and is carefully treasured by them both. If, nevertheless, a domestic jar should unfortunately take place, the husband repairs to the family burying-ground with the precious packet. There he lights a fire with a wood of a particular kind, fumigates the talisman, sprinkles it with water from a prescribed source, waves it round his head, and then stirring the needle in the bundle which represents himself he says, "I change the heart of this woman, that she may love me." If the wife still remains obdurate, he ties a sugar-cane to the bundle, and presents it to her through a third person. If she eats of the sugar-cane, she feels her love for her husband revive. On her side she has the right to operate in like manner on the bundle which represents herself, always provided that she does not go the burying-ground, which is strictly forbidden to women.[1]

12. Another beneficent use of homoeopathic magic is to heal or prevent sickness. In ancient Greece, when a man died of dropsy, his children were made to sit with their feet in water until the body was burned. This was supposed to prevent the disease from attacking them.[1] Similarly, on the principle of water to water, among the natives of the hills near Rajamahall in India, the body of a person who has died of dropsy is thrown into a river; they think that if the corpse were buried, the disorder would return and carry off other people.[2]

The ancient Hindus performed an elaborate ceremony, based on homoeopathic magic, for the cure of jaundice. Its main drift was to banish the yellow colour to yellow creatures and yellow things, such as the sun, to which it properly belongs, and to procure for the patient a healthy red colour from a living, vigorous source, namely a red bull.[3] Pliny tells of the stone-curlew or some similar bird to which the Greeks gave their name for jaundice, because if a jaundiced man saw it, the disease left him and slew the bird.[4] He mentions also a stone which was supposed to cure jaundice because its hue resembled that of a jaundiced skin.[5] In modern Greece jaundice is called the Golden Disease, and very naturally it can be healed by gold. To effect a perfect cure, take a piece of gold and put it in a measure of wine. Expose the latter to the stars for three nights; then drink three glasses of the mixture daily till it is used up.[6] In Germany yellow turnips, gold coins and rings, saffron and other yellow things are still esteemed remedies for jaundice, just as a stick of red sealing-wax carried on the person cures the red eruption popularly known as St. Anthony's fire, or the blood-stone allays bleeding.[7]

Similarly, the Toradyas of Central Celebes employ rings of red stones to staunch the bleeding of wounds of all sorts.[7a] The same principle of homoeopathic magic is employed by the Brahuis of Baluchistan to save the wheat crop when it is attacked by red rust;[7b] while in Europe there is an old superstition that if scarlet fever or smallpox were epidemic, red flannel worn around the neck, or next to the skin on any part of the body, warded away the disease. Even in the present day the peasantry of Wales cling very closely to the old superstition about a bit of red flannel as a preventive against fever, smallpox, and rheumatism.[7c]

13. One of the great merits of homoeopathic magic is that it enables the cure to be performed on the person of the doctor instead of on that of his victim, who is thus relieved of all trouble and inconvenience, while he sees his medical man writhe in anguish before him. For example, the peasants of Perche, in France, labour under the impression that a prolonged fit of vomiting is brought about by the patient's stomach becoming unhooked, as they call it, and so falling down. Accordingly, a practitioner is called in to restore the organ to its proper place. After hearing the symptoms he at once throws himself into the most horrible contortions, for the purpose of unhooking his own stomach. Having succeeded in the effort, he next hooks it up again in another series of contortions and grimaces, while the patient experiences a corresponding relief. Fee five francs.[1] In like manner a Dyak medicine-man, who has been fetched in a case of illness, will lie down and pretend to be dead. He is accordingly treated like a corpse, is bound up in mats, taken out of the house, and deposited on the ground. After about an hour the other medicine-men loose the pretended dead man and bring him to life; and as he recovers, the sick person is supposed to recover too.[2] A cure for a tumour, based on the principle of homoeopathic magic, is prescribed by Marcellus of Bordeaux, court physician to Theodosius the First, in his curious work on medicine. It is as follows. Take a root of vervain, cut it across, and hang one end of it round the patient's neck, and the other in the smoke of the fire. As the vervain dries up in the smoke, so the tumour will also dry up and disappear. If the patient should afterwards prove ungrateful to the good physician, the man of skill can avenge himself very easily by throwing the vervain into water; for as the root absorbs the moisture once more, the tumour will return.[3] The same sapient writer recommends you, if you are troubled with pimples, to watch for a falling star, and then instantly, while the star is still shooting from the sky, to wipe the pimples with a cloth or anything that comes to hand. Just as the star falls from the sky, so the pimples will fall from your body; only you must be very careful not to wipe them with your bare hand, or the pimples will be transferred to it.[4]

14. Further, homoeopathic and in general sympathetic magic plays a great
part in the measures taken by the rude hunter or fisherman to secure an abundant supply of food. On the principle that like produces like, many things are
done by him and his friends in deliberate imitation of the result which he seeks
to attain; and, on the other hand, many things are scrupulously avoided because they bear some more or less fanciful resemblance to others which would
really be disastrous.

Nowhere is the theory of sympathetic magic more systematically carried
into practice for the maintenance of the food supply than in the barren regions
of Central Australia. Here the tribes are divided into a number of totem clans,
each of which is charged with the duty of propagating and multiplying their
totem for the good of the community by means of magical ceremonies and incantations. The great majority of the totems are edible animals and plants,
and the general result supposed to be accomplished by these magical totemic
ceremonies or *intichiuma,* as the Arunta call them, is that of supplying the
tribe with food and other necessaries. Often the rites consist of an imitation
of the effect which the people desire to produce; in other words, their magic is
of the homoeopathic or imitative sort.

Thus among the Arunta the men of the witchetty grub totem perform a
series of elaborate ceremonies for multiplying the grub which the other members of the tribe use as food. One of the ceremonies is a pantomime representing the fully-developed insect in the act of emerging from the chrysalis. A
long narrow structure of branches is set up to imitate the chrysalis case of the
grub. In this structure a number of men, who have the grub for their totem,
sit and sing of the creature in its various stages. Then they shuffle out of it in a
squatting posture, and as they do so they sing of the insect emerging from the
chrysalis. This is supposed to multiply the numbers of the grubs.[1] Again, in
order to multiply emus, which are an important article of food, the men of the
emu totem in the Arunta tribe proceed as follows. They clear a small spot of
level ground, and opening veins in their arms they let the blood stream out
until the surface of the ground, for a space of about three square yards, is
soaked with it. When the blood has dried and caked, it forms a hard and fairly
impermeable surface, on which they paint the sacred design of the emu totem,
especially the parts of the bird which they like best to eat, namely, the fat and
the eggs. Round this painting the men sit and sing. Afterwards performers,
wearing head-dresses to represent the long neck and small head of the emu,
mimic the appearance of the bird as it stands aimlessly peering about in all directions.[2] Again, men of the hakea flower totem in the Arunta tribe perform a
ceremony to make the hakea tree burst into blossom. The scene of the ceremony is a little hollow, by the side of which grows an ancient hakea tree. In
the middle of the hollow is a small worn block of stone, supposed to represent

a mass of hakea flowers. Before the ceremony begins, an old man of the totem carefully sweeps the ground clean, and then strokes the stone all over with his hands. After that the men sit round the stone and chant invitations to the tree to flower much and to the blossoms to be filled with honey. Finally, at the request of the old leader, one of the young men opens a vein in his arm and lets the blood flow freely over the stone, while the rest continue to sing. The flow of blood is supposed to represent the preparation of the favourite drink of the natives, which is made by steeping the hakea flower in water. As soon as the stone is covered with blood the ceremony is complete.[3] Again, the men of the kangaroo totem in the Arunta tribe perform ceremonies for the multiplication of kangaroos at a certain rocky ledge, which, in the opinion of the natives, is full of the spirits of kangaroos ready to go forth and inhabit kangaroo bodies. A little higher up on the hillside are two blocks of stone, which represent a male and female kangaroo respectively. At the ceremony these two blocks are rubbed with a stone by two men. Then the rocky ledge below is decorated with alternate vertical stripes of red and white, to indicate the red fur and white bones of the kangaroo. After that a number of young men sit on the ledge, open veins in their arms, and allow the blood to spurtle over the edge of the rock on which they are seated. This pouring out of the blood of the kangaroo men on the rock is thought to drive out the spirits of the kangaroos in all directions, and so to increase the number of the animals. While it is taking place, the other men sit below watching the performers and singing songs which refer to the expected increase of kangaroos.[4] In the Kait- ish tribe, when the headman of the grass seed totem wishes to make the grass grow, he takes two sacred sticks or stones (*churinga*) of the well-known bull- roarer pattern, smears them with red-ochre, and decorates them with lines and dots of down to represent grass seed. Then he rubs the sticks or stones to- gether so that the down flies off in all directions. The down is supposed to carry with it some virtue from the sacred stick or stone whereby the grass seed is made to grow. For days afterwards the headman walks about by himself in the bush singing the grass seed and carrying one of the sacred bull-roarers (*churinga*) with him. At night he hides the implement in the bush and returns to camp, where he may have no intercourse with his wife. For during all this time he is believed to be so full of magic power, derived from the bull-roarer, that if he had intercourse with her the grass seed would not grow properly and his body would swell up when he tasted of it. When the seed begins to grow, he still goes on singing to make it grow more, but when it is fully grown he brings back the sacred implement to his camp hidden in bark; and having gathered a store of the seed he leaves it with the men of the other half of the tribe, saying, "You eat the grass seed in plenty, it is very good and grows in my country."[5]

15. The Indians of British Columbia live largely upon the fish which abound in their seas and rivers. If the fish do not come in due season, and the

Indians are hungry, a Nootka wizard will make an image of a swimming fish and put it into the water in the direction from which the fish generally appear. This ceremony, accompanied by a prayer to the fish to come, will cause them to arrive at once.[1] The islanders of Torres Straits use models of dugong and turtles to charm dugong and turtle to their destruction.[2] The Toradjas of Central Celebes believe that things of the same sort attract each other by means of their indwelling spirits or vital ether. Hence they hang up the jawbones of deer and wild pigs in their houses, in order that the spirits which animate these bones may draw the living creatures of the same kind into the path of the hunter.[3] In the island of Nias, when a wild pig has fallen into the pit prepared for it, the animal is taken out and its back is rubbed with nine fallen leaves, in the belief that this will make nine more wild pigs fall into the pit, just as the nine leaves fell from the tree.[4] In the East Indian islands of Saparoea, Haroekoe, and Noessa Laut, when a fisherman is about to set a trap for fish in the sea, he looks out for a tree, of which the fruit has been much pecked at by birds. From such a tree he cuts a stout branch and makes of it the principal post in his fish-trap; for he believes that just as the tree lured many birds to its fruit, so the branch cut from that tree will lure many fish to the trap.[5]

The western tribes of British New Guinea employ a charm to aid the hunter in spearing dugong or turtle. A small beetle, which haunts coco-nut trees, is placed in the hole of the spear-haft into which the spear-head fits. This is supposed to make the spear-head stick fast in the dugong or turtle, just as the beetle sticks fast to a man's skin when it bites him.[6] When a Cambodian hunter has set his nets and taken nothing, he strips himself naked, goes some way off, then strolls up to the net as if he did not see it, lets himself be caught in it, and cries, "Hillo! what's this? I'm afraid I'm caught." After that the net is sure to catch game.[7] A pantomime of the same sort has been acted within living memory in our Scottish Highlands. The Rev. James Macdonald, now of Reay in Caithness, tells us that in his boyhood when he was fishing with companions about Loch Aline and they had had no bites for a long time, they used to make a pretence of throwing one of their fellows overboard and hauling him out of the water, as if he were a fish; after that the trout or silloch would begin to nibble, according as the boat was on fresh or salt water.[8] Before a Carrier Indian goes out to snare martens, he sleeps by himself for about ten nights beside the fire with a little stick pressed down on his neck. This naturally causes the fall-stick of his trap to drop down on the neck of the marten.[9] Among the Galelareese, who inhabit a district in the northern part of Halmahera, a large island to the west of New Guinea, it is a maxim that when you are loading your gun to go out shooting, you should always put the bullet in your mouth before you insert it in the gun; for by so doing you practically eat the game that is to be hit by the bullet, which therefore cannot possibly miss the mark.[10] A Malay who has baited a trap for crocodiles, and is awaiting results, is careful in eating his curry always to begin by swallowing three lumps of rice successively; for this helps the bait to slide more easily down the crocodile's throat. He is equally scrupulous not to take any bones out of his curry; for, if he did, it seems clear that the sharp-pointed stick on which the bait is skewered would similarly work itself loose, and the crocodile would get off with the bait. Hence in these circumstances it is prudent for the hunter, before he begins his meal, to get somebody else to take the bones out of his curry, otherwise he may at any moment have to choose between swallowing a bone and losing the crocodile.[11]

16. This last rule is an instance of the things which the hunter abstains from doing lest, on the principle that like produces like, they should spoil his luck. For it is to be observed that the system of sympathetic magic is not merely composed of positive precepts; it comprises a very large number of negative precepts, that is, prohibitions. It tells you not merely what to do, but also what to leave undone. The positive precepts are charms: the negative precepts are taboos. In fact the whole doctrine of taboo, or at all events a large part of it, would seem to be only a special application of sympathetic magic, with its two great laws of similarity and contact. Though these laws are certainly not formulated in so many words nor even conceived in the abstract by the savage, they are nevertheless implicitly believed by him to regulate the course of nature quite independently of human will. He thinks that if he acts in a certain way, certain consequences will inevitably follow in virtue of one or other of these laws; and if the consequences of a particular act appear to him likely to prove disagreeable or dangerous, he is naturally careful not to act in that way lest he should incur them. In other words, he abstains from doing that which, in accordance with his mistaken notions of cause and effect, he falsely believes would injure him; in short, he subjects himself to a taboo. Thus taboo is so far a negative application of practical magic. Positive magic or sorcery says, "Do this in order that so and so may happen." Negative magic or taboo says, "Do not do this, lest so and so should happen." The aim of positive magic or sorcery is to produce a desired event; the aim of negative magic or taboo is to avoid an undesirable one. But both consequences, the desirable and the undesirable, are supposed to be brought about in accordance with the laws of similarity and contact. And just as the desired consequence is not really effected by the observance of a magical ceremony, so the dreaded consequence does not really result from the violation of a taboo. If the supposed evil necessarily followed a breach of taboo, the taboo would not be a taboo but a precept of morality or common sense. It is not a taboo to say, "Do not put your hand in the fire"; it is a rule of common sense, because the forbidden action entails a real, not an imaginary evil. In short, those negative precepts which we call taboo are just as vain and futile as those positive precepts which we call sorcery. The two things are merely opposite sides or poles of one great disastrous fallacy, a mistaken conception of the association of ideas. Of that fallacy, sorcery is the positive, and taboo the negative pole. If we give the general name of magic to the whole erroneous system, both theoretical and practical, then taboo may be defined as the negative side of practical magic.

17. Several examples of such negative magic can be cited. Thus, it is a rule with the Galelareese that when you have caught fish and strung them on a line, you may not cut the line through, or next time you go a-fishing your fishing-line will be sure to break.[1] Among the Esquimaux of Baffin Land boys are forbidden to play cat's cradle, because if they did so their fingers might in later life become entangled in the harpoon-line.[2] Here the taboo is obviously an application of the law of similarity, which is the basis of homoeopathic magic: as the child's fingers are entangled by the string in playing cat's cradle, so they will be entangled by the harpoon-line when he is a man and hunts whales. Again, among the Huzuls, who inhabit the wooded north-eastern slopes of the Carpathian Mountains, the wife of a hunter may not spin while her husband is eating, or the game will turn and wind like the spindle, and the hunter will be unable to hit it.[3] Here again the taboo is clearly derived from the law of similarity. So, too, in most parts of ancient Italy women were forbidden by law to spin on the highroads as they walked, or even to carry their spindles openly, because any such action was believed to injure the crops.[4] Probably the notion was that the twirling of the spindle would twirl the corn-stalks and prevent them from growing straight. So, too, among the Ainos of Saghalien a pregnant woman may not spin nor twist ropes for two months before her delivery, because they think that if she did so the child's guts might be entangled like the thread.[5] For a like reason in Bilaspore, a district of India, when the chief men of a village meet in council, no one present should twirl a spindle; for they think that if such a thing were to happen, the discussion, like the spindle, would move in a circle and never be wound up.[6] In the East Indian islands of Saparoea, Haroekoe, and Noessa Laut, any one who comes to the house of a hunter must walk straight in; he may not loiter at the door, for were he to do so, the game would in like manner stop in front of the hunter's snares and then turn back, instead of being caught in the trap.[7] For a similar reason it is a rule with the Toradjas of Central Celebes that no one may stand or loiter on the ladder of a house where there is a pregnant woman, for such delay would retard the birth of the child;[8] and in various parts of Sumatra the woman herself in these circumstances is forbidden to stand at the door or on the top rung of the house-ladder under pain of suffering hard labour for her imprudence in neglecting so elementary a precaution.[9] Malays engaged in the search for camphor eat their food dry and take care not to pound their salt fine. The reason is that the camphor occurs in the form of small grains deposited in the cracks of the trunk of the camphor-

tree. Accordingly it seems plain to the Malay that if, while seeking for camphor, he were to eat his salt finely ground, the camphor would be found
also in fine grains; whereas by eating his salt coarse he ensures that the
grains of the camphor will also be large.[10] Some of the Brazilian Indians
would never bring a slaughtered deer into their hut without first hamstring-
ing it, believing that otherwise they and their children would never be able
to run down their enemies.[11] Apparently they thought that by hamstring-
ing the animal they at the same stroke deprived their foemen of the use of
their legs. No Arikara Indian would break a marrow bone in a hut; for they
thought that were he to do so, their horses would break their legs in
the prairie.[12]

18. Among the taboos observed by savages none perhaps are more numerous than the prohibitions against eating certain foods, and many of these
are demonstrably derived from the law of similarity and are accordingly
examples of negative magic. Just as the savage eats many animals or plants
in order to absorb desirable qualities with which he believes them to be
endowed, so he avoids eating many others lest he acquire *un*desirable qualities which he attributes to them. In Madagascar, for example, soldiers are
forbidden to taste the flesh of hedgehog, "as it is feared that this animal,
from its propensity of coiling into a ball when alarmed, will impart a timid
shrinking disposition to those who partake of it." Again, no soldier is allowed
to eat an ox's knee, lest like an ox he become weak in the knees and unable
to march.[1] So too a Caffre has been known to refuse to eat two mice caught
at the same time in a single trap, alleging that if he were to do so his wife
would give birth to twins; yet he would eat freely of mice caught singly.[2]
Among the Zulus pig's flesh is not eaten by girls on any account; for they
think that if they eat it, a resemblance to the pig will appear among their
children; nor will Zulu men consume the entrails of cattle, lest their enemies
stab them in the bowels.[3]

19. The reader may have observed that in some of the foregoing examples
the magical influence is supposed to operate at long distance. Whatever
doubts science may entertain as to the possibility of action at a distance,
magic has none; faith in telepathy is one of its basic principles. Hence on
important occasions the behaviour of friends and relatives at a distance is
often regulated by a more or less elaborate code of rules, the neglect of
which by the one set of persons would, it is supposed, entail misfortune or
even death on the absent ones. In particular when a party of men are out
hunting or fighting, their kinsfolk at home are often expected to do certain
things or abstain from doing certain others, for the sake of ensuring the
safety and success of the distant warriors or hunters.

In setting out to look for the rare and precious eagle-wood on the mountains, Cham peasants enjoin their wives, whom they leave at home, not to
scold or quarrel in their absence, for such domestic brawls would lead to

their husbands' being rent in pieces by bears and tigers.[1] In Yule Island, Torres Straits, when the men are gone to fetch sago, a fire is lit and carefully kept burning throughout their absence; for the people believe that if it went out the voyagers would fare ill.[2] At the other end of the world the Lapps similarly object to extinguishing a brand in water while any of the family are out fishing, since to do so would spoil their luck.[3]

20. Among the Esquimaux of Alaska similar notions prevail. During the whaling season the women remain in comparative idleness, since it is considered inauspicious for them to sew while the men are out in the boats.[1] Moreover, even in England there may be found traces of this primitive belief that the good luck of fishermen at sea can be directly influenced by the conduct of their wives at home. Thus, at Flamborough in Yorkshire, while the men are at sea, their wives and other women disguise themselves in various ways, often wearing the clothes of their male relatives, and go about the village with music and laughter, receiving alms or wishes of God-speed from their neighbors.[1a] Similarly, while a Gilyak hunter is pursuing the game in the forest, his children at home are forbidden to make drawings on wood or sand; for they fear that if the children did so, the paths in the forest would become as "crossed up" as the lines in the drawings, so that the hunter would lose his way and never return.[2] Again, when a Nuba of north-eastern Africa goes to El Obeid for the first time, he tells his wife not to wash or oil herself and not to wear pearls round her neck during his absence, because she would thus draw down in him the most terrible misfortunes.[3]

Elephant-hunters in East Africa believe that, if their wives prove unfaithful in their absence, this gives the elephant power over his pursuer, who will accordingly be killed or severely wounded. Hence if a hunter hears of his wife's misconduct, he abandons the chase.[4]

Many of the indigenous tribes of Sarawak are firmly persuaded that were the wives to commit adultery while their husbands are searching for camphor in the jungle, the camphor obtained by the men would evaporate.[5] Further, the wives dare not touch a comb while their husbands are away collecting the camphor; for it they did so, the interstices between the fibres of the tree, instead of being filled with the precious crystals, would be empty like the spaces between the teeth of a comb.[6] While men of the Toaripi or Motumotu tribe of eastern New Guinea are away hunting, fishing, fighting, or on any long journey, the people who remain at home must observe strict chastity, and may not let the fire go out. Those of them who stay in the men's clubhouses must further abstain from eating certain foods and from touching anything that belongs to others.[7]

21. Where beliefs like these prevail as to the sympathetic connexion between friends at a distance, we need not wonder that above everything else war, with its stern yet stirring appeal to some of the deepest and tenderest of human emotions, should quicken in the anxious relations left behind a desire to turn the sympathetic bond to the utmost account for the benefit of the dear ones who may at any moment be fighting and dying far away. Hence, to secure an end so natural and laudable, friends at home are apt to resort to devices which will strike us as pathetic or ludicrous, according as we consider their object or the means adopted to effect it. Thus in some districts of Borneo, when the men are away on a warlike expedition, their mats are spread in their houses just as if they were at home, and the fires are kept up till late in the evening and lighted again before dawn, in order that the men may not be cold. Further, the roofing of the house is opened before daylight to prevent the distant husbands, brothers, and sons from sleeping too late, and so being surprised by the enemy.[1] While a Malay of the Peninsula is away at the wars, his pillows and sleeping-mat at home must be kept rolled up. If any one else were to use them, the absent warrior's courage would fail and disaster would befall him. His wife and children may not have their hair cut in his absence, nor may he himself have his hair shorn.[2]

Among the Shans of Burma the wife of an absent warrior has to observe certain rules. Every fifth day she rests and does no work. She fills an earthen goblet with water to the brim and puts flowers into it every day. If the water sinks or the flowers fade, it is an omen of death. Moreover, she may not sleep on her husband's bed during his absence, but she sweeps the bedding clean and lays it out every night.[3] In the island of Timor, while war is being waged, the high-priest never quits the temple; his food is brought to him or cooked inside; day and night he must keep the fire burning, for if he were to let it die out, disaster would befall the warriors and would continue so long as the the hearth was cold. Moreover, he must drink only hot water during the time the army is absent; for every draught of cold water would damp the spirits of the people, so that they could not vanquish the enemy.[4]

An old historian of Madagascar informs us that "while the men are at the wars, and until their return, the women and girls cease not day and night to dance, and neither lie down nor take food in their own houses. And although they are very voluptuously inclined, they would not for anything in the world have an intrigue with another man while their husband is at the war, believing firmly that if that happened, their husband would be either killed or wounded. They believe that by dancing they impart strength, courage, and good fortune to their husbands; accordingly during such times they give themselves no rest, and this custom they observe very religiously."[5] In the Babar Archipelago, and among the Wagogo of East Africa, when the men are at the wars the women at home are bound to chastity, and in the Babar Archipelago they must fast besides.[6] Under similar circumstances in the islands of Leti, Moa, and Lakor the women and children are forbidden to remain inside of the houses and to twine thread or weave.[7] When the men of the Yuki tribe of Indians in California were away fighting, the women at home did not sleep; they danced continually in a circle, chanting and waving leafy wands. For they said that if they danced all the time, their husbands would not grow tired.[8] At Masset the Haida women danced and sang war-songs all the time their husbands were away at the wars, and they had to keep everything about them in a certain order. It was thought that a wife might kill her husband by not observing these customs.[9] In the Kafir district of the Hindu Kush, while the men are out raiding, the women abandon their work in the fields and assemble in the villages to dance day and night. The dances are kept up most of each day and the whole of each night.[10]

Among the Bantu people of Southern Nigeria, while the men were away at the war their wives at home were forbidden to wash, and they remained very quiet and anxious, and held no festivities of any kind. If any of them during this time had illicit intercourse, it was believed that her husband would surely be killed, and if any of them had previously sinned in this way and had not confessed her fault before his departure, it was believed that he would incur great danger and would hear a shot whistle by his ears. If he, after all, returned in safety, he would sell his faithless wife into another country.[10a]

22. Among the many beneficent uses to which a mistaken ingenuity has applied the principle of homoeopathic or imitative magic is that of causing trees and plants to bear fruits in due season.

In the interior of Sumatra rice is sown by women who, while sowing, let their hair hang loose down their backs, in order that the rice may grow luxuriantly and have long stalks.[1] And Thomas Hardy was once told that the reason why certain trees in front of his house did not thrive was that he looked at them before breakfast on an empty stomach!

Among the Huzuls of the Carpathians, when a woman is planting cabbages, she winds many cloths about her head, in order that the heads of the cabbages may also be thick. And as soon as she sows parsley, she grasps the calf of her leg with both hands, saying, "May it be as thick as that!"[2] By similar reasoning the Malagasy think that only people with an even set of teeth should plant maize, for otherwise there will be empty spaces in the cob corresponding to those in the planter's teeth.[3]

23. In many parts of Europe dancing or leaping high in the air are approved homoeopathic methods of making the crops grow high. Thus in Swabia and among the Transylvanian Saxons it is a common custom for a man who has sown hemp to leap high on the field in the belief that this will make the hemp grow tall.[1] All over Baden until recently it was the custom that the farmer's wife gave the sower a dish of eggs or a cake baked with eggs either before or after the sowing, in order that he might be strengthened to leap as high as possible.[2] Of the same import, too, was the rule at Quellendorf, in Anhalt, that the first bushel of seed-corn had to be heaped up high;[3] while when Macedonian farmers have done digging their fields, they throw their spades into the air and, catching them again, exclaim "May the crops grow as high as the spade has gone!"[4]

24. The notion that a person can influence a plant homoeopathically by his act or conditions comes out clearly in a remark made by a Malay woman. Being asked why she stripped the upper part of her body naked in reaping the rice, she explained that she did it to make the rice-husks thinner, as she was tired of pounding thick-husked rice.[1] Clearly, she thought that the less clothing she wore the less husk there would be on the rice. Among the Minangkabauers of Sumatra, when a rice barn has been built a feast is held, of which a woman far advanced in pregnancy must partake. Her condition will obviously help the rice to be fruitful and multiply.[2] Among the Zulus a pregnant woman sometimes grinds corn, which is afterwards burnt among the half-grown crops in order to fertilise them.[3] For a similar reason in Syria when a fruit-tree does not bear, the gardener gets a pregnant woman to fasten a stone to one of its branches; then the tree will be sure to bear fruit, but the woman will run a risk of miscarriage,[4] having transferred her fertility, or part of it, to the tree. In Bohemia for a similar purpose the first apple of a young tree is sometimes plucked and eaten by a woman who has borne many children, for them the tree will be sure to bear many apples.[5] In the Zürcher Oberland, Switzerland, they think that a cherry-tree will bear abundantly if its first fruit is eaten by a woman who has just given birth to her first child.[6] In Macedonia the first fruit of a tree should not be eaten by a barren woman but by one who has many children.[7] The Nicobar Islanders think it lucky to get a pregnant woman and her husband to plant seed in gardens.[8] Among the Ilocans of Luzon the men sow bananas, but the sower must have a young child on his shoulder, or the bananas will bear no fruit.[9] When a tree bears no fruit, the Galelareese think it is a male, so they put a woman's petticoat on it in order to change its sex and render it naturally prolific.[10]

25. This belief in the noxious and infectious nature of certain personal qualities or accidents has given rise in turn to a number of prohibitions or rules of avoidance: people abstain from doing certain things lest they should homoeopathically infect the fruits of the earth with their own undesirable state or condition. Thus the Indians of Santiago Tepehuacan suppose that if a single grain of the maize which they are about to sow were eaten by an animal, the birds and the wild boars would come and devour all the rest, and nothing would grow. And if any of these Indians has ever in his life buried a corpse, he will never be allowed to plant a fruit-tree, for they say that the tree would wither. Moreover, they will not let such a man go fishing with them, for the fish would flee from him.[1] Clearly these Indians imagine that anybody who has buried a corpse is thereby tainted, so to say, with an

against whom the charm is directed.[2] When a Galla sees a tortoise, he will take off his sandals and step on it, believing that the soles of his feet are thereby made hard and strong like the shell of the animal.[3] The Wajaggas of Eastern Africa think that if they wear a piece of the wing-bone of a vulture tied round their leg they will be able to run and not grow weary, just as the vulture flies unwearied through the sky.[4] The Esquimaux of Baffin Land fancy that if part of the intestines of a fox is placed under the feet of a baby boy, he will become active and skilful in walking over thin ice like a fox.[5] The Lkuñgen Indians of Vancouver Island believed that the ashes of wasps rubbed on the faces of warriors before going to battle will make them as pugnacious as wasps, and that a decoction of wasps' nests or of flies administered internally to barren women will make them prolific like insects.[6] The Baronga of Delagoa Bay carry the powdered ashes of a serpent in a little bag as a talisman which guards them from snake-bites.[7] The Cholones of eastern Peru think that to carry the poison tooth of a serpent is a protection against the bite of a serpent, and that to rub the cheek with the tooth of an ounce is an infallible remedy for toothache and face-ache.[8] In order to strengthen her teeth some Brazilian Indians used to hang round a girl's neck at puberty the teeth of an animal which they called *capugouare,* that is "grass-eating."[9] When a thoroughbred mare has drunk at a trough, an Arab woman will hasten to drink any water that remains in order that she may give birth to strong children.[10] If a South Slavonian has a mind to pilfer and steal at market, he has nothing to do but to burn a blind cat, and then throw a pinch of its ashes over the person with whom he is higgling; after that he can take what he likes from the booth, and the owner will not be a bit the wiser, having become as blind as the deceased cat with whose ashes he has been sprinkled. The thief may even ask boldly "Did I pay for it?" and the deluded huckster will reply, "Why, certainly."[11] The ancient Greeks thought that to eat the flesh of the wakeful nightingale would prevent a man from sleeping; that to smear the eyes of a blear-sighted person with the gall of an eagle would give him the eagle's vision; and that a raven's eggs would restore the blackness of the raven to silvery hair. Only the person who adopted this last mode of concealing the ravages of time had to be most careful to keep his mouth full of oil all the time he applied the eggs to his venerable locks, else his teeth as well as his hair would be dyed raven black, and no amount of scrubbing and scouring would avail to whiten them again.[12] The hair-restorer was in fact a shade too powerful, and in applying it you might get more than you bargained for.

29. On the principle of homoeopathic magic, inanimate things, as well as plants and animals, may diffuse blessing or bane around them, according to their own intrinsic nature and the skill of the wizard to tap or dam, as the case may be, the stream of weal or woe. Thus, for example, the Galelareese think that when your teeth are being filed you should keep spitting

on a pebble, for this establishes a homoeopathic connexion between you
and the pebble, by virtue of which your teeth will henceforth be as hard
and durable as a stone. On the other hand, you ought not to comb a child
before it has teethed, for if you do, its teeth will afterwards be separated
from each other like the teeth of a comb.[1] Nor should children look at a
sieve, otherwise they will suffer from a skin disease, and will have as many
sores on their bodies as there are holes in the sieve.[2] In Samaracand women
give a baby sugar candy to suck and put glue in the palm of its hand, in order
that, when the child grows up, his words may be sweet and precious things
may stick to his hands as if they were glued.[3] The Greeks thought that a
garment made from the fleece of a sheep that had been torn by a wolf would
hurt the wearer, setting up an itch or irritation in his skin.[4] Among the Arabs
of Moab a childless woman often borrows the robe of a woman who has had
many children, hoping with the robe to acquire the fruitfulness of its owner.[5]
The Caffres of Sofala, in East Africa, had a great dread of being struck with
anything hollow, such as a reed or a straw, and greatly preferred being
thrashed with a good thick cudgel or an iron bar, even though it hurt very
much. For they thought that if a man were beaten with anything hollow, his
inside would waste away till he died.[6] Again, the Galelareese think that, if
you are imprudent enough to eat while somebody is sharpening a knife,
your throat will be cut that same evening, or next morning at latest.[7]
At critical times the Mahakam Dyaks of Central Borneo seek to strengthen
their souls by biting on an old sword or setting their feet upon it.[8] At
initiation a Brahman boy is made to tread with his right foot on a stone,
while the words are repeated, "Tread on this stone; like a stone be firm";[9]
and the same ceremony is performed, with the same words, by a Brahman
bride at her marriage.[10]

The common custom of swearing upon a stone may be based partly on a
belief that the strength and stability of the stone lend confirmation to an
oath. Thus the Old Danish historian Saxo Grammaticus tells us that "the
ancients, when they were to choose a king, were wont to stand on stones
planted in the ground, and to proclaim their votes, in order to foreshadow
from the steadfastness of the stones that the deed would be lasting."[11] There
was a stone at Athens on which the nine archons stood when they swore
to rule justly and according to the laws.[12] In Laconia an unwrought stone
was shewn which, according to the legend, relieved the matricide Orestes of
his madness as soon as he had sat down on it;[13] and Zeus is said to have
often cured himself of his love for Hera by sitting down on a certain rock
in the island of Leucadia.[14] In these cases it may have been thought that
the wayward and fighty impulses of love and madness were counteracted by
the steadying influence of a heavy stone.

30. But while a general magical efficacy may be supposed to reside in all
stones by reason of their common properties of weight and solidity, special

magical virtues are attributed to particular stones, or kinds of stone, in accordance with their individual or specific qualities of shape and colour. Thus in the Banks Islands a stone with little discs on it is deemed good for bringing in money; and if a man found a larger stone with a number of small ones under it, like a sow among her litter, he was sure that to offer money upon it would bring him pigs.[1]

The ancients set great store on the magical qualities of precious stones; indeed it has been maintained, with great show of reason, that such stones were used as amulets long before they were worn as mere ornaments.[2] Thus the Greeks gave the name of tree-agate to a stone which exhibits tree-like markings, and they thought that if two of these gems were tied to the horns or neck of oxen at the plough, the crop would be sure to be plentiful.[3] Again, they recognized a milk-stone which produced an abundant supply of milk in women if only they drank it dissolved in honey-mead.[4] In Lechrain down to modern times German women have attempted to increase their milk by stroking their breasts with a kind of alum which they call a milk-stone.[5] Again, the Greeks believed in a stone which cured snake-bites, and hence was named the snake-stone; to test its efficacy you had only to grind the stone to powder and sprinkle the powder on the wound.[6] The wine-coloured amethyst received its name, which means "not drunken," because it was supposed to keep the wearer of it sober.[7] In Albania people think that if the blood-stone is laid on a wound it will stop the flow of blood.[8]

31. Dwellers by the sea cannot fail to be impressed by the sight of its ceaseless ebb and flow, and are apt, on the principles of that rude philosophy of sympathy and resemblance which here engages our attention, to trace a subtle relation, a secret harmony, between its tides and the life of man, of animals, and of plants. In the flowing tide they see not merely a symbol, but a cause of exuberance, of prosperity, and of life, while in the ebbing tide they discern a real agent as well as a melancholy emblem of failure, of weakness, and of death. The Breton peasant fancies that clover sown when the tide is coming in will grow well, but that if the plant be sown at low water or when the tide is going out, it will never reach maturity and that the cows which feed on it will burst.[1] Another ancient belief, attributed to Aristotle, was that no creature can die except at ebb tide. The belief, if we can trust Pliny, was confirmed by experience, so far as regards human beings, on the coast of France.[2] Philostratus also assures us that at Cadiz dying people never yielded up the ghost while the water was high.[3] A like fancy still lingers in some parts of Europe. On the Cantabrian coast of Spain they think that persons who die of chronic or acute disease expire at the moment when the tide begins to recede.[4] In Portugal, all along the coast of Wales, and on some parts of the coast of Brittany, a belief is said to prevail that people are born when the tide comes in, and die when it goes out.[5] Dickens attests the existence of the same superstition in England. "People can't die, along the coast," said Mr. Peggotty, "except when the tide's pretty nigh out. They can't be born, unless it's pretty nigh in—not properly born till flood."[6] The belief that most deaths happen at ebb tide is said to be held along the east coast of England from Northumberland to Kent.[7] Shakespeare must have been familiar with it, for he makes Falstaff die "even just between twelve and one, e'en at the turning o' the tide."[8] We meet the belief again on the Pacific coast of North America among the Haidas of the Queen Charlotte Islands. Whenever a good Haida is about to die he sees a canoe manned by some of his dead friends, who come with the tide to bid him welcome to the spirit land. "Come with us now," they say, "for the tide is about to ebb and we must depart."[9] At the other extremity of America the same fancy has been noted among the Indians of Southern Chile. A Chilote Indian in the last stage of consumption, after preparing to die like a good Catholic, was heard to ask how the tide was running. When his sister told him that it was still coming in, he smiled and said that he had yet a little while to live.[10] At Port Stephens, in New South Wales, the natives always buried their dead at flood tide, never at ebb, lest the retiring water should bear the soul of the departed to some distant country.[11]

In San Cristoval, one of the Solomon Islands, a woman of the noble Araha clan may not leave the house in her pregnancy. Pregnant women of other clans may leave their houses, but only at high tide, because they believe that it is only at high tide that women give birth to offspring successfully.[11a] In Loango it is believed that people do not die when the tide is flowing, but only when it is ebbing.[11b] Similarly the coast-dwellers of the North Andaman Islands believe that the soul of a dying man goes out with the ebbing tide.[11c]

32. To ensure a long life the Chinese have recourse to certain complicated charms, which concentrate in themselves the magical essence emanating, on homoeopathic principles, from times and seasons, persons and things. The vehicles employed to transmit these happy and beneficial influences are no other than grave-clothes. These are provided by many Chinese in their life-time, and most people have them cut out and sewn by an unmarried girl or a very young woman, wisely calculating that, since such a person is likely to live a great many years to come, a part of her capacity to live long must surely pass into the clothes, and thus stave off for many years the time when they shall be put to their proper use. Further, the garments are made by preference in a year which has an intercalary month; for to the Chinese mind it seems plain that grave-clothes made in a year which is unusually long will possess the capacity of prolonging life in an unusually high degree. Amongst the clothes there is one robe in particular on which special pains have been lavished to imbue it with this priceless quality. It is a long silken gown of the deepest blue colour, with the word "longevity" embroidered all over it in thread of gold. To present an aged parent with one of these costly and splendid mantles, known as "longevity garments," is esteemed by the Chinese an act of filial piety and a delicate mark of attention. As the garment purports to prolong the life of its owner, he often wears it, especially on festive occasions, in order to allow the influence of longevity, created by the many golden letters with which it is bespangled, to work their full effect upon his person. On his birthday, above all, he hardly ever fails to don it, for in China common sense bids a man lay in a large stock of vital energy on his birthday, to be expended in the form of health and vigour during the rest of the year. Attired in the gorgeous pall, and absorbing its blessed influence at every pore, the happy owner receives complacently the congratulations of friends and relations, who warmly express their admiration of these magnificent cerements, and of the filial piety which prompted the children to bestow so beautiful and useful a present on the author of their being.[1]

33. Sometimes homoeopathic or imitative magic is called in to annul an evil omen by accomplishing it in mimicry. The effect is to circumvent destiny by substituting a mock calamity for a real one. It is related, for instance, that two missionaries were once journeying through Central Celebes, accompanied by some Toradjas. Unfortunately the note of a certain bird called *teka-teka* was heard to the left. This boded ill, and the natives insisted that they must either turn back or pass the night on the spot. When the missionaries refused to do either, an expedient was hit upon which allowed them to continue the journey in safety. A miniature hut was made out of a leafy branch, and in it were deposited a leaf moistened with spittle and a hair from the head of one of the party. Then one of the Toradjas said, "We shall pass the night here," and addressing the hair he spoke thus: "If any misfortune should happen through the cry of that bird, may it fall on you." In this way the evil omen was diverted from the real men and directed against their substitute the hair, and perhaps also the spittle, in the tiny hut.[1] When a Cherokee has dreamed of being stung by a snake, he is treated just in the same way as if he had really been stung; otherwise the place would swell and ulcerate in the usual manner, though perhaps years might pass before it did so. It is the ghost of a snake that has bitten him in sleep.[2] One night a Huron Indian dreamed that he had been taken and burned alive by his hereditary foes the Iroquois. Next morning a council was held on the affair, and the following measures were adopted to save the man's life. Twelve or thirteen fires were kindled in the large hut where they usually burned their prisoners to death. Every man seized a flaming brand and applied it to the naked body of the dreamer, who shrieked with pain. Thrice he ran round the hut, escaping from one fire only to fall into another. As each man thrust his blazing torch at the sufferer he said, "Courage, my brother, it is thus that we have pity on you." At last he was allowed to escape. Passing out of the hut he caught up a dog which was held ready for the purpose, and throwing it over his shoulder carried it through the wigwams as a sacred offering to the war-god, praying him to accept the animal instead of himself. Afterwards the dog was killed, roasted, and eaten, exactly as the Indians were wont to roast and eat their captives.[3]

CONTAGION

34. The most familiar example of Contagious Magic is the magical sympathy which is supposed to exist between a man and any severed portion of his person, such as his hair or nails; so that whoever gets possession of human hair or nails may work his will, at any distance, upon the person from whom they were cut.

Among the Australian tribes it was a common practice to knock out one or more of a boy's front teeth at those ceremonies of initiation to which every male member had to submit before he could enjoy the rights and privileges of a full-grown man.[1] The reason of the practice is obscure; all that concerns us here is the evidence of a belief that a sympathetic relation continued to exist between the lad and his teeth after the latter had been extracted from his gums. Thus among some of the tribes about the river Darling, in New South Wales, the extracted tooth was placed under the bark of a tree near a river or water-hole; if the bark grew over the tooth, or if the tooth fell into the water, all was well; but if it were exposed and the ants ran over it, the natives believed that the boy would suffer from a disease of the mouth.[2] Among the Murring and other tribes of New South Wales the extracted tooth was at first taken care of by an old man, and then passed from one headman to another, until it had gone all round the community, when it came back to the lad's father, and finally to the lad himself. But however it was thus conveyed from hand to hand, it might on no account be placed in a bag containing magical substances, for to do so would, they believed, put the owner of the tooth in great danger.[3]

The Basutos are careful to conceal their extracted teeth, lest these should fall into the hands of certain mythical beings called *baloi,* who haunt graves, and could harm the owner of the tooth by working magic on it.[4] In Sussex some forty years ago a maid-servant remonstrated strongly against the throwing away of children's cast teeth, affirming that should they be found and gnawed by any animal, the child's new tooth would be, for all the world, like the teeth of the animal that had bitten the old one. A similar belief has led to practices intended, on the principles of homoeopathic magic, to replace old teeth by new and better ones. Thus in many parts of the world it is customary to put extracted teeth in some place where they will be found by a mouse or a rat, in the hope that, through the sympathy which continues to subsist between them and their former owner, his other teeth may acquire the same firmness and excellence as the teeth of these rodents. Thus in Germany it is said to be an almost universal maxim among the people that when you have had a tooth taken out you should insert it in a mouse's hole. To do so with a child's milk-tooth which has fallen out will prevent the child from having toothache. Or you should go behind the stove and throw your tooth backwards over your head, saying, "Mouse, give me your iron tooth; I will give you my bone tooth." After that your other teeth will remain good. German children say, "Mouse, mouse, come out and bring me out a new tooth"; or "Mouse, I give you a little bone; give me a little stone"; or "Mouse, there is an old tooth for you; make me a new one."[5] Jewish children in South Russia used to throw their cast teeth on the roof with the same request to the mouse to give them an iron tooth for one of bone;[6] just as a Singhalese will throw them on the roof, saying, "Squirrel, dear squirrel, take this tooth and give me a dainty one!"[7] In Bohemia a child will sometimes throw its cast tooth behind the stove, asking the fox to give it an iron one instead.[8] An Armenian generally buries his extracted teeth at the edge of the hearth with the prayer: "Grandfather, take a dog's tooth and give me a golden tooth."[9] In the light of the preceding examples, we may conjecture that the grandfather here invoked is not so much the soul of a dead ancestor as a mouse or a rat.

35. Other parts which are commonly believed to remain in a sympathetic union with the body, after the physical connexion has been severed, are the navel-string and the afterbirth, including the placenta. So intimate, indeed, is the union conceived to be, that the fortunes of the individual for good or evil throughout life are often supposed to be bound up with one or other of these portions of his person, so that if his navel-string or afterbirth is preserved and properly treated, he will be prosperous; whereas if it be injured or lost, he will suffer accordingly. Thus among the Maoris, when the navel-string dropped off, the child was carried to a priest to be solemnly named by him. But before the ceremony of naming began, the navel-string was buried in a sacred place and a young sapling was planted over it. Ever afterwards that tree, as it grew, was a *tohu oranga* or sign of life for the child.[1] Among the Arunta of Central Australia the navel-string is swathed in fur-string and made into a necklace, which is hung around the child's neck. The necklace is supposed to facilitate the growth of the child, keep it quiet and contented, and avert illness generally.[2] In like manner, in the Yabim tribe of New Guinea the mother ties the navel-string to the net which carries the child, lest any one should use the string to the child's hurt.[3] At Rotuma in Fiji it has become almost obligatory for a young man, who wants the girls to respect him, to make a voyage in a white man's vessel; and mothers come alongside ships anchored in the roadstead and fasten their boy's navel-string to the vessel's chainplates. This will make sure of a voyage for the child when it has grown up. This, of course, must be a modern development, but it has all the strength of an ancient custom.[4] In Ceram the child sometimes wears the navel-string round its neck as an amulet;[5] and in the islands of Leti, Moa, and Lakor he carries it as a talisman in war or on a far journey.[6] Similarly in the islands of Saparoea, Haoekoe, and Noessa Laut, to the east of Amboyna, it is thought that a child born with a caul will enjoy in later years the gift of second sight.[7] So too in the Luang-Sermata islands a child born with a caul is counted lucky and can perceive and recognize the spirits of his ancestors.[8]

The people of Laos in Indo-China never consider the afterbirth as useless or throw it away in any corner: they believe that it remains in sympathetic connection with the individual, and according to its treatment will influence his lot in various ways. Attached to the highest branch of a tree in the court-yard, it becomes the prey of beneficent spirits, who will prepare for the child a happy life. Buried in the garden, it will secure the fidelity of the child to the house in which he was born: he will never leave it. Buried under the house ladder it will, oddly enough, secure the child from pains in his stomach.[8a]

In the Marshall Islands of the western Pacific the navel-string of a boy is thrown into the sea in order that he may become a good fisher: the navel-string of a girl is inserted in a leafy *pandanus* tree, in order that she may be diligent in plaiting *pandanus* fibre.[8b] In the Marquesas Islands, when a birth had taken place, the afterbirth was hastily buried under a frequented path in order that women passing over the spot might acquire from the afterbirth the gift of fecundity.[8c]

The Incas of Peru preserved the navel-string with the greatest care, and gave it to the child to suck whenever it fell ill.[9] In ancient Mexico they used to give a boy's navel-string to soldiers, to be buried by them on a field of battle, in order that the boy might thus acquire a passion for war. But the navel-string of a girl was buried beside the domestic hearth, because this was believed to inspire her with a love of home and a taste for cooking and baking.[10] Algonquin women hung the navel-string round the child's neck; if he lost it, they thought the child would be stupid and spiritless.[11]

36. Even in Europe many people still believe that a person's destiny is more or less bound up with that of his navel-string or afterbirth. Thus in Rhenish Bavaria the navel-string is kept for a while wrapt up in a piece of old linen, and then cut or pricked to pieces according as the child is a boy or a girl, in order that he or she may grow up to be a skilful workman or a good sempstress.[1] In Berlin the midwife commonly delivers the dried navel-string to the father with a strict injunction to preserve it carefully, for so long as it is kept the child will live and thrive and be free from sickness.[2] Again, in Europe children born with a caul are considered lucky;[3] in Holland, as in the East Indies, they can see ghosts.[4] The Icelanders also hold that a child born with a caul will afterwards possess the gift of second sight, that he will never be harmed by sorcery, and will be victorious in every contest he undertakes, provided he has the caul dried and carries it with him.[5]

37. A curious application of the doctrine of contagious magic is the relation commonly believed to exist between a wounded man and the agent of the wound, so that whatever is subsequently done by or to that agent must correspondingly affect the patient either for good or evil. Thus Pliny tells us that if you have wounded a man and are sorry for it, you have only to spit on the hand that inflicted the wound, and the sufferer's pain will be instantly relieved.[1] So, too, among the Lkuñgen Indians of British Columbia it is a rule that an arrow, or any other weapon that has wounded a man, must be hidden by his friends, who have to be careful not to bring it near the fire till the wound is healed. If a knife or an arrow which is still covered with a man's blood were thrown into the fire, the wounded man would suffer very much.[2] In the Yerkla-mining tribe of south-eastern Australia it is thought that if any one but the medicine-man touches the flint knife with which a boy has been subincised, the boy will thereby be made very ill. So seriously is this belief held that if the lad chanced thereafter to fall sick and die, the man who had touched the knife would be killed.[3] "It is constantly received and avouched," says Bacon, "that the anointing of the weapon that maketh the wound will heal the wound itself. In this experiment, upon the relation of men of credit (though myself, as yet, am not fully inclined to believe it), you shall note the points following: first, the ointment wherewith this is done is made of divers ingredients, whereof the strangest and hardest to come by are the moss upon the skull of a dead man unburied, and the fats of a boar and a bear killed in the act of generation." The precious ointment compounded out of these and other ingredients was applied, as the philosopher explains, not to the wound but to the weapon, and that even though the injured man was at a great distance and knew nothing about it. The experiment, he tells us, had been tried of wiping the ointment off the weapon without the knowledge of the person hurt, with the result that he was presently in a great rage of pain until the weapon was anointed again. Moreover, "it is affirmed that if you cannot get the weapon, yet if you put an instrument of iron or wood resembling the weapon into the wound, whereby it bleedeth, the anointing of that instrument will serve and work the effect."[4] Remedies of the sort which Bacon deemed worthy of his attention are still in vogue in the eastern counties of England. Thus in Suffolk if a man cuts himself with a bill-hook or a scythe he always takes care to keep the weapon bright, and oils it to prevent the wound from festering. If he runs a thorn into his hand, he oils or greases it when extracted. If a horse wounds its foot by treading on a nail, your Suffolk groom will invariably preserve the nail, clean it, and grease it every day, to prevent the foot from festering. Arguing in the same way, a Suffolk woman whose sister had burned her face with a flat-iron, observed that "the face would never heal till the iron had been put out of the way; and even if it did heal, it would be sure to break out again every time the iron was heated."[5] Similarly Essex rustics opine that, if a man has been stabbed with a knife, it is essential to his recovery that the knife should be greased and laid across the bed on which the sufferer is lying,[6] while in the Harz mountains they say that if you cut yourself, you ought to smear the knife or the scissors with fat and put the instrument away in a dry place in the name of the Father, of the Son, and of the Holy Ghost. As the knife dries, the wound heals.[7]

In the Kagoro tribe of Northern Nigeria, if a man is wounded by a spear or sword and the place refuses to heal, the weapon, if it can be obtained, is washed with water, which is drunk by the patient, who is then supposed to recover.[7a]

The train of reasoning which thus commends itself to English and German rustics, in common with the savages of Melanesia and America, is carried a step further by the aborigines of Central Australia, who conceive that under certain circumstances the near relations of a wounded man must grease themselves, restrict their diet, and regulate their behaviour in other ways in order to ensure his recovery. Thus when a lad has been circumcised and the wound is not yet healed, his mother may not eat opossum, or a certain kind of lizard, or carpet snake, or any kind of fat, for otherwise she would retard the healing of the boy's wound. Every day she greases her digging-sticks and never lets them out of her sight; at night she sleeps with them close to her head. No one is allowed to touch them. Every day also she rubs her body all over with grease, as in some way this is believed to help her son's recovery.[8] Another refinement of the same principle is due to the ingenuity of the German peasant. It is said that when one of his pigs or sheep breaks its leg, a farmer of Rhenish Bavaria or Hesse will bind up the leg of a chair with bandages and splints in due form. For some days thereafter no one may sit on that chair, move it, or knock up against it; for to do so would pain the injured pig or sheep and hinder the cure.[9] In this last case it is clear that we have passed wholly out of the region of contagious magic and into the region of homoeopathic or imitative magic; the chair-leg, which is treated instead of the beast's leg, in no sense belongs to the animal, and the application of bandages to it is a mere simulation of the treatment which a more rational surgery would bestow on the real patient.

38. The sympathetic connexion supposed to exist between a man and the weapon which has wounded him is probably founded on the notion that the blood on the weapon continues to feel with the blood in his body. Strained and unnatural as this idea may seem to us, it is perhaps less so than the belief that magic sympathy is maintained between a person and his clothes, so that whatever is done to the clothes will be felt by the man himself, even though he may be far away at the time. That is the reason the Papuans of Tumleo search most anxiously for the smallest scrap which they may have lost of their scanty garments,[1] and why other Papuans, travelling through the thick forest, will stop and carefully scrape from a bough any clot of red pomade which may have adhered to it from their greasy heads.[2] The witch in Theocritus, while she melted an image or lump of wax in order that her faithless lover might melt with love of her, did not forget to throw into the fire a bit of the hem of his cloak which she had managed to acquire.[3] In Prussia they say that if you cannot catch a thief, the next best thing is to get hold of a garment which he may have shed in his flight; for if you beat it soundly, the thief will fall sick.[4] This belief is deeply rooted in the popular mind of primitives. Thus the Kai of Northern New Guinea believe that everything with which a man comes in contact retains something of his soul-stuff, by working on which a sorcerer may do the man himself grievous hurt. This is the great source of anxiety to the natives of New Guinea. Hence the native is at great pains to remove any traces of his presence from any object with which he has been in contact. If upon his way through the forest he leaves a lock of his hair or a thread of his girdle on a thorny bush, he goes no further until he has removed every trace of it. He throws nothing away. Even when he is a guest at a friendly village he gathers the shells of the betel-nuts carefully in his pouch which he always carries about with him; or he throws the remains in the fire. Even the places where he sits retain something of his soul-stuff, so on rising he is careful to efface the traces of his person, either by stamping with his feet, or by poking with his stick, or by sprinkling them with water from a stream. Or on the spot he places certain leaves which are believed to possess the property of driving away his soul-stuff. The soul-stuff is thought of itself soon to depart, but it is desirable to hasten its departure, for once a magician gets possession of the soul-stuff the original owner of it is often supposed to be a doomed man.[4a]

39. Again, magic may be wrought on a man sympathetically not only through his clothes and severed parts of himself, but also through the impressions left by his body in sand or earth. In particular, it is a worldwide superstition that by injuring footprints you injure the feet that made them. Thus the natives of south-eastern Australia think that they can lame a man by placing sharp pieces of quartz, glass, bone, or charcoal in his footprints. Rheumatic pains are often attributed by them to this cause.

In New Britain it is thought that you can cause the sickness or death of a man by pricking his footprints with the sting of a sting-ray.[1] The Maoris imagine that they can work grievous harm to an enemy by taking up earth from his footprints, depositing it in a sacred place, and performing a ceremony over it.[2] On Savage Island a common form of witchcraft was to take up the soil on which an enemy had set his foot, and to carry it to a sacred place, where it was solemnly cursed, in order that the man might be afflicted with lameness.[3] The Galelareese think that if anybody sticks something sharp into your footprints while you are walking, you will be wounded in your feet.[4] In New Ireland a person who has been robbed looks for the footprints of the thief, and if he finds them he takes them up and performs ceremonies over them, which he supposes will disable the malefactor and so prevent him from doing further mischief.[4a]

In Izumo, a district of Japan, if a house has been robbed in the night while the inmates are asleep, when they wake in the morning they will look for the footprints of the burglars, and if they find them they will burn mugwort in them. By this operation it is hoped or believed that the burglar's feet will be made so sore that he cannot run far, and that the police may easily overtake him.[4b] The Ewe-speaking people of West Africa fancy they can drive an enemy mad by throwing a magic powder on his footprints.[5]

Similar practices prevail in various parts of Europe. Thus in Mecklenburg it is thought that if you drive a nail into a man's footprint he will fall lame; sometimes it is required that the nail should be taken from a coffin.[6] A like mode of injuring an enemy is resorted to in some parts of France.[7] It is said that there was an old woman who used to frequent Stow in Suffolk, and she was a witch. If, while she walked, any one went after her and stuck a nail or a knife into her footprint in the dust, the dame could not stir a step till it was withdrawn.[8] More commonly, it would seem, in Germany earth from the footprint is tied up in a cloth and hung in the chimney smoke; as it dries up, so the man withers away or his foot shrivels up.[9] The same practice and the same belief are said to be common in Matogrosso, a province of Brazil.[10] An old Danish mode of concluding a treaty was based on the same idea of the sympathetic connexion between a man and his footprints: the covenanting parties sprinkled each other's footprints with their own blood, thus giving a pledge of fidelity.[11] In ancient Greece superstitions of the same sort seem to have been current, for it was thought that if a horse stepped on the track of a wolf he was seized with numbness;[12] and a maxim ascribed to Pythagoras forbade people to pierce a man's footprints with a nail or a knife.[13]

40. But though the footprint is the most obvious it is not the only impression made by the body through which magic may be wrought on a man. The aborigines of south-eastern Australia believe that a man may be injured by burying sharp fragments of quartz, glass, and so forth in the mark made by his reclining body; the magical virtue of these sharp things enters his body and causes those acute pains which the ignorant European puts down to rheumatism.[1] To ensure the good behaviour of an ally with whom they have just held a conference, the Basutos cut and preserve the grass on which he sat during the interview.[2] Moors who write on the sand are careful to obliterate all the marks they have made, never leaving a stroke or dot in the sand when they have done writing.[3]

THE MAGICAL CONTROL

OF THE WEATHER

RAIN

41. Of the things which the public magician sets himself to do for the good of the tribe, one of the chief is to control the weather and especially to ensure an adequate fall of rain. In savage communities the rain-maker is a very important personage; and often a special class of magicians exists for the purpose of regulating the heavenly water-supply. The methods by which they attempt to discharge the duties of their office are commonly, though not always, based on the principle of homoeopathic or imitative magic. If they wish to make rain they simulate it by sprinkling water or mimicking clouds: if their object is to stop rain and cause drought, they avoid water and resort to warmth and fire for the sake of drying up the too abundant moisture.

Thus in a village near Dorpat, in Russia, when rain was much wanted, three men used to climb up the fir-trees of an old sacred grove. One of them drummed with a hammer on a kettle or small cask to imitate thunder; the second knocked two fire-brands together and made the sparks fly, to imitate lightning; and the third, who was called "the rain-maker," had a bunch of twigs with which he sprinkled water from a vessel on all sides.[1] To put an end to drought and bring down rain, women and girls of the village of Ploska are wont to go naked by night to the boundaries of the village and there pour water on the ground.[2] In Halmahera, or Gilolo, a large island to the west of New Guinea, a wizard makes rain by dipping a branch of a particular kind of tree in water and then scattering the moisture from the dripping bough over the ground.[3] In Ceram it is enough to dedicate the bark of a certain tree to the spirits, and lay it in water.[4] A Javanese mode of making rain is to imitate the pattering sound of rain-drops by brushing a coco-nut leaf over the sheath of a betel-nut in a mortar.[5] Amongst the Omaha Indians of North America, when the corn is withering for want of rain, the members of the sacred Buffalo Society fill a large vessel with water

38

and dance four times round it. One of them drinks some of the water and spirts it into the air, making a fine spray in imitation of a mist or drizzling rain. Then he upsets the vessel, spilling the water on the ground; whereupon the dancers fall down and drink up the water, getting mud all over their faces. Lastly, they squirt the water into the air, making a fine mist. This saves the corn.[6] At Takitount in Algeria, when the drought is severe, the people prepare a sacrificial banquet (zerda), in the course of which they dance, and filling their mouths with water spirt it into the air crying, "The rain and abundance!" Elsewhere in the course of these banquets it is customary for the same purpose to sprinkle water on children. At Tlemcen in time of drought water is thrown from terraces and windows on small girls who pass singing.[7] In the Wotjobaluk tribe of Victoria the rain-maker dipped a bunch of his own hair in water, sucked out the water and squirted it westward, or he twirled the ball round his head, making a spray like rain.[8] In Java, when rain is wanted, two men will sometimes thrash each other with supple rods till the blood flows down their backs; the streaming blood represents the rain, and no doubt is supposed to make it fall on the ground.[9] The people of Eggibiu, a district of Abyssinia, used to stage sanguinary conflicts with each other, village against village, for a week together every January for the purpose of procuring rain.[10] The prophets of Baal who, in the famous contest with Elijah, sought to procure rain by cutting themselves with knives till the blood gushed out, may have been acting on the same principle.[11]

42. There is a widespread belief that twin children possess magical powers over nature, especially over rain and weather. This curious notion prevails among some of the Indian tribes of British Columbia, and has led them often to impose singular taboos on the parents of twins, though the exact meaning of these restrictions is generally obscure. Thus the Tsimshian Indians believe that twins actually control the weather; they therefore pray to wind and rain, "Calm down, breath of the twins."[1] The Nutka Indians likewise believe that twins can make fair weather or foul and can cause rain by painting their faces black and then washing them—a representation, perhaps, of rain dripping from dark clouds.[2] Again, among the Thompson Indians twins were called "grizzly-bear children" or "hairy feet," because they were thought to be under the protection of the grizzly bear and to be endowed by him with special powers such as that of making fair or foul weather.[3] Similarly, the Shuswap Indians associate twins with the grizzly bear, for they call them "young grizzly bears." According to them, twins remain throughout life endowed with supernatural powers. In particular they can make good or bad weather. They produce rain by spilling water from a basket in the air; they make fine weather by shaking a small flat piece of wood attached to a stick by a string; they raise storms by strewing down on the ends of spruce branches.[4]

The Indians of Peru entertained similar notions as to the special relation in which twins stand to the rain and the weather. For they said that one of each pair of twins was a son of the lightning; and they called the lightning the lord and creator of rain, and prayed to him to send showers.[5]

The same power of influencing the weather is attributed to twins by the Baronga, a tribe of Bantu Negroes who inhabit the shores of Delagoa Bay in south-eastern Africa. They bestow the name of *Tilo*—that is, the sky—on a woman who has given birth to twins, and the infants themselves are called the children of the sky. Now when the storms which generally burst in the months of September and October have been looked for in vain, when a drought with its prospect of famine is threatening, and all nature, scorched and burnt up by a sun that has shone for six months from a cloudless sky, is panting for the beneficent showers of the South African spring, the women perform ceremonies to bring down the longed-for rain on the parched earth. Stripping themselves of all their garments, they assume in their stead girdles and head-dresses of grass, or short petticoats made of the leaves of a particular sort of creeper. Thus attired, uttering peculiar cries and singing ribald songs, they go about from well to well, cleansing them of the mud and impurities which have accumulated in them. The wells, it may be said, are merely holes in the sand where a little turbid unwholesome water stagnates. Further, the women must repair to the house of one of their gossips who has given birth to twins, and must drench her with water, which they carry in little pitchers. Having done so they go on their way, shrieking out their loose songs and dancing immodest dances. No man may see these leaf-clad women going their rounds. If they meet a man, they maul him and thrust him aside. When they have cleansed the wells, they must go and pour water on the graves of their ancestors in the sacred grove. It often happens, too, that at the bidding of the wizard they go and pour water on the graves of twins. For they think that the grave of a twin ought always to be moist, for which reason twins are regularly buried near a lake. If all their efforts to procure rain prove abortive, they will remember that such and such a twin was buried in a dry place on the side of a hill. "No wonder," says the wizard in such a case, "that the sky is fiery. Take up his body and dig him a grave on the shore of the lake." His orders are at once obeyed, for this is supposed to be the only means of bringing down the rain.[6] Lastly, the Hindus of the Central Provinces of India believe that a twin can save the crops from the ravages of hail and heavy rain if he will only paint his right buttock black and his left buttock some other color, and thus adorned go and stand in the direction of the wind.[7]

43. Many of the foregoing facts strongly support an interpretation which Oldenberg has given of the rules to be observed by a Brahman who would learn a particular hymn of the ancient Indian collection known as the Samaveda. The hymn, which bears the name of the Ṣakvarī song, was believed to embody the might of Indra's weapon, the thunderbolt; and hence, on account of the dreadful and dangerous potency with which it was thus charged, the bold student who essayed to master it had to be isolated from his fellow-men, and to retire from the village into the forest. Here for a space of time, which might vary, according to different doctors of the law, from one to twelve years, he had to observe certain rules of life, among which were the following. Thrice a day he had to touch water; he must wear black garments and eat black food; when it rained, he might not seek the shelter of a roof, but had to sit in the rain and say, "Water is the Şakvarī song"; when the lightning flashed he said, "That is like the Şakvarī song"; when the thunder pealed he said, "The Great One is making a great noise." He might never cross a running stream without touching water; he might never set foot on a ship unless his life were in danger, and even then he must be sure to touch water when he went on board; "for in water," so ran the saying, "lies the virtue of the Şakvarī song." When at last he was allowed to learn the song itself, he had to dip his hands in a vessel of water in which plants of all sorts had been placed. If a man walked in the way of all these precepts, the rain-god Parjanya, it was said, would send rain at the wish of that man. It is clear, as Professor Oldenberg well points out, that "all these rules are intended to bring the Brahman into union with water, to make him, as it were, an ally of the water powers, and to guard him against their hostility. The black garments and the black food have the same significance; no one will doubt that they refer to the rain-clouds when he remembers that a black victim is sacrificed to procure rain; 'it is black, for such is the nature of rain.' In respect of another rain-charm it is said plainly, 'He puts on a black garment edged with black, for such is the nature of rain.' We may therefore assume that here in the circle of ideas and ordinances of the Vedic schools there have been preserved magical practices of the most remote antiquity, which were intended to prepare the rain-maker for his office and dedicate him to it."[1]

44. In south-eastern Europe at the present day ceremonies are observed for the purpose of making rain which not only rest on the same general train of thought as the preceding, but even in their details resemble the ceremonies practised with the same intention by the Baronga of Delagoa Bay. Among the Greeks of Thessaly and Macedonia, when a drought has lasted a long time, it is customary to send a procession of children round to all the wells and springs of the neighbourhood. At the head of the procession walks a girl adorned with flowers, whom her companions drench with water at every halting-place, while they sing an invocation, of which the following is part:—

> Perperia, all fresh bedewed,
> Freshen all the neighbourhood;
> By the woods, on the highway,

> As thou goest, to God now pray:
> O my God, upon the plain,
> Send thou us a still, small rain;
> That the fields may fruitful be,
> And vines in blossom we may see;
> That the grain be full and sound,
> And wealthy grow the folks around.[1]

In time of drought the Servians strip a girl to her skin and clothe her from head to foot in grass, herbs, and flowers, even her face being hidden behind a veil of living green. Thus disguised she is called the Dodola, and goes through the village with a troop of girls. They stop before every house; the Dodola keeps turning herself round and dancing, while the other girls form a ring about her singing one of the Dodola songs, and the housewife pours a pail of water over her. One of the songs they sing runs thus:—

> We go through the village;
> The clouds go in the sky;
> We go faster,
> Faster go the clouds;
> They have overtaken us,
> And wetted the corn and the vine.

A similar custom is observed in Greece and Roumania.[2] In Roumania the rain-maker is called Paparuda or Babaruda. She is a gypsy girl, who goes naked except for a short skirt of dwarf elder (*Sambucus ebulus*) or of corn and vines. Thus scantily attired the girls go in procession from house to house, singing for rain, and are drenched by the people with buckets of water. The ceremony regularly takes place all over Roumania on the third Tuesday after Easter, but it may be repeated at any time of drought during the summer. But the Roumanians have another way of procuring rain. They make a clay figure to represent Drought, cover it with a pall, and place it in an open coffin. Girls crouch round the coffin and lament, saying, "Drought (*Scaloi*) is dead! Lord, give us rain!" Then the coffin is carried by children in funeral procession, with a burning wax candle before it, while lamentations fill the air. Finally, they throw the coffin and the candle into a stream or a well.[3] When rain is wanted in Bulgaria the people dress up a girl in branches of nut-trees, flowers, and the green stuff of beans, potatoes, and onions. She carries a nosegay of flowers in her hand, and is called Djuldjul or Peperuga. Attended by a train of followers she goes from house to house, and is received by the goodman with a kettleful of water, on which flowers are swimming. With this water he drenches her, while a song is sung:—

> The Peperuga flew;
> God give rain,
> That the corn, the millet, and the wheat may thrive.[4]

Similar rain-charms are practised in Armenia, except that there the representative of vegetation is an effigy or doll, not a person. At Kerak in Palestine, whenever there is a drought, the Greek Christians dress up a winnowing-fork in women's clothes. They call it "the bride of God." The girls and women carry it from house to house, singing doggerel songs.[5] We are not told that "the bride of God" is drenched with water or thrown into a stream, but the charm would hardly be complete without this feature. Similarly, when rain is much wanted, the Arabs of Moab attire a dummy in the robes and ornaments of a woman and call it "the Mother of the Rain." A woman carries it in procession past the houses of the village or the tents of the camp, singing:—

O Mother of the Rain, O Immortal, moisten our sleeping seeds.
Moisten the sleeping seeds of the sheikh, who is ever generous.
She is gone, the Mother of the Rain, to bring the storm; when she comes back,
   the crops are as high as the walls.
She is gone, the Mother of the Rain, to bring the winds; when she comes back, the
   plantations have attained the height of lances.
She is gone, the Mother of the Rain, to bring the thunders; when she comes back,
   the crops are as high as camels.[6]

Pavra, Naira, and Nahal Bhils perform an analogous ceremony. Boys and girls under nine years of age go from house to house on four successive nights, accompanied by men bearing torches which simulate lightning. The girls, who are drenched at each house, sing:—

Dondhya, Dondhya, give rain,
Make rice and pulse grow![6a]

45. Bathing is practised as a rain-charm in some parts of southern and western Russia. Sometimes after service in church the priest in his robes has been thrown down on the ground and drenched with water by his parishioners. Sometimes it is the women who, without stripping off their clothes, bathe in crowds on the day of St. John the Baptist, while they dip in the water a figure made of branches, grass, and herbs, which is supposed to represent the saint.[1] In Kursk, a province of southern Russia, when rain is much wanted, the women seize a passing stranger and throw him into the river, or souse him from head to foot.[2] An Armenian rain-charm is to throw the wife of a priest into the water and drench her.[3] The Arabs of North Africa fling a holy man, willy-nilly, into a spring as a remedy for drought.[4] In Minahassa, a province of North Celebes, the priest bathes as a rain-charm.[5] In Kumaon, a district of north-west India, when rain fails they sink a Brahman up to his lips in a tank or pond, where he repeats the name of a god of rain for a day or two. When this rite is duly performed, rain is sure to fall.[6] In the Solok district of Sumatra, when a drought has lasted a long time, a number of half-naked women take a half-witted man to a river; and there besprinkle him with water as a means of compelling the rain to fall.[7] In some parts of Bengal, when drought threatens the country, troops of children of all ages go from house to house and roll and tumble in puddles which have been prepared for the purpose by pouring water into the courtyards. This is supposed to bring down rain.[8]

46. Sometimes the means adopted for bringing about the desired result appear to be not so much imitative action as the pronouncement of effective curses and maledictions. Thus in Dubrajpur, a village in the Birbhum district of Bengal, when rain has been looked for in vain, people will throw dirt or filth on the houses of their neighbors, who abuse them for doing so. Or they drench the lame, halt, and blind, and are reviled for their pains by the victims. This vituperation is believed to accomplish the desired result by drawing down showers on the parched earth.[1] In the Shahpur district of the Punjab it is said to be customary in time of drought to spill a pot of filth on the threshold of a notorious old shrew, in order that the fluent stream of foul language in which she vents her feelings may accelerate the lingering rain.[2] Analogous is the ancient Greek usage whereby the sower of cummin had to curse and swear, or the crop would not turn out well.[3] Roman writers mention a similar custom observed by sowers of rue and basil;[4] and hedge doctors in Greece laid it down as a rule that in cutting black hellebore you should face eastward and curse.[5] Perhaps the bitter language was supposed to strengthen the bitter taste, and hence the medicinal virtue, of these plants.

47. Women are sometimes supposed to be able to make rain by ploughing or pretending to plough. In a district of Transylvania, when the ground is parched with drought, some girls strip themselves naked, and, led by an older woman, who is also naked, they steal a harrow and carry it across the fields to a brook, where they set it afloat. Next they sit on the harrow and keep a tiny flame burning on each corner of it for an hour. Then they leave the harrow in the water and go home.[1] A similar rain-charm is resorted to in some parts of India; naked women drag a plough across a field by night, while the men keep carefully out of the way, for their presence would break the spell.[2] The Tarahumare Indians of Mexico dip the plough in water before they use it, that it may draw rain.[3]

48. Sometimes the rain-charm operates through *the dead*. Thus in New Caledonia the rain-makers blackened themselves all over, dug up a dead body, took the bones to a cave, jointed them, and hung the skeleton over some taro leaves. Water was poured over the skeleton to run down on the leaves. They believed that the soul of the deceased took up the water, converted it into rain, and showered it down again.[1] In 1868 the prospect of a bad harvest, caused by a prolonged drought, induced the inhabitants of a village in the Tarashchansk district to dig up the body of a Raskolnik, or Dissenter, who had died in the preceding December. Some of the party beat the corpse, or what was left of it, about the head, exclaiming, "Give us rain!" while others poured water on it through a sieve.[2] Here the pouring of water through a sieve seems plainly an imitation of a shower, and reminds us of the manner in which Strepsiades in Aristophanes imagined that rain was made by Zeus.[3] An Armenian rain-charm is to dig up a skull and throw it into running water.[4] Among some of the Indian tribes in the region of the Orinoco it was customary for the relatives of a deceased person to disinter his bones a year after burial and scatter the ashes in the belief that the latter changed to rain, which the dead man sent in return for his obsequies.[5]

49. *Animals,* too, often play an important part in these weather-charms. Thus, when some of the Blackfoot Indians were at war in summer and wished to bring on a tempest, they would take a kit-fox skin and rub it with dirt and water.[1] The Thompson Indians of British Columbia think that when the loon calls loud and often, it will soon rain, and that to mimic the cry of the bird may bring the rain down.[2] Again, if Aino fishermen desire to bring on rain and wind, they pray to the skulls of raccoons and then throw water over one another.[3] In southern Celebes people try to make rain by carrying a cat tied in a sedan chair thrice round the parched fields, while they drench it with water from bamboo squirts. When the cat begins to miaul, they say, "O lord, let rain fall on us!"[4]

50. The intimate association of *frogs and toads* with water has earned for these creatures a widespread reputation as custodians of rain; and hence they often play a part in charms designed to draw needed showers from the sky. It is said, for instance, that the Aymara Indians of Peru and Bolivia often make little images of frogs and other aquatic animals and place them on hilltops as a means of inducing rainfall.[1] The Thompson River Indians of British Columbia and some people in Europe think that to kill a frog brings on rain,[2] while in the Central Provinces of India people of low caste will tie a frog to a rod covered with green leaves and branches of the *nim* tree and carry it from door to door singing:—

> Send soon, O frog, the jewel of water!
> And ripen the wheat and millet in the field.[3]

51. Sometimes, when the drought is long and their temper short, people will drop the usual hocus-pocus of magic altogether. Thus, when rain is wanted badly, the Feloupes of Senegambia cast down their fetishes and drag them about the fields, cursing them until the rain falls.[1] Similarly, when the spirits withhold rain or sunshine, the Comanches whip a slave; if the gods prove obstinate, the victim is almost flayed alive.[2]

The Chinese are adepts at the art of taking the kingdom of heaven by storm. Sometimes they threaten and beat the god if he does not give rain.[3] So too when the Siamese need rain, they set out their idols in the blazing sun; but if they want dry weather, they unroof the temples and let the rain pour down on the idols. They think that the discomfort to which the gods are thus subjected will induce them to grant the wishes of their worshippers.[4]

The reader may smile at the meteorology of the Far East; but precisely similar methods of procuring rain have been resorted to in Christian Europe within our own life-time. By the end of April 1893 there was great distress in Sicily for lack of water. The drought had lasted six months. Every day the sun rose and set in a sky of cloudless blue. The gardens of the Conca d'Oro, which surround Palermo with a magnificent belt of verdure, were withering. Food was becoming scarce. The people were in great alarm. All the most approved methods of procuring rain had been tried without effect. At last the peasants began to lose patience. Most of the saints were banished. At Palermo they dumped St. Joseph in a garden to see the state of things for himself, and they swore to leave him there in the sun till rain fell. Other saints were turned, like naughty children, with their faces to the wall. Others again, stripped of their beautiful robes, were exiled far from their parishes, threatened, grossly insulted, ducked in horse-ponds. At Caltanisetta the golden wings of St. Michael the Archangel were torn from his shoulders and replaced with wings of pasteboard; his purple mantle was taken away and a clout wrapt about him instead. At Licata the patron saint, St. Angelo, fared even worse, for he was left without any garments at all; he was reviled, he was put in irons, he was threatened with drowning or hanging. "Rain or the rope!" roared the angry people at him, as they shook their fists in his face.[5]

52. *Stones* are often supposed to possess the property of bringing on rain, provided they be dipped in water or sprinkled with it, or treated in some other appropriate manner. In a Samoan village a certain stone was carefully housed as the representative of the rain-making god, and in time of drought his priests carried the stone in procession and dipped it in a stream.[1] Among the Ta-ta-thi tribe of New South Wales, the rain-maker breaks off a piece of quartz-crystal and spits it towards the sky; the rest of the crystal he wraps in emu feathers, soaks both crystal and feathers in water, and carefully hides them.[2] In the Keramin tribe of New South Wales the wizard retires to the bed of a creek, drops water on a round flat stone, then covers up and conceals it.[3] At Sagami in Japan there is a stone which draws down rain whenever water is poured on it.[4] In Behar people think to put an end to drought by keeping a holy stone named Náráyan-chakra in a vessel of water.[5] The Turks of Armenia make rain by throwing pebbles into the water. At Egin the pebbles are hung in two bags in the Euphrates; there should be seventy thousand and one of them.[6] At Myndus in Asia Minor the number of the stones used for this purpose is seventy-seven thousand, and each of them should be licked before it is cast into the sea.[7] In some parts of Mongolia, when the people desire rain, they fasten a bezoar stone to a willow twig, and place it in pure water, uttering incantations or prayers at the same time.[8]

In the Thana District of the Bombay Presidency, in order to procure rain, stones are taken out of a pool and worshipped. They are then carried to every house in the village, and water is poured upon them by the inmates.[8a]

53. But customs of this sort are not confined to the wilds of Africa and Asia or the torrid deserts of Australia and the New World. They have been practised in the cool air and under the grey skies of Europe. There is a fountain called Barenton, of romantic fame, in those "wild woods of Broceliande," where, if legend be true, the wizard Merlin still sleeps his magic slumber in the hawthorn shade. Thither the Breton peasants used to resort when they needed rain. They caught some of the water in a tankard and threw it on a slab near the spring.[1] On Snowdon there is a lonely tarn called Dulyn, or the Black Lake, lying "in a dismal dingle surrounded by high and dangerous rocks." A row of stepping-stones runs out into the lake, and if any one steps on the stones and throws water so as to wet the farthest stone, which is called the Red Altar, "it is but a chance that you do not get rain before night, even when it is hot weather."[2] In these cases it appears probable that, as in Samoa, the stone is regarded as more or less divine. This appears from the custom sometimes observed of dipping the cross in the Fountain of Barenton to procure rain, for this is plainly a Christian substitute for the old pagan way of throwing water on the stone.[3] At various places in France it is, or used till lately to be, the practice to dip the image of a saint in water as a means of procuring rain. Thus, beside the old priory of Commagny, a mile or two to the south-west of Moulins-Engilbert, there is a spring of St. Gervais, whither the inhabitants go in procession to obtain rain or fine weather according to the needs of the crops. In times of great drought they throw into the basin of the fountain an ancient stone image of the saint that stands in a sort of niche from which the fountain flows.[4] At Collobrières and Carpentras, both in Provence, a similar practice was observed with the images of St. Pons and St. Gens respectively.[5] In several villages of Navarre prayers for rain used to be offered to St. Peter, and by way of enforcing them the villagers carried the image of the saint in procession to the river, where they thrice invited him to reconsider his resolution and to grant their prayers; then, if he was still obstinate, they plunged him in the water, despite the remonstrances of the clergy, who pleaded with as much truth as piety that a simple caution or admonition administered to the image would produce an equally good effect. After this the rain was sure to fall within twenty-four hours.[6] Catholic countries do not enjoy a monopoly of making rain by ducking holy images in water. In Mingrelia, when the crops are suffering from want of rain, they take a particularly holy image and dip it in water every day till a shower falls;[7] and in the Far East the Shans drench the images of Buddha with water when the rice is perishing of drought.[8] In all such cases

and fears to be overtaken by darkness, he will sometimes take a piece of twine, loop it, and look through the loop at the sun. Then he pulls the loop into a knot and says: "Wait until we get home, and we will give you the fat of a pig." After that he passes the string to the man behind him, and then it is thrown away.[3] Jerome of Prague, travelling among the heathen Lithuanians early in the fifteenth century, found a tribe which worshipped the sun and venerated a large iron hammer. The priests told him that once the sun had been invisible for several months, because a powerful king had shut it up in a strong tower; but the signs of the zodiac had broken open the tower with that very hammer and released the sun.[4] When the Golos, a tribe of the Bahr-el-Ghazal, are on the march, they will sometimes take a stone or a small ant-heap, about the size of a man's head, and place it in the fork of a tree in order to retard the sunset.[5] South African natives in travelling will put a stone in a fork of a tree or place some grass on the path with a stone over it, believing that this will cause their friends to keep the meal waiting till their arrival.[6] In this, as in the previous examples, the purpose apparently is to retard the sun. On the other hand, to make it go down faster, the Australians throw sand into the air and blow with their mouths towards the sun,[7] perhaps to waft the lingering orb westward and bury it under the sands into which it appears to sink at night.

58. As some people imagine they can hasten the sun, so others fancy they can jog the tardy moon. The natives of German New Guinea reckon months by the moon, and some of them have been known to throw stones and spears at the moon, in order to accelerate its progress and so to hasten the return of their friends, who were away from home, for twelve months working on a tobacco plantation.[1] The Malays think that a bright glow at sunset may throw a weak person into a fever. Hence they attempt to extinguish the glow by spitting out water and throwing ashes at it.[2] The Shuswap Indians of British Columbia believe that they can bring on cold weather by burning the wood of a tree that has been struck by lightning. The belief may be based on the observation that in their country cold follows a thunderstorm. Hence in spring, when these Indians are travelling over the snow on high ground, they burn splinters of such wood in the fire in order that the crust of the snow may not melt.[3]

WIND

59. Once more, the savage thinks he can make the wind blow or be still. When the day is hot and a Yakut has a long way to go, he takes a stone which he has chanced to find in an animal or fish, winds a horse-hair several times round it, and ties it to a stick. He then waves the stick about, uttering a spell. Soon a cool breeze begins to blow.[1] In order to procure a cool wind for nine days the stone should first be dipped in the blood of a bird or beast and then presented to the sun, while the sorcerer makes three turns contrary to the course of the luminary.[2] The Wind clan of the Omahas flap their blankets to start a breeze which will drive away the mosquitoes.[3] When a Persian peasant desires a strong wind to winnow his corn, he rubs a kind of bastard saffron and throws it up into the air; after that the breeze soon begins to blow.[4] If a Cherokee wizard desires to turn aside an approaching storm he faces it and recites a spell with outstretched hand. Then he gently blows towards the quarter to which he wishes it to go, waving his hand in the same direction, as if he were pushing the storm away.[5] In Santa Cruz the wizard makes wind by waving the branch of a tree and chanting the appropriate charm.[6] The natives of the island of Bibili, off German New Guinea, are reputed to make wind by blowing with their mouths. In stormy weather the Bogadjim people say, "The Bibili folk are at it again, blowing away."[7] Another way of making wind which is practised in New Guinea is to strike a "wind-stone" lightly with a stick; to strike it hard would bring on a hurricane.[8] So in Scotland witches used to raise the wind by dipping a rag in water and beating it thrice on a stone, saying:

> "I knok this rag upone this stane
> To raise the wind in the divellis name,
> It sall not lye till I please againe."[9]

The Kwakiutl Indians of British Columbia, as we have seen, believe that twins can summon any wind by merely moving their hands.[10] In Greenland a woman in child-bed and for some time after delivery is supposed to possess the power of laying a storm. She has only to go out of doors, fill her mouth with air, and coming back into the house blow it out again.[11] Even in Christian times, under the reign of Constantine, a certain Sopater suffered death at Constantinople on a charge of binding the winds by magic, because it happened that the corn-ships of Egypt and Syria were detained afar off by calms or head-winds, to the rage and disappointment of the hungry Byzantine rabble.[12] Finnish wizards used to sell wind to storm-stayed mariners. The wind was enclosed in three knots; if they undid the first knot, a moderate wind sprang up; if the second, it blew half a gale; if the third, a hurricane.[13] Indeed the Esthonians, whose country is divided from Finland only by an arm of the sea, still believe in the magical powers of their northern neighbours. The bitter winds that blow in spring from the north and north-east, bringing ague and rheumatic inflammations in their train, are set down by the simple Esthonian peasantry to the machinations of the Finnish wizards and witches. In particular they regard with special dread three days in spring to which they give the name of Days of the Cross; one of them falls on the Eve of Ascension Day. The people in the neighbourhood of Fellin fear to go out on these days lest the cruel winds from Lappland should smite them dead. A popular Esthonian song runs:

MAGICIANS AS KINGS

62. The foregoing evidence may satisfy us that in many lands and many races magic has claimed to control the great forces of nature for the good of man. If that has been so, the practitioners of the art must necessarily be personages of importance and influence in any society which puts faith in their extravagant pretensions, and it would be no matter for surprise if, by virtue of the reputation which they enjoy and of the awe which they inspire, some of them should attain to the highest position of authority over their credulous fellows. In point of fact magicians appear to have often developed into chiefs and kings.

63. Among the tribes of Central Australia the headmen are public magicians. Further, their most important function is to take charge of the sacred storehouse, usually a cleft in the rocks or a hole in the ground, where are kept the holy stones and sticks (*churinga*) with which the souls of all the people, both living and dead, are apparently supposed to be in a manner bound up. Thus while the headmen have certainly to perform what we should call civil duties, such as to inflict punishment for breaches of tribal custom, their principal functions are sacred or magical.[1]

Again, in the tribes of South-Eastern Australia the headman was often, sometimes invariably, a magician. Thus in the southern Wiradjuri tribe the headman was always a wizard or a medicine-man. There was one for each local division. He called the people together for the initiation ceremonies or to discuss matters of public importance.[2] In the Yerkla-mining tribe the medicine-men are the headmen; they are called *Mobung-bai,* from *mobung,* "magic." They decide disputes, arrange marriages, conduct the ceremonies of initiation, and in certain circumstances settle the formalities to be observed in ordeals of battle. "In fact, they wield authority in the tribe, and give orders where others only make requests." Again, in the Yuin tribe there was a headman for each local division, and in order to be fitted for his office he had, among other qualifications, to be a medicine-man; above all he must be able to perform magical feats at the initiation ceremonies.[3] Similarly in New Guinea the *nepu* or sorcerers are everywhere. Nothing happens without the sorcerer's intervention: wars, marriages, diseases, deaths, expeditions, fishing, hunting—always and everywhere the sorcerer. The *nepu* is not a chieftain, but he dominates over the chiefs, and we may say that the true authority, the only effective influence in New Guinea, is that of the *nepu*.[4]

According to a native Melanesian account, the origin of the power of chiefs lies in the belief that they have communication with mighty ghosts (*tindalo*), and wield that supernatural power (*mana*) whereby they can bring the influence of ghosts to bear.[5] A chief in the island of Paramatta informed a European that he had the power of making rain, wind, storm, thunder, lightning, and dry weather. He exhibited as his magical instrument a piece of bamboo with some parti-colored rags attached to it.[6] In the Marshall Bennet Islands to the east of New Guinea it was the duty of each chief of a clan to charm the gardens of his clan so as to make them productive. The charm consisted in turning up part of the soil with a long stick and muttering an appropriate spell.[7]

64. Still rising in the scale of culture we come to Africa, where both the chieftainship and the kingship are fully developed; and here the evidence for the evolution of the chief out of the magician, and especially out of the rain-maker, is comparatively plentiful. The chiefs of the Wa-Taturu, a people of East Africa, are said to be nothing but sorcerers, destitute of any direct political influence;[1] while among the Wa-Gogo of German East Africa the main power of the chiefs, we are told, is derived from their art of rain-making.[2] Again, in the powerful Masai nation of the same region the medicine-men (*laibon*) are not uncommonly the chiefs, and the supreme chief of the race is almost invariably a powerful medicine-man.[3] The Suk and Turkana, two other peoples of British East Africa, distinguish between their chiefs and their medicine-men, who wield great power; but very often the medicine-man is a chief by virtue of his skill in medicine or the occult arts.[4]

65. So too among the tribes of the Upper Nile the medicine-men are generally the chiefs.[1] Their authority rests above all upon their supposed power of making rain, for "rain is the one thing which matters to the people in those districts, as if it does not come down at the right time it means untold hardships for the community. It is therefore small wonder that men more cunning than their fellows should arrogate to themselves the power of producing it, or that having gained such a reputation, they should trade on the credulity of their simpler neighbours."

Again, among the Bongo, a tribe of the same region, the influence of the chiefs is said to rest in great part on a belief in their magical powers; for

more especially for their tact in magic and mysteries, in which they all deal to a very great extent. . . . In all tribes their doctors are conjurors—are magicians—are sooth-sayers, and I had like to have said high-priests, inasmuch as they superintend and conduct all their religious ceremonies; they are looked upon by all as oracles of the nation. In all councils of war and peace, they have a seat with the chiefs, are regularly consulted before any public step is taken, and the greatest deference and respect is paid to their opinions."[1] Similarly in California "the shaman was, and still is, perhaps the most important individual among the Maidu. In the absence of any definite system of government, the word of a shaman has great weight: as a class they are regarded with much awe, and as a rule are obeyed much more than the chief."[2] Among the Yokuts, another tribe of Californian Indians, the rain-makers exercised great influence. One of them by his insinuating address, eloquence, and jugglery spread his fame for a distance of two hundred miles, and cunningly availed himself of two years of drought to levy contributions far and wide from the trembling Indians, who attributed to his magic the fall of the rain.[3]

72. In South America also the magicians or medicine-men seem to have been on the highroad to chieftainship or kingship. Among the Lengua Indians of the Gran Chaco, for instance, every clan has its cazique or chief, but he possesses little authority. In virtue of his office he has to make many presents, so he seldom grows rich and is generally more shabbily clad than any of his subjects. "As a matter of fact the magician is the man who has most power in his hands, and he is accustomed to receive presents instead of to give them." It is the magician's duty to bring down misfortune and plagues on the enemies of his tribe, and to guard his own people against hostile magic. For these services he is well paid and by them he acquires a position of great influence and authority.[1] Among the Indians of Guiana also the magician or medicine-man (*piai, peaiman*) is a personage of great importance. Every village has one such spiritual guardian, who is physician, priest, and magician in one. His influence is immense. No Indian dare refuse him anything he takes a fancy to, from a trifle of food to a man's wife.[2]

73. Throughout the Malay region the rajah or king is commonly regarded with superstitious veneration as the possessor of supernatural powers, and there are grounds for thinking that he too, like apparently so many African chiefs, has been developed out of a simple magician. At the present day the Malays firmly believe that the king possesses a personal influence over the works of nature, such as the growth of the crops and the bearing of fruit-trees. The same prolific virtue is supposed to reside, though in a lesser degree, in his delegates, and even in the persons of Europeans who chance to have charge of districts. Thus in Selangor, one of the native states of the Malay Peninsula, the success or failure of the rice crops is often attributed to a change of district officers.[1] The Toorateyas of southern Celebes hold that the prosperity of the rice depends on the behaviour of their princes, and that bad government, by which they mean a government which does not conform to ancient custom, will result in a failure of the crops.[2]

74. The Dyaks of Sarawak believed that their famous English ruler, Rajah Brooke, was endowed with a certain magical virtue which, if properly applied, could render the rice-crops abundant. Once when a European remarked that the rice-crops of the Samban tribe were thin, the chief immediately replied that they could not be otherwise since Rajah Brooke had never visited them, and he begged that Mr. Brooke be induced to come and thus remove the sterility of the land.[1]

75. The belief that kings possess magical or supernatural powers by virtue of which they can fertilise the earth and confer other benefits on their subjects would seem to have been shared by the ancestors of all the Aryan races from India to Ireland, and it has left clear traces of itself in our own country down to modern times. Thus the ancient Hindoo law-book called *The Laws of Manu* describes as follows the effects of a good king's reign: "In that country where the king avoids taking the property of mortal sinners, men are born in due time and are long-lived. And the crops of the husbandmen spring up, each as it was sown, and the children die not, and no misshaped offspring is born."[1] In Homeric Greece it was thought that the reign of a good king caused the earth to bring forth wheat and barley, the trees to be loaded with fruit, the flocks to multiply, and the sea to yield fish.[2] Conversely, when the crops failed, the Burgundians used to blame their kings and depose them; and, in the time of the Swedish king Domalde, when a mighty famine broke out, the chiefs decided that the king himself was the cause of the scarcity, wherefore they slew him and smeared with his blood the altars of the gods.[3]

76. Perhaps the last relic of such superstitions which lingered about our English kings was the notion that they could heal scrofula by their touch. The disease was accordingly known as the King's Evil. Queen Elizabeth often exercised this miraculous gift of healing. On Midsummer Day 1633, Charles the First cured a hundred patients at one swoop in the chapel royal at Holyrood.[1] But it was under his son Charles the Second that the practice seems to have attained its highest vogue. It is said that in the course of his reign the Merry Monarch touched nearly a hundred thousand persons for scrofula. The cool-headed William the Third contemptuously refused to lend himself to the hocus-pocus; and when his palace was besieged by the usual unsavoury crowd, he ordered them to be turned away with a dole. However, the practise was continued, as might have been expected, by the dull bigot James the Second[2] and his dull daughter Queen Anne. In his childhood Dr. Johnson was touched for scrofula by the Queen, and he always retained a faint but solemn recollection of her as of a lady in diamonds with a long black hood.[3]

The kings of France also claimed to possess the same gift of healing by touch, which they are said to have derived from Clovis or from St. Louis, just as English kings inherited it from Edward the Confessor.[4] Similarly, down to the nineteenth century the West African tribe of the Walos, in Senegal, ascribed to their royal family a like power of healing by touch;[5] and the savage chiefs of Tonga were believed to heal scrofula and cases of indurated liver by the touch of their feet. This last cure, it may be added, was strictly homoeopathic, for the disease as well as the cure was thought to be caused by contact with the royal person or with anything that belonged to it.[6]

KINGS AS INCARNATE

LIFE-SPIRITS

77. But it is not merely as priests—that is, as intercessors between god and man—that kings are revered. Often *they are themselves regarded as gods,* able to bestow upon their subjects those blessings which are usually sought only by prayer and sacrifice offered to superhuman and invisible beings. They are expected, for instance, to give rain and sunshine in due season, to make the crops grow, and so on. Strange as this may appear to us, it is quite of a piece with early modes of thought. A primitive hardly conceives the distinction commonly drawn by more advanced peoples between the natural and the supernatural. To him the world is to a great extent worked by supernatural agents, that is, by personal beings acting on impulses and motives like his own, liable like him to be moved by appeals to their pity, their hopes, and their fears. In a world so conceived he sees no limit to his power of influencing the course of nature to his own advantage. Prayers, promises, or threats may secure him fine weather and an abundant crop from the gods; and if a god should happen, as he sometimes believes, to become incarnate in his own person, he need appeal to no higher being; he, the primitive, then possesses in himself all the powers necessary to further his own well-being and that of his fellow-men.

78. The notion of a man-god, or of a human being endowed with divine or supernatural powers, belongs essentially to that earlier period of religious history in which gods and men are still viewed as beings of much the same order, and before they are divided by the impassable gulf which, to later thought, opens out between them. Strange, therefore, as may seem to us the idea of a god incarnate in human form, it has nothing very startling for early man, who sees in a man-god or a god-man only a higher degree of the same supernatural powers which he arrogates in perfect good faith to himself. Nor does he draw any very sharp distinction between a god and a powerful sorcerer. His gods, as we have seen, are often merely invisible magicians who behind the veil of nature work the same sort of charms and incantations which the human magician works in a visible and bodily form among his fellows. And as the gods are commonly believed to exhibit themselves in the likeness of men to their worshippers, it is easy for the magician, with his supposed miraculous powers, to acquire the reputation of being an incarnate deity. Thus beginning as little more than a simple conjurer, the medicine-man or magician tends to blossom out into a full-blown god and king in one. In speaking of him as a god, however, we must beware of importing into the savage conception of deity those very abstract and complex ideas which *we* attach to the term. When the savage uses his word for god, he has in his mind a being of a certain sort: when the civilised man uses his word for god, he has in his mind a being of a very different sort. If we civilised men insist on limiting the name of God to that particular conception of the divine nature which we ourselves have formed, then we must confess that the savage has no god at all. But we shall adhere more closely to the facts of history if we allow most of the higher savages at least to possess a rudimentary notion of certain supernatural beings who may fittingly be called gods, though not in the full sense in which we use the word.

Incarnate gods are common in rude society. The incarnation may be temporary or permanent. In the former case—where it is commonly known as inspiration or possession—it reveals itself in supernatural knowledge rather than in supernatural power. Its usual manifestations are divination and prophecy rather than miracles. On the other hand, when the incarnation is not merely temporary, the god-man is usually expected to vindicate his character by working miracles. Only we have to remember that by men at this stage of thought miracles are not considered as breaches of natural law. Not conceiving the existence of natural law, primitive man cannot conceive a breach of it. A miracle is to him merely an unusually striking manifestation of a common power.

79. The belief in temporary incarnation or inspiration is world-wide. Certain persons are supposed to be possessed from time to time by a spirit or deity; while the possession lasts, their own personality lies in abeyance, the presence of the spirit is revealed by convulsive shiverings and shakings of the man's whole body, by wild gestures and excited looks, all of which are referred, not to the man himself, but to the spirit which has entered into him; and in this abnormal state all his utterances are accepted as the voice of the indwelling god or spirit. Thus, for example, in the Sandwich Islands, the king, personating the god, uttered the responses of the oracle from his concealment in a frame of wicker-work. But in the southern islands of the Pacific the god "frequently entered the priest, who, inflated as it were with the divinity, ceased to act or speak as a voluntary agent, but moved and spoke as entirely under supernatural influence. In this respect there was a striking resemblance between the rude oracles of the Polynesians, and those of the celebrated nations of ancient Greece. As soon as the god was supposed to have entered the priest, the latter became violently agitated, and worked himself up to the highest pitch of apparent frenzy, the muscles of the limbs seemed convulsed, the body swelled, the countenance became terrific, the features distorted, and the eyes wild and strained. In this state he often rolled on the earth, foaming at the mouth, as if labouring under the influence of the divinity by whom he was possessed, and, in shrill cries, and violent and often indistinct sounds, revealed the will of the god. The priests, who were attending, and versed in the mysteries, received, and reported to the people, the declarations which had been thus received. When the priest had uttered the response of the oracle, the violent paroxysm gradually subsided, and comparative composure ensued. The god did not, however, always leave him as soon as the communication had been made. Sometimes the same *taura,* or priest, continued for two or three days possessed by the spirit or deity; a piece of a native cloth, of a peculiar kind, worn round one arm, was an indication of inspiration, or of the indwelling of the god with the individual who wore it. The acts of the man during this period were considered as those of the god, and hence the greatest attention was paid to his expressions, and the whole of his deportment. . . . When *uruhia,* (under the inspiration of the spirit,) the priest was always considered as sacred as the god, and was called, during this period, *atua,* god, though at other times only denominated *taura* or priest."[1]

80. But examples of such temporary inspiration are so common in every part of the world and are now so familiar through books on ethnology that it is needless to multiply illustrations of the general principle.[1] It may be well, however, to refer to two particular modes of producing temporary inspiration, because they are perhaps less known than some others, and because we shall have occasion to refer to them later on. One of these modes of producing inspiration is by sucking the fresh blood of a sacrificed victim. In the temple of Apollo Diradiotes at Argos, a lamb was sacrificed by night once a month; a woman, who had to observe a rule of chastity, tasted the blood of the lamb, and thus being inspired by the god she prophesied or divined.[2] At Aegira in Achaia the priestess of Earth drank the fresh blood of a bull before she descended into the cave to prophesy.[3] At Rhetra, a great religious capital of the Western Slavs, the priest tasted the blood of the sacrificed oxen and sheep in order the better to prophesy.[4] The true test of a Dainyal or diviner among some of the Hindu Kush tribes is to suck the blood from the neck of a decapitated goat.[5]

Thus in the Mandaya tribe of the Davao district on Mindanao, one of the Philippine Islands, there is in each community one or more persons, generally women, who are known as *ballyan.* These priestesses or mediums are versed in all the ceremonies and dances which their ancestors have found effectual in overcoming evil influences, and in retaining the favour of the spirits. When the women are about to give an oracle they place the images of the gods, made of a certain kind of wood, upon a small altar. A hog is brought. The chief priestess kills it with a dagger, and she and all the other women drink of the flowing blood, in order to attract the prophetic spirit to themselves, and to give their auguries or the supposed utterances of their gods. Scarcely have they drunk the blood when they become as though possessed by an infernal spirit which agitates them and makes them tremble as does the body of a person with the ague or like one who shivers with the cold.[5a] In the Mundjhulas, a subdivision of the Gandmhali tribe in the Central Provinces in India there are certain devotees of the goddess Somlai in Sambalpur, on whom the inspiration of the goddess descends, making them shake and roll their heads. When they are in this state they are believed to drink the blood flowing from goats sacrificed in the temple.[5b]

81. The other mode of producing temporary inspiration consists in the use of a sacred tree or plant. Thus in the Hindu Kush a fire is kindled with twigs of the sacred cedar; and the Dainyal or sibyl, with a cloth over her head, inhales the thick pungent smoke till she is seized with convulsions and falls senseless to the ground. Soon she rises and raises a shrill chant, which is caught up and loudly repeated by her audience.[1] So Apollo's prophetess ate the sacred laurel and was fumigated with it before she prophesied.[2] The Bacchanals ate ivy, and their inspired fury was by some believed to be due to the exciting and intoxicating properties of the plant.[3] In Uganda the priest, in order to be inspired by his god, smokes a pipe of tobacco fiercely till he works himself into a frenzy; the loud excited tones in which he then talks are recognised as the voice of the god speaking through him.[4] In Madura, an island off the north coast of Java, each spirit has its regular medium, who is oftener a woman than a man. To prepare herself for the reception of the spirit she inhales the fumes of incense, sitting with her head over a smoking censer. Gradually she falls into a sort of trance accompanied by shrieks, grimaces, and violent spasms. The spirit is now supposed to have entered into her, and when she grows calmer her words are regarded as oracular, being the utterances of the indwelling spirit, while her own soul is temporarily absent.[5]

82. The person temporarily inspired is believed to acquire not merely divine knowledge but also, at least occasionally, divine power. In Cambodia, when an epidemic breaks out, the inhabitants of several villages unite and go with a band of music at their head to look for the man whom the local god is supposed to have chosen for his temporary incarnation. When found, the man is conducted to the altar of the god where the mystery of incarnation takes place. Then the man becomes an object of veneration to his fellows, who implore him to protect the village against the plague.[1] A certain image of Apollo, which stood in a sacred cave at Hylae near Magnesia, was thought to impart superhuman strength. Sacred men, inspired by it, leaped down precipices, tore up huge trees by the roots, and carried them on their backs along the narrowest defiles.[2] The feats performed by inspired dervishes belong to the same class.

83. Thus far we have seen that the savage, failing to discern the limits of his ability to control nature, ascribes to himself and to all men certain powers which we should now call supernatural. Further, we have seen that, over and above this general supernaturalism, some persons are supposed to be inspired for short periods by a divine spirit, and thus temporarily to enjoy the knowledge and power of the indwelling deity. From beliefs like these it is an easy step to the conviction that certain men are permanently possessed by a deity, or in some other undefined way are endued with so high a degree of supernatural power as to be ranked as gods and to receive the homage of prayer and sacrifice. Sometimes these human gods are restricted to purely supernatural or spiritual functions. Sometimes they exercise supreme political power in addition. In the latter case they are kings as well as gods, and the government is a theocracy. Thus in the Marquesas or Washington Islands there was a class of men who were deified in their lifetime. They were supposed to wield a supernatural power over the elements; they could give abundant harvests or smite the ground with barrenness; and they could inflict disease or death. Human sacrifices were offered to them to avert their wrath. There were not many of them, at the most one or two in each island. They lived in mystic seclusion. Their powers were sometimes, but not always, hereditary. A missionary has described one of these human gods from personal observation. The god was a very old man who lived in a large house within an enclosure. In the house was a kind of altar, and on the beams of the house and on the trees round it were hung human skeletons, head down. No one entered the enclosure except the persons dedicated to the service of the god; only on days when human victims were sacrificed might ordinary people penetrate into the precinct. This human god received more sacrifices than all the other gods; often he would sit on a sort of scaffold in front of his house and call for two or three human victims at a time. They were always brought, for the terror he inspired was extreme. He was invoked all over the island, and offerings were sent to him from every side.[1] In the Pelew Islands it is thought that every god can take possession of a man and speak through him. The possession may be either temporary or permanent; in the latter case the chosen person is called a *korong*. The god is free in his choice, so the position of *korong* is not hereditary. After the death of a *korong* the god is for some time unrepresented, until he suddenly makes his appearance in a new Avatar. The person thus chosen gives signs of the divine presence by behaving in a strange way; he gapes, runs about, and performs a number of senseless acts. At first people laugh at him, but his sacred mission is in time recognised, and he is invited to assume his proper position in the state. Generally this position is a distinguished one and confers on him a powerful influence over the whole community. In some of the islands the god is political sovereign of the land; and hence his new incarnation, however humble his origin, is raised to the same high rank, and rules, as god and king, over all the other chiefs.[2]

84. The ancient Egyptians, far from restricting their adoration to cats and dogs and such small deer, very liberally extended it to men. One of these human deities resided at the village of Anabis, and burnt sacrifices were offered to him on the altars; after which, says Porphyry, he would eat his dinner just as if he were an ordinary mortal.[1] In classical antiquity the Sicilian philosopher Empedocles gave himself out to be not merely a wizard but a god. He asserted that he could teach his disciples how to make the wind blow or be still, the rain to fall and the sun to shine, how to banish sickness and old age, and to raise the dead.[3]

85. The ancient Germans sometimes worshipped women as true and living goddesses. For example, in the reign of Vespasian a certain Veleda, of the tribe of the Bructeri, was commonly held to be a deity, and in that character reigned over her people, her sway being acknowledged far and wide. She lived in a tower on the river Lippe, a tributary of the Rhine. When the people of Cologne sent to make a treaty with her, the ambassadors were not admitted to her presence; the negotiations were conducted through a minister, who acted as the mouthpiece of her divinity and reported her oracular utterances.[1] So too among the Getae, down to the beginning of our era, there was always a man who personified a god and was called God by the people. He dwelt on a sacred mountain and acted as adviser to the king.[2]

86. Among the Barotse, a tribe on the upper Zambesi, there is an old but waning belief that a chief is a demigod, and in heavy thunderstorms the Barotse flock to his yard for protection from lightning.[1] The chief of Urua, a large region to the west of Lake Tanganyika, "arrogates to himself divine honours and power and pretends to abstain from food for days without feeling its necessity; and, indeed, declares that as a god he is altogether above requiring food and only eats, drinks, and smokes for the pleasure it affords him."[2] Among the Gallas, when a woman grows tired of the chores of housekeeping, she begins to talk incoherently and to demean herself extravagantly. This is a sign of the descent of the holy spirit Callo upon her. Immediately her husband prostrates himself and adores her; she ceases to bear the humble title of wife and is called "Lord"; domestic duties have no further claim on her, and her will is a divine law.[3]

The king of Loango is honoured by his people "as though he were a god; and he is called Sambee and Pango, which mean god. They believe that he can let them have rain when he likes; and once a year, in December, which is the time they want rain, the people come to beg of him to grant it to them." On this occasion the king, standing on his throne, shoots an arrow into the air,

which is supposed to bring on rain.[4] Much the same is said of the king of
Mombasa.[5] Down to a few years ago, when his spiritual reign on earth was
brought to an abrupt end by the carnal weapons of English marines and blue-
jackets, the king of Benin was the chief object of worship in his dominions.
"He occupies a higher post here than the Pope does in Catholic Europe; for
he is not only God's vicegerent upon earth, but a god himself, whose subjects
both obey and adore him as such, although I believe their adoration to arise
rather from fear than love."[6] The king of Iddah told the English officers of the
Niger Expedition, "God made me after his own image; I am all the same as
God; and he appointed me a king."[7]

87. Among the Hovas and other tribes of Madagascar there is said to be a
deep sense of the divinity of kings; and down to the acceptance of Christianity
in the nineteenth century, the Hova sovereigns were regularly called "the
visible God" and other terms of similar import were also applied to them.[1]
Similarly, the king whom the Sakkalava of the north often call also *Zanahari
antani,* God on earth, is surrounded by them with a veneration which resembles idolatry.[2]

88. There is no word in the Siamese language by which any creature of
higher rank or greater dignity than a monarch can be described; and the missionaries, when they speak of God, are forced to use the native word for
king.[1]

89. But perhaps no country in the world has been so prolific of human gods
as India; nowhere has the divine grace been poured out in a more liberal
measure on all classes of society from kings down to milkmen. Thus amongst
the Todas, a pastoral people of the Neilgherry Hills of southern India, the
dairy is a sanctuary, and the milkman who attends to it has been described as
a god. On being asked whether the Todas salute the sun, one of these divine
milkmen replied, "Those poor fellows do so, but I," tapping his chest, "I, a
God! why should I salute the sun?" Every one, even his own father, prostrates
himself before the milkman, and no one would dare to refuse him anything.
No human being, except another milkman, may touch him; and he gives
oracles to all who consult him, speaking with the voice of a god.[1]

Further, in India "every king is regarded as little short of a present god."[2]
The Hindu law-book of Manu goes farther and says that "even an infant king
must not be despised from an idea that he is a mere mortal; for he is a great
deity in human form."[3] There is said, indeed, to have been a sect in Orissa
that worshipped Queen Victoria as their chief divinity; and another in the
Punjab which adored, under the divine name of Nikkal Sen, the redoubtable
General Nicholson![4]

90. Sometimes, at the death of the human incarnation, the divine spirit
transmigrates into another man. In Bhotan the spiritual head of the government is a dignitary called the Dhurma Rajah, who is supposed to be a perpetual incarnation of the deity. At his death the new incarnate god shews him-

self in an infant by the refusal of his mother's milk and a preference for that of a cow.[1]

The Buddhist Tartars believe in a great number of living Buddhas, who officiate as Grand Lamas at the head of the most important monasteries. When one of these Grand Lamas dies his disciples do not sorrow, for they know that he will soon reappear, being born in the form of an infant. Their only anxiety is to discover the place of his birth. If at this time they see a rainbow they take it as a sign sent them by the departed Lama to guide them to his cradle.[2]

At the head of Taoism, the most numerous religious sect of China, is a pope who goes by the name of the Heavenly Master and is believed to be an incarnation and representative on earth of the god of heaven. His official title is *Chên-yen,* or "the True Man." When one of these pontiffs or incarnate deities departs this life, his soul passes into a male member of his family, the ancient house of Chang.[3]

91. From our survey of the religious position occupied by the king in rude societies we may infer that the claim to divine and supernatural powers put forward by the monarchs of great historical empires like those of Egypt, China, Mexico, and Peru, was not the simple outcome of inflated vanity or the empty expression of a grovelling adulation; it was merely a survival and extension of the old savage apotheosis of living kings. Thus, for example, as children of the Sun the Incas of Peru were revered like gods; they could do no wrong, and no one dreamed of offending against the person, honour, or property of the monarch or of any of the royal race. Hence, too, the Incas did not, like most people, look on sickness as an evil. They considered it a messenger sent from their father the Sun to call them to come and rest with him in heaven. Therefore the usual words in which an Inca announced his approaching end were these: "My father calls me to come and rest with him." They would not oppose their father's will by offering sacrifice for recovery, but openly declared that he had called them to his rest.[1] Issuing from the sultry valleys upon the lofty tableland of the Colombian Andes, the Spanish conquerors were astonished to find, in contrast to the savage hordes they had left in the sweltering jungles below, a people enjoying a fair degree of civilisation, practising agriculture, and living under a government which Humboldt has compared to the theocracies of Tibet and Japan. These were the Chibchas, Muyscas, or Mozcas, divided into two kingdoms, with capitals at Bogata and Tunja, but united apparently in spiritual allegiance to the high pontiff of Sogamozo or Iraca. By a long and ascetic novitiate, this ghostly ruler was reputed to have acquired such sanctity that the waters and the rain obeyed him, and the weather depended on his will.[2]

92. In China, if the emperor is not himself worshipped as a deity, he is nevertheless supposed by his subjects to be the lord and master of the gods; while in Japan, the Mikado was held to be an incarnation of the sun-goddess.

Once a year all the gods wait upon him, and spend a month at his court; and the name of that month is "without gods."[1]

93. The early Babylonian kings claimed to be gods in their lifetime;[1] while the Parthian monarchs of the Arsacid dynasty styled themselves brothers of the sun and moon and were worshipped as deities. It was esteemed sacrilege to strike even a private member of the Arsacid family in a brawl.[2]

The kings of Egypt were deified in their lifetime, sacrifices were offered to them, and their worship was celebrated in special temples and by special priests. Indeed the worship of the kings sometimes cast that of the gods into the shade. Thus in the reign of Merenra a high official declared that he had built many holy places in order that the spirits of the king, the ever-living Merenra, might be invoked "more than all the gods."[3] "It has never been doubted that the king claimed actual divinity; he was the 'great god,' the 'golden Horus,' and son of Ra. He claimed authority not only over Egypt, but over 'all lands and nations,' 'the whole world in its length and its breadth, the east and the west,' 'the entire compass of the great circuit of the sun,' 'the sky and what is in it, the earth and all that is upon it,' 'every creature that walks upon two or upon four legs, all that fly or flutter, the whole world offers her productions to him.' Whatever in fact might be asserted of the Sun-god, was dogmatically predicable of the king of Egypt. His titles were directly derived from those of the sun-god."[4] "In the course of his existence," we are told, "the king of Egypt exhausted all the possible conceptions of divinity which the Egyptians had framed for themselves. A superhuman god by his birth and by his royal office, he became the deified man after his death. Thus all that was known of the divine was summed up in him."[5] "The divinity of the king was recognised in all the circumstances of the public life of the sovereign. It was not enough to worship Pharaoh in the temple; beyond the limits of the sanctuary he remained the 'good god' to whom all men owed a perpetual adoration. The very name of the sovereign was sacred like his person; people swore by his name as by that of the gods, and he who took the oath in vain was punished."[6]

In the House of Commons under Elizabeth it was openly asserted "that absolute princes, such as the sovereigns of England, were a species of divinity."[6a]

DEPARTMENTAL KINGS

OF NATURE

94. *Neither his location nor his title allows us to suppose that the King of the Wood at Nemi had ever been a king in the common sense of the word. More likely he was a king of nature, and of a special side of nature, namely, the woods from which he took his title.* Instances of such departmental kings are not wanting.

95. On a hill at Bomma near the mouth of the Congo dwells Namvulu Vumu, King of the Rain and Storms.[1] Of some of the tribes on the Upper Nile we are told that they have no kings in the common sense; the only persons whom they acknowledge as such are the Kings of the Rain, *Mata Kodou,* who are credited with the power of giving rain at the proper time, that is in the rainy season. So, when the end of March draws on, each householder betakes himself to the King of the Rain and offers him a cow that he may make the blessed waters of heaven to drip on the brown and withered pastures. If no shower falls, the people assemble and demand that the king shall give them rain; and if the sky still continues cloudless, they rip up his belly, in which he is believed to keep the storms.[2]

Among tribes on the outskirts of Abyssinia a similar office exists and has been thus described by an observer: "The priesthood of the Alfai, as he is called by the Barea and Kunama, is a remarkable one; he is believed to be able to make rain. This office formerly existed among the Algeds and appears to be still common to the Nuba Negroes. The Alfai of the Barea, who is also consulted by the northern Kunama, lives near Tembadere on a mountain alone with his family. The people bring him tribute in the form of clothes and fruits, and cultivate for him a large field of his own. He is a kind of king, and his office passes by inheritance to his brother or sister's son. He is supposed to conjure down rain and to drive away the locusts. But if he disappoints the people's expectation and a great drought arises in the land, the Alfai is stoned to death, and his nearest relations are obliged to cast the first stone at him."[3]

96. In the backwoods of Cambodia live two mysterious sovereigns known as the King of the Fire and the King of the Water. Their royal functions are of a purely mystic or spiritual order; they have no political authority; they are simple peasants, living by the sweat of their brow and the offerings of the faithful. According to one account they live in absolute solitude, never meeting each other and never seeing a human face. They inhabit successively seven towers perched upon seven mountains, and every year they pass from one tower to another. People come furtively and cast within their reach what is needful for their subsistence. The kingship lasts seven years, the time necessary to inhabit all the towers successively; but many die before their time is out. The offices are hereditary in one or (according to others) two royal families, who enjoy high consideration, have revenues assigned to them, and are exempt from the necessity of tilling the ground. But naturally the dignity is not coveted, and when a vacancy occurs, all eligible men (they must be strong and have children) flee and hide themselves.

Like many other sacred kings, of whom we shall read in the sequel, the Kings of Fire and Water are not allowed to die a natural death, for that would lower their reputation. Accordingly when one of them is seriously ill, the elders hold a consultation and if they think he cannot recover they stab him to death. His body is burned and the ashes are piously collected and publicly honoured for five years. Part of them is given to the widow, and she keeps them in an urn, which she must carry on her back when she goes to weep on her husband's grave.

A reason for confining the royal dignity to the same family is that this family is in possession of certain famous talismans which would lose their virtue or disappear if they passed out of the family. These talismans are three: the fruit of a creeper called *Cui,* gathered ages ago at the time of the last deluge, but still fresh and green; a rattan, also very old but bearing flowers that never fade; and lastly, a sword containing a *Yan* or spirit, who guards it constantly and works miracles with it. The spirit is said to be that of a slave, whose blood chanced to fall upon the blade while it was being forged, and who died a voluntary death to expiate his involuntary offence. By means of the two former talismans the Water King can raise a flood that would drown the whole earth. If the Fire King draws the magic sword a few inches from its sheath, the sun is hidden and men and beasts fall into a profound sleep; were he to draw it quite out of the scabbard, the world would come to an end. To this wondrous brand sacrifices of buffaloes, pigs, fowls, and ducks are offered for rain. It is kept swathed in cotton and silk; and amongst the annual presents sent by the King of Cambodia were rich stuffs to wrap the sacred sword.[1]

These, then, are examples of what I have called departmental kings of nature. But it is a far cry to Italy from the forests of Cambodia and the sources of the Nile. And though Kings of Rain, Water, and Fire have been found, we have still to discover a King of the Wood to match the Arician priest who bore that title. Perhaps we shall find him, or at least survivals of him, nearer home—to wit, in such figures of European popular custom as the May King, Jack o' the Green, and the like. To understand such figures, however, we must first address ourselves to the wider question of the embodiment of the spirit of fertility in trees and foliage.

TREES AS EMBODIMENTS OF THE LIFE-SPIRIT

97. From the earliest times the worship of trees has played an important part in the religious life of European peoples. And, indeed, nothing could be more natural. For at the dawn of history Europe was covered with immense primaeval forests, in which the scattered clearings must have appeared like islets in an ocean of green. Down to the first century before our era the Hercynian forest stretched eastward from the Rhine for a distance at once vast and unknown; Germans whom Caesar questioned had travelled for two months through it without reaching the end.[1] In England, the wealds of Kent, Surrey, and Sussex are remnants of the great forest of Anderida, which once clothed the whole of the south-eastern portion of the island. Westward it seems to have stretched till it joined another forest that extended from Hampshire to Devon. In the forest of Arden it was said that down to modern times a squirrel might leap from tree to tree for nearly the whole length of Warwickshire.[2] The excavation of ancient pile-villages in the valley of the Po has shewn that long before the rise and probably the foundation of Rome the north of Italy was covered with dense woods of elms, chestnuts, and especially of oaks.[3] Archaeology is here confirmed by history; for classical writers contain many references to Italian forests which have now disappeared.[4] As late as the fourth century before our era Rome was divided from central Etruria by the dreaded Ciminian forest, which Livy compares to the woods of Germany. No merchant, if we may trust the Roman historian, had ever penetrated its pathless solitudes.[5] In Greece beautiful woods of pine, oak, and other trees still linger on the slopes of the high Arcadian mountains, still adorn with their verdure the deep gorge through which the Ladon hurries to join the sacred Alpheus; and were still, down to a few years ago, mirrored in the dark blue waters of the lonely lake of Pheneus; but they are mere fragments of the forests which clothed great tracts in antiquity, and which at a more remote epoch may have spanned the Greek peninsula from sea to sea.[6]

98. From an examination of the Teutonic words for "temple" Grimm has made it probable that amongst the Germans the oldest sanctuaries were natural woods.[1] However this may be, tree-worship is well attested for all the great European families of the Aryan stock. Amongst the Celts the oak-worship of the Druids is familiar to every one.[2] Sacred groves were common among the ancient Germans, and tree-worship is hardly extinct amongst their descendants at the present day.[3] How serious that worship was in former times may be gathered from the ferocious penalty appointed by the old German laws for such as dared to peel the bark of a standing tree. The culprit's navel was to be cut out and nailed to the part of the tree which he had peeled, and he was to be driven round and round the tree till all his guts were wound about its trunk.[4] The intention of the punishment clearly was to replace the dead bark by a living substitute taken from the culprit; it was a life for a life, the life of a man for the life of a tree. At Upsala, the old religious capital of Sweden, there was a sacred grove in which every tree was regarded as divine.[5] The heathen Slavs worshipped trees and groves. The Lithuanians were not converted to Christianity till towards the close of the fourteenth century, and amongst them at the date of their conversion the worship of trees was prominent. Some of them revered remarkable oaks and other great shady trees, from which they received oracular responses. Some maintained holy groves about their villages or houses, where even to break a twig would have been a sin. They thought that he who cut a bough in such a grove either died suddenly or was crippled in one of his limbs.[6] Proofs of the prevalence of tree-worship in ancient Greece and Italy are abundant.[7] In the sanctuary of Aesculapius at Cos, for example, it was forbidden to cut down the cypress-trees under a penalty of a thousand drachms.[8] But nowhere, perhaps, in the ancient world was this antique form of religion better preserved than in the heart of the great metropolis itself. In the Forum, the busy centre of Roman life, the sacred fig-tree of Romulus was worshipped down to the days of the empire, and the withering of its trunk was enough to spread consternation through the city.[9] Again, on the slope of the Palatine Hill grew a cornel-tree which was esteemed one of the most sacred objects in Rome. Whenever the tree appeared to a passer-by to be drooping, he set up a hue and cry which was echoed by the people in the street, and soon a crowd might be seen running helter-skelter from all sides with buckets of water, as if (says Plutarch) they were hastening to put out a fire.[10]

Among the tribes of the Finnish-Ugrian stock in Europe the heathen worship was performed for the most part in sacred groves, which were always enclosed with a fence. Such a grove often consisted merely of a glade or clearing with a few trees dotted about, upon which in former times the skins of the sacrificial victims were hung. The central point of the grove, at least among the tribes of the Volga, was the sacred tree, beside which everything else sank into insignificance. Before it the worshippers assembled and the priest offered his prayers, at its roots the victim was sacrificed, and its boughs sometimes served as a pulpit. No wood might be hewn and no branch broken in the grove, and women were generally forbidden to enter it. The Ostyaks and Woguls, two peoples of the Finnish-Ugrian stock in Siberia, had also sacred groves in which nothing might be touched, and where the skins of the sacrificed animals were suspended; but these groves were not enclosed with fences.[11]

99. But it is necessary to examine in some detail the notions on which the worship of trees and plants is based. To the savage the world in general is animate, and trees and plants are no exception to the rule. He thinks that they have souls like his own, and he treats them accordingly. "They say," writes the ancient vegetarian Porphyry, "that primitive men led an unhappy life, for their superstition did not stop at animals but extended even to plants. For why should the slaughter of an ox or a sheep be a greater wrong than the felling of a fir or an oak, seeing that a soul is implanted in these trees also?"[1] Similarly, the Hidatsa Indians of North America believe that every natural object has its spirit, or to speak more properly, its shade. To these shades some consideration or respect is due, but not equally to all. For example, the shade of the cottonwood, the greatest tree in the valley of the Upper Missouri, is supposed to possess an intelligence which, if properly approached, may help the Indians in certain undertakings; but the shades of shrubs and grasses are of little account.[2] In the Yasawu islands of Fiji a man will never eat a coco-nut without first asking its leave—"May I eat you, my chief?"[3] The Dyaks ascribe souls to trees, and do not dare to cut down an old tree. In some places, when an old tree has been blown down, they set it up, smear it with blood, and deck it with flags "to appease the soul of the tree."[4] According to Chinese belief, the spirits of plants are never shaped like plants but have commonly the form either of human beings or of animals, for example bulls and serpents. Occasionally at the felling of a tree the tree-spirit has been seen to rush out in the shape of a blue bull.[5]

100. If trees are animate, they are necessarily sensitive. When an oak is being felled "it gives a kind of shriekes or groanes, that may be heard a mile off, as if it were the genius of the oake lamenting."[1] The Ojibways "very seldom cut down green or living trees, from the idea that it puts them to pain, and some of their medicine-men profess to have heard the wailing of the trees under the axe."[2] Trees that bleed and utter cries of pain or indignation when they are hacked or burned occur very often in Chinese books, even in Standard Histories.[3] Old peasants in some parts of Austria still believe that forest-trees are animate, and will not allow an incision to be made in the bark without special cause; they have heard from their fathers that the tree feels the cut not less than a wounded man his hurt. In felling a tree they beg its pardon.[4] It is said that in the Upper Palatinate also old woodmen still secretly ask a fine, sound tree to forgive them before they cut it down.[5] So in Jarkino the woodman craves pardon of the tree he fells.[6] Among the Tigre-speaking tribes in the north of Abyssinia people are afraid to fell a green and fruit-bearing tree lest they incur the curse of God, which is heard in the groaning of the tree as it sinks to the ground. But if a man is bold enough to cut down such a tree, he will say to it, "Thy curse abide in thee," or he will allege that it was not he but an elephant or a rhinoceros that knocked it down.[7] Before a Karo Batak cuts down a tree, he will offer it betel and apologies; and if in passing the place afterwards he should see the tree weeping or, as we should say, exuding sap, he hastens to console it by sprinkling the blood of a fowl on the stump.[8]

With regard to the Kiwai of British New Guinea we are told that "even nowadays, when provided with iron axes, they show great reluctance in felling certain large trees, particularly if the tree stands by itself or is conspicuous in some other way. Such a tree is thought to be inhabited by one of the *etengena*, a group of sylvan beings. If it is necessary to cut down some tree in which an *etengena* may dwell, the being must be asked to remove to some other tree suggested to it. After a few days the man returns and prepares to begin the cutting, but if his arms feel very heavy so that he can hardly lift them, this is a sign that the *entengena* has not yet moved from the tree and has passed into his arms to prevent the felling of the tree."[8a]

101. The conception of trees and plants as animated beings naturally results in treating them as male and female, who can be married to each other in a real, and not merely a figurative or poetical sense of the word. For example, if a Hindu has planted a grove of mangos, neither he nor his wife may taste of the fruit until he has formally married one of the trees, as a bridegroom, to a tree of a different sort, commonly a tamarind-tree, which grows near it in the grove. If there is no tamarind to act as bride, a jasmine will serve the turn.[1] On Christmas Eve German peasants used to tie fruit-trees together with straw ropes to make them bear fruit, saying that the trees were thus married.[2] In the Moluccas, when the clove-trees are in blossom, they are treated like pregnant women. No noise may be made near them; no light or fire may be carried past them at night; no one may approach them with his hat on, lest the tree be alarmed and bear no fruit, or drop its fruit too soon, like the untimely delivery of a women who has been frightened in her pregnancy.[3] In some districts of Western Borneo there must be no talk of corpses or demons in the fields, else the spirit of the growing rice would be frightened and flee away to Java.[4] The Toboongkoos of Central Celebes will not fire a gun in a rice-field, lest the rice should be frightened away.[5] The Chams of Binh-Thuan, in Cochin-China, do not dare to touch the rice in the granary at mid-day, because the rice is then asleep, and it would be both rude and dangerous to disturb its noonday slumber.[6]

102. Sometimes it is the souls of the dead that are believed to animate trees. The Dieri tribe of South Australia regard as very sacred certain trees which are supposed to be their fathers transformed; hence they speak with reverence of those trees and take care not to cut them down or burn them.[1] The natives of Bontoc, a province in the north of Luzon, cut down the woods near their villages, but leave a few fine trees standing as the abode of the spirits of their ancestors (*anitos*); and they honour the spirits by depositing food under the trees.[2] The Dyaks believe that when a man dies by accident, as by drowning, it is a sign that the gods mean to exclude him from the realms of bliss. Accordingly his body is not buried, but carried into the forest and there laid down. The souls of such unfortunates pass into trees or animals or fish, and are much dreaded by the Dyaks, who abstain from using kinds of wood, or eating certain sorts of fish, because they are supposed to contain the souls of the dead.[3]

In Korea the souls of people who die of the plague or by the roadside, and of women who expire in childbed, invariably take up their abode in trees.[4] Among the Miao-Kia, an aboriginal race of southern and western China, a sacred tree stands at the entrance of every village, and the inhabitants believe that it is tenanted by the soul of their first ancestor and that it rules their destiny.[5] Among the Maraves of Southern Africa the burial-ground is always regarded as a holy place where neither a tree may be felled nor a beast killed, because everything is supposed to be tenanted by the souls of ancestors.[6] The Lkuñgen Indians of British Columbia fancy that trees are transformed men, and that the creaking of the branches in the wind is their voice.[7] A tree that grows on a grave is regarded by the South Slavonian peasant as a sort of fetish. Whoever breaks a twig from it hurts the soul of the dead, but gains thereby a magic wand, since the soul embodied in the twig will be at his service.[8] This reminds us of the story of Polydorus in Virgil,[9] and of the bleeding pomegranate that grew on the grave of the fratricides Eteocles and Polynices at Thebes.[10]

103. In most, if not all, of these cases the spirit is viewed as incorporate in the tree; it animates the tree and must suffer and die with it. But, according to another and probably later opinion, the tree is not the body, but merely the abode of the tree-spirit, which can quit it and return to it at pleasure. The inhabitants of Siaoo, an island of the Sangi group in the East Indies, believe in certain sylvan spirits who dwell in forests or in great solitary trees. At full moon the spirit comes forth from his lurking-place and roams about. He has a big head, very long arms and legs, and a ponderous body. In order to propitiate the wood-spirits people bring offerings of food, fowls, goats, and so forth to the places which they are supposed to haunt.[1] On the Tanga coast of East Africa mischievous sprites reside in great trees, especially in the fantastically shaped baobabs. Sometimes they appear in the shape of ugly black beings, but as a rule they enter unseen into people's bodies, from which, after causing much sickness and misery, they have to be cast out by the sorcerer.[2] The Warramunga tribe of Central Australia believe that certain trees are the abode of disembodied human spirits waiting to be born again. No woman will strike one of these trees with an axe, lest the blow might disturb one of the spirits, who might come forth from the tree and enter her body.[3] In the Galla region of East Africa, where the vegetation is magnificent, there are many sacred trees, the haunts of jinn. In many Galla tribes women may not tread on the shadow of sacred trees or even approach the trees.[4]

104. Not a few ceremonies observed at cutting down haunted trees are based on the belief that the spirits have it in their power to quit the trees at pleasure or in case of need. Thus when the Pelew Islanders are felling a tree, they conjure the spirit of the tree to leave it and settle on another.[1] The wily Negro of the Slave Coast, who wishes to fell an *ashorin* tree, but knows that he cannot do it so long as the spirit remains in the tree, places a little palm-oil on the ground as a bait, and then, when the unsuspecting spirit has quitted the tree to partake of this dainty, hastens to cut down its late abode.[2] When the Toboongkoos of Central Celebes are about to clear a piece of forest in order to plant rice, they build a tiny house and furnish it with tiny clothes and some food and gold. Then they call together all the spirits of the wood, offer them the little house with its contents, and beseech them to quit the spot. After that they may safely cut down the wood without fearing to wound themselves in so doing.[3]

The Sundanese of the Eastern Archipelago drive golden or silver nails into the trunk of a sacred tree for the sake of expelling the tree-spirit before they hew down his abode.[4] They seem to think that, though the nails will hurt him, his vanity will be soothed by the reflection that they are of gold or silver. In Rotti, an island to the south of Timor, when they fell a tree to make a coffin, they sacrifice a dog as compensation to the tree-spirit whose property they are thus making free with.[5] Before the Gayos of Northern Sumatra clear a piece of forest for the purpose of planting tobacco or sugar-cane, they offer a quid of betel to the spirit whom they call the Lord of the Wood, and beg his leave to quarter themselves on his domain.[6] When the Tagales of the Philippines are about to fell a tree which they believe to be inhabited by a spirit, they excuse themselves to the spirit, saying: "The priest has ordered us to do it; the fault is not ours, nor the will either."[7]

Before they cut down a great tree, the Indians in the neighborhood of Santiago Tepehuacan hold a festival in order to appease it.[8] So too when the Dyaks fell the jungle on the hills, they often leave a few trees standing on the hilltops as a refuge for the dispossessed tree-spirits.[9]

105. Even where no mention is made of wood-spirits, we may generally assume that when trees or groves are sacred and inviolable, it is because they are believed to be either inhabited or animated by sylvan deities. In Central India the *bar* tree (*Ficus Indica*) and the *pipal* (*Ficus religiosa*) are sacred, and every child learns the saying that "it is better to die a leper than pluck a leaf of a *pipal,* and he who can wound a *bar* will kick his little sister."[1] In Livonia there is a sacred grove in which, if any man fells a tree or breaks a branch, he will die within the year.[2] The Wotyaks have sacred groves. A Russian who ventured to hew a tree in one of them fell sick and died next day.[3] The heathen Cheremiss of South-Eastern Russia have sacred groves, and woe to him who dares to fell one of the holy trees. If the author of the sacrilege is unknown, they take a cock or a goose, torture it to death and then throw it on the fire, while they pray to the gods to punish the sinner and cause him to perish like the bird.[4] So in the island of Skye some two hundred and fifty years ago there was a holy lake, "surrounded by a fair wood, which none presumes to cut"; and those who ventured to infringe its sanctity by breaking even a twig either sickened on the spot or were visited afterwards by "some signal inconvenience."[5]

106. In classical art the sylvan deities are depicted in human shape, their woodland character being denoted by a branch or some equally obvious symbol.[1] But this change of shape does not affect the essential character of the tree-spirit. The powers which he exercised as a tree-soul incorporate in a tree, he still continues to wield as a god of trees. Trees considered as animate beings are credited with the power of making the rain to fall, the sun to shine, flocks and herds to multiply, and women to bring forth easily; and, the very same powers are attributed to tree-gods conceived as anthropomorphic beings or as actually incarnate in living men. When the missionary Jerome of Prague was persuading the heathen Lithuanians to fell their sacred groves, a multitude of women besought the Prince of Lithuania to stop him, saying that with the woods he was destroying the house of god from which they had been wont to get rain and sunshine.[2] The Mundaris in Assam think that if a tree in the sacred grove is felled the sylvan gods evince their displeasure by withholding rain.[3] In Cambodia each village or province has its sacred tree, the abode of a spirit. If the rains are late the people sacrifice to the tree.[4] In time of drought the elders of the Wakamba in East Africa assemble and take a calabash of cider and a goat to a baobab-tree, where they kill the goat but do not eat it.[5] When Ovambo women go out to sow corn they take with them in the basket of seed two green branches of a particular kind of tree (*Peltophorum africanum Sond.*), one of which they plant in the field along with the first seed sown. The branch is believed to have the power of attracting rain; hence in one of the native dialects the tree goes by the name of the "rain-bush."[6] Among the Mundaris every village has its sacred grove, and "the grove deities are held responsible for the crops, and are especially honoured at all the great agricultural festivals."[7] The Negroes of the Gold Coast are in the habit of sacrificing at the foot of certain tall trees, and they think that if one of these were felled all the fruits of the earth would perish.[8]

The same idea comes out in the German and French custom of the Harvest-May. This is a large branch or a whole tree, which is decked with ears of corn, brought home on the last waggon from the harvest-field, and fastened on the roof of the farmhouse or of the barn, where it remains for a year. Mannhardt has proved that this branch or tree embodies the tree-spirit conceived as the spirit of vegetation in general, whose vivifying and fructifying influence is thus brought to bear upon the corn in particular.[9] The Harvest-May of Germany has its counterpart in the *eiresione* of ancient Greece.[10] The *eiresione* was a branch of olive or laurel, bound about with ribbons and hung with a variety of fruits. This branch was carried in procession at a harvest festival and was fastened over the door of the house, where it remained for a year. The object of preserving the Harvest-May or the *eiresione* for a year is that the life-giving virtue of the bough may foster the growth of the crops throughout the year. By the end of the year the virtue of the bough is supposed to be exhausted and it is replaced by a new one. In Northern India the *Emolica officialis* is a sacred tree. On the eleventh of the month Phalgun (February) libations are poured at the foot of the tree, a red or yellow string is bound about the trunk, and prayers are offered to it for the fruitfulness of women, animals, and crops. Again, in Northern India the coco-nut is esteemed one of the most sacred fruits, and is called Sriphala, or the fruit of Sri, the goddess of prosperity.[11] In the town of Qua, near Old Calabar, there used to grow a palm-tree which ensured conception to any barren woman who ate a nut from its branches.[12] In Europe the May-tree or May-pole is apparently supposed to possess similar powers over both women and cattle. Thus in some parts of Germany on the first of May the peasants set up May-trees or May-bushes at the doors of stables and byres, one for each horse and cow; this is thought to make the cows yield much milk.[13] Of the Irish we are told that "they fancy a green bough of a tree, fastened on May-day against the house, will produce plenty of milk that summer."[14]

The Circassians regard the pear-tree as the protector of cattle. So they cut down a young pear-tree in the forest, branch it, and carry it home, where it is adored as a divinity. Almost every house has one such pear-tree. In autumn, on the day of the festival, the tree is carried into the house with great ceremony to the sound of music and amid the joyous cries of all the inmates, who compliment it on its fortunate arrival. It is covered with candles, and a cheese is fastened to its top. Round about it they eat, drink, and sing. Then they bid the tree good-bye and take it back to the courtyard, where it remains for the rest of the year, set up against the wall, without receiving any mark of respect.[15]

107. In the Tuhoe tribe of Maoris "the power of making women fruitful is ascribed to trees. These trees are associated with the navel-strings of definite mythical ancestors, as indeed the navel-strings of all children used to be hung upon them down to quite recent times. A barren woman had to embrace such a tree with her arms, and she received a male or a female child according as she embraced the east or the west side."[1] The common European custom of placing a green bush on May Day before or on the house of a beloved maiden probably originated in the belief of the fertilising power of the tree-spirit.[2] In some parts of Bavaria such bushes are set up also at the houses

fir-trees are raised at the doorway and elsewhere about the homestead; and very often small umbrageous arbours are constructed in the garden. In Stockholm the chief event of the day is setting up the May-pole. This consists of a straight and tall spruce-pine tree, stripped of its branches. "At times hoops and at others pieces of wood, placed crosswise, are attached to it at intervals; whilst at others it is provided with bows, representing, so to say, a man with his arms akimbo. From top to bottom not only the 'Maj Stång' (May-pole) itself, but the hoops, bows, etc., are ornamented with leaves, flowers, slips of various cloth, gilt eggshells, etc.; and on the top of it is a large vane, or it may be a flag."[2] Midsummer customs of the same sort used to be observed in some parts of Germany. Thus in the towns of the Upper Harz Mountains tall fir-trees, with the bark peeled off their lower trunks, were set up in open places and decked with flowers and eggs, which were painted yellow and red. Round these trees the young folk danced by day and the old folk in the evening.[3] In some parts of Bohemia also a May-pole or midsummer-tree is erected on St. John's Eve. The lads fetch a tall fir or pine from the wood and set it up on a height, where the girls deck it with nosegays, garlands, and red ribbons. It is afterwards burned.[4]

110. In all these cases, apparently, the custom is or was to bring in a new May-tree each year. However, in England the village May-pole seems as a rule, at least in later times, to have been permanent, not renewed annually.[1] Villages of Upper Bavaria renew their May-pole once every three, four, or five years. It is a fir-tree fetched from the forest, and amid all the wreaths, flags, and inscriptions with which it is bedecked, an essential part is the bunch of dark green foliage left at the top "as a memento that in it we have to do, not with a dead pole, but with a living tree from the greenwood."[2] We can hardly doubt that originally the practice everywhere was to set up a new May-tree every year. As the object of the custom was to bring in the fructifying spirit of vegetation, newly awakened in spring, the end would have been defeated if, instead of a living tree, green and sappy, an old withered one had been erected year after year or allowed to stand permanently. When, however, the meaning of the custom had been forgotten, and the May-tree was regarded simply as a centre for holiday merry-making, people saw no reason for felling a fresh tree every year, and preferred to let the same tree stand permanently, only decking it with fresh flowers on May Day. But even when the May-pole had thus become a fixture, the need of giving it the appearance of being a green tree, not a dead pole, was sometimes felt. Thus at Weverham in Cheshire "are two May-poles, which are decorated on this day (May Day) with all due attention to the ancient solemnity; the sides are hung with garlands, and the top terminated by a birch or other tall slender tree with its leaves on; the bark being peeled, and the stem spliced to the pole, so as to give the appearance of one tree from the summit."[3] Thus the renewal of the May-tree is like the renewal of the

Harvest-May; each is intended to secure a fresh portion of the fertilising spirit of vegetation, and to preserve it throughout the year. But whereas the efficacy of the Harvest-May is restricted to promoting the growth of the crops, that of the May-tree or May-branch extends also, as we have seen, to women and cattle. Lastly, it is worth noting that the old May-tree is sometimes burned at the end of the year. Thus in the district of Prague young people break pieces of the public May-tree and place them behind the holy pictures in their rooms, where they remain till next May Day, and are then burned on the hearth.[4] In Würtemberg the bushes which are set up on the houses on Palm Sunday are sometimes left there for a year and then burnt.[5] The *eiresione* (the Harvest-May of Greece) was perhaps burned at the end of the year.[6]

111. Now, there is an instructive class of cases in which the tree-spirit is represented simultaneously in vegetable form and in human form, which are set side by side as if for the express purpose of explaining each other. In these cases the human representative of the tree-spirit is sometimes a doll or puppet, sometimes a living person; but whether a puppet or a person, it is placed beside a tree or bough; so that together the person or puppet, and the tree or bough, form a sort of bilingual inscription, the one being, so to speak, a translation of the other. Thus in Bohemia, on the fourth Sunday in Lent, young people throw a puppet called Death into the water; then the girls go into the wood, cut down a young tree, and fasten to it a puppet dressed in white clothes to look like a woman; with this tree and puppet they go from house to house collecting gratuities and singing songs with the refrain:—

> "We carry Death out of the village,
> We bring Summer into the village."[1]

In some parts of our own country children go about asking for pence with some small imitations of May-poles, and with a finely-dressed doll which they call the Lady of the May.[2]

At Thann, in Alsace, a girl called the Little May Rose, dressed in white, carries a small May-tree, which is gay with garlands and ribbons. Her companions collect gifts from door to door, singing a song:—

> "Little May Rose turn round three times,
> Let us look at you round and round!
> Rose of the May, come to the greenwood away,
> We will be merry all.
> So we go from the May to the roses."

In the course of the song a wish is expressed that those who give nothing may lose their fowls by the marten, that their vine may bear no clusters, their tree no nuts, their field no corn; the produce of the year is supposed to depend on the gifts offered to these May singers.[3] In Brie (Isle de France) a May-tree is set up in the midst of the village; its top is crowned with flowers; lower down it is twined with leaves and twigs, still lower with huge green branches. The girls dance round it, and at the same time a lad wrapt in leaves and called Father May is led about.[4] In the small towns of the Franken Wald mountains in Northern Bavaria, on the second of May, a *Walber* tree is erected before a tavern, and a man dances round it, enveloped in straw from head to foot in such a way that the ears of corn unite above his head to form a crown. He is called the *Walber,* and used to be led in procession through the streets, which were adorned with sprigs of birch.[5]

Among the gypsies of Transylvania and Roumania the festival of Green George is the chief celebration of spring. Some of them keep it on Easter Monday, others on St. George's Day (the twenty-third of April). On the eve of the festival a young willow tree is cut down, adorned with garlands and leaves, and set up in the ground. Women with child place one of their garments under the tree, and leave it there over night; if next morning they find a leaf of the tree lying on the garment, they know that their delivery will be easy. Sick and old people go to the tree in the evening, spit on it thrice, and say, "You will soon die, but let us live." Next morning the gypsies gather about the willow. The chief figure of the festival is Green George, a lad who is concealed from top to toe in green leaves and blossoms. He throws a few handfuls of grass to the beasts of the tribe, in order that they may have no lack of fodder throughout the year. Then he takes three iron nails, which have lain for three days and nights in water, and knocks them into the willow; after which he pulls them out and flings them into a running stream to propitiate the water-spirits. Finally, a pretence is made of throwing Green George into the water, but in fact it is only a puppet made of branches and leaves which is ducked in the stream.[6]

112. Sometimes the representation of the tree- or vegetation-spirit by a tree, bough, or flower is sometimes entirely dropped, while the representation of him by a living person remains. In this case the representative character of the person is generally marked by dressing him or her in leaves or flowers; sometimes too it is indicated by the name he or she bears.

In Ruhla (Thüringen) as soon as the trees begin to grow green in spring, the children assemble on a Sunday and go out into the woods, where they choose one of their playmates to be the Little Leaf Man. They break branches from the trees and twine them about the child till only his shoes peep out from the leafy mantle. Holes are made in it for him to see through, and two of the children lead the Little Leaf Man that he may not stumble or fall. Singing and dancing they take him from house to house, asking for gifts of food such as eggs, cream, sausages, and cakes. Lastly, they sprinkle the Leaf Man with water and feast on the food they have collected.[1] At Röllshausen on the Schwalm, in Hesse, when afternoon service is over on Whitsunday, the schoolboys and schoolgirls go out into the wood and there clothe a boy from head to foot in leaves so that nobody would know him. He is called the Little Whitsuntide Man. A procession is then formed. Two boys lead their leaf-clad playfellow; two others precede him with a basket; and two girls with another basket bring up the rear. Thus they go from house to house singing hymns or popular songs and collecting eggs and cakes in the baskets. When they have feasted on these, they strip their comrade of his verdant envelope on an open place in front of the village.² In some parts of Rhenish Bavaria at Whitsuntide a boy or lad is swathed in the yellow blossom of the broom, the dark green twigs of the firs, and other foliage. Thus attired he is known as the Quack and goes from door to door, whirling about in the dance, while an appropriate song is chanted and his companions levy contributions.³ In the Fricktal, Switzerland, at Whitsuntide boys go out into a wood and swathe one of their number in leafy boughs. He is called the Whitsuntide-lout (*Pfingstlümmel*), and being mounted on horseback with a green branch in his hand he is led back into the village. At the village-well a halt is called and the leaf-clad lout is dismounted and ducked in the trough. Thereby he acquires the right of sprinkling water on everybody, and he exercises the right specially on girls and street urchins. The urchins march before him in bands begging him to give them a Whitsuntide wetting.⁴

113. In England the best-known example of these leaf-clad mummers is the Jack-in-the-Green, a chimney-sweeper who walks encased in a pyramidal framework of wickerwork, which is covered with holly and ivy, and surmounted by a crown of flowers and ribbons. Thus arrayed he dances on May Day at the head of a troop of chimney-sweeps, who collect pence.¹ In the neighbourhood of Ertingen (Würtemberg) a masker of the same sort, known as the Lazy Man (*Latzmann*), goes about the village on Midsummer Day; he is hidden under a great pyramidal or conical frame of wickerwork, ten or twelve feet high, which is completely covered with sprigs of fir. He has a bell which he rings as he goes, and he is attended by a suite of persons dressed up in character—a footman, a colonel, a butcher, an angel, the devil, the doctor, and so on. They march in Indian file and halt before every house, where each of them speaks in character, except the Lazy Man, who says nothing. With what they get by begging from door to door they hold a feast.²

114. Often the leaf-clad person who represents the spirit of vegetation is known as the king or queen, e.g., the May King, Whitsuntide King, Queen of the May.

At the village of Ellgoth in Silesia a ceremony called the King's Race is observed at Whitsuntide. A pole with a cloth tied to it is set up in a meadow, and the young men ride past it on horseback, each trying to snatch away the cloth as he gallops by. The one who succeeds in carrying it off and dipping it in the neighbouring River Oder is proclaimed king.¹ At Wahrstedt in Brunswick the boys at Whitsuntide choose by lot a king and a high-steward (*füstje-*

meier). The latter is completely concealed in a May-bush, wears a wooden crown wreathed with flowers, and carries a wooden sword. The king, on the other hand, is only distinguished by a nosegay in his cap, and a reed, with a red ribbon tied to it, in his hand. They beg for eggs from house to house, threatening that, where none are given, none will be laid by the hens throughout the year. In this custom the high-steward appears, for some reason, to have usurped the insignia of the king.[2] At Hildesheim, in Hanover, five or six young fellows go about on the afternoon of Whit-Monday cracking long whips in measured time and collecting eggs from the houses. The chief person of the band is the Leaf King, a lad swathed so completely in birchen twigs that nothing of him can be seen but his feet. A huge headdress of birchen twigs adds to his apparent stature. In his hand he carries a long crook, with which he tries to catch stray dogs and children.[3] At Grossvargula, near Langensalza, in the eighteenth century a Grass King used to be led about in procession at Whitsuntide. He was encased in a pyramid of poplar branches, the top of which was adorned with a royal crown of branches and flowers. He rode on horseback with the leafy pyramid over him, so that its lower end touched the ground, and an opening was left in it only for his face. Surrounded by a cavalcade of young fellows, he rode in procession to the town hall, the parsonage, and so on, where they all got a drink of beer. Then under the seven lindens of the neighbouring Sommerberg, the Grass King was stripped of his green casing; the crown was handed to the Mayor, and the branches were stuck in the flax fields in order to make the flax grow tall.[4]

115. Often the spirit of vegetation in spring is represented by a queen instead of a king. In the neighbourhood of Libchowic (Bohemia), on the fourth Sunday in Lent, girls dressed in white and wearing the first spring flowers, as violets and daisies, in their hair, lead about the village a girl who is called the Queen and is crowned with flowers. During the procession, which is conducted with great solemnity, none of the girls may stand still, but must keep whirling round continually and singing. In every house the Queen announces the arrival of spring and wishes the inmates good luck and blessings, for which she receives presents.[1] In German Hungary the girls choose the prettiest girl to be their Whitsuntide Queen, fasten a towering wreath on her brow, and carry her singing through the streets. At every house they stop, sing old ballads, and receive presents.[2] In the south-east of Ireland on May Day the prettiest girl used to be chosen Queen of the district for twelve months. She was crowned with wild flowers; feasting, dancing, and rustic sports followed, and were closed by a grand procession in the evening. During her year of office she presided over rural gatherings of young people at dances and merrymakings. If she married before next May Day, her authority was at an end, but her successor was not elected till that day came round.[3] The May Queen is common in France[4] and familiar in England.

116. Again the spirit of vegetation is sometimes represented by a king and queen, a lord and lady, or a bridegroom and bride. At Halford in south Warwickshire the children go from house to house on May Day, walking two and two in procession and headed by a King and Queen.[1] In a Bohemian village near Königgrätz on Whit-Monday the children play the king's game, at which a king and queen march about under a canopy, the queen wearing a garland, and the youngest girl carrying two wreaths on a plate behind them. They are attended by boys and girls called groomsmen and bridesmaids, and they go from house to house collecting gifts.[2] A regular feature in the popular celebration of Whitsuntide in Silesia used to be, and to some extent still is, the contest for the kingship. This contest took various forms, but the mark or goal was generally the May-tree or May-pole. Sometimes the youth who succeeded in climbing the smooth pole and bringing down the prize was proclaimed the Whitsuntide King and his sweetheart the Whitsuntide Bride.[3] Near Grenoble, in France, a king and queen are chosen on the first of May and are set on a throne for all to see.[4] At Fleuriers in Switzerland on the seventh of May 1843 a May-bridegroom (*Époux de Mai*) and his bride were escorted in a procession of over two hundred children, some of whom carried green branches of beech. A number of May Fools were entrusted with the delicate duty of going round with the hat. The proceeds of their tact and industry furnished a banquet in the evening, and the day ended with a children's ball.[5] In some Saxon villages at Whitsuntide a lad and a lass used to disguise themselves and hide in the bushes or high grass outside the village. Then the whole village went out with music "to seek the bridal pair." When they found the couple they all gathered round them, the music struck up, and the bridal pair was led merrily to the village.[6] In a parish of Denmark it used to be the custom at Whitsuntide to dress up a little girl as the Whitsun-bride (*pinse-bruden*) and a little boy as her groom.[7]

In Sweden the ceremonies associated elsewhere with May Day or Whitsuntide commonly take place at Midsummer. Accordingly we find that in some parts of the Swedish province of Blekinge they still choose a Midsummer's Bride, to whom the "church coronet" is occasionally lent. The girl selects for herself a Bridegroom, and a collection is made for the pair, who for the time being are looked on as man and wife. The other youths also choose each his bride.[8] In Sardinia the Midsummer couples are known as the Sweethearts of St. John, and their association with the growth of plants is clearly brought out by the pots of sprouting grain which form a principal part of the ceremony.

and places a flower of the plantain between her legs; then her husband comes and knocks the flower away with his genital member. Further, the parents go through the country, performing dances in the gardens of favoured friends, apparently for the purpose of causing the plantain-trees to bear fruit more abundantly.[2]

121. In various parts of Europe customs have prevailed both at spring and harvest which are clearly based on the same crude notion that the relation of the human sexes to each other can be so used as to quicken the growth of plants. For example, in the Ukraine on St. George's Day (the twenty-third of April) the priest in his robes, attended by his acolytes, goes out to the fields of the village, where the crops are beginning to shew green above the ground, and blesses them. After that the young married people lie down in couples on the sown fields and roll several times over on them, in the belief that this will promote the growth of the crops. In some parts of Russia the priest himself is rolled by women over the sprouting crop, and that without regard to the mud and holes which he may encounter in his beneficent progress.[1] In England it seems to have been customary for young couples to roll down a slope together on May Day.[2] In some parts of Germany at harvest the men and women who have reaped the corn roll together in the field.[3]

122. Again, the sympathetic relation supposed to exist between the commerce of the sexes and the fertility of the earth manifests itself in the belief that illicit love tends, directly or indirectly, to mar that fertility and to blight the crops. The Bahaus or Kayans, a tribe in the interior of Borneo, believe that adultery is punished by the spirits, who visit the whole tribe with failure of the crops and other misfortunes. Hence in order to avert these calamities from the innocent members of the tribe, the two culprits, with all their possessions, are put in quarantine on a gravel bank in the middle of the river; then in order thoroughly to disinfect them, pigs and fowls are killed, and with the blood priestesses smear the property of the guilty pair. Finally the two are set on a raft, with sixteen eggs, and allowed to drift down the stream. They may save themselves by swimming ashore, but this is perhaps a mitigation of an older sentence of death by drowning. Young people shower long grass-stalks, which stand for spears, at the shamefaced and dripping couple.[1] The Blu-u Kayans of the same region similarly imagine that an intrigue between an unmarried pair is punished by the spirits with failure of the harvest, of the fishing, and of the hunt. Hence the delinquents have to appease the wrath of the spirits by sacrificing a pig and some rice.[2] When it rains in torrents, the Galelareese of Halmahera say that brother and sister, or father and daughter, or in short some near relations are having illicit relations with each other, and that every human being must be informed of it, for then only will the rain cease to descend.[3]

123. In some parts of Africa, also, it is believed that breaches of sexual morality disturb the course of nature, particularly by blighting the fruits of the earth. Thus the Negroes of Loango suppose that the intercourse of a man with an immature girl is punished by God with drought and consequent famine, until the culprits atone for their sin by dancing naked before the king and an assembly of the people, who throw hot gravel and bits of glass at the pair.[1] Similar notions of the disastrous effects of sexual crimes may be detected among some of the civilised races of antiquity, who seem not to have limited the supposed sterilising influence of such offences to the fruits of the earth, but to have extended it also to women and cattle. Amongst the Bavili of Loango, it is believed that if a man breaks the marriage law by marrying a woman of his mother's clan, God will in like manner punish the crime by withholding the rains in their due season.[2] So too among the Hebrews we read how Job, passionately protesting his innocence before God, declares that he is no adulterer; "For that," says he, "were an heinous crime; yea, it were an iniquity to be punished by the judges: for it is a fire that consumeth unto Destruction, and would root out all mine increase." In this passage the Hebrew word translated "increase" commonly means "the produce of the earth";[3] and if we give the word its usual sense here, then Job affirms adultery to be destructive of the fruits of the ground, which is just what many savages still believe. Again, in Leviticus, after a list of sexual crimes, we read:[4] "Defile not ye yourselves in any of these things: for in all these the nations are defiled which I cast out from before you: and the land is defiled: therefore I do visit the iniquity thereof upon it, and the land vomiteth out her inhabitants." This passage appears to imply that the land itself was somehow physically tainted by sexual transgressions so that it could no longer support the inhabitants.

124. It would seem that the ancient Greeks and Romans entertained similar notions. According to Sophocles the land of Thebes suffered from blight, from pestilence, and from the sterility both of women and of cattle under the reign of Oedipus, who had unwittingly slain his father and wedded his mother.[1] The Celts of ancient Ireland similarly believed that incest blighted the fruits of the earth. According to legend Munster was afflicted in the third century of our era with a failure of the crops and other misfortunes. When the nobles enquired into the matter, they were told that these calamities were the result of an incest which the king had committed with his sister.[2]

125. If we ask why it is that similar beliefs should logically lead, among different peoples, to such opposite modes of conduct as strict chastity and more or less open debauchery, the reason, as it presents itself to the primitive mind, is perhaps not very far to seek. If rude man identifies himself, in a manner, with nature; if he fails to distinguish the impulses and processes in himself from the methods which nature adopts to ensure the reproduction of plants and animals, he may leap to one of two conclusions. Either he may infer that by yielding to his appetites he will thereby assist in the multiplication of plants and animals; or he may imagine that the vigour which he refuses to expend in reproducing his own kind, will form as it were a store of energy whereby other creatures, whether vegetable or animal, will somehow benefit in propagating their species. Thus from the same crude philosophy, the same primitive notions of nature and life, the savage may derive by different channels a rule either of profligacy or of asceticism.

THE DIVINE NUPTIALS

126. Magical dramas designed to stimulate the growth of plants by the real or mock marriage of men and women who masquerade as spirits of vegetation have played a great part in the popular festivals of Europe, and based as they are on a very crude conception of natural law, it is clear that they must have been handed down from a remote antiquity. We shall hardly, therefore, err in assuming that they date from a time when the forefathers of the civilised nations of Europe were still barbarians. But if these old spells and enchantments for the growth of leaves and blossoms, of grass and flowers and fruit, have lingered down to our own time in the shape of pastoral plays and popular merry-makings, it is not reasonable to suppose that they survived in less attenuated forms some two thousand years ago among the civilised peoples of antiquity? Or, to put it otherwise, is it not likely that in certain festivals of the ancients we may be able to detect the equivalents of our May Day, Whitsuntide, and Midsummer celebrations, with this difference, that in those days the ceremonies had not yet dwindled into mere shows and pageants, but were still religious or magical rites, in which the actors consciously supported the high parts of gods and goddesses? May not the priest who bore the title of King of the Wood at Nemi and his mate the goddess of the grove have been serious counterparts of the merry mummers who play the King and Queen of May, the Whitsuntide Bridegroom and Bride in modern Europe? and may not their union have been yearly celebrated in a *theogamy* or divine marriage? Such dramatic weddings of gods and goddesses, as we shall see presently, were carried out as solemn religious rites in many parts of the ancient world; hence there is no intrinsic improbability in the supposition that the sacred grove at Nemi may have been the scene of an annual ceremony of this sort. No ancient writer mentions that this was done in the grove at Nemi; but our knowledge of the Arician ritual is so scanty that the want of information on this head can hardly count as a fatal objection to the theory. That theory, in the absence of direct evidence, must necessarily be based on the analogy of similar customs practised elsewhere. Some modern examples of such customs, more or less degenerate, were described above. Here we shall consider their ancient counterparts.

127. At Babylon the imposing sanctuary of Bêl rose like a pyramid above the city in a series of eight towers or stories, planted one on the top of the other. On the highest tower, reached by an ascent which wound about all the rest, there stood a spacious temple, and in the temple a great bed, magnificently draped and cushioned, with a golden table beside it. In the temple no image was to be seen, and no human being passed the night there, save a single woman, whom, according to the priests, the god chose from among all the women of Babylon. They said that the deity himself came into the temple at night and slept in the great bed; and the woman, as a consort of the god, might have no intercourse with mortal man.[1]

128. At Thebes in Egypt a woman slept in the temple of Ammon as the consort of the god and, like the human wife of Bêl at Babylon, she was said to have no commerce with a man.[1] In Egyptian texts she is often mentioned as "the divine consort," and usually she was no less a personage than the Queen of Egypt herself. For, according to the Egyptians, their monarchs were actually begotten by the god Ammon, who assumed for the time being the form of the reigning king, and in that disguise had intercourse with the queen. The divine procreation is carved and painted in great detail on the walls of two of the oldest temples in Egypt, those of Deir el Bahari and Luxor; and the inscriptions attached to the paintings leave no doubt as to the meaning of the scenes.

129. At Athens the god of the vine, Dionysus, was annually married to the Queen, and it appears that the consummation of the divine union, as well as the espousals, was enacted at the ceremony; but whether the part of the god was played by a man or an image we do not know. We learn from Aristotle that the ceremony took place, not at the sanctuary in the marshes, but in the old official residence of the King, known as the Cattle-stall, which stood near the Prytaneum or Town-hall on the north-eastern slope of the Acropolis.[1] Its object can hardly have been any other than that of ensuring the fertility of the vines and other fruit-trees, of which Dionysus was the god. Thus both in form and in meaning the ceremony would answer to the nuptials of the King and Queen of May. Again, the story, dear to poets and artists, of the forsaken and sleeping Ariadne, waked and wedded by Dionysus, resembles so closely the little drama acted by French peasants of the Alps on May Day, that, considering the character of Dionysus as a god of vegetation, we can hardly help regarding it as the reflection of a spring ceremony like the French one. The chief difference between the French and the Greek ceremonies appears to have been that in the former the sleeper was a forsaken bridegroom, in the latter a forsaken bride; and the group of stars in the sky, in which fancy saw Ariadne's wedding crown,[2] may have been only a translation to heaven of the garland worn by the Greek girl who played the Queen of May.

130. The marriage of Zeus and Hera was acted at annual festivals in various parts of Greece,[1] and it is at least a fair conjecture that Zeus and Hera at these festivals were the Greek equivalents of the Lord and Lady of the May. Homer's glowing picture of Zeus and Hera couched on fresh hyacinths and crocuses,[2] like Milton's description of the dalliance of Zephyr with Aurora, "as he met her once a-Maying," was perhaps painted from the life.

The sacred marriage of Zeus and Hera had, as was natural, its counterpart among the northern kinsfolk of the Greeks. In Sweden every year a life-size image of Frey, the god of fertility, both animal and vegetable, was drawn about the country in a waggon attended by a beautiful girl who was called the god's wife. She acted also as his princess in the great temple at Upsala.[3]

131. Thus the custom of marrying gods either to images or to human beings was widespread among the nations of antiquity. The ideas on which such a custom is based are too crude to allow us to doubt that the civilised Babylonians, Egyptians, and Greeks inherited it from their barbarous or savage forefathers. This presumption is strengthened when we find rites of a similar kind in vogue among the lower races. Thus, for example, we are told that once upon a time the Wotyaks of the Malmyz district in Russia were distressed by a series of bad harvests. They did not know what to do, but at last concluded that their powerful but mischievous god Keremet must be angry at being unmarried. So a deputation of elders visited the Wotyaks of Cura and came to an understanding with them on the subject. Then they returned home, laid in a large stock of brandy, and having made ready a gaily decked waggon and horses, they drove in procession with bells ringing, as they do when they are fetching home a bride, to the sacred grove at Cura. There they ate and drank merrily all night, and next morning they cut a square piece of turf in the grove and took it home with them. After this, though it fared well with the people of Malmyz, it fared ill with the people of Cura; for in Malmyz the bread was good, but in Cura it was bad. Hence the men of Cura who had consented to the marriage were blamed and roughly handled by their indignant fellow-villagers. "What they meant by this marriage ceremony," says the writer who reports it, "it is not easy to imagine. Perhaps, as Bechterew thinks, they meant to marry Keremet to the kindly and fruitful Mukylćin, the Earth-wife, in order that she might influence him for good."[1] This carrying of turf, like a bridge, in a waggon from a sacred grove resembles the Plataean custom of carting an oak log as a bride from an ancient oak forest; and we have seen ground for thinking that the Plataean ceremony, like its Wotyak counterpart, was intended as a charm to secure fertility. When wells are dug in Bengal, a wooden image of a god is made and married to the goddess of water.[2]

132. Often the bride destined for the god is not a log or a clod, but a living woman of flesh and blood. The Indians of a village in Peru have been known to marry a beautiful girl, about fourteen years of age, to a stone shaped like a human being, which they regarded as a god (*huaca*). All the villagers took part in the marriage ceremony, which lasted three days, and was attended with much revelry. The girl thereafter remained a virgin and sacrificed to the idol for the people. They shewed her the utmost reverence and deemed her divine.[1] The Blackfoot Indians of North America used to worship the Sun as their chief god, and they held a festival every year in his honour. Four days before the new moon of August the tribe halted on its march, and all hunting was suspended. Bodies of mounted men were on duty day and night to carry

out the orders of the high priest of the Sun. He enjoined the people to fast and
to take vapour baths during the four days before the new moon. Moreover,
with the help of his council, he choose the Vestal who was to represent the
Moon and to be married to the Sun at the festival. She might be either a virgin
or a woman who had had but one husband. Any girl or woman found to have
discharged the sacred duties without fulfilling the prescribed conditions was
put to death. On the third day of preparation, after the last purification had
been observed, they built a round temple of the Sun. Posts were driven into
the ground in a circle; these were connected with cross-pieces, and the whole
was covered with leaves. In the middle stood the sacred pole, supporting the
roof. A bundle of many small branches of sacred wood, wrapped in a splendid
buffalo robe, crowned the summit of the temple. The entrance was on the east,
and within the sanctuary stood an altar on which rested the head of a buffalo.
Beside the altar was the place reserved for the Vestal. Here, on a bed prepared for her, she slept "the sleep of war," as it was called. Her other duties
consisted in maintaining a sacred fire of fragrant herbs, in presenting a
lighted pipe to her husband the Sun, and in telling the high priest the dream
she dreamed during "the sleep of war." On learning it the priest had it proclaimed to the whole nation to the beat of drum.[2] Every year about the middle
of March, when the season for fishing with the drag-net began, the Algon-
quins and Hurons married their nets to two young girls, aged six or seven. At
the wedding feast the net was placed between the two maidens, and was exhorted to take courage and catch many fish. The reason for choosing the
brides so young was to make sure that they were virgins.[3] The Oraons of
Bengal worship the earth as a goddess, and annually celebrate her marriage
with the Sun-god at the time when the sāl-tree is in blossom, the roles of bride
and groom being played by the priest and his wife.[4]

133. At the village of Bas Doda, in the Gurgaon district of North-Western
India, a fair is held on the twenty-sixth of the month Chait and the two following days. We are told that formerly girls of the Dhinwar class used to be married to the god at these festivals, and that they always died soon afterwards.
(Of late years the practice is said to have been discontinued.)[1] Among the
Ewe-speaking peoples of the Slave Coast in West Africa human wives of gods
are very common. In Dahomey they swarm, and it has even been estimated
that every fourth woman is devoted to the service of some deity. The chief
business of these female votaries is prostitution. In every town there is at least
one seminary where the handsomest girls, between ten and twelve years of
age, are trained. They stay for three years, learning the chants and dances
peculiar to the worship of the gods, and prostituting themselves to the priests
and the inmates of the male seminaries. At the end of their noviciate they become public harlots. But no disgrace attaches to their profession, for it is believed that they are married to the god, and that their excesses are caused and
directed by him. Strictly speaking, they should confine their favours to the

male worshippers at the temple, but in practice they bestow them indiscriminately. Children born of such unions belong to the deity. As the wives of a god, these sacred women may not marry. But they are not bound to the service of the divinity for life. Some only bear his name and sacrifice to him on their birthdays.[2]

134. It deserves to be remarked that the supernatural being to whom women are married is often a god or spirit of water. Thus Mukasa, the god of the Victoria Nyanza lake, who was propitiated by the Baganda every time they undertook a long voyage, had virgins provided for him to serve as his wives. Like the Vestals they were bound to chastity, but unlike the Vestals they seem to have been often unfaithful. The custom lasted until Mwanga was converted to Christianity.[1] In Kengtung, one of the principal Shan states of Upper Burma, the spirit of the Nawng Tung lake is regarded as very powerful, and is propitiated with offerings in the eighth month (about July) of each year. A remarkable feature of the worship of this spirit consists in the dedication to him of four virgins in marriage. Custom requires that this should be done once in every three years. It was actually done by the late king or chief (Sawbwa), in 1893, but down to 1901 the rite had not been performed by his successor.[2] When the Arabs conquered Egypt they learned that at the annual rise of the Nile the Egyptians were wont to deck a young virgin in gay apparel and throw her into the river as a sacrifice, in order to obtain a plentiful inundation. The Arab general abolished the barbarous custom.[3] It is said that under the Tang dynasty the Chinese used to marry a young girl to the Yellow River once a year by drowning her in the water. For this purpose the witches chose the fairest damsel they could find and themselves superintended the fatal marriage.[4] A usage of the same sort is reported to have prevailed in the Maldive Islands before the conversion of the inhabitants to Islam. The famous Arab traveller Ibn Batutah has described the custom and the manner in which it came to an end. He was assured by several trustworthy natives, whose names he gives, that when the people of the islands were idolaters there appeared to them every month an evil spirit among the jinn, who came from across the sea in the likeness of a ship full of burning lamps. The wont of the inhabitants, as soon as they perceived him, was to take a young virgin, and, having adorned her, to lead her to a heathen temple that stood on the shore, with a window looking out to sea. There they left the damsel for the night, and when they came back in the morning they found her a maid no more, and dead. Every month they drew lots, and he upon whom the lot fell gave up his daughter to the jinnee of the sea.[5]

135. Ibn Batutah's narrative of the demon lover and his mortal brides closely resembles a well-known type of folk-tale, of which versions have been found from Japan and Annam in the East to Senegambia, Scandinavia, and Scotland in the West. The story varies in details from people to people, but as commonly told it runs thus. A certain country is infested by a many-headed serpent, dragon, or other monster, which would destroy the whole people if a human victim, generally a virgin, were not delivered up to him periodically. Many victims have perished, and at last it has fallen to the lot of the king's own daughter to be sacrificed. She is exposed to the monster, but the hero of the tale, generally a young man of humble birth, interposes in her behalf, slays the monster, and receives the hand of the princess as his reward. In many of the tales the monster, who is sometimes described as a serpent, inhabits the water of a sea, a lake, or a fountain. In other versions he is a serpent or dragon who takes possession of the springs of water, and only allows the water to flow or the people to make use of it on condition of receiving a human victim.[1]

It would probably be a mistake to dismiss all these tales as pure inventions of the story-teller. Rather we may suppose that they reflect a real custom of sacrificing girls or women to be the wives of water-spirits, who are very often conceived as great serpents or dragons.

136. Now, besides the King of the Wood, an important figure in the grove at Nemi was the water-nymph Egeria, who was worshipped by pregnant women because she, like Diana, could grant them an easy delivery. From this it seems fairly safe to conclude that, like many other springs, the water of Egeria was credited with a power of facilitating conception as well as delivery. The votive offerings found on the spot, which clearly refer to the begetting of children, may possibly have been dedicated to Egeria rather than to Diana, or perhaps we should rather say that the water-nymph Egeria is only another form of the great nature-goddess Diana herself, the mistress of sounding rivers as well as of umbrageous woods,[1] who had her home by the lake and her mirror in its calm waters, and whose Greek counterpart Artemis loved to haunt meres and springs.[2] The identification of Egeria with Diana is confirmed by a statement of Plutarch that Egeria was one of the oak-nymphs[3] whom the Romans believed to preside over every green oak-grove;[4] for while Diana was a goddess of the woodlands in general she appears to have been intimately associated with oaks in particular, especially at her sacred grove of Nemi.[5] Perhaps, then, Egeria was the fairy of a spring that flowed from the roots of a sacred oak. This would explain the more than mortal wisdom with which, according to tradition, Egeria inspired her royal husband or lover Numa. When we remember how very often in early society the king is held responsible for the fall of rain and the fruitfulness of the earth, it seems hardly rash to conjecture that in the legend of the nuptials of Numa and Egeria we have a reminiscence of a sacred marriage which the old Roman kings regularly contracted with a goddess of vegetation and water for the purpose of enabling him to discharge his divine or magical functions. In such a rite the part of the goddess might be played either by an image or a woman, and if by a woman, probably by the Queen. If there is any truth in this conjecture, we may suppose that the King and Queen of Rome impersonated the god and goddess at their marriage, exactly as the King and Queen of Egypt appear to have done.[6]

137. The legend of Numa and Egeria points to a sacred grove rather than to a house as the scene of the nuptial union, celebrated annually as a charm to ensure the fertility not only of the earth but of man and beast. Now, according to some accounts, the scene of the marriage was no other than the sacred grove of Nemi, and on quite independent grounds we have been led to suppose that in that same grove the King of the Wood was wedded to Diana. The coincidence suggests that the legendary union of the Roman king with Egeria may have been a reflection or duplicate of the union of the King of the Wood with Egeria or her double Diana. This does not imply that the Roman kings ever served as Kings of the Wood in the Arician grove, but only that they may originally have been invested with a sacred character of the same general kind, and may have held office on similar terms.

Our knowledge of the Roman kingship is far too scanty to allow us to affirm any one of these propositions with confidence; but at least there are some scattered hints or indications of a similarity in all these respects between the priests of Nemi and the kings of Rome, or perhaps rather between their remote predecessors in the dark ages which preceded the dawn of legend.

138. In the first place, it would seem that the Roman king personated no less a deity than Jupiter himself. For down to imperial times victorious generals celebrating a triumph, and magistrates presiding at the games in the Circus, wore the costume of Jupiter, which was borrowed for the occasion from his great temple on the Capitol; and it has been held with a high degree of probability both by ancients and moderns that in so doing they copied the traditionary attire and insignia of the Roman kings.[1] They rode a chariot drawn by four laurel-crowned horses through the city, where every one else went on foot;[2] they wore purple robes embroidered or spangled with gold; in the right hand they bore a branch of laurel and in the left hand an ivory sceptre topped with an eagle; a wreath of laurel crowned their brows; their face was reddened with vermilion; and over their head a slave held a heavy crown of massy gold fashioned in the likeness of oak leaves.[3] In this attire the assimilation of the man to the god comes out above all in the eagle-topped sceptre, the oaken crown, and the reddened face. For the eagle was the bird of Jove, and the face of his image standing in his four-horse chariot on the Capitol was in like manner regularly dyed red on festivals.[4]

Thus, we may fairly assume that on certain solemn occasions Roman generals and magistrates personated the supreme god, and that in so doing they revived the practice of the early kings. To us moderns such mimicry might appear impious, but it was otherwise with the ancients. To their thinking gods and men were akin, for many families traced their descent from a divinity, and the deification of a man probably seemed as little extraordinary to them as the canonisation of a saint seems to a modern Catholic. The Romans in particular were quite familiar with the spectacle of men masquerading as spirits; for at the funerals of great houses all the illustrious dead of the family were personated by men specially chosen for their resemblance to the departed. These representatives wore masks fashioned and painted in the likeness of the originals: they were dressed in rich robes of office, resplendent with purple and gold, such as the dead nobles had worn in their lifetime: like them, they rode in chariots through the city preceded by the rods and axes, and attended by all the pomp and heraldry of high station; and when at last the funeral procession, after threading its way through the crowded streets, defiled into the Forum, the maskers solemnly took their seats on ivory chairs placed for them on the platform of the Rostra, in the sight of the people, recalling no doubt to the old, by their silent presence, the memories of an illustrious past, and firing the young with the ambition of a glorious future.[5]

139. According to a tradition which we have no reason to reject, Rome was founded by settlers from Alba Longa, a city situated on the slope of the Alban hills, overlooking the lake and the Campagna.[1] Hence if the Roman kings claimed to be representatives or embodiments of Jupiter, the god of the sky and of the thunder, it is natural to suppose that the kings of Alba, from whom the founder of Rome traced his descent, may have set up the same claim before them; and, indeed, the Roman annals record that one of them, Romulus, Remulus, or Amulius Silvius by name, set up for being a god in his own person, the equal or superior of Jupiter. To support his pretensions and overawe his subjects, he constructed machines whereby he mimicked the clap of thunder and the flash of lightning. Diodorus relates that in the season of fruitage, when thunder is loud and frequent, the king commanded his soldiers to drown the roar of heaven's artillery by clashing their swords against their shields. But he paid the penalty of his impiety, for he perished, he and his house, struck by a thunderbolt in the midst of a dreadful storm. Swollen by the rain, the Alban lake rose in flood and drowned his palace. But still, says an ancient historian, when the water is low and the surface unruffled by a breeze, you may see the ruins of the palace at the bottom of the clear lake.[2] This legend points to a real custom observed by the early kings of Greece and Italy, who like their fellows in Africa down to modern times may have been expected to produce rain and thunder for the good of the crops.[3] The priestly king Numa passed for an adept in the art of drawing down lightning from the sky.[4] Mock thunder, we know, has been made by various peoples as a rain-charm in modern times; why should it not have been made by kings in antiquity? At Rome the sluices of heaven were opened by means of a sacred stone, and the ceremony appears to have formed part of the ritual of Jupiter Elicius, the god who elicits from the clouds the flashing lightning and the dripping rain.[5] And who so well fitted to perform the ceremony as the king, the living representative of the sky-god?

140. The conclusion which we have reached as to the kings of Rome and

Alba probably holds good of all the kings of ancient Latium: each of them, we may suppose, represented or embodied the local Jupiter. For we can hardly doubt that of old every Latin town or settlement had its own Jupiter, as every town and almost every church in modern Italy has its own Madonna; and like the Baal of the Semites the local Jupiter was commonly worshipped on high places. Wooded heights, round which the rain-clouds gather, were indeed the natural sanctuaries for a god of the sky, the rain, and the oak. At Rome he occupied one summit of the Capitoline hill, while the other summit was assigned to his wife Juno, whose temple, with the long flight of stairs leading up to it, has for ages been appropriately replaced by the church of St. Mary "in the altar of the sky" (*in Araceli*).[1] That both heights were originally wooded seems certain, for down to imperial times the saddle which joins them was known as the place "between the two groves."[2]

141. If the kings of Rome aped Capitoline Jove, their predecessors the kings of Alba probably laid themselves out to mimic the great Latian Jupiter, who had his seat above the city on the summit of the Alban Mountain. Latinus, the legendary ancestor of the dynasty, was said to have been changed into Latian Jupiter after vanishing from the world in the mysterious fashion characteristic of the old Latin kings.[1] The sanctuary of the god on the top of the mountain was the religious centre of the Latin League, as Alba was its political capital till Rome wrested the supremacy from its ancient rival. Apparently no temple, in our sense of the word, was ever erected to Jupiter on this his holy mountain; as god of the sky and thunder he appropriately received the homage of his worshippers in the open air. The massive wall, of which some remains still enclose the old garden of the Passionist monastery, seems to have been part of the sacred precinct which Tarquin the Proud, the last king of Rome, marked out for the solemn annual assembly of the Latin League.[2] The god's oldest sanctuary on this airy mountain-top was a grove.[3]

142. Since, then, we have seen reason to suppose that the Roman kings personated Jupiter, while Egeria is expressly said to have been an oak-nymph, the story of their union in the sacred grove raises a presumption that at Rome in the regal period a ceremony was periodically performed exactly analogous to that which was annually celebrated at Athens down to the time of Aristotle.[1] The marriage of the King of Rome to the oak-goddess, like the wedding of the vine-god to the Queen of Athens, must have been intended to quicken the growth of vegetation by homoeopathic magic. Of the two forms of the rite we can hardly doubt that the Roman was the older, and that long before the northern invaders met with the vine on the shores of the Mediterranean their forefathers had married the tree-god to the tree-goddess in the vast oak forests of Central and Northern Europe.

NOTES

1 1. Strabo, v. 3, 12.

2 1. J. Marquardt, *Römische Staatsverwaltung*² (Leipzig 1885), iii. 321 ff.
2. Plato, *Politicus,* 290 E; Aristotle, *Constitution of Athens,* 57; Lysias, *Orationes,* vi. 4; G. Gilbert, *Handbuch der griechischen Staatsaltertümer*² (Leipzig 1893), i. 281 ff.
3. Aristotle, *Politics,* viii (vi). 8, 20, p. 1302B. 26 ff.; Gilbert, *op. cit.,* ii. 323 f.
4. This was the case at ELIS (H. Roehl, *Inscriptiones Graecae antiquissimae* [Berlin 1882], No. 112); in Cos (Dittenberger, *Sylloge*², No. 616); at CHIOS (ib., No. 570); at MITYLENE (P. Cauer, *Delectus Inscriptionum Graecarum*² [Leipzig 1883], Nos. 428, 431); at CYME (Plutarch, *Quaest. Graec.,* 2); and possibly also in SIPHNOS (Isocrates, *Or.,* xiv. 36).
5. Herodotus, vi. 56.

3 1. Strabo, xii. 3, 37; xii. 5, 3.
2. J. Grimm, *Deutsche Rechtsaltertümer*³ (Göttingen 1881), 343.
3. Li-ki, tr. Legge (*SBE,* xxvii–xxviii), *passim.*
4. W. Ellis, *History of Madagascar* (London n.d.), i. 359 f.
5. P. Paulitschke, *Ethnographie Nordost-Afrikas: die geistige Cultur der Danakil, Galla und Somal* (Berlin 1896), 129.
6. Brasseur de Bourbourg, *Histoire des nations civilisées du Mexique et de l'Amérique Centrale* (Paris 1857–59), i. 94.

6 1. See Theocritus, ii; Vergil, *Eclogues,* viii. 78–82; Ovid, *Heroides,* vi. 91 f.; id., *Amores,* iii. 7, 29 f.
2. P. Jones, *History of the Ojebway Indians* (London n.d.), 146.
3. C. Lumholtz, *Unknown Mexico* (London 1903), i. 485 f.
4. P. J. de Arriaga, *Extirpacion de la Idolatria del Piru* (Lima 1621), 25 f.
5. *Reports of the Cambridge Anthropol. Exped. to Torres Straits,* v (Cambridge 1904), 324 f.
6. J. Batchelor, *The Ainu and their Folklore* (London 1901), 329–31.
7. J. J. M. de Groot, *The Religious System of China,* v (Leyden 1907), 920 f.

101

8. C. J. Forbes, *British Burma* (London 1878), 232.
9. A. Hillebrandt, *Vedische Opfer und Zauber* (Strasburg 1897), 177.
10. E. Doutté, *Magie et religion dans l'Afrique du Nord* (Algiers 1908), 61 f.
10a. P. A. Talbot, *The Peoples of Southern Nigeria* (London 1926), ii. 182.
10b. P. Güssfeldt, *et al.*, *Die Loango-Expedition, 1873–1876* (Stuttgart 1909), III. ii, 337.
10c. A. D. Nock, in *Archiv für Religionswissenschaft*, 24 (1926), 172.

7   1. G. Maspero, *Histoire ancienne de l'Orient classique: les origines* (Paris 1895), 213 f.
1a. E. A. W. Budge, *Osiris and the Egyptian Resurrection* (London 1911), ii. 177 f.
2. M. Jastrow, *The Religion of Babylonia and Assyria* (Boston 1898), 268, 286.

8   1. *Ib.*, 286 f.
2. E. A. W. Budge, *Egyptian Magic* (London 1899), 77 ff.

9   1. E. W. Nelson, in *Eighteenth Ann. Report of the Bureau of Amer. Ethnology* (1899), 435.
2. J. Teit, in *Memoirs of the Am. Mus. Nat. History: The Jessup North Pacific Expedition*, i., No. 4 (April 1900), 314.
3. J. R. Swanton, *Contributions to the Ethnology of the Haida* (Leyden-New York 1905), 47 ff.
4. S. Powers, *Tribes of California* (Washington 1877), 318.
5. C. Lumholtz, in *Mem. Am. Mus. Nat. History*, iii (May 1900), 52.
6. P. J. de Arriaga, *op. cit.*, 37.
7. A. Delegorgue, *Voyage dans l'Afrique Australe* (Paris 1847), ii. 325 f.
8. E. Casalis, *The Basutos* (London 1861), 251.
9. Capt. Binger, *Du Niger au golfe de Guinée* (Paris 1892), ii. 230.
10. W. G. Aston, *Shinto* (London 1905), 331.
11. R. Taylor, *Te Ika A Maui, or New Zealand and its Inhabitants*[2] (London 1870), 213.

10   1. W. Caland, *Altindisches Zauberritual* (Amsterdam 1900), 119; Hymns of the Atharva-Veda, tr. Blomfield (*SBE* xlii), 358 f.
2. W. H. Keating, *Narrative of an Expedition to the Source of St. Peter's River* (London 1825), ii. 159.
3. See Theocritus, ii. 28 f.; Vergil, *Ecl.*, viii. 81 f.

11   1. Father Lambert, *Moeurs et Superstitions des Néo-Calédoniens* (Nouméa 1900), 97 f.

12   1. Plutarch, *De sera numinis vindicata*, 14.
2. T. Shaw, in *Asiatic Researches*, 4 (1809), 69.
3. Caland, *op. cit.*, 75 ff.

4. Pliny, *NH*, xxx. 94.
5. *Ib.*, xxxvii. 170.
6. Personal communication from R. C. Bosanquet.
7. A. Wuttke, *Der deutsche Volksaberglaube*[2] (Berlin 1869), 302, ¶477.
7a. N. Adriani and A. C. Kruijt, *Die Bare'e-sprekende Toradja's van Midden-Celebei* (Batavia 1912), 350.
7b. D. Bray, in *Census of India*, 1911, iv. 68.
7c. M. Trevelyan, *Folk-Lore and Folk-Stories of Wales* (London 1909), 311.

13 1. P. Chapiseau, *Le Folk-lore de la Beuce et du Perche* (Paris 1902), i. 172 f.
2. H. Ling Roth, *The Natives of Sarawak and British North Borneo* (London 1896), i. 280.
3. Marcellus, *De medicamentis*, xv. 82.
4. *Ib.*, xxiv. 10.

14 1. B. Spencer and F. J. Gillen, *The Native Tribes of Central Australia* (London 1899), 176.
2. *Ib.*, 179 ff.
3. *Ib.*, 184 ff.
4. *Ib.*, 193 ff., 199 ff., 206 f.
5. Id., *The Northern Tribes of Central Australia* (London 1904), 291–94.

15 1. F. Boas, in *Sixth Ann. Report on the North-Western Tribes of Canada* (1890), 45.
2. A. C. Haddon, in *JAI*, 19 (1890), 427.
3. A. C. Kruijt, in *Vorslagen en Med. d. konink. Akad. v. Wetenschappen, Afdeeling Letterkunde*, IV. iii (1899), 203 f.
4. J. W. Thomas, in *Tijdschrift v. Indische Taal- Land en Volkenkunde* 26 : 277.
5. Van Schmid, in *Tijdschrift voor Neerlands-Indië*, 1843, ii. 601 f.
6. B. A. Hely, in *British New-Guinea, Ann. Report for 1894–95*, p. 56.
7. E. Aymonier, in *Cochinchine française*, No. 16 (Saigon 1883), 157.
8. J. Macdonald, *Religion and Myth* (London 1893), 5.
9. A. G. Monce, *Au pays de l'Ours Noir* (Paris-Lyons 1897), 71.
10. M. J. van Baarda, in *Bijdragen tot de Taal- Land en Volkenkunde van Nederl. Indië*, 45 (1895), 502.
11. W. W. Skeat, *Malay Magic* (London 1900), 300.

17 1. M. J. van Baarda, *op. cit.*, 507.
2. F. Boas, in *Bull. Am. Mus. Nat. History*, 15, i (1901), 161.
3. R. F. Kaindl, in *Globus*, 76 (1899), 273.
4. Pliny, *NH*, xxviii. 20.
5. B. Pilsudski, in *Anthropos*, 5 (1910), 763.
6. E. M. Gordon, *Indian Folk-Tales* (London 1908), 82 f.
7. Van Schmid, in *Tijdschr. v. Neerlands-Indië*, 1843, ii. 604.

8. A. C. Kruijt, in *Med. Zendel.*, 40 (1896), 262 f.; 44 (1900), 235.
9. C. Snouck Hurgronje, *De Atjehers* (Batavia-Leyden 1893–94), i. 409.
10. W. W. Skeat, *op. cit.*, 213.
11. A. Thevet, *Les Singularitez de la France Antarctique, autrement nommée Amérique* (Antwerp 1558), 93.
12. Maximilian zu Wied, *Reise in das innere Nord-America* (Coblenz 1839–41), ii. 247.

18   1. H. F. Standing, in *Antanarivo Annual and Madagascar Magazine*, 2 (reprinted 1896), 261.
2. D. Kidd, *Savage Childhood* (London 1906), 48.
3. H. Callaway, *Nursery Tales, Traditions and Histories of the Zulus*, i (Natal-London 1868), 280 ff.

19   1. E. Aymonier, in *RHR*, 24 (1891), 278.
2. A. C. Haddon, *Head-hunters* (London 1901), 259.
3. C. Leemius, *De Lapponibus Finmarchiae* (Copenhagen 1767), 500.

20   1. *Report of the Internat. Polar Exped. to Point Barrow, Alaska* (Washington 1883), 39.
1a. A. H. Armytage, *Flamborough, Village and Heathland* (Saffron Walden 1880), 143.
2. P. Labbé, *Un Bagne Russe, l'Ile de Sakhaline* (Paris 1903), 268.
3. *Missions Catholiques*, 14 (1882), 460.
4. P. Reichard, *Deutsch-Ostafrika* (Leipzig 1892), 427.
5. Private communication from Dr. C. Hose, formerly Resident Magistrate of the Baram district, Sarawak.
6. W. H. Furness, *Home-life of the Borneo Head-hunters* (Philadelphia 1902), 169.
7. J. Chalmers, in *JAI*, 27 (1898), 327.

21   1. H. Ling Roth, in *JAI*, 22 (1893), 56.
2. W. W. Skeat, *op. cit.*, 524.
3. *Indian Antiquary*, 21 (1892), 120.
4. H. O. Forbes, in *JAI*, 13 (1884), 414.
5. De Flacourt, *Histoire de la Grande Isle Madagascar* (Paris 1658), 97 f.
6. H. Cole, in *JAI*, 32 (1902), 312, 317.
7. J. G. F. Riedel, *De sluik- en kroesharige rassen tusschen Selebes en Papua* (The Hague 1886), 377.
8. S. Powers, *Tribes of California* (Washington 1877), 129 f.
9. J. R. Swanton, *Contributions to the Ethnology of the Haida* (Leyden-New York 1905), 55 f.
10. G. S. Robertson, *The Kafirs of the Hindu Kush* (London 1896), 335, 621–26.
10a. P. A. Talbot, *The Peoples of Southern Nigeria* (London 1926), iii. 856.

22 1. A. L. van Hasselt, *Volksbeschrijving van Midden-Sumatra* (Leyden 1882), 323.
2. R. F. Kaindl, in *Globus*, 76 (1899), 276.
3. H. F. Standing, in *Antanarivo Annual and Madagascar Magazine*, 2 (reprinted 1896), 257.

23 1. E. Meier, *Deutsche Sagen, Sitten und Gebräuche aus Schwaben* (Stuttgart 1852), 499.
2. E. H. Meyer, *Badisches Volksleben im 19ten Jahrhundert* (Strasburg 1900), 421 f.
3. O. Hartung, in *Zeitschrift d. Vereins für Volkskunde*, 7 (1897), 149 f.
4. G. F. Abbott, *Macedonian Folklore* (Cambridge 1903), 122.

24 1. W. W. Skeat, *op. cit.*, 248.
2. J. L. van der Toorn, in *BTLVNI*, 39 (1890), 67.
3. D. Kidd, *Savage Childhood* (London 1906), 291.
4. Eijub Abela, in *ZDPV*, 7 (1884), 112, ¶202.
5. J. V. Grohman, *Aberglauben und Gebräuche aus Böhmen und Mähren* (Prague 1864), 143, ¶1053.
6. E. Hoffman-Krayer, in *Schweizer. Archiv f. Volkskunde*, 11 (1907), 263.
7. G. F. Abbott, *op. cit.*, 122.
8. *Census of India, 1901*, iii. 206.
9. F. Blumentritt, in *Globus*, 48, No. 12, p. 202.
10. M. J. van Baarda, in *BTLVNI*, 45 (1895), 489.

25 1. *Bull. Soc. Géogr. de Paris, IIme Sér.*, ii (1834), 181 ff.
2. E. Modigliani, *Un Viaggio a Nias* (Milan 1890), 590.
3. D. Grangeon, in *Missions Catholiques*, 28 (1896), 83.
4. J. Mooney, *Myths of the Cherokee* (Washington 1900), 425 ff.
5. R. Southey, *History of Brazil*, ii (London 1817), 37.
6. F. Boas, in *Sixth Ann. Report on the North-Western Tribes of Canada* (1890), 25.
7. B. Spencer and F. J. Gillen, *The Northern Tribes of Central Australia* (London 1904), 624 ff.
8. Id., *The Native Tribes of Central Australia* (London 1899), 552.

26 1. F. S. Krauss, *Volksglaube und religiöser Brauch der Südslaven* (Munster i.W. 1890), 146.
2. J. Knebel, in *Tijdschrift voor Indische Taal- Land en Volkenkunde*, 40 (1898), 506.
3. W. Crooke, *Popular Religion and Folklore of Northern India* (Westminster 1896), i. 261.
4. P. J. de Arriaga, *Extirpacion de la Idolatria del Piru* (Lima 1621), 22.
5. R. F. Kaindl, in *Globus*, 61 (1892), 282.
6. J. Brand, *Popular Antiquities of Great Britain* (London 1882–83), iii. 278 f.

7. A. Wuttke, *Der deutsche Volksaberglaube*[2] (Berlin 1869), 126 f.
8. Aelian, *Nat. animalium*, i. 38.

27 1. F. S. Krauss, *op. cit.*, 140.
2. Father Lambert, *Moeurs et Superstitions des Néo-Calédoniens* (Nouméa 1900), 30 f.
3. Hesiod, *Works and Days*, 750 ff. (But the lines are not free of ambiguity.)
4. E. Doutté, *Magie et religion dans l'Afrique du Nord* (Algiers 1908), 302 ff.

28 1. B. Shaw, *Memorials of South Africa* (London 1840), 66.
2. A. Leared, *Morocco and the Moors* (London 1876), 272.
3. P. Paulitschke, *Ethnographie Nordost-Afrikas* (Berlin 1896), 27.
4. M. Merker, *Rechstverhältnisse und Sitten der Wadschagga* (Gotha 1902), 21.
5. F. Boas, in *Bull. Am. Mus. Nat. Hist.*, 15, i (1901), 160.
6. Id., in *Sixth Ann. Report on the North-Western Tribes of Canada* (1890), 25.
7. H. A. Junod, *Les Ba-ronga* (Neuchatel 1898), 472.
8. E. Poeppig, *Reise in Chile, Peru und auf dem Amazonenstrome* (Leipzig 1835–36), ii. 323.
9. A. Thevet, *Cosmographie universelle* (Paris 1575), ii. 946 [980].
10. A. Jaussen, *Coutumes des Arabes au pays de Moab* (Paris 1908), 36.
11. F. S. Krauss, *op. cit.*, 147.
12. Aelian, *Nat. animalium*, i. 42, 43, 48.

29 1. M. J. van Baarda, in *BTLVNI*, 45 (1895), 483.
2. *Ib.*, 534.
3. E. Chavannes, *Documents sur les Tou-Kiue occidentaux* (St. Petersburg 1903), 134.
4. Aelian, *Nat. anim.*, i. 38.
5. Jaussen, *op. cit.*, 35.
6. J. Dos Santos, "Eastern Ethiopia," in G. McCall Theal's *Records of South-Eastern Africa* ([London] 1901), vii. 224.
7. M. J. van Baarda, *op. cit.*, 468.
8. A. W. Nieuwenhuis, *Quer durch Borneo*, ii (Leyden 1907), 173.
9. Grihya-Sútras, tr. Oldenberg (*SBE* xxx), 146.
10. Id., *SBE* xxix. 168, 282 f.
11. *The First Nine Books of . . . Saxo Grammaticus*, tr. O. Elton (London 1894), 16.
12. Aristotle, *Const. Ath.*, vii. 55; Plutarch, *Solon*, 25; Pollux, viii. 86.
13. Pausanias, iii. 22,1. (Cp. ii. 31,4)
14. Ptolemaeus, *apud* Photius, Bibliotheca, 153 Bekker.

30 1. R. H. Codrington, *The Melanesians* (Oxford 1891), 181 ff.
2. W. Ridgeway, *The Early Age of Greece* (Cambridge 1901), i. 330.
3. Orphica, *Lithica*, 230 ff.

4. *Ib.*, 189 ff.
5. K. von Leoprechting, *Aus dem Lechrain* (Munich 1855), 92.
6. Orphica, *Lithica*, 335 ff.
7. Pliny, *NH*, xxxvii. 124.
8. J. G. von Hahn, *Albanesische Studien* (Jena 1854), i. 158.

31   1. P. Sébillot, *Légendes, croyances et superstitions de la mer* (Paris 1886), i. 136.
    2. Pliny, *NH*, ii. 220.
    3. Philostratus, *Vita Apolon.*, v. 2.
    4. Sébillot, *op. cit.*, i. 132.
    5. *Ib.*, i. 129–32; M. E. James, in *Folk-Lore*, 9 (1898), 189.
    6. *David Copperfield*, Chap. xxx.
    7. W. Henderson, *Folk-Lore of the Northern Counties of England* (London 1879), 58.
    8. *Henry V*, Act II, Scene 3.
    9. C. Harrison, in *JAI*, 21 (1892), 17 f.
  10. C. Martin, in *Zeitschrift für Ethnologie*, 4 (1877), 179.
  11. A. W. Howitt, *The Native Tribes of S. E. Australia* (London 1904), 465.
  11a. C. E. Fox, *The Threshold of the Pacific* (London 1924), 337.
  11b. P. Güssfeldt, *et al.*, *Die Loango-Expedition, 1873–1876* (Stuttgart 1909), III. ii, 325.
  11c. A. R. Brown, *The Andaman Islanders* (Cambridge 1922), 175.

32   1. J. J. M. de Groot, *The Religious System of China* (Leyden 1892–), i. 60–63.

33   1. N. Adriani and A. C. Kruijt, in *Med Zendel.*, 42 (1898), 524.
    2. J. Mooney, in *Seventh Ann. Report of the Amer. Bureau of Ethnology* (1891), 352; id., in *Nineteenth Ann. Report*, i (1900), 295.
    3. *Relations des Jésuites* (1642), 86 ff.

34   1. A. W. Howitt, *op. cit.*, 538 ff.; B. Spencer and F. J. Gillen, *The Native Tribes of Central Australia* (London 1899), 213 f., 450 ff.; id., *The Northern Tribes of Central Australia* (London 1904), 18, 329, 588 ff.
    2. F. Bonney, in *JAI*, 13 (1884), 128.
    3. Howitt, *op. cit.*, 561.
    4. Porte, in *Missions Catholiques*, 28 (1896), 312.
    5. A. Wuttke, *Der deutsche Volksaberglaube*[2] (Berlin, 1869), 330. ¶526; F. Panzer, *Beitrag zur deutschen Mythologie* (Munich 1848–55), ii. 307.
    6. S. Weissenberg, in *Globus*, 88 (1903), 317.
    7. A. A. Perera, in *Indian Antiquary*, 32 (1903), 435.
    8. J. V. Grohmann, *Aberglauben und Gebräuche aus Böhmen und Mähren* (Prague 1864), 55, 111, ¶825.
    9. M. Abeghian, *Der armenische Volksglaube* (Leipzig 1899), 68.

35 1. R. Taylor, *Te Ika A Maui, or New Zealand and its Inhabitants*[2] (London 1870), 184.

2. B. Spencer and F. J. Gillen, *The Native Tribes of Central Australia* (London 1899), 467.

3. M. Krieger, *New Guinea* (Berlin [1899]), 165.

4. Personal communication from L. Fison (5/29/1901).

5. J. G. F. Riedel, *De sluik– en kroesharige rassen tusschen Selebes en Papua* (The Hague 1886), 135.

6. *Ib.*, 391.

7. Riedel, *op. cit.*, 73 f.

8. *Ib.*, 326.

8a. G. Maupetit, in *Bull. et Mém. Soc. d'Anthropologie de Paris,* 6 (1912), 473.

8b. P. A. Erdland, *Die Marshall-Insulaner* (Munster 1914), 125, 338.

8c. M. Radiguet, *Les derniers sauvages* (Paris 1882), 173.

9. Garcilasso de la Vega, *Royal Commentaries on the Yncas,* tr. C. Markham (London 1867–71), i. 186.

10. B. de Sahagun, *Histoire générale des choses de la Nouvelle Empire,* tr. Jourdanet-Simeon (Paris 1880), 310.

11. *Relations des Jésuites* (1639), p. 44.

36 1. *Bavaria, Landes– und Volkskunde des Königsreichs Bayern,* IV. ii, 346.

2. E. Krause, in *Zeitschrift für Ethnologie,* 15 (1883), 84.

3. H. Ploss, *Das Kind*[2] (Leipzig 1884), i. 12 ff.

4. J. Grimm, *Deutsche Mythologie*[4] (Berlin 1875–78), ii. 728, n. 1.

5. M. Bartels, in *Zeitschrift für Ethnologie,* 32 (1900), 70 f.

37 1. Pliny, *NH,* xxviii. 36.

2. F. Boas, in *Sixth Ann. Report on the North-Western Tribes of Canada* (1890), 25.

3. A. W. Howitt, *op. cit.,* 667.

4. Francis Bacon, *Natural History,* cent. x, ¶998.

5. W. W. Groome, in *Folk-Lore,* 6 (1895), 126; E. S. Hartland, *The Legend of Perseus* (London 1894–96), ii. 169–72.

6. C. Partridge, *Cross River Natives* (London 1905), 295.

7. H. Pröhle, *Harzbilder* (Leipzig 1855), 82.

7a. A. J. N. Tremearne, in *JRAI,* 42 (1912), 161.

8. Spencer and Gillen, *Native Tribes,* 250.

9. F. Panzer, *op. cit.,* ii. 302.

38 1. M. J. Erdweg, in *Mitt. d. Anthropol. Ges. in Wien,* 32 (1902), 287.

2. B. Hagen, *Unter den Papua's* (Wiesbaden 1899), 269.

3. Theocritus, ii. 53 f.

4. Hartland, *op. cit.,* ii. 86 ff.

4a. R. Neuhauss, *Deutsch Neu-Guinea* (Berlin 1911), iii. 117.

39 1. R. Parkinson, *Dreissig Jahre in der Südsee* (Stuttgart 1907), 605.
2. E. Best, in *Journal of the Polynesian Society,* 9 (1900), 196.
3. B. C. Thomson, *Savage Island* (London 1902), 97.
4. M. J. van Baarda, in *BTLVNI,* 45 (1895), 512.
4a. P. F. Hess, in *Anthropos,* 10–11 (1915–16), 48.
4b. Lafcadio Hearn, *Glimpses of Unfamiliar Japan* (London 1905), ii. 604.
5. A. B. Ellis, *The Ewe-Speaking Peoples of the Slave-Coast* (London 1890), 94.
6. K. Bartsch, *Märchen und Gebräuche aus Meklenburg* (Vienna 1879–80), ii. 329 ff.
7. J. L. M. Nogués, *Les Moeurs d'autrefois en Saintonge et en Aunis* (Saintes 1890), 169 f.
8. Lady E. C. Gordon, ed., *County Folklore: Suffolk* (London 1893), 201.
9. Bartsch, *op. cit.,* ii. 330, 334; R. Andree, *Ethnographische Parallelen und Vergleiche, N. F.* (Leipzig 1889), 8, 11.
10. K. von den Steinen, *Unter den Naturvölkern Zentral-Brasiliens* (Berlin 1894), 558.
11. Saxo Grammaticus, tr. Elton (London 1894), 28 ff.
12. Aelian, *De natura animalium,* i. 36.
13. Mullach, ed., *Fragmenta Philosophrum Graecorum* (Paris 1875), i. 510.

40 1. Howitt, *op. cit.,* 366.
2. E. Casalis, *The Basutos* (London 1861), 273.
3. J. Richardson, *Travels in the Great Desert of Sahara* (London 1848), ii. 65.

41 1. W. Mannhardt, *Antike Wald– und Feldkulte* (Berlin 1877), 342, n.
2. K. von Bruchhausen, in *Globus,* 76 (1899), 253.
3. C. F. H. Campen in *Tijdschrift voor Indische Taal- Land en Volkenkunde,* 27 (1882), 447.
4. J. G. F. Riedel, *op. cit.,* 114.
5. G. A. J. Hazen, in *Tijdschr. v. Ind. Taal- Land en Volkenkunde,* 46 (1903), 298.
6. J. O. Dorsey, in *Third Ann. Report of the Amer. Bureau of Ethnology* (1884), 347.
7. Doutté, *op. cit.,* 583.
8. Howitt, *op. cit.,* 398.
9. J. Kreemer, in *Mend. Zendel.,* 30 (1886), 113.
10. Coulbeaux, in *Missions Catholiques,* 30 (1898), 455.
11. I Kings, 18 : 28.

42 1. F. Boas, in *Fifth Ann. Report on the North-Western Tribes of Canada* (1889), 51.
2. Id., in *Sixth Ann. Report* (1890), 39 f.
3. J. Teit, *The Thompson Indians of British Columbia* (New York 1900), 310 f.

4. Boas, in *Sixth Report*, 92.

5. P. J. de Arriaga, *Extirpacion de la idolatria del Piru* (Lima 1621), 16 f., 30, 130 f.

6. H. A. Junod, *Les Ba-ronga* (Neuchatel 1898), 412, 416 f.

7. M. N. Venketswami, in *Indian Antiquary*, 28 (1899), 111.

43 1. Grihya-Sutras, tr. Oldenberg, ii (*SBE* xxx), 72 f.

44 1. Lucy Garnett, *The Women of Turkey and their Folklore* (London 1890), 123 f.

2. W. Mannhardt, *Der Baumkultus der Germanen und ihre-Nachbarstämme* (Berlin 1875), 329 ff.; W. R. S. Ralston, *Songs of the Russian People*[2] (London 1872), 227 ff.; E. Gerard, *The Land beyond the Forest* (Edinburgh 1888), ii. 13.

3. E. Fischer, in *Globus*, 98 (1908), 14 f.

4. M. Abeghian, *op. cit.*, 93 f.

5. S. I. Curtiss, *Primitive Semitic Religion To-day* (Chicago 1902), 114

6. A. Jaussen, *Coutumes des Arabes au pays de Moab* (Paris 1908), 326, 328.

6a. J. Abbot, *The Keys of Power* (London 1932), 340.

45 1. J. Polek, in *Zeitschrift d. Vereins f. Volkskunde*, 3 (1893), 85.

2. Mannhardt, *op. cit.*, 331.

3. Abeghian, *op. cit.*, 93.

4. Doutté, *op. cit.*, 584.

5. J. G. F. Riedel, in *Tijdschr. v. Ind. Taal- Land en Volkenkunde*, 18 (1873), 524.

6. *North Indian Notes and Queries*, 3. 134, ¶285.

7. J. L. van der Toorn, in *BTLVNI*, 39 (1890), 93.

8. Sarat Chandra Mitra, in *Journal of the Anthropol. Soc. of Bombay*, 3 (1893), 25, 27.

46 1. *Loc. cit.*

2. *Punjab Notes and Queries*, 1. 102, ¶791.

3. Theophrastus, *Historia plantarum*, vii. 3, 3; ix. 8, 8; Plutarch, *Quaest. Conviv.*, vii. 2, 3; Pliny, *NH*, xix. 120.

4. Palladius, *De re rustica*, iv. 9; Pliny, *op. cit.*, xix. 120.

5. Theophrastus, *op. cit.*, ix. 8, 8.

47 1. Mannhardt, *op. cit.*, 553; Gerard, *op. cit.*, ii. 40.

2. *Punjab Notes and Queries*, 3. 41, ¶173; 115, ¶513.

3. C. Lumholtz, *Unknown Mexico* (London 1903), i. 330

48 1. G. Turner, *Samoa, A Hundred Years Ago and Long Before* (London 1884), 345 f.

2. Ralston, *op. cit.*, 425 f.; P. von Stenin, in *Globus*, 57 (1890), 285.

3. Aristophanes, *Clouds*, 373.

4. Abeghian, *op. cit.*, 93.

5. A. Caulin, *Historia coro-graphica* . . . *dela Nueva Andalucia, etc.* (1779), 92.

49 1. G. B. Grinnell, *Blackfoot Lodge Tales* (London 1893), 262.

2. Teit, *op. cit.*, 374.

3. J. Batchelor, *The Ainu and their Folklore* (London 1901), 334.

4. B. F. Matthes, in *Verslagen en Med. d. kon. Akad. v. Wetenschappen, Afeeling Letterkunde,* Ser. II. ii (1885), 169.

50 1. D. Forbes, in *Journal of the Ethnological Soc. of London,* 2 (1870), 237, n. On the supposed relation of frogs and toads to water in America, see further E. J. Payne, *History of the New World called America* (Oxford 1892), i. 420 f.; 425 f.

2. Teit, *op. cit.*, 346; A. Kuhn, *Gebräuche und Märchen aus Westfalen* (Leipzig 1859), ii. 80; Gerard, *op. cit.*, 11. 13.

3. M. N. Venketswami, in *Indian Antiquary,* 29 (1899), 111.

51 1. L. J. B. Bérenger-Féraud, *Les Peuplades de la Sénégambie* (Paris 1879), 291.

2. H. H. Bancroft, *The Native Races of the Pacific States* (London 1875–76), i. 520.

3. Rizzolati, in *Annales de la Propagation de la Foi,* 16 (1844), 350; Retord, *ib.*, 28 (1856), 102.

4. Bruguière, *ib.*, 5 (1831), 131.

5. G. Pitré, *Usi e costumi, credenze e pregiudizi del popolo siciliano,* iii (Palermo 1889), 142–44.

52 1. Turner, *op. cit.*, 145.

2. A. L. P. Cameron, in *JAI,* 14 (1885), 362.

3. *Loc. cit.*

4. W. G. Aston, *Shinto* (London 1905), 330.

5. W. Crooke, *Popular Religion and Folklore of Northern India* (Westminster 1896), i. 75 f.

6. Private communication from J. Rendel Harris.

7. W. R. Paton, in *Folk-Lore,* 12 (1901), 216.

8. G. Timkowski, *Travels of the Russian Mission through Mongolia to China* (London 1827), i. 402 f.

8a. S. C. Roy, *The Birhors* (Ranchi 1925), 369 f.

53 1. J. Rhys, *Celtic Heathendom* (London 1888), 184.

2. *Ib.*, 185 f.

3. *Ib.*, 187.

4. G. Herve, in *Bull. Soc. Anthropol. de Paris,* IV. iii (1892), 530.

5. L. J. B. Bérenger-Féraud, *Superstitions et survivances* (Paris 1896), i. 427.

6. *Ib.*, i. 477; P. Sébillot, *Le Folk-lore de France* (Paris 1904–07), ii 376 ff.
7. Lamberti, in *Voyages au Nord*, vii (Amsterdam 1725), 174.
8. W. S. Hallett, *A Thousand Miles on an Elephant in the Shan States* (London–Edinburgh 1890), 264.

54 1. Pausanias, ii. 25, 10; Marcus Antoninus, v. 7; Petronius, 44; Tertullian, *Apol.*, 40; P. Cauer, *Delectus inscriptionum graecarum*[2] (Leipzig 1883), No. 162.
2. Pausanias, viii. 38, 4.
3. Apollodorus, *Bibl.*, i. 9, 7; Vergil, *Aen.*, vi. 585 (and Servius *in loc.*).
4. Festus, s. vv. *aquaelicium, manalem lapidem;* Nonius Marcellus, s. v. *trullum* (p. 637, ed. Quicherat); Servius, Vergil, *Aen.*, iii. 175.
5. Diodorus Siculus, v. 55.

55 1. P. Jones, *History of the Ojebway Indians* (London, n. d.), 84.
2. W. Smythe and F. Lowe, *Narrative of a Journey from Lima to Para* (London 1836), 230.
3. J. Gumilla, *Histoire de l'Orénoque* (Avignon 1758), iii. 243 f.
4. A. G. Morice, in *Proc. Canadian Institute, Toronto*, III. viii (1888–89), 154.
5. A. Moret, *Le rituel du culte divin journalier en Égypte* (Paris 1902), 90 f.
6. Lambert, *Moeurs et superstitions des Néo-Calédoniens* (Neuméa 1900), 193 f.
7. *Ib.*, 296 f.
8. R. H. Codrington, *The Melanesians* (Oxford 1891), 184.

56 1. Festus, s. v. *October equus.*
2. II Kings, 23 : 11.
3. Pausanias, iii. 20, 4.
4. Xenophon, *Cyropaed.*, viii. 3, 24; Philostratus, *Vita Apollon.*, i. 31, 2; Ovid, *Fasti*, i. 385 f.; Pausanias, iii. 20, 4.
5. Herodotus, i. 216; Strabo, xi. 8, 6. See further J. Negelein, in *Zeitschrift für Ethnologie*, 33 (1901), 62 ff.
5a. P. S. Walleser, in *Anthropos*, 8 (1913), 1053.

57 1. H. R. Schoolcraft, *The American Indians* (Buffalo 1851), 97 ff.; W. W. Gill, *Myths and Songs of the South Pacific* (London 1876), 61 f.
2. F. Boas, in *Bull. Amer. Mus. Nat. Hist.*, 15 (1901), 151.
3. J. Chalmers, *Pioneering in New Guinea* (London 1887), 172.
4. Aeneas Silvius, *Opera* (Basle 1571), 418.
5. S. L. Cummins, in *JAI*, 34 (1904), 164.
6. D. Kidd, *Savage Childhood* (London 1906), 147 f.; E. Gottschling, in *JAI* 35 (1905), 381.
7. E. M. Curr, *The Australian Race* (Melbourne-London 1886–87), iii. 145.

58 1. K. Vetter, in B. Hagen's *Unter den Papua's* (Wiesbaden 1899), 287.
2. W. W. Skeat, *Malay Magic* (London 1900), 92 ff.
3. G. M. Dawson, in *Trans. Royal Soc. Canada*, 9 (1901), sect. ii. 38.

59 1. J. G. Gmelin, *Reise durch Sibirien* (Göttingen 1751–52), ii. 510.
2. C. H. Cottrell, *Recollections of Siberia* (London 1842), 140.
3. J. O. Dorsey, in *Third Ann. Report of the Amer. Bureau of Ethnology* (1884), 241.
4. J. Richardson, *A Dictionary of Persian, Arabic and English* (London 1829), iii f.
5. J. Mooney, in *Sixth Ann. Report of the Am. Bur. of Ethnol.* (1891), 387 f.
6. R. H. Codrington, *op. cit.*, 200 f.
7. B. Hagen, *op. cit.*, 269.
8. W. Monckton, in *Journal of the Polynesian Society*, 5 (1896), 186.
9. J. G. Dalyell, *The Darker Superstitions of Scotland* (Edinburgh 1834), 248.
10. F. Boas, in *Sixth Ann. Report on the North-Western Tribes of Canada* (1890), 39 f.
11. H. Egede, *Description of Greenland*[2] (London 1818), 196 n.
12. Eunapius, *Vitae sophistorum*; Aedesius, 463 Didot.
13. Olaus Magnus, *Historia de gentium septentrionalium variis conditionibus* (Basle 1567), iii. 15.
14. R. H. Dana, *Two Years before the Mast* (New York 1840), Chap. vi.
14a. P. Güssfeld, *et al., Die Loango-Expedition 1873–1876*, III (Stuttgart 1909), ii. 336.
14b. A. R. Colquhoun, *Across Chryse* (London 1883), 52.
14c. S. J. Hickson, *A Naturalist in North Celebes* (London 1889), 14.

60 1. J. Scheffer, *Lapponia* (Frankfort 1673), 144; C. F. Gordon Cumming, *In the Hebrides* (London 1883), 254 f.; M. Cameron, in *Folk-Lore*, 14 (1903), 301 f. Cp. Shakespeare, *Macbeth*, Act. I, Scene 3, line 11: "But, my loving master, if any wind will not serve, then I wish I were in Lapland, to buy a good wind of one of the honest witches, that sell so many winds there and so cheap."
2. C. Leemius, *De Lapponibus Finmarchiae, etc.* (Copenhagen 1767), 454.
3. *Odyssey*, x. 19 ff.
4. J. Chalmers, *Pioneering in New Guinea* (London 1887), 177.
5. H. Klose, *Togo unter deutscher Flagge* (Berlin 1899), 189.

61 1. Hymns of the Atharva-Veda, tr. Blomfield (*SBE*, xlii), 249.
2. Livinhac, in *Annales de la Propagation de la Foi*, 53 (1881), 209.
3. H. Ling Roth, *The Natives of Sarawak and British North Borneo* (London 1896), i. 201.
4. P. Sébillot, *Coutumes populaires de la Haute-Bretagne* (Paris 1886), 302 ff.

5. Holzmayer, in *Verh. d. gel. Estnischen Ges. zu Dorpat*, VII, ii. 54.
6. A. Kuhn and W. Schwartz, *Nord-deutsche Sagen, Märchen und Gebräuche* (Leipzig 1848), 454, ¶406; W. Mannhardt, *Die Götter der deutschen und nordischen Völker* (Berlin 1860), 99; id., *Antike Wald- und Feldkulte* (Berlin 1877), 85.
7. W. C. Harris, *The Highlands of Ethiopia* (London 1844), i. 352.
8. Herodotus, iv. 173; Aulus Gellius, xvi. 11.

63 1. B. Spencer and F. J. Gillen, *The Native Tribes of Central Australia* (London 1899), 9–15, 154, 159–205; id., *The Northern Tribes of Central Australia* (London 1904), 20–27, 285–97, 309 f., 316; A. W. Howitt, *The Native Tribes of S.E. Australia* (London 1904), 320–26.
2. Howitt, *op. cit.*, 303.
3. *Ib.*, 313.
4. Guis, in *Missions Catholiques*, 36 (1904), 334.
5. R. H. Codrington, *The Melanesians* (Oxford 1891), 52.
6. C. Ribbe, *Zwei Jahren unter den Kannibalen der Salomo-Inseln* (Dresden 1903), 173 f.
7. C. G. Seligman, *The Melanesians of New Guinea* (Cambridge 1910), 702.

64 1. O. Baumann, *Durch Masailand zur Nilquelle* (Berlin 1894), 173.
2. H. Cole, in *JAI*, 32 (1902), 321.
3. H. Johnston, *The Uganda Protectorate* (London 1902), ii. 830.
4. *Ib.*, ii. 851.

65 1. *Ib.*, ii. 779.
2. G. Schweinfurth, *The Heart of Africa*[3] (London 1878), i. 144 f.

66 1. Johnston, *op. cit.*, ii. 555.
2. G. Casati, *Ten Years in Equatoria* (London-New York 1891), ii. 57; cp. i. 134.
3. E. Torday and T. A. Joyce, in *JAI*, 37 (1907), 140.

67 1. O. Lenz, *Skizzen aus Westafrika* (Berlin 1878), 87.

68 1. D. Kidd. *The Essential Kafir* (London 1904), 114.

69 1. H. Hecquard, *Reise an der Küste und in das Innere von West Afrika* (Leipzig 1854), 78.
2. A. Bastian, *Loango-Küste* (Jena 1874–75), i. 354; ii. 230.
3. J. L. Wilson, *Western Africa* (London 1856), 129 ff.; Mary Kingsley, in *JAI*, 29 (1899), 62.
4. P. Kollmann,*The Victoria Nyanza* (London 1899), 168.
5. Legével de Lacombe, *Voyage à Madagascar* (Paris 1840), i. 229 f.

70 1. Scholiast on Apollonius Rhodius, *Argonautica*, ii. 1248.
2. Ammianus Marcellinus, xxviii. 5, 14.
3. Plutarch, *De Iside et Osiride*, 73.
4. G. Turner, *Samoa, A Hundred Years Ago and Long Before* (London 1884), 304 f.
5. A. Pfizmayer, in *Sitzb. phil-hist. Kl. Kaiserl. Akad. d. Wiss. zu Wien*, 57 (1868), 483 f.
6. Havard, in *Annales de la Propagation de la Foi*, 7 (1834), 470–73.

71 1. G. Catlin, *Manners, Customs and Conditions of the North American Indians*[4] (London 1844), i. 40 f.
2. R. B. Dixon, in *Bull. Am. Mus. Nat. Hist.*, 17, iii (1905), 267.
3. S. Powers, *Tribes of California* (Washington 1877), 372 ff.

72 1. G. Kurze, in *Mitt. d. Geogr. Ges. zu Jena*, 23 (1905), 19, 29.
2. E. F. im Thurm, *Among the Indians of Guiana* (London 1883), 211, 213 f., 328, 333 ff.

73 1. W. W. Skeat, *Malay Magic* (London 1900), 36.
2. G. Maan, in *Tijdschrift voor Indische Taal- Land en Volkenkunde*, 46 (1903), 339.

74 1. H. Low, *Sarawak* (London 1848), 259 ff.

75 1. *The Laws of Manu*, tr. Bühler, ix. 246 f. (*SBE*, xxv. 385).
2. *Odyssey*, xix. 109–14.
3. Snorre Sturlason, *Chronicle of the Kings of Norway*, tr. Laing, Saga I, Chaps. 18, 47. Cp. F. Liebrecht, *Zur Volkskunde* (Heilbronn 1879), 7.

76 1. J. G. Dalyell, *The Darker Superstitions of Scotland* (Edinburgh 1834), 62 ff.
2. T. B. Macaulay, *History of England*, Chap. xiv.
3. James Boswell, *Life of Samuel Johnson*, Chap. i.
4. T. J. Pettigrew, *Superstitions connected with . . . Medicine* (London (1844), 117–54.
5. Baron Roger, in *Bull. Soc. Géogr. de Paris*, 8 (1827), 351.
6. W. Mariner, *An Account of the Natives of the Tonga Islands*[2] (London 1818), i. 434 n.

79 1. W. Ellis, *Polynesian Researches*[2] (London 1832–36), i. 372–75.

80 1. For examples see E. B. Tylor, *Primitive Culture*[2] (London 1873), ii. 131 f.
2. Pausanias, ii. 24, 1.
3. Pliny, *NH*, xxviii. 147.
4. F. J. Mone, *Geschichte des Heidentums im nördlichen Europa* (Leipzig 1822–23), i. 188.

5. J. Biddulph, *Tribes of the Hindoo Kush* (Calcutta 1880), 96.

5a. Cole Fay-Cooper, *The Wild Tribes of the Davao District, Mindanao* (Chicago 1913), 174 ff.

5b. R. V. Russell, *Tribes and Castes of the Central Provinces* (Nagpur 1902), iii. 18.

81   1. Biddulph, *op. cit.*, 97.
     2. Lucian, *Bis accus.*, 1; Tzetzes, *Scol. on Lycophron*, 6; Plutarch, *E apud Delphos*, 2; id., *De Pythiae oraculis*, 6.
     3. Plutarch, *Quaest. Rom.*, 112.
     4. J. Roscoe, in *JAI*, 32 (1902), 42.
     5. C. Lekkerkerker, in *Tijdschrift v. Ind. Taal- Land en Volkenk.*, 45 (1902), 252 f.

82   1. J. Moura, *Le Royaume de Cambodge* (Paris 1883), i. 177 f.
     2. Pausanias, x. 32, 6.

83   1. C. S. Stewart, *A Visit to the South Seas* (London 1832), i. 244 f.
     2. J. Kubary, in Bastian's *Allerlei aus Volks- und Menschenkunde* (Berlin 1888), i. 30 f.

84   1. Porphyry, *De abstinentia*, iv. 9; Eusebius, *Praep. ev.*, iii. 12.
     2. Diogenes Laertius, *Vit. philosoph.*, viii. 56–62; H. Diels, *Die Fragmente der Vorsokratiker*[3], i. (Berlin 1906), 205.

85   1. Tacitus, *Germania*, 8; id., *Hist.*, iv. 61, 65; v. 22; Cp. K. Müllenhoff, *Deutsche Altertumskunde* (Berlin 1870–1900), iv. 208 ff.
     2. Strabo, vii. 3, 5.

86   1. P. S. Arnot, *Garengauze* (London [1889]), 78.
     2. V. L. Cameron, *Across Africa* (London 1877), ii. 69.
     3. Massaya, in *Ann. de la Propagation de la Foi*, 30 (1858), 51.
     4. "The Strange Adventures of Andrew Battel," in Pinkerton's *Voyages and Travels*, xvi. 330; Poyart, *ib.*, xvi. 577; O. Dapper, *Description de l'Afrique* (Amsterdam 1686), 335.
     5. Dapper, *op. cit.*, 400.
     6. J. Adams, *Remarks on the Country extending from Cape Palmas to the River Congo* (London 1823), 111.
     7. W. Allen and E. R. H. Thompson, *Narrative of the Expedition to the River Niger in 1841* (London 1848), i. 288.

87   1. J. Sibree, in *JAI*, 21 (1892), 218.
     2. V. Noel, in *Bull. Soc. Géogr. de Paris, IIme sér.*, 20 (1843), 56.

88   1. E. Young, *The Kingdom of the Yellow Robe* (Westminster 1898), 142 f.

89   1. W. E. Marshall, *Travels among the Todas* (London 1873), 136 f., 141 f.; F. Metz, *Tribes inhabiting the Neilgherry Hills*[2] (Mangalore 1864), 19 ff.; W. H. R. Rivers, *The Todas* (London 1906), 448 f.

2. Monier Williams, *Religious Life and Thought in India* (London 1883), 259.
3. *The Laws of Manu*, vii. 8 (tr. Bühler, *SBE*, xxv. 217).
4. Monier Williams, *op. cit.*, 259 f.

90 1. W. Robinson, *Descriptive Account of Assam* (London-Calcutta 1841), 342 f.
2. L. A. Waddell, *The Buddhism of Tibet* (London 1895), 245 ff.
3. Danicourt, in *Ann. de la Prop. de la Foi*, 30 (1858), 15–20; J. H. Gray, *China* (London 1878), i. 103 f.

91 1. Garcilasso de la Vega, *First Part of the Royal Commentaries of the Yncas*, Book II, Chaps. 8, 15 (tr. Markham, i. 131, 155).
2. A. von Humboldt, *Researches concerning the Institutions and Monuments of the Ancient Inhabitants of America* (London 1814), iii. 106 ff.; T. Waitz, *Anthropologie der Naturvölker* (Leipzig 1860–77), iv. 352 ff.

92 1. *Manners and Customs of the Japanese in the Nineteenth Century:* from recent Dutch visitors to Japan and the German of Dr. Ph. Fr. von Scebold (London 1841), 141 ff.

93 1. [See: R. Labat, *Le caractère religieux de la royauté assyro-babylonienne* (Paris 1939); I. Engnell, *Studies in Divine Kingship in the Ancient Near East* (Uppsala 1943); C. J. Gadd, *Ideas of Divine Rule in the Ancient East* (London 1948), 33–62; H. Frankfort, *Kingship and the Gods* (Chicago 1948); T. H. Gaster, in *Review of Religion*, 9 (1945), 267–81.]
2. Ammianus Marcellinus, xxiii. 6, ¶6.
3. A. Erman, *Die ägyptische Religion* (Berlin 1905), 39 f.
4. P. le Page Renouf, in *Proc. Soc. Biblical Archaeology*, 12 (1890), 355.
5. A. Moret, *Du Caractère religieux de la royauté pharaonique* (Paris 1902), 378 f.; *ib.*, 313 f.
6. *Ib.*, 306.
6a. D. Hume, *History of England*, v. 441.

95 1. A. Bastian, *Loango-Küste* (Jena 1874–75), ii. 230.
2. Brun-Rollet, *Le Nil blanc et le Soudan* (Paris 1855), 227 ff.
3. W. Munzinger, *Ostafrikanische Studien* (Schaffhausen 1864), 474.

96 1. A. Bastian, in *Zeitschr. d. Ges. für Erdkunde zu Berlin*, 1 (1866), 37.

97 1. Caesar, *Bell. Gall.*, vi. 25.
2. O. Elton, *Origins of English History* (London 1882), 3, 106 f., 224.
3. W. Helbig, *Die Italiker in der Poebene* (Leipzig 1879), 25 f.
4. H. Nissen, *Italische Landeskunde,* i (Berlin 1883), 431 ff.
5. Livy, ix. 36–38.
6. C. Neumann and J. Partsch, *Physikalische Geogr. von Griechenland* (Breslau 1885), 357 ff.

98 1. J. Grimm, *Deutsche Mythologie*⁴ (Berlin 1875–78), i. 53 ff.
2. Pliny, *NH*, xvi. 249 ff.; Maximus Tyrius, *Dissert.*, viii. 8.
3. Tacitus, *Germania*, 9, 39, 40, 43; id., *Ann.*, ii. 12; iv. 73; id., *Hist.*, iv. 14; Grimm, *op. cit.*, 541 ff.
4. W. Mannhardt, *Der Baumkultus der Germanen und ihrer Nachbarstämme* (Berlin 1875), 26 ff.
5. Adam of Bremen, *Descr. insularum Aquilonia*, 27 (in Migne, *PL*, cxlvi, col. 644).
6. M. Cromer, *De origine et rebus gestis Polonorum* (Basle 1568), 241; Fabricius, *Livonicae historiae compendiosa series* (Riga-Leipzig 1848), 441.
7. C. Bötticher, *Der Baumkultus der Hellenen* (Berlin 1856); L. Preller, *Römische Mythologie*³ (Berlin 1881–83), i. 105–14.
8. *Classical Review*, 19 (1905), 331, referring to an inscription found in Cos.
9. Pliny, *NH*, xv. 77; Tacitus, *Ann.*, xiii. 58.
10. Plutarch, *Romulus*, 20.
11. K. Rhamm, in *Globus*, 67 (1895), 343, 348 (based on J. Krohn, *Soumen suvum pakanillinen jumalen palvelus* [Helsingfors 1894]).

99 1. Porphyry, *De abstinentia*, i. 6.
2. W. Matthews, *Ethnography and Philology of the Hidatsa Indians* (Washington 1877), 48 f.
3. Private communication from L. Fison (11/3/1898).
4. C. Hupe, in *Tijdschrift voor Neerlands-Indië*, 1846, dl. iii, 158.
5. J. J. M. de Groot, *The Religious System of China*, iv (Leyden 1901), 272 ff.

100 1. J. Aubrey, *Remaines of Gentilisme and Judaisme* (London 1881), 247.
2. P. Jones, *History of the Ojebway Indians* (London, n.d.), 104.
3. De Groot, *op. cit.*, iv. 274.
4. A. Peter, *Volksthümliche aus Österreichisch-Schlesien* (Troppau 1865–67), ii. 30.
5. P. Wagler, *Die Eiche in alter und neuer Zeit*, ii (Berlin 1891), 56, n. 1.
6. A. Bastian, *Die Völker des östlichen Asiens* (Leipzig-Jena 1866–71), ii. 475 f., iii. 251 f., iv. 42 f.
7. T. Noeldeke, in *Zeitschrift für Assyriologie*, 24 (1910), 298.
8. J. H. Neumann, in *Med. Zendel.*, 48 (1904), 724 f.
8a. C. Landtmann, *The Kiwai Papuans of British New Guinea* (London 1927), 65.

101 1. W. H. Sleeman, *Rambles and Recollections of an Indian Official* (Westminster 1893), i. 38 f.
2. U. Jahn, *Die deutschen Opfergebräuche bei Ackerbau und Viehzucht* (Breslau 1884), 214 ff.
3. Van Schmid, in *TNI*, 1843, dl. ii. 605.
4. E. L. M. Kühr, in *BTLVNI*, 47 (1897), 58 f.

5. A. C. Kruijt, in *Med. Zendel.*, 44 (1900), 221.

6. D. Grangeon, in *Missions Catholiques*, 28 (1896), 83.

102 1. A. W. Howitt, in *JAI*, 20 (1891), 89.

2. A. Schadenberg, in *Verh. Berliner Ges. f. Anthropol., Ethnol., und Urgeschichte, 1880*, p. 40.

3. F. Grabowsky, in *Internat. Archiv f. Ethnologie*, 2 (1889), 181.

4. Mrs. Bishop, *Korea and her Neighbours* (London 1898), i. 106 f.

5. *La Mission Lyonnaise d'exploration commerciale en Chine, 1895–97* (Lyons 1898), 361.

6. *Zeitschrift für allgemeine Erdkunde*, 6 (1856), 273.

7. F. Boas, in *Sixth Ann. Report on the North-Western Tribes of Canada* (1890), 28.

8. F. S. Krauss, *Volksglaube und religiöser Brauch der Südslaven* (Munster 1890), 36.

9. *Aeneid*, iii. 22 ff.

10. Philostratus, *Imagines*, ii. 29.

103 1. B. C. A. J. van Dinter, in *Tijdschr. v. Indische Taal Land en Volkenk.*, 41 (1899), 379 f.

2. O. Baumann, *Usambra und seine Nachbargebiete* (Breslau 1891), 57 ff.

3. B. Spencer and F. J. Gillen, *The Northern Tribes of Central Australia* (London 1904), 162, 330 f.

4. P. Paulitschke, *Ethnographie Nordost-Afrikas* (Berlin 1896), 34 ff.; Coulbeaux, in *Missions Catholiques*, 30 (1898), 418.

104 1. J. Kubary, *Ethnographische Beiträge zur Kenntniss des Karolinen Archipels*, iii (Leyden 1895), 228.

2. A. B. Ellis, *The Yoruba-speaking Peoples of the Slave Coast* (London 1894), 115.

3. A. C. Kruijt, in *Med. Zendel.*, 44 (1900), 220 f.

4. J. Habbema, in *BTLVNI*, 41 (1900), 113 ff.

5. G. Heijmering, in *Tidjschr. v. Neerlands-Indië*, 1844, dl. i, 358.

6. C. Snouck Hurgronje, *Het Gayoland en zijne Bewoners* (Batavia 1903), 351.

7. F. Blumentritt, *Versuch einer Ethnographie der Philippinen* (Gotha 1882), 13.

8. *Bull. Soc. Géogr. de Paris, IIme sér.*, ii (1834), 182 f.

9. H. Ling Roth, *The Natives of Sarawak and British North Borneo* (London 1896), 184.

105 1. E. C. Luard, in *Census of India, 1901*, xix (Lucknow 1902), 76.

2. J. Grimm, *op. cit.*, i. 497; ii. 540 f.

3. M. Buch, *Die Wotjäken* (Stuttgart 1882), 124.

4. P. von Stenin, in *Globus*, 58 (1890), 204.

5. J. G. Dalyell, *Darker Superstitions of Scotland* (Edinburgh 1834), 400.

106 1. On the representations of Silvanus, the Roman wood-god, see H. Jordan in L. Preller's *Römische Mythologie*³ (Berlin 1881–83), 393 n.; A. Baumeister, *Denkmäler des Klassischen Altertums* (Munich 1855–88), iii. 1665 f.

2. Aeneas Sylvius, *Opera* (Basle 1571), 418, wrongly numbered 420.

3. E. T. Dalton, *Descriptive Ethnology of Bengal* (Calcutta 1872), 186.

4. E. Aymonier, in *Cochinchine française*, No. 16 (Saigon 1883), 175 f.

5. L. Decle, *Three Years in Savage Africa* (London 1898), 489.

6. H. Schinz, *Deutsch-Südwest Afrika* (Oldenburg-Leipzig [1891]), 295 f.

7. Dalton, *op. cit.*, 188.

8. Villault, *Relation des costes appellées Guinée* (Paris 1669), 266 f.; Labat, *Voyage du chevalier des Marchais en Guinée, etc.* (Paris 1730), i. 338.

9. W. Mannhardt, *Baumkultus*, 190 ff.

10. Id., *Antike Wald- und Feldkulte* (Berlin 1877), 212 ff.

11. W. Crooke, *Popular Religion and Folk-lore of Northern India* (Westminster 1896), ii. 102.

12. T. J. Hutchinson, *Impressions of Western Africa* (London 1858), 128.

13. Mannhardt, *Baumkultus*, 161.

14. W. Camden, *Britannia*, ed. R. Gough (London 1779), ii. 659.

15. J. Potocki, *Voyage dans les steps d'Astrakhan et du Caucase* (Paris 1829), i. 309.

107 1. W. Foy, in *Archiv für Religionswissenschaft*, 10 (1907), 551. For details, see W. H. Goldie, in *Trans. and Proc. New Zealand Institute*, 37 (1904), 93 ff.

2. Mannhardt, *Baumkultus*, 163 ff.

3. *Bavaria, Landes- und Volkskunde des Königreichs Bayern* (Munich 1860–67), i. 373.

4. F. S. Krauss, *op. cit.*, 35.

5. W. Radloff, *Proben der Volkslitteratur der nördlichen türkischen Stämme*, ii (St. Petersburg 1885).

6. Mannhardt, *Baumkultus*, 51 f.

7. C. Bötticher, *op. cit.*, 30 f.

108 1. J. Brand, *Popular Antiquities of Great Britain* (London 1882–83), i. 212 f.

2. T. F. Thistleton Dyer, *Popular British Customs* (London 1876), 233.

3. R. Chambers, *Book of Days* (London-Edinburgh 1886), i. 578; Dyer, *op. cit.*, 237 f.

4. E. Cortet, *Essai sur les fêtes religieuses* (Paris 1867), 167 ff.

5. *Revue des traditions populaires*, 2 (1887), 200.

6. *Folk-Lore*, 1 (1890), 518 ff.

7. W. R. S. Ralston, *Songs of the Russian People*² (London 1892), 234 f.

109 1. L. Lloyd, *Peasant Life in Sweden* (London 1870), 235.

2. *Ib.*, 257 ff.

3. H. Pröhle, *Harzbilder* (Leipzig 1855), 19 f.
4. F. Reinsberg-Düringsfeld, *Fest-Kalender aus Böhmen* (Prague n.d.), 308 f.

110 1. W. Hone, *Every Day Book* (London [1827]), i. 547 ff.; Chambers, *op. cit.*, i. 571.
2. *Bavaria, Landes- und Volkskunde des Königreichs Bayern* (Munich 1860–67), i. 372.
3. Hone, *op. cit.*, ii. 597 f.
4. Reinsberg-Düringsfeld, *op. cit.*, 217; Mannhardt, *Baumkultus*, 566.
5. Mannhardt, *loc. cit.*
6. Aristophanes, *Plutus*, 1054; Mannhardt, *Antike Wald- u. Feldkulte*, 222 f.

111 1. Mannhardt, *Baumkultus*, 156.
2. Chambers, *op. cit.*, i. 573.
3. Mannhardt, *op. cit.*, 312.
4. *Ib.*, 314.
5. *Ib.*, 312 f.
6. H. von Wislocki, *Volksglaube u. relig. Brauch d. Zigeuner* (Munster 1891), 148 f.

112 1. Mannhardt, *op. cit.*, 320.
2. W. Kolbe, *Hessische Volks-Sitten und Gebräuche im Lichte der heidnischen Vorzeit²* (Marburg 1888), 70.
3. Mannhardt, *op. cit.*, 318.
4. E. Hoffmann-Krayer, in *Schweiz. Archiv f. Volkskunde*, 11 (1907), 252.

113 1. Mannhardt, *op. cit.*, 322; Hone, *op. cit.*, i. 583 ff.; Dyer, *op. cit.*, 230 f.
2. Mannhardt, *op. cit.*, 325.

114 1. F. Tetzner, in *Globus*, 68 (1900), 340.
2. R. Andree, *Braunschweiger Volkskunde* (Brunswick 1896), 249 f.
3. K. Seifart, *Sagen, Märchen . . . u. Gebräuche aus . . . Hildesheim²* (Hildesheim 1889), 180 f.
4. Mannhardt, *op. cit.*, 347 f.

115 1. *Ib.*, 344.
2. *Ib.*, 343 f.
3. Dyer, *op. cit.*, 270 f.
4. Mannhardt, *op. cit.*, 344 ff.

116 1. Private communication from Miss A. Wyse of Halford.
2. Mannhardt, *op. cit.*, 422.
3. P. Drechsler, *Sitte, Brauch u. Volksglaube in Schlesien*, i (Leipzig 1903), 125 ff.

4. Mannhardt, *op. cit.*, 423.
5. E. Hoffmann-Krayer, in *Schweiz. Archiv f. Volkskunde*, 11 (1907), 257 f.
6. Mannhardt, *op. cit.*, 431 f.
7. H. F. Feilberg, in *Folk-Lore*, 6 (1895), 194 f.
8. L. Lloyd, *op. cit.*, 257.

117 1. Mannhardt, *op. cit.*, 437.
2. *Ib.*, 438.
3. *Ib.*, 439 f.

119 1. H. H. Bancroft, *Native Races of the Pacific States* (London 1856–76), ii. 719 f., iii. 507.
2. P. J. de Arriaga, *Extirpacion de la Idolatria del Piru* (Lima 1621), 36 ff.
3. G. A. Wilken, in *De Indische Gido*, June 1884, p. 958.
3a. G. Tessmann, *Die Pangwe* (Berlin 1913), i. 90 f.

120 1. Maimonides, as quoted in D. Chwolson, *Die Ssabier und der Ssabismus* (St. Petersburg 1856), ii. 475. (The "Nabataean treatise" is now recognized as a forgery, but the superstitions it describes may nonetheless be genuine.)
2. J. Roscoe, in *JAI*, 32 (1902), 32–35, 38, 80.

121 1. Mannhardt, *op. cit.*, 480 f.; id., *Mythologische Forschungen* (Strasburg 1884), 341.
2. J. Brand, *Popular Antiquities of Great Britain* (London 1882–83), i. 181.
3. Mannhardt, *Baumkultus*, 481; id., *Mythol. Forsch.*, 340. Cp. T. Siebs, in *Zeitschrift für Volkskunde*, 3 (1893), 277.

122 1. A. W. Nieuwenhuis, *Quer durch Borneo* (Leyden 1904–07), i. 367.
2. *Ib.*, ii. 99.
3. M. J. van Baarda, in *BTLVNI*, 45 (1895), 514.

123 1. R. E. Dennett, *At the Back of the Black Man's Mind* (London 1906), 53, 67–71.
2. *Ib.*, 52.
3. Job 31 : 11 f. (Revised Standard Version).
4. Lev. 18 : 24 f.

124 1. *Oedipus Tyrannus*, 22 ff., 95 ff.
2. J. Rhys, *Celtic Heathendom* (London-Edinburgh 1888), 308 ff.

127 1. Herodotus, i. 181 f.

128 1. Herodotus, i. 182.

129 1. Aristotle, *Constitution of Athens*, iii. 5; Demosthenes, *Contra Neaer.*, 73–78; Hesychius, s.vv. *Dionysou gamos* and *gerarai;* Et. Magn., s.v.

gerarai; Pollux, viii. 108; A. Mommsen, *Feste der Stadt Athen im Altertum* (Leipzig 1898), 391 ff.

2. Hyginus, *Astron.,* i. 5.

130   1. At Knossos (Crete): Diodorus Siculus, v. 72; at Samos: Lactantius, *Inst.,* i. 17; at Athens: Photius, *Lex.,* s.v. *hieron gamon;* Et. Magn. s.v. *hieromnemones.* A fragment of Pherekydes relating to the marriage of Zeus and Hera will be found in B. P. Grenfell and A. S. Hunt, eds., *New Classical and other Greek and Latin Papyri* (Oxford 1897), 23.

2. *Iliad,* xiv. 347 ff.

3. J. Grimm, *Deutsche Mythologie*[4] (Berlin 1875–78), i. 176; P. Hermann, *Nordische Mythologie* (Leipzig 1903), 198 ff., 217, 520, 529.

131   1. M. Buch, *op. cit.,* 137.

2. E. A. Gait, in *Census of India, 1901,* vi, pt. ii (Calcutta 1902), 190.

132   1. P. J. de Arriaga, *Extirpacion de la Idolatria del Piru* (Lima 1621), 20.

2. Lacombe, in *Missions Catholiques,* 2 (1869), 359 f.

3. *Relations des Jésuites,* 1636, p. 109; *ib.,* 1639, p. 95.

4. F. Hahn, in *Journal of the Asiatic Soc. of Bengal,* 72, pt. ii (1904), 12.

133   1. W. Crooke, *Popular Religion and Folklore of Northern India* (Westminster 1868), ii. 118.

2. A. B. Ellis, *The Ewe-speaking Peoples of the Slave Coast* (London 1890), 139 ff.

134   1. H. Johnston, *The Uganda Protectorate* (London 1902), ii. 607.

2. J. G. Scott and J. P. Hardiman, *Gazetteer of Upper Burma and the Shan States,* ii (Rangoon 1901), 439.

3. E. W. Lane, *Manners and Customs of the Modern Egyptians,* Chap. xxvi (quoting the Arab historian Makrizi).

4. The *North China Herald,* May 4, 1906, p. 235.

5. *Voyages d'Ibn Batuta,* ed. B. R. Sanguinetti (Paris 1853–58), iv. 126 ff.

135   1. For a list of these tales, see J. G. Frazer on Pausanias, ix. 26, 7. Compare E. S. Hartland, *The Legend of Perseus* (London 1894–96), where, however, the institution of the sacred marriage is overlooked.

136   1. Catullus, xxxiv. 9 ff.

2. Wernicke, in Pauly-Wissowa, *RE,* ii. coll. 1343, 1351.

3. Plutarch, *De fortuna Romanorum,* 9. The late A. B. Cook suggested (*Classical Review,* 18 [1904], 366; *Folk-Lore,* 16 [1905], 283 f.) that the name *Egeria* (spelt *Aegeria* by Valerius Maximus, i. 2, 1) actually derived from a root *aeg* underlying German *Eiche,* English *oak,* etc.

4. Festus, s.v. *querquetulanae.*

5. Ovid, *Fasti,* iii. 273 ff.; Cicero, *De legibus,* i. 1, 4; Livy, i. 19, 5; Plutarch, *Numa,* 4, 8, 13, 15; Juvenal, *Sat.,* iii. 12.

6. See above, ¶128.

would then personify and epitomize the "spirit" or character of a living community, as it exists at a specific moment in time; whereas the god would personify or epitomize the "essence" of that community conceived as an ideal, continuous entity, of which the living generation is but the present phase. Thus the king would be but an avatar of a preterpunctual, perpetual being; but as such he would be that being's real incarnation, and his divine qualities and powers would be inherent, not conferred. He would be not merely exercising the functions of a god; he would be himself the god in his immediate, as distinct from his continuous, aspect. To put the matter in contemporary terms: the king would be the reigning sovereign of Great Britain, while the god would be "the Crown."

An illuminating illustration of this relationship is afforded by the concept of the *devaraja,* or "god-king" in ancient Cambodia. "The *devaraja,*" we are informed, "is not the deified sovereign, but rather the permanent principle and essence of kingship." But—and this is the significant point—that "essence of kingship" is conceived to be concretized and punctualized in the basic self of each successive ruler, and it may even be symbolized by an image or idol.

A close parallel is the ancient Egyptian belief that every pharaoh was an embodiment of the god Horus; and the picture may be further clarified by reference to contemporary African usage. The king of the Loango, for instance, is styled *pango,* which means "god." He is thus, as a Christian might put it, "very God of very God," co-substantial and of the same essence. Similarly, the king of Ganda is called *Llare,* "Almighty God," and is believed to control the punctual and immediate manifestations of nature. Here again, he is not a deputy or vicar, but an incarnation. "God" is likewise the title of the king of Ruanda; while among the Kaffitshos, he bears the name of the chief deity, Heql. In the same way, too, the people of Landa hail their king with the cry, "Greetings to our god"; and when the chief of the Biu dies, it is said that "God has fallen."

Ancient and primitive peoples tend to articulate this intrinsic parallelism under the figure of genealogical descent or actual conferment of properties and status. Thus, the Egyptian pharaoh is a son of the god Re^e; the Babylonian king is suckled at the breasts of the goddess Ishtar; and the Hebrew monarch is formally adopted by Jehovah at the moment of his installation: "I have installed my king on Zion, my holy hill. . . . Jehovah hath said unto me, 'Thou art my son, this day have I begotten thee' " (Psalm 2 : 6–7). Alternatively, the emblems of kingship are believed to be stored on high and to be bestowed, as an act of divine favor, upon each succeeding sovereign. In the Babylonian Story of Etana, it is said expressly that, during a period of divine displeasure, when the city of Kish was left without a king, crown and sceptre remained in the treasuries of Anu, the supreme god; while Hammurabi, king of Babylon, declares that the insignia of royalty were conferred on him by the god Sin. Similarly, in Psalm 110 (which appears to have been composed for an enthronement ceremony), "Jehovah sends forth the sceptre of thy prowess." So deeply, indeed, does this notion of *conferment* take root that it in turn gives rise to a secondary set of symbols: the "power and the glory" are *rubbed into* the king by unction or anointment, or *pressed upon* him by the laying on of hands, or *passed to* him by a symbolic clasping of the divine hand.

It is most important that these forms of expression be clearly apprehended for what they are, for otherwise we are in danger of letting them obscure the true nature of the underlying idea. This, indeed, is what has very largely happened in recent studies of "divine kingship." What is metaphorical has been taken all too often at face value, and on this basis elaborate theories have been constructed in which the king is represented to be the actual offspring of a "sacred marriage" or a human being specifically selected and delegated by a superior deity. The truth is, however, that he is nothing other than the deity himself in the latter's punctual aspect, the imagery of physical descent or special selection and designation being simply a concession to empirical forms of articulation.

3. *The priestly kings of Africa* have now been studied in greater detail. See especially: C. Petersson, *Chiefs and Gods. Religious and Social Elements in the South Eastern Bantu Kingship* (Lund 1953); T. Irstam, *The King of Ganda* (Stockholm 1944); P. Hadfield, *Traits of Divine Kingship in Africa* (London 1949); C. G. Seligman, *Egypt and Negro Africa* (London 1934); W. T. H. Beukes, *Der Häuptling in der Gesellschaft der Süd-Ost- und Zentral-Bantuvölker* (Hamburg 1931); K. A. Busia, *The Position of a Chief in the Modern Political System of Ashanti* (London 1951); M. Glucjman, "The Kingdom of the Zulu of South Africa," in *The African Political Systems* (London 1948), 22–55; M. D. W. Jeffreys, "The Divine Umandri King," in *Africa*, 8 (1938), 346–54; E. J. and J. D. Krige, *The Realm of a Rain-Queen* (London 1947); S. S. Dornan, "Rainmaking in S. Africa," in *Bantu Studies*, 3 (1927–29), 188–95; id., "The Killing of the Divine King in S. Africa," in *South African Journal of Science*, 15 (1918), 394–99; E. E. Evans-Pritchard, *The Divine Kingship of the Shilluk of the Nilotic Sudan* (Cambridge 1948). — According to Audrey Richards, *Hunger and Work in a Savage Tribe* (London 1932), the S. Bantu chief derives his authority from the fact that he is the food-provider of the community; while H. Boemer-Kuper asserts (*Africa*, 10 [1938], 58–74, 176–207) that the Swazi chief derives his from his function as military leader and from the fact that he is the wealthiest man in the group. A clear distinction should be drawn, however, between the purely pragmatic basis on which a chief is chosen, or the esteem which he claims by virtue of his social position and economic superiority, and the "spiritual" or "numinous" power with which, once he is recognized, he is believed to be innately endowed. It is with the latter alone that Frazer is concerned.

5. *Magic.* Among recent studies of magic the following are especially significant: E. de Martino, *Il mondo magico* (Turin 1948); H. Webster, *Magic: A Sociological Study* (Stanford 1948); H. Aubin, *L'homme et la magie* (Paris 1952); K. Beth, *Religion und Magie*[2] (Leipzig 1927); S. Seligmann, *Die magischen-Heil- und Schutzmittel aus der unbelebten Natur* (Stuttgart 1927); L. Thorndike, *A History of Magic and Experimental Science during the First Thirteen Centuries of our Era* (New York 1929–38); L. Deubner, *Magie und Religion* (Freiburg i.B. 1922); C. Clemen, "Wesen und Ursprung der Magie," in *Archiv für Religionspsychologie*, 2–3 (1921), 108–35.

19. *Animal flesh proscribed for homoeopathic reasons.* See on this: R. Andree, *Ethnographische Parallelen und Vergleiche*, i (Stuttgart 1878), 114–27 T. H. Gaster, *The Holy and the Profane* (New York 1955), 204 f. — The Loango proscribe the consumption of goat meat, lest the consumer's skin tend likewise to "scale": A. Bastian, *Die deutsche Expedition an der Loango-Küste* (Jena 1874–75), i. 185. — The Sea Dyaks of Borneo will not eat pork lest they contract a skin disease (scrofula?) to which pigs (cp. Italian *scrofa*) are thought to be liable: F. H. von Kittlitz, *Denkwürdigkeiten einer Reise* (1858), iii. 105. — The Caribs avoid pork for fear of getting "pigs' eyes," and tortoises lest they become clumsy: T. Waitz, *Anthropologie der Naturvölker* (Leipzig 1860–77), iii. 384. — It is not improbable that some of these traditional taboos really underlie the dietary provisions of the Mosaic Code, though this is but one factor.

21. *Taboos during wartime.* See in general: Holsti, "Some Superstitious Customs in Primitive Warfare," in *Festskrift tillegnad Westermarck* (Helsingfors 1912), 137 f.; F. Schwally, *Semitische Kriegsaltertümer* (Leipzig 1901), 46 f. — Among the early Arabs, sexual intercourse was taboo to warriors: Aghāni, xiv. 67, xv. 161; Al-Aḥtal, *Diwan*, 120.2; Mas'udi, vi. 63–65; *Frag. Hist. Ar.*, 247; W. R. Smith, *Religion of the Semites*[3] (London 1927), 455, 640 f. — Among the Hebrews, the word "consecrate" (*q-d-sh*) was used in the sense of "prepare for war": Jer. 22.7; 51.27 f.; Joel 4.9. Cp. also I Sam. 21.4–5; II Sam. 11.11. — The taboo upon consorting with women in wartime is but one application of the general idea that the very sight of women debilitates: see Stith Thompson, *Motif-Index*, C 212; T. H. Gaster, *Thespis* (New York 1950), 328.

23. *Leaping as a fertility-charm.* At Cambridge, England, it is still a popular folk custom that adults perform a ritual act of skipping on Good Friday: R. F. Rattray, *From Primitive to Modern Religion* (London [1949]), 25. — In a hymn to Zeus Kouros discovered at Palaikastro, in Crete, and dating from the third or second century B.C., the god is invoked to "leap for our herds and full pails," and some scholars have thought that this is an invitation to the deity to join his worshippers in a rite of leaping for fertility: see R. C. Bosanquet, in *Annual of the British School at Athens*, 15 (1908–09), 339 ff.; Gilbert Murray, *ib.*, 357 ff.; Jane Harrison, *Themis* (Cambridge 1912), 3 ff.; Aly, in *Philologus*, 71 (1912), 469 ff.; W. M. L. Hutchinson, in *Classical Review*, 27 (1913), 132 ff.; Latte, *De saltationibus Graecorum* (1913), 21. — It has likewise been suggested that the real function of the Salii, i.e., leapers, who performed in the forum at Rome during the month of March was to execute a ritual leaping for fertility.

26. *Use of corpses in magical practice.* For further literature see: T. J. Pettigrew, *On Superstitions connected with the History and Practise of Medicine and Surgery* (Philadelphia 1844), 100; E. S. McCartney, "Folklore Heirlooms," in *Papers of the Michigan Acad. of Science, Arts and Letters*, 16 (1931), 189–90; V. S. Lean, *Collectanea* (Bristol-London 1902–04), ii. 583; F. D. Bergen, "Current Superstitions," *Memoirs of the American Folk-Lore Society*, 4 (1876), 131. — A popular recipe from Kentucky prescribes: "If you have a goitre on your neck, rub a dead person's hand over it three times. As the body decays, the

goitre will disappear": D. L. and L. B. Thomas, *Kentucky Superstitions* (Princeton 1920), 105. This practise, which is also attested from Storington, England
(*Folk-Lore Record* I [1878], 48), can be traced back to Pliny (*NH*, xxviii. 45).
— In Thomas Hardy's story, "The Withered Arm" (included in *Wessex Tales*),
touching the neck of a man who has been hanged is said to effect a cure. This
finds a parallel in the belief of certain S. African primitives that the left hand
and foot of a person ritually slain can, if decocted, prove effective for magical
purposes. A trial for murder committed to this end was reported in the New York
Herald Tribune of June 6, 1957. This, too, has an analogy in Pliny's statements
that the hair of a crucified man protects from quartan fever (*NH*, xxviii. 41) and
that the noose used by a suicide when applied to the temples, cures headache
(xxviii. 49).

A magical papyrus in the British Museum says that in cases of theft by an unknown person, the culprit's eye will appear bruised and inflamed if a sorcerer
taps his own ear with a hammer made out of the wood of a gibbet. A similar
procedure survived in the seventeenth century at Holstein, Germany: E. Riess
in *Trans. Am. Philological Association*, 25 (1895), 52. See on this subject: G.
Kittredge, *Witchcraft in Old and New England* (Cambridge 1929), 151, 470 f.,
n. 126; Stith Thompson, *Motif-Index*, D 1500.1.26. — The noose used by a
suicide is likewise credited with the power of protecting from mishap: Kittredge,
op. cit., 142, 461, Stith Thompson, *op. cit.*, D 1384.2.

The idea underlying all these practices is that the vitality which quits the dead
may be transferred to the living. Comparable therefore is the notion attested in
Jewish folklore that a barren woman may induce conception by applying to her
own person the water or soap with which a corpse has been washed: R. Patai
in Talpioth, 5 (1953), 248, n. 2 [Hebrew]. The use for this purpose of criminals
already condemned to death is simply a short cut in the interests of "economy."
Analogous is the use of them as human scapegoats, concerning which see below
on ❡ 462.

28. *Animal properties transferred to man.* Here belongs also the practice of
giving newborn children the names of powerful or even of obnoxious animals
as a means of warding off demons who might be seeking to attack them. For
examples see: R. Andree, *Ethnographische Parallelen und Vergleiche*, i (Stuttgart 1879), 177; *Zeitschrift d. Ges. f. Erdkunde zu Berlin*, 1 (1866), 386; Th.
Bent, quoted in E. Clodd, *Tom Tit-Tot* (London 1898), 94. (It is quite mistaken
to regard such names as evidence of totemism!)

30. *Transference of properties from stones.* An arresting example of this is
afforded by the widespread practice of supplying expectant mothers with a so-
called eagle-stone (*aetites*) which they wear around their necks or carry upon
their persons as a protective amulet. The object in question is a ferruginous
pebble, usually found in streams, which, when rattled, reveals the presence of a
smaller stone inside it and thus serves as a very natural symbol of pregnancy.
See: Aelian, *De nat. animal.*, i. 35; Levret, *Essai sur les accouchements* (1776),
52; S. Seligmann, *Der böse Blick* (1910), 215–17; W. B. McDaniel, *Birth and
Infancy in Ancient Rome and Modern Italy* (Coconut Grove, Florida 1948),

12–13; *Notes and Queries,* VI, iii (1880), 327, 509; iv (1881), 297. The practice is mentioned by Plutarch (V. 95, Didot), and the properties of the stone are duly described by both Pliny (*HN,* xxx. 14; xxxvi. 39) and Dioscorides (v. 161). In Germany and Italy, it is not uncommon to bind it to the left hip of a pregnant woman: *Handwörterbuch deutsch. Abergl.,* v. 133 f.; McDaniel, *loc. cit.;* E. Canziani, in *Folk-Lore,* 39 (1928), 211. In the Middle Ages, such a stone was carefully preserved in Durham Cathedral: Bede, *Historia Eccles. Gentis Angliae,* ed. Smith (1722), 740.

31. *Death at ebb-tide.* On this superstition, see further: F. D. Bergen, *Current Superstitions* (1896), 126, No. 1184 [New England]. Pliny says (*NH,* ii. 220) that the belief was tested along the "Gallic ocean" but found to hold true only for human beings. In Boulogne, *s'en aller avec la marée* is a popular euphemism for "to die": A. S. Rapoport, *Superstitions of Sailors* (London 1928), 42. See also: P. Sébillot, *Folklore de la France* (Paris 1904–07), ii. 19 f.; Rutilius Benincasa, *Almanaco perpetuo,* pt. iv, tract. 5, c. 14; Ferraris, *Prompta Bibliotheca,* §36; Tusser's *Five Hundred Points of Good Husbandrie* (1557), c. xiv, verse 4; *Notes and Queries,* V. vi (1876), 186, 305, 356; E. S. McCartney, *op. cit.,* 173 f.

CONTAGIOUS MAGIC

Like his assumption of "homoeopathy," Frazer's theory of a Law of Contagion as a principle of magic is open to question. The practices which he cites in support of this contention can be otherwise explained.

What is really involved would seem to be the primitive notion of what we may call *the extended self.* The primitive believes that the self, or identity, of a person is not limited to his physical being but embraces also everything associated with it and everything that can evoke his presence in another person's mind. Thus, the shadow, name, footprint, gait, dress, excreta, portrait, etc., of a person are just as much an essential and integral part of him as his body, the more so since they can bear evidence of him even when he is corporeally absent. To "contact" any of these things is therefore just as effective a method of affecting him (for good or ill) as to work on his actual body. To bless or curse his name, for example, or to perform acts with portions of his clothing, will "touch" him—that is, "him" in his full, extended being—just as much as to punch him or caress him. Hence it is incorrect and oversimplified to say that one can use a man's garment in magic because of some property attaching to it materially because, having once been in contact with him, it can ever afterwards "influence" him. The truth is rather that the garment is itself a part of him. In other words, it is a question not of conveyance of properties or influences, but rather of identity.

34. *Hair as seat of the soul.* See further: Schredelseker, *De superstitionibus quae ad crines pertinent* (Heidelberg 1913); S. Reinach, *Samson* (1912), 23 ff.; Waser, in *ARW* 16 (1913), 381; Güntert, in *Sitzb. Heidelb. Akad. Wiss.,* 6 (1915), 11 f.; A. Abt, *Apologie des Apuleius* (Giessen 1908), 179 ff.; O. Gruppe, *Griech. Mythologie* (Munich 1906), 187, n. 2; 882, nn. 2 ff.; G. A. Wilken, *Ueber das Haaropfer* (Amsterdam 1886–87), 78 f. — According to L. Sommer,

Das Haar in Religion u. Aberglauben d. Griechen (Munich 1918), this belief underlies the practice of swearing by the beard.

As to the belief that it is unlucky to cut a baby's hair, see the instances quoted in *Notes and Queries*, I. vi (1852), 312; II. xii (1861), 500; IV. vi (1870), 130, 204, 376; VI. vi (1882), 249, 416. Note also the superstition reported from Bottesford Moors, England, that if a child's nails are cut before it is one year old, it will grow up to be a thief: *N & Q.*, I. vi (1852), 71. This, of course, is simply a later rationalization of the time-honored taboo.

36. Caul. See further: H. Ploss, *Das Kind* (Leipzig 1911–12), i. 37 ff., 54 f.; G. F. Abbott, *Macedonian Folklore* (Cambridge 1903), 139; A. S. Rapoport, *Superstitions of Sailors* (London 1928), 264; McCartney, *op. cit.*, 113 ff. Medieval comments on the subject will be found in Levinius Lemnius, *De miraculis occultis naturae* (1593), Bk. ii, c. 8. — The caul is always regarded as beneficial in averting demons; E. Crawley, *The Mystic Rose*[2] (London 1927), i. 151–52; Van Gennep, *Les rites de passage* (Paris 1909), 72 f.; Ploss-Bartels, *Weib*[2], ch. 53; P. Sartori, *Sitte u. Brauch* (Leipzig 1910–14), i. 23; J. Trachtenberg, *Jewish Magic and Superstition* (New York 1939), 134.

38. Sympathetic magic of clothes. A striking example of the "sympathetic" quality popularly attached to garments is the Italian belief that if menstrual cloths are put in the wash above and not underneath the clothes of a man, the man will suffer atrocious pains: Z. Zanetti, *La medicina delle nostre donne* (Città di Castello 1892), 97 f., 101. — On the magic of clothes, see in general: E. Crawley, *Dress, Drink and Drums* (London 1931).

39. Footprint. Italian witches gather dust from footprints on Tuesdays and Fridays in order to work mischief with it: M. Cox, *Introduction to Folk-Lore* (London 1897), 217. — An ancient German method of discomfiting a rival in love was to rub out his left footprint with one's right foot, and vice-versa, saying meanwhile, "I tread on thee and am over thee": W. Kroll, *Antiker Aberglaube* (Hamburg 1897), 23. — Not impossibly, superstitions of this kind underlie the legend in the Koran (Sura 20.96) that when Moses rebuked Aaron for his share in the incident of the Golden Calf, he accompanied his words by throwing dust from "the footprints of an angel" (i.e., Gabriel) at the offensive object.

41. Elijah on Mount Carmel. On the rain-making rites performed by the priests of Baal in their contest with Elijah (I Kings, ch. 18), see R. de Vaux, in *Bulletin du Musée de Beyrouth*, vol. 5. The practise of gashing the flesh was prominent in the mystery-cult of Cybele and Attis and of the "Syrian Goddess": Apuleius, *Met.*, iii. 27; Lucian, *De Dea Syria*, 50; id., *Luc. sive Asin.*, 37; Iamblichus, *De mysteriis*, iii. 4; H. Hepding, *Attis* (Giessen 1903), 159 f.; H. Graillot, *Le culte de Cybèle* (Paris 1912), 305–06; F. Cumont, *Les religions orientales, etc.*[4] (Paris 1919), 50 f. Eisele, in *Neue Jahrbüch*, 23 (1909), 625 ff., suggests that in the cult of Cybele it was designed to fructify the earth by bringing "new blood" to it; but to this O. Gruppe objects (*Literatur z. Religionsgesch. u. Antiken Mythologie*, 1906–17 [Leipzig 1921], 181 f.) that the practice came into that cult only in the sixth century B.C., when Cybele was no longer regarded as an earth-goddess. It was, he says, simply an orgiastic gesture.

42. *Twins control weather.* See Rendell Harris, *The Cult of the Heavenly Twins* (Cambridge 1906) and *Boanerges* (Cambridge 1913), where this theme is fully worked out, albeit with certain excesses. — In Classical mythology, the Dioscuri, or Heavenly Twins, were credited with the power of allaying storms: Homeric Hymns, xxxviii. 15–18; Theocritus, xxii. 1, 7–21.

44. *Drenching as rain-charm.* On the Macedonian custom to which Frazer refers see G. Eckert, "Das Regenmädchen. Eine mazedonisch-kaukasische Parallele," in *Tribus* (Jahrb. d. Linden Museums), 51 (1952), 98–101. — On the subject in general, see A. J. Reinach in *Rev. et. d'éthnogr. et de sociologie*, 1 (1908), 297; M. H. Morgan, "Rain Gods and Rain Charms," in *Trans. and Proc. Amer. Philos. Soc.*, 32. 83 ff.; E. Samter, "Altrömische Regenzauber," in *ARW* 21 (1919), 317 f.; U. Holmberg, *Die Wassergottheiten der finnisch-ugrischen Völker* (Helsinki 1913), 181 ff.; Kölbing, in *Zeitschrift für vergl. Litteraturgeschichte*, 9. 442 ff.; A. Lang, *Myth, Ritual and Religion* (London 1887), ii. 190 f.; Stith Thompson, *op. cit.*, d 2143.1.1. — On the Rumanian custom of burying an effigy of "Drought," see M. Beza, *Paganism in Roumanian Folklore* (London 1928), 27 ff. Beza insists, however, that the image is called not Scalojan (Drought) but Kalojan, and that this is a popular distortion of *kalos Ionannês* (beautiful John), a pious substitute for the older pagan *kalos Adonis* (beautiful Adonis), an exclamation known from a fragment of Sappho (No. 94, ed. Wharton) to have been used in the cult of that god. According to this interpretation, the rite is not specifically a rain-charm but simply a survival of the familiar burial of the vegetation-spirit (Osiris, Attis, Carnival, etc.). The burial and mourning for Adonis by women is indeed mentioned by Plutarch, *Alcibiades*, 18.

On the Palestinian rain-maiden, known as "Mother of the Downpour" (*Umm el-gheith*), see G. Dalman, *Arbeit und Sitte in Palästina*, I. i (Gütersloh 1928), 134 ff.

The custom of sprinkling water on the ground as a rain-charm is attested also in ancient Assyria: Bezold, in *Zeitschrift für Assyrologie*, 26 (1912), 120 f. Analogous is the custom of ritually shedding tears, concerning which see M. Canney, "The Magic of Tears," in *Journal of the Manchester Egyptian and Oriental Society*, 12 (1926), 47–54. The famous words of Psalms 126 : 5, "They that sow in tears shall reap in joy," are interpreted by Canney (*Expository Times*, Oct. 1925, p. 44) as a reference to this practice.

On the other hand, the widespread custom of aspersing people with water at New Year is purely purificatory, being often combined with the aspersion of buildings and implements and with passing through *fire*.

47. *Besprinkling the plough as a rain-charm.* The custom of the Tarahumare Indians whereby the plough is dipped in water as a rain-charm has parallels in several parts of the world. Thus in ancient India the foremost ox of the team was sprinkled with water before the first ploughing of the season: *Zeitschrift d. Vereins für Volkskunde*, 14.7, 137 f.; and the besprinkling of the plough is likewise not uncommon in German popular usage: P. Sartori, *Sitte und Brauch* (Leipzig 1910–14), ii. 61, nn. 9–10. — But such rites of aspersion are observed also in connection with many other agricultural operations: A. Dieterich, *Mutter Erde*[3] (Berlin 1925), 96 f.; *Zeits. d. Ver. f. Volkskunde*, 7.1750. In Baden, Germany, it takes place also at sowing: E. H. Meyer, *Badisches Volksleben im neunzehnten Jahrhundert* (Strassburg 1900), 420.

50. *Frogs in rain-charms.* On the Vedic hymn (Rig Veda vii. 103) to which Frazer alludes, see L. von Schroeder, *Mysterium und Mimus* (Leipzig 1908), 395 ff. Von Schroeder adds that the hymn is still recited in India as a rain-charm! — In the Malay peninsula, the swinging of a frog is thought to cause rain: *JRAS*, South. Br. 3.88. — In parts of Germany, it is believed that if frogs are killed rain will ensue, and at Whitsuntide rites are performed involving the use of frogs as a means of inducing rainfall: S. Gesemann, *Regenzauber in Deutschland* (Braunschweig 1913), 79 f. — Bones of frogs and toads interred in a Roman tomb of the third century near Abu Shusa in Palestine are interpreted by R. Giveon, *Bull. of the Israel Exploration Soc.*, 19 (1955), 238 ff., as relics of a rain-charm. See also *ERE* i. 516b.

52. *"Rain-stones."* On the subject in general, see: M. Éliade, *Traité d'histoire des religions* (Paris 1949), 199 f.; J. G. Frazer, *Folklore in the Old Testament* (London 1919), ii. 58 f.; W. J. Perry, *Children of the Sun*[2] (London 1926), 392; G. F. Kung, *The Magic of Jewels and Charms* (Philadelphia 1915), 5 f., 34; G. A. Wainright, *The Sky-Religion in Egypt* (Cambridge 1938), 76; R. Eisler, in *Philologus*, 68 (1909), 42, n. 222; Wagenvoort, in *Studi e Materiale di Storia delle Religioni*, 14 (1938), 53n.; J. Rendell Harris, in *Folk-Lore*, 15 (1905), 427 ff., 434 ff.; *Notes and Queries*, III, vi (1864), 338. — At Üskub, in a time of drought, both Christians and Moslems set upright a fallen altar of Jupiter Optimus Maximus and poured wine over it: Hasluck, *Annual of the British School at Athens*, 21 (1914–16), 78. Parallels from Africa, India, and Mexico are cited by Margaret Murray in *Zeits. Aeg. Spr.*, 51 (1913), 131, and from Turkey by Eisler, *Philologus* 68 (1909), 194.

54. *Lapis manalis.* According to L. Deubner, *Neue Jahrb.*, 27 (1911), 334, n. 3, the *lapis manalis* was originally a "rain-stone" and came later to be integrated into the cult of Jupiter in order to give sanction to traditional prayers and sacrifices associated with it. But Festus, c. 128, suggests a different explanation. The stone, he says, was called *manalis* because it covered the mouth of the netherworld (*ostium Orci*), through which the spirits of the dead, called *manes*, ascended at stated times to the world of men. Whether or not the etymology is correct or merely an ingenious afterthought, this would connect the *lapis manalis* with the widespread ancient belief that the nether waters, usually personified as a dragon, were forcibly held down by a giant stone placed over them when the divine hero defeated that monster. Thus in the Babylonian Epic of Creation (*Enuma elish*, 1.71) the god Ea establishes his dwellingplace over the subjugated waters (*apsu*); Marduk does likewise after subduing Tiamat (vi. 62–64); and he is described in a Babylonian liturgical text as "the lord who dwells in a fane in the midst of the ocean" (*bêlu ša ina â-ki-it ina qa-bal tam-tim āš-bu*): E. Ebeling, *Tod und Leben nach den Vorstellungen der Babylonier* (Berlin 1931), 25, No. 5, rev. 4 (where, however, the passage is differently interpreted). The city of Babylon, the central fane of this god, was established on the nether waters: E. Burrows, *Orientalia*, 1 (1932), 251; so too was the temple of E-ninu at Lagash and that of E-engurak at Eridu: Jacobsen, *Journal of Near Eastern Studies*, 5 (1946), 145, n. 28. In Egyptian myth Ra was said to have placed a stone forty cubits long over the defeated monster Apep: P. le Page Renouf in *Trans. Soc. Bibl. Archaeology*, 8 (1883), 217. In a Hittite text describing the discomfiture of the dragon Illuyankas (Goetze, *ANET* 125 f.) the victorious god takes his seat on a throne placed "above the well." Lucian, *De Dea Syria*, 13, says that the shrine of "Juno" at Hierapolis was erected by Deucalion over a chasm which received the waters of the deluge. In Psalm 29 : 10, Yahweh is said to sit enthroned "above the stormflood"—a passage usually misunderstood. In rabbinic litera- ture, the foundation stone of Solomon's Temple is said to hold down the sub- terranean waters of the deluge: Mishnah, Yômâ, 5.2; Pal. Targum, Ex. 28.30; Mishnah, *Middoth* 2.6; Pesiqta de Rab Kahana, p. 27; Feuchtwang, in *Monats- schrift. Ges. Wiss. Judenthums* 1910. 724 f.

Fulgentius, p. 359, cites many other instances of cylindrical stones dragged across borders in time of drought.

55. The Egyptian ceremony called "the circumambulation of the wall" (*phrr ḥ 'inb*) wherein a Pharaoh walked around the walls of a temple, was as old as the time of Menes, legendary founder of the United Kingdom: S. A. B. Mercer, *The Religion of Ancient Egypt* (London 1949), 351. It may be questioned, how- ever, whether it had anything to do with influencing the course of the sun, as asserted by Frazer (on the authority of Moret); it may just as well connect with the familiar practice of periodically redefining the boundaries of a sanctuary or demain by walking round them; see K. Sethe, *Untersuchungen zur Geschichte und Altertumskunde Aegyptens*, iii (Berlin 1905), 133–35; J. Vandier, *La religion égyptienne* (Paris 1949), 181 f. For instances of this practice (which survives in the "beating of the bounds" in English parishes), see T. H. Gaster, *Thespis* (New York 1950), 179 f.

56. *Chariot of the sun.* The belief that the sun rides in a chariot does not occur in Homer, though Dawn is said to possess steeds (*Odyssey* 23.244). The idea first appears in the Homeric Hymns (ii. 63, 88; iv. 69; xxviii. 14; xxxi. 9) and in Hesiod (fr. 67 Rzach); later, however, it becomes a commonplace: Allen- Sikes-Halliday, *The Homeric Hymns*[2] (Oxford 1936), 433; A. B. Cook, *Zeus* ii (Cambridge 1925), 96, 552. — Shamash, the Babylonian god of the sun, was sometimes styled "the charioteer" (*rakib narkabti*): M. Jastrow, *Religion of Babylonia and Assyria* (Boston 1898), 461; and this is possibly the meaning of the divine name Rkb-il in inscriptions of the eighth century B.C. from Zenčirli, in northwest Syria: *ANET*[2], 500 f. — For the idea in Norse mythology, see J. A. MacCulloch, *Celtic Mythology* (Boston 1918), 198; and for Teutonic parallels, see K. Helm, *Altgermanische Religions geschichte*, i (Heidelberg 1913), i. 178, 256. — On the charioteer of the sun in folktales, cf. Stith Thompson, *Motif- Index*, A 724; O. Howey, *The Horse in Magic and Myth* (London 1923), 114 ff.

For Hindu parallels, see N. M. Penzer, *The Ocean of Story* (London 1923), i. 143, n. 2; ii. 150 f.

59. *Whistling for the wind.* On this widespread superstition, see: Heims, *Seespuk*[2] (Leipzig 1888), 54 f.; F. Liebrecht, *Zur Volkskunde* (Heilbronn 1879), 332 [Norway]; G. Kittredge, *Witchcraft*, 160, 478 f. and nn. 77–78; Stith Thompson, *Motif-Index*, D 2142.0.6. The idea forms a central motif in one of M. R. James' ghost stories.

60. *Wind tied in a bag.* Cf. *Odyssey*, 10.1–76; Ovid, *Met.*, 14.223–32; Apollodorus, *Epitome*, vii. 10 ff.; Hyginus, *Fab.*, 125. — On the theme in general see R. Stroemberg, "The Aeolus Episode and Greek Wind Magic," in *Symbolae Phil. Goteb.*, 1950. 71–84; and for a Teutonic parallel, see Grimm-Stallybrass, *Teutonic Mythology* (London 1880), 1087. — Not impossibly there is an allusion to this concept in Proverbs 30 : 4: "Who gathered the wind in his garment?" for the question is propounded along with other riddles which appear to possess a mythological basis: T. H. Gaster, in *Standard Dict. of Folklore*, etc., 987b. — On the motif in folktales, see Stith Thompson, *Motif-Index*, C 322.1.

75. The belief that *the fertility of the land is bound up with the health of the king* appears as early as the fourteenth century B.C. in the *Poem of Keret* from Ras Shamra-Ugarit, in N. Syria. When that monarch falls ill, corn and rain fail: *ANET*, 148 (iii); T. H. Gaster, in *Jewish Quarterly Review*, 37 (1946–47), 285 ff.

76. *Touching for "King's Evil."* The first English king who "touched" patients to cure scrofula was Edward the Confessor, in 1058: Baker, *Chronicles of the Kings of England* (London 1679), 18. In *The London Gazette* of March 12, 1712, Queen Anne solemnly announced her intention to "touch" for the disease, and the practice was discontinued only by George I in 1714. — On the subject in general see E. Law Hussey, "On the Cure of Scrofulous Diseases attributed to the Royal Touch," in *Archaeological Journal*, No. 39.

81. *Laurel induces inspiration.* See Ogle, "The Laurel in Ancient Religion and Literature," in *Amer. Journal of Philology*, 31 (1910), 287 f.; A. Abt, *Apologie des Apuleius*, 77 ff. — According to J. Reid, in *Journal of Roman Studies*, 2 (1912), 45 ff., the Roman lustral use of the laurel was borrowed from the Greeks.

86. *Shooting arrows to produce rain.* See also L. Spence, *An Introduction to Mythology* (New York 1921), 28 ff. — But arrows are also shot to drive off demons who *create* storms, as among the ancient Getae (Herodotus, iv. 94), Calydonians (i. 172), and Psylli (iv. 173), and the modern Bulgarians (Kazarow, in *Klio*, 12 [1912], 356 f.).

87. Significant also in this connection is the fact that in Ethiopic a common term for "god" is *emlak*, actually a plural of the regular Semitic word for "king."

97. G. Stara Tedde, "I boschi sacri dell'antica Roma," in *Bull. Comiss. arch. comm. di Roma,* 33 (1905), 189 ff., lists twenty-eight sacred groves in the vicinity of Rome alone.

98. *Natural sanctuaries.* Leeuwen, in *Mnemosyne,* 34 (1906), 181 ff., argues that in Homer (e.g., *Iliad,* 1. 39; 6. 93) the Greek word *nêos* (sanctuary) means a *natural* preserve rather than a constructed edifice; and A. L. Frothingham, in *AJA,* 18 (1914), 302 ff., maintains that this was likewise the original meaning of Latin *templum.* See further K. D. White, "The Sacred Grove," in *Greece and Rome,* N. S. 1 (1954), 112–27, where the "Minoan" cult of trees and pillars is illustrated from analogies in the ancient Near East. On the subject in general, see: J. Toutain, "Les cavernes sacrés dans l'antiquité grecque," in *Ann. Mus. Guimet,* 39 (1913); P. Saintyves, *Les grottes dans les cultes magico-religieux* (1919).

100. *Sacred trees.* The sacrosanct character of certain trees in the ancient Near East is well illustrated by the episode in the Babylonian Epic of Gilgamesh (tablets iii–v) dealing with the bold assault made by that hero and his companion Enkidu upon the sacred cedar-grove guarded by the monster Humbaba-Huwawa ("Whoof-whoof"?). — To this day, among the Moslems of Palestine, branches of trees beside a shrine may not be cut: T. Canaan, in *Journal of the Palestine Oriental Society,* 4 (1924), 36.

107. *Fertilizing properties of apples.* The practice adopted by the Kara-Kirghiz of rolling on the ground near an apple-tree as a means of inducing pregnancy may be connected more specifically with fertilizing properties ascribed to that particular fruit; see on this, Aigremont, *Volkserotik und Pflanzenwelt* (Halle n.d.), 59 ff.; K. Helbig, in *Zeits. f. neutestamentliche Wissenschaft,* 44 (1953), 111–17; B. O. Foster, "Notes on the Symbolism of the Apple in Classical Antiquity," in *Harvard Studies in Classical Philology,* 10 (1899), 39–55; E. S. McCartney, "How the Apple Became the Token of Love," in *Trans. and Proc. Amer. Phil. Assoc.,* 56 (1925), 70–81. — Similarly in Oriental Jewish folklore, women are advised to induce conception by washing hands and face in water mixed with the sap of an apple-tree: R. Patai, in *Talpiôth,* 5 (1953), 248 [Hebrew]. — Analogous, too, is the custom of throwing apples as a sign of love. Basically, this is a means of conveying fertility: see D. L. and L. B. Thomas, *Kentucky Superstitions* (Princeton 1920), 25–26, 41.

108–110. *Eiresionê and maypole.* On the *eiresionê,* see M. Nilsson, *Greek Popular Religion* (New York 1940), 36 f. — Analogous is the Jewish custom of carrying a *lulab*—that is, a palm-branch twined with willows and myrtle-leaves— at the autumnal Feast of Ingathering (or Booths), which concludes the agricultural year. This is interpreted as a fulfillment of the Biblical commandment (Leviticus 23 : 40) to take the fruit of a goodly tree, etc., on that occasion. The precise application of the commandment to something like an *eiresionê* is, however, a later development, which may have come in during the Greek age. — Among the Swazis of S. E. Africa, "the big Incwala begins with the 'fetching of the holy trees' [*luskewane*], a bush with leaves that keep green very long." It is

fetched by young unmarried men, and the underlying symbolism is clearly indicated by the words of a lullaby sung meanwhile, viz., "We lull him, *shiwayo,
shiwayo.* The Child grows; we rock him, *shiwayo* . . . He who is as big as the
world": H. Kuper, *An African Aristocracy* (Oxford 1947), 209 ff. — At the
close of the nineteenth century, it was customary at Banga, in Georgia, to bring
a felled oak into church during the last days of April: C. F. Lehmann, in *Die
Zeit*, 2 (1902), 468. — Early forms of this usage may perhaps be recognized in
the custom associated with the mysteries of Attis whereby a pine-log (mythically
identified with that god) was introduced into the precincts of the temple at the
spring equinox. March 22, says the Calendar of Philocalus, was therefore known
among Roman adherents of the cult as *Arbor Intrat*, "Day when the Log Comes
In." According to Firmicus Maternus (*De errore prof. rel.*, 27. 2), the sacred
poles of Attis were burned from year to year. — A Hittite text (*KUB* xxv. 31)
mentions the burning of the *eyan*, or sacred pole, together with other appurten-
ances of the temple, as part of the ritual of the summer festival of Puruli: see
T. H. Gaster, *Thespis*, 376 f. Similarly, in Herefordshire, England, the "Bush,"
i.e., the hawthorn or blackthorn bush, which, with the mistletoe bough, had been
hung in the farmhouse kitchen since the last new year, was ceremonially burned
on January 1. During the operation, a new one was made. It was believed that
without this ceremony there would be no crops: A. Wright, *British Calendar
Customs* (London 1938), ii. 22–23. — See also O. Lauffer, *Der Weinachtsbaum
und sein Ursprung aus dem volkstümlichen Geisterglauben der Mittwinterzeit*
(1933).

119. *Sex rites at seasonal festivals.* Among certain African peoples sexual
intercourse is ordained not only at calendar crises relating to vegetation but also
as a means of reinvigorating the community at *any* time of trouble or distress:
see H. Junod, *The Life of a South African Tribe* (Neuchâtel 1913), i. 153, 292;
O. Petersson, *Chiefs and Gods* (Lund 1953), 220. So too among the Ronga, a
clan of the S. E. Bantu, the headman and his wife must copulate when a new
village is founded: Junod, *op. cit.*, 295; and among the Bantu in general sexual
license is a common concomitant of initiation: H. Fehlinger, *Sexual Life of
Primitive People*, tr. S. Herbert (London 1921), 23. — On sex rites, cf. R.
Goodland, *A Bibliography of Sex Rites and Customs* (London 1931).

121. *Rolling.* An analogous custom, known as *rebolada*, is observed in May,
before the reaping of flax, at Arçal, near Valença da Minho, and at Santo Tirso,
Portugal: R. Gallop, *Portugal, A Book of Folkways* (Cambridge 1936), 11. —
For the custom in Germany, see: L. Strackerjan, *Aberglaube und Sagen aus dem
Herzogthum Oldenburg* (Oldenburg 1867), ii. 125; Lüpkes, *Ostfriesische Volkskunde* (Emden [1908]), 184. — An instance from Mexico is cited in *Globus*,
86. 356.

123. *Human conduct affects fertility.* In prayers of the Hittite king, Mursilis
II, a twenty-year blight is attributed to the sins of the royal house: see A. Goetze,
in *Kleinasiatische Forschungen*, 1 (1930), 175. Similar ideas appear in Mesopotamian texts: see R. Labat, *Le caractère religieux de la royauté assyro-babylonienne* (Paris 1939), 121 f. — In folktales, the idea receives the moral twist that

crops fail during the reign of a wicked king: Stith Thompson, *Motif-Index*, Q 552. 3.

As for the impact of *sexual* misconduct upon the fertility of the soil, it is significant that in several passages of the Old Testament (e.g., Isa. 24 : 5; Jer. 3 : 1, 2, 9; Psalm 106 : 38), lechery and adultery are said to defile the soil in exactly the same way as a woman might be defiled if involved in those offenses, the same Hebrew word (*ḥ-n-p*) being employed. — See also ¶76.

On the subject in general, see James G. Frazer, *Folklore in the Old Testament* (London 1919), i. 82 ff.; R. Patai, in *Jewish Quarterly Review*, New Series, 30 (1939), 59–69; id., *Man and Temple* (London 1947), 151–52; Marie Delcourt, *Stérilités mystérieuses et naissances maléfiques dans l'antiquité classique* (Paris 1938), 17 f.

But it is not only sexual misbehavior that is believed to affect vegetation and fecundity. In the Biblical story of Cain and Abel, *blood shed in homicide* renders the soil barren: Gen. 4 : 11–12. Similarly, in Numbers 35 : 33 it is stated explicitly that "blood pollutes the land"; while in the farewell song of Moses (Deut. 32 : 43), Yahweh's championship of His people is said to extend to avenging their spilled blood and "expiating" their soil from the taint of it. — In the Ugaritic (North Canaanite) *Poem of Aqhat*, our extant text of which dates from the fourteenth century B.C., the murder of that youth is revealed to his father and sister by the sudden infertility of the soil: see T. H. Gaster, *Thespis* (New York 1950), 296.

127. On *the sacred marriage in ancient Mesopotamia*, see E. Douglas van Buren, in *Orientalia*, 13 (1944), 1 ff.; R. Labat, *Le caractère religieux de la royauté assyro-babylonienne* (Paris 1939), 256 ff. Reisner, *Hymnen* viii, obv. 8, describes how Marduk, god of Babylon, "hastes to the wedding" at the Akîtu, or New Year festival. The espousals of the god Ningirsu and the goddess Baú are mentioned in an earlier Sumerian inscription of Gudea of Lagash (*KB* III. i, 59 iii. 6 ff.). Išme-Dagan, a king of the Isin dynasty, declares himself to be the groom of the goddess Innina: S. Langdon, *Sumerian Liturgical Texts*, 143. 9. Bridal gifts were offered to the goddess of Ur (*RA* 9 [1912], pl. vii. 56). A bridal hymn for the marriage of the king to the goddess during the epoch of Isin-Larsa is published by Langdon, *JRAS*, 1926, 15–42.

128. On *the sacred marriage in ancient Egypt*, see A. Moret, *Du caractère religieux de la royauté pharaonique* (Paris 1902), 48–73.

134–35. *The marriage of girls to rivers* (or to dragons who control them) is a frequent motif of folktales: Stith Thompson, *Motif-Index*, B 11. 10. The marriage is usually designed to appease the dragon against causing a flood, and is thus but a particular variation of the theme of annual or periodic sacrifice of girls or boys to the same end—an idea familiar especially from the Classical legend of the Minotaur: see G. Freytag, in *Am Urquell*, 1 (1890), 179 ff., 197; Frazer, *Pausanias*, vol. v, p. 145.

The idea occurs already in ancient Near Eastern literature. In the Egyptian "Astarte Papyrus" (*ANET*, 17; Gaster, in *Bibliotheca Orientalis* 5 [1952], 82 ff.), that goddess offers herself to the draconic "Sir Sea" (**Yam**) in order to end his depredations; and this seems also to underlie certain incidents in the Ugaritic Poem of Baal. Indeed, in one passage of the latter (II AB, iv–v. 120–vi. 15) the god Baal forbids the architect of his new palace to cut windows in it lest Yam crawl through them and abduct his brides! Similarly, in a Hittite myth, the goddess ("Ishtar") pretends to offer herself to the sea-dragon Hedammu in order to arrest his assaults upon the earth (Gaster, *loc. cit.*). — In Egypt, images of the goddess of the Nile (called *rpât*, "princess") were thrown into the river. They are mentioned at the end of the Papyrus Harris, dating from the reign of Ramses II (c. 1170 B.C.). A. Moret (*La mise à mort du dieu en Égypte* [Paris 1927], 11) thinks they symbolized a "sacred marriage" designed to promote fertility through the river.

Thévenot, *Relation d'un voyage au Levant*, 301, says he saw a male and female wooden effigy thrown ceremonially into the Nile on August 18, 1657. On August 15, a conical figurine made of mould and called *aruseh*, "bride," is still thrown into the Nile off the isle of Rodah, near Cairo, at the annual ceremony of "opening the dyke": Palanque, *Le Nil aux temps pharaoniques*, 85; Savary, *Lettres sur l'Égypte*, xiv.

136. On *the marriage of the nymph Egeria to Numa* in a grove outside the Porta Capena, see: Livy, 1. 21, 3; Ovid, *Fasti*, 3. 274; Martial, 10. 35, 13–14; Juvenal, 3. 11–20; Statius, *Silv.*, 5. 3, 289–91; Sulpicius, 67–68.

138. On *the eagle-topped sceptre* of Roman kings, see Mayor on Juvenal, 10. 43. Such sceptres were later carried by consuls: Prudentius, *c. Symm.* 1. 349; Ammianus Marc., 29. 2, §15. They are figured on coins and diptychs. — The eagle was regarded as a symbol of apotheosis: cf. Isid., 18, 2, 5: *quod per victoriam quasi ad supernam magnitudinem accederent.* — For the eagle as a general symbol of kingship, see: Henderson, *Survivals of Belief among the Celts* (1911), 93; O. Gruppe, in *Bursians Jahrbuch*, 186 (1921), 138 f.; A. S. Pease on Cicero, *De Divinatione*, vol. i, p. 129 b. — On the eagle as the bird of Zeus, see G. E. Mylonas, in *Classical Journal*, 41 (1946), 203–07; as the bird of Jupiter, see Pease, *op. cit.*, 290 ff. — According to H. Usener, in *Rhein. Mus.*, 60. 24 f., the bird personifies lightning. It should be observed, however, that in Roman Syria it was the common emblem of a *solar* deity: R. Dussaud, in *Rev. arch.*, 1 (1903), 134–43; F. Cumont, in *Rev. de l'histoire des religions*, 62 (1910), 147. The winged solar disk is associated with an eagle at the Phoenician holy place of 'Ain el-Ḥayat: S. A. Cook, *The Religion of Ancient Palestine in the Light of Archaeology* (London 1930), 48, pl. viii, 1. Similarly, on a N. Syrian bronze, the eagle stands on a discoid base inscribed HÊLIOS (Sun): A. B. Cook, *Zeus*, i, 604, fig. 473. On a seal of Zeus Dolichenus from Beirut, the eagle is actually substituted for the usual solar disc: M. Lidzbarski, *Ephemeris für Semitische Epigraphik*, (Giessen 1902–15), iii. 198. Similarly, in Levantine art of the Graeco-Roman age, the eagle perched on the omphalos has solar implications: Sittl, in *Jahrb. f. Klass. Phil.*, Suppl. 14. — The eagle is likewise the bird of Odin and carries his messages: Hopf, *Thierorakel und Orakelthier in alter und neuer Zeit* (Stuttgart 1888), 11. — On the eagle in early Hittite religion, see H. G. Güterbock, *Siegel aus Boghazköy* (*Archiv für Orientforschung*, Beiheft 7), 18 f.; S. Alp, *Personennamen in der heth. Hieroglyphenschrift* (Ankara 1950), 28. — There seems no reason to seek any more esoteric connection between the eagle and the king, or the eagle and the king of the gods, than that the bird was regarded as king of the fowl of heaven: cf. Ziegler, in *Rhein Mus.*, 68 (1913), 336 ff. This was commonly acknowledged among the Greeks: Aeschylus, *Agam.*, 113; Pindar, *Pyth.*, 1. 13; Aristophanes, *Knights*, 1087; Callimachus, *Hymns*, 1. 68, etc.

PART II

TABOO AND THE PERILS

OF THE SOUL

SAFEGUARDING

THE LIFE-SPIRIT

143. *At a certain stage of early society the king or priest is often thought to be endowed with supernatural powers or to be an incarnation of a deity, and consistently with this belief the course of nature is supposed to be more or less under his control, and he is held responsible for bad weather, failure of the crops, and similar calamities. To some extent it appears to be assumed that the king's power over nature, like that over his subjects and slaves, is exerted through definite acts of will; and therefore if drought, famine, pestilence, or storms arise, the people attribute the misfortune to the negligence or guilt of their king, and punish him accordingly with stripes and bonds, or, if he remains obdurate, with deposition and death. Sometimes, however, the course of nature, while regarded as dependent on the king, is supposed to be partly independent of his will. His person is considered, if we may express it so, as the dynamical centre of the universe, from which lines of force radiate to all quarters of the heaven; so that any motion of his—the turning of his head, the lifting of his hand—instantaneously affects and may seriously disturb some part of nature. He is the point of support on which hangs the balance of the world, and the slightest irregularity on his part may overthrow the delicate equipoise. The greatest care must, therefore, be taken both by and of him; and his whole life, down to its minutest details, must be so regulated that no act of his, voluntary or involuntary, may disarrange or upset the established order of nature.*

144. Of this class of monarchs the Mikado, the spiritual emperor of Japan, is or rather used to be a typical example. He is an incarnation of the sun goddess, the deity who rules the universe, gods and men included; once a year all the gods wait upon him and spend a month at his court.[1] The Mikado receives from his people and assumes in his official proclamations and decrees the title of "manifest or incarnate deity" (*Akitsu Kami*) and he

145

claims a general authority over the gods of Japan.[2] For example, in an official decree of the year 646 the emperor is described as "the incarnate god who governs the universe."[3]

145. Similar priestly or rather divine kings are found, at a lower level of barbarism, on the west coast of Africa. At Shark Point near Cape Padron, in Lower Guinea, lives the priestly king Kukulu, alone in a wood. He may not touch a woman nor leave his house; indeed he may not even quit his chair, in which he is obliged to sleep sitting, for if he lay down no wind would arise and navigation would be stopped. He regulates storms, and in general maintains a wholesome and equable state of the atmosphere.[1] On Mount Agu in Togo, there lives a fetish or spirit called Bagba, who is of great importance for the whole of the surrounding country. The power of giving or withholding rain is ascribed to him, and he is lord of the winds. His priest dwells in a house on the highest peak of the mountain, where he keeps the winds bottled up in huge jars. Applications for rain, too, are made to him. Yet though his power is great and he is indeed the real chief of the land, the rule of the fetish forbids him ever to leave the mountain, and he must spend the whole of his life on its summit. Only once a year may he come down to make purchases in the market; but even then he may not set foot in the hut of any mortal man, and must return to his place of exile the same day. The business of government in the villages is conducted by subordinate chiefs, who are appointed by him.[2] In the West African kingdom of Congo there was a supreme pontiff called Chitomé or Chitombé, whom the Negroes regarded as a god on earth and all-powerful in heaven. Hence before they would taste the new crops they offered him the first-fruits, fearing that manifold misfortunes would befall them if they broke this rule. When he left his residence to visit other places within his jurisdiction, all married people had to observe strict continence the whole time he was out; for it was supposed that any act of incontinence would prove fatal to him. And if he were to die a natural death, they thought that the world would perish, and the earth, which he alone sustained by his power and merit, would immediately be annihilated.[3] Amongst the semi-barbarous nations of the New World, at the date of the Spanish conquest, there were found hierarchies or theocracies like those of Japan; in particular, the high pontiff of the Zapotecs in Southern Mexico appears to have presented a close parallel to the Mikado. A powerful rival to the king himself, this spiritual lord governed Yopaa, one of the chief cities of the kingdom, with absolute dominion. He was looked on as a god whom the earth was not worthy to hold nor the sun to shine upon. He profaned his sanctity if he even touched the ground with his foot. A rule of continence was regularly imposed on the Zapotec priests, especially upon the high pontiff; but "on certain days in each year, which were generally celebrated with feasts and dances, it was customary for the high priest to become drunk. While in this state, seeming to belong neither to heaven nor to earth, one of the most beautiful of the virgins consecrated to the service of the gods was brought to him." If the child she bore him was a son, he was brought up as a prince of the blood, and the eldest son succeeded his father on the pontifical throne.[4]

146. Such a king or priest, it is clear, must be regarded by his subjects as a source both of infinite blessing and of infinite danger. What he gives he can refuse; and so close is the dependence of nature on his person, so delicate the balance of the system of forces whereof he is the centre, that the least irregularity on his part may set up a tremor which may shake the earth to its foundations. And if nature may be disturbed by the slightest involuntary act of the king, it is easy to conceive the convulsion which his death might provoke.

A king of this sort lives hedged in by a ceremonious etiquette, a network of prohibitions and observances, of which the intention is not to contribute to his dignity, much less to his comfort, but to restrain him from conduct which, by disturbing the harmony of nature, might involve himself, his people, and the universe in one common catastrophe.

Of the supernaturally endowed kings of Loango it is said that the more powerful a king is, the more taboos is he bound to observe; they regulate all his actions, his walking and his standing, his eating and drinking, his sleeping and waking.[1] To these restraints the heir to the throne is subject from infancy; but as he advances in life the number of abstinences and ceremonies which he must observe increases, "until at the moment that he ascends the throne he is lost in the ocean of rites and taboos."[2] In the crater of an extinct volcano, enclosed on all sides by grassy slopes, lie the scattered huts and yam-fields of Riabba, the capital of the native king of Fernando Po. This mysterious being lives in the lowest depths of the crater, surrounded by a harem of forty women, and covered, it is said, with old silver coins. He has never seen a white man and, according to the firm conviction of all the Boobies, or aborigines of the islands, the sight of a pale face would cause his instant death. He cannot bear to look upon the sea; indeed it is said that he may never see it even in the distance, and that therefore he wears away his life with shackles on his legs in the dim twilight of his hut. Certain it is that he has never set foot on the beach. With the exception of his musket and knife, he uses nothing that comes from the whites; European cloth never touches his person, and he scorns tobacco, rum, and even salt.[3]

Among the Ewe-speaking peoples of the Slave Coast, in West Africa, "the king is at the same time high priest. In this quality he was, particularly in former times, unapproachable by his subjects. Only by night was he allowed to quit his dwelling in order to bathe and so forth. None but his representative, the so-called 'visible king,' with three chosen elders might converse with him, and even they had to sit on an ox-hide with their backs turned to him. He might not see any European nor any horse, nor might he look upon the sea, for which reason he was not allowed to quit his capital even for a few moments. (These rules have been disregarded in recent times.)"[4] The king of Dahomey himself is subject to the prohibition of beholding the sea,[5] and so are the kings of Loango[6] and Great Ardra in Guinea.[7] The sea is the fetish of the Eyeos, to the north-west of Dahomey, and they and their king are threatened with death by their priests if ever they dare to look on it.[8] It is believed that the king of Cayor in Senegal would infallibly die within the year if he were to cross a river or an arm of the sea.[9] In Mashonaland down to recent times the chiefs would not cross certain rivers, particularly the Rurikwi and the Nyadiri; and the custom was still strictly observed by at least one chief within the last few years.[10] So among the Mahafalys and Sakalavas in the south of Madagascar some kings are forbidden to sail on the sea or to cross certain rivers.[11] The horror of the sea is not peculiar to kings. The Basutos are said to share it instinctively, though they have never seen salt water, and live hundreds of miles from the Indian Ocean.[12] The Egyptian priests loathed the sea, and called it the foam of Typhon; they were forbidden to set salt on their table, and they would not speak to pilots because they got their living by the sea; hence too they would not eat fish, and the hieroglyphic symbol for hatred was a fish.[13] When the Indians of the Peruvian Andes were sent by the Spaniards to work in the hot valleys of the coast, the vast ocean which they saw before them as they descended the Cordillera was dreaded by them as a cause of disease; hence they prayed to it that they might not fall ill. This they all did without exception, even the little children.[14] Similarly the inland people of Lampong in Sumatra are said to pay a kind of adoration to the sea, and to make it an offering of cakes and sweetmeats when they behold it for the first time, deprecating its power of doing them mischief.[15]

The ancient kings of Ireland were subject to certain quaint prohibitions or taboos, on the due observance of which the prosperity of the people and the country, as well as their own, was supposed to depend. Thus, for example, the sun might not rise on the king of Ireland in his bed at Tara, the old capital of Erin; he was forbidden to alight on Wednesday at Magh Breagh, to traverse Magh Cuillinn after sunset, to incite his horse at Fan-Chomair, to go in a ship upon the water the Monday after Bealltaine (May Day), and to leave the track of his army upon Ath Maighne the Tuesday after All-Hallows'. If the kings strictly observed these and many other customs, which were enjoined by immemorial usage, it was believed that they would never meet with mischance or misfortune, and would live for ninety years without experiencing the decay of old age; that no epidemic or mortality would occur during their reigns; and that the seasons would be favourable and the earth yield its fruit in abundance; whereas, if they set the ancient usages at naught, the country would be visited with plague, famine, and bad weather.[16] Among the Karen-nis of Upper Burma a chief attains his position, not by hereditary right, but on account of his habit of abstaining from rice and liquor. The mother, too, of a candidate for the chieftainship must have eschewed these things and lived solely on yams and potatoes so long as she was with child. During that time she may not eat any meat nor drink water from a common well. And if her son is to be qualified for the office of chief he must continue to observe these habits.[17]

RESTRICTIONS IMPOSED ON PRIESTS

147. Of the taboos imposed on *priests* we may see a striking example in the rules of life prescribed for the Flamen Dialis at Rome, who has been interpreted as a living image of Jupiter, or a human embodiment of the sky-spirit. They were such as the following:—The Flamen Dialis might not ride or even touch a horse, nor see an army under arms, nor wear a ring which was not broken, nor have a knot on any part of his garments; no fire except a sacred fire might be taken out of his house; he might not touch wheaten flour or leavened bread; he might not touch or even name a goat, a dog, raw meat, beans,[1] and ivy; he might not walk under a vine; the feet of his bed had to be daubed with mud; his hair could be cut only by a free man and with a bronze knife, and his hair and nails when cut had to be buried under a lucky tree; he might not touch a dead body nor enter a place where one was burned; he might not see work being done on holy days; he might not be uncovered in the open air; if a man in bonds were taken into his house, the captive had to be unbound and the cords had to be drawn up through a hole in the roof and so let down into the street. His wife, the Flaminica, had to observe nearly the same rules, and others of her own besides. She might not ascend more than three steps of the kind of staircase called Greek; at a certain festival she might not comb her hair; the leather of her shoes might not be made from a beast that had died a natural death, but only from one that had been slain or sacrificed; if she heard thunder she was tabooed till she had offered an expiatory sacrifice.[2]

Among the Todas of Southern India the holy milkman of the highest class (*palol*), who acts as priest of the sacred dairy, must live at the sacred dairy and may never visit his home or any ordinary village. He must be celibate; if he is married he must leave his wife. On no account may any ordinary person touch him; such a touch would so defile his holiness that he would forfeit his office. It is only on two days a week, namely Mondays and Thursdays, that a mere layman may even approach him. He never cuts his hair or pares his nails so long as he holds office; he never crosses a river by a bridge, but wades through a ford and only certain fords; if a death occurs in his clan, he may not attend any of the funeral ceremonies, unless he first resigns his office and descends from the exalted rank of milkman to that of a mere common mortal.[3]

OUTWARD FORMS OF THE SPIRIT

148. *What is the nature of the danger which threatens the king's life, and which it is the intention of these curious restrictions to guard against? What does early man understand by death? To what causes does he attribute it? And how does he think it may be forefended?*

As the savage commonly explains the processes of inanimate nature by supposing that they are produced by living beings working in or behind them, so he explains the phenomena of life itself. If an animal lives and moves, it can only be, he thinks, because there is a little animal inside which moves it: if a man lives and moves, it can only be because he has a little man or animal inside who moves him. The animal inside the animal, the man inside the man, is the soul. And as the activity of an animal or man is explained by the presence of the soul, so the repose of sleep or death is explained by its absence; sleep or trance being the temporary, death being the permanent absence of the soul. Hence if death be the permanent absence of the soul, the way to guard against it is either to prevent the soul from leaving the body, or, if it does depart, to ensure that it shall return. The precautions adopted by savages to secure one or other of these ends take the form of certain prohibitions or taboos.

149. According to the Nootkas of British Columbia the soul has the shape of a tiny man; its seat is the crown of the head. So long as it stands erect, its owner is hale and hearty; but when from any cause it loses its upright position, he loses his senses.[1] Among the Indian tribes of the Lower Fraser River, man is held to have four souls, of which the principal one has the form of a mannikin, while the other three are shadows of it.[2] The Malays conceive the human soul (*semangat*) as a little man, mostly invisible and of the bigness of a thumb, who corresponds exactly in shape, proportion, and even in complexion to the man in whose body he resides. This mannikin is of a thin unsubstantial nature, though not so impalpable but that it may cause displacement on entering a physical object, and it can flit quickly from place to place; it is temporarily absent from the body in sleep, trance, and disease, and permanently absent after death.[3]

The ancient Egyptians believed that every man has a soul (*ka*) which is his exact counterpart or double, with the same features, the same gait, even the same dress as the man himself. Many of the monuments dating from the eighteenth century onwards represent various kings appearing before divinities, while behind the king stands his soul or double portrayed as a little man with the king's features. So exact is the resemblance of the mannikin to the man, in other words, of the soul to the body, that, as there are fat bodies and thin bodies, so there are fat souls and thin souls;[4] as there are heavy bodies and light bodies, long bodies and short bodies, so there are heavy souls and light souls, long souls and short souls. The people of Nias (an island to the west of Sumatra) think that every man, before he is born, is asked how long or how heavy a soul he would like, and a soul of the desired weight or length is measured out to him. The length of a man's life is proportioned to the length of his soul; children who die young had short souls.[5] The Fijian conception of the soul as a tiny human being comes out clearly in the customs observed at the death of a chief among the Nakelo tribe. When he dies, certain men, who are the hereditary under-takers, call him, as he lies, oiled and ornamented, on fine mats, saying, "Rise, sir, the chief, and let us be going. The day has come over the land." Then they conduct him to the river side, where the ghostly ferryman comes to ferry Nakelo ghosts across the stream. As they thus attend the chief on his last journey, they hold their great fans close to the ground to shelter him, because, as one of them explained to a missionary, "His soul is only a little child."[6] People in the Punjab who tattoo themselves believe that at death the soul, "the little entire man or woman" inside the mortal frame, will go to heaven blazoned with the same tattoo patterns which adorned the body in life.[7] Like many other peoples, the natives of Yap, one of the Caroline Islands in the Pacific, conceive of the soul (ya'al) as an invisible body dwelling within the visible body and resembling it in form exactly.[7a]

150. The soul is commonly supposed to escape by the natural orifices of the body, especially the mouth and nostrils. Hence in Celebes they sometimes fasten fish-hooks to a sick man's nose, navel, and feet, so that if his soul should try to escape it may be hooked and held fast.[1] When a Sea Dyak sorcerer or medicine-man is initiated, his fingers are likewise supposed to be furnished with fish-hooks with which he will hereafter clutch the human soul in the act of flying away, and restore it to the body of the sufferer.[2] The Calchaquis Indians to the west of Paraguay used to plant arrows in the ground about a sick man to keep death from getting at him.[3] When any one yawns in their presence the Hindus always snap their thumbs, believing that this will hinder the soul from issuing through the open mouth.[4] The Marquesans used to hold the mouth and nose of a dying man, in order to keep him in life by preventing his soul from escaping,[5] and the same custom is reported of the New Caledonians.[6] On the other hand, the Itonamas in South America seal up the eyes, nose, and mouth of a dying person, in case his ghost should get out and carry off others;[7] and for a similar reason the people of Nias, who fear the spirits of the recently deceased and identify them with the breath, seek to confine the vagrant soul in its earthly tabernacle by bunging up the nose or tying up the jaws of the corpse.[8] Before leaving a corpse the Wakelbura in Australia used to place hot coals in its ears in order to keep the ghost in the body, until they had got such a good start that he could not overtake them.[9] Esquimaux mourners plug their nostrils with deerskin, hair, or hay for several days,[10] probably to prevent their souls from following that of their

But in order that a man's soul should quit his body it is not necessary that he should be asleep. *It may quit him in his waking hours, and then sickness, insanity or death will ensue.* The Lolos, an aboriginal tribe of western China, believe that the soul leaves the body in chronic illness. In that case they read a sort of elaborate litany, calling on the soul by name and beseeching it to return from the hills, the vales, the rivers, the forests, the fields, or from wherever it may be straying. At the same time cups of water, wine, and rice are set at the door for the refreshment of the weary wandering spirit. When the ceremony is over, they tie a red cord round the arm of the sick man to tether the soul, and this cord is worn by him until it decays and drops off.[13] So among the Kenyahs of Sarawak a medicine-man has been known to recall the stray soul of a child, and to fasten it firmly in its body by tying a string round the child's right wrist, and smearing its little arm with the blood of a fowl.[14] The Ilocanes of Luzon think that a man may lose his soul in the woods or gardens, and that he who has thus lost his soul loses also his senses. Hence before they quit the woods or the fields they call to their soul, "Let us go! let us go!" lest it should loiter behind or go astray. And when a man becomes crazed or mad, they take him to the place where he is supposed to have lost his soul and invite the truant spirit to return to his body.[15] Some of the Congo tribes believe that when a man is ill, his soul has left his body and is wandering at large. The aid of the sorcerer is then invoked to capture the vagrant spirit and restore it to the invalid.[16] Pining, sickness, great fright, and death are ascribed by the Battas (or Bataks) of Sumatra to the absence of the soul from the body. At first they try to beckon the wanderer back and to lure him, like a fowl, by strewing rice. This they follow in turn by more elaborate gifts.[17] The Tobungkus of Central Celebes believe that sickness is caused by the departure of the soul. To recover the wanderer a priest will set out food in the courtyard of the sufferer's house and then invoke the soul, promising it many fine things if only it will come back. When he thinks it has complied with his request, he catches it in a cloth which he keeps ready for the purpose. This cloth he afterwards claps on the sick man's head.[18] Similarly the Greeks told how the soul of Hermotimos of Clazomenae used to quit his body and roam far and wide, bringing back intelligence of what he had seen on his rambles until one day, when his spirit was abroad, his enemies contrived to seize his deserted body and committed it to the flames.[19] Parallels to this tale are to be found in Indian and Malayan folklore.

The departure of the soul is not always voluntary. It may be extracted from the body by ghosts, demons, or sorcerers. Hence, when a funeral is passing the house, the Karens of Burma tie their children with a special kind of string to a particular part of the house, lest the souls of the children should leave their bodies and go into the corpse which is passing.[20] On the return of a Burmese or Shan family from a burial, old men tie up the wrists of each member of the family with string, to prevent his or her "butterfly" or soul from escaping; and this string remains till it is worn out and falls off.[21] The Bahnars of eastern Cochin-China think that when a man is sick of a fever his soul has gone away with the ghosts to the tombs;[22] while in the East Indian island of Keisar it is deemed imprudent to go near a grave at night, lest the ghosts should catch and keep the soul of the passer-by.[23]

153. Often the abduction of a man's soul is set down to demons. The Annamites believe that when a man meets a demon and speaks to him, the demon inhales the man's breath and soul.[1]

If Galelareese mariners are sailing past certain rocks or come to a river where they never were before, they must wash their faces, for otherwise the spirits of the rocks or the river would snatch away their souls.[2] When a Dyak is about to leave a forest through which he has been walking alone, he never forgets to ask the demons to give him back his soul, for it may be that some forest-devil has carried it off. For the abduction of a soul may take place without its owner being aware of his loss, and it may happen either while he is awake or asleep.[3]

Among the Alfoors or Toradjas of Poso, in Central Celebes, a wooden puppet is offered to the demon as a substitute for the soul which he has abstracted, and the patient must touch the puppet in order to identify himself with it.[4] Similarly the Mongols make up a horse of birch-bark and a doll, and invite the demon to take the doll instead of the patient and to ride away on the horse.[5] A Yakut shaman, rigged out in his professional costume, with his drum in his hand, will boldly descend into the lower world and haggle with the demon who has carried off a sick man's soul. Not uncommonly the demon proves amenable to reason, and in consideration of the narrow circumstances of the patient's family will accept a more moderate ransom than he at first demanded.[6]

154. Demons are especially feared by persons who have just entered a new house. Hence at a house-warming among the Alfoors of Minahassa in Celebes the priest performs a ceremony for the purpose of restoring their souls to the inmates. He hangs up a bag at the place of sacrifice and then goes through a list of the gods. There are so many of them that this takes him the whole night through without stopping. In the morning he offers the gods an egg and some rice. By this time the souls of the household are supposed to be gathered in the bag. So the priest takes the bag, and holding it on the head of the master of the house, says, "Here you have your soul; go (soul) to-morrow away again." He then does the same, saying the same words, to the housewife and all the other members of the family.[1]

155. Sometimes the lost soul is brought back in a visible shape. In Melanesia a woman, knowing that a neighbour was at the point of death, heard a rustling in her house, as of a moth fluttering, just at the moment when a noise of weeping and lamentation told her that the soul was flown. She caught the fluttering thing between her hands and ran with it, crying out that she had caught the soul. But though she opened her hands above the mouth of the corpse, it did not revive.[1] In Lepers' Island, one of the New Hebrides, for ten days after a birth the father is careful not to exert himself or the baby would suffer for it. If during this time he goes away to any distance, he will bring back with him on his return a little stone representing the infant's soul. Arrived at home he cries, "Come hither," and puts down the stone in the house. Then he waits till the child sneezes, at which he cries, "Here it is"; for now he knows that the little soul has not been lost after all.[2] In Amboyna, the sorcerer, to recover a soul detained by demons, plucks a branch from a tree, and waving it to and fro as if to catch something, calls out the sick man's name. Returning he strikes the patient over the head and body with the branch, into which the lost soul is supposed to have passed, and from which it returns to the patient.[3]

156. Again, souls may be extracted from their bodies or detained on their wanderings not only by ghosts and demons but also by men, especially by sorcerers. In Fiji, if a criminal refused to confess, the chief sent for a scarf with which "to catch away the soul of the rogue." At the sight or even at the mention of the scarf the culprit generally made a clean breast. For if he did not, the scarf would be waved over his head till his soul was caught in it, when it would be carefully folded up and nailed to the end of a chief's canoe; and for want of his soul the criminal would pine and die.[1] The sorcerers of Danger Island used to set snares for souls. The snares were made of stout cinet, about fifteen to thirty feet long, with loops on either side of different sizes, to suit the different sizes of souls; for fat souls there were large loops, for thin souls there were small ones.

Among the Sereres of Senegambia, when a man wishes to revenge himself on his enemy he goes to the *fitaure* (chief and priest in one) and prevails on him to conjure the soul of his enemy into a large jar of red earthenware, which is then deposited under a consecrated tree. The man whose soul is shut up in the jar soon dies.[2] In some parts of West Africa, indeed, wizards are continually setting traps to catch souls that wander from their bodies during sleep; and when they have caught one, they tie it up over the fire, and as it shrivels in the heat the owner sickens.[3]

A Karen wizard will catch the wandering soul of a sleeper and transfer it to the body of a dead man. The latter, therefore, comes to life as the former dies. But the friends of the sleeper in turn engage a wizard to steal the soul of another sleeper, who dies as the first sleeper comes to life. In this way an indefinite succession of deaths and resurrections is supposed to take place.[4]

Nowhere perhaps is the art of abducting human souls more carefully cultivated or carried to higher perfection than in the Malay Peninsula. Here the methods by which the wizard works his will are various, and so too are his motives. Sometimes he desires to destroy an enemy, sometimes to win the love of a cold or bashful beauty. Some of the charms operate entirely without contact; in others, the receptacle into which the soul is to be lured has formed part of, or at least touched, the person of the victim. Thus, to take an instance of the latter sort of charm, the following are the directions given for securing the soul of one whom you wish to render distraught. When the moon, just risen, looks red above the eastern horizon, go out, and standing in the moonlight, with the big toe of your right foot on the big toe of your left, make a speaking-trumpet of your right hand and recite through it the following words:

"OM.   I loose my shaft, I loose it and the moon clouds over,
I loose it, and the sun is extinguished.
I loose it, and the stars burn dim.
But it is not the sun, moon, and stars that I shoot at,
It is the stalk of the heart of that child of the congregation, So-and-so.

Cluck! cluck! soul of So-and-so, come and walk with me,
Come and sit with me,
Come and sleep and share my pillow.
Cluck! cluck! soul."

Repeat this thrice and after every repetition blow through your hollow fist.[5]

157. But the spiritual dangers which we have described are not the only ones that beset the primitive. Often he regards his shadow or reflection as his soul, and as such it is necessarily a source of potential danger to him. For if it is trampled upon, struck, or stabbed, he will feel the injury as if it were done to his person; and if it is detached from him entirely (as he believes that it may be) he will die. In the island of Wetar there are magicians who can make a man ill by stabbing his shadow with a pike or hacking it with a sword.[1] In the Babar Islands the demons get power over a man's soul by holding fast his shadow, or by striking and wounding it.[2] Among the Tolindoos of Central Celebes to tread on a man's shadow is an offence, because it is supposed to make the owner sick;[3] and for the same reason the Toboongkoos of that region forbid their children to play with their shadows.[4] The Ottawa Indians thought they could kill a man by making certain figures on his shadow.[5] The Baganda of central Africa regarded a man's shadow as his ghost; hence they used to kill or injure their enemies by stabbing or treading on their shadows.[6] Among the Bavili of West Africa it used to be considered a crime to trample on or even to cross the shadow of another, especially if the shadow were that of a married woman.[7] Some Caffres are very unwilling to let anybody stand on their shadow, believing that they can be influenced for evil through it.[8] They think that "a sick man's shadow dwindles in intensity when he is about to die; for it has such an intimate relation to the man that it suffers with him."[9] The natives of Nias tremble at the sight of a rainbow, because they think it is a net spread by a powerful spirit to catch their shadows.[10] The Indian tribes of the Lower Frazer River believe that man has four souls, of which the shadow is one, though not the principal, and that sickness is caused by the absence of one of them. Hence no one will let his shadow fall on a sick shaman, lest the latter should purloin it to replace his own lost soul.[11] At a funeral in China, when the lid is about to be placed on the coffin, most of the bystanders, with the exception of the nearest kin, retire a few steps or even withdrawn to another room, for a person's health is believed to be endangered by allowing his shadow to be enclosed in a coffin.[12]

In view of these notions, the primitive makes it a rule to shun the shadow of certain persons whom for various reasons he regards as sources of dangerous influence. Among the dangerous classes he commonly ranks mourners and women, especially his mother-in-law. The Shuswap Indians of British Columbia think that the shadow of a mourner falling on a person makes him sick.[13] Among the Kurnai tribe of Victoria novices at initiation were cautioned not to let a woman's shadow fall across them, as this would make them thin, lazy, and stupid.[14]

The awe and dread with which the primitive often contemplates his mother-in-law are among the most familiar facts of anthropology. In the Yuin tribes of New South Wales the rule which forbade a man to hold any communication with his wife's mother was very strict. It was a ground of divorce if his shadow happened to fall on her; in that case he had to leave his wife, and she returned to her parents.[15]

Where the shadow is so intimately bound up with a man's life that the loss of it entails debility or death, it is but natural that its diminution should be regarded with solicitude and apprehension, as betokening a corresponding decrease in the vital energy of its owner. The Baganda of central Africa used to judge of a man's health by the length of his shadow. They said, "So-and-so is going to die, his shadow is very small"; or, "He is in good health, his shadow is large."[16] Similarly the Caffres of South Africa think that a man's shadow grows very small or vanishes at death. When her husband is away at the wars, a woman hangs up his sleeping-mat; if its shadow grows less, she says her husband has been killed; if it remains unchanged, she says he is unscathed.[17] The loss of the shadow, real or apparent, has often been regarded as a cause or precursor of death. Whoever entered the sanctuary of Zeus on Mount Lycaeus in Arcadia was believed to lose his shadow and to die within the year.[18] In Lower Austria on the evening of St. Sylvester's day—the last day of the year—the company seated round the table mark whose shadow is not cast on the wall, and believe that the seemingly shadowless person will die next year.

Nowhere, perhaps, does the equivalence of the shadow to the life or soul come out more clearly than in some customs practised to this day in south-eastern Europe. In modern Greece, when the foundation of a new building is being laid, it is the custom to kill a cock, a ram, or a lamb, and to let its blood flow on the foundation-stone, under which the animal is afterwards buried. The object of the sacrifice is to give strength and stability to the building. But sometimes, instead of killing an animal, the builder entices a man to the foundation-stone, secretly measures his body, or a part of it, or his shadow, and buries the measure under the foundation-stone; or he lays the foundation-stone upon the man's shadow. It is believed that the man will die within the year.[19] In the island of Lesbos it is deemed enough if the builder merely casts a stone at the shadow of a passer-by; the man whose shadow is thus struck will die, but the building will be solid.[20] The Roumanians of Transylvania think that he whose shadow is thus immured will die within forty days; so persons passing by a building which is in course of erection may hear a warning cry, "Beware lest they take thy shadow!" In the nineteenth century there were still shadow-traders whose business it was to provide architects with the shadows necessary for securing their walls![21]

158. As some peoples believe a man's soul to be in his shadow, so other (or the same) peoples believe it to be in his reflection in water or a mirror.

When the Motumotu of New Guinea first saw their likeness in a looking-glass they thought they were seeing their souls.[1] An Aztec mode of keeping sorcerers from the house was to leave a vessel of water with a knife in it behind the door. When a sorcerer entered he was so much alarmed at seeing his reflection in the water transfixed by a knife that he turned and fled.[2] The Basutos say that a crocodile has the power of killing a man by dragging his reflection under water;[3] while in Saddle Island, Melanesia, there is a pool "into which if any one looks he dies; the malignant spirit takes hold upon his life by means of his reflection on the water."[4]

We can now understand why it was a maxim both in ancient India and in ancient Greece not to look at one's reflection in water, and why the Greeks regarded it as an omen of death if a man dreamed of seeing himself so reflected.[5] Further, we can now explain the widespread custom of covering up mirrors or turning them to the wall when a death has taken place in the house. It is feared that the soul, projected out of the person in the shape of his reflection in the mirror, may be carried off by the ghost of the departed, which is commonly supposed to linger about the house until the burial. The reason why sick people should not see themselves in a mirror, and why the mirror in a sick-room is therefore often covered up[6] likewise becomes plain: in time of sickness, when the soul might take flight so easily, it is particularly dangerous to project it out of the body by means of the reflection in a mirror. The rule is therefore precisely parallel with that observed by some peoples of not allowing sick people to sleep;[7] in sleep the soul is thought to be projected out of the body, and there is always a risk that it may not return.

159. As with shadows and reflections, so with *portraits;* they are often believed to contain the soul of the person portrayed. People who hold this belief are naturally loth to have their likenesses taken. For many years no Yankton Dakota would consent to have his picture taken lest one of his "apparitions" should remain after death in the picture instead of going to the spirit-land.[1] An Indian whose portrait the Prince of Wied wished to get refused to let himself be drawn, because he believed it would cause his death.[2] The Mandan Indians also thought they would soon die if their portraits fell into the hands of another; they wished at least to have the artist's picture as a kind of hostage.[3] Similarly when Dr. Catat and some companions had photographed the royal family in the Bara country on the west coast of Madagascar, they found themselves accused of taking the souls of the natives for the purpose of selling them when they returned to France![4] In former times, no Siamese coins were ever stamped with the image of the king, "for there was a strong prejudice against the making of portraits in any medium." Europeans who travel into the jungle have, even at the present time, only to point a camera at a crowd to procure its instant dispersal.[5]

Beliefs of the same sort still linger in various parts of Europe. Not so long ago it was reported that some old women in the Greek island of Carpathus were very angry at having their likenesses drawn, thinking that in consequence they would pine and die.[6] Again, it is a German superstition that if you have your portrait painted, you will soon die;[7] while some people in Russia object to having their silhouettes cut, fearing that this will entail their death before the year is out.[8] And in the West of Scotland may still be found persons "who refuse to have their likenesses taken lest it prove unlucky; [they] give as instances the cases of several of their friends who never had a day's health after being photographed."[9]

TABOOED ACTS

160. *If every person was at such pains to save his own soul from the perils which threatened it on so many sides, how much more carefully must* he *have been guarded upon whose life hung the welfare and even the existence of the whole people, and whom therefore it was the common interest of all to preserve? Therefore we should expect to find the king's life protected by a system of precautions or safeguards still more numerous and minute than those which in primitive society every man adopts for the safety of his own soul. Now in point of fact the life of the early kings is regulated, as we have seen and shall see more fully presently, by a very exact code of rules. May we not then conjecture that these rules are in fact the very safeguards which we should expect to find adopted for the protection of the king's life? An exam-*

ination of the rules themselves confirms this conjecture. For from this it appears that some of the rules observed by the kings are identical with those observed by private persons out of regard for the safety of their souls; and even of those which seem peculiar to the king, many, if not all, are most readily explained on the hypothesis that they are nothing but safeguards or lifeguards of the king.

As the object of the royal taboos is to isolate the king from all sources of danger, their general effect is to compel him to live in a state of seclusion, more or less complete, according to the number and stringency of the rules he observes. Now of all sources of danger none are more dreaded by the savage than magic and witchcraft, and he suspects all strangers of practising these black arts. To guard against the baneful influence exerted voluntarily or involuntarily by strangers is therefore an elementary dictate of savage prudence. Hence before strangers are allowed to enter a district, or at least before they are permitted to mingle freely with the inhabitants, certain ceremonies are often performed by the natives of the country for the purpose of disarming them of their magical powers, of counteracting the baneful influence which is believed to emanate from them, or of disinfecting, so to speak, the tainted atmosphere by which they are supposed to be surrounded. In the interior of Yorubs (West Africa), for instance, the sentinels at the gates of towns often oblige European travellers to wait till nightfall before they admit them, fearing that if strangers were admitted by day the devil would enter behind them.[1] The whole Mahafaly country in Madagascar used to be tabooed to strangers of the white race, the natives imagining that the intrusion of a white man would immediately cause the death of their king.[2] "More dreaded," says a traveller in central Borneo, "than the evil spirits of the neighborhood are those that accompany travellers from a distance. When a company from the middle Mahakam river visited me among the Biu-u Kayans in 1897, no woman showed herself outside her house without a burning bundle of *plehiding* bark, the stinking smoke of which drives away evil spirits."[3] In Laos, before a stranger can be accorded hospitality, the master of the house must offer sacrifice to the ancestral spirits; otherwise the spirits would be offended and send disease on the inmates.[4] When strangers land on the Ongtong Java Islands, they are first received by the sorcerers, sprinkled with water, anointed with oil, and girt with dried pandanus leaves. At the same time sand and water are thrown about in all directions, and the newcomer and his boat are wiped with green leaves. Only after this ceremony are the strangers introduced by the sorcerers to the chief.[5]

Sometimes the dread of strangers and their magic is too great to allow of their reception on any terms at all. Thus when Speke arrived at a certain village, the natives shut their doors against him, "because they had never before seen a white man nor the tin boxes that the men were carrying; 'Who

knows,' they said, 'but that these very boxes are the plundering Watuta transformed and come to kill us? You cannot be admitted.' "[6]

The fear thus entertained of alien visitors is often mutual. Entering a
strange land the savage feels that he is treading enchanted ground, and he
takes steps to guard against the demons that haunt it and the magical arts of
its inhabitants. Thus on going to a strange land the Maoris performed certain
ceremonies to make it *noa* (common), lest it might have been previously *tapu*
(sacred).[7] Before Stuhlmann and his companions entered the territory of the
Wanyamwesi in central Africa, one of his men killed a white cock and buried
it in a pot just at the boundary.[8] In Australia, when a strange tribe has been
invited into a district and is approaching the encampment of the tribe which
owns the land, "the strangers carry lighted bark or burning sticks in their
hands, for the purpose, they say, of clearing and purifying the air."[9] It is said
that just before Greek armies advanced to the shock of battle, a man bearing
a lighted torch stepped out from either side and threw his torch into the space
between the hosts. Then they retired unmolested, for they were thought to be
sacred to Ares and inviolable.[10] Now some peoples fancy that when they advance to battle the spirits of their fathers hover in the van.[11] Hence fire thrown
out in front of the line of battle may be meant to disperse these shadowy combatants, leaving the issue of the fight to be determined by more substantial
weapons than ghosts can wield. Similarly the fire which is sometimes borne
at the head of an army is perhaps in some cases intended to dissipate the evil
influences, whether magical or spiritual, with which the air of the enemy's
country may be conceived to teem.

Again, it is thought that a man who has been on a journey may have contracted some magic evil from the strangers with whom he has been brought
into contact. Hence, on returning home, before he is readmitted to the society
of his tribe and friends, he has to undergo certain purificatory ceremonies.
Thus the Bechuanas "cleanse or purify themselves after journeys by shaving
their heads, etc., lest they should have contracted from strangers some evil
by witchcraft or sorcery."[12] In some parts of western Africa when a man returns home after a long absence, before he is allowed to visit his wife, he must
wash his person with a particular fluid, and receive from the sorcerer a certain mark of his forehead, in order to counteract any magic spell which a
stranger woman may have cast on him in his absence, and which might be
communicated through him to the women of his village.[13] Among the Kayans
of Borneo, men who have been absent on a long journey are secluded for four
days in a small hut specially made for the purpose before they are allowed to
re-enter their own homes.[14]

When such precautions are taken on behalf of the people in general against
the malign influence supposed to be exercised by strangers, it is no wonder
that special measures are adopted to protect the king from the same insidious
danger. In the Middle Ages, the envoys to a Tartar Khan were obliged to pass

between two fires before they were admitted to his presence, and the gifts they brought were also carried between the fires. The reason assigned for the custom was that the fire purged away untoward influences which the strangers might exercise.[15] Before any strangers were admitted to the presence of Lobengula, king of the Matabeles, they had to be treated with a sickly green medicine, which was profusely sprinkled over them by means of a cow's tail.[16] The king of Loango might not look upon the house of a white man.[17]

161. In the opinion of savages the acts of eating and drinking are attended with special danger; for at these times the soul may escape from the mouth or be extracted by the magic arts of an enemy who happens to be present. Precautions are therefore taken to guard against these dangers. Thus among the Battas of Sumatra one may find the whole house shut up on the occasion of a feast, in order that the soul may stay and enjoy the good things set before it.[1] In Shoa, one of the southern provinces of Abyssinia, the doors of the house are scrupulously barred at meals against the evil eye, and a fire is invariably lighted, else devils would enter and there would be no blessing on the meat.[2] Whenever an Abyssinian of rank drinks, a servant holds a cloth before him to guard him from the evil eye.[3] The Tuaregs never eat or drink in the presence of anyone else.[4] In Fiji persons who suspected others of plotting against them avoided eating in their presence, or were careful to leave no fragment of food behind.[5]

If these are the ordinary precautions taken by common people, the precautions taken by kings are extraordinary. The king of Loango may not be seen eating or drinking by man or beast under pain of death.[6] The rules observed by the neighboring king of Coango were similar; it was thought that the king would die if any of his subjects were to see him drink.[7] The king of Susa, a region to the south of Abyssinia, presides daily at the feast in the long banqueting-hall, but is hidden by a curtain from the gaze of his subjects.[8] In the palace of the ancient Persian kings there were two dining-rooms opposite each other; in one of them the king dined, in the other his guests.[9]

162. In some of the preceding cases the intention of eating and drinking in strict seclusion may perhaps be to hinder evil influences from entering the body rather than to prevent the escape of the soul. This certainly is the motive of some drinking customs observed by natives of the Congo region. Thus we are told of these people that "there is hardly a native who would dare to swallow a liquid without first conjuring the spirits. One of them rings a bell all the time he is drinking; another crouches down and places his left hand on the earth; another veils his head; another puts a stalk of grass or a leaf in his hair, or marks his forehead with a line of clay. This fetish custom assumes very varied forms. To explain them, the black is satisfied to say that they are an energetic mode of conjuring spirits." In this part of the world a chief will commonly ring a bell at each draught of beer which he swallows, and at the same moment a lad stationed in front of him brandishes a spear "to keep at bay the spirits which might try to sneak into the old chief's body by the same road as the *massanga* (beer)."¹ The same motive of warding off evil spirits probably explains the custom observed by some African sultans of veiling their faces. The Sultan of Darfur wraps up his face with a piece of white muslin, which goes round his head several times, covering his mouth and nose first, and then his forehead, so that only his eyes are visible. The same custom of veiling the face as a mark of sovereignty is said to be observed in other parts of central Africa.² The Sultan of Bornu never shewed himself to his people and only spoke to them from behind a curtain.³ The king of Chonga, a town on the right bank of the Niger above Egga, may not be seen by his subjects nor by strangers. At an interview he sits in his palace concealed by a mat which hangs like a curtain, and from behind it he converses with his visitor.⁴

The king of Jebu, on the Slave Coast of West Africa, is surrounded by a great deal of mystery. Until lately his face might not be seen even by his own subjects, and if circumstances compelled him to communicate with them he did so through a screen which concealed him from view. Now, though his face may be seen, it is customary to hide his body; and at audiences a cloth is held before him so as to conceal him from the neck downwards, and it is raised so as to cover him altogether whenever he coughs, sneezes, spits, or takes snuff. His face is partially hidden by a conical cap with hanging strings of beads.⁵ In New South Wales for some time after his initiation into the tribal mysteries, a young blackfellow (whose soul at this time is in a critical state) must always cover his mouth with a rug when a woman is present.⁶ We have already seen how common is the notion that the life or soul may escape by the mouth or nostrils.

163. By an extension of the like precaution kings are sometimes forbidden ever to leave their palaces; or, if they are allowed to do so, their subjects are forbidden to see them abroad.

The fetish king of Benin, who was worshipped as a deity, might not quit his palace.¹ The king of Onitsha, on the Niger, "does not step out of his house into the town unless a human sacrifice is made to propitiate the gods: on this account he never goes out beyond the precincts of his premises."² Indeed, we are told that he may not quit his palace under pain of death or of giving up one or more of his slaves to be executed in his presence. Yet, once a year, at the Feast of Yams, the king is allowed, and even required by custom, to dance before his people outside the high mud wall of the palace.³ Similarly the Tomas or Habes, a hardy race of mountaineers who inhabit Mount Bandiagara in Nigeria, revere a great fetish doctor called the Ogom, who is not suffered to quit his house on any pretext.⁴ The kings of Ethiopia were adored as gods, but were mostly kept shut up in their palaces.⁵ On the mountainous coast of Pontus there dwelt in antiquity a rude and warlike people named the Mosyni or Mosynoeci, through whose rugged terrain the Ten Thousand marched on their famous retreat from Asia to Europe. These barbarians kept their king in close custody at the top of a high tower, from which after his election he was never more allowed to descend. Here he dispensed justice to his people; but if he offended them, they stopped his rations for a day or even starved him to death.[6]

TABOOED PERSONS

164. *The divine person who epitomizes the corporate life of his group is a source of danger as well as of blessing; he must not only be guarded, he must also be guarded against. His sacred organism, so delicate that a touch may disorder it, is also, as it were, electrically charged with a powerful magical or spiritual force which may discharge itself with fatal effect on whatever comes in contact with it. Accordingly the isolation of the man-god is quite as necessary for the safety of others as for his own. His magical virtue is in the strictest sense contagious; his divinity is a fire which, under proper restraints, confers endless blessings, but, if rashly touched or allowed to break bounds, burns and destroys what it touches. Hence the disastrous effects supposed to attend a breach of taboo; the offender has thrust his hand into the divine fire, which shrivels and consumes him on the spot.*

Examples of this principle are legion. We have already seen that the Mikado's food was cooked daily in new pots and served up in new dishes; both pots and dishes were of common clay, and were usually broken after use lest any one else should touch them. Indeed, it was believed that if he did so, his mouth and throat would become swollen and inflamed. The same ill effect was thought to be experienced by anyone who dared to put on the Mikado's clothes; he would have swellings and pains all over his body.[1] Similarly, the Nubas in eastern Africa believe they would die if they ventured to enter the house of their priestly king; however, they can evade the penalty of their intrusion by baring the left shoulder and getting the king to lay his hand on it. And were any man to sit on a stone which the king has consecrated to his own use, the transgressor would die within the year.[2] The Cazembes, in the interior of Angola, regard their king (the *Muata* or *Mambo*) as so holy that no one can touch him without being killed by the magical power which pervades his sacred person.[3] A Maori woman having eaten of some fruit, and being afterwards told that the fruit had been taken from a tabooed place, exclaimed that the spirit of the chief, whose sanctity had been thus profaned, would kill her. This was in the afternoon, and next day by twelve o'clock she was dead.[4] An observer who knows the Maoris well, says, "Tapu [taboo] is an awful weapon. I have seen a strong young man die the same day he was tapued; the victims die under it as though their strength ran out as water."[5] A Maori chief's tinderbox was once the means of killing several persons; for, having been lost by him, and found by some men who used it to light their pipes, they died of fright on learning to whom it had belonged. So, too, the garments of a high New Zealand chief will kill any one else who wears them.[6]

165. In primitive society the rules of ceremonial purity observed by divine kings, chiefs, and priests agree in many respects with the rules observed by homicides, mourners, women in childbed, girls at puberty, hunters and fishermen, and so on. To us these various classes of persons appear to differ totally in character and condition; some of them we should call holy, others we might pronounce unclean and polluted. But the savage makes no such moral distinction between them; the conceptions of holiness and pollution are not yet differentiated in his mind. To him the common feature of all these persons is that they are dangerous and in danger, and the danger in which they stand and to which they expose others is what we should call spiritual or ghostly, and therefore imaginary. The danger, however, is not less real because it is imaginary; imagination acts upon man as really as does gravitation, and may kill him as certainly as a dose of prussic acid. To seclude these persons from the rest of the world so that the dreaded spiritual danger shall neither reach them, nor spread from them, is the object of the taboos which they have to observe. These taboos act, so to say, as electrical insulators to preserve the spiritual force with which these persons are charged from suffering or inflicting harm by contact with the outer world.

For example, sacred kings and priests in Polynesia were not allowed to touch food with their hands, and had therefore to be fed by others and as we have just seen, their vessels, garments, and other property might not be used by others on pain of disease and death. Now precisely the same observances are exacted by some savages from girls at their first menstruation, women after childbirth, homicides, mourners, and all persons who have come into contact with the dead.[1] Among the Maoris, for example, any one who had handled a corpse, helped to convey it to the grave, or touched a dead man's bones, was cut off from all intercourse and almost all communication with mankind. He could not enter any house, or come into contact with any person or thing, without utterly bedevilling them. He might not even touch food with his hands, which had become so frightfully tabooed or unclean as to be quite useless. Food would be set for him on the ground, and he would then sit or kneel down, and, with his hands carefully held behind his back, gnaw at it as best he could. In some cases he would be fed by another person, who with outstretched arm contrived to do it without touching the tabooed man; but the feeder was himself subjected to many severe restrictions, little less onerous than those which were imposed upon the other.[2]

This particular taboo would seem to have been universal in Polynesia. Thus in Samoa "those who attended the deceased were most careful not to handle food, and for several days were fed by others as if they were helpless infants."[3] Again, in Wallis Island "contact with a corpse subjects the hands to the law of taboo until they are washed, which is not done for several weeks. Before that purification has taken place, the tabooed persons may not themselves put food to their mouths; other people render them that service."[4] A rule of the same sort is or was observed in various parts of Melanesia. Thus in Fiji the taboo for handling a dead chief lasted from one to ten months according to his rank; for a commoner it lasted not more than four days. It was commonly resorted to by the lazy and idle; for during the time of their seclusion they were not only provided with food, but were actually fed by attendants or ate their food from the ground.[5] Similarly in the Motu tribe of New Guinea a man is tabooed, generally for three days, after handling a corpse, and while the taboo lasts he may not touch food with his hands;[6] while in the Ba-Pedi and Ba-Thonga tribes of South Africa men who have dug a grave may not touch food with their fingers till the rites of their purification are accomplished; meantime they eat with the help of special spoons. If they broke this rule, it is thought that they would be consumptive.[7] In Annam mourners are not allowed to marry or to have any sexual relations whatever. The prohibition formerly extended to the whole period of mourning, but it is now restricted to the three days after the death, during which it is absolute, and during these days they are further forbidden to chew betel, to drink alcohol, and to eat flesh.[7a]

166. As the garments which have been touched by a sacred chief kill those who handle them, so do the things which have been touched by a menstruous woman. Hence, during their menstrual periods, Australian women are forbidden under pain of death to touch anything that men use, or even to walk on a path that men frequent.[1] They are also secluded at childbirth, and all vessels then used by them are burned.[2] In Uganda, pots which a woman touches while the impurity of menstruation is upon her have to be destroyed; spears and shields defiled by her touch are, however, merely purified.[3] No Esquimaux of Alaska will willingly drink out of the same cup or eat out of the same dish that has been used by a woman at her confinement until it has been purified by certain incantations.[4] Among some of the Indians of North America women at menstruation are forbidden to touch men's utensils, which would be so defiled by their touch that their subsequent use would be attended by certain mischief or misfortune.[5] Among the Bribri Indians of Costa Rica a menstruous woman is regarded as unclean. The only plates she may use for her food are banana leaves, which, when she has done with them, she throws away in some sequestered spot; for were a cow to find them and eat them, it would waste away. And she drinks out of a special vessel for a like reason: if any one drank out of the same cup after her, he would surely die.[6]

Among many peoples similar restrictions are imposed on women in childbed. Thus, in Tahiti a woman was secluded for two or three weeks after delivering a child and was confined in a temporary hut erected on sacred ground.[7] Similarly in Manahiki, an island of the South Pacific, for ten days after her delivery a woman was not allowed to handle food and had to be fed by some other person.[8] In the Sinaugolo tribe of British New Guinea, for about a month after her confinement a woman may not prepare or handle food; she may not even cook for herself, and when she eats food prepared for her by friends she must use a sharpened stick to transfer it to her mouth.[9] Similarly in the island of Kadiak, off Alaska, a woman about to be delivered retires to a low hovel built of reeds, where she must remain for twenty days after the birth of her child, no matter what the season may be, and she is considered so unclean that no one will touch her, and food is reached to her on sticks.[10] In the Ba-Pedi and Ba-Thonga tribes of South Africa a woman in childbed may not touch food with her hands all the time of her seclusion; she must eat with the help of a wooden spoon. They think that if she touched her victuals she might infect them with her bloody flux, and that having partaken of such tainted food she would fall into a consumption.[11]

Among the Maoris when a male child is born to a chief all his tribe rejoice. But the mother is separated from the inhabitants of the settlement, to prevent her coming in contact with persons engaged in cultivating the sweet potato (*kumara*), lest anything belonging to the mother should be accidentally touched by them, and lest the sweet potato should be affected by her state of *tapu* (taboo); for the sacredness of any nursing mother (*rehu-wahine*) is greatly feared.[11a]

Restrictions and taboos like those laid on menstruous and lying-in women are imposed by some savages on lads at the initiatory rites which celebrate the attainment of puberty; hence we may infer that at such times young men are supposed to be in a state like that of women at menstruation and in childbed. Thus, among the Creek Indians a lad at initiation had to abstain for twelve moons from picking his ears or scratching his head with his fingers; he had to use a small stick for these purposes. For four moons he must have a fire of his own to cook his food at; and a little girl, a virgin, might cook for him. During the fifth moon any person might cook for him, but he must serve himself first, and use one spoon and pan. On the fifth day of the twelfth moon he gathered corn cobs, burned them to ashes, and with the ashes rubbed his body all over. At the end of the twelfth moon he sweated under blankets, and then bathed in water, which ended the ceremony. While the ceremonies lasted, he might touch no one but lads who were undergoing a like course of initiation.[12] Caffre boys at a circumcision live secluded in a special hut; they are smeared from head to foot with white clay; they wear tall head-dresses with horn-like projections and short skirts like those of ballet-dancers. When their wounds are healed, all the vessels which they had used during their seclusion and the boyish mantles which they had hitherto worn are burned, together with the hut, and the boys rush away from the burning hut without looking back, "lest a fearful curse should cling to them." After that they are bathed, anointed, and clad in new garments.[13]

167. Once more, warriors are conceived by the savage to move, so to say, in an atmosphere of spiritual danger which constrains them to practise a variety of superstitious observances quite different in their nature from those rational precautions which, as a matter of course, they adopt against foes of flesh and blood. The general effect of these observances is to place the warrior, both before and after victory, in the same state of seclusion or spiritual quarantine in which, for his own safety, primitive man puts his human gods and other dangerous characters. Thus when the Maoris went out on the war-path they were sacred or taboo in the highest degree, and they and their friends at home had to observe strictly many curious customs over and above the numerous taboos of ordinary life. They became, in the irreverent language of Europeans who knew them in the old fighting days, "tabooed an inch thick"; and as for the leader of the expedition, he was quite unapproachable.[1] Similarly, when the Israelites marched forth to war they were bound by certain rules of ceremonial purity identical with rules observed by Maoris and Australian blackfellows on the war-path. The vessels they used were sacred, and they had to practise continence and a custom of personal cleanliness of which the original motive, if we may judge from the avowed motive of savages who conform to the same custom, was a fear lest the enemy should obtain the refuse of their persons, and thus be enabled to work their destruction by magic.[2] Among some Indian tribes of North America a young warrior in his first campaign had to conform to certain customs, of which two were identical with the observances imposed by the same Indians on girls at their first menstruation: the vessels he ate and drank out of might be touched by no other person, and he was forbidden to scratch his head or any other part of his body with his fingers; if he could not help scratching himself, he had to do it with a stick.[3] The latter rule, like the one which forbids a tabooed person to feed himself with his own fingers, seems to rest on the supposed sancitity or pollution, whichever we choose to call it, of the tabooed hands. The first four times that an Apache Indian goes out on the war-path, he is bound to refrain from scratching his head with his fingers and from letting water touch his lips. Hence he scratches his head with a stick, and drinks through a hollow reed or cane. Stick and reed are attached to the warrior's belt and to each other by a leathern thong.[4] The rule not to scratch their heads with their fingers, but to use a stick for the purpose instead, was regularly observed by Ojibways on the war-path.[5] With regard to the Creek Indians and kindred tribes we are told they "will not cohabit with women while they are out at war; they religiously abstain from every kind of intercourse even with their own wives, for the space of three days and nights before they go to war, and so after they return home, because they are to sanctify themselves."[6] "An Indian, intending to go to war, will commence by blacking his face, permitting his hair to grow long, and neglecting his personal appearance, and also will frequently fast, sometimes for two or three days together, and refrain from all intercourse with the other sex."[7] Among the Ba-Pedi and Ba-Thonga tribes of South Africa not only have the warriors to abstain from women, but the people left behind in the villages are also bound to continence; they think that any incontinence on their part would cause thorns to grow on the ground traversed by the warriors, and that success would not attend the expedition.[8]

Similarly with regard to the Kiwai Papuans of British New Guinea we read that "before going to war a man must not cohabit with his wife, which under the circumstances is a bad thing, and may cause his death. During the days preceding a fighting expedition the warriors eat in the men's house, and at least in the notions of certain people must avoid having their food cooked by women who are used to sexual intercourse. The young warriors abstain from playing with the girls and do not even speak to them."[8a] So again the Melanesians of New Britain "were very particular in preserving chastity during or before a fight, and they believed that if a man slept with his wife he would be killed or wounded."[8b]

Why exactly so many savages have made it a rule to refrain from women in time of war, we cannot say for certain, but we may conjecture that their motive was a superstitious fear lest, on the principles of sympathetic magic, close contact with women should infect them with feminine weakness and cowardice.[9] Similarly some savages imagine that contact with a woman in childbed enervates warriors and enfeebles their weapons. Indeed the Kayans of central Borneo go so far as to hold that to touch a loom or women's clothes would so weaken a man that he would have no success in hunting, fishing, and war.[10] Hence it is not merely sexual intercourse with women that the savage warrior sometimes shuns; he is careful to avoid the sex altogether. Thus among the hill tribes of Assam, not only are men forbidden to cohabit with their wives during or after a raid, but they may not eat food cooked by a woman; nay, they should not address a word even to their own wives. Once a woman, who unwittingly broke the rule by speaking to her husband while he was under the war taboo, sickened and died when she learned the awful crime she had committed.[11]

168. If the reader still doubts whether the rules of conduct which we have just been considering are based on superstitious fears or dictated by a rational prudence, his doubts will probably be dispelled when he learns that rules of the same sort are often imposed even more stringently on warriors after the victory has been won and when all fear of the living corporeal foe is at an end. In such cases one motive for the inconvenient restrictions laid on the victors in their hour of triumph is probably a dread of the angry ghosts of the slain; and that the fear of the vengeful ghosts does influence the behaviour of the slayers is often expressly affirmed. In the island of Timor, when a warlike expedition has returned in triumph bringing the heads of the vanquished foe, the leader of the expedition is forbidden by religious custom to return at once to his own house. A special hut is prepared for him, in which he has to reside for two months, undergoing bodily and spiritual purification.[1] In some Dyak tribes men returning from an expedition in which they have taken human heads are obliged to keep to themselves and to abstain from a variety of things for several days; they may not touch iron nor eat salt or fish with bones, and they may have no intercourse with women.[2]

In Logea, an island off the south-eastern extremity of New Guinea, men who have killed or assisted in killing enemies shut themselves up for about a week in their houses. They must avoid all intercourse with their wives and friends, and they may not touch food with their hands. They may eat vegetable food only, which is brought to them cooked in special pots. The intention of these restrictions is to guard the men against the smell of the blood of the slain; for it is believed that if they smelt the blood, they would fall ill and die.[3] In the Toaripi or Montumotu tribe of south-eastern New Guinea a man who has killed another may not go near his wife, and may not touch food with his fingers. He is fed by others, and only with certain kinds of food. These observances last till the new moon.[4]

Again, among the Southern Massim of British New Guinea a warrior who has taken a prisoner or slain a man remains secluded in his house for six days. During the first three he may eat only roasted food and has to cook for himself. Then he bathes and blackens his face for the remainder of the time.[5] Among the Basutos "warriors who have killed an enemy are purified. The chief has to wash them, sacrificing an ox in the presence of the whole army. They are furthermore anointed with the gall of the animal, which prevents the ghost of the enemy from pursuing them any further."[6] So too among the Bechuanas a man who has killed another, whether in war or in single combat, is not allowed to enter the village until he has been purified;[7] while some South African tribes require the slayer of a very gallant foe in war to observe a period of forced seclusion before rejoining his household. When a Nandi of British East Africa has killed a member of another tribe, he paints one side of his body, spear, and sword red, and the other side white. For four days after the slaughter he is considered unclean and may not go home. He has to build a small shelter by a river and live there.[8] Herero warriors on their return from battle may not approach the sacred hearth until they have been shriven from the guilt of bloodshed. They crouch in a circle round the hearth, but at some distance from it, while the chief besprinkles their brows and temples with water in which branches of a holy bush have been placed.[9] In the Washington group of the Marquesas Islands, the man who has slain an enemy in battle becomes tabooed for ten days, during which he may not engage in sexual intercourse with his wife and may not meddle with fire. Hence another has to make fire and cook for him. Nevertheless he is treated with marked distinction and receives presents of pigs.[10] Among the Natchez of North America young braves who had taken their first scalps were obliged to observe certain rules of abstinence for six months;[11] while when a Choctaw had killed an enemy and taken his scalp, he went into mourning for a month. If, during this time, his head itched, he might not scratch it except with a little stick which he wore fastened to his wrist for the purpose.[12]

Thus we see that warriors who have taken the life of a foe in battle are temporarily cut off from free intercourse with their fellows, and especially with their wives, and must undergo certain rites of purification before they are readmitted to society. Now if the purpose of their seclusion and of the expiatory rites which they have to perform is, as we have been led to believe, no other than to shake off, frighten, or appease the angry spirit of the slain man, we may safely conjecture that the similar purification of homicides and murderers, who have imbrued their hands in the blood of a fellow-tribesman, had at first the same significance, and that the idea of a moral or spiritual regeneration symbolised by the washing, the fasting, and so on, was merely a later interpretation put upon the old custom by men who had outgrown the primitive modes of thought in which the custom originated. The conjecture will be confirmed if we can shew that savages have actually imposed certain restrictions on the murderer of a fellow-tribesman from a definite fear that he is haunted by the ghost of his victim. This we can do with regard to the Omahas, a tribe of the Siouan stock in North America. Among these Indians the kinsmen of a murdered man had the right to put the murderer to death, but sometimes they waived their right in consideration of presents which they consented to accept. When the life of the murderer was spared, he had to observe certain stringent rules for a period which varied from two to four years. He must walk barefoot, and he might eat no warm food, nor raise his voice, nor look around. He was compelled to pull his robe about him and to have it tied at the neck even in hot weather; he might not let it hang loose or fly open. He might not move his hands about, but had to keep them close to his body. He might not comb his hair, and it might not be blown about by the wind. When the tribe went out hunting, he was obliged to pitch his tent about a quarter of a mile from the rest of the people "lest the ghost of his victim should raise a high wind, which might cause damage." Only one of his kindred was allowed to remain with him at his tent. No one wished to eat with him, for they said, "If we eat with him whom Wakanda hates, Wakanda will hate us." Sometimes he wandered at night crying and lamenting his offence. At the end of his long isolation the kinsmen of the murdered man heard his crying and said, "It is enough. Begone, and walk among the crowd. Put on moccasins and wear a good robe."[13] Here the reason alleged for keeping the murderer at a considerable distance from the hunters gives the clue to all the other restrictions laid on him: he was haunted and therefore dangerous. The ancient Greeks believed that the soul of a man who had just been killed was wroth with his slayer and troubled him; wherefore it was needful even for the involuntary homicide to depart from his country for a year until the anger of the dead man had cooled down; nor might the slayer return until sacrifice had been offered and ceremonies of purification performed. If his victim chanced to be a foreigner, the homicide had to shun the native country of the dead man as well as his own.[14] The legend of the matricide Orestes, how he roamed from place to place pursued by the Furies of his murdered mother, and none would sit at meat with him, or take him in, till he had been purified,[15] reflects faithfully the real Greek dread of such as were still haunted by an angry ghost. When the turbulent people of Cynaetha, after perpetrating an atrocious massacre, sent an embassy to Sparta, every Arcadian town through which the envoys passed on their journey ordered them out of its walls at once; and the Mantineans, after the embassy had departed, even instituted a solemn purification of the city and its territory by carrying sacrificial victims round them both.[16]

169. In savage society the hunter and fisherman have often to observe rules of abstinence and to submit to ceremonies of purification. On the strength of the material we have already adduced, we may assume with some probability that this custom is actuated principally by a fear of the spirits of the beasts, birds, or fish which he has killed or intends to kill. For the savage commonly conceives animals to be endowed with "souls" and intelligences like his own, and hence he naturally treats them with similar respect.

Thus the Indians of Nutka Sound used to prepare themselves for catching whales by fasting for an entire week, during which time they also bathed several times a day and rubbed their bodies with shells and bushes. They were required also to abstain from any commerce with women for the like period. Indeed, a chief who failed to catch a whale has been known to attribute his failure to breach of this last injunction.[1] Among the Motu of Port Moresby, in New Guinea, chastity is enjoined before fishing and wallaby-hunting; it is believed that men who have been unchaste will be unable to catch the fish and wallabies, which will turn about and jeer at their pursuers.[2] In the Pelew Islands, fishermen are likewise debarred from intercourse with women, on the grounds that it would have an adverse effect on the fishing. The same taboo is said to be observed in all the other islands of the South Sea.[3]

In the island of Nias the hunters sometimes dig pits, cover them lightly over with twigs, grass, and leaves, and then drive the game into them. While they are engaged in digging the pits, they have to observe a number of taboos. They may not spit, or the game would turn back in disgust from the pits. They may not laugh, or the sides of the pit would fall in. They may eat no salt, prepare no fodder for swine, and in the pit they may not scratch themselves, for if they did, the earth would be loosened and would collapse. And the night after digging the pit they may have no intercourse with a woman, or all their labour would be in vain.[4] In the Motumotu tribe of New Guinea a man will not see his wife the night before he starts on a major fishing or hunting expedition; if he did, he would have no luck.[5] A Carrier Indian of British Columbia was wont to separate from his wife for a full month before he set traps for bears, and during that time he might not drink from the same vessel. Neglect of these precautions, it was held, would cause the game to escape from the snare.[6] And among the natives of the Gazelle Peninsula in New Guinea men who are engaged in making fish-traps avoid women and observe strict continence.[7]

TABOOED THINGS

170. But it is not only by certain acts that the soul or sacred person can be imperilled. The danger extends to bringing it into contact with certain material objects deemed potentially noxious—a concept with survives widely in popular superstitions.

171. In its most extreme form the taboo against such contact is general and universal, as when the awful sanctity attaching to kings leads to a prohibition against touching their persons. It was unlawful, for example, to lay hands on the person of a Spartan king;[1] and no one might touch the body of the king or queen of Tahiti.[2]

Especially noxious and dangerous are objects made of iron. Thus, in 1800 King Tieng-tsong-tai-Oang of Korea died of a tumour in the back, no one dreaming of employing the lancet, which would probably have saved his life. It is said that one king suffered terribly from an abscess in the lip, till his physician called in a jester, whose pranks made the king laugh heartily, and so the abscess burst.[3] Roman and Sabine priests might not be shaved with iron but only with bronze razors or shears;[4] and whenever an iron graving-tool was brought into the sacred grove of the Arval Brothers at Rome for the purpose of cutting an inscription in stone, an expiatory sacrifice of a lamb and a pig must be offered, which was repeated when the graving-tool was removed from the grove.[5] As a general rule iron might not be brought into Greek sanctuaries.[6] In Crete sacrifices were offered to Menedemus without the use of iron, because (so the legend ran) Menedemus had been killed by an iron weapon in the Trojan war.[7] To this day a Hottentot priest never uses an iron knife, but always a sharp splint of quartz, in sacrificing an animal or circumcising a boy.[8] Among the Ovambo of south-west Africa custom requires that lads be circumcised with a sharp flint; if none be to hand, the operation may be performed with iron only if the iron is subsequently buried.[9] In Uap, one of the Caroline Islands, wood of the hibiscus tree, which was used to make the fire-drill, had to be cut with shell knives or shell axes, never with iron or steel.[10] The men who made the need-fire in Scotland had to divest themselves of all metal.[11] There was hardly any belief, we are told, that had a stronger hold on the mind of a Scottish Highlander than that on no account whatever should iron be put in the ground on Good Friday. Hence no grave was dug and no field ploughed on that day. It has been suggested that the belief was based on that rooted aversion to iron which fairies are known to feel. These touchy beings live underground, and might resent having the roof pulled from over their heads on the hallowed day.[12] Again, in the Highlands of Scotland the shoulder-blades of sheep are employed in divination, being consulted as to future marriages, births, death, and funerals; but the forecasts thus made will not be accurate unless the flesh has been removed from the bones without the use of any iron.[13] Amongst the Jews no iron tool was used in building the Temple at Jerusalem or in making an altar.[14] The old wooden bridge (*Pons Sublicius*) at Rome, which was considered sacred, was made and had to be kept in repair without the use of iron or bronze.[15] It was expressly provided by law that the temple of Jupiter Liber at Furfo might be repaired with iron tools.[16] The council chamber at Cyzicus was constructed of wood without any iron nails, the beams being so arranged that they could be taken out and replaced.[17] The late Rajah Vijyanagram, a member of the Viceroy's Council, and described as one of the most enlightened and estimable of Hindu princes, would not allow iron to be used in the construction of buildings within his territory, believing that its use would inevitably be followed by small-pox and other epidemics.[18]

This superstitious objection to iron perhaps dates from that early time in the history of society when iron was still a novelty, and as such was viewed by many with suspicion and dislike. For everything new is apt to excite the awe and dread of the primitive. When, for instance, the introduction of iron plowshares into Poland happened to be followed by a succession of bad harvests, the farmers attributed the disaster to the newfangled implements and discarded them for the old wooden ones.[19] To this day the Baduwis of Java, who live chiefly by husbandry, will use no iron tools in tilling their fields.[20]

The disfavor in which iron is held by the gods and their ministers has another side. As their dislike of it is supposed to be so great that they will not approach persons and things protected by the obnoxious metal, iron may obviously be employed as a charm for banning ghosts and other dangerous spirits. Thus, in Morocco it is considered a great protection against demons; hence it is usual to place an iron knife or dagger under a sick man's pillow.[21] The Singhalese peasant will not dare to carry good food, such as cakes or roast meat, from one place to another without putting an iron nail on it to prevent a demon from taking possession of it and thus harming the consumer.[22] Among the Maravars, an aboriginal race of southern India, a knife or other iron object lies beside a woman after childbirth to keep off the devil.[23] The use of iron as a means to exorcise demons was forbidden by the Coptic church.[24] In India "the mourner who performs the ceremony of putting fire into the dead person's mouth carries with him a piece of iron: it may be a key or a knife, or a simple piece of iron, and during the whole time of his separation (for he is unclean for a certain time, and no one will either touch him or eat or drink with him, neither can he change his clothes) he carries the piece of iron about with him to keep off the evil spirit."[25] When a woman dies in childbed in the island of Salsette, they put a nail or other piece of iron in the folds of her dress; this is done especially if the child survives her. The intention plainly is to prevent her spirit from coming back; for they believe that a dead mother haunts the house and seeks to carry away her child.[26] In the

as a cure for headache and other ailments, they are very careful not to spill any of the blood on the ground, but sprinkle it on each other.[18] Among the Latuka of central Africa the earth on which a drop of blood has fallen at childbirth is carefully scraped up with an iron shovel, put into a pot along with the water used in washing the mother, and buried tolerably deep outside the house on the left-hand side.[19] In West Africa, if a drop of your blood has fallen on the ground, you must carefully cover it up, rub and stamp it into the soil; if it has fallen on the side of a canoe or a tree, the place is cut out and the chip destroyed.[20]

The general explanation of the reluctance to shed blood on the ground is probably to be found in the belief that the soul is in the blood, and that therefore any ground on which it may fall necessarily becomes taboo or sacred. In New Zealand anything upon which even a drop of a high chief's blood chances to fall becomes taboo or sacred to him. For instance, a party of natives having come to visit a chief in a fine new canoe, the chief got into it, but in doing so a splinter entered his foot, and the blood trickled on the canoe, which at once became sacred to him. The owner jumped out, dragged the canoe ashore opposite the chief's house, and left it there. Again, a chief in entering a missionary's house knocked his head against a beam, and the blood flowed. The natives said that in former times the house would have belonged to the chief.[21] As usually happens with taboos of universal application, the prohibition to spill the blood of a tribesman on the ground applies with particular stringency to chiefs and kings, and is observed in their case long after it has ceased to be observed in the case of others.

174. Among many peoples the head is peculiarly sacred on the grounds that it is the seat of a spirit which is very sensitive to injury or disrespect. Thus the Yorubas of the Slave Coast hold that every man has three spiritual inmates, of whom the first, called Olori, dwells in the head and is the man's protector, guardian, and guide. Offerings are made to this spirit, chiefly of fowls, and some of the blood mixed with palm-oil is rubbed on the forehead.[1] If a Siamese touch the head of another with his foot, both of them must build chapels to the earth-spirit to avert the omen. Nor does the guardian spirit of the head like to have the hair washed too often; it might injure or incommode him. Indeed, it was a grand solemnity when the king of Burma's head was washed with water drawn from the river.[2] The head of the king of Persia was cleaned only once a year, on his birthday.[3] Roman women washed their heads annually on the thirteenth of August, Diana's day.[4]

The son of a Marquesan high priest has been seen to roll on the ground in an agony of rage and despair, begging for death, because some one had desecrated his head and deprived him of his divinity by sprinkling a few drops of water on his hair.[5] But it was not the Marquesan chiefs only whose heads were sacred. The head of every Marquesan was taboo, and might neither be touched nor stepped over by another; even a father might not step over the head of his sleeping child;[6] women were forbidden to carry or touch anything that had been in contact with, or had merely hung over, the head of their husband or father.[7] In Cambodia the head of every person must be respected, and most especially the head of the king. No one may touch the head of a nursling at the breast; formerly, if any one were so malicious as to do so he was put to death, for only thus could the sacrilege be atoned for.[7a] Again the Wa-Singi of Kenya perform a great ceremony at the circumcision of youths. During the whole of this ceremony they have to take particular care not to touch each others' heads or their hair falls off, so they cover their heads with a cloth or skin.[7b]

175. When the head was considered so sacred that it might not even be touched without grave offence, it is obvious that the cutting of the hair must have been a delicate and difficult operation. The difficulties and dangers which, on the primitive view, beset the operation are of two kinds. There is first the danger of disturbing the spirit of the head, which may be injured in the process and may revenge itself upon the person who molests him. Secondly, there is the difficulty of disposing of the shorn locks. For the savage believes that the sympathetic connexion which exists between himself and every part of his body continues to exist even after the physical connexion has been broken, and that therefore he will suffer from any harm that may befall the severed parts of his body, such as the clippings of his hair or the parings of his nails. Accordingly he takes care that these severed portions of himself shall not be left in places where they might either be exposed to accidental injury or fall into the hands of malicious persons who might work magic on them to his detriment or death. Such dangers are common to all, but sacred persons have more to fear from them than ordinary people, so the precautions taken by them are proportionately stringent. The simplest way of evading the peril is not to cut the hair at all; and this is the expedient adopted where the risk is thought to be more than usually great. The Frankish kings were never allowed to crop their hair; from their childhood upwards they had to keep it unshorn.[1] To poll the long locks that floated on their shoulders would have been to renounce their right to the throne.

Among the Hos, a Negro tribe of Togoland in West Africa, "there are priests on whose head no razor may come during the whole of their lives. The god who dwells in the man forbids the cutting of his hair on pain of death. If the hair is at last too long, the owner must pray to his god to allow him at least to clip the tips of it. The hair is in fact conceived as the seat and lodging-place of his god, so that if it were shorn the god would lose his abode in the priest."[2] Men of the Tsetsaut tribe in British Columbia do not cut their hair, believing that if they cut it they would quickly grow old.[3] Elsewhere men travelling abroad have been in the habit of leaving their hair unshorn until their return. The reason for this custom is probably the danger to which a traveller is believed to be exposed from the magic arts of the strangers among whom he sojourns; if they got possession of his shorn hair, they might work his destruction through it. The Egyptians when on a journey kept their hair uncut until they returned home.[4] "At Tâif when a man returned from a journey his first duty was to visit the Rabba and poll his hair."[5] Achilles kept his yellow hair unshorn, because his father had vowed to offer it to the River Sperchius if ever his son came home from the wars beyond the sea.[6]

Again, men who have taken a vow of vengeance sometimes keep their hair uncut until they have fulfilled that vow. On one occasion a Hawaiian taboo is said to have lasted a full thirty years, "during which the men were not allowed to trim their beards."[7] While his vow lasted, a nazirite might not have his hair cut: "All the days of the vow of his separation there shall no razor come upon his head."[8] In Uganda a child's hair may not be cut until the child has received a name. Should any of it be rubbed or plucked off accidentally, it is refastened to the head with string or by being knotted to other hair.[9] Similarly, in some parts of Germany, it is thought that if a child's hair is combed in its first year, the child will be unlucky;[10] or that if a boy's hair is cut before his seventh year he will have no courage.[11]

When it indeed becomes necessary to crop the hair, measures are taken to lessen the dangers which are supposed to attend the operation. Thus in some parts of New Zealand the most sacred day of the year was that appointed for hair-cutting; the people assembled in large numbers from all the neighborhood.[12] Sometimes a Maori chieftain's hair was shorn by his wife, who was then tabooed for a week as a consequence of having touched his sacred locks.[13] The hair and nails of the Mikado could be cut only while he was asleep,[14] perhaps because his soul being then absent from his body, there was less chance of injuring it with the shears.

176. The same feeling perhaps gave rise to the European rule that a child's nails should not be pared during the first year, but that if it is absolutely necessary to shorten them they should be bitten off by the mother or nurse.[1] For in all parts of the world a young child is believed to be especially exposed to supernatural dangers, and particular precautions are taken to guard it against them; in other words, the child is subject to a number of taboos, of which the rule just mentioned is one. "Among the Hindus the usual custom seems to be that the nails of a firstborn child are cut at the age of six months. With other children a year or two is allowed to elapse."[2] The Slave, Hare, and Dogrib Indians of Northwest America do not pare the nails of female children until they are four years of age.[3]

177. But even when the hair and nails have been safely cut there remains the difficulty of disposing of them, for their owner believes himself liable to suffer from any harm that may befall them. The notion that a man may be bewitched by means of the clippings of his hair, the parings of his nails, or any other severed portion of his person is almost world-wide.

The Huzuls of the Carpathians imagine that if mice get a person's shorn

hair and make a nest of it, the person will suffer from headache or even become idiotic.[1] Similarly in Germany it is a common notion that if a bird finds
a person's cut hair and builds a nest in it, the person will suffer from headache.[2]

It is thought also that cut or combed-out hair may disturb the weather by
producing rain and hail, thunder and lightning. In the Tyrol, witches are supposed to use cut or combed-out hair to make hailstorms or thunderstorms.[3]
Tlingit Indians have been known to attribute stormy weather to the rash act
of a girl who had combed her hair outdoors.[4] The Romans held similarly that
no one on shipboard should cut his hair or nails except in a storm—that is,
when the mischief had already been done.[5] The Makoko of the Anzikos
begged the missionaries to give him half of their beards as a rain-charm.[6]

To preserve the cut hair and nails from injury and from misuse by sorcerers, it is necessary to deposit them in some safe place. Hence the natives of
the Maldives carefully keep and bury them, with a little water, in the cemeteries.[7] The shorn tresses of the Vestal virgins were hung on an ancient lotus-
tree.[8] In Morocco women often hang their cut hair on a tree near the grave of
a wonder-working saint; for they think thus to rid themselves of headache or
guard against it.[9] In parts of Germany, the clippings used frequently to be
buried under an elder-bush.[10] In the Aru Islands, as soon as a child is able to
run alone, a female relative shears a lock of its hair and lays it on a banana-
tree.[11] Indians of the Yukon territory do not throw away their cut hair and
nails but tie them up in little bundles and place them in the crotches of trees
or wherever they are out of the way of animals.[12]

Sometimes the severed hair and nails are preserved, not to prevent them
from falling into the hands of a magician, but that the owner may have them
at the resurrection of the body, to which some races look forward. Thus the
Armenians hide them in places esteemed holy, such as a crack in a church
wall, a pillar of the house, or a hollow tree. They believe that a man who has
not so stored them away will have to hunt for them on the great day.[13] To the
same end the Macedonians bury them in a hole,[14] and devout Moslems in
Morocco hide them in a secret place.[15] In the village of Drumconrath, near
Abbeyleix, in Ireland, there used to be some old women who, having ascertained from Scripture that the hairs of their heads were all numbered by the
Almighty, expected to have to account for them at the Day of Judgment. In
order to be able to do so they stuffed the severed hair away in the thatch of
their cottages![16]

178. On the same principles of sympathetic magic the spittle is part of the
man, and whatever is done to it will have a corresponding effect on him. Special precautions are therefore taken to keep it out of the reach of sorcerers or
enemies; and such precautions apply, of course, with double force in the case
of kings and chiefs. In the Sandwich Islands chiefs were attended by a confi-
dential servant bearing a portable spittoon, and the deposit was carefully

buried every morning to keep it away from sorcerers.[1] On the Slave Coast of Africa, for the same reason, whenever a king or chief expectorates, the saliva is scrupulously gathered up and hidden or buried.[2] Page-boys, who carry tails of elephants, hasten to sweep up or cover with sand the spittle of the king of Ashanti;[3] an attendant used to perform a similar service for the king of Congo;[4] and a custom of the same sort used to prevail at the court of the Muata Jamwo in the interior of Angola.[5] Among the Guaycurus and Payaguas of Brazil, when a chief spat, those around him received the saliva on their hands,[6] probably to prevent it from being misused by magicians. "The saliva of the king of Hawaii was carefully preserved in a spittoon, in the edges of which were set the teeth of his ancestors. Should his enemies get possession of any of it, they were supposed to have the power to occasion his death, by sorcery and prayer."[6a]

179. As might have been expected, the superstitions of the savage cluster thick about the subject of food; and he abstains from eating many animals and plants, wholesome enough in themselves, which for one reason or another he fancies would prove dangerous or fatal to the eater. Examples of such abstinence are too familiar and far too numerous to quote. But if the ordinary man is thus deterred by superstitious fear from partaking of various foods, the restraints of this kind which are laid upon sacred or tabooed persons, such as kings and priests, are still more numerous and stringent. We have already seen that the Flamen Dialis was forbidden to eat or even name several plants and animals, and that the flesh diet of Egyptian kings was restricted to veal and goose.[1] In antiquity many priests and many kings of barbarous peoples abstained wholly from a flesh diet.[2] The *Gangas* or fetish priests of the Loango Coast are forbidden to eat or even see a variety of animals and fish, in consequence of which their flesh diet is extremely limited; often they live only on herbs and roots, though they may drink fresh blood.[3] The heir to the throne of Loango is forbidden from infancy to eat pork; from early childhood he is interdicted the use of the *cola* fruit in company; at puberty he is taught by a priest not to partake of fowls except such as he has himself killed and cooked; and so the number of taboos goes on increasing with his years.[4] In Fernando Po the king after installation is forbidden to eat *cocco* (*arum acaule*), deer, and porcupine, which are the ordinary foods of the people.[5] The head chief of the Masai may eat nothing but milk, honey, and the roasted livers of goats; for if he partook of any other food he would lose his power of soothsaying and of compounding charms.[6] Among the Murrams of Manipur "there are many prohibitions in regard to the food, both animal and vegetable, which the chief should eat; and the Murrams say that the chief's post must be a very uncomfortable one."[7] So, too, in the village of Tomil, in Yap (one of the Caroline Islands) there are five men who for a hundred days in the year may eat only fish and taro, may not chew betel, and must observe strict continence.

If they fail to do so, it is believed, immature girls would attain puberty too soon.[8]

180. We have seen that among the many taboos which the Flamen Dialis at Rome had to observe, there was one that forbade him to have a knot on any part of his garments, and another that obliged him to wear no ring unless it were broken.[1] In like manner Moslem pilgrims to Mecca are in a state of sanctity or taboo and may wear on their persons neither knots nor rings.[2] These rules are probably of kindred significance, and may conveniently be considered together. To begin with knots, many people in different parts of the world entertain a strong objection to having any knot about their person at certain critical seasons, particularly childbirth, marriage, and death. Thus among the Saxons of Transylvania, when a woman is in travail all knots on her garments are untied, because it is believed that this will facilitate her delivery, and with the same intention all the locks in the house, whether on doors or boxes, are unlocked.[3] The Lapps think that a lying-in woman should have no knot on her garments, because a knot would have the effect of making the delivery difficult and painful.[4] In ancient India it was a rule to untie all knots in a house at the moment of childbirth.[5] Roman religion required that women who took part in the rites of Juno Lucina, the goddess of childbirth, should have no knot tied on their persons.[6] In the Toumbuluh tribe of North Celebes a ceremony is performed in the fourth or fifth month of a woman's pregnancy, and after it her husband is forbidden, among many other things, to tie any fast knots and to sit with his legs crossed over each other.[7] In the Kaitish tribe of central Australia the father of a newborn child goes out into the scrub for three days, away from his camp, leaving his girdle and armbands behind him, so that he has nothing tied tightly round any part of his body. This freedom from constriction is supposed to benefit his wife.[8]

In all these cases the idea seems to be that the tying of a knot would "tie up" the woman—that is, impede her delivery or delay her convalescence.

Again, a Toumbuluh man abstains not only from tying knots, but also from sitting with crossed legs during his wife's pregnancy. The train of thought is the same in both cases. Whether you cross threads in tying a knot, or only cross your legs in sitting at your ease, you are equally, on the principles of homoeopathic magic, crossing or thwarting the free course of things, and your action cannot but check and impede whatever may be going forward in your neighbourhood. Of this important truth the Romans were fully aware. To sit beside a pregnant woman or a patient under medical treatment with clasped hands, says the grave Pliny, is to cast a malignant spell over the person, and it is worse still if you nurse your leg or legs with your clasped hands, or lay one leg over the other. Such postures were regarded by the old Romans as a let and hindrance to business of every sort, and at a council of war or a meeting of magistrates, at prayers and sacrifices, no man was suffered to cross his legs or clasp his hands.[9] The stock instance of the dreadful consequences that might flow from doing one or the other was that of Alcmena, who travailed with Hercules for seven days and seven nights, because the goddess Lucina sat in front of the house with clasped hands and crossed legs, and the child could not be born until the goddess had been beguiled into changing her attitude.[10] It is a Bulgarian superstition that if a pregnant woman is in the habit of sitting with crossed legs, she will suffer much in childbed.[11]

The converse underlies a practice observed by some peoples of opening all locks, doors, and so on, while a birth is taking place in the house. This custom obtains, for instance, among the Germans of Transylvania, in Voigtland and Mecklenburg,[12] and in the north-western districts of Argyllshire, Scotland.[13] The old Roman custom of presenting women with a key as a symbol of easy delivery[14] perhaps points to a similar notion. In the island of Calsette near Bombay, when a woman is in difficult labor, all locks of doors or drawers are opened with a key to facilitate delivery.[15] Among the Mandelings of Sumatra, the lids of all chests, boxes, pans, and so forth are opened; if this does not produce the desired result, the anxious husband has to strike the projecting ends of some of the house-beams in order to loosen them.[16] At a difficult birth the Battas of the same island make a search through the possessions of husband and wife and untie everything that is bundled up.[17]

The magical effect of knots in tramelling and obstructing human activity was believed to be manifested at marriage no less than at birth. The persons who help a Syrian bridegroom to don his wedding garments take care that no knot is tied on them and no button buttoned, for they believe that unless this were done he might be deprived of his nuptial rights by magical means.[18] The fear of such charms is likewise diffused all over North Africa. To render a bridegroom impotent the enchanter has only to tie a knot in a handkerchief which he has previously slipped into the bridegroom's attire.[19]

The maleficent power of knots may be manifested also in the infliction of sickness, disease, and all kinds of misfortune. Babylonian witches and wizards of old hoped to strangle their victim, seal his mouth, wrack his limbs, and tear his entrails by merely tying knots in a cord, while at each knot they muttered a spell. But happily the evil could be undone by simply undoing the knots.[20] We hear of a man in one of the Orkney Islands who was utterly ruined by nine knots cast on a blue thread; and it would seem that sick people in Scotland sometimes prayed to the devil to restore them to health by loosing the secret knot that was doing all the mischief.[21] In the Koran there is an allusion to the mischief of "those who puff into the knots," and an Arab commentator on the passage explains that the words refer to women who practise magic by tying knots in cords, and then blowing and spitting upon them. He goes on to relate how, once upon a time, a wicked Jew bewitched the prophet Mohammed himself by tying nine knots on a string, which he then hid in a well. So the prophet fell ill, and nobody knows what might have happened if the archangel Gabriel had not opportunely revealed to the holy man the place where the knotted cord was concealed. The trusty Ali soon fetched the baleful thing from the well; and the prophet recited over it certain charms, which were specially revealed to him for the purpose. At every verse of the charms a knot untied itself, and the prophet experienced a certain relief.[22]

There are certain beneficent knots to which a positive power of healing is ascribed. Pliny tells us that some folk cured diseases of the groin by taking a thread from a web, tying seven or nine knots on it, and then fastening it to the patient's groin; but to make the cure effectual it was necessary to name some widow as each knot was tied.[23] The ancient Assyrians seem to have made much use of knotted cords as a remedy for ailments and disease. The cord with its knots, which were sometimes twice seven in number, was tied round the head, neck, or limbs of the patient, and then after a time cut off and thrown away, carrying with it, as was apparently supposed, the aches and pains of the sufferer. Sometimes the magic cord which was used for this beneficent purpose consisted of a double strand of black and white wool; sometimes it was woven of the hair of a virgin kid.[24] A modern Arab cure for fever reported from the ruins of Nineveh is to tie a cotton thread with seven knots on it round the wrist of the patient, who must wear it for seven or eight days or till such time as the fever passes, after which he may throw it away.[25]

A Scottish cure for a sprained leg or arm is to cast nine knots in a black thread round the suffering limb, while you say:

> "The Lord rade,
> And the foal slade;
> He lighted
> And he righted,
> Set joint to joint,
> Bone to bone,
> And sinew to sinew.
> Heal, in the Holy Ghost's name!"[26]

In Gujarat, if a man takes seven cotton threads, goes to a place where an owl is hooting, strips naked, ties a knot at each hoot, and fastens the knotted thread round the right arm of a man sick of the fever, the malady will leave him.[27]

Again, knots may be used by an enchantress to win a lover and attach him firmly to herself. Thus the love-sick maid in Virgil seeks to draw Daphnis to her from the city by spells and by tying three knots on each of three strings of different colours.[28] So an Arab maiden, who had lost her heart to a certain man, tried to gain his love and bind him to herself by tying knots in his whip; but her jealous rival undid the knots.[29] On the same principle magic knots may be employed to stop a runaway. In Swaziland you may often see grass tied in knots at the side of the footpaths. Every one of these knots tells of a domestic tragedy. A wife has run away from her husband, and he and his friends have gone in pursuit, binding up the paths, as they call it, in this fashion to prevent the fugitive from doubling back over them.[30]

A similar power to bind and hamper spiritual as well as bodily activities is ascribed by some people to rings. Thus in the Greek island of Carpathus, people never button the clothes they put upon a dead body and they are careful to remove all rings from it; "for the spirit, they say, can even be detained in the little finger, and cannot rest."[31] Here it is plain that even if the soul is not definitely supposed to issue at death from the finger-tips, yet the ring is conceived to exercise a certain constrictive influence which detains and imprisons the immortal spirit in spite of its efforts to escape from the tabernacle of clay; in short the ring, like the knot, acts as a spiritual fetter. Nobody might enter the ancient Arcadian sanctuary of the Mistress at Lycosura with a ring on his or her finger.[32] Persons who consulted the oracle of Faunus had to be chaste, to eat no flesh, and to wear no rings.[33]

On the other hand, the same constriction which hinders the egress of the soul may prevent the entrance of evil spirits; hence we find rings used as amulets against demons, witches, and ghosts. In the Tyrol it is said that a woman in childbed should never take off her wedding-ring, or spirits and witches will have power over her.[34] Among the Lapps, the person who is about to place a corpse in the coffin receives from the husband, wife, or children of the deceased a brass ring, which he must wear fastened to his right arm until the corpse is safely deposited in the grave. The ring is believed to serve the person as an amulet against any harm which the ghost might do to him.[35] The Huzuls of the Carpathians sometimes milk a cow through a wedding-ring to prevent witches from stealing its milk.[36] In India iron rings are often worn as an amulet against disease or to counteract the malignant influence of the planet Saturn. A coral ring is used in Gujarat to ward off the baleful influence of the sun, and in Bengal mourners touch it as a form of purification.[37] A Masai mother who has lost one or more children at an early age will put a copper ring on the second toe of her next infant's right foot to guard it against sickness.[38] Masai men also wear on the middle finger of the right hand a ring made out of the hide of a sacrificial victim; it is supposed to protect the wearer from witchcraft and disease of every kind.[39]

Before leaving the subject of knots I may be allowed to hazard a conjecture as to the meaning of the famous Gordian knot, which Alexander the Great, failing in his efforts to untie it, cut through with his sword. In Gordium, the ancient capital of the kings of Phrygia, there was preserved a waggon of which the yoke was fastened to the pole by a strip of cornel-bark or a vine-shoot twisted and tied in an intricate knot. Tradition ran that the waggon had been dedicated by Midas, the first king of the dynasty, and that whoever untied the knot would be ruler of Asia.[40] Perhaps the knot was a talisman with which the fate of the dynasty was believed to be bound up in such a way that whenever the knot was loosed the reign of the dynasty would come to an end. We have seen that the magic virtue ascribed to knots is naturally enough supposed to last only so long as they remain tied. If the Gordian knot was the talisman of the Phrygian kings, the local fame it enjoyed, as guaranteeing to them the rule of Phrygia, might easily be exaggerated by distant rumour into a report that the sceptre of Asia itself would fall to him who should undo the wondrous knot.[41]

TABOOED WORDS

181. Taboos are applied not only to acts and objects but also to words, and to none more than to names. Primitive man regards his name as a vital portion of himself and guards it accordingly. For this reason many savages at the present day take great pains to conceal their real names, lest these should give to evil-minded persons a handle by which to injure their owners. Thus among the tribes of south-eastern Australia "when the new name is given at initiation, the child's name becomes secret, not to be revealed to strangers or to be mentioned by friends";[1] while among those living in the center of that continent every man, woman and child has, besides a personal name which is in common use, a secret or sacred name which is bestowed by the older men upon him or her soon after birth, and which is known to none but the fully initiated members of the group. This secret name is never mentioned except upon the most solemn occasions; to utter it in the hearing of women or of men of another group would be a most serious breach of tribal custom, as serious as the most flagrant case of sacrilege among ourselves. When mentioned at all, the name is spoken only in a whisper, and not until the most elaborate precautions have been taken that it shall be heard by no one but members of the group. "The native thinks that a stranger knowing his secret name would have special power to work him ill by means of magic."[2]

The same fear seems to have led to a custom of the same sort amongst the ancient Egyptians. Every Egyptian received two names, which were known respectively as the true name and the good name, or the great name and the little name; and while the good or little name was made public, the true or great name appears to have been carefully concealed.[3] Similarly in Abyssinia at the present day it is customary to conceal the real name which a person receives at baptism and to call him only by a sort of nickname which his mother gives him on leaving the church. A Brahman child receives two names, one for common use, the other a secret name which none but his father and mother should know. The latter is only used at ceremonies such as marriage. The custom is intended to protect the person against magic, since a charm only becomes effectual in combination with the real name.[4] Similarly, among the hill tribes of Assam each individual has a private name which may not be revealed. Should any one imprudently allow his private name to be known, the whole village is tabooed for two days and a feast is provided at the expense of the culprit.[5]

In North America superstitions of the same sort are current. The Navahos of New Mexico are most unwilling to reveal their Indian names or those of their friends; they generally go by some Mexican name which they have received from the whites.[6] "No Apache will give his name to a stranger, fearing some hidden power may thus be placed in the stranger's hand to his [own] detriment."[7] The Tonkawe Indians of Texas will give their children Comanche and English names in addition to their native names, which they are unwilling to communicate to others; for they believe that when somebody calls a person by his or her native name after death the spirit of the deceased may hear it, and may be prompted to take revenge on such as disturbed his rest; whereas if the spirit be called by a name drawn from another language, it will pay no heed.[8] Blackfoot Indians believe that they would be unfortunate in all their undertakings if they were to speak their names.[9] When the Canadian Indians were asked their names, they used to hang their heads in silence or answer that they did not know.[10] When an Ojibway is asked his name, he will look at some bystander and ask him to answer.[11]

Sometimes the embargo laid on personal names is not permanent; it is conditional on circumstances, and when these change it ceases to operate. Thus when the Nandi men are away on a foray, nobody at home may pronounce the names of the absent warriors; they must be referred to as birds. Should a child so far forget itself as to mention one of the distant ones by name, the mother would rebuke it, saying, "Don't talk of the birds who are in the heavens."[12] Among the Bangala of the Upper Congo, while a man is fishing and when he returns with his catch, his proper name is in abeyance and nobody may mention it. Whatever the fisherman's real name may be, he is called *mwele* without distinction. The reason is that the river is full of spirits, who, if they heard the fisherman's real name, might so work against him that he would catch little or nothing. Even when he has caught his fish and landed with them, the buyer must still not address him by his proper name, but must only call him *mwele;* for even then, if the spirits were to hear his proper name, they would either bear it in mind and serve him out another day, or they might so mar the fish he had caught that he would get very little for them. Hence the fisherman can extract heavy damages from anybody who mentions his name, or can compel the thoughtless speaker to relieve him of the fish at a good price so as to restore his luck.[13]

When it is deemed necessary that a man's real name should be kept secret, it is often customary, as we have seen, to call him by a surname or nickname. As distinguished from the real or primary names, these secondary names are apparently held to be no part of the man himself, so that they may be freely used and divulged to everybody without endangering his safety thereby. Sometimes in order to avoid the use of his own name a man will be called after his child. Thus we are informed that "the Gippsland blacks objected strongly to let any one outside the tribe know their names, lest their enemies, learning them, should make them vehicles of incantation, and so charm their lives away. As children were not thought to have enemies, they used to speak of a man as 'the father, uncle, or cousin of So-and-so,' naming a child; but on all occasions abstained from mentioning the name of a grown-up person."[14] Similarly among the Nufoors of Dutch New Guinea, grown-up persons who are related by marriage may not mention each other's names, but it is lawful to mention the names of children; hence in order to designate a person whose name they may not pronounce they will speak of him or her as the father or mother of So-and-so.[15] The Alfoors of Poso, in Celebes, will not pronounce their own names. Among them, accordingly, if you wish to ascertain a person's name, you ought not to ask the man himself, but should enquire of others. But if this is impossible, for example, when there is no one else near, you should ask him his child's name, and then address him as the "Father of So-and-so." Nay, these Alfoors are shy of uttering the names even of children, so when a boy or girl has a nephew or niece, he or she is addressed as "Uncle of So-and-so," or "Aunt of So-and-so."[16] Among the Kukis and Zemis or Kacha Nagas of Assam parents drop their own names after the birth of a child and are named Father and Mother of So-and-so. Childless couples go by the names of "the childless father," "the childless mother," "the father of no child," "the mother of no child."[17] A Hindu woman will not name her husband. If she has to refer to him she will designate him as the father of her child or by some other periphrasis.[18] The widespread custom of naming a father after his child has sometimes been supposed to spring from a desire on the father's part to assert his paternity, apparently as a means of obtaining those rights over his children which had previously, under a system of mother-kin, been possessed by the mother.[19] But this explanation does not account for the parallel custom of naming the mother after her child, which seems commonly to co-exist with the practice of naming the father after the child. Still less, if possible, does it apply to the customs of calling childless couples the father and mother of children which do not exist, of naming people after their younger brothers, and of designating children as the uncles and aunts of So-and-so, or as the fathers and mothers of their first cousins. But all these practices are explained in a simple and natural way if we suppose that they originate in a reluctance to utter the real names of persons addressed or directly referred to. That reluctance is probably based partly on a fear of attracting the notice of evil spirits, partly on a dread of revealing the name to sorcerers, who would thereby obtain a handle for injuring the owner of the name.

182. It might naturally be expected that the reserve so commonly maintained with regard to personal names would be dropped or at least relaxed among relations and friends. But the reverse of this is often the case. It is precisely the persons most intimately connected by blood and especially by marriage to whom the rule applies with the greatest stringency. Such people are often forbidden, not only to pronounce each other's names, but even to utter ordinary words which resemble or have a single syllable in common with these names. The persons who are thus mutually debarred from mentioning each other's names are especially husbands and wives, a man and his wife's parents, and a woman and her husband's father. For example, among the Caffres of South Africa a woman may not publicly pronounce the birth-name of her husband or of any of his brothers, nor may she use the interdicted word in its ordinary sense. If her husband, for instance, be called u-Mpaka, from *impaka,* a small feline animal, she must speak of that beast by some other name.[1] Further, a Caffre wife is forbidden to pronounce even mentally the names of her father-in-law and of all her husband's male relatives in the ascending line; and whenever the emphatic syllable of any of their names occurs in another word, she must avoid it by substituting either another term or another syllable in its place. Hence this custom has given rise to an almost distinct woman's language, which the Caffres call *Ukuteta Kwabafazi* or "female speech."[2] A Caffre man, on his side, may not mention the name of his mother-in-law, nor may she pronounce his; but he is free to utter words in which the emphatic syllable of her name occurs.[3] Among the Kondes, who live at the northwestern end of Lake Nyassa, a woman may not mention the name of her father-in-law; indeed she may not even speak to him nor see him.[4] Among the Barea and Bogos of Eastern Africa a woman never mentions her husband's name; a Bogo wife would rather be unfaithful to him than commit the monstrous sin of allowing his name to pass her lips.[5] Among the Haussas "the first-born son is never called by his parents by his name; indeed they will not even speak with him if other people are present. The same rule holds good of the first husband and the first wife."[6] In antiquity Ionian women would not call their husbands by their names.[7] While the rites of Ceres were being performed in Rome, no one might name a father or a daughter.[8] Among the South Slavs at the present day husbands and wives will not mention each other's names, and a young wife may not call any of her housemates by their true names; she must invent or at least adopt other names for them.[9] After marriage an Aino wife may not mention her husband's name; to do so would be deemed equivalent to killing him.[10] Among the Sgaus, a Karen tribe of Burma, children never mention their parents' names.[11] A Toda man may not utter the names of his mother's brother, his grandfather and grandmother, his wife's mother, and of the man from whom he has received his wife, who is usually the wife's father.[12] In southern India wives believe that to tell their husbands' names or to pronounce them even in a dream would bring them to an untimely end. Further, they may not mention the names of their parents, parents-in-law, brothers-in-law, and sisters-in-law.[13] Among the Ojibways husbands and wives never mention each other's names;[14]

among the Omahas a man and his parents-in-law will on no account utter each other's names in company.[15] In the Nishinam tribe of California "a husband never calls his wife by name on any account, and it is said that divorces have been produced by no other provocation than that."[16] In the Booandik tribe of South Australia persons connected by marriage, except husbands and wives, spoke to one another in a low whining voice and employed words different from those in common use.[17]

183. The custom of abstaining from all mention of the names of the dead was observed in antiquity by the Albanians of the Caucasus,[1] and at the present day is in full force among several primitive tribes. Thus we are told that one of the customs most rigidly observed among the Australian aborigines is never to mention the name of a deceased person.[2] The chief motive for this abstinence appears to be a fear of evoking the ghost, although the natural unwillingness to revive past sorrows undoubtedly operates also to draw the veil of oblivion over the names of the dead.[3] If a Katabara black dies, his tribesmen never mention his name, but call him *Wurponum*, "the dead," and in order to explain who it is that has died, they speak of his father, mother, brothers, and so forth.[4] Of the tribes on the Lower Murray River we are informed that when a person dies "they carefully avoid mentioning his name; but if they are compelled to do so, they pronounce it in a very low whisper, so faint that they imagine the spirit cannot hear their voice."[5] Among some tribes of north-western Australia a dead man's name is never mentioned after his burial and he is spoken of only as "that one"; otherwise they think that he would return and frighten them at night in camp.[6]

The same reluctance to utter the names of the dead appears to prevail among all the Indian tribes of America, from Hudson Bay Territory to Patagonia; while among the Abipones of Paraguay to mention the departed by name was a serious crime, which often led to bloodshed.[7] The practice is reported also of peoples so widely separated as the Samoyeds of Siberia and the Todas of southern India; the Mongols of Tartary and the Tuaregs of the Sahara; the Ainos of Japan and the Wa-Kamba and Nandi of central Africa; the Tinguianes of the Philippines and the inhabitants of the Nicobar Islands, of Borneo, Madagascar, and Tasmania.[8] In all cases, even where it is not expressly stated, the fundamental reason is probably the avoidance of the ghost.

184. The same fear of the ghost, which moves people to suppress his old name, naturally leads all persons who bear a similar name to exchange it for another, lest its utterance should attract the attention of the ghost, who cannot reasonably be expected to discriminate between all the different applications of the same name. Thus we are told that in the Adelaide and Encounter Bay tribes of South Australia the repugnance to mentioning the names of those who have died lately is carried so far, that persons who bear the same name as the deceased abandon it, and either adopt temporary

themselves they designate it by another name, because they say that, were they to call the snake too often by its real name, they would lose control over the creature, and it would come out of the water and eat them all up.[1] For this reason, too, the sacred books of the Mongols, which narrate the miraculous deeds of the divinities, are allowed to be read only in spring or summer; because at other seasons the reading of them would bring on tempests or snow.[2] Nowhere was this crude conception of the secrecy and magical virtue of the divine name more firmly held or more fully developed than in ancient Egypt, where the superstitions of a dateless past were embalmed in the hearts of the people hardly less effectually than the bodies of cats and crocodiles and the rest of the divine menagerie in their rock-cut tombs. The conception is well illustrated by a story which tells how the subtle Isis wormed his secret name from Ra, the great Egyptian god of the sun. Isis, so runs the tale, was a woman mighty in words, and she was weary of the world of men, and yearned after the world of the gods. And she meditated in her heart, saying, "Cannot I by virtue of the great name of Ra make myself a goddess and reign like him in heaven and earth?" For Ra had many names, but the great name which gave him all power over gods and men was known to none but himself. Now the god was by this time grown old; he slobbered at the mouth and his spittle fell upon the ground. So Isis gathered up the spittle and the earth with it, and kneaded thereof a serpent and laid it in the path where the great god passed every day to his double kingdom after his heart's desire. And when he came forth according to his wont, attended by all his company of gods, the sacred serpent stung him, and the god opened his mouth and cried, and his cry went up to heaven. And the company of gods cried, "What aileth thee?" and the gods shouted, "Lo and behold!" But he could not answer; his jaws rattled, his limbs shook, the poison ran through his flesh as the Nile floweth over the land. When the great god had stilled his heart, he cried to his followers, "Come to me, O my children, offspring of my body. I am a prince, the son of a prince, the divine seed of a god. My father devised my name; my father and my mother gave me my name, and it remained hidden in my body since my birth, that no magician might have magic power over me. I went out to behold that which I have made, I walked in the two lands which I have created, and lo! something stung me. What it was, I know not. Was it fire? was it water? My heart is on fire, my flesh trembleth, all my limbs do quake. Bring me the children of the gods with healing words and understanding lips, whose power reacheth to heaven." Then came to him the children of the gods, and they were very sorrowful. And Isis came with her craft, whose mouth is full of the breath of life, whose spells chase pain away, whose word maketh the dead to live. She said, "What is it, divine Father? what is it?" The holy god opened his mouth, he spake and said, "I went upon my way, I walked after my heart's desire in the two regions which I have made to behold that which I have created, and lo! a serpent that I saw not stung me. Is it fire? is it water? I am colder than water, I am hotter than fire, all my limbs sweat, I tremble, mine eye is not steadfast, I behold not the sky, the moisture bedeweth my face as in summer-time." Then spake Isis, "Tell me thy name, divine Father, for the man shall live who is called by his name." Then answered Ra, "I created the heavens and the earth, I ordered the mountains, I made the great and wide sea, I stretched out the two horizons like a curtain. I am he who openeth his eyes and it is light, and who shutteth them and it is dark. At his command the Nile riseth, but the gods know not his name. I am Khepera in the morning, I am Ra at noon, I am Tum at eve." But the poison was not taken away from him; it pierced deeper, and the great god could no longer walk. Then said Isis to him, "That was not thy name that thou spakest unto me. Oh tell it me, that the poison may depart; for he shall live whose name is named." Now the poison burned like fire, it was hotter than the flame of fire. The god said, "I consent that Isis shall search into me, and that my name shall pass from my breast into hers." Then the god hid himself from the gods, and his place in the ship of eternity was empty. Thus was the name of the great god taken from him, and Isis, the witch, spake, "Flow away poison, depart from Ra. It is I, even I, who overcome the poison and cast it to the earth; for the name of the great god hath been taken away from him. Let Ra live and let the poison die." Thus spake great Isis, the queen of the gods, she who knows Ra and his true name.[3]

In Egypt attempts like that recorded of Isis to appropriate the power of a high god by possessing herself of his name were not mere legends told of the mythical beings of a remote past; every Egyptian magician aspired to wield like powers by similar means. For it was believed that he who possessed the true name possessed the very being of god or man, and could force even a deity to obey him as a slave obeys his master. Thus the art of the magician consisted in obtaining from the gods a revelation of their sacred names, and he left no stone unturned to accomplish his end. When once a god in a moment of weakness or forgetfulness had imparted to the wizard the wondrous lore, the deity had no choice but to submit humbly to the man or pay the penalty of his contumacy.[4] In one papyrus we find the god Typhon thus adjured: "I invoke thee by thy true names, in virtue of which thou canst not refuse to hear me"; and in another the magician threatens Osiris that if the god does not do his bidding he will name him aloud in the port of Busiris.[5] So in the Lucan the Thessalian witch whom Sextus Pompeius consulted before the battle of Pharsalia threatens to call up the Furies by their real names if they will not do her bidding.[6] In modern Egypt the magician still works his old enchantments by the same ancient means; only the name of the god by which he conjures is different. The man who knows "the most great name" of God can, we are told, by the mere

utterance of it kill the living, raise the dead, transport himself instantly
wherever he pleases, and perform any other miracle.[7] Similarly among the
Arabs of North Africa at the present day "the power of the name is such
that when one knows the proper names the jinn can scarcely help answering the call and obeying; they are the servants of the magical names; in this
case the incantation has a constraining quality which is for the most part very
strongly marked. When Ibn el Hâdjdj et-Tlemsânî relates how the jinn
yielded up their secrets to him, he says, 'I once met the seven kings of the
jinn in a cave and I asked them to teach me the way in which they attack
men and women, causing them to fall sick, smiting them, paralysing them,
and the like. They all answered me: "If it were anybody but you we would
teach that to nobody, but you have discovered the bonds, the spells, and
the names which compel us; were it not for the names by which you have
constrained us, we would not have answered to your call." ' "[8] So, too, "the
Chinese of ancient times were dominated by the notion that beings are
intimately associated with their names, so that a man's knowledge of the
name of a spectre might enable him to exert power over the latter and to
bend it to his will."[9]

The belief in the magic virtue of divine names was shared by the Romans.
When they sat down before a city, the priests addressed the guardian deity
of the place in a set form of prayer or incantation, inviting him to abandon
the beleaguered city and come over to the Romans, who would treat him
as well or better than he had ever been treated in his old home. Hence the
name of the guardian deity of Rome was kept a profound secret, lest the
enemies of the republic might lure him away, even as the Romans themselves had induced many gods to desert, like rats, the falling fortunes of
cities that had sheltered them in happier days.[10] Nay, the real name, not
merely of its guardian deity, but of the city itself, was wrapt in mystery and
might never be uttered, not even in the sacred rites. A certain Valerius
Soranus, who dared to divulge the priceless secret, was put to death or
came to a bad end,[11] and down to modern times the Cheremiss of the
Caucasus keep the names of their communal villages secret from motives
of superstition.[12]

If the reader has had the patience to follow this long and perhaps tedious
examination of the superstitions attaching to personal names, he will probably agree that the mystery in which the names of royal personages are so
often shrouded is no isolated phenomenon, no arbitrary expression of
courtly servility and adulation, but merely the particular application of a
general law of primitive thought, which includes within its scope common
folk and gods as well as kings and priests.

NOTES

144 1. *Manners and Customs of the Japanese in the Nineteenth Century* (London 1841), 141 ff.
2. W. G. Aston, *Shinto* (London 1905), 41.
3. M. Revon, *Le Shintoisme*, i (Paris 1907), 190, n. 2.

145 1. A. Bastian, *Die deutsche Expedition an der Loango-Küste* (Jena 1874–75), i. 287 ff.
2. H. Klose, *Togo unter deutscher Flagge* (Berlin 1899), 189, 268.
3. J. B. Labat, *Relation historique de l'Éthiopie occidentale* (Paris 1732), i. 254 ff.
4. G. H. Bancroft, *Native Races of the Pacific States* (London 1875–76), ii. 142 f.

146 1. Bastian, *op. cit.*, i. 355.
2. O. Dapper, *Description de l'Afrique* (Amsterdam 1686), 336.
3. O. Baumann, *Eine afrikanische Tropen-Insel, Fernando Pio und die Bube* (Vienna-Olmütz 1888), 103 f.
4. G. Zündel, in *Zeitschrift d. Gesell. f. Erdkunde zu Berlin*, 12 (1877), 402.
5. Béraud, in *Bull. Soc. Géogr. de Paris, Vme sér.*, 12 (1866), 377.
6. Bastian, *op. cit.*, i. 263.
7. Bosman's "Guinea," in Pinkerton's *Voyages and Travels*, xvi. 500.
8. A. Dalzell, *History of Dahomey* (London 1793), 15.
9. J. B. L. Durand, *Voyage en Sénégal* (Paris 1802), 55.
10. W. S. Taberer, in *Journal of the African Society*, 15 (1905), 320.
11. A. Van Gennep, *Tabu et totémisme à Madagascar* (Paris 1904), 113.
12. Father Porte, in *Missions Catholiques*, 28 (1896), 235.
13. Plutarch, *De Iside et Osiride*, 32.
14. P. J. de Arriaga, *Extirpacion de la Idolatria del Piru* (Lima 1621), 11, 132.
15. W. Marsden, *History of Sumatra* (London 1811), 301.
16. John O'Donovan, ed., *The Book of Rights* (Dublin 1847), 3–8.
17. J. G. Scott, *Gazetteer of Upper Burma and the Shan States*, II, i (Rangoon 1901), 308.

147 1. Egyptian priests likewise abstained from beans: Herodotus ii. 37; Plutarch, *op. cit.*, 5.
2. Aulus Gellius, x. 15; Plutarch, *Quaest. Rom.*, 109–12 [with H. J. Rose's notes]; Pliny, *NH*, xxviii. 146; Macrobius, *Sat.*, i. 16, 8 f.
3. W. H. R. Rivers, *The Todas* (London 1906), 98–103.

149 1. F. Boas, in *Sixth Ann. Report on the North-Western Tribes of Canada* (1890), 44.
2. Id., *Ninth Ann. Report* (1892), 461.
3. W. W. Skeat, *Malay Magic* (London 1900), 47.
4. W. W. Gill, *Myths and Songs of the South Pacific* (London 1876), 171.
5. H. Sundermann, in *Allgemeine Missions-Zeitschrift*, 11 (1884), 455.
6. Private communication from L. Fison (12/3/98).
7. H. A. Rose in *Indian Antiquary*, 31 (1902), 298.
7a. S. Walleser, in *Anthropos*, 8 (1913), 610 f.

150 1. B. F. Matthes. *Over de Bissues of heidensche priesters en priesteressen der Boeginezen* (Amsterdam 1872), 24.
2. H. Ling Roth, in *JAI*, 21 (1892), 115.
3. R. Southey, *History of Bengal* (London 1817–19), iii. 396.
4. *Punjab Notes and Queries*, ii. 114, ¶665.
5. M. Radiguet, *Les derniers sauvages* (Paris 1882), 245; C. Clavel, *Les Marquisiens* (Paris 1885), 42, n.
6. Guaguiére, in *Ann. de la Propagation de la Foi*, 32 (1860), 439.
7. T. J. Hutchinson, *Trans. Ethnol. Soc. of London*, N. S. 3 (1863), 322 f.
8. E. Modigliani, *Un Viaggio a Nias* (Milan 1890), 283.
9. A. W. Howitt, *The Native Tribes of S. E. Australia* (London 1904), 473.
10. F. Boas, *Sixth Ann. Report of the Am. Bureau of Ethnology* (1888), 613 ff.; J. Murdoch, *Ninth Ann. Report* (1892), 425.
11. G. F. Lyon, *Private Journal* (London 1824), 370.
12. B. F. Matthes, *Bijdragen tot de Ethnologie van Zuid-Celebes* (The Hague 1875), 54.
13. J. L. van der Toorn, in *BTLVNI*, 39 (1890), 56.
14. Cp. Herodas, iii. 3 f [with Headlam-Knox's note *in loc.*].

151 1. K. von den Steinen, *Unter den Naturvölken Zentral-Brasiliens* (Berlin 1894), 511 f.
2. F. Boas, in *Seventh Ann. Report on the North-Western Tribes of Canada* (1891), 14.
3. R. H. Codrington, *The Melanesians* (Oxford 1891), 207 ff.
4. Pliny, *NH*, vii. 174; Herodotus, iv. 14 f.; Maximus Tyrius, Diss., xvi. 2.
5. G. A. Wilken, in *De Indische Gias*, 1884, p. 944.
6. J. van der Toorn, *op. cit.*, 56 ff.

152 1. E. F. im Thurm, *Among the Indians of Guiana* (London 1883), 344 ff.
2. V. Frič, in *Globus*, 89 (1908), 233.

3. Shway Yoe, *The Burman, his Life and Notions* (London 1882), ii. 100.
4. A. B. Ellis, *The Ewe-speaking Peoples of the Slave Coast of West Africa* (London 1890), 20.
5. J. G. F. Riedel, *De sluik- en kroesharige rassen tusschen Selebes en Papua* (The Hague 1886), 267.
6. H. Ling Roth, in *JAI*, 21 (1892), 112.
7. Yoe, *op. cit.*, ii. 103; R. G. Woodthorpe, in *JAI*, 26 (1897), 23; Riedel, *op. cit.*, 440; A. C. Hollis, *The Masai* (Oxford 1905), 308. The rule is mentioned, and a mystic reason given for it, in the Indic Satapatha Brahmana, v, 371 in Eggeling's translation.
8. Private communication from L. Fison (8/3/98).
9. K. von den Steinen. *op. cit.*, 340.
10. Van der Toorn, *op. cit.*, 50.
11. W. W. Rockhill, in *The American Anthropologist*, 4 (1891), 183.
12. W. R. S. Ralston, *Songs of the Russian People*[2] (London 1872), 117 f.
13. A. Henry, in *JAI*, 33 (1903), 102.
14. C. Hose and W. McDougall, in *JAI*, 31 (1901), 183 ff.
15. De los Reyes y Florentino, in *Mitt. d. kon. k. geogr. Gesell. in Wien*, 31 (1888), 569 f.
16. H. Ward, *Five Years with the Congo Cannibals* (London 1890), 53 f.
17. M. Joustra, in *Med. Zendel.*, 46 (1902), 408.
18. A. C. Kruijt, *ib.*, 44 (1900), 225.
19. Pliny, *NH*, vii. 174; Plutarch, *De genio Socratis*, 22; Lucian, *Muscae encomium*, 7. Cp. E. Rohde, *Psyche*[3] (Tübingen-Leipzig 1903), ii. 91 f.
20. E. B. Cross, in *JAOS*, 4 (1854), 311.
21. R. G. Woodthorpe, in *JAI*, 26 (1897), 23.
22. Guerlach, in *Missions Catholiques*, 19 (1887), 525 ff.
23. Riedel, *op. cit.*, 414.

153 1. A. Landes, in *Cochinchine française*, No. 23 (Saigon 1885), 80.
2. M. J. van Baarda, in *BTLVNI*, 45 (1895), 509.
3. M. T. H. Perelaer, *Ethnographische Beschrijving der Dajak* (Zalt-Bommel 1870), 26.
4. A. C. Kruijt, in *Med. Zendel.*, 39 (1895), 5–8.
5. J. G. Gmelin, *Reise durch Sibirien* (Göttingen 1751–52), ii. 359 f.
6. V. Priklonski, in *Globus*, 59 (1891), 81 ff.

154 1. P. N. Wilken, in *Med. Zendel.*, 7 (1863), 146 f. It is not clear why the priest, after restoring the soul, tells it to go away again.

155 1. R. H. Codrington, *op. cit.*, 267.
2. *Ib.*, 229.
3. Riedel, *op. cit.*, 77 f.

156 1. T. Williams, *Fiji and the Fijians*[2] (London, 1860), i. 250.
2. L. J. B. Bérenger-Féraud, *Les peuples de la Sénégambie* (Paris 1879), 277.
3. Mary Kingsley, *Travels in W. Africa* (London 1897), 461 ff.
4. E. B. Cross, in *JAOS*, 4 (1854), 307.
5. W. W. Skeat, *op. cit.*, 566 f.

157 1. Riedel, *op. cit.*, 440.
2. *Ib.*, 340.
3. N. Adriani and A. C. Kruijt, in *Med. Zendel.*, 42 (1898), 511.
4. Kruijt, *ib.*, 44 (1900), 226.
5. *Ann. de la Prop. de la Foi*, 4 (1830), 481.
6. Private communication from J. Roscoe (5/26/1904).
7. R. E. Dennett, *At the Back of the Black Man's Mind* (London 1906), 79.
8. D. Kidd, *The Essential Kafir* (London 1904), 84.
9. id., *Savage Childhood* (London 1906), 68.
10. E. Modigliani, *Un Viaggio a Nias* (Milan 1890), 620, 624.
11. F. Boas, *Ninth Ann. Report on the North-Western Tribes of Canada* (1894), 461 f.
12. J. J. M. de Groot, *The Religious System of China*, i (Leyden 1892), 94, 210 f.
13. F. Boas, in *Sixth Ann. Report* (1890), 92, 94.
14. A. W. Howitt, in *JAI*, 14 (1885), 316.
15. Id., *The Native Tribes of S. E. Australia* (London 1904), 266.
16. Private communication from J. Roscoe (5/26/1904).
17. D. Kidd, *The Essential Kafir*, 83, 303; id., *Savage Childhood*, 69.
18. Pausanias, viii. 38, 6; Polybius, xvi. 12, 7; Plutarch, *Quaest. Graec.*, 39.
19. B. Schmidt, *Das Volksleben der Neugriechen* (Leipzig 1871), 196 ff.
20. Georgeakis and Pineau, *Folk-lore de Lesbos* (Paris 1894), 346 f.
21. E. Gerard, *The Land Beyond the Forest* (Edinburgh-London 1888), ii. 17 f.

158 1. J. Chalmers, *Pioneering in New Guinea* (London 1887), 170.
2. B. de Sahagun, *Histoire générale des choses de la Nouvelle Espagne* (Paris 1880), 315.
3. T. L. Fairclough, in *Journal of the African Society*, No. 14 (1905), 201.
4. R. H. Codrington, *op. cit.*, 186.
5. *Laws of Manu*, iv. 38; Artemidorus, *Oneirocrit.*, ii. 7.
6. *Folk-lore Journal*, 6 (1888), 145 ff.; *Punjab Notes and Queries*, ii. 61.
7. J. G. Frazer, in *JAI*, 15 (1886), 82 ff.

159 1. J. O. Dorsey, in *The Amer. Anthropologist*, 2 (1889), 143.
2. Maximilian zu Weid, *Reise in das innere Nord-America* (Coblenz 1839–41), i. 417.
3. *Ib.*, ii. 166.

4. *The Times* (London), 24 March, 1891.

5. E. Young, *The Kingdom of the Yellow Robe* (Westminster 1898), 140.

6. *Blackwood's Magazine*, Feb. 1886, p. 235.

7. J. A. E. Kohler, *Volksbrauch, Aberglauben, Sagen u. andere alte Ueber-lieferungen im Voigtlande* (Leipzig 1867), 423.

8. Ralston, *op. cit.*, 117.

9. J. Napier, *Folk-Lore, or Superstitious Beliefs in the West of Scotland* (Paisley 1879), 142. Further examples of this superstition are cited by R. Andree, *Ethnographische Parallelen und Vergleiche*, II (Leipzig 1889), 18 f.

160 1. P. Bouche, *La Côte des Esclaves et de Dahomey* (Paris 1885), 133.

2. A. van Gennep, *Tabou et totémisme à Madagascar* (Paris 1904), 42.

3. A. W. Nieuwenhuis, *Quer durch Borneo* (Leyden 1904–07), ii. 102.

4. E. Aymonier, *Notes sur les Laos* (Saigon 1885), 196.

5. R. Parkinson, in *Internat. Archiv f. Ethnogr.*, 10 (1897), 112.

6. J. A. Grant, *A Walk across Africa* (Edinburgh-London 1864), 104 f.

7. E. Shortland, *Traditions and Superstitions of the New Zealanders*[2] (London 1856), 103.

8. Fr. Stuhlmann, *Mit Emin Pascha ins Herz von Afrika* (Berlin 1894), 94.

9. R. B. Smyth, *Aborigines of Victoria* (Melbourne-London 1878), i. 134.

10. Scholiast on Euripides, *Phoenissae*, 1377.

11. Conon, *Narrationes*, 18; Pausanias, iii. 19, 12; D. Kidd, *The Essential Kafir*, 307.

12. J. Campbell, *Travels in South Africa* (London 1822), ii. 205.

13. L. Magyar, *Reisen in Süd-Afrika* (Budapest-Leipzig 1859), 203.

14. Nieuwenhuis, *op. cit.*, i. 165.

15. De Plano Carpini, *Historia Mongolorum*, ed. D'Avezac (Paris 1838), Chap. iii, ¶3, p. 627; cap. ult., ¶1, x, p. 744; Appendix, p. 775.

16. Collard, in *Bull. soc. géogr. de Paris, VIme sér.*, 20 (1880), 393.

17. Bastian, *op. cit.*, i. 268 f.

161 1. J. B. Neumann, in *Tijdschr. van het Nederl. Aardrijskundig Genootschap.* II ser., dl. iii (1886), 300.

2. W. C. Harris, *The Highlands of Aethiopia* (London 1844), iii. 171 f.

3. Th. Lefebvre, *Voyage en Abyssinie* (Paris 1895), i, p. lxxii.

4. Ebn-el-Dyn el-Eghouâthy, in *Bull. soc. géogr. de Paris, IIIme sér.*, i (1834), 200.

5. T. Williams, *Fiji and the Fijians*[2], i. 249.

6. A. Bastian, *Loango-Küste*, i. 262 ff.

7. Proyart's "History of Loango, etc." in *Pinkerton's Voyages and Travels*, xvi. 584.

8. Harris, *op. cit.*, iii. 78.

9. Heraclides Commanus, quoted by Athenaeus, iv. 26.

162 1. *Notes analytiques sur les collections ethnographiques du Musée du Congo*, I. Les arts, religion (Brussels 1900–06), 164.

2. Mohammed Ibn-Omar el-Tounsy, *Voyage au Daufour* (Paris 1845), 203.

3. Ibn Batutah, *Voyages*, ed. C. Defrémery and B. R. Sanguinetti (Paris 1853–58), iv. 441.

4. Mattei, *Bas-Niger, Bênoné, Dahomey* (Paris 1895), 90 f.

5. A. B. Ellis, *The Toruba-speaking Peoples of the Slave Coast* (London 1894), 170.

6. A. W. Howitt, in *JAI*, 13 (1884), 456.

163 1. H. Ling Roth, *Great Benin* (Halifax, England 1903), 74.

2. S. Crowther and J. C. Taylor, *The Gospel on the Banks of the Niger* (London 1859), 433.

3. *Ib.*, 379; Matthei, *op. cit.*, 67–72.

4. *Bull. soc. géogr. de Paris, VIIIme sér.*, 20 (1899), 223.

5. Strabo, xvii. 2, 2.

6. Xenophon, *Anabasis*, v. 4, 26; Scymus Chius in *Geogr. Graec. Minores*, ed. Müller, i. 234; Diodorus Siculus, xiv. 30, 6 f.; Apollonius Rhodius, *Argon.*, ii. 1026 (with Scholiast *in loc.*); Pomponius Mela, i. 106, p. 29 Parthey; Nicolaus Damascenus, quoted by Stobaeus, xliv. 41.

164 1. Kaempfer's "History of Japan," in *Pinkerton's Voyages and Travels*, vii. 717.

2. *Missions Catholiques*, 14 (1882), 460; 15 (1883), 450.

3. F. T. Valden, *Six Years of a Traveller's Life in Western Africa* (London 1861), ii. 251 f.

4. W. Brown, *New Zealand and its Aborigines* (London 1845), 76, 177 ff.

5. E. Tregear, in *JAI*, 19 (1890), 100.

6. R. Taylor, *Te Ika a Mau, or New Zealand and Its Inhabitants*[2] (London 1870), 164.

165 1. W. Ellis, *Polynesian Researches*[2] (London 1830–56), iv. 388.

2. *Old New Zealand, by a Pakeha Maori* (London 1884), 104–14. Cp. also: G. F. Angus, *Savage Life and Scenes in Australia and New Zealand* (London 1847), ii. 90; E. Dieffenbach, *Travels in New Zealand* (London 1843), ii. 104 f.

3. G. Turner, *Samoa, a Hundred Years ago and Long before* (London 1884), 145.

4. *Annales de la Propagation de la Foi*, 13 (1841), 19; cf. also J. Cook, *Voyages* (London 1809), vii. 147.

5. C. Wilkes, *Narrative of the U. S. Exploring Expedition*, New ed. (New York 1851), iii. 99 f.

6. W. G. Lawes, in *JAI*, 8 (1879), 370.

7. H. A. Junod, in *Rev. d'ethnogr. et de sociologie*, 1 (1910), 153.

7a. P. Giran, *Magie et religion Annamites* (Paris 1912), 405.

166   1. W. E. Armit, in *JAI*, 9 (1880), 459.
2. W. Ridley, *ib*, 2 (1873), 268.
3. Private communication from J. Roscoe and Miller (6/24/1897), subsequently corrected by the Prime Minister of Uganda and in conversation with Roscoe (6/20/1902).
4. *Report of the Internat. Polar Expedition to Point Barrow, Alaska* (Washington 1885), 46.
5. A. Mackenzie, *Voyages from Montreal through the Continent of North America* (London 1861), p. cxxiii.
6. H. Pittier de Fabrega, in *Sitzb. d. kaiserl. Akad. d. Wiss. zu Wien*, 138 (1898), phil.-hist. K1., 20.
7. J. Wilson, *Missionary Voyage to the S. Pacific Ocean* (London 1799), 354.
8. Turner, *op. cit.*, 276.
9. C. G. Seligman, in *JAI*, 32 (1902), 302. For the seclusion of brides in Uganda, see J. Roscoe, *ib.*, 37.
10. V. Lisiansky, *A Voyage Round the World* (London 1814), 201.
11. H. A. Junod, in *Revue d'ethnogr. et de sociologie*, 1 (1910), 153.
11a. E. Shortland, *Maori Religion and Mythology* (London 1882), 40.
12. B. Hawkins, in *Collections of the Georgia Historical Society*, iii, i (Savannah 1848), 78 ff. In the Turbal tribe of southern Queensland, boys who were undergoing the rite of initiation were not allowed to scratch themselves with their fingers, but they might do so with a stick: A. W. Howitt, *The Native Tribes of S. E. Australia* (London 1904), 596.
13. L. Alberti, *De Kaffirs* (Amsterdam 1810), 76 ff.; D. Kidd, *The Essential Kafir* (London 1904), 208.

167   1. *Old New Zealand, by a Pakeha Maori* (London 1884), 96, 114 f.
2. Deuteronomy, 23 : 9–14; I Sam., 21 : 5. For a similar custom among the Melanesians, see Codrington, *The Melanesians*, 203 n.; J. Macdonald, in *JAI*, 20 (1891), 131. So too among the Miranha Indians of Brazil: J. B. Spix and C. F. Martins, *Reise in Brasilien* (Munich 1823–31), iii. 1251, n. On the subject in general, see F. Schwally, *Semitische Kriegsaltertümer* (Leipzig 1901), 67 f.
3. *Narrative of the Captivity and Adventures of John Turner* (London 1830), 122.
4. J. G. Bourke, *On the Border with Crook* (New York 1891), 133.
5. J. G. Kohl, *Kitschi-Gami* (Bremen 1859), ii. 168.
6. J. Adair, *History of the American Indians* (London 1775), 163.
7. Major M. Marston, in Jedidiah Morses's *Report to the Secretary of War of the United States on Indian Affairs* (New Haven 1822), Appendix, p. 130.
8. H. A. Junod, *op. cit.*, 149.
8a. G. Landtmann, in *JAI*, 46 (1916), 323.
8b. G. Brown, *Melanesians and Polynesians* (London 1910), 154.

4. J. Adair, *History of the American Indians* (London 1775), 134, 117. The reference is to the Creeks, Cherokees and other S. E. tribes.

5. Schlömann, in *Verh. d. Berlin. Ges. f. Anthropol., Ethnologie und Urgeschichte*, 1894, p. 67.

6. Lev. 17 : 10–14; cp. Deut. 12 : 23–25.

7. Servius on Vergil, *Aen.*, v. 79; cp. id., on *Aen.*, iii. 67.

8. J. Wellhausen, *Reste arabischen Heidentums* (Berlin 1887), 217.

9. J. J. M. de Groot, *Religious System of China* (Leyden 1892), iv. 80–82.

10. A. Goudswaard, *De Papoewa's van de Geelvinksbaai* (Schiedam 1863), 77.

11. H. Yule, trans. *The Book of Marco Polo* (London 1875), i. 335.

12. A. Fynche, *Burma, Past and Present* (London 1878), i. 217 n.

13. J. Roscoe, in *JAI*, 22 (1902), 50.

14. Sir Walter Scott, note 2 to *Peveril of the Peak*, Chap. 2.

15. C. Latham, in *Folk-Lore Record*, 1 (1878), 17.

16. *Native Tribes of S. Australia* (Adelaide 1879), 230; E. J. Eyre, *Journals of Expeditions of Discovery into Central Australia* (London 1845), ii. 335; R. B. Smyth, *Aborigines of Victoria* (Melbourne-London 1878), i. 75, n.

17. D. Collins, *Account of the English Colony of New South Wales* (London 1798), 580.

18. *Native Tribes of S. Australia*, 224 ff.; G. F. Angus, *Savage Life and Scenes in Australia and New Zealand* (London 1847), i. 110 f.

19. Fr. Stuhlmann, *op. cit.*, 795.

20. Mary Kingsley, *Travels in W. Africa*, 440, 447.

21. R. Taylor, *op. cit.*, 194 f.

174 1. A. B. Ellis, *The Yoruba-speaking Peoples of the Slave Coast* (London 1894), 125 ff.

2. A. Bastian, *Die Völker des östlichen Asiens* (Leipzig-Jena 1866–71), ii. 256, iii. 71, 230, 235 f.

3. Herodotus, ix. 110.

4. Plutarch, *Quaest. Rom.*, 100.

5. Matthias G***, *Lettres sur les Isles Marquises* (Paris 1843), 50.

6. Langsdorff, *op. cit.*, i. 115 f.

7. M. Radiguet, *Les derniers sauvages* (Paris 1882), 156.

7a. R. Verneau and Pennatier, in *L'Anthropologie*, 36 (1921), 317.

7b. C. W. Hobley, *Ethnology of the A-kamba* (Cambridge 1910), 73.

175 1. Agathias, *Hist.* i. 3; J. Grimm, *Deutsche Rechtsalterthümer*[3] (Göttingen 1881), 239 ff.

2. J. Spieth, *Die Ewe-Stämme* (Berlin 1906), 229.

3. F. Boas, in *Tenth Ann. Report on the North-Western Tribes of Canada* (1895), 45.

4. Diodorus Siculus, i. 18.

5. W. Robertson Smith, *Kinship and Marriage in Early Arabia* (Cambridge 1885), 152 ff.

6. *Iliad,* xxiii. 141 ff.

7. W. Ellis, *Polynesian Researches*[3] (London 1832–36), iv. 387.

8. Numbers 6 : 5.

9. J. Roscoe, in *JAI,* 32 (1902), 30.

10. O. Knoop, *Volkssagen, Erzählungen, Aberglauben, Gebräuche und Märchen aus dem östlichen Hinterpommern* (Posen 1885), 157, ¶23.

11. Wolf, *op. cit.,* i. 209, ¶57.

12. E. Shortland, *Traditions and Superstitions of the New Zealanders*[2] (London 1856), 108 ff.

13. G. F. Angus, *Savage Life and Scenes in Australia and New Zealand* (London 1847), ii. 90 f.

14. Kaempfer, "History of Japan," in Pinkerton's *Voyages and Travels,* vii. 716 f. (It should be observed, however, that this account has been questioned by M. Revon, *Le Shintoïsme* [Paris 1907], i. 191, n. 3.)

176   1. J. A. Köhler, *Volksbrauch, Aberlauben, Sagen u. andere alte Ueberlieferungen im Voigtlande* (Leipzig 1867), 424; F. Panzer, *Beitrag zur deutschen Mythologie* (Munich 1848–55), i. 258, ¶23; J. W. Wolf, *Beiträge zur deutschen Mythologie* (Göttingen-Leipzig 1852–57), i. 208, ¶45, 209, ¶53; E. Krause, in *Zeitschrift für Ethnologie,* 15 (1883), 84; W. Henderson, *Folk-lore of the Northern Counties* (London 1879), 16 ff. (See also *Notes and Queries,* I, vi (1852), 71; II, xii (1861), 500; IV, vi (1870), 130, 204, 376.)

2. *Punjab Notes and Queries,* 2. 205, ¶1092.

3. G. Gibbs, in *Annual Report of the Smithsonian Institute, 1866,* p. 305; W. Dall, *Alaska and its Resources* (London 1870), 202.

177   1. R. F. Kaindl, in *Globus,* 69 (1896), 94.

2. [*Handwörterbuch d. deutsch. Aberglaube,* s.v. *Haar.*]

3. I. V. Zingerle, *Sitten, Bräuche und Meinungen des Tiroler Volkes*[3] (Innsbruck 1871), ¶¶176, 179.

4. A. Krause, *Die Tlinkit-Indianer* (Jena 1885), 300.

5. Petronius, *Satyricon,* 104.

6. A. Bastian, *Loango-Küste,* i. 231 f.

7. F. Pyrard, *Voyage to the East Indies, the Maldives, the Moluccas, and Brazil,* tr. A. Gray (Hakluyt Society 1887), i. 110 f.

8. Pliny, *NH,* xvi. 235; Festus. s. v. *capillatum vel capillarem arborem.*

9. M. Quedenfelt, in *Verh. d. Berlin. Ges. f. Anthropol.,* 1886, p. 680.

10. A. Wuttke, *Der deutsche Volksaberglaube*[2] (Berlin 1869), 294 ff., ¶464.

11. J. G. F. Riedel, *De sluik- en kroesharige rassen tusschen Selebes en Papua* (The Hague 1886), 265.

12. W. Dall, *Alaska and its Resources* (London 1870), 54.

13. M. Abeghian, *Der armenische Volksglaube* (Leipzig 1899), 68.

14. G. F. Abbott, *Macedonian Folklore* (Cambridge 1903), 214.

15. Quendenfelt, *loc. cit.*

16. Private communication from Miss A. H. Singleton (2/24/1904).

178 1. W. Ellis, *Polynesian Researches*[2], i. 365.

2. A. B. Ellis, *The Ewe-speaking Peoples of the Slave Coast of West Africa* (London 1890), 99.

3. C. de Mensignac, *Recherches ethnogr. sur la salive et le crachet* (Bordeaux 1892), 48.

4. *Mission evangelica al reyno de Congo* (Madrid 1649), 70 *verso*.

5. R. Andree, *Ethnographische Parallelen und Vergleiche*, II (Leipzig 1889), 13.

6. R. Southey, *History of Brazil*, i[2] (London 1822), 127, 138.

6a. J. J. Jarves, *History of the Hawaiian or Sandwich Islands* (Boston 1843), 197.

179 1. See above, ¶147.

2. Porphyry, *De abstinentia*, iii. 18.

3. A. Bastian, *op. cit.*, ii. 170.

4. O. Dapper, *Description de l'Afrique* (Amsterdam 1686), 336.

5. T. J. Hutchinson, *Impressions of W. Africa* (London 1858), 198.

6. M. Merker, *Die Masai* (Berlin 1904), 21.

7. G. Watt, in *JAI*, 16 (1887), 360 (quoting Col. W. J. M'Culloch).

8. A. Senfft, in Petermann's *Mitteilungen*, 49 (1903), 54.

180 1. Aulus Gellius, x. 15. 6, 9.

2. E. Doutté, *Magie et Religion dans l'Afrique du Nord* (Algiers 1908), 87 f.

3. J. Hillner, *Volksthümlicher Brauch und Glaube bei Geburt und Taufe im Siebenbürger Sachsenlande* (program of the high school at Schässburg, Transylvania, 1876–77), 15.

4. C. Lemmius, *De Lapponibus Finmarchiae, etc.* (Copenhagen 1767), 495.

5. W. Caland, *Altindisches Zauberritual* (Amsterdam 1900), 108.

6. Servius on Vergil, *Aen.*, iii. 518.

7. J. G. F. Riedel, in *Internat. Archiv für Ethnographie*, 8 (1895), 95 f.

8. B. Spencer and F. J. Gillen, *The Northern Tribes of Central Australia* (London 1904), 606 ff.

9. Pliny, *NH*, xxviii. 59; cp. E. Rohde, *Psyche*[3] (Tübingen-Leipzig 1903), ii. 76, n. 1.

10. Ovid, *Met.*, ix. 285 f.

11. A. Strausz, *Die Bulgaren* (Leipzig 1898), 293.

12. Wuttke, *op. cit.*, 355, ¶574.

13. J. G. Campbell, *Superstitions of the Highlands and Islands of Scotland* (Glasgow 1900), 37, n. 1.

14. Festus, p. 56 Müller.

15. G. F. D'Penha, in *Indian Antiquary*, 28 (1899), 115.

16. H. Ris, in *BTLVNI*, 46 (1896), 503.

17. J. H. Meerwaldt, in *Med. Zendel.*, 49 (1905), 110.
18. Eijūb Abēla, in *Zeitschrift d. deutsch. Palästina-Vereins*, 7 (1884), 91 ff.
19. Doutté, *op. cit.*, 288–92.
20. M. Jastrow, *Religion of Babylonia and Assyria* (Boston 1898), 268, 270.
21. J. G. Dalyell, *Darker Superstitions of Scotland* (Edinburgh 1834), 307.
22. Al Baidāwi on Koran 113 : 4.
23. *NH*, xxviii. 48.
24. R. C. Thompson, *Semitic Magic* (London 1908), 164 ff.
25. *Ib.*, 168.
26. R. Chambers, *Popular Rhymes of Scotland*, New Edition (London, n. d.), 349. (This is a Christianized version of a very ancient spell for curing a lame horse. It was based on an incident in the myth of the old Norse god Balder; see J. Grimm, *Teutonic Mythology*, tr. F. Stallybrass [London 1880], 224, 1232.
27. W. Crooke, *Popular Religion and Folklore of Northern India* (Westminster 1896), i. 279.
28. Vergil, *Ecl.*, viii. 78–80.
29. J. Wellhausen, *Reste arabischen Heidentums²* (Berlin 1897), 163.
30. D. Kidd, *The Essential Kafir* (London 1904), 263.
31. *Blackwood's Magazine*, Feb. 1886, p. 238.
32. Dittenberger, *Sylloge²*, No. 939.
33. Ovid, *Fasti*, iv. 657 f. [with Frazer's note].
34. Zingerle, *op. cit.*, 3.
35. J. Scheffer, *Lapponia* (Frankfort 1673), 313.
36. R. F. Kaindl, *Die Huzulen* (Vienna 1894), 89.
37. Crooke, *op. cit.*, ii. 13, 16.
38. M. Merker, *op. cit.*, 143.
39. *Ib.*, 200 ff. 250.
40. Arrian, *Anabasis*, ii. 3; Quintus Curtius, iii. 1; Justin, xi. 7; Scholiast on Euripides, *Hippolytus*, 671.
41. Public talismans, on which the safety of the state was supposed to depend, were common in antiquity; see C. A. Lobeck, *Aglaophamus* (Königsberg 1829), 278 ff., and J. G. Frazer on Pausanias, viii. 47, 5.

181 1. A. W. Howitt, *The Native Tribes of S. E. Australia* (London 1904), 736.
2. B. Spencer and F. J. Gillen, *The Native Tribes of Central Australia* (London 1899), 139; id., *The Northern Tribes of Central Australia* (London 1904), 584 f.
3. E. Lefébvre, in *Mélusine*, 8 (1897), coll. 226 f.
4. Griyha Sutras, tr. Oldenberg (*SBE*, xxix-xxx), i 50, 183, 395; ii, 55, 215, 281; W. Caland, *Altindisches Zauberritual* (Amsterdam 1900), 162, n. 20.

5. T. C. Hodson, in *JAI*, 36 (1906), 97.
6. H. Schoolcraft, *Indian Tribes of the United States* (Philadelphia 1853–56), iv. 217.
7. J. G. Bourke, in *Folk-Lore*, 2 (1891), 423.
8. A. S. Gatschet, *The Karankawa Indians: Archaeological and Ethnological Papers of the Peabody Museum, Harvard University*, I, ii. 69.
9. G. B. Grinnell, *Blackfoot Lodge Tales* (London 1893), 194.
10. *Relations des Jésuites*, 1633, p. 3.
11. P. Jones, *History of the Ojebway Indians* (London, n. d.), 162; A. P. Reid, in *JAI*, 3 (1874), 107.
12. A. C. Hollis, *The Nandi* (Oxford 1909), 43.
13. J. H. Weeks, in *JAI*, 39 (1909), 128, 459.
14. E. M. Curr, *The Australian Race* (Melbourne-London 1886–87), iii. 545.
15. Th. J. F. van Hasselt, in *Tijdschrift v. Ind. Taal- Land en Volkendunde*, 45 (1902), 278.
16. A. C. Kruijt, in *Med. Zendel.*, 45 (1896), 273 f.
17. L. A. Waddell, in *Journal Asiatic Soc. of Bengal*, 59 (1901), iii. 52, 69.
18. W. Crooke, *Popular Religion and Folk-Lore of N. India* (Westminster 1896), ii. 5 f.
19. G. A. Wilken, *Handleiding voor de vergelijkende Volkenkunde van Nederlandsch-Indië* (Leyden 1893), 216–19; E. B. Tylor, in *JAI*, 18 (1889), 248–50. Wilken's view is rejected by A. C. Kruijt, who explains the custom by the fear of attracting evil spirits to the person named. For yet another interpretation, see E. Crawley, *The Mystic Rose*[2] (London 1927), 164 f.

182
1. J. Shooter, *The Kafirs of Natal* (London 1857), 221.
2. Col. Maclean, *Compendium of Kafir Laws and Customs* (Cape Town 1860), 92 f.; D. Leslie, *Among the Zulus and Amatongas*[2] (Edinburgh 1875), 141 f., 172; D. Kidd, *The Essential Kafir* (London 1904), 236–43.
3. Maclean, *op. cit.*, 93; Leslie, *op. cit.*, 141, 172–80; A. Werner, in *Journal of the African Society*, No. 15 (April 1905), 346–56.
4. A. Merensky, in *Verh. Berlin. Ges. f. Anthropologie*, 1893, p. 296.
5. W. Munzinger, *Ostafrikanische Studien* (Schaffhausen 1864), 526.
6. G. A. Krause, in *Globus*, 69 (1896), 375.
7. Herodotus, i. 146.
8. Servius on Vergil, *Aen.*, iv. 58.
9. K. Rhamm, in *Globus*, 82 (1902), 192.
10. J. Batchelor, *The Ainu and their Folklore* (London 1901), 226, 249 f., 252.
11. Bringaud, in *Missions Catholiques*, 20 (1888), 308.
12. W. H. R. Rivers, *The Todas* (London 1906), 626.
13. E. Thurston, *Ethnographic Notes in S. India* (Madras 1906), 533.
14. P. Jones, *op. cit.*, 162.

15. E. James, *Expedition from Pittsburgh to the Rocky Mountains* (London 1823), i. 232.
16. S. Powers, *Tribes of California* (Washington 1877), 315.
17. Mrs. James Smith, *The Booandik Tribe* (Adelaide 1880), 5.

183 1. Strabo, xi. 4, 8.
2. G. Grey, *Journals of Two Expeditions of Discovery in N. W. and W. Australia* (London 1841), ii. 232, 257; D. Collins, *Account of the English Colony in New South Wales* (London 1804), 390; S. Gason, in *Native Tribes of S. Australia* (Adelaide 1879), 275; J. D. Lang, *Queensland* (London 1861), 367, 387 f.; C. Lumholtz, *Among Cannibals* (London 1889), 279.
3. On this latter motive, see A. W. Howitt, *Kamilaroi and Kurnai* (Melbourne 1880), 249; F. Bonney, in *JAI*, 13 (1884), 127.
4. A. W. Howitt, *The Native Tribes of S. E. Australia* (London 1904), 469.
5. G. F. Angas, *Savage Life and Scenes in Australia and New Zealand* (London 1847), i. 94.
6. E. Clement, in *Internat. Archiv f. Ethnographie*, 16 (1904), 9.
7. M. Dobrizhoffer, *Historia de Abiponibus* (Vienna 1784), ii. 301, 498.
8. P. S. Pallas, *Reise durch verschiedene Provinzen des russischen Reichs* (St. Petersburg 1771–76), ii. 76; W. E. Marshall, *Travels among the Todas* (London 1873), 177; De Plano Carpini, *Relation des Mongoles ou Tartares*, ed. D'Avezac (Paris 1838), c. iii, ¶3; H. Duveyrier, *Exploration du Sahara: les Touareg du nord* (Paris 1864), 415; J. Batchelor, *op. cit.*, 252, 564; J. M. Hillebrandt, in *Zeitschr. f. Ethnologie*, 10 (1878), 405 (Akamba); A. C. Hollis, *The Nandi* (Oxford 1909), 71; F. Blumentritt, *Versuch einer Ethnographie der Philippinen* (Gotha 1882), 38; N. Fontana, in *Asiatick Researches*, 3 (1799), 155 (Nicobar Islands); W. H. Furness, *Folk-Lore in Borneo* (Wallingford, Pennsylvania, 1899), 26; A. van Gennep, *Tabou et totémisme à Madagascar* (Paris 1904), 70 f.; J. Bonwick, *Daily Life of the Tasmanians* (London 1870), 97, 145, 183.

184 1. W. Wyatt, in *Native Tribes of S. Australia* (Adelaide 1879), 165.
2. D. Collins, *op. cit.*, 392.
3. P. Beveridge, in *Trans. Royal Soc. of Victoria*, vi. 20 f.
4. *Journal of the Royal Geographical Society*, 1 (1832), 46 f.

185 1. E. J. Eyre, *Journal of Expeditions of Discovery into Central Australia* (London 1845), ii. 354 f.
2. J. Macgillivray, *Narrative of the Voyage of H.M.S. Rattlesnake* (London 1852), ii. 10 f.
3. H. E. A. Meyer, in *Native Tribes of S. Australia*, 199.
4. M. Dobrizhoffer, *Historia de Abiponibus* (Vienna 1784), ii. 199, 301.

186 1. E. J. Jessen, *De Finnorum Lapponumque Norwegicorum religione pagana* (Copenhagen 1767), 33 f.
2. E. W. Nelson, in *Eighteenth Ann. Report, Am. Bureau of Ethnology*, i (1899), 363 f., 379, 424 f.

187 1. A. Cecchi, *De Zeila alle frontiere del Caffa*, ii (Rome 1885), 551.
2. J. Roscoe, in *JAI*, 37 (1907), 96.
3. De la Loubère, *Du royaume de Siam* (Amsterdam 1691), i. 306; Pallegoix, *Royaume Thai ou Siam* (Paris 1854), i. 260.
4. J. S. Polack, *Manners and Customs of the New Zealanders* (London 1840), ii. 127, n. 43.
5. A. Fytche, *Burma Past and Present* (London 1878), i. 238.
6. J. Edkins, *Religion in China*[2] (London 1878), 35.
7. Isabella L. Bishop (Bird), *Korea and her Neighbours* (London 1898), i. 48.
8. E. Aymonier, *Le Cambodge*, i (Paris 1900), 58.
9. D. Leslie, *Among the Zulus and Amatongas*[2] (Edinburgh 1875), 172–79; J. Macdonald, in *JAI*, 20 (1891), 131.
10. Polack, *op. cit.*, i. 37 f., ii. 126 f.
11. J. Cook, *Voyages* (London 1809), vi. 155; W. Ellis, *Polynesian Researches*[2] (London 1832–36), iii. 101.
12. Lucian, *Lexiphanes*, 10. But the custom was not very ancient; see A. Mommsen, *Feste der Stadt Athen im Altertum* (Leipzig 1898), 253 f.
13. G. Kaibel, *Epigrammata Graeca ex lapidibus conlecta* (Berlin 1878), No. 865; *Ephemeris Archaiologike*, 1883, col. 79 f. See on this entire subject W. R. Paton, "The Holy Names of the Eleusinian Priests," in *Papers and Transactions of the International Folk-lore Congress*, 1891, pp. 202–14.

188 1. B. Spencer and F. J. Gillen, *Northern Tribes of Central Australia* (London 1904), 227.
2. G. Timkowski, *Travels of the Russian Mission through Mongolia to China* (London 1827), ii. 348.
3. A. Wiedemann, *Die Religion der alten Aegypter* (Munster i. W. 1890), 29–32; E. A. W. Budge, *The Gods of the Egyptians* (London 1904), i. 360 f.
4. G. Maspero, *Études de mythologie et d'archéologie égyptienne* (Paris 1893), ii. 297 f.
5. E. Lefèbvre, in *Mélusine*, 8 (1897), coll. 227 ff.; E. A. W. Budge, *Egyptian Magic* (London 1899), 157 ff.
6. Lucan, *Pharsalia*, vi. 730 ff.
7. E. W. Lane, *Manners and Customs of the Modern Egyptians* (London 1875), Chap. xii, p. 273.
8. E. Doutté, *Magie et religions dans l'Afrique du nord* (Algiers 1908), 130.
9. J. J. M. de Groot, *The Religious System of China*, vi (Leyden 1910), 1126.

10. Pliny, *NH*, xxviii. 18; Macrobius, *Sat.*, iii. 9; Servius on Vergil, *Aen.*, ii. 351; Plutarch, *Quaest. Rom.*, 61.
11. Pliny, *NH*, iii. 65; Solinus, i. 4 f.; Macrobius, *Sat.*, iii. 9, 3–5; Servius on Vergil, *Aen*, i. 277; Joannes Lydus, *De mensibus*, iv. 50.
12. T. de Pauly, *Description ethnographique des peuples de la Russie* (St. Petersburg 1862): *Peuples ouralo-altaïques*, 24.

ADDITIONAL NOTES

TABOO

In connection with Frazer's treatment of *taboo* three general points may be raised:

(a) Taboo is not always, as he supposes, a formal ritual or social prohibition. It exists also on the level of purely psychological aversion, an expression of the normal instinct of recoil involved in the sensation of awe. That is to say, a man may avoid and regard as taboo any person or thing which he deems awesome or uncanny, but he may do so merely out of an automatic sense of apprehension rather than as the result of a legal ban.

(b) In scrutinizing Frazer's examples, a careful distinction should be made between taboos and avoidances. There are many things which people avoid (e.g., going near fire) not out of a sense of awe or "numinosity" but simply out of caution born of experience.

(c) It might be useful, for purely practical classification, to distinguish between taboos imposed for the benefit of the subject and those imposed for the benefit of the object. In some cases persons or things are tabooed in order to prevent impairment of their inherent qualities by contact with the "profane"; while in others the purpose is to prevent "infection" of human beings by persons or things believed to be potentially noxious. Thus, in avoiding consumption of certain animals, or travel on certain days, the object is to avoid contagion. The taboo is a kind of quarantine. But the prohibition against entering a "holy of holies," or wearing dirty clothes at worship, etc., is motivated rather by the desire to prevent impairment of the divine and ultramundane by mortal pollution.

149. *Separable Soul.* See also: J. Bolte and G. Polivka, *Anmerkungen zu den Kinder– und Hausmärchen der Brüder Grimm* (Leipzig 1913–18), iii. 440; A. H. Krappe, in N. M. Penzer, *The Ocean of Story* (London 1923), viii. 107; J. A. MacCulloch, *Childhood of Fiction* (London 1905), 118 ff; Stith Thompson, *Motif-Index*, E 710.

150. For the idea that *the departing soul hangs on the lips*, see Headlam-Knox on Hero[n]das, 3. 4; Meleager, in *Anthol. Pal.*, v. 197; Seneca, *Epist.*, 30. 14. — An offshoot of this idea was the custom of kissing the mouth of the dying in order to receive his soul. Joseph thus kissed Jacob on his deathbed:

Genesis 50 : 1. Anna, sister of Dido, rushed forward to the pyre to catch the latter's last breath in a kiss: Vergil, *Aeneid*, 4. 684. Alexander Pope has Heloise cry out to Abelard: "Suck my last breath and catch my flying soul"; while Shelley invokes Adonais: "O let thy breath flow from thy dying soul/Even to my mouth and heart, that I may suck!" — See in general: E. Rohde, *Psyche*[3] (Tübingen 1903), 25; E. Riess, in *Classical Review*, 10 (1896), 409; T. J. Duncan, in *Classical Journal*, 25 (1929), 230–34; M. Cox, *Introduction to Folk-Lore* (London 1897), 42 f.; R. B. Onians, *The Origins of European Thought concerning the Body* (Cambridge 1952), 128. According to an emendation proposed by Leonard A. Magnus, this belief is also to be found in the Russian *Armament of Igor*, line 554; cp. p. 81 of Magnus' edition (London 1915).

151. *The soul as a bird.* See in general: G. Weichert, *Der Seelenvogel in der alten Literatur und Kunst* (Leipzig 1902); V. Aptowitzer, *Die Seele als Vogel* (Breslau 1925); A. B. Cook, *Zeus*, ii (Cambridge 1925), 524, 697 n., 1132; O. Gruppe, *Griech. Mythol.* (Munich 1906), 1502, n. 1, 1618, n. 1; Waser, in *ARW*, 16 (1913), 337 ff.; O. Dähnhardt, *Natursagen* (Leipzig 1907–12), iii. 476 f. EGYPT: L. Klebs, in *Zs. Äg. Spr.*, 61 (1926), 104–08; W. Spiegelberg, in *Orientalistische Literaturzeitung*, 29 (1926), 393–95. TEUTONIC: Grimm-Stallybrass, *Teutonic Mythology* (London 1880), 828 f.; F. Nork, *Die Sitten und Gebräuche der Deutschen u. ihrer Nachbarvölker: Das Kloster*, xii (Stuttgart 1849), 271. CZECH: K. Schwenk, *Die Mythologie der Slawer* (Frankfurt a. M. 1853), 274 f. SILESIAN: Kühnau, in *Mitt. d. Sachs. Ges. f. Volkskunde*, 16 (1906), 96 f. PRE-ISLAMIC ARABS: G. Jacob, *Das Leben der vorislâmischen Beduinen* (Berlin 1899), 122, n. 2.

It is a popular belief in parts of Great Britain that a white bird or pigeon is a sign of the departing soul: *The Gentleman's Magazine*, 92 (1822), i, 311; Byron, *Don Juan*, Canto II, stanza 94; *Notes and Queries*, VI. vi (1882), 269, 452 f. In Thornton Wilder's *The Bridge of San Luis Rey*, there is a discussion whether "the soul can be seen, like a dove, fluttering away at the moment of death"; see E. S. McCartney, in *Proc. Michigan Acad. Sc. Arts and Letters*, 16 (1931), 164.

Gregory of Tours in his *Dialogues*, c. iv, 10, says that the monks at a monastery in Nuria saw a dove issue from the mouth of their dying abbot and fly to heaven: Migne, *Patrologia Latina*, 71, col. 386. St. Benedict saw the soul of his sister Scholastica depart as a dove; *ib.*, 66, col. 196; and a dove issued from the mouth of Polycarp when he was slain: *Letter of the Smyrnaeans on the Martyrdom of S. Polycarp*, 16.

152. The primitive notion is well expressed both by the colloquial expressions, "to be beside onself," "to jump out of one's skin," and by the etymology of the word *ecstasy*, viz., standing outside (of oneself). On the latter, see T. Achelis, *Die Ekstase in ihrer kulturellen Bedeutung* (1902).

156. In Hebrew, "to steal the heart" means to get a man into one's power: Genesis 31 : 20,26; while according to D. S. Margoliouth (Temple Bible: *Proverbs* [London 1902], 118), the converse expression, "to guard the heart," in Proverbs 4 : 23 alludes to the belief that it can be stolen. "Stealers of the heart," in the sense of hostile persons who will despoil a corpse and thus prevent its after-life, are mentioned in the Egyptian Book of the Dead, Chaps. 26–30; see also W. Spiegelberg, "Das Herz als zweites Wesen des Menschens," in *Zs. für Aeg. Spr.*, 66 (1930), 35–37.

157. *The soul as shadow or reflection.* See: J. Negelein, "Bild, Spiegel und Schatten im Volksglauben," in *Archiv für Religionswiss.*, 5 (1902), 1–37; A. Löwinger, in *Mitt. zur. jüd. Volkskunde*, 1910. In Numbers 14 : 9 the expression, "their shadow is departed from them" (Revised Standard Version, wrongly, "their protection is removed from them") is thought to mean "they are doomed to die"; while in Job 15 : 29 the Greek (Septuagint) Version reads: "He will not be rich, and his wealth will not endure, neither will *his shadow be stretched out upon the ground.*" — On similar beliefs in ancient Egypt, see S. Birch, "On the Shade or Shadow of the Dead," in *Trans. Soc. Bibl. Arch.*, 8 (1885), 386–97. — "New England (Indian) tribes called the soul *chemung*, "shadow." In Tasmanian, Quiche, and Eskimo languages, and in several dialects of Costa Rica, as among the Zulus and Abipones, one word expresses both soul and shade"; M. Cox, *Introduction to Folk-lore* (London 1897), 67 f. Cp. also Greek *skia*, Latin *umbra*, etc.

Widespread is the belief that the absence of one's shadow on a wall betokens imminent death. Thus, in ancient Greece, it was held that if one ventured into the inner fane of Lycaean Zeus, one would lose his shadow and die within a year: Pausanias, viii. 38, 6; Plutarch, *Quaest. Graec.*, 39. Similarly, in Silesia, superstition asserts that he who does not see his shadow on the wall on Christmas Eve will die during the year: P. Drechsler, *Sitte, Brauch und Volksglauben in Schlesien* (Leipzig 1905–06), i. 31; while Jewish folklore entertains the same fancy about the absence of the shadow from the wall of the synagogue on the sixth day (Hosh'annâ Rabbâ) of the Feast of Booths. The Japanese likewise hold that the fading of the shadow betokens imminent death, and a proverb runs: "Do not tread on a shadow, for a shadow is a life"; G. H. Simon, in *Journal of American Folklore*, 65 (1952), 192.

Widespread also is the belief that *the soul resides in the pupil of the eye.* In Hebrew, the pupil is called *îshôn*, "little man," and with this may be compared the German *Männlein im Auge* and the Spanish *la niña del ojo.* See: J. Grimm, *Teutonic Mythology*, tr. F. Stallybrass (London 1880), iii. 1181; V. S. Lean, *Collectanea* (Bristol-London 1902–04), ii. 579; E. B. Tylor, *Primitive Culture* (London 1920), i. 431; K. F. Smith, "Pupula Duplex," in *Studies in Honor of Basil L. Gildersleeve* (Baltimore 1902), 287 ff.; E. S. McCartney, in *Papers of the Michigan Acad. of Science, Arts and Letters*, 16 (1931), 187 ff.; A. le Roy, *Les Pygmées* (1928), 187; Waser, in *Archiv für Religionswissenschaft*, 16 (1913), 381 f.

158–59. On the *burning or destruction of portraits* as a means of magically encompassing a man's death, see: Berkusky, in *Archiv für Anthropol.*, N. F. 11 (1912), 88 f.; L. Bianchi, in *Hess. Blätter f. Volkskunde*, 13 (1914), 111; Penquitt, *De Didonis Vergilianae exitu* (Diss., Königsberg 1910), 35 ff.

THE PRIMITIVE CONCEPT OF THE "SOUL"

Frazer's assertion that primitive peoples believe in a separable or external soul, which leaves the body during sleep, sickness, or stress, and which can likewise be extracted from it by magical means, is gravely misleading. For what in fact the primitive believes to depart or be extracted under such conditions is not the *soul*—that is, the entire psychic side of the self—but something far nearer what we should call *consciousness*. What a man is then thought to lose is the normal control of his faculties, not his "spiritual" being or vitality.

Similarly, it is quite mistaken to speak (as do Frazer and many later anthropologists) of a primitive belief that the individual possesses several *souls,* for this implies that he is thought to possess several manifestations of the same thing, several vessels of the same essential spiritual essence. What he really believes is, however, that the total self is a complex of several different spiritual elements— a notion which we ourselves endorse when we use such several and subtly differentiated terms as: character, personality, individuality, identity, identification, name, temper, disposition, mood, vital spark, sensibility, talent, reputation, and the like. To him, the broad twofold distinction between corporeal and psychic would be grossly oversimplified.

The ancient Egyptians, when they spoke of multiple psychic elements in man (e.g., the *ka,* the *ba,* the *ab,* etc.) were really expressing the same idea; to blanket such intuitive distinctions with a single over-all term is thoroughly to distort the picture.

TABOO ON STRANGERS

The reason why strangers are avoided and have to be "purified" is simply that they have not been subjected to the ritual disciplines recognized by the natives and do not stand under the protection of the powers with whom the natives are in communion and alliance. Accordingly, they *may* (not necessarily *do*) impart impurity or danger which has not been previously "hanselled" or counteracted, as in the case of their hosts. The measures adopted in receiving them should therefore be considered as preventive, not curative. Sometimes, indeed, the desired end is believed to be achieved by a different procedure: host and guest enter into a bond of temporary alliance with each other's gods. Thus, when Abraham visited the city of Salem, the local priest-king Melchizedek proffered food and drink so that by partaking of them his guest might enter into commensal communion with the local god El 'Elyon, "God Most High" (Gen. 14); and the same procedure was followed in the cases of Abimelech the Philistine and Isaac, of Jethro the Kenite and Moses, and of the Israelites as a whole and the inhabitants of Gibeon (Joshua 9 : 14).

TABOOS IN MOURNING

A distinction should be drawn between taboos imposed upon mourners themselves and those imposed on others in relation to them. The latter, it may be conceded, are inspired by the belief that persons who have been in contact with death are potentially dangerous and contagious. The former, however, do not depend—as Frazer seems to suppose—on any property attaching to the deceased. Rather are they based on the idea that death itself is a visitation which, though it may claim one particular victim, besets the community *as a whole*. All members of that community are therefore partially infected by it, and it is this state of suspended animation or "mortification" that is really expressed in the restrictive observances of mourning, e.g., fasts, abstinences.

171. *Iron in magic.* See: A. Abt, *Die Apologie des Apuleius,* 86; Th. Höpfner, *Griechisch-aeg. Offenbarungszauber* (Leipzig 1921), §596; O. Gruppe, *Griech. Mythol.,* 895; E. Norden, *Aeneis VI* (Leipzig 1916), 163, 201; S. Eitrem, *Papyri Osloenses,* I (Oslo 1925), 56 f.; I. Scheftelowitz, *Altpaläst. Bauernglaube* (Hanover 1925), 66 f.; W. Kroll, *Antiker Aberglaube* (Hamburg 1897), 7 f.; E. Clodd, *Tom Tit-Tot* (London 1898), 33 ff.; I. Goldziher, in *ARW,* 10 (1907), 41 ff. [Arabic]; E. Westermarck, *Pagan Survivals in Mohammedan Civilisation* (London 1933), 9; F. T. Elworthy, *The Evil Eye* (London 1895), 220 ff.; A. B. Cook, in *Journal of Hellenic Studies,* 20 (1900), 20 ff.; M. Eliade, *Forgerons et Alchimistes* (Paris 1957), 26 ff., 70, 188.

In the *Testament of Solomon* (ed. Connybeare, *JQR* 11. 18), a demon is scared by iron. In an Aramaic incantation from Nippur, the reciter wears iron armor to forefend the demons: J. A. Montgomery, *Aramaic Incantation Texts from Nippur* (Philadelphia 1913), No. 2. In England, a red-hot poker is plunged into the churn to prevent witches from interfering with the making of butter: M. Cox, *Introduction to Folklore* (London 1897), 8. Iron horseshoes are likewise apotropaic: *ib.,* 16. Arabs cry, "Iron! Iron!" when encountering a *jinn:* E. W. Lane, *Arabian Society in the Middle Ages* (London 1883), 36. Hindus carry a piece of iron when visiting the sick, in order to frighten away the demon of disease: Clodd, *op. cit.,* 35. In German and Slavonic folk custom, iron is waved in the air to keep off the demons of whirlwind: F. Nork, *Die Sitten u. Gebr. der Deutschen* (Stuttgart 1849), 535. Mohammed's mother had a piece of iron bound on her hand and throat at the time of his birth: Sprenger, *Mohammed*[2] (Berlin 1861–69), i. 142. Iron is placed in the bed of a woman in labor in Germany and Italy: S. Seligmann, *Der böse Blick* (Berlin 1910), ii. 8; G. Finamore, *Tradizioni popolari abruzzesi* (Palermo 1890), 69. This practice is known also to the Jews, but was considered heathenish by the rabbis.

173. *Blood as the vehicle of the soul or intelligence.* See further: W. Wundt, *Elements of Folk Psychology,* tr. Schaub (London 1916), 208 ff.; O. Gruppe, *Griech. Mythol.* (Munich 1906), 728, n. 5; J. Wellhausen, *Reste des arabischen Heidenthums* (Berlin 1897), 9 ff.; E. Rohde, *Psyche*[1] (Tübingen 1921), iii. 176; Theophrastus, *De sens.,* 10.25 f. — The pre-Islamic Arabs forbade the consumption of blood, and held that kings and nobles could requite those who drank it from their corpses by causing hydrophobia and demonic possession: W. R. Smith, *Religion of the Semites*[3] (London 1927), 369.

The belief that *the suet, or fat of the omentum, is the seat of vitality* underlies the prohibition, in Leviticus 7 : 22, against eating it. In Psalm 17 : 10, the expression "they have shut tight their midriff" is used to describe insensitive persons; while in Arabic, "midriff" or "suet" is a virtual synonym for "feeling":

T. H. Gaster, *The Holy and the Profane* (New York 1955), 208 f. — The Greeks too held that the center of vitality lay in the diaphragm: A. Platt, in *Journal of Philology*, 19 (1890), 46; while Australian primitives regard kidney fat as the seat of the soul: E. Crawley, *The Idea of the Soul* (London 1909), 235.

174. On the idea that *the head is the seat of "genius" or animating principle,* see R. B. Onians, *The Origins of European Thought about the Body* (Cambridge 1951), 95 ff, though allowance must be made for a certain amount of exaggeration in this treatment of the subject; K. Bethe, in *Rhein Mus.* 62 (1907), 465, would thus account for the Homeric expression *amenêna karêna* (Odyssey 10. 521, 536; 11. 29, 49); but L. Radermacher (*ARW* 11 [1908], 414) objects that it refers simply to the fact that people were counted *per capita!* — Among the Romans the forehead was deemed sacred to the *genius natalis,* and one touched it in praying to him: Servius, on Vergil, *Ecl.,* 6. 3 and *Aen.,* 3. 607. — See further J. A. MacCulloch, in *ERE,* s. v. Head.

178. *Spittle.* See: F. W. Nicolson, "The Saliva Superstition in Classical Literature," in *Harvard Studies in Classical Philology,* 8 (1897), 23–40; Volgraff, in *Mnemosyne,* 42 (1914), 410 f.; A. Abt, *Die Apologie des Apuleius,* 260 f.; C. de Monsignac, *Récherches ethnographiques sur la salive et le crachet* (Bordeaux 1892), 41 ff.; E. S. Hartland, *The Legend of Perseus* (London 1894–96), ii. 258 ff.; J. E. Crombie, in *Trans. Internat. Folklore Congress,* 1891; B. Schmidt, in *Neue Jahrb.,* 31 (1913), 591 f. [modern Greece]. — On the use of spitting in charms, see Kirby Smith on Tibullus, I. ii. 54; Mayor on Juvenal, 7. 112; T. H. Gaster, in *Orientalia,* 11 (1942), 64. — Ida Lublinski (in *ARW* 22 [1923–24], 154 ff.; *Zs. f. Völkerpsychologie,* 6 [1930], 36) makes the interesting suggestion that the idea that blood, faeces, spittle, etc., were animate or the seats of animation originated in observation of the dead who could not bleed, excrete, urinate, etc.

180. *Magical use of knots.* On the subject in general, see Kirby Smith on Tibullus, I. viii, 5.

On the untying of knots *at childbirth,* see: W. B. McDaniel, *Conception, Birth and Infancy in Ancient Rome and Modern Italy* (Coconut Grove, Florida 1948), 16; E. S. McCartney, in *Papers of the Michigan Acad. of Science, Arts and Letters,* 16 (1931), 110 f.; *Handwörterbuch d. deutsch. Aberglaube,* V. 19; F. Liebrecht, *Zur Volkskunde* (Heilbronn 1879), 322 [Norway], 360 [Scotland]; J. G. Frazer, *Pausanias,* vol. v, p. 95; *Zs. für vergl. Volkskunde,* 17. 168 [W. Russia]; *Philologus,* 57 (1898), 131; Stith Thompson, *Motif-Index,* T 582. 3. — Knots are similarly avoided *on graveclothes:* e.g., P. Sartori, *Sitte u. Brauch* (Leipzig 1910), i. 133, n. 15.

Taboo on crossing legs or clasping hands. For this taboo in England, see *Notes and Queries,* I, ii (1850), 407 f. In parts of Italy it is forbidden to keep hands clasped or fingers knit in the room in which a birth takes place: A. de Jorio, *La mimica degli antichi* (Naples 1832), 203.

181. *Magic of names.* In primitive thought, the name of a person is not merely an appellation, but denotes what he is to the world outside of himself—that is, his "outer" as distinguished from his "inner" being. Thus, the "name of God" in the Bible is His outward manifestation in the world, and in the Semitic languages, "name" and "posterity" are virtual synonyms. To bless or curse the name is therefore more than to invoke verbal benediction or malediction; it is to compass or invoke the prosperity or ruin of a person in his human relations.

Because the name is thus an integral part of the self, the attitude of primitive peoples towards bestowing their own upon their living relatives (descendants) is necessarily ambivalent: on the one hand, it is thought to subtract something from the vitality of him who originally bore it; on the other, to guarantee his continuance or revitalize his debilitated being. See on this: R. Andree, *Ethnographische Parallelen und Vergleiche*, i (Stuttgart 1878), 165–84; H. Ploss, *Das Kind*[3] (Leipzig 1884), i. 142 ff.

On ancient ideas concerning the name, see: E. Lefébvre, "La vertu et la vie du nom en Egypte," in *Mélusine*, 8 (1897), 229–31; G. Contenau, "De la valeur du nom chez les babyloniens," in *Revue de l'histoire des religions* (1920), 316–22; W. Kroll, "Namenaberglaube bei Griechen und Römern," in *Mitt. d. Schles. Ges. für Volkskunde*, 16 (1914), 179 ff.; Abt, *Apologie des Apuleius*, 44, 150 f.

The custom of not divulging the name of a child until it has been protected by baptism is recorded from West Sussex, England, as late as the nineteenth century: E. Clodd, *Tom Tit-Tot* (London 1898), 91. — In the Cyclades, a child is called Iron Dragon (see above, §171) or the like before christening in order to avert evil spirits: *ib.*, 94. So too in Tonkin and Siam: Andree, *op. cit.*, 177. For a similar usage in Britain, see *Notes and Queries*, III. xi. 175, 202; IV. v. 543; vi. 17.

In time of illness, it is customary among many peoples to change the patient's name in order thereby to change his identity and foil the hovering demons. This is attested, for instance, among the Mongols (J. von Klaproth, *Reise in den Kaukasus* [Halle-Berlin 1812], i. 253), the Arabs (C. A. Doughty, *Arabia Deserta* [Cambridge 1888], i. 329) and the Baholoho (R. Schmitz, *Baholoho* [Brussels 1911], 327).

On the magical power attaching to the name of a god or demon, see: W. Heitmüller, *Im Namen Jesu* (Göttingen 1903); L. R. Farnell, *Evolution of Religion* (London 1905), 185; F. Dornseiff, *Das Alphabet im Mystik u. Magie*[3] (Leipzig 1925), 51, n. 1; S. Eitrem, *Papyri Osloenses* I (1925), 98.

In connection with the idea that the names of especially numinous beings (e.g., Yahweh among the Israelites) are "ineffable," it is worth noting that, according to S. Schott (in *Studium Generale*, 6 [1953], 237–58), the name of the Pharaoh was regarded as ineffable after the Eighteenth Dynasty.

PART III

DEATH AND RESURRECTION:

THE RHYTHM OF NATURE

THE SUCCESSION

OF KINGS AND SEASONS

189. *At an early stage of his intellectual development man deems himself naturally immortal, and imagines that were it not for the baleful arts of sorcerers, who cut the vital thread prematurely short, he would live for ever. But in time the sad truth of human mortality was borne in upon our primitive philosopher with a force of demonstration which no prejudice could resist and no sophistry dissemble. Nevertheless, even if he reluctantly acknowledged the existence of beings at once superhuman and supernatural, he was as yet far from suspecting the width and the depth of the gulf which divided him from them. The gods with whom his imagination now peopled the darkness of the unknown were indeed admitted by him to be his superiors in knowledge and in power, in the joyous splendour of their life and in the length of its duration. But, though he knew it not, these glorious and awful beings were merely, like the spectre of the Brocken, the reflections of his own diminutive personality exaggerated into gigantic proportions by distance and by the mists and clouds of ignorance upon which they were cast.*

Man in fact created gods in his own likeness and being himself mortal he naturally supposed his creatures to be in the same sad predicament. Thus the Greenlanders believed that a wind could kill their most powerful god, and that he would certainly die if he touched a dog.[1] In answer to the enquiries of Colonel Dodge, a North American Indian stated that the world was made by the Great Spirit. Being asked which Great Spirit he meant, the good one or the bad one, "Oh, neither of *them*," replied he, "the Great Spirit that made the world is dead long ago. He could not possibly have lived as long as this."[2] A tribe in the Philippine Islands told the Spanish conquerors that the grave of the Creator was upon the top of Mount Cabunian.[3] Heitsi-eibib, a god or divine hero of the Hottentots, died several times and

The Dinka are a congeries of independent tribes in the valley of the White Nile, whose territory, lying mostly on the eastern bank of the river and stretching from the sixth to the twelfth degree of North Latitude, has been estimated to comprise between sixty and seventy thousand square miles. They worship a supreme being whose name of Dengdit means literally Great Rain, and the human rain-maker (*bain*) is a very important personage among the Dinka to this day; indeed the men in authority whom travellers dub chiefs or sheikhs are in fact the actual or potential rain-makers of the tribe or community. Each of them is believed to be animated by the spirit of a great rain-maker, which has come down to him through a succession of rain-makers; and in virtue of this inspiration a successful rain-maker enjoys very great power and is consulted on all important matters. Yet, in spite, or rather in virtue, of the high honour in which he is held, no Dinka rain-maker is allowed to die a natural death of sickness or old age; for the Dinka believe that if such an untoward event were to happen, the tribe would suffer from disease and famine, and the herds would not yield their increase. So when a rain-maker feels that he is growing old and infirm, he tells his children that he wishes to die. Among the Agar Dinka a large grave is dug and the rain-maker lies down in it on his right side with his head resting on a skin. He is surrounded by his friends and relatives, including his younger children; but his elder children are not allowed to approach the grave lest in their grief and despair they should do themselves a bodily injury. For many hours, generally for more than a day, the rain-maker lies without eating or drinking. From time to time he speaks to the people, recalling the past history of the tribe, reminding them how he has ruled and advised them, and instructing them how they are to act in the future. Then, when he has concluded his admonition, he tells them that it is finished and bids them cover him up. So the earth is thrown down on him as he lies in the grave, and he soon dies of suffocation. Even if a rain-maker is quite young he will be put to death should he seem likely to perish of disease. Further, every precaution is taken to prevent a rain-maker from dying an accidental death, for such an end, though not nearly so serious a matter as death from illness or old age, would be sure to entail sickness on the tribe. As soon as a rain-maker is killed, his valuable spirit is supposed to pass to a suitable successor, whether a son or other near blood relation.[4b]

In the Central African kingdom of Unyoro down to recent years custom required that as soon as the king fell seriously ill or began to break up from age, he should die by his own hand; for, according to an old prophecy, the throne would pass away from the dynasty if ever the king were to die a natural death. He killed himself by draining a poisoned cup. If he faltered or were too ill to ask for the cup, it was his wife's duty to administer the poison.[5] When the king of Kibanga, on the Upper Congo, seems near his end, the sorcerers put a rope round his neck, which they draw gradually tighter till he dies.[6] If the king of Gingiro happens to be wounded in war, he is put to death by his comrades, or, if they fail to kill him, by his kinsfolk, however hard he may beg for mercy. They say they do it that he may not die by the hands of his enemies.[7] The Jukos are a heathen tribe of the Benue river, a great tributary of the Niger. In their country "the town of Gatri is ruled by a king who is elected by the big men of the town as follows. When in the opinion of the big men the king has reigned long enough, they give out that 'the king is sick'—a formula understood by all to mean that they are going to kill him, though the intention is never put more plainly. They then decide who is to be the next king. How long he is to reign is settled by the influential men at a meeting; the question is put and answered by each man throwing on the ground a little piece of stick for each year he thinks the new king should rule. The king is then told, and a great feast prepared, at which the king gets drunk on guinea-corn beer. After that he is speared, and the man who was chosen becomes king."[8]

It appears to have been a Zulu custom to put the king to death as soon as he began to have wrinkles or grey hairs. At least this seems implied in the following passage written by one who resided for some time at the court of the notorious Zulu tyrant Chaka, in the early part of the nineteenth century: "The extraordinary violence of the king's rage with me was mainly occasioned by that absurd nostrum, the hair oil, with the notion of which Mr. Farewell had impressed him as being a specific for removing all indications of age. From the first moment of his having heard that such a preparation was attainable, he evinced a solicitude to procure it, and on every occasion never forgot to remind us of his anxiety respecting it; more especially on our departure on the mission his injunctions were particularly directed to this object. It will be seen that it is one of the barbarous customs of the Zoolas in their choice or election of their kings that he must neither have wrinkles nor grey hairs, as they are both distinguishing marks of disqualification for becoming a monarch of a warlike people. It is also equally indispensable that their king should never exhibit those proofs of having become unfit and incompetent to reign; it is therefore important that they should conceal these indications so long as they possibly can. Chaka had become greatly apprehensive of the approach of grey hairs; which would at once be the signal for him to prepare to make his exit from this sublunary world, it being always followed by the death of the monarch."[9] The writer to whom we are indebted for this instructive anecdote of the hair-oil omits to specify the mode in which a grey-haired and wrinkled Zulu chief used "to make his exit from this sublunary world"; but on analogy we may conjecture that he did so by the simple and perfectly sufficient process of being knocked on the head.

The custom of putting kings to death as soon as they suffered from any personal defect prevailed two centuries ago in the Caffre kingdom of Sofala, to the north of the present Zululand. These kings of Sofala were regarded as gods by their people, being entreated to give rain or sunshine, according as each might be wanted. Nevertheless, as we learn from an old Portuguese historian,[10] a slight bodily blemish, such as the loss of a tooth, was considered a sufficient cause for putting one of these god-men to death.

The king of Sofala who dared to survive the loss of his front tooth was thus a bold reformer like Ergamenes, king of Ethiopia. We may conjecture that the ground for putting the Ethiopian kings to death was, as in the case of the Zulu and Sofala kings, the appearance on their person of any bodily defect or sign of decay; and that the oracle which the priests alleged as the authority for the royal execution was to the effect that great calamities would result from the reign of a king who had any blemish on his body; just as an oracle warned Sparta against a "lame reign," that is, the reign of a lame king.[11] It is some confirmation of this conjecture that the kings of Ethiopia were chosen for their size, strength, and beauty long before the custom of killing them was abolished.[12] To this day the Sultan of Wadai must have no obvious bodily defect, and the king of Angoy cannot be crowned if he has a single blemish, such as a broken or a filed tooth or the scar of an old wound.[13] According to the Book of Acaill and many other authorities no king who was afflicted with a personal blemish might reign over Ireland at Tara. Hence, when the great King Cormac Mac Art lost one eye by an accident, he at once abdicated.[14] It is only natural, therefore, to suppose, especially with the other African examples before us, that any bodily defect or symptom of old age appearing on the person of the Ethiopian monarch was the signal for his execution.

Many days' journey to the north-east of Abomey, the old capital of Dahomey, lies the kingdom of Eyeo. "The Eyeos are governed by a king, no less absolute than the king of Dahomey, yet subject to a regulation of state, at once humiliating and extraordinary. When the people have conceived an opinion of his ill-government, which is sometimes insidiously infused into them by the artifice of his discontented ministers, they send a deputation to him with a present of parrots' eggs, as a mark of its authenticity, to represent to him that the burden of government must have so far fatigued him that they consider it full time for him to repose from his cares and indulge himself with a little sleep. He thanks his subjects for their attention to his ease, retires to his own apartment as if to sleep, and there gives directions to his women to strangle him. This is immediately executed, and his son quietly ascends the throne upon the usual terms of holding the reins of government no longer than whilst he merits the approbation of the people."[15]

The Bambara, a large tribe in the French territory of Upper Senegal and Niger, have an ancient tradition that formerly their kings were only allowed to reign so long as they retained their strength and vigour. When they noticed that the king's strength was failing, they said "The grass is withering!

The grass is beginning to wither," which had a sinister significance for the ageing king whose hair was beginning to grow grey.[15a]

Among the Banyankole, a pastoral people of the Uganda Protectorate, the king is known by the title of Mugabe. "No Mugabe ever allowed himself to grow old . . . he had to put an end to his life before his powers, either mental or physical, began to deteriorate. It was even thought undesirable that the Mugabe should look old, and treatment was applied to prevent his hair from growing grey. As soon as he felt his strength diminishing he knew it was time to end his life, and he called his chiefs, and also his sons, who never came to see him except on this occasion . . . when all was ready, he summoned the royal medicine-man and asked for the king's poison. This was always kept in readiness in the shell of a crocodile's egg. The white of the egg was dried and powdered and mixed with the dried nerve from the pointed end of an elephant's tusk and some other ingredients, the exact mixture being kept strictly secret. This had only to be mixed with a little water or beer to be ready for use, and when the Mugabe drank it he fell dead in a few moments."[15b]

The old Prussians acknowledged as their supreme lord a ruler who governed them in the name of the gods, and was known as God's Mouth (*Kirwaido*). When he felt himself weak and ill, if he wished to leave a good name behind him, he had a great heap made of thorn-bushes and straw, on which he mounted and delivered a long sermon to the people, exhorting them to serve the gods and promising to go to the gods and speak for the people. Then he took some of the perpetual fire which burned in front of the holy oak-tree, and lighting the pile with it burned himself to death.[16]

191. Some peoples appear to have thought it unsafe to wait for even the slightest symptom of decay and have preferred to kill the king while he was still in the full vigour of life. Accordingly, they have fixed a term beyond which he might not reign, and at the close of which he must die, the term fixed upon being short enough to exclude the probability of his degenerating physically in the interval. In some parts of southern India the period fixed was twelve years. Thus, according to an old traveller, in the province of Quilacare, about twenty leagues to the north-east of Cape Comorin, "there is a Gentile house of prayer, in which there is an idol which they hold in great account, and every twelve years they celebrate a great feast to it, whither all the Gentiles go as to a jubilee. This temple possesses many lands and much revenue: it is a very great affair. This province has a king over it, who has not more than twelve years to reign from jubilee to jubilee. His manner of living is in this wise, that is to say: when the twelve years are completed, on the day of this feast there assemble together innumerable people, and much money is spent in giving food to Bramans. The king has a wooden scaffolding made, spread over with silken hangings: and on that day he goes to bathe at a tank with great ceremonies and sound of music, after that he comes to the idol and prays to it, and mounts on to the scaffolding, and there before all the people he takes some very sharp knives, and begins to cut off his nose, and then his ears, and his lips, and all his members, and as much flesh off himself as he can; and he throws it away very hurriedly until so much of his blood is spilled that he begins to faint, and then he cuts his throat himself. And he performs this sacrifice to the idol, and whoever desires to reign other twelve years and undertake this martyrdom for love of the idol, has to be present looking on at this: and from that place they raise him up as king."[1]

The king of Calicut, on the Malabar coast, bears the title of Samorin or Samory, which in the native language is said to mean "God on earth."[2] He "pretends to be of a higher rank than the Brahmans, and to be inferior only to the invisible gods; a pretention that was acknowledged by his subjects, but which is held as absurd and abominable by the Brahmans, by whom he is only treated as a Sudra."[3] Formerly the Samorin had to cut his throat in public at the end of a twelve years' reign. But towards the end of the seventeenth century the rule had been modified as follows: "Many strange customs were observed in this country in former times, and some very odd ones are still continued. It was an ancient custom for the Samorin to reign but twelve years, and no longer. If he died before his term was expired, it saved him a troublesome ceremony of cutting his own throat, on a publick scaffold erected for the purpose. He first made a feast for all his nobility and gentry, who are very numerous. After the feast he saluted his guests, and went on the scaffold, and very decently cut his own throat in the view of the assembly, and his body was, a little while after, burned with great pomp and ceremony, and the grandees elected a new Samorin. Whether that custom was a religious or a civil ceremony, I know not, but it is now laid aside. And a new custom is followed by the modern Samorins, that jubilee is proclaimed throughout his dominions, at the end of twelve years, and a tent is pitched for him in a spacious plain, and a great feast is celebrated for ten or twelve days, with mirth and jollity, guns firing night and day, so at the end of the feast any four of the guests that have a mind to gain a crown by a desperate action, in fighting their way through 30 or 40,000 of his guards, and kill the Samorin in his tent, he that kills him succeeds him in his empire. In anno 1695, one of those jubilees happened, and the tent pitched near Pennany, a seaport of his, about fifteen leagues to the southward of Calicut. There were but three men that would venture on that desperate action, who fell in, with sword and target, among the guard, and, after they had killed and wounded many, were themselves killed. One of the desperados had a nephew of fifteen or sixteen years of age, that kept close by his uncle in the attack on the guards, and, when he saw him fall, the youth got through the guards into the tent, and made a stroke at his Majesty's head, and had certainly despatched him if a large brass lamp which was burning over his head had not marred the blow; but, before he could make another, he was killed by the guards; and, I believe, the same Samorin reigns yet. I chanced to come that time along the coast and heard the guns for two or three days and nights successively."[4]

When kings were bound to suffer death, whether at their own hands or at the hands of others, on the expiration of a fixed term of years, it was natural that they should seek to delegate the painful duty, along with some of the privileges of sovereignty, to a substitute who should suffer vicariously in their stead. This expedient appears to have been resorted to by some of the princes of Malabar. Thus we are informed by a native authority on that country that "in some places all powers both executive and judicial were delegated for a fixed period to natives by the sovereign. This institution was styled *Thalavettiparothiam* or authority obtained by decapitation. . . . It was an office tenable for five years during which its bearer was invested with supreme despotic powers within his jurisdiction. On the expiry of the five years the man's head was cut off and thrown up in the air amongst a large concourse of villagers, each of whom vied with the other in trying to catch it in its course down. He who succeeded was nominated to the post for the next five years."[5] A similar delegation of the duty of dying for his country was perhaps practised by the Sultans of Java. At least such a custom would explain a strange scene which was witnessed at the court of one of these sultans by the famous traveller Ibn Batuta, a native of Tangier, who visited the East Indies in the first half of the fourteenth century. He says: "During my audience with the Sultan I saw a man who held in his hand a knife like that used by a grape-gleaner. He placed it on his own neck and spoke for a long time in a language which I did not understand. After that he seized the knife with both hands at once and cut his throat. His head fell to the ground, so sharp was the blade and so great the force with which he used it. I remained dumbfounded at his behaviour, but the Sultan said to me, 'Does any one do like that in your country?' I answered, 'Never did I see such a thing.' He smiled and replied, 'These people are our slaves, and they kill themselves for love of us.' Then he commanded that they should take away him who had slain himself and should burn him. The Sultan's officers, the grandees, the troops, and the common people attended the cremation. The sovereign assigned a liberal pension to the children of the deceased, to his wife, and to his brothers; and they were highly honoured because of his conduct. A person, who was present at the audience when the event I have described took place, informed me that the speech made by the man who sacrificed himself set forth his devotion to the monarch. He said that he wished to immolate himself out of affection for the sovereign, as his father had done for love of the prince's father, and as his grandfather had done out of regard for the prince's grandfather."[6]

When once kings, who had hitherto been bound to die a violent death at the end of a term of years, conceived the happy thought of dying by deputy in the persons of others, they would very naturally put it in practice; and accordingly we need not wonder at finding so popular an expedient, or traces of it, in many lands. Thus, for example, the Bhuiyas are an aboriginal race of north-eastern India, and one of their chief seats is Keonjhur. At the installation of a Rajah of Keonjhur a ceremony is observed which has been described as follows by an English officer who witnessed it: "Then the sword, a very rusty old weapon, is placed in the Raja's hands, and one of the Bhuiyas, named Anand Kopat, comes before him, and kneeling sideways, the Raja touches him on the neck as if about to strike off his head, and it is said that in former days there was no fiction in this part of the ceremony. The family of the Kopat hold their lands on the condition that the victim when required shall be produced. Anand, however, hurriedly arose after the accolade and disappeared. He must not be seen for three days; then he presents himself again to the Raja as miraculously restored to life."[7] Here the custom of putting the king's proxy to death has dwindled, probably under English influence, to a mere pretence; but elsewhere it survives, or survived till recent times, in full force. Cassange, a native state in the interior of Angola, is ruled by a king, who bears the title of Jaga. When a king is about to be installed in office, some of the chiefs are despatched to find a human victim, who may not be related by blood or marriage to the new monarch. When he comes to the king's camp, the victim is provided with everything he requires, and all his orders are obeyed as promptly as those of the sovereign. On the day of the ceremony the king takes his seat on a perforated iron stool, his chiefs, councillors, and the rest of the people forming a great circle round about him. Behind the king sits his principal wife, together with all his concubines. An iron gong, with two small bells attached to it, is then struck by an official, who continues to ring the bells during the ceremony. The victim is then introduced and placed in front of the king, but with his back towards him. Armed with a scimitar the king then cuts open the man's back, extracts his heart, and having taken a bite out of it, spits it out and gives it to be burned. The councillors meantime hold the victim's body so that the blood from the wound spouts against the king's breast and belly, and, pouring through the hole in the iron stool, is collected by the chiefs in their hands, who rub their breasts and beards with it, while they shout, "Great is the king and the rites of the state!" After that the corpse is skinned, cut up, and cooked with the flesh of an ox, a dog, a hen, and some other animals. The meal thus prepared is served first to the king, then to the chiefs and councillors, and lastly to all the people assembled. Any man who refused to partake of it would be sold into slavery together with his family.[8] The distinction with which the human victim is here treated before his execution suggests that he is a substitute for the king.

Scandinavian traditions contain some hints that of old the Swedish kings reigned only for periods of nine years, after which they were put to death or had to find a substitute to die in their stead. Thus Aun or On, king of Sweden, is said to have sacrificed to Odin for length of days and to have been answered by the god that he should live so long as he sacrificed one of his sons every ninth year. He sacrificed nine of them in this manner, and would have sacrificed the tenth and last, but the Swedes would not allow him. So he died and was buried in a mound at Upsala.[9] Another indication of a similar tenure of the crown occurs in a curious legend of the disposition and banishment of Odin. Offended at his misdeeds, the other gods outlawed and exiled him, but set up in his place a substitute, Oller by name, a cunning wizard, to whom they accorded the symbols both of royalty and of godhead. The deputy bore the name of Odin, and reigned for nearly ten years, when he was driven from the throne, while the real Odin came to his own again. His discomfited rival retired to Sweden and was afterwards slain in an attempt to repair his shattered fortunes.[10] As gods are often merely men who loom large through the mists of tradition, we may conjecture that this Norse legend preserves a confused reminiscence of ancient Swedish kings who reigned for nine or ten years together, then abdicated, delegating to others the privilege of dying for their country. The great festival which was held at Upsala every nine years may have been the occasion on which the king or his deputy was put to death. We know that human sacrifices formed part of the rites.[11]

LIMITING THE KING'S REIGN

192. There are some grounds for believing that the reign of many ancient Greek kings was limited to eight years, or at least that at the end of every period of eight years a new consecration, a fresh outpouring of the divine grace, was regarded as necessary in order to enable them to discharge their civil and religious duties. Thus it was a rule of the Spartan constitution that every eighth year the ephors should choose a clear and moonless night and sitting down observe the sky in silence. If during their vigil they saw a meteor or shooting star, they inferred that the king had sinned against the deity, and they suspended him from his functions until the Delphic or Olympic oracle should reinstate him in them. This custom, which has all the air of great antiquity, was not suffered to remain a dead letter even in the last period of the Spartan monarchy; for in the third century before our era a king, who had rendered himself obnoxious to the reforming party, was actually deposed on various trumped-up charges, among which the allegation that the ominous sign had been seen in the sky took a prominent place.[1] When we compare this custom with the evidence to be presently adduced of an eight years' tenure of the kingship in Greece, we shall probably agree with K. O. Müller[2] that the quaint Spartan practice was much more than a mere antiquarian curiosity; it was the attenuated survival of an institution which may once have had great significance, and it throws an important light on the restrictions and limitations anciently imposed by religion on the Dorian kingship.

If the tenure of the regal office was formerly limited among the Spartans to eight years, we may naturally ask, why was that precise period selected as the measure of a king's reign? The reason is probably to be found in those astronomical considerations which determined the early Greek calendar. The difficulty of reconciling lunar with solar time is one of the standing puzzles which has taxed the ingenuity of men who are emerging from barbarism. Now an octennial cycle is the shortest period at the end of which sun and moon really mark time together after overlapping, so to say, throughout the whole of the interval. Thus, for example, it is only once in every eight years that the full moon coincides with the longest or shortest day; and as this coincidence can be observed with the aid of a simple dial, the observation is naturally one of the first to furnish a base for a calendar which shall bring lunar and solar times into tolerable, though not exact, harmony.[3] But in early days the proper adjustment of the calendar is a matter of religious concern, since on it depends a knowledge of the right seasons for propitiating the deities whose favour is indispensable to the welfare of the community. No wonder, therefore, that the king, as the chief priest of the state, or as himself a god, should be liable to deposition or death at the end of an astronomical period. When the great luminaries had run their course on high, and were about to renew the heavenly race, it might well be thought that the king should renew his divine energies, or prove them unabated, under pain of making room for a more vigorous successor. In southern India, the king's reign and life terminated with the revolution of the planet Jupiter round the sun. In Greece, on the other hand, the king's fate seems to have hung in the balance at the end of every eight years, ready to fly up and kick the beam as soon as the opposite scale was loaded with a falling star.[4]

Whatever its origin may have been, the cycle of eight years appears to have coincided with the normal length of the king's reign in other parts of the ancient world besides Sparta. Thus Minos, king of Knossos in Crete, is said to have held office for periods of eight years together. At the end of each period he retired for a season to commune with his divine father Zeus on Mount Ida, rendering him an account of his stewardship and receiving instructions for the future.[5] The tradition implies plainly that at the end of every eight years the king's sacred powers needed to be renewed by intercourse with the godhead.[6]

Without being unduly rash we may surmise that the tribute of seven youths and seven maidens whom the Athenians were bound to send to Minos every eight years had some connection with the renewal of the king's power for another octennial cycle; and it is likewise not without significance that many solemn rites were celebrated by the Greeks at intervals of eight years.[7]

193. In the province of Lagos, which forms part of Southern Nigeria, the Ijebu tribe of the Yoruba race is divided into two branches, which are known respectively as the Ijebu Ode and the Ijebu Remon. The Ode branch of the tribe is ruled by a chief who bears the title of Awujale and is surrounded by a great deal of mystery. Down to recent times his face might not be seen even by his own subjects, and if circumstances obliged him to communicate with them he did so through a screen which hid him from view. The other or Remon branch of the Ijebu tribe is governed by a chief, who ranks below the Awujale. Mr. John Parkinson was informed that in former times this subordinate chief used to be killed with ceremony after a rule of three years. As the country is now under British protection the custom of putting the chief to death at the end of a three years' reign has long been abolished, and Mr. Parkinson was unable to ascertain any particulars on the subjects.[1]

194. At Babylon, within historical times, the tenure of the kingly office was in practice lifelong, yet in theory it would seem to have been merely annual. For every year at the festival of Zagmuk the king had to renew his power by seizing the hands of the image of Marduk in his great temple of Esagila at Babylon. Even when Babylon passed under the power of Assyria, the monarchs of that country were expected to legalise their claim to the throne every year by coming to Babylon and performing the ancient ceremony at the New Year festival, and some of them found the obligation so burdensome that rather than discharge it they renounced the title of king altogether and contented themselves with the humbler one of Governor.[1] Further, it would appear that in remote times, though not within the historical period, the kings of Babylon or their barbarous predecessors forfeited not merely their crown but their life at the end of a year's tenure of office. At least this is the conclusion to which the following evidence seems to point. According to the historian Berosus, who as a Babylonian priest spoke with ample knowledge, there was annually celebrated in Babylon a festival called the Sacaea. It began on the sixteenth day of the month Lous, and lasted for five days. During these five days masters and servants changed places, the servants giving orders and the masters obeying them. A prisoner condemned to death was dressed in the king's robes, seated on the king's throne, allowed to issue whatever commands he pleased, to eat, drink, and enjoy himself, and to lie with the king's concubines. But at the end of the five days he was stripped of his royal robes, scourged, and hanged or impaled. During his brief term of office he bore the title of Zoganes.[2] This custom might perhaps have been explained as merely a grim jest perpetrated in a season of jollity at the expense of an unhappy criminal. But one circumstance—the leave given to the mock king to enjoy the king's concubines—is decisive against this interpretation. Considering the jealous seclusion of an oriental despot's harem we may be quite certain that permission to invade it would never have been granted by the despot, least of all to a condemned criminal, except for the very gravest cause. This cause could hardly be other than that the condemned man was about to die in the king's stead, and that to make the substitution perfect it was necessary he should enjoy the full rights of royalty during his brief reign. There is nothing surprising in this substitution. The rule that the king must be put to death either on the appearance of any symptom of bodily decay or at the end of a fixed period is certainly one which, sooner or later, the kings would seek to abolish or modify. We have observed that in Ethiopia and in Sofala the rule was boldly set aside by enlightened monarchs; and that in Calicut the old custom of killing the king at the end of twelve years was changed into a permission granted to any one at the end of the twelve years' period to attack the king, and, in the event of killing him, to reign in his stead; though, as the king took care at these times to be surrounded by his guards, the permission was little more than a form. Another way of modifying the stern old rule is seen in the Babylonian custom just described. When the time drew near for the king to be put to death (in Babylon this appears to have been at the end of a single year's reign) he abdicated for a few days, during which a temporary king reigned and suffered in his stead. At first the temporary king may have been an innocent person, possibly a member of the king's own family; but with the growth of civilisation the sacrifice of an innocent person would be revolting to the public sentiment, and accordingly a condemned criminal would be invested with the brief and fatal sovereignty. In the sequel we shall find other examples of a dying criminal representing a dying god. For we must not forget that, as the case of the Shilluk kings clearly shews, the king is slain in his character of a god or a demigod, his death and resurrection, as the only means of perpetuating the divine life unimpaired, being deemed necessary for the salvation of his people and the world.

A vestige of a practice of putting the king to death at the end of a year's reign appears to have survived in the festival called Macahity, which used to be celebrated in Hawaii during the last month of the year. About a hundred years ago a Russian voyager described the custom as follows: "The taboo Macahity is not unlike to our festival of Christmas. It continues a whole month, during which the people amuse themselves with dances, plays, and sham-fights of every kind. The king must open this festival wherever he is. On this occasion his majesty dresses himself in his richest cloak and helmet, and is paddled in a canoe along the shore, followed sometimes by many of his subjects. He embarks early, and must finish his excursion at sun-rise. The strongest and most expert of the warriors is chosen to receive him on his landing. This warrior watches the canoe along the beach; and as soon as the king lands, and has thrown off his cloak, he darts his spear at him, from a distance of about thirty paces, and the king must either catch the spear in his hand, or suffer from it: there is no jesting in the business. Having caught it, he carries it under his arm, with the sharp end downwards, into the temple or *heavoo*. On his entrance, the assembled multitude begin their sham-fights, and immediately the air is obscured by clouds of spears, made for the occasion with blunted ends. Hamamea [the king] has been frequently advised to abolish this ridiculous ceremony, in which he risks his life every year; but to no effect. His answer always is, that he is as able to catch a spear as any one on the island is to throw it at him. During the Macahity, all punishments are remitted throughout the country; and no person can leave the place in which he commences these holidays, let the affair be ever so important."[3]

That a king should regularly have been put to death at the close of a year's reign will hardly appear improbable when we learn that to this day there is still a kingdom in which the reign and the life of the sovereign are limited to a single day. In Ngoio, a province of the ancient kingdom of Congo in West Africa, the rule obtains that the chief who assumes the cap of sovereignty is always killed on the night after his coronation. The right of succession lies with the chief of the Musurongo; but we need not wonder that he does not exercise it, and that the throne stands vacant. "No one likes to lose his life for a few hours' glory on the Ngoio throne."[4]

THE SLAYING OF THE KING IN LEGEND

195. If a custom of putting kings to death at the end of a set term has prevailed in many lands, it is natural enough that reminiscences of it should survive in tradition long after the custom itself has been abolished. In the *High History of the Holy Grail* we read how Lancelot roamed through strange lands and forests seeking adventures till he came to a fair and wide plain lying without a city that seemed of right great lordship. As he rode across the plain the people came forth from the city to welcome him with the sound of flutes and viols and many instruments of music. When he asked them what meant all this joy, " 'Sir,' said they, 'all this joy is made along of you, and all these instruments of music are moved to joy and sound of gladness for your coming.' 'But wherefore for me?' saith Lancelot. 'That shall you know well betimes,' say they. 'This city began to burn and to melt in one of the houses from the very same hour that our king was dead, nor might the fire be quenched, nor ever will be quenched until such time as we have a king that shall be lord of the city and of the honour thereunto belonging, and on New Year's Day behoveth him to be crowned in the midst of the fire, and then shall the fire be quenched, for otherwise may it never be put out nor extinguished. Wherefore have we come to meet you to give you the royalty, for we have been told that you are a good knight.' 'Lords,' saith Lancelot, 'of such a kingdom have I no need, and God defend me from it.' 'Sir,' say they, 'you may not be defended thereof, for you come into this land at hazard, and great grief would it be that so good a land as you see this is were burnt and melted away by the default of one single man, and the lordship is right great, and this will be right great worship to yourself, that on New Year's Day you should be crowned in the fire and thus save this city and this great people, and thereof shall you have great praise.' Much marvelleth Lancelot of this that they say. They come round about him on all sides and lead him into the city. The ladies and damsels are mounted to the windows of the great houses and make great joy, and say the one to another 'Look at the new king here that they are leading in. Now will he quench the fire on New Year's Day.' 'Lord!' say the most part, 'what great pity is it of so comely a knight that he shall end on such-wise!' 'Be still!' say the others. 'Rather should there be great joy that so fair city as is this should be saved by his death, for prayer will be made throughout all the kingdom for his soul for ever!' Therewith they lead him to the palace with right great joy and say that they will crown him. Lancelot found the palace all strewn with rushes and hung about with curtains of rich cloths of silk, and the lords of the city all apparelled to do him homage. But he refuseth right stoutly, and saith that their king nor their lord will he never be in no such sort. Thereupon behold you a dwarf that entereth into the city, leading one of the fairest dames that be in any kingdom, and asketh whereof this joy and this murmuring may be. They tell him they are fain to make the knight king, but that he is not minded to allow them, and they tell him the whole manner of the fire. The dwarf and the damsel are alighted, then they mount up to the palace. The dwarf calleth the provosts of the city and the greater lords. 'Lords,' saith he, 'sith that this knight is not willing to be king, I will be so willingly, and I will govern the city at your pleasure and do whatsoever you have devised to do.' 'In faith, sith that the knight refuseth this honour and you desire to have it, willingly will we grant it you, and he may go his way and his road, for herein do we declare him wholly quit.' Therewithal they set the crown on the dwarf's head, and Lancelot maketh great joy thereof. He taketh his leave, and they commend him to God, and so remounteth he on his horse and goeth his way through the midst of the city all armed. The dames and damsels say that he would not be king for that he had no mind to die so soon."[1]

A story of the same sort is told of Ujjain, the ancient capital of Malwa in Western India, where the renowned King Vikramaditya is said to have held his court, gathering about him a circle of poets and scholars.[2] Tradition has it that once on a time an arch-fiend, with a legion of devils at his command, took up his abode in Ujjain, the inhabitants of which he vexed and devoured. Many had fallen a prey to him, and others had abandoned the country to save their lives. The once populous city was fast being converted into a desert. At last the principal citizens, meeting in council, besought the fiend to reduce his rations to one man a day, who would be duly delivered up to him in order that the rest might enjoy a day's repose. The demon closed with the offer, but required that the man whose turn it was to be sacrificed should mount the throne and exercise the royal power for a single day, all the grandees of the kingdom submitting to his commands, and everybody yielding him the most absolute obedience. Necessity obliged the citizens to accept these hard terms; their names were entered on a list; every day one of them in his turn ruled from morning to night, and was then devoured by the demon.

Now it happened by great good luck that a caravan of merchants from

Gujerat halted on the banks of a river not far from the city. They were attended by a servant who was no other than Vikramaditya. At nightfall the jackals began to howl as usual, and one of them said in his own tongue, "In two hours a human corpse will shortly float down this river, with four rubies of great price at his belt, and a turquois ring on his finger. He who will give me that corpse to devour will bear sway over the seven lands." Vikramaditya, knowing the language of birds and beasts, understood what the jackal said, gave the corpse to the beast to devour, and took possession of the ring and the rubies. Next day he entered the town, and, traversing the streets, observed a troop of horse under arms, forming a royal escort, at the door of a potter's house. The grandees of the city were there, and with them was the garrison. They were in the act of inducing the son of the potter to mount an elephant and proceed in state to the palace. But strange to say, instead of being pleased at the honour conferred on their son, the potter and his wife stood on the threshold weeping and sobbing most bitterly. Learning how things stood, the chivalrous Vikramaditya was touched with pity, and offered to accept the fatal sovereignty instead of the potter's son, saying that he would either deliver the people from the tyranny of the demon or perish in the attempt. Accordingly he donned the kingly robes, assumed all the badges of sovereignty, and, mounting the elephant, rode in great pomp to the palace, where he seated himself on the throne, while the dignitaries of the kingdom discharged their duties in his presence. At night the fiend arrived as usual to eat him up. But Vikramaditya was more than a match for him, and after a terrific combat the fiend capitulated and agreed to quit the city. Next morning the people on coming to the palace were astonished to find Vikramaditya still alive. They thought he must be no common mortal, but some superhuman being, or the descendant of a great king. Grateful to him for their deliverance they bestowed the kingdom on him, and he reigned happily over them.[3]

Tales of the foregoing sort might be dismissed as fictions designed to amuse a leisure hour, were it not for their remarkable agreement with beliefs and customs which, as we have seen, still exist, or are known to have existed in former times. That agreement can hardly be accidental. We seem to be justified, therefore, in assuming that stories of the kind really rest on a basis of facts, however much these facts may have been distorted or magnified in passing through the mind of the story-teller, who is naturally more concerned to amuse than instruct his hearers. Even the legend of a line of kings of whom each reigned for a single day, and was sacrificed at night for the good of the people, will hardly seem incredible when we remember that to this day a kingdom is held on a similar tenure in west Africa, though under modern conditions the throne stands vacant. And while it would be vain to rely on such stories for exact historical details, yet they may help us in a general way to understand the practical working of an institution which to civilised men

he returned to the palace, and the real King thereupon invested him with a new white gown and turban. After receiving them the slave renounced his pseudo-royal privileges until the following year.[7a]

At the installation of a prince of Carinthia, a peasant, in whose family the office was hereditary, ascended a marble stone which stood surrounded by meadows in a spacious valley; on his right stood a black mother-cow, on his left a lean ugly mare. A rustic crowd gathered about him. Then the future prince, dressed as a peasant and carrying a shepherd's staff, drew near, attended by courtiers and magistrates. On perceiving him the peasant called out, "Who is this whom I see coming so proudly along?" The people answered, "The prince of the land." The peasant was then prevailed on to surrender the marble seat to the prince on condition of receiving sixty pence, the cow and mare, and exemption from taxes. But before yielding his place he gave the prince a light blow on the cheek.[8]

In the foregoing cases the temporary king is appointed annually in accordance with a regular custom. But in other cases the appointment is made only to meet a special emergency, such as to relieve the real king from some actual or threatened evil by diverting it to a substitute, who takes his place on the throne for a short time. Thus Shah Abbas the Great, the most eminent of all the kings of Persia, who reigned from 1586 to 1628 A.D., being warned by his astrologers in the year 1591 that a serious danger impended over him, attempted to avert the omen by abdicating the throne and appointing a certain unbeliever named Yusoofee, probably a Christian, to reign in his stead. The substitute was accordingly crowned, and for three days, if we may trust the Persian historians, he enjoyed not only the name and the state but the power of the king. At the end of his brief reign he was put to death: the decree of the stars was fulfilled by this sacrifice; and Abbas, who reascended his throne in a most propitious hour, was promised by his astrologers a long and glorious reign.[9]

197. A point to notice about the temporary kings described in the foregoing pages is that in two places (Cambodia and Jambi) they come of a stock which is believed to be akin to the royal family. If the view here taken of the origin of these temporary kingships is correct, we can easily understand why the king's substitute should sometimes be of the same race as the king. When the king first succeeded in getting the life of another accepted as a sacrifice instead of his own, he would have to shew that the death of that other would serve the purpose quite as well as his own would have done. Now it was as a god or demigod that the king had to die; therefore the substitute who died for him had to be invested, at least for the occasion, with the divine attributes of the king. But no one could so well represent the king in his divine character as his son, who might be supposed to share the divine afflatus of his father. No one, therefore, could so appropriately die for the king and, through him, for the whole people, as the king's son.

As was seen earlier, Aun, King of Sweden, is said to have sacrificed nine of his sons to Odin at Upsala that his own life might be spared. After he had sacrificed his second son he received from the god an answer that he should live so long as he gave him one of his sons every ninth year. When he had sacrificed his seventh son, he still lived, but was so feeble that he could not walk but had to be carried in a chair. Then he offered up his eighth son, and lived nine years more, lying in his bed. After that he sacrificed his ninth son, and lived another nine years, but so that he drank out of a horn like a weaned child. He now wished to sacrifice his only remaining son to Odin, but the Swedes would not allow him. So he died and was buried in a mound at Upsala.[1]

In ancient Greece there seems to have been at least one kingly house of great antiquity of which the eldest sons were always liable to be sacrificed in place of their royal sires. When Xerxes was marching through Thessaly at the head of his mighty host to attack the Spartans at Thermopylae, he came to the town of Alus. Here he was shewn the sanctuary of Laphystian Zeus, about which his guides told him a strange tale. It ran somewhat as follows. Once upon a time the king of the country, by name Athamas, married a wife Nephele, and had by her a son called Phrixus and a daughter named Helle. Afterwards he took to himself a second wife called Ino, by whom he had two sons, Learchus and Melicertes. But his second wife was jealous of her step-children, Phrixus and Helle, and plotted their death. She went about very cunningly to compass her bad end. First of all she persuaded the women of the country to roast the seed corn secretly before it was committed to the ground. So next year no crops came up and the people died of famine. Then the king sent messengers to the oracle at Delphi to enquire the cause of the dearth. But the wicked step-mother bribed the messenger to give out as the answer of the god that the dearth would never cease till the children of Athamas by his first wife had been sacrificed to Zeus. When Athamas heard that, he sent for the children, who were with the sheep. But a ram with a fleece of gold opened his lips, and speaking with the voice of a man warned the children of their danger. So they mounted the ram and fled with him over land and sea. As they flew over the sea, the girl slipped from the animal's back, and falling into water was drowned. But her brother Phrixus was brought safe to the land of Colchis, where reigned a child of the Sun. Phrixus married the king's daughter, and she bore him a son Cytisorus. And there he sacrificed the ram with the golden fleece to Zeus the God of Flight; but some will have it that he sacrificed the animal to Laphystian Zeus. The golden fleece itself he gave to his wife's father, who nailed it to an oak tree, guarded by a sleepless dragon in a sacred grove of Ares. Meanwhile at home an oracle had commanded that King Athamas himself should be sacrificed as an expiatory offering for the whole country. So

Phoenicians call El, being king of the land and having an only-begotten son called Jeoud (for in the Phoenician tongue Jeoud signifies 'only-begotten'), dressed him in royal robes and sacrificed him upon an altar in a time of war, when the country was in great danger from the enemy."[6] When the king of Moab was besieged by the Israelites and hard beset, he took his eldest son, who should have reigned in his stead, and offered him for a burnt offering on the wall.[7]

With the preceding evidence before us we may safely infer that a custom of allowing a king to kill his son, as a substitute or vicarious sacrifice for himself, would be in no way exceptional or surprising. And it would be entirely in accordance with analogy if, long after the barbarous custom had been dropped by others, it continued to be observed by kings, who remain in many respects the representatives of a vanished world, solitary pinnacles that topple over the rising waste of waters under which the past lies buried. We have seen that in Greece two families of royal descent remained liable to furnish human victims from their number down to a time when the rest of their fellow countrymen and countrywomen ran hardly more risk of being sacrificed than passengers in Cheapside at present run of being hurried into St. Paul's or Bow Church and immolated on the altar. A final mitigation of the custom would be to substitute condemned criminals for innocent victims. Such a substitution is known to have taken place in the human sacrifices annually offered in Rhodes to Baal,[8] and we have seen good grounds for believing that the criminal, who perished on the cross or the gallows at Babylon, died instead of the king in whose royal robes he had been allowed to masquerade for a few days.

SUCCESSION TO THE KINGSHIP

198. To the view that in early times, and among barbarous races, kings have frequently been put to death at the end of a short reign, it may be objected that such a custom would tend to the extinction of the royal family. The objection may be met by observing, first, that the kingship is often not confined to one family, but may be shared in turn by several; second, that the office is frequently not hereditary, but is open to men of any family, even to foreigners, who may fulfil the requisite conditions, such as marrying a princess or vanquishing the king in battle; and, third, that even if the custom did tend to the extinction of a dynasty, that is not a consideration which would prevent its observance among people less provident of the future and less heedful of human life than ourselves. Many races, like many individuals, have indulged in practices which must in the end destroy them. Not to mention such customs as collective suicide and the prohibition of marriage, both of which may be set down to religious mania, it is recorded by the first missionaries that the Polynesians killed two-thirds of their children.[1] In some parts of East Africa the proportion of infants massacred at birth is said to be the same. Only children born in certain presentations are allowed to live.[2] The Jagas, a conquering tribe in Angola, are reported to have put to death all their children, without exception, in order that the women might not be cumbered with babies on the march. They recruited their numbers by adopting boys and girls of thirteen or fourteen years of age, whose parents they had killed and eaten.[3] Among the Mbaya Indians of South America the women used to murder all their children except the last, or the one they believed to be the last. If one of them had another child afterwards, she killed it.[4] We need not wonder that this practice entirely destroyed a branch of the Mbaya nation, who had been for many years the most formidable enemies of the Spaniards.[5] Among the Lengua Indians of the Gran Chaco the missionaries discovered what they describe as "a carefully planned system of racial suicide, by the practice of infanticide, by abortion, and other methods."[6]

199. The explanation here given of the custom of killing divine persons assumes, or at least is readily combined with, the idea that the soul of the slain divinity is transmitted to his successor. Of this transmission I have no direct proof except in the case of the Shilluk, among whom the practice of killing the divine king prevails in a typical form, and with whom it is a fundamental article of faith that the soul of the divine founder of the dynasty is immanent in every one of his slain successors. But if this is the only actual example of such a belief which I can adduce, analogy seems to render it probable that a similar succession to the soul of the slain god has been supposed to take place in other instances, though direct evidence of it is wanting. For it has been already shewn that the soul of the incarnate deity is often supposed to transmigrate at death into another incarnation;[1] and if this takes place when the death is a natural one, there seems no reason why it should not take place when the death has been brought about by violence. Certainly the idea that the soul of a dying person may be transmitted to his successor is perfectly familiar to primitive peoples. In Nias the eldest son usually succeeds his father in the chieftainship. But if from any bodily or mental defect the eldest son is disqualified for ruling, the father determines in his lifetime which of his sons shall succeed him. In order, however, to establish his right of succession, it is necessary that the son upon whom his father's choice falls shall catch in his mouth or in a bag the last breath, and with it the soul, of the dying chief. For whoever catches his last breath is chief equally with the appointed successor. Hence the other brothers, and sometimes also strangers, crowd round the dying man to catch his soul as it passes. The houses in Nias are raised above the ground on posts, and it has happened that when the dying man lay with his face on the floor, one of the candidates has bored a hole in the floor and sucked in the chief's last breath through a bamboo tube. When the chief has no son, his soul is caught in a bag, which is fastened to an image made to represent the deceased; the soul is then believed to pass into the image.[2]

Amongst the Takilis or Carrier Indians of North-West America, when a corpse was burned the priest pretended to catch the soul of the deceased in his hands, which he closed with many gesticulations. He then communicated the captured soul to the dead man's successor by throwing his hands towards and blowing upon him.[3] Amongst the Seminoles of Florida when a woman died in childbed the infant was held over her face to receive her parting spirit.[4] When infants died within a month or two of birth, the Huron Indians did not lay them in bark coffins on poles, as they did with other corpses, but buried them beside the paths, in order that they might secretly enter into the wombs of passing women and be born again.[5] The Tonquinese cover the face of a dying person with a handkerchief, and at the moment when he breathes his last, they fold up the handkerchief carefully, thinking that they have caught the soul in it.[6] The Romans caught the breath of dying friends in their mouths, and so received into themselves the soul of the departed.[7] The same custom is said to be still practised in Lancashire.[8]

200. In conformity with this general principle, provision is often made for the ghostly succession of kings and chiefs. On the seventh day after the death of a king of Gingiro the sorcerers bring to his successor, wrapt in a piece of silk, a worm which they say comes from the nose of the dead king; and they make the new king kill the worm by squeezing its head between his teeth.[1] The ceremony seems to be intended to convey the spirit of the deceased monarch to his successor.

Every year at the new moon of September the king of Sofala in eastern Africa used to perform obsequies for the kings, his predecessors, on the top of a high mountain, where they were buried. In the course of the lamentations for the dead, the soul of the king who had died last used to enter into a man who imitated the deceased monarch, both in voice and gesture. The living king conversed with this man as with his dead father, consulting him in regard to the affairs of the kingdom and receiving his oracular replies.[2]

Sometimes it would appear that the spiritual link between a king and the souls of his predecessors is formed by the possession of some part of their persons. In southern Celebes, for example, the royal regalia often consist of corporeal portions of deceased rajahs, which are treasured as sacred relics and confer the right to the throne.[3] Similarly among the Sakalavas of southern Madagascar a vertebra of the neck, a nail, and a lock of hair of a deceased king are placed in a crocodile's tooth and carefully kept along with the similar relics of his predecessors in a house set apart for the purpose. The possession of these relics constitutes the right to the throne.[4]

Among the Masai of East Africa, when an important chief has been dead and buried for a year, his eldest son or other successor removes the skull of the deceased, while he at the same time offers a sacrifice and a libation with goat's blood, milk, and honey. He then carefully secretes the skull, the possession of which is understood to confirm him in power and to impart to him some of the wisdom of his predecessor.⁵ When the Alake or king of Abeokuta in West Africa dies, the principal men decapitate his body, and placing the head in a large earthen vessel deliver it to the new sovereign; it becomes his fetish and he is bound to pay it honours.⁶ Similarly, when the Jaga or king of Cassange, in Angola, has been put to death an official extracts a tooth from the deceased monarch and presents it to his successor, who deposits it along with the teeth of former kings in a box, which is the sole property of the crown and without which no Jaga can legitimately exercise the regal power.⁷ Sometimes, in order apparently that the new sovereign may inherit more surely the magical and other virtues of the royal line, he is required to eat a piece of his dead predecessor. Thus at Abeokuta not only was the head of the late king presented to his successor, but the tongue was cut out and given him to eat. A custom of the same sort is still practised at Ibadan, a large town in the interior of Lagos, West Africa. When the king dies his head is cut off and sent to his nominal suzerain, the Alafin of Oyo, the paramount king of Yoruba land; but his heart is eaten by his successor.⁸

THE MUMMERS' PLAY

201. The custom of periodically killing the human representatives of the tree-spirit has left unmistakeable traces in the rural festivals of the peasantry in Northern Europe.

At Niederpöring, in Lower Bavaria, the Whitsuntide representative of the tree-spirit—the so-called *Pfingstl*—had finally to wade into the brook up to his middle; whereupon one of his attendants, standing on the bridge, pretended to cut off his head.¹ At Wurmlingen, in Swabia, a score of young fellows dress themselves on Whit-Monday in white shirts and white trousers, with red scarves round their waists and swords hanging from the scarves. They ride on horseback into the wood, led by two trumpeters blowing their trumpets. In the wood they cut down leafy oak branches, in which they envelop from head to foot him who was the last of their number to ride out of the village. His legs, however, are encased separately, so that he may be able to mount his horse again. Further, they give him a long artificial neck, with an artificial head and a false face on the top of it. Then a May-tree is cut, generally an aspen or beech about ten feet high; and being decked with coloured handkerchiefs and ribbons it is entrusted to a special "May-bearer." The cavalcade then returns with music and song to the village. Amongst the personages who figure in the procession are a Moorish king with a sooty face and a crown on his head, a Dr. Iron-Beard, a corporal, and an executioner. They halt on the village green, and each of the characters makes a speech in rhyme. The executioner announces that the leaf-clad man has been condemned to death, and cuts off his false head. Then the riders race to the May-tree, which has been set up a little way off. The first man who succeeds in wrenching it from the ground as he gallops past keeps it with all its decorations. The ceremony is observed every second or third year.[2]

In Saxony and Thüringen there is a Whitsuntide ceremony called "chasing the Wild Man out of the bush," or "fetching the Wild Man out of the Wood." A young fellow is enveloped in leaves or moss and called the Wild Man. He hides in the wood and the other lads of the village go out to seek him. They find him, lead him captive out of the wood, and fire at him with blank muskets. He falls like dead to the ground, but a lad dressed as a doctor bleeds him, and he comes to life again. At this they rejoice, and, binding him fast on a waggon, take him to the village, where they tell all the people how they have caught the Wild Man. At every house they receive a gift.[3] In the Erzgebirge the following custom was annually observed at Shrovetide about the beginning of the seventeenth century. Two men disguised as Wild Men, the one in brushwood and moss, and the other in straw, were led about the streets, and at last taken to the market-place, where they were chased up and down, shot and stabbed. Before falling they reeled about with strange gestures and spirted blood on the people from bladders which they carried. When they were down, the huntsmen placed them on boards and carried them to the ale-house, the miners marching beside them and winding blasts on their mining tools as if they had taken a noble head of game.[4] A very similar Shrovetide custom is still observed near Schluckenau in Bohemia. A man dressed up as a Wild Man is chased through several streets till he comes to a narrow lane across which a cord is stretched. He stumbles over the cord and, falling to the ground, is overtaken and caught by his pursuers. The executioner runs up and stabs with his sword a bladder filled with blood which the Wild Man wears round his body; so the Wild Man dies, while a stream of blood reddens the ground. Next day a straw-man, made up to look like the Wild Man, is placed on a litter, and, accompanied by a great crowd, is taken to a pool into which it is thrown by the executioner. The ceremony is called "burying the Carnival."[5]

But perhaps, for our purpose, the most instructive of these mimic executions is the following Bohemian one, which has been described by Mannhardt. In some places of the Pilsen district (Bohemia) on Whit-Monday the King is dressed in bark, ornamented with flowers and ribbons; he wears a crown of gilt paper and rides a horse, which is also decked with flowers. Attended by a judge, an executioner, and other characters, and followed by a train of soldiers, all mounted, he rides to the village square, where a hut or arbour of green boughs has been erected under the May-trees, which are firs, freshly cut, peeled to the top, and dressed with flowers and ribbons. Here the girls of the village are criticised, a frog is beheaded (as a rain-charm, in Mannhardt's view), and then the cavalcade rides to a place previously determined upon, in a straight, broad street. Here they draw up in two lines and the King takes to flight. He is given a short start and rides off at full speed, pursued by the whole troop. If they fail to catch him he remains King for another year, and his companions must pay his score at the ale-house in the evening. But if they overtake and catch him he is scourged with hazel rods or beaten with the wooden swords and compelled to dismount. Then the executioner asks, "Shall I behead this King?" The answer is given, "Behead him"; the executioner brandishes his axe, and with the words, "One, two, three, let the King headless be!" he strikes off the King's crown. Amid the loud cries of the bystanders the King sinks to the ground; then he is laid on a bier and carried to the nearest farmhouse.[6]

In most of the personages who are thus slain in mimicry it is impossible not to recognise representatives of the tree-spirit or spirit of vegetation, as he is supposed to manifest himself in spring. The bark, leaves, and flowers in which the actors are dressed, and the season of the year at which they appear, shew that they belong to the same class as the Grass King, King of the May, Jack-in-the-Green, and other representatives of the vernal spirit of vegetation which we examined in an earlier chapter. As if to remove any possible doubt on this head, we find that in two cases these slain men are brought into direct connexion with May-trees, which are the impersonal, as the May King, Grass King, and so forth, are the personal representatives of the tree-spirit.

But what is the object of slaying the spirit of vegetation at any time and above all in spring, when his services are most wanted? The only probable answer to this question seems to be given in the explanation already proposed of the custom of killing the divine king or priest. The divine life, incarnate in a material and mortal body, is liable to be tainted and corrupted by the weakness of the frail medium in which it is for a time enshrined; and if it is to be saved from the increasing enfeeblement which it must necessarily share with its human incarnation as he advances in years, it must be detached from him before, or at least as soon as, he exhibits signs of decay, in order to be transferred to a vigorous successor. This is done by killing the old representative of the god and conveying the divine spirit from him to a new incarnation. The killing of the god, that is, of his human incarnation, is therefore merely a necessary step to his revival or resurrection in a better form. Far from being an extinction of the divine spirit, it is only the beginning of a purer and stronger manifestation of it. In every one of these instances the life of the god-man is prolonged on condition of his shewing, in a severe physical contest of fight or flight, that his bodily strength is not decayed.

"Burying the Carnival"

202. Besides the ceremonies already described there are two kindred sets of observances in which the simulated death of a divine or supernatural being is a conspicuous feature. In one of them the being whose death is dramatically represented is a personification of the Carnival; in the other it is Death himself. The former ceremony falls naturally at the end of the Carnival, either on the last day of that merry season, namely Shrove Tuesday, or on the first day of Lent, namely Ash Wednesday. The date of the other ceremony—the Carrying or Driving out of Death, as it is commonly called—is not so uniformly fixed. Generally it is the fourth Sunday in Lent, which hence goes by the name of Dead Sunday; but in some places the celebration falls a week earlier, in others, as among the Czechs of Bohemia, a week later, while in certain German villages of Moravia it is held on the first Sunday after Easter. Perhaps, as has been suggested, the date may originally have been variable, depending on the appearance of the first swallow or some other herald of the spring. We shall first take examples of the mimic death of the Carnival, which always falls before the other in the calendar.

At Frosinone, in Latium, about half-way between Rome and Naples, the dull monotony of life in a provincial Italian town is agreeably broken on the last day of the Carnival by the ancient festival known as the *Radica*. About four o'clock in the afternoon the town band, playing lively tunes and followed by a great crowd, proceeds to the Piazza del Plebiscito, where is the Sub-Prefecture as well as the rest of the Government buildings. Here, in the middle of the square, the eyes of the expectant multitude are greeted by the sight of an immense car decked with many-coloured festoons and drawn by four horses. Mounted on the car is a huge chair, on which sits enthroned the majestic figure of the Carnival, a man of stucco about nine feet high with a rubicund and smiling countenance. Enormous boots, a tin helmet like those which grace the heads of officers of the Italian marine, and a coat of many colours embellished with strange devices, adorn the outward man of this stately personage. His left hand rests on the arm of the chair, while with his right he gracefully salutes the crowd, being moved to this act of civility by a string which is pulled by a man who modestly shrinks from publicity under the mercy-seat. And now the crowd, surging excitedly round the car, gives vent to its feelings in wild cries of joy, gentle and simple being mixed up together and all dancing furiously the *Saltarello*. A special feature of the festival is that every one must carry in his hand what is called a *radica* ("root"), by which is meant a huge leaf of the aloe or rather the agave. Any one who ventured into the crowd without such a leaf would be unceremoniously hustled out of it, unless indeed he bore as a substitute a large cabbage at the end of a long stick or a bunch of grass curiously plaited. When the multitude, after a short turn, has escorted the slow-moving car to the gate of the Sub-Prefecture, they halt, and the car, jolting over the uneven ground, rumbles into the courtyard. A hush now falls on the crowd, their subdued voices sounding, according to the description of one who has heard them, like the murmur of a troubled sea. All eyes are turned anxiously to the door from which the Sub-Prefect himself and the other representatives of the majesty of the law are expected to issue and pay their homage to the hero of the hour. A few moments of suspense and then a storm of cheers and hand-clapping salutes the appearance of the dignitaries, as they file out and, descending the staircase, take their place in the procession. The hymn of the Carnival is now thundered out, after which, amid a deafening roar, aloe leaves and cabbages are whirled aloft and descend impartially on the heads of the just and the unjust, who lend fresh zest to the proceedings by engaging in a free fight. When these preliminaries have been concluded to the satisfaction of all concerned, the procession gets under weigh. The rear is brought up by a cart laden with barrels of wine and policemen, the latter engaged in the congenial task of serving out wine to all who ask for it, while a most internecine struggle, accompanied by a copious discharge of yells, blows, and blasphemy, goes on among the surging crowd at the cart's tail in their anxiety not to miss the glorious opportunity of intoxicating themselves at the public expense. Finally, after the procession has paraded the principal streets in this majestic manner, the effigy of Carnival is taken to the middle of a public square, stripped of his finery, laid on a pile of wood, and burnt amid the cries of the multitude, who thundering out once more the song of the Carnival fling their so-called "roots" on the pyre and give themselves up without restraint to the pleasures of the dance.[1]

In the Abruzzi a pasteboard figure of the Carnival is carried by four gravediggers with pipes in their mouths and bottles of wine slung at their shoulderbelts. In front walks the wife of the Carnival, dressed in mourning and dissolved in tears. From time to time the company halts, and while the wife addresses the sympathising public, the grave-diggers refresh the inner man with a pull at the bottle. In the open square the mimic corpse is laid on a pyre, and to the roll of drums, the shrill screams of the women, and the gruffer cries of the men a light is set to it. While the figure burns, chestnuts are thrown about among the crowd. Sometimes the Carnival is represented by a strawman at the top of a pole which is borne through the town by a troop of mummers in the course of the afternoon. When evening comes on, four of the mummers hold out a quilt or sheet by the corners, and the figure of the Carnival is made to tumble into it. The procession is then resumed, the performers weeping crocodile tears and emphasising the poignancy of their grief by the help of saucepans and dinner bells. Sometimes, again, in the Abruzzi the dead Carnival is personified by a living man who lies in a coffin, attended by another who acts the priest and dispenses holy water in great profusion from a bathing tub.[2] In Malta the death of the Carnival used to be mourned by women on the last day of the merry festival. Clad from head to foot in black mantles, they carried through the streets of the city the linen effigy of a corpse, stuffed with straw or hay and decked with leaves and oranges. As they carried it, they chanted dirges, stopping after every verse to howl like professional mourners. The custom came to an end about the year 1737.[3]

A ceremony of the same sort is observed in Provence on Ash Wednesday. An effigy called Caramantran, whimsically attired, is drawn in a chariot or borne on a litter, accompanied by the populace in grotesque costumes, who carry gourds full of wine and drain them with all the marks, real or affected, of intoxication. At the head of the procession are some men disguised as judges and barristers, and a tall gaunt personage who masquerades as Lent; behind them follow young people mounted on miserable hacks and attired as mourners who pretend to bewail the fate that is in store for Caramantran. In the principal square the procession halts, the tribunal is constituted, and Caramantran placed at the bar. After a formal trial he is sentenced to death amid the groans of the mob; the barrister who defended him embraces his client for the last time: the officers of justice do their duty: the condemned is set with his back to a wall and hurried into eternity under a shower of stones. The sea or a river receives his mangled remains.[4] At Lussac in the department of Vienne young people, attired in long mourning robes and with woebegone countenances, carry an effigy down to the river on Ash Wednesday and throw it into the river, crying, "Carnival is dead! Carnival is dead!"[5] Throughout nearly the whole of the Ardennes it was and still is customary on Ash Wednesday to burn an effigy which is supposed to represent the Carnival, while appropriate verses are sung round about the blazing figure. Very often an attempt is made to fashion the effigy in the likeness of the husband who is reputed to be least faithful to his wife of any in the village. As might perhaps have been anticipated, the distinction of being selected for portraiture under these painful circumstances has a slight tendency to breed domestic jars, especially when the portrait is burnt in front of the house of the gay deceiver whom it represents, while a powerful chorus of caterwauls, groans, and other melodious sounds bears public testimony to the opinion which his friends and neighbours entertain of his private virtues. In some villages of the Ardennes a young man of flesh and blood, dressed up in hay and straw, used to act the part of Shrove Tuesday (*Mardi Gras*), as the personification of the Carnival is often called in France after the last day of the period which he personates. He was brought before a mock tribunal, and being condemned to death was placed with his back to a wall, like a soldier at a military execution, and fired at with blank cartridges. At Vrigne-aux-Bois one of these harmless buffoons, named Thierry, was accidentally killed by a wad that had been left in a musket of the firing-party. When poor Shrove Tuesday dropped under the fire, the applause was loud and long, he did it so naturally; but when he did not get up again, they ran to him and found him a corpse. Since then there have been no more of these mock executions in the Ardennes.[6] In Franche-Comté people used to make an effigy of Shrove Tuesday on Ash Wednesday, and carry it about the streets to the accompaniment of songs. Then they brought it to the public square, where the offender was tried in front of the town-hall. Judges muffled in old red curtains and holding big books in their hands pronounced sentence of death. The mode of execution varied with the place. Sometimes it was burning, sometimes drowning, sometimes decapitation. In the last case the effigy was provided with tubes of blood, which spouted gore at the critical moment, making a profound impression on the minds of children, some of whom wept bitterly at the sight. Meantime the onlookers uttered piercing cries and appeared to be plunged in the deepest grief. The proceedings generally wound up in the evening with a ball, which the young married people were obliged to provide for the public entertainment; otherwise their slumbers were apt to be disturbed by the discordant notes of a cat's concert chanted under their windows.[7]

In Normandy on the evening of Ash Wednesday it used to be the custom to hold a celebration called the Burial of Shrove Tuesday. A squalid effigy scantily clothed in rags, a battered old hat crushed down on his dirty face, his great round paunch stuffed with straw, represented the disreputable old rake who after a long course of dissipation was now about to suffer for his sins. Hoisted on the shoulders of a sturdy fellow, who pretended to stagger under the burden, this popular personification of the Carnival promenaded the streets for the last time in a manner the reverse of triumphal. Preceded by a drummer and accompanied by a jeering rabble, among whom the urchins and all the tag-rag and bobtail of the town mustered in great force, the figure was carried about by the flickering light of torches to the discordant din of shovels and tongs, pots and pans, horns and kettles, mingled with hootings, groans, and hisses. From time to time the procession halted, and a champion of morality accused the broken-down old sinner of all the excesses he had committed and for which he was now about to be burned alive. The culprit, having nothing to urge in his own defence, was thrown on the heap of straw, a torch was put to it, and a great blaze shot up, to the delight of the children who frisked round it screaming out some old popular verses about the death of the Carnival. Sometimes the effigy was rolled down the slope of a hill before being burnt.[8] At Saint-Lô the ragged effigy of Shrove Tuesday was followed by his widow, a big burly lout dressed as a woman with a crape veil, who emitted sounds of lamentation and woe in a stentorian voice. After being carried about the streets on a litter attended by a crowd of maskers, the figure was thrown into the River Vire.[9]

In Upper Brittany the burial of Shrove Tuesday or the Carnival is sometimes performed in a ceremonious manner. Four young fellows carry a strawman or one of their companions, and are followed by a funeral procession. A show is made of depositing the pretended corpse in the grave, after which the bystanders make believe to mourn, crying out in melancholy tones, "Ah! my poor little Shrove Tuesday!" The boy who played the part of Shrove Tuesday bears the name for the whole year.[10] At Lesneven in Lower Brittany it was formerly the custom on Ash Wednesday to burn a straw-man, covered with rags, after he had been promenaded about the town. He was followed by a representative of Shrove Tuesday clothed with sardines and cods' tails.[11] At Pontaven in Finistère an effigy representing the Carnival used to be thrown

selves in all their finery with flowers in their hair. Thus attired they repaired to the neighbouring town, carrying puppets which were adorned
with leaves and covered with white cloths. These they took from house to
house in pairs, stopping at every door where they expected to receive something, and singing a few lines in which they announced that it was Mid-Lent
and that they were about to throw Death into the water. When they had
collected some trifling gratuities they went to the river Regnitz and flung
the puppets representing Death into the stream. This was done to ensure a
fruitful and prosperous year; further, it was considered a safeguard against
pestilence and sudden death.[3] At Nuremberg girls of seven to eighteen years
of age go through the streets bearing a little open coffin, in which is a doll
hidden under a shroud. Others carry a beech branch, with an apple fastened
to it for a head, in an open box. They sing, "We carry Death into the water,
it is well," or "We carry Death into the water, carry him in and out again."[4]
In other parts of Bavaria the ceremony took place on the Saturday before
the fifth Sunday in Lent, and the performers were boys or girls, according
to the sex of the last person who died in the village. The figure was thrown
into water or buried in a secret place, for example, under moss in the
forest, that no one might find Death again. Then early on Sunday morning
the children went from house to house singing a song in which they announced the glad tidings that Death was gone.[5] In some parts of Bavaria
down to 1780 it was believed that a fatal epidemic would ensue if the custom of "Carrying out Death" were not observed.[6]

In some villages of Thüringen, on the fourth Sunday of Lent, the children used to carry a puppet of birchen twigs through the village, and then
threw it into a pool, while they sang, "We carry the old Death out behind
the herdsman's old house; we have got Summer, and Kroden's (?) power is
destroyed."[7] The custom of "Carrying out Death" was practised also in
Saxony. At Leipsic the bastards and public women used to make a straw
effigy of Death every year at Mid-Lent. This they carried through all the
streets with songs and shewed it to the young married women. Finally they
threw it into the river Parthe. By this ceremony they professed to make the
young wives fruitful, to purify the city, and to protect the inhabitants for
that year from plague and other epidemics.[8]

Ceremonies of the same sort are observed at Mid-Lent in Silesia. Thus
in many places the grown girls with the help of the young men dress up a
straw figure with women's clothes and carry it out of the village towards
the setting sun. At the boundary they strip it of its clothes, tear it in
pieces, and scattered the fragments about the fields. This is called "Burying
Death." As they carry the image out, they sing that they are about to bury
death under an oak, that he may depart from the people. Sometimes the
song runs that they are bearing death over hill and dale to return no more.
In the Polish neighborhood of Gross-Strehlitz the puppet is called Goik.

It is carried on horseback and thrown into the nearest water. The people think that the ceremony protects them from sickness of every sort in the coming year. In some Polish parts of Upper Silesia the effigy, representing an old woman, goes by the name of Marzana, the goddess of death. It is made in the house where the last death occurred, and is carried on a pole to the boundary of the village, where it is thrown into a pond or burnt.[9]

In Bohemia the children go out with a straw-man, representing Death, to the end of the village, where they burn it, singing—

> "Now carry we Death out of the village,
> The new Summer into the village,
> Welcome, dear Summer,
> Green little corn."[10]

At Tabor in Bohemia the figure of Death is carried out of the town and flung from a high rock into the water, while they sing—

> "Death swims on the water,
> Summer will soon be here,
> We carried Death away for you,
> We brought the Summer.
> And do thou, O holy Marketa,
> Give us a good year
> For wheat and for rye."[11]

In other parts of Bohemia they carry Death to the end of the village, singing—

> "We carry Death out of the village,
> And the New Year into the village.
> Dear Spring, we bid you welcome,
> Green grass, we bid you welcome."

Behind the village they erect a pyre, on which they burn the straw figure, reviling and scoffing at it the while. Then they return, singing—

> "We have carried away Death,
> And brought Life back.
> He has taken up his quarters in the village,
> Therefore sing joyous songs."[12]

The preceding evidence shews that the effigy of Death is often regarded with fear and treated with marks of hatred and abhorrence. Thus the anxiety of the villagers to transfer the figure from their own to their neighbours' land, and the reluctance of the latter to receive the ominous guest, are proof enough of the dread which it inspires. Further, in Lusatia and Silesia the puppet is sometimes made to look in at the window of a house, and it is believed that someone in the house will die within the year unless his life is redeemed by the payment of money.[13] Again, after throwing the effigy

quiries, however, elicited the information that at the end of every week in Lent one of the feather legs was pulled off the puppet, and that the puppet was finally destroyed on the last day of Lent.[10]

"Bringing in Summer"

205. In the preceding ceremonies the return of Spring, Summer, or Life, as a sequel to the expulsion of Death, is only implied or at most announced. In the following ceremonies it is plainly enacted. Thus in some parts of Bohemia the effigy of Death is drowned by being thrown into the water at sunset; then the girls go out into the wood and cut down a young tree with a green crown, hang a doll dressed as a woman on it, deck the whole with green, red, and white ribbons, and march in procession with their *Lito* (Summer) into the village, collecting gifts and singing—

> "Death swims in the water,
> Spring comes to visit us,
> With eggs that are red,
> With yellow pancakes.
> We carried Death out of the village,
> We are carrying Summer into the village."[1]

In many Silesian villages the figure of Death, after being treated with respect, is stript of its clothes and flung with curses into the water, or torn to pieces in a field. Then the young folk repair to a wood, cut down a small fir-tree, peel the trunk, and deck it with festoons of evergreens, paper roses, painted egg-shells, motley bits of cloth, and so forth. The tree thus adorned is called Summer or May. Boys carry it from house to house singing appropriate songs and begging for presents. Among their songs is the following—

> "We have carried Death out,
> We are bringing the dear Summer back,
> The Summer and the May
> And all the flowers gay."

Sometimes they also bring back from the wood a prettily adorned figure, which goes by the name of Summer, May, or the Bride; in the Polish districts it is called Dziewanna, the goddess of spring.[2]

In these cases Death is represented by the puppet which is thrown away, Summer or Life by the branches or trees which are brought back. But sometimes a new potency of life seems to be attributed to the image of Death itself, and by a kind of resurrection it becomes the instrument of the general revival. Thus in some parts of Lusatia women alone are concerned in carrying out Death, and suffer no male to meddle with it. Attired in mourning, which they wear the whole day, they make a puppet of straw, clothe it in a white shirt, and give it a broom in one hand and a scythe in the other. Singing songs and pursued by urchins throwing stones, they carry the puppet to the village boundary, where they tear it in pieces. Then they cut down a fine tree, hang the shirt on it, and carry it home singing.[3] Here the transference of the shirt worn by the effigy of Death to the tree clearly indicates that the tree is a kind of revivification, in a new form, of the destroyed effigy. This comes out also in the Transylvanian and Moravian customs: the dressing of a girl in the clothes worn by the Death, and the leading her about the village to the same song which had been sung when the Death was being carried about, shew that she is intended to be a kind of resuscitation of the being whose effigy has just been destroyed. These examples therefore suggest that the Death whose demolition is represented in these ceremonies cannot be regarded as the purely destructive agent which we understand by Death. If the tree which is brought back as an embodiment of the reviving vegetation of spring is clothed in the shirt worn by the Death which has just been destroyed, the object certainly cannot be to check and counteract the revival of vegetation: it can only be to foster and promote it. Therefore the being which has just been destroyed—the so-called Death—must be supposed to be endowed with a vivifying and quickening influence, which it can communicate to the vegetable and even the animal world. This ascription of a life-giving virtue to the figure of Death is put beyond a doubt by the custom, observed in some places, of taking pieces of the straw effigy of Death and placing them in the fields to make the crops grow, or in the manger to make the cattle thrive. Thus in Spachendorf, a village of Austrian Silesia, the figure of Death, made of straw, brushwood, and rags, is carried with wild songs to an open place outside the village and there burned, and while it is burning a general struggle takes place for the pieces, which are pulled out of the flames with bare hands. Each one who secures a fragment of the effigy ties it to a branch of the largest tree in his garden, or buries it in his field, in the belief that this causes the crops to grow better.[4] In the Troppau district of Austrian Silesia the straw figure which the boys make on the fourth Sunday in Lent is dressed by the girls in woman's clothes and hung with ribbons, necklace, and garlands. Attached to a long pole it is carried out of the village, followed by a troop of young people of both sexes, who alternately frolic, lament, and sing songs. Arrived at its destination—a field outside the village—the figure is stripped of its clothes and ornaments; then the crowd rushes at it and tears it to bits, scuffling for the fragments. Every one tries to get a wisp of the straw of which the effigy was made, because such a wisp, placed in the manger, is believed to make the cattle thrive.[5] Or the straw is put in the hens' nest, it being supposed that this prevents the hens from carrying away their eggs, and makes them brood much better.[6] The same attribution of a fertilising power to the figure of Death appears in the belief that if the bearers of the figure, after throwing it away, beat cattle with their sticks, this will render the beasts fat or prolific. Perhaps the sticks had been previously used to beat the Death, and so had acquired the fertilising power ascribed to the effigy. We have seen, too, that at Leipsic a straw effigy of Death was shewn to young wives to make them fruitful.

It seems hardly possible to separate from the May-trees the trees or branches which are brought into the village after the destruction of the Death. The bearers who bring them in profess to be bringing in the Summer,[6] therefore the trees obviously represent the Summer; indeed in Silesia they are commonly called the Summer or the May, and the doll which is sometimes attached to the Summer-tree is a duplicate representative of the Summer, just as the May is sometimes represented at the same time by a May-tree and a May Lady. Further, the Summer-trees are adorned like May-trees with ribbons and so on; like May-trees, when large, they are planted in the ground and climbed up; and like May-trees, when small, they are carried from door to door by boys or girls singing songs and collecting money.[7] And as if to demonstrate the identity of the two sets of customs the bearers of the Summer-tree sometimes announce that they are bringing in the Summer and the May. The customs, therefore, of bringing in the May and bringing in the Summer are essentially the same; and the Summer-tree is merely another form of the May-tree, the only distinction (besides that of name) being in the time at which they are respectively brought in; for while the May-tree is usually fetched in on the first of May or at Whitsuntide, the Summer-tree is fetched in on the fourth Sunday in Lent. Therefore, if the May-tree is an embodiment of the tree-spirit or spirit of vegetation, the Summer-tree must likewise be an embodiment of the tree-spirit or spirit of vegetation. But we have seen that the Summer-tree is in some cases a revivification of the effigy of Death. It follows, therefore, that in these cases the effigy called Death must be an embodiment of the tree-spirit or spirit of vegetation. This inference is confirmed, first, by the vivifying and fertilising influence which the fragments of the effigy of Death are believed to exercise both on vegetable and on animal life; for this influence, as we saw in the first part of this work, is supposed to be a special attribute of the tree-spirit. It is confirmed, secondly, by observing that the effigy of Death is sometimes decked with leaves or made of twigs, branches, hemp, or a threshed-out sheaf of corn; and that sometimes it is hung on a little tree and so carried about by girls collecting money,[8] just as is done with the May-tree and the May Lady, and with the Summer-tree and the doll attached to it. In short we are driven to regard the expulsion of Death and the bringing in of Summer as, in some cases at least, merely another form of that death and revival of the spirit of vegetation in spring which we saw enacted in the killing and resurrection of the Wild Man. The burial and resurrection of the Carnival is probably another way of expressing the same idea. The interment of the representative of the Carnival under a dung-heap is natural, if he is supposed to possess a quickening and fertilising influence like that ascribed to the effigy of Death. The Esthonians, indeed, who carry the straw figure out of the village in the usual way on Shrove Tuesday, do not call it the Carnival, but the Wood-spirit (*Metsik*), and they clearly indicate the identity of the effigy with the wood-spirit by fixing it to the top of a tree in the wood, where it remains for a year, and is besought almost daily with prayers and offerings to protect the herbs; for like a true wood-spirit the *Metsik* is a patron of cattle. Sometimes the *Metsik* is made of sheaves of corn.[9]

Thus we may fairly conjecture that the names Carnival, Death, and Summer are comparatively late and inadequate expressions for the beings personified or embodied in the customs with which we have been dealing. The very abstractness of the names bespeaks a modern origin; for the personification of times and seasons like the Carnival and Summer, or of an abstract notion like Death, is hardly primitive. But the ceremonies themselves bear the stamp of a dateless antiquity; therefore we can hardly help supposing that in their origin the ideas which they embodied were of a more simple and concrete order. The notion of a tree, perhaps of a particular kind of tree (for some savages have no word for tree in general), or even of an individual tree, is sufficiently concrete to supply a basis from which by a gradual process of generalisation the wider idea of a spirit of vegetation might be reached. But this general idea of vegetation would readily be confounded with the season in which it manifests itself; hence the substitution of Spring, Summer, or May for the tree-spirit or spirit of vegetation would be easy and natural. Again, the concrete notion of the dying tree or dying vegetation would by a similar process of generalisation glide into a notion of Death in general; so that the practice of carrying out the dying or dead vegetation in spring, as a preliminary to its revival, would in time widen out into an attempt to banish Death in general from the village or district. The view that in these spring ceremonies Death meant originally the dying or dead vegetation of winter has the high support of W. Mannhardt; and he confirms it by the analogy of the name Death as applied to the spirit of the ripe corn. Commonly the spirit of the ripe corn is conceived, not as dead, but as old, and hence it goes by the name of the Old Man or the Old Woman. But in some places the last sheaf cut at harvest, which is generally believed to be the seat of the corn spirit, is called "the Dead One": children are warned against entering the corn-fields because Death sits in the corn; and, in a game played by Saxon children in Transylvania at the maize harvest, Death is represented by a child completely covered with maize leaves.[10]

THE BATTLE OF SUMMER AND WINTER

206. Sometimes in the popular customs of the peasantry the contrast between the dormant powers of vegetation in winter and their awakening vitality in spring takes the form of a dramatic contest between actors who play the parts respectively of Winter and Summer. Thus in the towns of Sweden on May Day two troops of young men on horseback used to meet as if for mortal combat. One of them was led by a representative of Winter clad in furs, who threw snowballs and ice in order to prolong the cold weather. The other troop was commanded by a representative of Summer covered with fresh leaves and flowers. In the sham fight which followed the party of Summer came off victorious, and the ceremony ended with a feast.[1] Again, in the region of the middle Rhine, a representative of Summer clad in ivy combats a representative of Winter clad in straw or moss and finally gains a victory over him. The vanquished foe is thrown to the ground and stripped of his casing of straw, which is torn to pieces and scattered about, while the youthful comrades of the two champions sing a song to commemorate the defeat of Winter by Summer. Afterwards they carry about a summer garland or branch and collect gifts of eggs and bacon from house to house. Sometimes the champion who acts the part of Summer is dressed in leaves and flowers and wears a chaplet of flowers on his head. In the Palatinate this mimic conflict takes place on the fourth Sunday in Lent.[2] All over Bavaria the same drama used to be acted on the same day, and it was still kept up in some places down to the middle of the nineteenth century or later. While Summer appeared clad all in green, decked with fluttering ribbons, and carrying a branch in blossom or a little tree hung with apples and pears, Winter was muffled up in cap and mantle of fur and bore in his hand a snow-shovel or a flail. Accompanied by their respective retinues dressed in corresponding attire, they went through all the streets of the village, halting before the houses and singing staves of old songs, for which they received presents of bread, eggs, and fruit. Finally, after a short struggle, Winter was beaten by Summer and ducked in the village well or driven out of the village with shouts and laughter into the forest.[3] In some parts of Bavaria the boys who play the parts of Winter and Summer act their little drama in every house that they visit, and engage in a war of words before they come to blows, each of them vaunting the pleasures and benefits of the season he represents and disparaging those of the other. The dialogue is in verse. A few couplets may serve as specimens:—

SUMMER

"Green, green are meadows wherever I pass
And the mowers are busy among the grass."

WINTER

"White, white are the meadows wherever I go,
And the sledges glide hissing across the snow."

SUMMER

"I'll climb up the tree where the red cherries glow,
And Winter can stand by himself down below."

WINTER

"With you I will climb the cherry-tree tall,
Its branches will kindle the fire in the hall."

SUMMER

"O Winter, you are most uncivil
To send old women to the devil."

WINTER

"By that I make them warm and mellow,
So let them bawl and let them bellow."

SUMMER

"I am the Summer in white array,
I'm chasing the Winter far, far away."

WINTER

"I am the Winter in mantle of furs,
I'm chasing the Summer o'er bushes and burs."

SUMMER

"Just say a word more, and I'll have you bann'd
At once and for ever from Summer Land."

WINTER

"O Summer, for all your bluster and brag,
You'd not dare to carry a hen in a bag."

SUMMER

"O Winter, your chatter no more can I stay,
I'll kick and I'll cuff you without delay."

Here ensues a scuffle between the two little boys, in which Summer gets the best of it, and turns Winter out of the house. But soon the beaten champion of Winter peeps in at the door and says with a humbled and crestfallen air:—

"O Summer, dear Summer, I'm under your ban,
For you are the master and I am the man."

To which Summer replies:—

" 'Tis a capital notion, an excellent plan,
If I am the master and you are the man.
So come, my dear Winter, and give me your hand,
We'll travel together to Summer Land."[4]

In Wachtl and Brodek, a German village and a little German town of Moravia, encompassed by Slavonic people on every side, the great change that comes over the earth in spring is still annually mimicked. The long village of Wachtl, with its trim houses and farmyards, nestles in a valley surrounded by pretty pine-woods. Here, on a day in spring, about the time of the vernal equinox, an elderly man with a long flaxen beard may be seen going from door to door. He is muffled in furs, with warm gloves on his hands and a bearskin cap on his head, and he carries a threshing flail. This is the personification of Winter. With him goes a younger beardless man dressed in white, wearing a straw hat trimmed with gay ribbons on his head, and carrying a decorated May-tree in his hands. This is Summer. At every house they receive a friendly greeting and recite a long dialogue in verse, Winter punctuating his discourse with his flail, which he brings down with rude vigour on the backs of all within reach.[5] Amongst the Slavonic population near Ungarisch Brod, in Moravia, the ceremony took a somewhat different form. Girls dressed in green marched in procession round a May-tree. Then two others, one in white and one in green, stepped up to the tree and engaged in a dialogue. Finally, the girl in white was driven away, but returned afterwards clothed in green, and the festival ended with a dance.[6]

Among the central Esquimaux of North America the contest between representatives of summer and winter, which in Europe has long degenerated into a mere dramatic performance, is still kept up as a magical ceremony of which the avowed intention is to influence the weather. In autumn, when storms announce the approach of the dismal Arctic winter, the Esquimaux divide themselves into two parties called respectively the ptarmigans and the ducks, the ptarmigans comprising all persons born in winter, and the ducks all persons born in summer. A long rope of sealskin is then stretched out, and each party laying hold of one end of it seeks by tugging with might and main to drag the other party over to its side. If the ptarmigans get the worst of it, then summer has won the game and fine weather may be expected to prevail through the winter.[7] The Indians of Canada seem also to have imagined that persons are endowed with distinct natural capacities according as they are born in summer or winter, and they turned the distinction to account in much the same fashion as the Esquimaux. When they wearied of the long frosts and the deep snow which kept them prisoners in their huts and prevented them from hunting, all of them who were born in summer rushed out of their houses armed with burning brands and torches which they hurled against the One who makes Winter; and this was supposed to produce the desired effect of mitigating the cold. But those Indians who were born in winter abstained from taking part in the ceremony, for they believed that if they meddled with it the cold would increase instead of diminishing.[8] We may surmise that in the corresponding European ceremonies, which have just been described, it was formerly deemed necessary that the actors, who played the parts of Winter and Summer, should have been born in the seasons which they personated.

MOCK FUNERALS

207. In Russia funeral ceremonies like those of "Burying the Carnival" and "Carrying out Death" are celebrated under the names, not of Death or the Carnival, but of certain mythic figures, Kostrubonko, Kostroma, Kupalo, Lada, and Yarilo. These Russian ceremonies are observed both in spring and at midsummer. Thus "in Little Russia it used to be the custom at Eastertide to celebrate the funeral of a being called Kostrubonko, the deity of the spring. A circle was formed of singers who moved slowly around a girl who lay on the ground as if dead, and as they went they sang,—

> 'Dead, dead is our Kostrubonko!
> Dead, dead is our dear one!'

until the girl suddenly sprang up, on which the chorus joyfully exclaimed,—

> 'Come to life, come to life has our Kostrubonko!
> Come to life, come to life has our dear one!' "[1]

On the Eve of St. John (Midsummer Eve) a figure of Kupalo is made of straw and "is dressed in woman's clothes, with a necklace and a floral crown. Then a tree is felled, and, after being decked with ribbons, is set up on some chosen spot. Near this tree, to which they give the name of Marena [Winter or Death], the straw figure is placed, together with a table, on which stand spirits and viands. Afterwards a bonfire is lit, and the young men and maidens jump over it in couples, carrying the figure with them. On the next day they strip the tree and the figure of their ornaments, and throw them both into a stream." On St. Peter's Day, the twenty-ninth of June, or on the following Sunday, "the Funeral of Kostroma" or of Lada or of Yarilo is celebrated in Russia. In the Governments of Penza and Simbirsk the funeral used to be represented as follows. A bonfire was kindled on the twenty-eighth of June, and on the next day the maidens chose one of their number to play the part of Kostroma. Her companions saluted her with deep obeisances, placed her on a board, and carried her to the bank of a stream. There they bathed her in the water, while the oldest girl made a basket of lime-tree bark and beat it like a drum. Then they returned to the village and ended the day with processions, games, and dances. In the Murom district Kostroma was represented by a straw figure dressed in woman's clothes and flowers. This was laid in a trough and carried with songs to the bank of a lake or river. Here the crowd divided into two sides, of which the one attacked and the other defended the figure. At last the assailants gained the day, stripped the figure of its dress and ornaments, tore it in pieces, trod the straw of which it was made under foot, and flung it into the stream; while the defenders of the figure hid their faces in their hands and pretended to bewail the death of Kostroma. In the district of Kostroma the burial of Yarilo was celebrated on the twenty-ninth or thirtieth of June. The people chose an old man and gave him a small coffin containing a Priapus-like figure representing Yarilo. This he carried out of the town, followed by women chanting dirges and expressing by their gestures grief and despair. In the open fields a grave was dug, and into it the figure was lowered amid weeping and wailing, after which games and dances were begun, "calling to mind the funeral games celebrated in old times by the pagan Slavonians."[1] In Little Russia the figure of Yarilo was laid in a coffin and carried through the streets after sunset surrounded by drunken women, who kept repeating mournfully, "He is dead! he is dead!" The men lifted and shook the figure as if they were trying to recall the dead man to life. Then they said to the women, "Women, weep not. I know what is sweeter than honey." But the women continued to lament and chant, as they do at funerals. "Of what was he guilty? He was so good. He will arise no more. O how shall we part from thee? What is life without thee? Arise, if only for a brief hour. But he rises not, he rises not." At last the Yarilo was buried in a grave.[2]

These Russian customs are plainly of the same nature as those which in Austria and Germany are known as "Carrying out Death." Therefore if the interpretation here adopted of the latter is right, the Russian Kostrubonko, Yarilo, and the rest must also have been originally embodiments of the spirit of vegetation, and their death must have been regarded as a necessary preliminary to their revival. The revival as a sequel to the death is enacted in the first of the ceremonies described, the death and resurrection of Kostrubonko. The reason why in some of these Russian ceremonies the death of the spirit of vegetation is celebrated at midsummer may be that the decline of summer is dated from Midsummer Day, after which the days begin to shorten, and the sun sets out on his downward journey—

> "To the darksome hollows
> Where the frosts of winter lie."

Such a turning-point of the year, when vegetation might be thought to share the incipient though still almost imperceptible decay of summer, might very well be chosen by primitive man as a fit moment for resorting to those magic rites by which he hopes to stay the decline, or at least to ensure the revival, of plant life.

NOTES

189 1. C. Meiners, *Geschichte der Religionen* (Hanover 1806–07), i. 48.
2. R. I. Dodge, *Our Wild Indians* (Hartford, Connecticut, 1886), 112.
3. F. Blumentritt, in *Mitteilingen der Weiner geographischen Gesellschaft*, 1882, p. 198.
4. J. E. Alexander, *Expedition of Discovery into the Interior of Africa* (London 1838), i. 166.
5. Callimachus, *Hymn to Zeus*, 9 f.; Diodorus Siculus, iii. 61; Lucian, *Philopseudes*, 3; id., *Jupiter Tragoedus*, 45; id., *Philopatris*, 10; Porphyry, *Vita Pythagorae*, 17; Cicero, *De natura decorum*, iii. 21, 53; Pomponius Mela, iii. 7, 112; Minucius Feliz, *Octavius*, 21.
6. Plutarch, *De Iside et Osiride*, 35; Philocorus, fr. 22 (in *FHG*, i. 378). Cp. C. Petersen, in *Philologus*, 15 (1860), 77–91.
7. Porphyry, *op. cit.*, 16.
8. Philocorus, fr. 184 (in *FHG*, ii. 414).
9. C. Lobeck, *Aglaophamus* (Königsberg 1829), 574 f.
10. G. Maspero, *Histoire ancienne des peuples de l'Orient classique: les origines* (Paris 1895), 108–11, 116–18. On the mortality of the Egyptian gods, see further A. Moret, *Le rituel du culte divin journalier en Egypte* (Paris 1902), 219 ff.

190 1. See above, ¶96.
2. W. W. Reade, *Savage Africa* (London 1863), 362.
3. Diodorus Siculus, iii. 6; Strabo, xvii. 2, 3.
4. R. Lepsius, *Letters from Egypt, Ethiopia and the Peninsula of Sinai* (London 1853), 202, 204.
4a. P. W. Hoffmayr, in *Anthropos*, 6 (1911), 120–22; C. G. Seligman, *The Cult of Nyaking and the Divine Kings of the Shilluk* (Khartoum 1911); id., in *ERE*, s.v. *Shilluk*.
4b. For this account of the Dinka the author is indebted to C. G. Seligman, who kindly placed manuscript notes at his disposal.
5. *Emin Pasha in Central Africa* (London 1888), 91.
6. Gullemé, in *Annales de la Propagation de la Foi*, 60 (1888), 258.

7. F. B. Tellez, ed., *The Travels of the Jesuits in Ethiopia* (London 1710), 197.

8. H. Pope-Henessy, in *JAI*, 30 (1900), 29.

9. N. Isaacs, *Travels and Adventures in Eastern Africa* (London 1836), i. 295 f.

10. J. dos Santos, "Eastern Ethiopia," in G. M. Theal's *Records of S. E. Africa*, vii (London 1901), 194 ff.

11. Xenephon, *Hellenica*, iii. 3, 3; Plutarch, *Agesilaus*, 3; id., *Lysander*, 22; Pausanias, iii. 8, 9.

12. Herodotus, iii. 20; Aristotle, *Politics*, iv. 4, 4; Athenaeus, xiii. 20.

13. G. Nachtigal, *Sahara und Sudan*, iii (Leipzig 1889), 225.

14. P. W. Joyce, *Social History of Ancient Ireland* (London 1903), i. 311.

15. A. Dalzel, *History of Dahomy* (London 1793), 12 f., 156 f.

15a. L. Tauxier, *La Religion Bambara* (Paris 1927), 219, n.

15b. J. Roscoe, *The Bayankole* (Cambridge 1923), 50 ff.

16. Simon Gruneau, *Preussische Chronik*, ed. M. Perlbach (Leipzig 1876), i. 97.

191   1. Duarte Barbosa, *A Description of the Coasts of E. Africa and Malabar in the Beginning of the Sixteenth Century* (London, Hakluyt Society, 1866), 172 ff.

2. L. di Varthema, *Travels*, tr. J. W. Jones and G. P. Badger (London, Hakluyt Society, 1863), 134.

3. F. Buchanan, "Journey from Madras through the Countries of Mysore, Canara and Malabar," in Pinkerton's *Voyages and Travels*, viii. 735.

4. A. Hamilton, "A New Account of the East Indies," *ib.*, viii. 374.

5. T. K. Goppel Panikar, *Malabar and its Folk* (Madras [1901]), 120 f.

6. C. Deffrémery and B. R. Sanguinetti, eds., *Voyage d'Ibn Batoutah* (Paris 1853–58), iv. 246 f.

7. E. T. Dalton, *Descriptive Ethnology of Bengal* (Calcutta 1872), 146.

8. F. T. Valdez, *Six Years of a Traveller's Life in W. Africa* (London 1861), ii. 158 f. (The title *Marquita* is here rendered approximately as "chief"; the writer does not explain it.)

9. *Ynglinga Saga*, 29 (= *The Heimskringla*, tr. S. Laing [London 1844], i. 239 f.).

10. Saxo Grammaticus, *Historia Danica*, iii. 129–31 Müller.

11. Adam of Bremen, *Descriptio insularum Aquilonis*, 27 (in Migne, *PL*, cxlvi, 644).

192   1. Plutarch, *Agis*, 11.

2. *Die Dorier*[2] (Breslau 1844), ii. 96.

3. I. Ideler, *Handbuch der mathematischen und technischen Chronologie* (Berlin 1825–26), ii. 605 ff. On the religious and political import of the eight-year cycle in ancient Greece, see especially K. O. Müller, *Orchomenos und die Minyer*[2] (Breslau 1844), 213–18; id., *Die Dorier*[2], i. 254 f., 333 f., 440; ii. 96, 483.

4. The same train of thought may perhaps explain an ancient Greek

custom which appears to have required that a homicide be exiled and do penance for eight or nine years: see fully, W. H. Roscher, "Die enneadischen und hebdomadischen Fristen und Wochen der ältesten Griechen," in *Abh. Sächs. Ges. d. Wiss., phil. –hist. Kl.*, 21 No. 4 (1903), 24 ff.

5. *Odyssey,* xix. 178 f. Homer's expression (*enneôros basileus*) is often taken to mean that Minos ruled for *nine* years. It must be remembered, however, that in reckoning intervals of time numerically the Greeks included both of the terms separated by the intervals, whereas we include only one of them. Hence what is here meant is a period of *eight* years.

6. L. Preller, *Griech. Mythologie*[3] (Berlin 1875), iii. 119–23; W. H. Roscher, *Ueber Selene und Verwandtes* (Leipzig 1895), 3; A. B. Cook, in *Classical Review*, 17 (1903), 406–12; id., in *Folk-Lore*, 15 (1904), 272.

7. Censorinus, *De die natali*, 18. 6.

193 1. J. Parkinson, in *The Empire Review*, 15 (1908), 290 f. See also A. B. Ellis, *The Yoruba-speaking Peoples of the Slave Coast* (London 1894), 170.

194 1. M. Jastrow, *The Religion of Babylonia and Assyria* (Boston 1898), 680; C. Brockelmann, in *Zeitschrift für Assyriologie*, 16 (1902), 391 f., 396 f.

2. Athenaeus, xiv. 44; Dio Chrysostom, *Orationes*, iv. pp. 69 ff. (i, p. 76 Dindorf).

3. V. Lisiansky, *A Voyage round the World in the years 1803–06* (London 1814), 118 f.

4. R. E. Dennett, *At the Back of the Black Man's Mind* (London 1906), 120.

195 1. *The High History of the Holy Grail*, tr. S. Evans (London 1898), i. 200–03.

2. C. Wilford, in *Asiatick Researches*, 9 (1809), 117 ff.; C. Lassen, *Indische Alterthumuskunde*, ii[2] (Leipzig 1858–74), 752 ff., 794 ff. Vikramaditya is commonly supposed to have lived in the first century B.C., but according to H. Oldenberg (*Die Literatur des alten Indien* [Stuttgart-Berlin 1903], 215 f.), he was a purely legendary person.

3. "Histoire des rois d'Hindoustan après les Pandaras, traduite du texte hindoustani de Mir Cher-i Ali Afsos, par M. l'abbé Bertrand," in *Journal Asiatique*, IVme sér., 3 (1844), 248–57. The story is told briefly by Mrs. Postans in her volume, *Cutch* (London 1839), 21 f. Cp. Lassen, *op. cit.*, 798.

196 1. E. Aymonier, *Notice sur le Cambodge* (Paris 1875), 61; J. Moura, *Le royaume de Cambodge* (Paris 1883), i. 327 f.

2. De la Loubère, *Du royaume de Siam* (Amsterdam 1691), i. 56 f.

3. E. Chavannes, *Documents sur les Tou-Kive* (*Turcs*) *occidentaux* (St. Petersburg 1903), 133, n.

4. C. B. Klunzinger, *Bilder aus Oberägypten, der Wüste und dem Rothen Meere* (Stuttgart 1877), 180 f.

5. E. Carew, *Survey of Cornwall* (London 1811), 322.

6. J. W. Boers, in *Tijdschrift voor Neerlands-Indië*, 1840, dl. i, 372 ff.

7. *Punjab Notes and Queries*, 1 (1884), 86, ¶674.

7a. J. R. Wilson-Hoffenden, in *Journal of the African Society*, 27 (1928), 385 f.

8. Aeneas Sylvius, *Opera* (Basle 1571), 409 ff.; E. Goldmann, *Die Einführung der deutschen Herzogsgeschlechter Kärntens in den Slovenischen Stammesverband* (Breslau 1903).

9. J. Malcolm, *History of Persia* (London 1815), i. 527 f.

197   1. *Ynglinga Saga*, 29; H. M. Chadwick, *The Cult of Othin* (London 1899), 4, 27.

2. Herodotus, vii. 197; Apollodorus, i. 9, 1 f. [with Frazer's note *in loc.*].

3. Plato, *Minos*, 315 C.

4. Plutarch, *Quaest. Graec.*, 38; Antoninus Liberalis, *Transform.*, 10; Ovid, *Met.*, iv. 1 f.

5. Pausanias, ix. 34, 5 ff.; Apollonius Rhodius, *Argonautica*, iii. 265 f.; Apollodorus, *Bibl.*, i. 9, 1.

6. Quoted by Eusebius, *Praep. Ev.*, i. 10, 29 f.

7. II Kings 3 : 27.

8. Porphyry, *De abstinentia*, ii. 54.

198   1. W. Ellis, *Polynesian Researches*[2] (London 1832–36), i. 251 ff.

2. Picarda, in *Missions Catholiques*, 18 (1886), 284.

3. *The Strange Adventures of Andrew Battell* (London, Hakluyt Society, 1901), 32, 84 f.

4. F. de Azara, *Voyages dans l'Amérique méridionale* (Paris 1809), ii. 115–17.

5. R. Southey, *History of Brazil*, iii (London 1819), 385.

6. W. B. Grubb, *An Unknown People in an Unknown Land* (London 1911), 233.

199   1. See above, ¶190.

2. J. T. Nieuwenhuisen and H. C. B. Rosenberg, in *Verh. Batav. Gen. van Kunsten en Wetenschappen*, 30 (1863), 85; H. von Rosenberg, *Der Malayische Archipel* (Leipzig 1878), 160; L. Chatelin, in *Tijdschr. v. Ind. Taal- Land- en Volkenkunde*, 26 (1880), 142 f.; H. Sundermann, in *Allgemeine Missions-Zeitschrift*, 11 (1884), 443; E. Modigliani, *Un Viaggio a Nias* (Milan 1890), 479 f.

3. C. Wilkes, *Narrative of the U. S. Exploring Expedition* (London 1845), iv. 453.

4. D. G. Brinton, *Myths of the New World*[2] (New York 1876), 270 f.

5. *Relations des Jésuites*, 1636, p. 130.

6. A. Bastian, *Die Völker des östlichen Asien* (Leipzig-Jena 1866–71), iv. 386.
7. Servius on Vergil, *Aen.*, iv. 685; Cicero, *In Verr.*, ii. 5, 45.
8. J. Harland and T. K. Wilkinson, *Lancashire Folk-lore* (London 1882), 7 f.

200   1. F. B. Tellez, ed., *The Travels of the Jesuits in Ethiopia* (London 1710), 198.
     2. J. dos Santos, "Eastern Ethiopia," in G. M. Theal's *Records of S. E. Africa*, vii. 196.
     3. See above, ¶75.
     4. A. Grandidier, in *Bull. soc. géogr. de Paris, VIme sér.*, 3 (1872), 402 f.
     5. H. Johnston, *The Uganda Protectorate* (London 1902), ii. 828.
     6. Holley, in *Missions Catholiques*, 13 (1881), 353. See also W. Macgregor, in *Journal of the African Society*, No. xii (1904), 471 f.
     7. F. T. Valdez, *op. cit.*, iii. 161 f.
     8. Holley, in *Ann. de la Prop. de la Foi*, 54 (1882), 87.
     9. Private communication from H. G. Parsons (Lyons, 9/28/1903).

201   1. F. Panzer, *Beitrag zur deutschen Mythologie* (Munich 1848–53), i. 235 f.; W. Mannhardt, *Der Baumkultus der Germanen und ihrer Nachbarstämme* (Berlin 1875), 320 f.
     2. Mannhardt, *op. cit.*, 349 f.
     3. *Ib.*, 353 f.
     4. *Ib.*, 336.
     5. *Loc. cit.*
     6. *Ib.*, 353 f.

202   1. G. Targioni-Tozzetti, *Saggio di novelline, canti ed usanze popolari della Cicciara* (Palermo 1891), 89–95. At Palermo an effigy of the Carnival (*Nannu*) was burnt at midnight on Shrove Tuesday, 1878; see G. Pitré, *Usi e costumi, credenze e pregiudizi del popolo siciliano* (Palermo 1889), i. 117–19.
     2. G. Finamore, *Credenze, usi e costumi abruzzesi* (Palermo 1890), 111. For parallels, see Pitrè, *op. cit.*, 96–100.
     3. R. Wünsch, *Das Frühlingsfest der Insel Malta* (Leipzig 1902), 29 f.
     4. A. de Nore, *Coutumes, mythes et traditions des provinces de France* (Paris-Lyons 1846), 37 ff. The name *Caramantran* is thought to be compounded of *carême entrant*, "Lent coming in." It is said that Caramantran is sometimes burnt: E. Cortet, *Essai sur les fêtes religieuses* (Paris 1867), 107.
     5. L. Pineau, *Folk-lore du Poitou* (Paris 1892), 493.
     6. A. Meyrac, *Traditions, légendes et contes des Ardennes* (Charleville 1890), 63.
     7. C. Beauquier, *Les mois en Franche-Comté* (Paris 1900), 30.
     8. J. Lecoeur, *Esquisses du boscage normand* (Condé-sur-Noireua 1883–87), ii. 148 ff.

ADDITIONAL NOTES

189. The attitude of the primitive towards immortality and after-life has been admirably summarized by Ernst Cassirer, *An Essay on Man* (New York 1953), 111, in the dictum: "If anything is [to him] in need of proof, it is not the fact of immortality but the fact of death." (It may be of interest here to record that this was said independently to the present writer, and in the same words, by Prof. Carlo Diano, in private conversation at Padua on March 23, 1952.)

192. *Eight-year cycle.* The eight-year tenure of Spartan kings and of Minos, legendary king of Crete, is bound up with ancient astronomical theories which regarded that period as constituting a single major "life-lease"; see A. Schmidt, *Handbuch d. griech. Chronologie* (Jena 1888), 56 ff.; W. H. Roscher, "Die enneadischen und hebdomadischen Fristen und Wochen der ältesten Griechen," in *Abh. Sachs. Ges. Wiss.*, Phil.–hist. Kl., 21/iv (1903); O. Gruppe, *Griech. Mythologie* (Munich 1906), 957, n. 1; id., *Literatur zur Religionsgesch. u. antiken Mythologie*, 1906–17 (Leipzig 1921), 276 ff.; A. B. Cook, *Zeus*, ii (Cambridge 1925), 259 ff., 440, n. 2. — It is this that accounts for the octennial Delphic solemnities at Stepterion, Herois, and Charila (Cook, *op. cit.*, 240 ff.), and for the octennial celebration of the Pythian games (Schol., *Od.*, 3.267; Schol., Pindar, *Pyth.*, iii.). — The Illyrians likewise had an eight-year cycle (Strabo, 315), and there are traces of it in Jewish practise in the custom whereby the king has to read the Law to the people every eighth year, i.e., virtually reconfirm his authority for a new "lease." — Not improbably, the familiar use of "seven years" to indicate a long period in folktales and folk-songs goes back ultimately to this basis.

Pertinent in this connection is the fact that "nine-year old" is sometimes used in Greek to denote "initially adult," e. g., Theocritus, 26. 28; Paton-Hicks, *Inscr. of Cos*, No. 27; Callimachus, *Hymns*, iii. 14.

On the subject in general, see B. L. van der Waerden, "Das grosse Jahr und die ewige Wiederkehr," in *Hermes*, 52 (1952), 129–57.

194. On the *ritual humiliation and subsequent reinstatement of the king at the Babylonian Akîtu (Zagmuk) festival*, see: A. J. Wensinck, in *Acta Orientalia*,

278

1 (1923), 183 ff.; S. Langdon, *The Epic of Creation* (Oxford 1923), 26; I. Engnell, *Studies in Divine Kingship in the Ancient Near East* (Uppsala 1943), 35; G. Furlani, in *Studi e Materialie di Storia delle Religioni*, 4 (1928), 1–16, 305–07; R. Labat, *Le caractère religieux de la royauté assyro-babylonienne* (Paris 1939), 87 ff.; F. Thureau-Dangin, *Rituels accadiens* (Paris 1921), 144, lines 415 ff.; T. H. Gaster, *Thespis* (New York 1950), 32, 36.

On the mock king at the Sacaea see R. Labat, *Le caractère religieux de la royauté assyro-babylonienne* (Paris 1939), 99 ff. and (but with caution) S. Langdon, in *Journal of the Royal Asiatic Society*, 1924. 65–72.

196. *Temporary kings (survivals)*. At Downside College, near Bath, England, it used to be the custom to elect a temporary "king" on Christmas Eve. He reigned for fourteen days—probably the original intercalary period; see J. S. Morgan, in *Notes and Queries*, IV. iv (1869), 585. — Analogous is the boy-bishop (*Episcopus puerorum*) who ruled annually at Mainz from St. Nicholas' Day (Dec. 6) until Holy Innocents' Day (Jan. 4): F. A. Dürr, *Commentatio historica de Episcopo Puerorum* (Mainz 1755). — There was a similar boy-bishop at Salisbury: Molini and Green, in *Notes and Queries*, IV. v (1870), 257. — Analogous also is the "mock rabbi" in popular celebrations of the Jewish feast of Purim in March: T. H. Gaster, *Festivals of the Jewish Year* (New York 1953), 219, 226 f.

201. *The Mummers' Play*. See: R. Tiddy, *The Mummers' Play* (Oxford 1923); P. Toschi, *Le origini del teatro italiano* (Turin 1955). For representative texts of the English plays, see also: *Folk-Lore*, 1928, 270–81 (Berkshire); 1929, 262–77 (Berkshire, Derbyshire, Cumberland, Isle of Man); 1921, 181–94 (Derbyshire); 1932, 97 ff. (Frodsham "Soul-Caking" play); 1935, 361–73 (Bisley, Minchenhampton); *Notes and Queries*, II. vi (1861), 271 f. (Worcestershire); *Tales and Traditions of Tenby* (Tenby 1858), 34–38. — On the connection of the Mummers' Play with the origins both of comedy and of tragedy, see F. M. Cornford, *The Origin of Attic Comedy* (New York, Anchor Books, 1957); H. Coote Lake, in *Folk-Lore*, 42 (1931), 141–49.

202. On European Carnival celebrations, see also Toschi, *op. cit.*; H. Donteville, *La mythologie française* (Paris 1948).

PART IV

DYING AND REVIVING GODS

MYTHIC EMBODIMENTS

OF FERTILITY

208. *The spectacle of the great changes which annually pass over the face of the earth has powerfully impressed the minds of men in all ages, and stirred them to meditate on the causes of transformations so vast and wonderful. Their curiosity has not been purely disinterested; for even the savage cannot fail to perceive how intimately his own life is bound up with the life of nature, and how the same processes which freeze the stream and strip the earth of vegetation menace him with extinction. At a certain stage of development men seem to have imagined that the means of averting the threatened calamity were in their own hands, and that they could hasten or retard the flight of the seasons by magic art. Accordingly they performed ceremonies and recited spells to make the rain to fall, the sun to shine, animals to multiply, and the fruits of the earth to grow. In course of time the slow advance of knowledge, which has dispelled so many cherished illusions, convinced at least the more thoughtful portion of mankind that the alternations of summer and winter, of spring and autumn, were not merely the result of their own magical rites, but that some deeper cause, some mightier power, was at work behind the shifting scenes of nature. They now pictured to themselves the growth and decay of vegetation, the birth and death of living creatures, as effects of the waxing or waning strength of divine beings, of gods and goddesses, who were born and died, who married and begot children, on the pattern of human life.*

Thus the old magical theory of the seasons was displaced, or rather supplemented, by a religious theory. For although men now attributed the annual cycle of change primarily to corresponding changes in their deities, they still thought that by performing certain magical rites they could aid the god, who was the principle of life, in his struggle with the opposing principle of death. They imagined that they could recruit his failing energies and even raise him from the dead. The ceremonies which they observed for this purpose

283

were in substance a dramatic representation of the natural processes which they wished to facilitate; for it is a familiar tenet of magic that you can produce any desired effect by merely imitating it. And as they now explained the fluctuations of growth and decay, of reproduction and dissolution, by the marriage, the death, and the rebirth or revival of the gods, their religious or rather magical dramas turned in great measure on these themes. They set forth the fruitful union of the powers of fertility, the sad death of one at least of the divine partners, and his joyful resurrection. Thus a religious theory was blended with a magical practice. The combination is familiar in history. Indeed, few religions have ever succeeded in wholly extricating them- selves from the old trammels of magic. The inconsistency of acting on two opposite principles, however it may vex the soul of the philosopher, rarely troubles the common man; indeed he is seldom even aware of it. His affair is to act, not to analyse the motives of his action. If mankind had always been logical and wise, history would not be a long chronicle of folly and crime.

Of the changes which the seasons bring with them, the most striking within the temperate zone are those which affect vegetation. The influence of the seasons on animals, though great, is not nearly so manifest. Hence it is natural that in the magical dramas designed to dispel winter and bring back spring the emphasis should be laid on vegetation, and that trees and plants should figure in them more prominently than beasts and birds. Yet the two sides of life, the vegetable and the animal, were not dissociated in the minds of those who observed the ceremonies. Indeed they commonly believed that the tie between the animal and the vegetable world was even closer than it really is; hence they often combined the dramatic representa- tion of reviving plants with a real or a dramatic union of the sexes for the purpose of furthering at the same time and by the same act the multiplication of fruits, of animals, and of men. To them the principle of life and fertility, whether animal or vegetable, was one and indivisible. To live and to cause to live, to eat food and to beget children, these were the primary wants of men in the past, and they will be the primary wants of men in the future so long as the world lasts. Other things may be added to enrich and beautify human life, but unless these wants are first satisfied, humanity itself must cease to exist. These two things, therefore, food and children, were what men chiefly sought to procure by the performance of magical rites for the regulation of the seasons.

Nowhere, apparently, have these rites been more widely and solemnly celebrated than in the lands which border the Eastern Mediterranean. Under the names of Osiris, Tammuz, Adonis, and Attis, the peoples of Egypt and Western Asia represented the yearly decay and revival of life, especially of vegetable life, which they personified as a god who annually died and rose again from the dead. In name and detail the rites varied from place to place: in substance they were the same.

TAMMUZ

209. In the pantheon of the Sumerians of Southern Babylonia Tammuz appears to have been one of the oldest, though certainly not one of the most important figures.[1] His name consists of a Sumerian phrase meaning "true son" or, in a fuller form, "true son of the deep water,"[2] and among the inscribed Sumerian texts which have survived the wreck of empires are a number of hymns in his honour.

In the religious literature of Babylonia Tammuz appears as the youthful spouse or lover of Ishtar, the great mother goddess, the embodiment of the reproductive energies of nature. The references to their connexion with each other in myth and ritual are both fragmentary and obscure, but we gather from them that Tammuz was believed to die, passing away from the cheerful earth to the gloomy subterranean world, and that his divine mistress journeyed in quest of him "to the land from which there is no returning, to the house of darkness, where dust lies on door and bolt." During her absence the passion of love ceased to operate: men and beasts alike forgot to reproduce their kinds: all life was threatened with extinction. So intimately bound up with the goddess were the sexual functions of the whole animal kingdom that without her presence they could not be discharged. A messenger of the great god Ea was accordingly despatched to rescue the goddess on whom so much depended. The stern queen of the infernal regions, Allatu or Eresh-Kigal by name, reluctantly allowed Ishtar to be sprinkled with the Water of Life and to depart, in company probably with her lover Tammuz, that the two might return together to the upper world, and that with their return all nature might revive.

Laments for the departed Tammuz are contained in several Babylonian hymns, which liken him to plants that quickly fade. He is

> "A tamarisk that in the garden has drunk no water,
>   Whose crown in the field has brought forth no blossom.
> A willow that rejoiced not by the watercourse,
>   A willow whose roots were torn up.
> A herb that in the garden had drunk no water."

His death appears to have been annually mourned, to the shrill music of flutes, by men and women about midsummer in the month named after him, the month of Tammuz. The dirges were seemingly chanted over an effigy of the dead god, which was washed with pure water, anointed with oil, and clad in a red robe, while the fumes of incense rose into the air, as if to stir his dormant senses by their pungent fragrance and wake him from the sleep of death.

ADONIS

210. The worship of Adonis was practised by the Semitic peoples of Babylonia and Syria, and the Greeks borrowed it from them as early as the seventh century B.C.[1] The name Adonis is simply the Semitic *Adon,* "lord," a title of honour by which his worshippers addressed him, but, through a misunderstanding, the Greeks converted it into a proper name.

The tragical story and the melancholy rites of Adonis are better known to us from the descriptions of Greek writers than from the fragments of Babylonian literature or the brief reference of the prophet Ezekiel, who saw the women of Jerusalem weeping for Tammuz at the north gate of the temple.[2] Mirrored in the glass of Greek mythology, the oriental deity appears as a comely youth beloved by Aphrodite. In his infancy the goddess hid him in a chest, which she gave in charge to Persephone, queen of the nether world. But when Persephone opened the chest and beheld the beauty of the babe, she refused to give him back to Aphrodite, though the goddess of love went down herself to hell to ransom her dear one from the power of the grave. The dispute between the two goddesses of love and death was settled by Zeus, who decreed that Adonis should abide with Persephone in the under world for one part of the year, and with Aphrodite in the upper world for another part. At last the fair youth was killed in hunting by a wild boar, or by the jealous Ares, who turned himself into the likeness of a boar in order to compass the death of his rival. Bitterly did Aphrodite lament her loved and lost Adonis.[3]

211. The myth of Adonis was localized and his rites were celebrated with much solemnity at two places in Western Asia, viz., Byblus on the coast of Syria, and Paphos in Cyprus.

Byblus was the more ancient; indeed, it claimed to be the oldest city in Phoenicia and to have been founded by the supreme god El himself.[1] The city stood on a height beside the sea[2] and contained a great sanctuary of Astarte[3] where the rites of Adonis were celebrated.[4] The entire city, in fact, was sacred to him,[5] and the river Nahr Ibrahim, which falls into the sea a little to the south of Byblus, bore in antiquity the name of Adonis.[6] This was the kingdom of Cinyras who is said to have founded a sanctuary of Aphrodite, that is, of Astarte, at a place on Mount Lebanon, distant a day's journey from the capital.[7] The spot was probably Aphaca, at the source of the river Adonis, half-way between Byblus and Baalbec; for at Aphaca there was a famous grove and sanctuary of Astarte which Constantine destroyed on account of the flagitious character of the worship.[8] The site of the temple has been discovered by modern travellers near the miserable village which still bears the name of Afka at the head of the wild, romantic, wooded gorge of the Adonis. The hamlet stands among groves of noble walnut-trees on the brink of the lyn. A little way off the river rushes from a cavern at the foot of a mightly amphitheatre of towering cliffs to plunge in a series of cascades into the awful depths of the glen. The deeper it descends, the ranker and denser grows the vegetation, which, sprouting from the crannies and fissures of the rocks, spreads a green veil over the roaring or murmuring stream in the tremendous chasm below. There is something delicious, almost intoxicating, in the freshness of these tumbling waters, in the sweetness and purity of the mountain air, in the vivid green of the vegetation. The temple, of which some massive hewn blocks and a fine column of Syenite granite still mark the site, occupied a terrace facing the source of the river and commanding a magnificent prospect. Across the foam and the roar of the waterfalls you look up to the cavern and away to the top of the sublime precipices above. So lofty is the cliff that the goats which creep along its ledges to browse on the bushes appear like ants to the spectator hundreds of feet below. Seaward the view is especially impressive when the sun floods the profound gorge with golden light, revealing all the fantastic buttresses and rounded towers of its mountain rampart, and falling softly on the varied green of the woods which clothe its depths. It was here that, according to the legend, Adonis met Aphrodite for the first or the last time,[9] and here his mangled body was buried.[10] A fairer scene could hardly be imagined for a story of tragic love and death. Yet, sequestered as the valley is and must always have been, it is not wholly deserted. A convent or a village may be observed here and there standing out against the sky on the top of some beetling crag, or clinging to the face of a nearly perpendicular cliff high above the foam and the din of the river; and at evening the lights that twinkle through the gloom betray the presence of human habitations on slopes which might seem inaccessible to man. In antiquity the whole of the lovely vale appears to have been dedicated to Adonis, and to this day it is haunted by his memory; for the heights which shut it in are crested at various points by ruined monuments of his worship, some of them overhanging dreadful abysses, down which it turns the head dizzy to look and see the eagles wheeling about their nests far below. One such monument exists at Ghineh. The face of a great rock, above a roughly hewn recess, is here carved with figures of Adonis and Aphrodite. He is portrayed with spear in rest, awaiting the attack of a bear, while she is seated in an attitude of sorrow.[11] Her grief-stricken figure may well be the mourning Aphrodite of the Lebanon described by Macrobius,[12] and the recess in the rock is perhaps her lover's tomb. Every year, in the belief of his worshippers, Adonis was wounded to death on the mountains, and every year the face of nature itself was dyed with his sacred blood. So year by year the Syrian damsels lamented his untimely fate,[13] while the red anemone, his flower, bloomed among the cedars of Lebanon, and the river ran red to the sea, fringing the winding shores of the blue Mediterranean, whenever the wind set inshore, with a sinuous band of crimson.

river, and even the sea, for a great way with a blood-red hue, and the crimson stain was believed to be the blood of Adonis, annually wounded to death by the boar on Mount Lebanon.[6] Again, the scarlet anemone is said to have sprung from the blood of Adonis, or to have been stained by it;[7] and as the anemone blooms in Syria about Easter, this may be thought to show that the festival of Adonis, or at least one of his festivals, was held in spring. The name of the flower is probably derived from Naaman ("darling"), which seems to have been an epithet of Adonis. The Arabs still call the anemone "wounds of the Naaman."[8] The red rose also was said to owe its hue to the same sad occasion; for Aphrodite, hastening to her wounded lover, trod on a bush of white roses; the cruel thorns tore her tender flesh, and her sacred blood dyed the white roses for ever red.[9] It would be idle, perhaps, to lay much weight on evidence drawn from the calendar of flowers, and in particular to press an argument so fragile as the bloom of the rose. Yet so far as it counts at all, the tale which links the damask rose with the death of Adonis points to a summer rather than to a spring celebration of his passion. In Attica, certainly, the festival fell at the height of summer. For the fleet which Athens fitted out against Syracuse, and by the destruction of which her power was permanently crippled, sailed at midsummer, and by an ominous coincidence the sombre rites of Adonis were being celebrated at the very time. As the troops marched down to the harbour to embark, the streets through which they passed were lined with coffins and corpse-like effigies, and the air was rent with the noise of women wailing for the dead Adonis. The circumstance cast a gloom over the sailing of the most splendid armament that Athens ever sent to sea.[10] Many ages afterwards, when the Emperor Julian made his first entry into Antioch, he found in like manner the gay, the luxurious capital of the East plunged in mimic grief for the annual death of Adonis: and if he had any presentiment of coming evil, the voices of lamentation which struck upon his ear must have seemed to sound his knell.[11]

The resemblance of these ceremonies to European ceremonies which I have described elsewhere[12] is obvious. From the similarity of these customs to each other and to the spring and midsummer customs of modern Europe we should naturally expect that they all admit of a common explanation. Hence, if the explanation which I have adopted of the latter is correct, the ceremony of the death and resurrection of Adonis must also have been a dramatic representation of the decay and revival of plant life. The inference thus based on the resemblance of the customs is confirmed by the following features in the legend and ritual of Adonis. His affinity with vegetation comes out at once in the common story of his birth. He was said to have been born from a myrrh-tree, the bark of which bursting, after a ten months' gestation, allowed the lovely infant to come forth. According to some, a boar rent the bark with his tusk and so opened a passage for the babe. A faint rationalistic colour was given to the legend by saying that his mother was a woman named Myrrh, who had been turned into a myrrh-tree soon after she had conceived the child.[13] The use of myrrh as incense at the festival of Adonis may have given rise to the fable.[14] We have seen that incense was burnt at the corresponding Babylonian rites,[15] just as it was burnt by the idolatrous Hebrews in honour of the Queen of Heaven,[16] who was no other than Astarte. Again, the story that Adonis spent half, or according to others a third, of the year in the lower world and the rest of it in the upper world, is explained most simply and naturally by supposing that he represented vegetation, especially the corn, which lies buried in the earth half the year and reappears above ground the other half. Certainly of the annual phenomena of nature there is none which suggests so obviously the idea of death and resurrection as the disappearance and reappearance of vegetation in autumn and spring. The annual death and revival of vegetation is a conception which readily presents itself to men in every stage of savagery and civilization; and the vastness of the scale on which this ever-recurring decay and regeneration takes place, together with man's intimate dependence on it for subsistence, combine to render it the most impressive annual occurrence in nature, at least within the temperate zones. It is no wonder that a phenomenon so important, so striking, and so universal should, by suggesting similar ideas, have given rise to similar rites in many lands. We may, therefore, accept as probable an explanation of the Adonis worship which accords so well with the facts of nature and with the analogy of similar rites in other lands. Moreover, the explanation is countenanced by a considerable body of opinion amongst the ancients themselves, who again and again interpreted the dying and reviving god as the reaped and sprouting grain.[17]

The character of Tammuz or Adonis as a corn-spirit comes out plainly in an account of his festival given by an Arabic writer of the tenth century. In describing the rites and sacrifices observed at the different seasons of the year by the heathen Syrians of Harran, he says: "Tammuz (July). In the middle of this month is the festival of el-Bûgât, that is, of the weeping women, and this is the Tâ-uz festival, which is celebrated in honour of the god Tâ-uz. The women bewail him, because his lord slew him so cruelly, ground his bones in a mill, and then scattered them to the wind. The women (during this festival) eat nothing which has been ground in a mill, but limit their diet to steeped wheat, sweet vetches, dates, raisins, and the like."[18] Tâ-uz, who is no other than Tammuz, is here like Burns's John Barleycorn—

"They wasted o'er a scorching flame
The marrow of his bones;
But a miller us'd him worst of all—
For he crush'd him between two stones."

This concentration, so to say, of the nature of Adonis upon the cereal crops is characteristic of the stage of culture reached by his worshippers in historical times. They had left the nomadic life of the wandering hunter and herdsman far behind them; for ages they had been settled on the land, and had depended for their subsistence mainly on the products of tillage. The berries and roots of the wilderness, the grass of the pastures, which had been matters of vital importance to their ruder forefathers, were now of little moment to them: more and more their thoughts and energies were engrossed by the staple of their life, the corn; more and more accordingly the propitiation of the deities of fertility in general and of the corn-spirit in particular tended to become the central feature of their religion. The aim they set before themselves in celebrating the rites was thoroughly practical. It was no vague poetical sentiment which prompted them to hail with joy the rebirth of vegetation and to mourn its decline. Hunger, felt or feared, was the mainspring of the worship of Adonis.

It has been suggested that the mourning for Adonis was essentially a harvest rite designed to propitiate the corn-god, who was then either perishing under the sickles of the reapers, or being trodden to death under the hoofs of the oxen on the threshing-floor. While the men slew him, the women wept crocodile tears at home to appease his natural indignation by a show of grief for his death.[19] The theory fits in well with the dates of the festivals, which fell in spring or summer; for spring and summer, not autumn, are the seasons of the barley and wheat harvests in the lands which worshipped Adonis. Further, the hypothesis is confirmed by the practice of the Egyptian reapers, who lamented, calling upon Isis, when they cut the first corn;[20] and it is recommended by the analogous customs of many hunting tribes, who testify great respect for the animals which they kill and eat.

Thus interpreted the death of Adonis is not the natural decay of vegetation in general under the summer heat or the winter cold; it is the violent destruction of the corn by man, who cuts it down on the field, stamps it to pieces on the threshing-floor, and grinds it to powder in the mill. That this was indeed the principal aspect in which Adonis presented himself in later times to the agricultural peoples of the Levant, may be admitted; but whether from the beginning he had been the corn and nothing but the corn, may be doubted. At an earlier period he may have been to the herdsman, above all, the tender herbage which sprouts after rain, offering rich pasture to the lean and hungry cattle. Earlier still he may have embodied the spirit of the nuts and berries which the autumn woods yield to the savage hunter and his squaw. And just as the husbandman must propitiate the spirit of the corn which he consumes, so also the herdsman must appease the spirit of the grass and leaves which his cattle munch, and the hunter must soothe the spirit of the roots which he digs, and of the fruits which he gathers from the bough.

214. Perhaps the best proof that Adonis was a deity of vegetation, and especially of the corn, is furnished by the gardens of Adonis, as they were called. These were baskets or pots filled with earth, in which wheat, barley, lettuces, fennel, and various kinds of flowers were sown and tended for eight days, chiefly or exclusively by women. Fostered by the sun's heat, the plants shot up rapidly, but having no root they withered as rapidly away, and at the end of eight days were carried out with the images of the dead Adonis, and flung with them into the sea or into springs.[1]

These gardens of Adonis are most naturally interpreted as representatives of Adonis or manifestations of his power; they represented him, true to his original nature, in vegetable form, while the images of him, with which they were carried out and cast into the water, portrayed him in his later human shape. All these Adonis ceremonies, if I am right, were originally intended as charms to promote the growth or revival of vegetation; and the principle by which they were supposed to produce this effect was homoeopathic or imitative magic.

215. Such "gardens" are still planted; first, by a primitive people as a regular agricultural rite, and, second, by European peasants at midsummer. Amongst the Oraons and Mundas of Bengal, when the time comes for planting out the rice which has been grown in seed-beds, a party of young people of both sexes go to the forest and cut a young Karma-tree, or the branch of one. Bearing it in triumph they return dancing, singing, and beating drums, and plant it in the middle of the village dancing-ground. A sacrifice is offered to the tree; and next morning the youth of both sexes, linked arm-in-arm, dance in a great circle round the Karma-tree, which is decked with strips of coloured cloth and sham bracelets and necklets of plaited straw. As a preparation for the festival, the daughters of the headman of the village cultivate blades of barley in a peculiar way. The seed is sown in moist, sandy soil, mixed with turmeric, and the blades sprout and unfold of a pale-yellow or primrose colour. On the day of the festival the girls take up these blades and carry them in baskets to the dancing-ground, where, prostrating themselves reverentially, they place some of the plants before the Karma-tree. Finally, the Karma-tree is taken away and thrown into a stream or tank.[1] The meaning of planting these barley blades and then presenting them to the Karma-tree is hardly open to question. Trees are supposed to exercise a quickening influence upon the growth of crops, and amongst the very people in question—the Mundas or Mundaris—"the grove deities are held responsible for the crops."[2] Therefore, when at the season for planting out the rice the Mundas bring in a tree and treat it with so much respect, their object can only be to foster thereby the growth of the rice which is about to be planted out; and the custom of causing barley blades to sprout rapidly and then presenting them to the tree must be intended to subserve the same purpose, perhaps by reminding the tree-spirit of his duty towards the crops, and stimulating his activity by this visible example of rapid vegetable growth. The throwing of the Karma-tree into the water is to be interpreted as a rain-charm. Whether the barley blades are also thrown into the water is not said; but if my interpretation of the custom is right, probably they are so. A distinction between this Bengal custom and the Greek rites of Adonis is that in the former the tree-spirit appears in his original form as a tree; whereas in the Adonis worship he appears in human form, represented as a dead man, though his vegetable nature is indicated by the gardens of Adonis, which are, so to say, a secondary manifestation of his original power as a tree-spirit.

Gardens of Adonis are cultivated also by the Hindus, with the intention apparently of ensuring the fertility both of the earth and of mankind. Thus at Oodeypoor in Rajputana a festival is held "in honour of Gouri, or Isani, the goddess of abundance." The rites begin when the sun enters the sign of the Ram, the opening of the Hindu year. An image of the goddess Gouri is made of earth, and a smaller one of her husband Iswara, and the two are placed together. A small trench is next dug, barley is sown in it, and the ground watered and heated artificially till the grain sprouts, when the women dance round it hand in hand, invoking the blessing of Gouri on their husbands. After that the young corn is taken up and distributed by the women to the men, who wear it in their turbans. Every wealthy family, or at least every subdivision of the city, has its own image. These and other rites, known only to the initiated, occupy several days, and are performed within doors. Then the images of the goddess and her husband are decorated and borne in procession to a beautiful lake, whose deep blue waters mirror the cloudless Indian sky, marble palaces, and orange groves. Here the women, their hair decked with roses and jessamine, carry the image of Gouri down a marble staircase to the water's edge, and dance round it singing hymns and love-songs. Meantime the goddess is supposed to bathe in the water. No men take part in the ceremony; even the image of Iswara, the husband-god, attracts little attention.[3] In these rites the distribution of the barley shoots to the men, and the invocation of a blessing on their husbands by the wives, point clearly to the desire of offspring as one motive for observing the custom. The same motive probably explains the use of gardens of Adonis at the marriage of Brahmans in the Madras Presidency. Seeds of five or nine sorts are mixed and sown in earthen pots, which are made specially for the purpose and are filled with earth. Bride and bridegroom water the seeds both morning and evening for four days; and on the fifth day the seedlings are thrown, like the real gardens of Adonis, into a tank or river.[4]

In the Himalayan districts of North-Western India the cultivators sow barley, maize, pulse, or mustard in a basket of earth on the twenty-fourth day of the fourth month (*Asárh*), which falls about the middle of July.

Then on the last day of the month they place amidst the new sprouts small clay images of Mahadeo and Parvati and worship them in remembrance of the marriage of those deities. Next day they cut down the green stalks and and wear them in their head-dress.[5] Similar is the barley feast known as Jâyî or Jawâra in Upper India and as Bhujariya in the Central Provinces. On the seventh day of the light half of the month Sâwan grains of barley are sown in a pot of manure, and spring up so quickly that by the end of the month the vessel is full of long, yellowish-green stalks. On the first day of the next month, Bhâdon, the women and girls take the stalks out, throw the earth and manure into water, and distribute the plants among their male friends, who bind them in their turbans and about their dress.[6] At the temple of the goddess Padmavati, near Pandharpur in the Bombay Presidency, a Nine Nights' festival is held in the bright half of the month Ashvin (September–October). At this time a bamboo frame is hung in front of the image, and from it depend garlands of flowers and strings of wheaten cakes. Under the frame the floor in front of the pedestal is strewn with a layer of earth in which wheat is sown and allowed to sprout.[7] A similar rite is observed in the same month before the images of two other goddesses, Ambabai and Lakhubai, who also have temples at Pandharpur.[8]

The person at whose house these baskets were prepared is obliged to remain bare-headed from the commencement of the ceremony. After the baskets have been floated down the stream his relatives present him with a turban and he puts it on as a sign that all is completed.[8a]

Again, among the Oraons of Chota Nagpur in India, "In the month of Bhado (August) seven days before the Karam festival, the Oraon maidens of the village carry two basketfuls of sand to their own dormitory, deposit this sand on the floor of their dormitory, scatter over this sand a few handfuls of barley-seeds, and cover them over with a thin layer of sand. Every night up till the Karam festival on the eleventh night of the moon, the maidens sprinkle water over the sand and sit up late at night singing songs and watching the seeds germinating. On the morning following the Karam festival, the maidens take up the seeds with shoots sprouting out of them, and distribute these germinated barley-seeds to the young Oraons of the village who all assemble at the village akhra at the time and also to such other Oraons of the village who may happen to be present at the akhra at the time. When the youth have received these mystic presents, the youth of both sexes dance together at the akhra. Although the meaning of this rite is no longer remembered by the people, it looks like a magical ceremony designed to improve the fecundity of the young people, and also perhaps to stimulate the growth of the standing crops of the fields."[8b]

Among the Bhils of Malwa, a district of north-western India, it is customary on the day when they begin their autumnal sowing to perform the mock marriage of two wooden dolls. All the ceremonies of marriage are

Jesus Christ passed upon the Cross. Beginning at the eighteenth and ending at the twenty-first hour of Italian time two priests preached alternately on the Passion. Anciently the sermons were delivered in the open air on the place called the Calvary: at last, when the third hour was about to strike, at the words *emisit spiritum* Christ died, bowing his head amid the sobs and and tears of the bystanders. Immediately afterwards in some places, three hours afterwards in others, the sacred body was unnailed and deposited in the coffin. In Castronuovo, at the Ave Maria, two priests clad as Jews, representing Joseph of Arimathea and Nicodemus, with their servants in costume, repaired to the Calvary, preceded by the Company of the Whites. There, with doleful verses and chants appropriate to the occasion, they performed the various operations of the Deposition, after which the procession took its way to the larger church. . . . In Salaparuta the Calvary is erected in the church. At the announcement of the death, the Crucified is made to bow his head by means of machinery, while guns are fired, trumpets sound, and amid the silence of the people, impressed by the death of the Redeemer, the strains of a melancholy funeral march are heard. Christ is removed from the Cross and deposited in the coffin by three priests. After the procession of the dead Christ the burial is performed, that is, two priests lay Christ in a fictitious sepulchre, from which at the mass of Easter Saturday the image of the risen Christ issues and is elevated upon the altar by means of machinery."[2] Scenic representations of the same sort, with variations of detail, are exhibited at Easter in the Abruzzi,[3] and probably in many other parts of the Catholic world.[4]

When we reflect how often the Church has skilfully contrived to plant the seeds of the new faith on the old stock of paganism, we may surmise that the Easter celebration of the dead and risen Christ was grafted upon a similar celebration of the dead and risen Adonis, which, as we have seen reason to believe, was celebrated in Syria at the same season. The type, created by Greek artists, of the sorrowful goddess with her dying lover in her arms, resembles and may have been the model of the *Pietà* of Christian art, the Virgin with the dead body of her divine Son in her lap, of which the most celebrated example is the one by Michael Angelo in St. Peter's.

THE MOTHER GODDESS

218. In Cyprus it appears that before marriage all women were formerly obliged by custom to prostitute themselves to strangers at the sanctuary of the goddess, whether she went by the name of Aphrodite, Astarte, or what not.[1] Similar customs prevailed in many parts of Western Asia. Whatever its motive, the practice was clearly regarded, not as an orgy of lust, but as a solemn religious duty performed in the service of that great Mother Goddess of Western Asia whose name varied, while her type remained constant, from place to place. Thus at Babylon every woman, whether rich or poor, had once in her life to submit to the embraces of a stranger at the temple of Mylitta, that is, of Ishtar or Astarte, and to dedicate to the goddess the wages earned by this sanctified harlotry.[2] At Heliopolis or Baalbec in Syria, the custom of the country required that every maiden should prostitute herself to a stranger at the temple of Astarte, and matrons as well as maids testified their devotion to the goddess in the same manner. The emperor Constantine abolished the custom, destroyed the temple, and built a church in its stead.[3] In Phoenician temples women prostituted themselves for hire in the service of religion, believing that by this conduct they propitiated the goddess and won her favour.[4] "It was a law of the Amorites, that she who was about to marry should sit in fornication seven days by the gate."[5]

At Byblus the people shaved their heads in the annual mourning for Adonis. Women who refused to sacrifice their hair had to give themselves up to strangers on a certain day of the festival, and the money which they thus earned was devoted to the goddess.[6] A Greek inscription found at Tralles in Lydia proves that the practice of religious prostitution survived in that country as late as the second century of our era. It records of a certain woman, Aurelia Aemilia by name, not only that she herself served the god in the capacity of a harlot at his express command, but that her mother and other female ancestors had done the same before her; and the publicity of the record, engraved on a marble column which supported a votive offering, shows that no stain attached to such a life and such a parentage.[7] In Armenia the noblest families dedicated their daughters to the service of the goddess Anaitis in her temple at Acilisena, where the damsels acted as prostitutes for a long time before they were given in marriage. Nobody scrupled to take one of these girls to wife when her period of service was over.[8] Again, the goddess Ma was served by a multitude of sacred harlots at Comana in Pontus, and crowds of men and women flocked to her sanctuary from the neighbouring cities and country to attend the biennial festivals or to pay their vows to the goddess.[9]

219. If we survey the whole of the evidence on this subject, some of which has still to be laid before the reader, we may conclude that a great Mother Goddess, the personification of all the reproductive energies of nature, was worshipped under different names but with a substantial similarity of myth and ritual by many peoples of Western Asia; that associated with her was a lover, or rather series of lovers, divine yet mortal, with whom she mated year by year, their commerce being deemed essential to the propagation of animals and plants, each in their several kind; and further, that the fabulous union of the divine pair was simulated and, as it were, multiplied on earth by the real, though temporary, union of the human sexes at the sanctuary of the goddess for the sake of thereby ensuring the fruitfulness of the ground and the increase of man and beast.[1]

220. At Paphos the custom of religious prostitution is said to have been in-

tions are abundantly proved by the votive offerings found at her ancient shrine among the wooded hills. On the other hand, the patricians, who afterwards invaded the country, brought with them father-kin in its strictest form, and consistently enough paid their devotions rather to Father Jove than to Mother Juno.

A parallel to what I conjecture to have been the original relation of the Flaminica to her husband the Flamen may to a certain extent be found among the Khasis of Assam, who preserve to this day the ancient system of mother-kin in matters of inheritance and religion. For among these people the propitation of deceased ancestors is deemed essential to the welfare of the community, and of all their ancestors they revere most the primaeval ancestress of the clan. Accordingly in every sacrifice a priest must be assisted by a priestess; indeed, we are told that he merely acts as her deputy, and that she "is without doubt a survival of the time when, under the matriarchate, the priestess was the agent for the performance of all religious ceremonies." It does not appear that the priest need be the husband of the priestess; but in the Khyrim State, where each division has its own goddess to whom sacrifices are offered, the priestess is the mother, sister, niece, or other maternal relation of the priest. It is her duty to prepare all the sacrificial articles, and without her assistance the sacrifice cannot take place.[5] Here, then, as among the ancient Romans on my hypothesis, we have the superiority of the priestess over the priest based on a corresponding superiority of the goddess or divine ancestress over the god or divine ancestor; and here, as at Rome, a priest would clearly have to vacate office if he had no woman of the proper relationship to assist him in the performance of his sacred duties.

222. Cinyras is said to have been famed for his exquisite beauty[1] and to have been wooed by Aphrodite herself.[2] Thus it would appear, as scholars have already observed,[3] that Cinyras was in a sense a duplicate of his handsome son Adonis, to whom the inflammable goddess also lost her heart. Further, these stories of the love of Aphrodite for members of the royal house of Paphos can hardly be dissociated from the corresponding legend told of Pygmalion, the Phoenician king of Cyprus, who is said to have fallen in love with an image of Aphrodite and taken it to his bed.[4] When we consider that Pygmalion was the father-in-law of Cinyras, that the son of Cinyras was Adonis, and that all three, in successive generations, are said to have been concerned in a love-intrigue with Aphrodite, we can hardly help concluding that the early Phoenician kings of Paphos, or their sons, regularly claimed to be not merely the priests of the goddess but also her lovers, in other words, that in their official capacity they personated Adonis. At all events Adonis is said to have reigned in Cyprus,[5] and it appears to be certain that the title of Adonis was regularly borne by the sons of all the Phoenician kings of the island.[6] It is true that the title strictly signified no more than "lord"; yet the legends which con-

nect these Cyprian princes with the goddess of love make it probable that they claimed the divine nature as well as the human dignity of Adonis. The story of Pygmalion points to a ceremony of a sacred marriage in which the king wedded the image of Aphrodite, or rather of Astarte. If this was so, the tale was in a sense true, not of a single man only, but of a whole series of men. As the custom of religious prostitution at Paphos is said to have been founded by King Cinyras and observed by his daughters, we may surmise that the kings of Paphos played the part of the divine bridegroom in a less innocent rite than the form of marriage with a statue; in fact, that at certain festivals each of them had to mate with one or more of the sacred harlots of the temple, who played Astarte to his Adonis. The fruit of their union would rank as sons and daughters of the deity, and would in time become the parents of gods and goddesses, like their fathers and mothers before them. In this manner Paphos, and perhaps all sanctuaries of the great Asiatic goddess where sacred prostitution was practised, might be well stocked with human deities, the offspring of the divine king by his wives, concubines, and temple harlots. Any one of these might probably succeed his father on the throne[7] or be sacrificed in his stead whenever stress of war or other grave junctures called, as they sometimes did, for the death of a royal victim. Such a tax, levied occasionally on the king's numerous progeny for the good of the country, would neither extinguish the divine stock nor break the father's heart, who divided his paternal affection among so many.

EXCURSUS: THE BURNED GOD

223. A constant feature in the myth of Adonis was his premature and violent death. If, then, the kings of Paphos regularly personated Adonis, we must ask whether they imitated their divine prototype in death as in life. Tradition varied as to the end of Cinyras. Some thought that he slew himself on discovering his incest with his daughter;[1] others alleged that, like Marsyas, he was defeated by Apollo in a musical contest and put to death by the victor.[2] Yet he cannot strictly be said to have perished in the flower of his youth if he lived, as Anacreon averred, to the ripe age of one hundred and sixty.[3] If we must choose between the two stories, it is perhaps more likely that he died a violent death than that he survived to an age which surpassed that of Thomas Parr by eight years, though it fell far short of the antediluvian standard. The life of eminent men in remote ages is exceedingly elastic and may be lengthened or shortened, in the interests of history, at the taste and fancy of the historian.

224. If a custom of putting a king or his son to death in the character of a god has left small traces of itself in Cyprus, the vestiges of that gloomy rite are clearer in Phoenicia itself and in the Phoenician colonies, which lay more remote from the highways of Grecian commerce. At all events, a custom of

was believed to have perished by a voluntary death on a pyre. For on many a beach and headland of the Aegean, where the Phoenicians had their trading factories, the Greeks may have watched the bale-fires of Melqarth blazing in the darkness of night, and have learned with wonder that the strange foreign folk were burning their god. In this way the legend of the voyages of Hercules and his death in the flames may be supposed to have originated. Yet with the legend the Greeks borrowed the custom of burning the god; for at the festivals of Hercules a pyre used to be kindled in memory of the hero's fiery death on Mount Oeta.[4] We may surmise, though we are not expressly told, that an effigy of Hercules was regularly burned on the pyre.

227. The theory that kings or princes were formerly burned to death in the character of gods is singularly confirmed by another and wholly independent line of argument.

Near the sea, within a day's march of Tarsus, might be seen in antiquity the ruins of a great ancient city named Anchiale, and outside its walls stood a monument called the monument of Sardanapalus, on which was carved in stone the figure of the monarch. He was represented snapping the fingers of his right hand, and the gesture was explained by an accompanying inscription, engraved in Assyrian characters, to the following effect:—"Sardanapalus, son of Anacyndaraxes, built Anchiale and Tarsus in one day. Eat, drink, and play, for everything else is not worth that," by which was implied that all other human affairs were not worth a snap of the fingers.[1] The story that Tarsus was founded by Sardanapalus may well be apocryphal,[2] but there must have been some reason for his association with the city. On the present hypothesis that reason is to be found in the traditional manner of his death. To avoid falling into the hands of the rebels, who laid siege to Nineveh, he built a huge pyre in his palace, heaped it up with gold and silver and purple raiment, and then burnt himself, his wife, his concubines, and his eunuchs in the fire.[3] The story is false of the historical Sardanapalus, that is, of the great Assyrian king Ashurbanipal, but it is true of his brother Shamashshumukin. Being appointed king of Babylon by Ashurbanipal, he revolted against his suzerain and benefactor, and was besieged by him in his capital. The siege was long and the resistance desperate, for the Babylonians knew that they had no mercy to expect from the ruthless Assyrians. But they were decimated by famine and pestilence, and when the city could hold out no more, King Shamashshumukin, determined not to fall alive into the hands of his offended brother, shut himself up in his palace, and there burned himself to death, along with his wives, his children, his slaves, and his treasures, at the very moment when the conquerors were breaking in the gates.[4] Not many years afterwards the same tragedy was repeated at Nineveh itself by Saracus or Sinsharishkun, the last king of Assyria. Besieged by the rebel Nabopolassar, king of Babylon, and by Cyaxares, king of the Medes, he burned himself in his palace. That was the end of Nineveh and of the Assyrian empire.⁵ Thus Greek history preserved the memory of the catastrophe, but transferred it from the real victims to the far more famous Ashurbanipal, whose figure in after ages loomed vast and dim against the setting sun of Assyrian glory.

228. Another Oriental monarch who prepared at least to die in the flames was Croesus, king of Lydia. Herodotus tells how the Persians under Cyrus captured Sardes, the Lydian capital, and took Croesus alive, and how Cyrus caused a great pyre to be erected, on which he placed the captive monarch in fetters, and with him twice seven Lydian youths. Fire was then applied to the pile, but at the last moment Cyrus relented, a sudden shower extinguished the flames, and Croesus was spared.¹ But it is most improbable that the Persians, with their profound reverence for the sanctity of fire, should have thought of defiling the sacred element with the worst of all pollutions, the contact of dead bodies.² Such an act would have seemed to them sacrilige of the deepest dye. For to them fire was the earthly form of the heavenly light, the eternal, the infinite, the divine; death, on the other hand, was in their opinion the main source of corruption and uncleanness. Hence they took the most stringent precautions to guard the purity of fire from the defilement of death. If a man or a dog died in a house where the holy fire burned, the fire had to be removed from the house and kept away for nine nights in winter or a month in summer before it might be brought back; and if any man broke the rule by bringing back the fire within the appointed time, he might be punished with two hundred stripes.³ As for burning a corpse in the fire, it was the most heinous of all sins, an invention of Ahriman, the devil; there was no atonement for it, and it was punished with death.⁴ Nor did the law remain a dead letter. Down to the beginning of our era the death penalty was inflicted on all who threw a corpse or cow-dung on the fire, nay, even on such as blew on the fire with their breath.⁵ It is hard, therefore, to believe that a Persian king should have commanded his subjects to perpetrate a deed which he and they viewed with horror as the most flagitious sacrilege conceivable.

Another and in some respects truer version of the story of Croesus and Cyrus has been preserved by two older witnesses—namely, by the Greek poet Bacchylides, who was born some forty years after the event, and by a Greek artist who painted the scene on a red-figured vase about, or soon after, the time of the poet's birth. Bacchylides tells us that when the Persians captured Sardes in 546 B.C., Croesus, unable to brook the thought of slavery, caused a pyre to be erected in front of his courtyard, mounted it with his wife and daughters, and bade a page apply a light to the wood. A bright blaze shot up, but Zeus extinguished it with rain from heaven, and Apollo of the Golden Sword wafted the pious king and his daughters to the happy land beyond the North Wind.⁶ In like manner the vase-painter clearly represents the burning of Croesus as a voluntary act, not as a punishment inflicted on him by the conqueror. He lets us see the king enthroned upon the pyre with a wreath of laurel on his head and a sceptre in one hand, while with the other he is pouring a libation. An attendant is in the act of applying to the pile two objects which have been variously interpreted as torches to kindle the wood or whisks to sprinkle holy water. The demeanour of the king is solemn and composed: he seems to be performing a religious rite, not suffering an ignominious death.[7]

Thus we may fairly conclude that in the extremity of his fortunes Croesus prepared to meet death like a king or a god in the flames. It was thus that Hercules, from whom the old kings of Lydia claimed to be sprung,[8] ascended from earth to heaven: it was thus that Zimri, king of Israel, passed beyond the reach of his enemies: it was thus that Shamashshumukin, king of Babylon, escaped a brother's vengeance: it was thus that the last king of Assyria expired in the ruins of his capital; and it was thus that, sixty-six years after the capture of Sardes, the Carthaginian king Hamilcar sought to retrieve a lost battle by a hero's death.

229. These events and these traditions seem to prove that under certain circumstances Oriental monarchs deliberately chose to burn themselves to death. What were these circumstances? and what were the consequences of the act? If the intention had merely been to escape from the hands of a conqueror, an easier mode of death would naturally have been chosen. There must have been a special reason for electing to die by fire. The legendary death of Hercules, the historical death of Hamilcar, and the picture of Croesus enthroned in state on the pyre and pouring a libation, all combine to indicate that to be burnt alive was regarded as a solemn sacrifice, nay, more than that, as an apotheosis which raised the victim to the rank of a god.[1] For it is to be remembered that Hamilcar as well as Hercules was worshipped after death. Fire, moreover, was regarded by the ancients as a purgative so powerful that properly applied it could burn away all that was mortal of a man, leaving only the divine and immortal spirit behind. Hence we read of goddesses who essayed to confer immortality on the infant sons of kings by burning them in the fire by night; but their beneficent purpose was always frustrated by the ignorant interposition of the mother or father, who peeping into the room saw the child in the flames and raised a cry of horror, thus disconcerting the goddess at her magic rites. This story is told of Isis in the house of the king of Byblus, of Demeter in the house of the king of Eleusis, and of Thetis in the house of her mortal husband Peleus.[2] In a slightly different way the witch Medea professed to give back to the old their lost youth by boiling them with a hellbroth in her magic cauldron;[3] and when Pelops had been butchered and served up at a banquet of the gods by his cruel father Tantalus, the divine beings, touched with pity, plunged his mangled remains in a kettle, from which after decoction he emerged alive and young.[4] "Fire," says Jamblichus, "destroys the material part of sacrifices, it purifies all things that are brought near it, releasing them from the bonds of matter and, in virtue of the purity of its nature, making them meet for communion with the gods. So, too, it releases us from the bondage of corruption, it likens us to the gods, it makes us meet for their friendship, and it converts our material nature into an immaterial."[5] Thus we can understand why kings and commoners who claimed or aspired to divinity should choose death by fire. It opened to them the gates of heaven. The quack Peregrinus, who ended his disreputable career in the flames at Olympia, gave out that after death he would be turned into a spirit who would guard men from the perils of the night; and, as Lucian remarked, no doubt there were plenty of fools to believe him.[6] According to one account, the Sicilian philosopher Empedocles, who set up for being a god in his lifetime, leaped into the crater of Etna in order to establish his claim to godhead.[7] There is nothing incredible in the tradition. The crack-brained philosopher, with his itch for notoriety, may well have done what Indian fakirs[8] and the brazen-faced mountebank Peregrinus did in antiquity, and what Russian peasants and Chinese Buddhists have done in modern times. There is no extremity to which fanaticism or vanity, or a mixture of the two, will not impel its victims.

ATTIS

230. Another of those gods whose supposed death and resurrection struck deep roots into the faith and ritual of Western Asia is Attis. He was to Phrygia what Adonis was to Syria. Like Adonis, he appears to have been a god of vegetation, and his death and resurrection were annually mourned and rejoiced over at a festival in spring.[1] The legends and rites of the two gods were so much alike that the ancients themselves sometimes identified them.

Attis was said to have been a fair young shepherd or herdsman beloved by Cybele, the Mother of the Gods, a great Asiatic goddess of fertility, who had her chief home in Phrygia. Some held that Attis was her son. His birth, like that of many other heroes, is said to have been miraculous. His mother, Nana, was a virgin, who conceived by putting a ripe almond or a pomegranate in her bosom.

Two different accounts of his death were current. According to the one, he was killed by a boar, like Adonis.[2] According to the other, he unmanned himself under a pine-tree and bled to death on the spot.[3] The latter is said to have been the local story told by the people of Pessinus, a great seat of the worship of Cybele, and the whole legend of which the story forms a part is stamped with a rudeness and savagery that speaks strongly for its antiquity. Both tales might claim the support of custom or rather both were probably invented to explain certain customs observed by the worshippers. The story of the self-mutilation of Attis is clearly an attempt to account for the self-mutilation of his priests, who regularly castrated themselves on entering the service of the goddess. The story of his death by the boar may have been told to explain why his worshippers, especially the people of Pessinus, abstained from eating swine.[4] In like manner the worshippers of Adonis abstained from pork, because a boar had killed their god.[5]

The worship of the Phrygian Mother of the Gods was adopted by the Romans in 204 B.C. towards the close of their long struggle with Hannibal. For their drooping spirits had been opportunely cheered by a prophecy, alleged to be drawn from that convenient farrago of nonsense, the Sibylline Books, that the foreign invader would be driven from Italy if the great Oriental goddess were brought to Rome. Accordingly ambassadors were despatched to her sacred city Pessinus in Phrygia. The small black stone which embodied the mighty divinity was entrusted to them and conveyed to Rome, where it was received with great respect and installed in the temple of Victory on the Palatine Hill. It was the middle of April when the goddess arrived,[6] and she went to work at once. For the harvest that year was such as had not been seen for many a long day, and in the very next year Hannibal and his veterans embarked for Africa. As he looked his last on the coast of Italy, fading behind him in the distance, he could not foresee that Europe, which had repelled the arms, would yet yield to the gods, of the Orient. The vanguard of the conquerors had already encamped in the heart of Italy before the rearguard of the beaten army fell sullenly back from its shores.

We may conjecture, though we are not told, that the Mother of the Gods brought with her the worship of her youthful lover or son to her new home in the West. Certainly the Romans were familiar with the Galli, the emasculated priests of Attis, before the close of the Republic. These unsexed beings, in their Oriental costume, with little images suspended on their breasts, appear to have been a familiar sight in the streets of Rome, which they traversed in procession, carrying the image of the goddess and chanting their hymns to the music of cymbals and tambourines, flutes and horns, while the people, impressed by the fantastic show and moved by the wild strains, flung alms to them in abundance, and buried the image and its bearers under showers of roses.[7] A further step was taken by the Emperor Claudius when he incorporated the Phrygian worship of the sacred tree, and with it probably the orgiastic rites of Attis, in the established religion of Rome.[8]

231. The great spring festival of Cybele and Attis is best known to us in the form in which it was celebrated at Rome; but as we are informed that the Roman ceremonies were also Phrygian,[1] we may assume that they differed hardly, if at all, from their Asiatic original. The order of the festival seems to have been as follows.[2]

(a) On the twenty-second day of March, a pine-tree was cut in the woods and brought into the sanctuary of Cybele, where it was treated as a great divinity. The duty of carrying the sacred tree was entrusted to a guild of Tree-bearers. The trunk was swathed like a corpse with woollen bands and decked with wreaths of violets, for violets were said to have sprung from the blood of Attis, as roses and anemones sprang from the blood of Adonis; and the effigy of a young man, doubtless that of Attis himself, was tied to the middle of the stem.

(b) On the second day of the festival, the twenty-third of March, the chief ceremony seems to have been a blowing of trumpets.

(c) The third day, the twenty-fourth of March, was known as the Day of Blood: the Archigallus or high-priest drew blood from his arms and presented it as an offering. Nor was he alone in making this bloody sacrifice. Stirred by the wild barbaric music of clashing cymbals, rumbling drums, droning horns, and screaming flutes, the inferior clergy whirled about in the dance with waggling heads and streaming hair, until, rapt into a frenzy of excitement and insensible to pain, they gashed their bodies with potsherds or slashed them with knives in order to bespatter the altar and the sacred tree with their flowing blood. The ghastly rite probably formed part of the mourning for Attis and may have been intended to strengthen him for the resurrection. The Australian aborigines cut themselves in like manner over the graves of their friends for the purpose, perhaps, of enabling them to be born again.[3] Further, we may conjecture, though we are not expressly told, that it was on the same Day of Blood and for the same purpose that the novices sacrificed their virility. Wrought up to the highest pitch of religious excitement they dashed the severed portions of themselves against the image of the cruel goddess. These broken instruments of fertility were afterwards reverently wrapt up and buried in the earth or in subterranean chambers sacred to Cybele,[4] where, like the offering of blood, they may have been deemed instrumental in recalling Attis to life and hastening the general resurrection of nature, which was then bursting into leaf and blossom in the vernal sunshine. Some confirmation of this conjecture is furnished by the savage story that the mother of Attis conceived by putting in her bosom a pomegranate sprung from the severed genitals of a man-monster named Agdestis, a sort of double of Attis.[5]

If there is any truth in this conjectural explanation of the custom, we can readily understand why other Asiatic goddesses of fertility were served in like manner by eunuch priests. These feminine deities required to receive from their male ministers, who personated the divine lovers, the means of discharging their beneficent functions: they had themselves to be impregnated by the life-giving energy before they could transmit it to the world. Goddesses thus ministered to by eunuch priests were the great Artemis of Ephesus[6] and the great Syrian Astarte of Hierapolis,[7] whose sanctuary, frequented by swarms of pilgrims and enriched by the offerings of Assyria and Babylonia, of Arabia and Phoenicia, was perhaps in the days of its glory the most popular in the East.[8] Now the unsexed priests of this Syrian goddess resembled those of Cybele so closely that some people took them to be the same.[9] And the mode in which they dedicated themselves to the religious life was similar. The greatest festival of the year at Hierapolis fell at the beginning of spring, when multitudes thronged to the sanctuary from Syria and the regions round about. While the flutes played, the drums beat, and the eunuch priests slashed themselves with knives, the religious excitement gradually spread like a wave among the crowd of onlookers, and many a one did that which he little thought to do when he came as a holiday spectator to the festival. For man after man, his veins throbbing with the music, his eyes fascinated by the sight of the streaming blood, flung his garments from him, leaped forth with a shout, and seizing one of the swords which stood ready for the purpose, castrated himself on the spot. Then he ran through the city, holding the bloody pieces in his hand, till he threw them into one of the houses which he passed in his mad career. The household thus honoured had to furnish him with a suit of female attire and female ornaments, which he wore for the rest of his life.[10] When the tumult of emotion had subsided, and the man had come to himself again, the irrevocable sacrifice must often have been followed by passionate sorrow and lifelong regret. This revulsion of natural human feeling after the frenzies of a fanatical religion is powerfully depicted by Catullus in a celebrated poem.[11]

The parallel of these Syrian devotees confirms the view that in the similar worship of Cybele the sacrifice of virility took place on the Day of Blood at the vernal rites of the goddess, when the violets, supposed to spring from the red drops of her wounded lover, were in bloom among the pines. Indeed the story that Attis unmanned himself under a pine-tree[12] was clearly devised to explain why his priests did the same beside the sacred violet-wreathed tree at his festival.

At all events, we can hardly doubt that the Day of Blood witnessed the mourning for Attis over an effigy of him which was afterwards buried.[13] The image thus laid in the sepulchre was probably the same which had hung upon the tree. Throughout the period of mourning the worshippers fasted from bread, nominally because Cybele had done so in her grief for the death of Attis, but really perhaps for the same reason which induced the women of Harran to abstain from eating anything ground in a mill while they wept for Tammuz. To partake of bread or flour at such a season might have been deemed a wanton profanation of the bruised and broken body of the god. Or the fast may possibly have been a preparation for a sacramental meal.[14]

(d) But when night had fallen, the sorrow of the worshippers was turned to joy. For suddenly a light shone in the darkness: the tomb was opened: the god had risen from the dead; and as the priest touched the lips of the weeping mourners with balm, he softly whispered in their ears the glad tidings of salvation. The resurrection of the god was hailed by his disciples as a promise that they too would issue triumphant from the corruption of the grave.[15]

(e) On the morrow, the twenty-fifth day of March, which was reckoned the vernal equinox, the divine resurrection was celebrated with a wild outburst of glee. At Rome, and probably elsewhere, the celebration took the form of a carnival. It was the Festival of Joy (*Hilaria*). A universal licence prevailed. Every man might say and do what he pleased. People went about the streets in disguise. No dignity was too high or too sacred for the humblest citizen to assume with impunity.[16]

(f) Next day, the twenty-sixth of March, was given to repose, which must have been much needed after the varied excitements and fatigues of the preceding days.[17] Finally, the Roman festival closed on the twenty-seventh of March with a procession to the brook Almo. The silver image of the goddess, with its face of jagged black stone, sat in a wagon drawn by oxen. Preceded by the nobles walking barefoot, it moved slowly, to the loud music of pipes and tambourines, out by the Porta Capena, and so down to the banks of the Almo, which flows into the Tiber just below the walls of Rome. There the high-priest, robed in purple, washed the wagon, the image, and the other sacred objects in the water of the stream. On returning from their bath, the wain and the oxen were strewn with fresh spring flowers. All was mirth and gaiety. No one thought of the blood that had flowed so lately. Even the eunuch priests forgot their wounds.[18]

232. Such, then, appears to have been the annual solemnization of the death and resurrection of Attis in spring. But besides these public rites, his worship is known to have comprised certain secret or mystic ceremonies, which probably aimed at bringing the worshipper, and especially the novice, into closer communication with his god. Our information as to the nature of these mysteries and the date of their celebration is unfortunately very scanty, but they seem to have included a sacramental meal and a baptism of blood. In the sacrament the novice became a partaker of the mysteries by eating out of a drum and drinking out of a cymbal, two instruments of music which figured prominently in the thrilling orchestra of Attis.[1] The fast which accompanied the mourning for the dead god may perhaps have been designed to prepare the body of the communicant for the reception of the blessed sacrament by purging it of all that could defile by contact the sacred elements.[2] In the baptism the devotee, crowned with gold and wreathed with fillets, descended into a pit, the mouth of which was covered with a wooden grating. A bull, adorned with garlands of flowers, its forehead glittering with gold leaf, was then driven on to the grating and there stabbed to death with a consecrated spear. Its hot reeking blood poured in torrents through the apertures, and was received with devout eagerness by the worshipper on every part of his person and garments, till he emerged from the pit, drenched, dripping, and scarlet from head to foot, to receive the homage, nay the adoration, of his fellows as one who had been born again to eternal life and had washed away his sins in the blood of the bull.[3] For some time afterwards the fiction of a new birth was kept up by dieting him on milk like a new-born babe.[4] The regeneration of the worshipper took place at the same time as the regeneration of his god, namely at the vernal equinox.[5]

233. The original character of Attis as a tree-spirit is brought out plainly by the part which the pine-tree plays in his legend, his ritual, and his monuments.[1] The story that he was a human being transformed into a pine-tree is only one of those transparent attempts at rationalizing old beliefs which meet us so frequently in mythology. The bringing in of the pine-tree from the woods, decked with violets and woollen bands, is like bringing in the May-tree or Summer-tree in modern folk-custom; and the effigy which was attached to the pine-tree was only a duplicate representative of the tree-spirit Attis. After being fastened to the tree, the effigy was kept for a year and then burned.[2] The same thing appears to have been sometimes done with the May-pole; and in like manner the effigy of the corn-spirit, made at harvest, is often preserved till it is replaced by a new effigy at next year's harvest.[3] The original intention of such customs was no doubt to maintain the spirit of vegetation in life throughout the year. Why the Phrygians should have worshipped the pine above other trees we can only guess. Perhaps the sight of its changeless, though sombre, green cresting the ridges of the high hills above the fading splendour of the autumn woods in the valleys may have seemed to their eyes to mark it out as the seat of a diviner life, of something exempt from the sad vicissitudes of the seasons, constant and eternal as the sky which stooped to meet it. Further, pine-cones were regarded as symbols or rather instruments of fertility. Hence at the festival of the Thesmophoria they were thrown, along with pigs and other agents or emblems of fecundity, into the sacred vaults of Demeter for the purpose of quickening the ground and the wombs of women.[4]

234. Like tree-spirits in general, Attis was apparently thought to wield power over the fruits of the earth or even to be identical with the corn. One of his epithets was "very fruitful": he was addressed as the "reaped green (or yellow) ear of corn"; and the story of his sufferings, death, and resurrection was interpreted as the ripe grain wounded by the reaper, buried in the granary, and coming to life again when it is sown in the ground.[1] A statue of him in the Lateran Museum at Rome clearly indicates his relation to the fruits of the earth, and particularly to the corn; for it represents him with a bunch of ears of corn and fruit in his hand, and a wreath of pine-cones, pomegranates, and other fruits on his head, while from the top of his Phrygian cap ears of corn are sprouting.[2] On a stone urn, which contained the ashes of an Archigallus or high-priest of Attis, the same idea is expressed in a slightly different way. The top of the urn is adorned with ears of corn carved in relief, and it is surmounted by the figure of a cock, whose tail consists of ears of corn.[3] Cybele in like manner was conceived as a goddess of fertility who could make or mar the fruits of the earth; for the people of Augustodunum (Autun) in Gaul used to cart her image about in a wagon for the good of the fields and vineyards, while they danced and sang before it,[4] and we have seen that in Italy an unusually fine harvest was attributed to the recent arrival of the Great Mother.[5] The bathing of the image of the goddess in a river may well have been a rain-charm to ensure an abundant supply of moisture for the crops. Or perhaps, as Hepding has suggested, the union of Cybele and Attis, like that of Aphrodite and Adonis, was dramatically represented at the festival, and the subsequent bath of the goddess was a ceremonial purification of the bride, such as is often observed at human marriages.[6] In like manner Aphrodite is said to have bathed after her union with Adonis,[7] and so did Demeter after her intercourse with Poseidon.[8] Hera washed in the springs of the river Burrha after her marriage with Zeus;[9] and every year she recovered her virginity by bathing in the spring of Canathus.[10] However that may be, the rules of diet observed by the worshippers of Cybele and Attis at their solemn fasts are clearly dictated by a belief that the divine life of these deities manifested itself in the fruits of the earth, and especially in such of them as are actually hidden by the soil. For while the devotees were allowed to partake of flesh, though not of pork or fish, they were forbidden to eat seeds and the roots of vegetables, but they might eat the stalks and upper parts of the plants.[11]

235. From inscriptions it appears that both at Pessinus and Rome the high-priest of Cybele regularly bore the name of Attis.[1] It is therefore a reasonable conjecture that he played the part of his namesake, the legendary Attis, at the annual festival. We have seen that on the Day of Blood he drew blood from his arms, and this may have been an imitation of the self-inflicted death of Attis under the pine-tree. It is not inconsistent with this supposition that Attis was also represented at these ceremonies by an effigy; for instances can be shown in which the divine being is first represented by a living person and afterwards by an effigy, which is then burned or otherwise destroyed.[2] Perhaps we may go a step farther and conjecture that this mimic killing of the priest, accompanied by a real effusion of his blood, was in Phrygia, as it has been elsewhere, a substitute for a human sacrifice which in earlier times was actually offered. We know from Strabo[3] that the priests of Pessinus were at one time potentates as well as priests; they may, therefore, have belonged to that class of divine kings or popes whose duty it was to die each year for their people and the world. The name of Attis, it is true, does not occur among the names of the old kings of Phrygia, who seem to have borne the names of Midas and Gordias in alternate generations; but a very ancient inscription carved in the rock above a famous Phrygian monument, which is known as the Tomb of Midas, records that the monument was made for, or dedicated to, King Midas by a certain Ates, whose name is doubtless identical with Attis, and who, if not a king himself, may have been one of the royal family.[4] It is

worthy of note also that the name Atys, which, again, appears to be only an- other form of Attis, is recorded as that of an early king of Lydia;[5] and that a son of Croesus, king of Lydia, not only bore the name Atys but was said to have been killed, while he was hunting a boar, by a member of the royal Phrygian family, who traced his lineage to King Midas and had fled to the court of Croesus because he had unwittingly slain his own brother.[6] Scholars have recognized in this story of the death of Atys, son of Croesus, a mere double of the myth of Attis;[7] and in view of the facts which have come before us in the present inquiry it is a remarkable circumstance that the myth of a slain god should be told of a king's son. May we conjecture that the Phrygian priests who bore the name of Attis and represented the god of that name were themselves members, perhaps the eldest sons, of the royal house, to whom their fathers, uncles, brothers, or other kinsmen deputed the honour of dying a violent death in the character of gods, while they reserved to themselves the duty of living, as long as nature allowed them, in the humbler character of kings? Be that as it may, the god they personated was a deity of vegetation whose divine life manifested itself especially in the pine-tree and the violets of spring; and if they died in the character of that divinity, they corresponded to the mummers who are still slain in mimicry by European peasants in spring, and to the priest who was slain long ago in grim earnest on the wooded shore of the Lake of Nemi.

Excursus: The Hanged God

236. A reminiscence of the manner in which these old representatives of the deity were put to death is perhaps preserved in the famous story of Marsyas. He was said to be a Phrygian satyr or Silenus, according to others a shepherd or herdsman, who played sweetly on the flute. A friend of Cybele, he roamed the country with the disconsolate goddess to soothe her grief for the death of Attis.[1] The composition of the Mother's Air, a tune played on the flute in honour of the Great Mother Goddess, was attributed to him by the people of Celaenae in Phrygia.[2] Vain of his skill, he challenged Apollo to a musical contest, he to play on the flute and Apollo on the lyre. Being van- quished, Marsyas was tied up to a pine-tree and flayed or cut limb from limb either by the victorious Apollo or by a Scythian slave.[3] His skin was shown at Celaenae in historical times. It hung at the foot of the citadel in a cave from which the river Marsyas rushed with an impetuous and noisy tide to join the Maeander.[4] So the Adonis bursts full-born from the precipices of the Leb- anon; so the blue river of Ibreez leaps in a crystal jet from the red rocks of the Taurus; so the stream, which now rumbles deep underground, used to gleam for a moment on its passage from darkness to darkness in the dim light of the Corycian cave. In all these copious fountains, with their glad promise of fertility and life, men of old saw the hand of God and worshipped him beside the rushing river with the music of its tumbling waters in their

ears. At Celaenae, if we can trust tradition, the piper Marsyas, hanging in his cave, had a soul for harmony even in death; for it is said that at the sound of his native Phrygian melodies the skin of the dead satyr used to thrill, but that if the musician struck up an air in praise of Apollo it remained deaf and motionless.[5]

In this Phrygian satyr, shepherd, or herdsman who enjoyed the friendship of Cybele, practised the music so characteristic of her rites,[6] and died a violent death on her sacred tree, the pine, may we not detect a close resemblance to Attis, the favourite shepherd or herdsman of the goddess, who is himself described as a piper,[7] is said to have perished under a pine-tree, and was annually represented by an effigy hung, like Marsyas, upon a pine? We may conjecture that in old days the priest who bore the name and played the part of Attis at the spring festival of Cybele was regularly hanged or otherwise slain upon the sacred tree, and that this barbarous custom was afterwards mitigated into the form in which it is known to us in later times, when the priest merely drew blood from his body under the tree and attached an effigy instead of himself to its trunk.

237. In the holy grove at Upsala men and animals were sacrificed by being hanged upon the sacred trees.[1] The human victims dedicated to Odin were regularly put to death by hanging or by a combination of hanging and stabbing, the man being strung up to a tree or a gallows and then wounded with a spear. Hence Odin was called the Lord of the Gallows or the God of the Hanged, and he is represented sitting under a gallows tree.[2] Indeed he is said to have been sacrificed to himself in the ordinary way, as we learn from the weird verses of the *Havamal,* in which the god describes how he acquired his divine power by learning the magic runes:

> "I know that I hung on the windy tree
> For nine whole nights,
> Wounded with the spear, dedicated to Odin,
> Myself to myself."[3]

The Bagobos of Mindanao, one of the Philippine Islands, used annually to sacrifice human victims for the good of the crops in a similar way. Early in December, when the constellation Orion appeared at seven o'clock in the evening, the people knew that the time had come to clear their fields for sowing and to sacrifice a slave. The sacrifice was presented to certain powerful spirits as payment for the good year which the people had enjoyed, and to ensure the favour of the spirits for the coming season. The victim was led to a great tree in the forest; there he was tied with his back to the tree and his arms stretched high above his head, in the attitude in which ancient artists portrayed Marsyas hanging on the fatal tree. While he thus hung by the arms, he was slain by a spear thrust through his body at the level of the armpits. Afterwards the body was cut clean through the middle at the waist, and the upper part was apparently allowed to dangle for a little from the tree, while the under part wallowed in blood on the ground. The two portions were finally cast into a shallow trench beside the tree. Before this was done, anybody who wished might cut off a piece of flesh or a lock of hair from the corpse and carry it to the grave of some relation whose body was being consumed by a ghoul. Attracted by the fresh corpse, the ghoul would leave the mouldering old body in peace. These sacrifices have been offered by men now living.[4]

238. In Greece the great goddess Artemis herself appears to have been annually hanged in effigy in her sacred grove of Condylea among the Arcadian hills, and there accordingly she went by the name of the Hanged One.[1] Indeed a trace of a similar rite may perhaps be detected even at Ephesus, the most famous of her sanctuaries, in the legend of a woman who hanged herself and was thereupon dressed by the compassionate goddess in her own divine garb and called by the name of Hecate.[2] Similarly, at Melite in Phthia, a story was told of a girl named Aspalis who hanged herself, but who appears to have been merely a form of Artemis. For after her death her body could not be found, but an image of her was discovered standing beside the image of Artemis, and the people bestowed on it the title of Hecaerge or Far-shooter, one of the regular epithets of the goddess. Every year the virgins sacrificed a young goat to the image by hanging it, because Aspalis was said to have hanged herself.[3] The sacrifice may have been a substitute for hanging an image or a human representative of Artemis. Again, in Rhodes the fair Helen was worshipped under the title of Helen of the Tree, because the queen of the island had caused her handmaids, disguised as Furies, to string her up to a bough.[4] That the Asiatic Greeks sacrificed animals in this fashion is proved by coins of Ilium, which represent an ox or cow hanging on a tree and stabbed with a knife by a man, who sits among the branches or on the animal's back.[5] At Hierapolis also the victims were hung on trees before they were burnt.[6] With these Greek and Scandinavian parallels before us we can hardly dismiss as wholly improbable the conjecture that in Phrygia a man-god may have hung year by year on the sacred but fatal tree.

239. The tradition that Marsyas was flayed and that his skin was exhibited at Celaenae down to historical times may well reflect a ritual practice of flaying the dead god and hanging his skin upon the pine as a means of effecting his resurrection, and with it the revival of vegetation in spring. Similarly, in ancient Mexico the human victims who personated gods were often flayed and their bloody skins worn by men who appear to have represented the dead deities come to life again.[1] When a Scythian king died, he was buried in a grave along with one of his concubines, his cup-bearer, cook, groom, lacquey, and messenger, who were all killed for the purpose, and a great barrow was heaped up over the grave. A year afterwards fifty of his servants and fifty of his best horses were strangled; and their bodies, having been disembowelled and cleaned out, were stuffed with chaff, sewn up, and set on scaffolds round about the barrow, every dead man bestriding a dead horse, which was bitted and bridled as in life.[2] These strange horsemen were no doubt supposed to mount guard over the king. The setting up of their stuffed skins might be thought to ensure their ghostly resurrection.

That some such notion was entertained by the Scythians is made probable by the account which the medieval traveller De Plano Carpini gives of the funeral customs of the Mongols. The traveller tells us that when a noble Mongol died, the custom was to bury him seated in the middle of a tent, along with a horse saddled and bridled, and a mare and her foal. Also they used to eat another horse, stuff the carcase with straw, and set it up on poles. All this they did in order that in the other world the dead man might have a tent to live in, a mare to yield milk, and a steed to ride, and that he might be able to breed horses. Moreover, the bones of the horse which they ate were burned for the good of his soul.[3] When the Arab traveller Ibn Batuta visited Peking in the fourteenth century, he witnessed the funeral of an emperor of China who had been killed in battle. The dead sovereign was buried along with four young female slaves and six guards in a vault, and an immense mound like a hill was piled over him. Four horses were then made to run round the hillock till they could run no longer, after which they were killed, impaled, and set up beside the tomb.[4] When an Indian of Patagonia dies, he is buried in a pit along with some of his property. Afterwards his favourite horse, having been killed, skinned, and stuffed, is propped up on sticks with its head turned towards the grave. At the funeral of a chief four horses are sacrificed, and one is set up at each corner of the burial-place. The clothes and other effects of the deceased are burned; and to conclude all, a feast is made of the horses' flesh.[5] The Scythians certainly believed in the existence of the soul after death and in the possibility of turning it to account. This is proved by the practice of one of their tribes, the Taurians of the Crimea, who used to cut off the heads of their prisoners and set them on poles over their houses, especially over the chimneys, in order that the spirits of the slain men might guard the dwellings.[6]

When the Sea Dyaks of Sarawak return home successful from a head-hunting expedition, they bring the head ashore with much ceremony, wrapt in palm leaves. "On shore and in the village, the head, for months after its arrival, is treated with the greatest consideration, and all the names and terms of endearment of which their language is capable are abundantly lavished on it; the most dainty morsels, culled from their abundant though inelegant repast, are thrust into its mouth, and it is instructed to hate its former friends, and that, having been now adopted into the tribe of its captors, its spirit must be always with them; sirih leaves and betel-nut are given to it, and finally a cigar is frequently placed between its ghastly and pallid lips. None of this disgusting mockery is performed with the intention of ridicule, but all to propitiate the spirit by kindness, and to procure its good wishes for the tribe, of whom it is now supposed to have become a member."⁷ Amongst these Dyaks the "Head-Feast," which has been just described, is supposed to be the most beneficial in its influence of all their feasts and ceremonies. "The object of them all is to make their rice grow well, to cause the forest to abound with wild animals, to enable their dogs and snares to be successful in securing game, to have the streams swarm with fish, to give health and activity to the people themselves, and to ensure fertility to their women. All these blessings, the possessing and feasting of a fresh head are supposed to be the most efficient means of securing. The very ground itself is believed to be benefited and rendered fertile, more fertile even than when the water in which fragments of gold presented by the Rajah have been washed, has been sprinkled over it."⁸

In like manner, if my conjecture is right, the man who represented the father-god of Phrygia used to be slain and his stuffed skin hung on the sacred pine in order that his spirit might work for the growth of the crops, the multiplication of animals, and the fertility of women. So at Athens an ox, which appears to have embodied the corn-spirit, was killed at an annual sacrifice, and its hide, stuffed with straw and sewn up, was afterwards set on its feet and yoked to a plough as if it were ploughing, apparently in order to represent, or rather to promote, the resurrection of the slain corn-spirit at the end of the threshing.⁹ This employment of the skins of divine animals for the purpose of ensuring the revival of the slaughtered divinity might be illustrated by other examples.¹⁰ Perhaps the hide of the bull which was killed to furnish the regenerating bath of blood in the rites of Attis may have been put to a similar use.

HYACINTH

240. Another mythical being who has been supposed to belong to the class of gods here discussed is Hyacinth.¹ He too has been interpreted as the vegetation which blooms in spring and withers under the scorching heat of the summer sun. Though he belongs to Greek, not to Oriental mythology, some account of him may not be out of place in the present discussion. According to the legend, Hyacinth was the youngest and handsomest son of the ancient king Amyclas, who had his capital at Amyclae in the beautiful vale of Sparta. One day playing at quoits with Apollo, he was accidentally killed by a blow of the god's quoit. Bitterly the god lamented the death of his friend. The hyacinth—"that sanguine flower inscribed with woe"—sprang from the blood of the hapless youth, as anemones and roses from the blood of Adonis, and violets from the blood of Attis:² like these vernal flowers it heralded the advent of another spring and gladdened the hearts of men with the promise of a joyful resurrection. The flower is usually supposed to be not what we call a hyacinth, but a little purple iris with the letters of lamentation (*AI*, which in Greek means "alas") clearly inscribed in black on its petals. In Greece it blooms in spring after the early violets but before the roses.[3] One spring, when the hyacinths were in bloom, it happened that the red-coated Spartan regiments lay encamped under the walls of Corinth. Their commander gave the Amyclean battalion leave to go home and celebrate as usual the festival of Hyacinth in their native town. But the sad flower was to be to these men an omen of death; for they had not gone far before they were enveloped by clouds of light-armed foes and cut to pieces.[4]

The tomb of Hyacinth was at Amyclae under a massive altar-like pedestal, which supported an archaic bronze image of Apollo. In the left side of the pedestal was a bronze door, and through it offerings were passed to Hyacinth, as to a hero or a dead man, not as to a god, before sacrifices were offered to Apollo at the annual Hyacinthian festival. Bas-reliefs carved on the pedestal represented Hyacinth and his maiden sister Polyboea caught up to heaven by a company of goddesses.[5] The annual festival of the Hyacinthia was held in the month of Hectombeus, which seems to have corresponded to May.[6] The ceremonies occupied three days. On the first the people mourned for Hyacinth, wearing no wreaths, singing no paeans, eating no bread, and behaving with great gravity. It was on this day probably that the offerings were made at Hyacinth's tomb. Next day the scene was changed. All was joy and bustle. The capital was emptied of its inhabitants, who poured out in their thousands to witness and share the festivities at Amyclae. Boys in high-girt tunics sang hymns in honour of the god to the accompaniment of flutes and lyres. Others, splendidly attired, paraded on horseback in the theatre: choirs of youths chanted their native ditties: dancers danced: maidens rode in wicker carriages or went in procession to witness the chariot races: sacrifices were offered in profusion: the citizens feasted their friends and even their slaves.[7] This outburst of gaiety may be supposed to have celebrated the resurrection of Hyacinth and perhaps also his ascension to heaven, which, as we have seen, was represented on his tomb. However, it may be that the ascension took place on the third day of the festival; but as to that we know nothing. The sister who went to heaven with him was by some identified with Artemis or Persephone.[8]

241. It is highly probable, as Erwin Rohde perceived,[1] that Hyacinth was an old aboriginal diety of the underworld who had been worshipped at Amyclae long before the Dorians invaded and conquered the country. If that was so, the story of his relation to Apollo must have been a comparatively late invention, an attempt of the newcomers to fit the ancient god of the land into their own mythical system, in order that he might extend his protection to them. On this theory it may not be without significance that sacrifices at the festival were offered to Hyacinth, as to a hero, before they were offered to Apollo.[2] Further, on the analogy of similar deities elsewhere, we should expect to find Hyacinth coupled, not with a male friend, but with a female consort. That consort may perhaps be detected in his sister Polyboea, who ascended to heaven with him. The new myth, if new it was, of the love of Apollo for Hyacinth would involve a changed conception of the aboriginal god, which in its turn must have affected that of his spouse. For when Hyacinth came to be thought of as young and unmarried there was no longer room in his story for a wife, and she would have to be disposed of in some other way. What was easier for the myth-maker than to turn her into his unmarried sister? However we may explain it, a change seems certainly to have come over the popular idea of Hyacinth; for whereas on his tomb he was portrayed as a bearded man, later art represented him as the pink of youthful beauty.[3] But it is perhaps needless to suppose that the sisterly relation of Polyboea to him was a late modification of the myth. The stories of Cronus and Rhea, of Zeus and Hera, of Osiris and Isis, remind us that in old days gods, like kings, often married their sisters, and probably for the same reason, namely, to ensure their own title to the throne under a rule of female kinship which treated women and not men as the channel in which the blood royal flowed.[4] It is not impossible that Hyacinth may have been a divine king who actually reigned in his lifetime at Amyclae and was afterwards worshipped at his tomb. The representation of his triumphal ascent to heaven in company with his sister suggests that, like Adonis and Persephone, he may have been supposed to spend one part of the year in the under-world of darkness and death, and another part in the upper-world of light and life. And as the anemones and the sprouting corn marked the return of Adonis and Persephone, so the flowers to which he gave his name may have heralded the ascension of Hyacinth.

OSIRIS

242. In ancient Egypt the god whose death and resurrection were annually celebrated with alternate sorrow and joy was Osiris, the most popular of all Egyptian deities; and there are good grounds for classing him in one of his aspects with Adonis and Attis as a personification of the great yearly vicissitudes of nature, especially of the corn. But the immense vogue which he enjoyed for many ages induced his devoted worshippers to heap upon him the attributes and powers of many other gods; so that it is not always easy to strip him, so to say, of his borrowed plumes and to restore them to their proper owners.

The story of Osiris is told in a connected form only by Plutarch, whose narrative has been confirmed and to some extent amplified in modern times by the evidence of the monuments.[1]

Osiris was the offspring of an intrigue between the earth-god Geb and the sky-goddess Nut. When the sun-god Ra perceived that his wife Nut had been unfaithful to him, he declared with a curse that she should be delivered of the child in no month and no year. But the goddess had another lover, the god Thoth, and he, playing at draughts with the moon, won from her a seventy-second part of every day, and having thus compounded five whole days he added them to the Egyptian year of three hundred and sixty days. On these five days, regarded as outside the year of twelve months—that is, as "epagomenal"—the curse of the sun-god did not rest, and accordingly Osiris was born on the first of them. But he was not the only child of his mother. On the second of the supplementary days she gave birth to the elder Horus, on the third to the god Set, on the fourth to the goddess Isis, and on the fifth to the goddess Nephthys. Afterwards Set married his sister Nephthys, and Osiris his sister Isis.

Reigning as a king on earth, Osiris reclaimed the Egyptians from savagery, gave them laws, and taught them to worship the gods. Before his time the Egyptians had been cannibals. But Isis, the sister and wife of Osiris, discovered wheat and barley growing wild, and Osiris introduced the cultivation of these grains amongst his people, who forthwith took kindly to a corn diet. Moreover, Osiris is said to have been the first to gather fruit from trees, to train the vine to poles, and to tread the grapes. Eager to communicate these beneficent discoveries to all mankind, he committed the whole government of Egypt to his wife Isis, and travelled over the world, diffusing the blessings of civilization and agriculture wherever he went. In countries where a harsh climate or niggardly soil forbade the cultivation of the vine, he taught the inhabitants to console themselves for the want of wine by brewing beer from barley. Loaded with the wealth that had been showered upon him by grateful nations, he returned to Egypt, and on account of the benefits he had conferred on mankind he was unanimously hailed and worshipped as a deity. But his brother Set with seventy-two others plotted against him. Having taken the measure of his good brother's body by stealth, the bad brother fashioned and highly decorated a coffer of the same size, and once when they were all drinking and making merry he brought in the coffer and jestingly promised to give it to the one whom it should fit exactly. They all tried one after the other, but it fitted none of them. Last of all Osiris stepped into it and lay down. On that the conspirators ran and slammed the lid down on him, nailed it fast, soldered it with molten lead, and flung the coffer into the Nile. This happened on the seventeenth day of the month Athyr, when the sun is in the sign of the Scorpion, and in the eight-and-twentieth year of the reign or the life of Osiris. When Isis heard of it she sheared off a lock of her hair, put on mourning attire, and wandered disconsolately up and down, seeking the body.

By the advice of the god of wisdom she took refuge in the papyrus swamps of the Delta. There she conceived a son while she fluttered in the form of a hawk over the corpse of her dead husband. The infant was the younger Horus, who in his youth bore the name of Harpocrates, that is, the child Horus. Him Buto, the goddess of the north, hid from the wrath of his wicked uncle Set. Yet she could not guard him from all mishap; for one day when Isis came to her little son's hiding-place she found him stretched lifeless and rigid on the ground: a scorpion had stung him. Then Isis prayed to the sun-god Ra for help. The god hearkened to her and staid his bark in the sky, and sent down Thoth to teach her the spell by which she might restore her son to life. She uttered the words of power, and straightway the poison flowed from the body of Horus, air passed into him, and he lived. Then Thoth ascended up into the sky and took his place once more in the bark of the sun, and the bright pomp passed onward jubilant.

Meantime the coffer containing the body of Osiris had floated down the river and away out to sea, till at last it drifted ashore at Byblus, on the coast of Syria. Here a fine *erica*-tree shot up suddenly and enclosed the chest in its trunk. The king of the country, admiring the growth of the tree, had it cut down and made into a pillar of his house; but he did not know that the coffer with the dead Osiris was in it. Word of this came to Isis and she journeyed to Byblus, and sat down by the well, in humble guise, her face wet with tears. To none would she speaks till the king's handmaidens came, and them she greeted kindly, and braided their hair, and breathed on them from her own divine body a wondrous perfume. When the queen beheld the braids of her handmaidens' hair and smelt the sweet smell that emanated from them, she sent for the stranger woman and took her into her house and made her the nurse of her child. Isis gave the babe her finger instead of her breast to suck, and at night she began to burn all that was mortal of him away, while she herself in the likeness of a swallow fluttered round the pillar that contained her dead brother, twittering mournfully. The queen spied what she was doing and shrieked out when she saw her child in flames, and thereby she hindered him from becoming immortal. Then the goddess revealed herself and begged for the pillar of the roof, and they gave it her, and she cut the coffer out of it, and fell upon it and embraced it and lamented so loud that the younger of the king's children died of fright on the spot. But the trunk of the tree she wrapped in fine linen, and poured ointment on it, and gave it to the king and queen, and the wood stands in a temple of Isis and is worshipped by the people of Byblus to this day. And Isis put the coffer in a boat and took the eldest of the king's children with her and sailed away. As soon as they were alone, she opened the chest, and laying her face on the face of her brother she kissed him and wept. But the child came behind her softly and saw what she was about, and she turned and looked at him in anger, and the child could not bear her look and died; but some say that it was not so, but that he fell into the sea and was drowned. It is he whom the Egyptians sing of at their banquets under the name of Maneros.

But Isis put the coffer by and went to see her son Horus at the city of Buto, and Set found the coffer as he was hunting a boar one night by the light of a full moon. And he knew the body, and rent it into fourteen pieces, and scattered them abroad. But Isis sailed up and down the marshes in a shallop made of papyrus, looking for the pieces; and that is why when people sail in shallops made of papyrus, the crocodiles do not hurt them, for they fear or respect the goddess. And that is the reason, too, why there are many graves of Osiris in Egypt, for she buried each limb as she found it. But others will have it that she buried an image of him in every city, pretending it was his body, in order that Osiris might be worshipped in many places, and that if Set searched for the real grave he might not be able to find it. However, the genital member of Osiris had been eaten by the fishes, so Isis made an image of it instead, and the image is used by the Egyptians at their festivals to this day. "Isis," writes the historian Diodorus Siculus, "recovered all the parts of the body except the genitals; and because she wished that her husband's grave should be unknown and honoured by all who dwell in the land of Egypt, she resorted to the following device. She moulded human images out of wax and spices, corresponding to the stature of Osiris, round each one of the parts of his body. Then she called in the priests according to their families and took an oath of them all that they would reveal to no man the trust she was about to repose in them. So to each of them privately she said that to them alone she entrusted the burial of the body, and reminding them of the benefits they had received she exhorted them to bury the body in their own land and to honour Osiris as a god. She also besought them to dedicate one of the animals of their country, whichever they chose, and to honour it in life as they had formerly honoured Osiris, and when it died to grant it obsequies like his. And because she would encourage the priests in their own interest to bestow the aforesaid honours, she gave them a third part of the land to be used by them in the service and worship of the gods. Accordingly it is said that the priests, mindful of the benefits of Osiris, desirous of gratifying the queen, and moved by the prospect of gain, carried out all the injunctions of Isis. Wherefore to this day each of the priests imagines that Osiris is buried in his country, and they honour the beasts that were consecrated in the beginning, and when the animals die the priests renew at their burial the mourning for Osiris. But the sacred bulls, the one called Apis and the other Mnevis, were dedicated to Osiris, and it was ordained that they should be worshipped as gods in common by all the Egyptians; since these animals above all others had helped the discoverers of corn in sowing the seed and procuring the universal benefits of agriculture."[2]

Such is the myth or legend of Osiris, as told by Greek writers and eked out by more or less fragmentary notices or allusions in native Egyptian literature. A long inscription in the temple at Denderah has preserved a list of the god's graves, and other texts mention the parts of his body which were treasured as holy relics in each of the sanctuaries. Thus his heart was at Athribis, his backbone at Busiris, his neck at Letopolis, and his head at Memphis. As often happens in such cases, some of his divine limbs were miraculously multiplied. His head, for example, was at Abydos as well as at Memphis, and his legs, which were remarkably numerous, would have sufficed for several ordinary mortals.

According to native Egyptian accounts, which supplement that of Plutarch, when Isis had found the corpse of her husband Osiris, she and her sister Nephthys sat down beside it and uttered a lament which in after ages became the type of all Egyptian lamentations for the dead. "Come to thy house," they wailed, "Come to thy house. O god On! come to thy house, thou who hast no foes. O fair youth, come to thy house, that thou mayest see me. I am thy sister, whom thou lovest; thou shalt not part from me. O fair boy, come to thy house. . . . I see thee not, yet doth my heart yearn after thee and mine eyes desire thee. Come to her who loves thee, who loves thee, Unnefer, thou blessed one! Come to thy sister, come to thy wife, to thy wife, thou whose heart stands still. Come to thy housewife. I am thy sister by the same mother, thou shalt not be far from me. Gods and men have turned their faces towards thee and weep for thee together. . . . I call after thee and weep, so that my cry is heard to heaven, but thou hearest not my voice; yet am I thy sister, whom thou didst love on earth; thou didst love none but me, my brother! my brother!"[3] This lament for the fair youth cut off in his prime reminds us of the laments for Adonis. The title of Unnefer or "the Good Being" bestowed on him marks the beneficence which tradition universally ascribed to Osiris; it was at once his commonest title and one of his names as king.[4]

The lamentations of the two sad sisters were not in vain. In pity for her sorrow the sun-god Ra sent down from heaven the jackal-headed god Anubis, who, with the aid of Isis and Nephthys, of Thoth and Horus, pieced together the broken body of the murdered god, swathed it in linen bandages, and observed all the other rites which the Egyptians were wont to perform over the bodies of the departed. Then Isis fanned the cold clay with her wings: Osiris revived, and thenceforth reigned as king over the dead in the other world.[5] There he bore the titles of Lord of the Underworld, Lord of Eternity, Ruler of the Dead. There, too, in the great Hall of the Two Truths, assisted by forty-two assessors, one from each of the principal districts of Egypt, he presided as judge at the trial of the souls of the departed, who made their solemn confession before him, and, their heart having been weighed in the balance of justice, received the reward of virtue in a life eternal or the appropriate punishment of their sins.[6]

243. In the resurrection of Osiris the Egyptians saw the pledge of a life everlasting for themselves beyond the grave. They believed that every man would live eternally in the other world if only his surviving friends did for his body what the gods had done for the body of Osiris. Hence the ceremonies observed by the Egyptians over the human dead were an exact copy of those which Anubis, Horus, and the rest had performed over the dead god. "At every burial there was enacted a representation of the divine mystery which had been performed of old over Osiris, when his son, his sisters, his friends were gathered round his mangled remains and succeeded by their spells and manipulations in converting his broken body into the first mummy, which they afterwards reanimated and furnished with the means of entering on a new individual life beyond the grave. The mummy of the deceased was Osiris; the professional female mourners were his two sisters Isis and Nephthys; Anubis, Horus, all the gods of the Osirian legend gathered about the corpse."[1]

244. Thus every dead Egyptian was identified with Osiris and bore his name. From the Middle Kingdom onwards it was the regular practice to address the deceased as "Osiris So-and-So," as if he were the god himself, and to add the standing epithet "true of speech," because true speech was characteristic of Osiris.[1] The thousands of inscribed and pictured tombs that have been opened in the valley of the Nile prove that the mystery of the resurrection was performed for the benefit of every dead Egyptian;[2] as Osiris died and rose again from the dead, so all men hoped to arise like him from death to life eternal. In an Egyptian text it is said of the departed that "as surely as Osiris lives, so shall he live also; as surely as Osiris did not die, so shall he not die; as surely as Osiris is not annihilated, so shall he too not be annihilated." The dead man, conceived to be lying, like Osiris, with mangled body, was comforted by being told that the heavenly goddess Nut, the mother of Osiris, was coming to gather up his poor scattered limbs and mould them with her own hands into a form immortal and divine. "She gives thee thy head, she brings thee thy bones, she sets thy limbs together and puts thy heart in thy body." Thus the resurrection of the dead was conceived, like that of Osiris, not merely as spiritual but also as bodily. "They possess their heart, they possess their senses, they possess their mouth, they possess their feet, they possess their arms, they possess all their limbs."[3]

245. If we may trust Egyptian legend, the trials and contests of the royal house did not cease with the restoration of Osiris to life and his elevation to the rank of presiding deity in the world of the dead. When Horus the younger, the son of Osiris and Isis, was grown to man's estate, the ghost of his royal and murdered father appeared to him and urged him, like another Hamlet, to avenge the foul unnatural murder upon his wicked uncle. Thus encouraged, the youth attacked the miscreant. The combat was terrific and lasted many days. Horus lost an eye in the conflict and Set suffered a still more serious mutilation. At last Thoth parted the combatants and healed their wounds; the eye of Horus he restored by spitting on it. According to one account the great battle was fought on the twenty-sixth day of the month of Thoth. Foiled in open war, the artful uncle now took the law on his virtuous nephew. He brought a suit of bastardy against Horus, hoping thus to rob him of his inheritance and to get possession of it himself; nay, not content with having murdered his good brother, the unnatural Set carried his rancour even beyond the grave by accusing the dead Osiris of certain high crimes and misdemeanours. The case was tried before the supreme court of the gods in the great hall at Heliopolis. Thoth, the god of wisdom, pleaded the cause of Osiris, and the august judges decided that "the word of Osiris was true." Moreover, they pronounced Horus to be the true-begotten son of his father. So that prince assumed the crown and mounted the throne of the lamented Osiris. However, according to another and perhaps later version of the story, the victory of Horus over his uncle was by no means so decisive, and their struggles ended in a compromise, by which Horus reigned over the Delta, while Set became king of the upper valley of the Nile from near Memphis to the first cataract. Be that is it may, with the accession of Horus began for the Egyptians the modern period of the world, for on his throne all the kings of Egypt sat as his successors.[1]

These legends of a contest for the throne of Egypt may perhaps contain a reminiscence of real dynastical struggles which attended an attempt to change the right of succession from the female to the male line. For under a rule of female kinship the heir to the throne is either the late king's brother, or the son of the late king's sister, while under a rule of male kinship the heir to the throne is the late king's son. In the legend of Osiris the rival heirs are Set and Horus, Set being the late king's brother, and Horus the late king's son; though Horus indeed united both claims to the crown, being the son of the king's sister as well as of the king.

246. Thus according to what seems to have been the general native tradition Osiris was a good and beloved king of Egypt, who suffered a violent death but rose from the dead and was henceforth worshipped as a deity. In harmony with this tradition he was regularly represented by sculptors and painters in human and regal form as a dead king, swathed in the wrappings of a mummy, but wearing on his head a kingly crown and grasping in one of his hands, which were left free from the bandages, a kingly sceptre.[1] Two cities above all others were associated with his myth or memory. One of them was Busiris in Lower Egypt, which claimed to possess his backbone; the other was Abydos in Upper Egypt, which gloried in the possession of his head.[2] Encircled by the nimbus of the dead yet living god, Abydos, originally an obscure place, became from the end of the Old Kingdom the holiest spot in Egypt; his tomb there would seem to have been to the Egyptians what the Church of the Holy Sepulchre at Jerusalem is to Christians. It was the wish of every pious man that his dead body should rest in hallowed earth near the grave of the glorified Osiris. Few indeed were rich enough to enjoy this inestimable privilege; for, apart from the cost of a tomb in the sacred city, the mere transport of mummies from great distances was both difficult and expensive. Yet so eager were many to absorb in death the blessed influence which radiated from the holy sepulchre that they caused their surviving friends to convey their mortal remains to Abydos, there to tarry for a short time, and then to be brought back by river and interred in the tombs which had been made ready for them in their native land. Others had cenotaphs built or memorial tablets erected for themselves near the tomb of their dead and risen Lord, that they might share with him the bliss of a joyful resurrection.[3]

247. It is natural to suppose that the various events of the agricultural year were celebrated by the Egyptian farmer with some simple religious rites designed to secure the blessing of the gods upon his labours. These rustic ceremonies he would continue to perform year after year at the same season, while the solemn festivals of the priests continued to shift, with the shifting calendar, from summer through spring to winter, and so backward through autumn to summer. The rites of the husbandman were stable because they rested on direct observation of nature: the rites of the priest were unstable because they were based on a false calculation. Yet many of the priestly festivals may have been nothing but the old rural festivals disguised in the course of ages by the pomp of sacerdotalism and severed, by the error of the calendar, from their roots in the natural cycle of the seasons.

248. These conjectures are confirmed by the little we know both of the popular and of the official Egyptian religion. Thus we are told that the Egyptians held a festival of Isis at the time when the Nile began to rise. They believed that the goddess was then mourning for the lost Osiris, and that the tears which dropped from her eyes swelled the impetuous tide of the river.[1] Now if Osiris was in one of his aspects a god of the corn, nothing could be more natural than that he should be mourned at midsummer. For by that time the harvest was past, the fields were bare, the river ran low, life seemed to be suspended, the corn-god was dead. At such a moment people who saw the handiwork of divine beings in all the operations of nature might well trace the swelling of the sacred stream to the tears shed by the goddess at the death of the beneficent corn-god her husband.

249. The sign of the rising waters on earth was accompanied by a sign in heaven. For in the early days of Egyptian history, some three or four thousand years before the beginning of our era, the splendid star of Sirius, the brightest of all the fixed stars, appeared at dawn in the east just before sunrise about the time of the summer solstice, when the Nile begins to rise.[1] The Egyptians called it Sothis, and regarded it as the star of Isis,[2] just as the Babylonians deemed the planet Venus the star of Astarte. To both peoples apparently the brilliant luminary in the morning sky seemed the goddess of life and love come to mourn her departed lover or spouse and to wake him from the dead. Hence the rising of Sirius marked the beginning of the sacred Egyptian year,[3] and was regularly celebrated by a festival which did not shift with the shifting official year.[4]

250. The cutting of the dams and the admission of water into the canals and fields is a great event in the Egyptian year. At Cairo the operation generally takes place between the sixth and the sixteenth of August, and till lately was attended by ceremonies which deserve to be noticed, because they were probably handed down from antiquity. An ancient canal, known by the name of the Khalíj, formerly passed through the native town of Cairo. Near its entrance the canal was crossed by a dam of earth, very broad at the bottom and diminishing in breadth upwards, which used to be constructed before or soon after the Nile began to rise. In front of the dam, on the side of the river, was reared a truncated cone of earth called the *'arooseh* or "bride," on the top of which a little maize or millet was generally sown. This "bride" was commonly washed down by the rising tide a week or a fortnight before the cutting of the dam. Tradition runs that the old custom was to deck a young virgin in gay apparel and throw her into the river as a sacrifice to obtain a plentiful inundation.[1] Certainly human sacrifices were offered for a similar purpose by the Wajagga of German East Africa down to recent years. These people irrigate their fields by means of skilfully constructed channels, through which they conduct the water of the mountain brooks and rivers to the thirsty land. They imagine that the spirits of their forefathers dwell in the rocky basins of these rushing streams, and that they would resent the withdrawal of the water to irrigate the fields if compensation were not offered to them. The water-rate paid to them consisted of a child, uncircumcised and of unblemished body, who was decked with ornaments and bells and thrown into the river to drown, before they ventured to draw off the water into the irrigation channel. Having thrown him in, his executioners shewed a clean pair of heels, because they expected the river to rise in flood at once on receipt of the water-rate.[2] In similar circumstances the Njamus of British East Africa sacrifice a sheep before they let the water of the stream flow into the ditch or artificial channel. The fat, dung, and blood of the animal are sprinkled at the mouth of the ditch and in the water; thereupon the dam is broken down and the stream pours into the ditch. The sacrifice may only be offered by a man of the Il Mayek clan, and for two days afterwards he wears the skin of the beast tied round his head. No one may quarrel with this man while the water is irrigating the crops, else the people believe that the water would cease to flow in the ditch; more than that, if the men of the Il Mayek clan were angry and sulked for ten days, the water would dry up permanently for that season. Hence the Il Mayek clan enjoys great consideration in the tribe, since the crops are thought to depend on their good will and good offices. Ten elders assist at the sacrifice of the sheep, though they may take no part in it. They must all be of a particular age; and after the ceremony they may not cohabit with their wives until harvest, and they are obliged to sleep at night in their granaries. Curiously enough, too, while the water is irrigating the fields, nobody may kill waterbuck, eland, oryx, zebra, rhinoceros, or hippopotamus. Anybody caught red-handed in the act of breaking this game-law would at once be cast out of the village.[3]

Whether the "bride" who used to figure at the ceremony of cutting the dam in Cairo was ever a live woman or not, the intention of the practice appears to have been to marry the river, conceived as a male power, to his bride the corn-land, which was soon to be fertilized by his water. The ceremony was therefore a charm to ensure the growth of the crops. As such it probably dated, in one form or another, from ancient times. At Cairo the time-honoured ceremony came to an end in 1897, when the old canal was filled up. An electric tramway now runs over the spot where for countless ages crowds of worshippers or holiday-makers had annually assembled to witness the marriage of the Nile.[4]

251. The next great operation of the agricultural year in Egypt is the sowing of the seed in November, when the water of the inundation has retreated from the fields. With the Egyptians, as with many peoples of antiquity, the committing of the seed to the earth assumed the character of a solemn and mournful rite. On this subject I will let Plutarch speak for himself. "What," he asks, "are we to make of the gloomy, joyless, and mournful sacrifices, if it is wrong either to omit the established rites or to confuse and disturb our conceptions of the gods by absurd suspicions? For the Greeks also perform many rites which resemble those of the Egyptians and are observed about the same time. Thus at the festival of the Thesmophoria in Athens women sit on the ground and fast. And the Boeotians open the vaults of the Sorrowful One, naming that festival sorrowful because Demeter is sorrowing for the descent of the Maiden. The month is the month of sowing about the setting of the Pleiades.[1] The Egyptians call it Athyr, the Athenians Pyanepsion, the Boeotians the month of Demeter. . . . It was that time of year when they saw some of the fruits vanishing and failing from the trees, while they sowed others grudgingly and with difficulty, scraping the earth with their hands and huddling it up again, on the uncertain chance that what they deposited in the ground would ever ripen and come to maturity. Thus they did in many respects like those who bury and mourn their dead."[2] Yet they sorrowed not without hope, perhaps a sure and certain hope, that the seed which they thus committed with sighs and tears to the ground would yet rise from the dust and yield fruit a hundredfold to the reaper. "They that sow in tears shall reap in joy. He that goeth forth and weepeth, bearing precious seed, shall doubtless come again with rejoicing, bringing his sheaves with him."[3]

252. The Egyptian harvest, as we have seen, falls not in autumn but in spring, in the months of March, April, and May. To the husbandman the time of harvest, at least in a good year, must necessarily be a season of joy: in bringing home his sheaves he is requited for his long and anxious labours. Yet if the old Egyptian farmer felt a secret joy at reaping and garnering the grain, it was essential that he should conceal the natural emotion under an air of profound dejection. For was he not severing the body of the corn-god with his sickle and trampling it to pieces under the hoofs of his cattle on the threshing-floor? Accordingly we are told that it was an ancient custom of the Egyptian corn-reapers to beat their breasts and lament over the first sheaf cut, while at the same time they called upon Isis.[1] The invocation seems to have taken the form of a melancholy chant, to which the Greeks gave the name of Maneros. Similar plaintive strains were chanted by corn-reapers in Phoenicia and other parts of Western Asia.[2] Probably all these doleful ditties were lamentations for the corn-god killed by the sickles of the reapers. In Egypt the slain deity was Osiris, and the name *Maneros* applied to the dirge appears to be derived from certain words meaning "Come to thy house," which often occur in the lamentations for the dead god.

253. Ceremonies of the same sort have been observed by other peoples, probably for the same purpose. Thus we are told that among all vegetables corn (*selu*), by which is apparently meant maize, holds the first place in the household economy and the ceremonial observance of the Cherokee Indians, who invoke it under the name of "the Old Woman" in allusion to a myth that it sprang from the blood of an old woman killed by her disobedient sons. "Much ceremony accompanied the planting and tending of the crop. Seven grains, the sacred number, were put into each hill, and these were not afterwards thinned out. After the last working of the crop, the priest and an assistant—generally the owner of the field—went into the field and built a small enclosure in the centre. Then entering it, they seated themselves upon the ground, with heads bent down, and while the assistant kept perfect silence the priest, with rattle in hand, sang songs of invocation to the spirit of the corn. Soon, according to the orthodox belief, a loud rustling would be heard outside, which they would know was caused by the 'Old Woman' bringing the corn into the field, but neither must look up until the song was finished. This ceremony was repeated on four successive nights, after which no one entered the field for seven other nights, when the priest himself went in, and, if all the sacred regulations had been properly observed, was rewarded by finding young ears upon the stalks. The corn ceremonies could be performed by the owner of the field himself, provided he was willing to pay a sufficient fee to the priest in order to learn the songs and ritual. Care was always taken to keep a clean trail from the field to the house, so that the corn might be encouraged to stay at home and not go wandering elsewhere. Most of these customs have now fallen into disuse excepting among the old people, by many of whom they are still religiously observed. Another curious ceremony, of which even the memory is now almost forgotten, was enacted after the first working of the corn, when the owner or priest stood in succession at each of the four corners of the field and wept and wailed loudly. Even the priests are now unable to give a reason for this performance, which may have been a lament for the bloody death of Selu," the Old Woman of the Corn.[1] In these Cherokee practices the lamentations and the invocations of the Old Woman of the Corn resemble the ancient Egyptian customs of lamenting over the first corn cut and calling upon Isis, herself probably in one of her aspects an Old Woman of the Corn. Further, the Cherokee precaution of leaving a clear path from the field to the house resembles the Egyptian invitation to Osiris, "Come to thy house." So in the East Indies to this day people observe elaborate ceremonies for the purpose of bringing back the Soul of the Rice from the fields to the barn.[2] The Nandi of British East Africa perform a ceremony in September when the eleusine grain is ripening. Every woman who owns a plantation goes out with her daughters into the cornfields and makes a bonfire of the branches and leaves of certain trees (the *Solanum campylanthum* and *Lantana salvifolia*). After that they pluck some of the eleusine, and each of them puts one grain in her necklace, chews another and rubs it on her forehead, throat, and breast. "No joy is shown by the womenfolk on this occasion, and they sorrowfully cut a basketful of the corn which they take home with them and place in the loft to dry."[3]

Just as the Egyptians lamented at cutting the corn, so the Karok Indians of California lament at hewing the sacred wood for the fire in the assembly-room. The wood must be cut from a tree on the top of the highest hill. In lopping off the boughs the Indian weeps and sobs piteously, shedding real tears, and at the top of the tree he leaves two branches and a top-knot, resembling a man's head and outstretched arms. Having descended from the tree, he binds the wood in a faggot and carries it back to the assembly-room, blubbering all the way. If he is asked why he thus weeps at cutting and fetching the sacred fuel, he will either give no answer or say simply that he does it for luck.[4] We may suspect that his real motive is to appease the wrath of the tree-spirit, many of whose limbs he has amputated, though he took care to leave him two arms and a head.

The conception of the corn-spirit as old and dead at harvest is very clearly embodied in a custom observed by the Arabs of Moab. When the harvesters have nearly finished their task and only a small corner of the field remains to be reaped, the owner takes a handful of wheat tied up in a sheaf. A hole is dug in the form of a grave, and two stones are set upright, one at the head and the other at the foot, just as in an ordinary burial. Then the sheaf of wheat is laid at the bottom of the grave, and the sheikh pronounces these words, "The old man is dead." Earth is afterwards thrown in to cover the sheaf, with a prayer, "May Allah bring us back the wheat of the dead."[5]

254. Such, then, were the principal events of the farmer's calendar in ancient Egypt, and such the simple religious rites by which he celebrated them. But we have still to consider the Osirian festivals of the official calendar, so far as these are described by Greek writers or recorded on the monuments. In examining them it is necessary to bear in mind that on account of the movable year of the old Egyptian calendar the true or astronomical dates of the official festivals must have varied from year to year, at least until the adoption of the fixed Alexandrian year in 30 B.C. From that time onward, apparently, the dates of the festivals were determined by the new calendar, and so ceased to rotate throughout the length of the solar year. At all events Plutarch, writing about the end of the first century, implies that they were then fixed, not movable; for though he does not mention the Alexandrian calendar, he clearly dates the festivals by it. Moreover, the long festal calendar of Esne, an important document of the Imperial age, is obviously based on the fixed Alexandrian year; for it assigns the mark for New Year's Day to the day which corresponds to the twenty-ninth of August, which was the first day of the Alexandrian year, and its references to the rising of the Nile, the position of the sun, and the operations of agriculture are all in harmony with this supposition.[1] Thus we may take it as fairly certain that from 30 B.C. onwards the Egyptian festivals were stationary in the solar year.

255. Herodotus tells us that the grave of Osiris was at Sais in Lower Egypt and that there was a lake there upon which the sufferings of the god were displayed as a mystery by night.[1] This commemoration of the divine passion was held once a year: the people mourned and beat their breasts at it to testify their sorrow for the death of the god; and an image of a cow, made of gilt wood with a golden sun between its horns, was carried out of the chamber in which it stood the rest of the year.[2] The cow no doubt represented Isis herself, for cows were sacred to her, and she was regularly depicted with the horns of a cow on her head,[3] or even as a woman with the head of a cow.[4] It is probable that the carrying out of her cow-shaped image symbolized the goddess searching for the dead body of Osiris; for this was the native Egyptian interpretation of a similar ceremony observed in Plutarch's time about the winter solstice, when the gilt cow was carried seven times round the temple.[5] A great feature of the festival was the nocturnal illumination. People fastened rows of oil-lamps to the outside of their houses, and the lamps burned all night long. The custom was not confined to Sais, but was observed throughout the whole of Egypt.[6]

256. This universal illumination of the houses on one night of the year suggests that the festival may have been a commemoration not merely of the dead Osiris but of the dead in general, in other words, that it may have been a night of All Souls.[1] For it is a widespread belief that the souls of the dead revisit their old homes on one night of the year; and on that solemn occasion people prepare for the reception of the ghosts by laying out food for them to eat, and lighting lamps to guide them on their dark road from and to the grave.

The Esquimaux of St. Michael and the lower Yukon River in Alaska hold a festival of the dead every year at the end of November or the beginning of December, as well as a greater festival at intervals of several years. At these seasons, food, drink, and clothes are provided for the returning ghosts in the *kashim* or clubhouse of the village, which is illuminated with oil lamps. Every man or woman who wishes to honour a dead friend sets up a lamp on a stand in front of the place which the deceased used to occupy in the clubhouse.

These lamps, filled with seal oil, are kept burning day and night till the festival is over. They are believed to light the shades on their return to their old homes and back again to the realm of the dead.[2]

The Miztecs of Mexico believed that the souls of the dead came back in the twelfth month of every year, which corresponded to our November. On this day of All Souls the houses were decked out to welcome the spirits. Jars of food and drink were set on a table in the principal room, and the family went forth with torches to meet the ghosts and invite them to enter.[3] The Indians of Santiago Tepehuacan believe that the souls of their dead return to them on the night of the eighteenth of October, the festival of St. Luke, and they sweep the roads in order that the ghosts may find them clean on their passage.[4]

In the Bilaspore district of the Central Provinces, India, "the festival known as the Fortnight of the Manes—*Pitr Pāk*—occurs about September. It is believed that during this fortnight it is the practice of all the departed to come and visit their relatives. The homes are therefore cleaned, and the spaces in front of the house are plastered and painted in order to be pleasing to those who are expected. Cakes are prepared, and with certain ceremony these are offered to the unseen hovering spirit.[5]

The Bghais, a Karen tribe of Burma, hold an annual feast for the dead at the new moon which falls near the end of August or the beginning of September. All the villagers who have lost relatives within the last three years take part in it. Food and drink are set out on tables for the ghosts, and new clothes for them are hung up in the room.[6] The great festival of the dead in Cambodia takes place on the last day of the month Phatrabot (September-October), but ever since the moon began to wane everybody has been busy preparing for it. In every house cakes and sweetmeats are set out, candles burn, incense sticks smoke, and the whole is offered to the ancestral shades with an invocation which is thrice repeated: "O all you our ancestors who are departed, deign to come and eat what we have prepared for you, and to bless your posterity and make it happy."[7] In Tonquin, as in Sumba, the dead revisit their kinsfolk and their old homes at the New Year. From the hour of midnight, when the New Year begins, no one dares to shut the door of his house for fear of excluding the ghosts, who begin to arrive at that time.[8] In Siam and Japan also the souls of the dead revisit their families for three days in every year, and the lamps which the Japanese kindle in multitudes on that occasion to light the spirits on their way have procured for the festival the name of the Feast of Lanterns. It is to be observed that in Siam, as in Tonquin and Sumba, the return of the ghosts takes place at the New Year.[9]

The Chewsurs of the Caucasus believe that the souls of the departed revisit their old homes on the Saturday night of the second week in Lent. This gathering of the dead is called the "Assembly of Souls." The people spare no expense to treat the unseen guests handsomely. Beer is brewed and loaves of various shapes baked specially for the occasion.[10] The Armenians celebrate the memory of the dead on many days of the year, burning incense and lighting tapers in their honour. One of their customs is to keep a "light of the dead" burning all night in the house in order that the ghosts may be able to enter. For if the spirits find the house dark, they spit down the chimney and depart, cursing the churlish inmates.[11]

The ancient Iranians held a similar feast of the dead, called Farwadigan, during the five days at the end of the year. Says the Arab geographer Al-Biruni (c. 1000 A.D.): "During this time the people put food in the halls of the dead and drink on the roofs of the houses, believing that the spirits of the dead come out from the places of their reward or punishment, go to the dishes laid out for them, and imbibe their strength or suck their taste. They fumigate their houses with juniper, that the dead may enjoy its scent. The spirits of the pious then dwell among their families and, though invisible, occupy themselves with family affairs."[12]

Similar beliefs survive to this day in many parts of Europe and find expression in similar customs. The day of the dead or of All Souls (as we call it) is commonly the second of November. In the Vosges Mountains, good Christians are invited by the solemn sound of church bells to pray for the repose of the dead. While the bells are ringing, it is customary in some families to uncover beds and open windows, doubtless in order to let the poor souls enter and rest.[13] In Bruges, Dinant, and other towns of Belgium holy candles burn all night on the Eve of All Souls, and the bells toll till midnight, or even till morning. People, too, often set lighted candles on the graves. At Scherpenheuvel the houses are illuminated, and the people walk in procession carrying lighted candles. A very common custom in Belgium is to eat "soul-cakes" or "soul-bread" on the eve of the day of All Souls.[14] In Lechrain, a district of Southern Bavaria, on the Eve of All Souls people proceed to visit the graves and to offer soul-cakes to the hungry souls. Next morning, before eight o'clock, commence the vigil, requiem, and solemn visitation of the graves. On that day every household offers a plate of meal, oats, and spelt on a side-altar in the church; while in the middle of the edifice a bier is set, covered with a pall, and surrounded by lighted tapers and vessels of holy water.[15]

Similar beliefs and customs obtain in the Tyrol. There too "soul-lights"— that is, lamps filled with lard or butter—are lighted and placed on the hearth so that the poor souls, escaped from the fires of purgatory, may smear the melted grease upon their burns and so alleviate their pangs![16]

The Letts used to entertain and feed the souls of the dead for four weeks from Michaelmas (September 29) to the day of St. Simon and St. Jude (October 28). At this season the people were wont to prepare food of all sorts for the spirits and set it on the floor of a room, which had been well heated and swept for the purpose. Late in the evening the master of the house went into the room, tended the fire, and called upon his departed kinsfolk by their names to come and eat and drink.[17]

On All Saints' Day, the first of November, shops and streets in the Abruzzi are filled with candles, which people buy in order to kindle them in the evening on the graves of their relations. For all the dead come to visit their homes that night, the Eve of All Souls, and they need lights to show them the way. For their use, too, lights are kept burning in the houses all night. Before people go to sleep they place on the table a lighted lamp or candle and a frugal meal of bread and water. The dead issue from their graves and stalk in procession through every street of the village.[18]

In our own country the old belief in the annual return of the dead long lingered in the custom of baking "soul-cakes" and eating them or distributing them to the poor on All Souls' Day. Peasant girls used to go from farmhouse to farmhouse on that day, singing,

> "Soul, soul, for a soul cake,
> Pray you, good mistress, a soul cake."[19]

In Shropshire down to the seventeenth century it was customary on All Souls' Day to set on the table a high heap of soul-cakes, and most visitors to the house took one of them.[20]

257. The foregoing evidence lends some support to the conjecture—for it is only a conjecture—that the great festival of Osiris at Sais, with its accompanying illumination of the houses, was a night of All Souls, when the ghosts of the dead swarmed in the streets and revisited their old homes, which were lit up to welcome them back again. Herodotus, who briefly describes the festival, omits to mention its date, but we can determine it with some probability from other sources. Thus Plutarch tells us that Osiris was murdered on the seventeenth of the month Athyr, and that the Egyptians accordingly observed mournful rites for four days from the seventeenth of Athyr.[1] Now in the Alexandrian calendar, which Plutarch used, these four days corresponded to the thirteenth, fourteenth, fifteenth, and sixteenth of November, and this date answers exactly to the other indications given by Plutarch, who says that at the time of the festival the Nile was sinking, the north winds dying away, the nights lengthening, and the leaves falling from the trees. During these four days a gilt cow swathed in a black pall was exhibited as an image of Isis. This, no doubt, was the image mentioned by Herodotus in his account of the festival.[2] On the nineteenth day of the month the people went down to the sea, the priests carrying a shrine which contained a golden casket. Into this casket they poured fresh water, and thereupon the spectators raised a shout that Osiris was found. After that they took some vegetable mould, moistened it with water, mixed it with precious spices and incense, and moulded the paste into a small moon-shaped image, which was then robed and ornamented.[3] Thus it appears that the purpose of the ceremonies described by

Plutarch was to represent dramatically, first, the search for the dead body of Osiris, and, second, its joyful discovery, followed by the resurrection of the dead god who came to life again in the new image of vegetable mould and spices.[4] It is probable that the boy who figured in the sacred drama played the part, not of Osiris, but of his son Horus; but as the death and resurrection of the god were celebrated in many cities of Egypt, it is also possible that in some places the part of the god come to life was played by a living actor instead of by an image. An early Christian writer describes how the Egyptians, with shorn heads, annually lamented over a buried idol of Osiris, smiting their breasts, slashing their shoulders, ripping open their old wounds, until, after several days of mourning, they professed to find the mangled remains of the god, at which they rejoiced.[5] However the details of the ceremony may have varied in different places, the pretence of finding the god's body, and probably of restoring it to life, was a great event in the festal year of the Egyptians. The shouts of joy which greeted it are described or alluded to by many ancient writers.[6]

258. The funeral rites of Osiris, as they were observed at his great festival in the sixteen provinces of Egypt, are described in a long inscription of the Ptolemaic period, which is engraved on the walls of the god's temple at Denderah, the Tentyra of the Greeks, a town of Upper Egypt situated on the western bank of the Nile about forty miles north of Thebes.[1] Unfortunately, while the information thus furnished is remarkably full and minute on many points, the arrangement adopted in the inscription is so confused and the expression often so obscure that a clear and consistent account of the ceremonies as a whole can hardly be extracted from it. Moreover, we learn from the document that the ceremonies varied somewhat in the several cities, the ritual of Abydos, for example, differing from that of Busiris. Without attempting to trace all the particularities of local usage I shall briefly indicate what seem to have been the leading features of the festival, so far as these can be ascertained with tolerable certainty.[2]

The rites lasted eighteen days, from the twelfth to the thirtieth of the month Khoiak, and set forth the nature of Osiris in his triple aspect as dead, dismembered, and finally reconstituted by the union of his scattered limbs. In the first of these aspects he was called Chent-Ament (Khenti-Amenti), in the second Osiris-Sep, and in the third Sokari (Seker). Small images of the god were moulded of sand or vegetable earth and corn, to which incense was sometimes added; his face was painted yellow and his cheek-bones green. These images were cast in a mould of pure gold, which represented the god in the form of a mummy, with the white crown of Egypt on his head. The festival opened on the twelfth day of Khoiak with a ceremony of ploughing and sowing. Two black cows were yoked to the plough, which was made of tamarisk wood, while the share was of black copper. A boy scattered the seed. One end of the field was sown with barley, the other with spelt, and the middle with flax. During the operation of the chief celebrant recited the ritual chapter of "the sowing of the fields." At Busiris on the twentieth of Khoiak sand and barley were put in the god's "garden," which appears to have been a sort of large flower-pot. This was done in the presence of the cow-goddess Shenty, represented seemingly by the image of a cow made of gilt sycamore wood with a headless human image in its inside. "Then fresh inundation water was poured out of a golden vase over both the goddess and the 'garden,' and the barley was allowed to grow as the emblem of the resurrection of the god after his burial in the earth, 'for the growth of the garden is the growth of the divine substance.' "[3] On the twenty-second of Khoiak, at the eighth hour, the images of Osiris, attended by thirty-four images of deities, performed a mysterious voyage in thirty-four tiny boats made of papyrus, which were illuminated by three hundred and sixty-five lights. On the twenty-fourth of Khoiak, after sunset, the effigy of Osiris in a coffin of mulberry wood was laid in the grave, and at the ninth hour of the night the effigy which had been made and deposited the year before was removed and placed upon boughs of sycamore.[4] Lastly, on the thirtieth day of Khoiak they repaired to the holy sepulchre, a subterranean chamber over which appears to have grown a clump of Persea-trees. Entering the vault by the western door, they laid the coffined effigy of the dead god reverently on a bed of sand in the chamber. So they left him to his rest, and departed from the sepulchre by the eastern door.[5]

259. In the foregoing account of the festival, drawn from the great inscription of Denderah, the burial of Osiris figures prominently, while his resurrection is implied rather than expressed. This defect of the document, however, is amply compensated by a remarkable series of bas-reliefs which accompany and illustrate the inscription. These exhibit in a series of scenes the dead god lying swathed as a mummy on his bier, then gradually raising himself up higher and higher, until at last he has entirely quitted the bier and is seen erect between the guardian wings of the faithful Isis, who stands behind him, while a male figure holds up before his eyes the *crux ansata,* the Egyptian symbol of life.[1] The resurrection of the god could hardly be portrayed more graphically. Even more instructive, however, is another representation of the same event in a chamber dedicated to Osiris in the great temple of Isis at Philae. Here we see the dead body of Osiris with stalks of corn springing from it, while a priest waters the stalks from a pitcher which he holds in his hand. The accompanying inscription sets forth that "this is the form of him whom one may not name, Osiris of the mysteries, who springs from the returning waters." Taken together, the picture and the words seem to leave no doubt that Osiris was here conceived and represented as a personification of the corn which springs from the fields after they have been fertilized by the inundation.[2] This, according to the inscription, was the kernel of the mysteries, the innermost secret revealed to the initiated. So in the rites of Demeter at Eleusis a reaped ear of corn was exhibited to the worshippers as the central mystery of their religion.³ We can now fully understand why at the great festival of sowing in the month of Khoiak the priests used to bury effigies of Osiris made of earth and corn. When these effigies were taken up again at the end of a year or of a shorter interval, the corn would be found to have sprouted from the body of Osiris, and this sprouting of the grain would be hailed as an omen, or rather as the cause, of the growth of the crops. The corn-god produced the corn from himself: he gave his own body to feed the people: he died that they might live.

260. And from the death and resurrection of their great god the Egyptians drew not only their support and sustenance in this life, but also their hope of a life eternal beyond the grave. This hope is indicated in the clearest manner by the very remarkable effigies of Osiris which have come to light in Egyptian cemeteries. Thus in the Valley of the Kings at Thebes there was found the tomb of a royal fan-bearer who lived about 1500 B.C. Among the rich contents of the tomb there was a bier on which rested a mattress of reeds covered with three layers of linen. On the upper side of the linen was painted a life-size figure of Osiris; and the interior of the figure, which was waterproof, contained a mixture of vegetable mould, barley, and a sticky fluid. The barley had sprouted and sent out shoots two or three inches long.¹ Again, in the cemetery at Cynopolis "were numerous burials of Osiris figures. These were made of grain wrapped up in cloth and roughly shaped like an Osiris, and placed inside a bricked-up recess at the side of the tomb, sometimes in small pottery coffins, sometimes in wooden coffins in the form of a hawk-mummy, sometimes without any coffins at all."² These corn-stuffed figures were bandaged like mummies with patches of gilding here and there, as if in imitation of the golden mould in which the similar figures of Osiris were cast at the festival of sowing.³ Again, effigies of Osiris, with faces of green wax and their interior full of grain, were found buried near the necropolis of Thebes.⁴ Finally, we are told by Professor Erman that between the legs of mummies "there sometimes lies a figure of Osiris made of slime; it is filled with grains of corn, the sprouting of which is intended to signify the resurrection of the god."⁵ We cannot doubt that, just as the burial of corn-stuffed images of Osiris in the earth at the festival of sowing was designed to quicken the seed, so the burial of similar images in the grave was meant to quicken the dead, in other words, to ensure their spiritual immortality.

261. The foregoing survey of the myth and ritual of Osiris may suffice to prove that in one of his aspects the god was a personification of the corn, which may be said to die and come to life again every year. Through all the pomp and glamour with which in later times the priests had invested his worship, the conception of him as the corn-god comes clearly out in the festival of his death and resurrection, which was celebrated in the month of Khoiak and at a later period in the month of Athyr. That festival appears to have been essentially a festival of sowing, which properly fell at the time when the husbandman actually committed the seed to the earth. On that occasion an effigy of the corn-god, moulded of earth and corn, was buried with funeral rites in the ground in order that, dying there, he might come to life again with the new crops. The ceremony was, in fact, a charm to ensure the growth of the corn by sympathetic magic, and we may conjecture that as such it was practised in a simple form by every Egyptian farmer on his fields long before it was adopted and transfigured by the priests in the stately ritual of the temple. In the modern, but doubtless ancient, Arab custom of burying "the Old Man," namely, a sheaf of wheat, in the harvest-field and praying that he may return from the dead,[1] we see the germ out of which the worship of the corn-god Osiris was probably developed.

The details of his myth fit in well with this interpretation of the god. He was said to be the offspring of Sky and Earth.[2] What more appropriate parentage could be invented for the corn which springs from the ground that has been fertilized by the water of heaven? It is true that the land of Egypt owed its fertility directly to the Nile and not to showers; but the inhabitants must have known or guessed that the great river in its turn was fed by the rains which fell in the far interior. Again, the legend that Osiris was the first to teach men the use of corn[3] would be most naturally told of the corn-god himself. Further, the story that his mangled remains were scattered up and down the land and buried in different places may be a mythical way of expressing either the sowing or the winnowing of the grain. The latter interpretation is supported by the tale that Isis placed the severed limbs of Osiris on a corn-sieve.[4] Or more probably the legend may be a reminiscence of a custom of slaying a human victim, perhaps a representative of the corn-spirit and distributing his flesh or scattering his ashes over the fields to fertilize them. In modern Europe the figure of Death is sometimes torn in pieces, and the fragments are then buried in the ground to make the crops grow well,[5] and in other parts of the world human victims are treated in the same way.[6] With regard to the ancient Egyptians we have it on the authority of Manetho that they used to burn red-haired men and scatter their ashes with winnowing fans,[7] and it is highly significant that this barbarous sacrifice was offered by the kings at the grave of Osiris.[8] We may conjecture that the victims represented Osiris himself, who was annually slain, dismembered, and buried in their persons that he might quicken the seed in the earth.

262. Possibly in prehistoric times the kings themselves played the part of the god and were slain and dismembered in that character. Set as well as Osiris is said to have been torn in pieces after a reign of eighteen days, which was commemorated by an annual festival of the same length.[1] According to one story Romulus, the first king of Rome, was cut in pieces by the senators, who buried the fragments of him in the ground;[2] and the traditional day of his death, the seventh of July, was celebrated with certain curious rites, which were apparently connected with the artificial fertilization of the fig.[8]

Again, Greek legend told how Pentheus, king of Thebes, and Lycurgus, king of the Thracian Edonians, opposed the vine-god Dionysus, and how the impious monarchs were rent in pieces, the one by the frenzied Bacchanals, the other by horses.[4] These Greek traditions may well be distorted reminiscences of a custom of sacrificing human beings, and especially divine kings, in the character of Dionysus, a god who resembled Osiris in many points and was said like him to have been torn limb from limb.[5] We are told that in Chios men were rent in pieces as a sacrifice to Dionysus;[6] and since they died the same death as their god, it is reasonable to suppose that they personated him. The story that the Thracian Orpheus was similarly torn limb from limb by the Bacchanals seems to indicate that he too perished in the character of the god whose death he died.[7] It is significant that the Thracian Lycurgus, king of the Edonians, is said to have been put to death in order that the ground, which had ceased to be fruitful, might regain its fertility.[8] In some Thracian villages at Carnival time a custom is still annually observed, which may well be a mitigation of an ancient practice of putting a man, perhaps a king, to death in the character of Dionysus for the sake of the crops. A man disguised in goatskins and fawnskins, the livery of Dionysus, is shot at and falls down as dead. A pretence is made of flaying his body and of mourning over him, but afterwards he comes to life again. Further, a plough is dragged about the village and seed is scattered, while prayers are said that the wheat, rye, and barley may be plentiful. One town (Viza), where these customs are observed, was the capital of the old Thracian kings. In another town (Kosti, near the Black Sea) the principal masker is called the king. He wears goatskins or sheepskins, and is attended by a boy who dispenses wine to the people. The king himself carries seed, which he casts on the ground before the church, after being invited to throw it on two bands of married and unmarried men respectively. Finally, he is stripped of the skins and thrown into the river.[9]

Further, we read of a Norwegian king, Halfdan the Black, whose body was cut up and buried in different parts of his kingdom for the sake of ensuring the fruitfulness of the earth. He is said to have been drowned at the age of forty through the breaking of the ice in spring. What followed his death is thus related by the old Norse historian Snorri Sturluson: "He had been the most prosperous (literally, blessed with abundance) of all kings. So greatly did men value him that when the news came that he was dead and his body removed to Hringariki and intended for burial there, the chief men from Raumariki and Westfold and Heithmörk came and all requested that they might take his body with them and bury it in their various provinces; they thought that it would bring abundance to those who obtained it. Eventually it was settled that the body was distributed in four places. The head was laid in a barrow at Steinn in Hringariki, and each party took away their own share and buried it. All these barrows are called Halfdan's barrows."[10]

Taken all together, these legends point to a widespread practice of dismembering the body of a king or magician and burying the pieces in different parts of the country in order to ensure the fertility of the ground and probably also the fecundity of man and beast.

263. To return to the human victims whose ashes the Egyptians scattered with winnowing-fans,[1] the red hair of these unfortunates was probably significant. If I am right, the custom of sacrificing such persons was not a mere way of wreaking a national spite on fair-haired foreigners, whom the black-haired Egyptians of old, like the black-haired Chinese of modern times, may have regarded as red-haired devils. For in Egypt the oxen which were sacrificed had also to be red; a single black or white hair found on the beast would have disqualified it for the sacrifice.[2] If, as I conjecture, these human sacrifices were intended to promote the growth of the crops—and the winnowing of their ashes seems to support this view—red-haired victims were perhaps selected as best fitted to personate the spirit of the ruddy grain. For when a god is represented by a living person, it is natural that the human representative should be chosen on the ground of his supposed resemblance to the divine original. Hence the ancient Mexicans, conceiving the maize as a personal being who went through the whole course of life between seed-time and harvest, sacrificed new-born babes when the maize was sown, older children when it had sprouted, and so on till it was fully ripe, when they sacrificed old men.[3] A name for Osiris was the "crop" or "harvest";[4] and the ancients sometimes explained him as a personification of the corn.[5]

264. But Osiris was more than a spirit of the corn; he was also a tree-spirit, and this may perhaps have been his primitive character, since the worship of trees is naturally older in the history of religion than the worship of the cereals. However that may have been, to an agricultural people like the Egyptians, who depended almost wholly on their crops, the corn-god was naturally a far more important personage than the tree-god, and attracted a larger share of their devotion. The character of Osiris as a tree-spirit was represented very graphically in a ceremony described by Firmicus Maternus.[1] A pine-tree having been cut down, the centre was hollowed out, and with the wood thus excavated an image of Osiris was made, which was then buried like a corpse in the hollow of the tree. It is hard to imagine how the conception of a tree as tenanted by a personal being could be more plainly expressed. The image of Osiris thus made was kept for a year and then burned, exactly as was done with the image of Attis which was attached to the pine-tree.[2] The ceremony of cutting the tree, as described by Firmicus Maternus, appears to be alluded to by Plutarch.[3] It was probably the ritual counterpart of the mythical discovery of the body of Osiris enclosed in the *erica*-tree.[4]

In the hall of Osiris at Denderah the coffin containing the hawk-headed mummy of the god is clearly depicted as enclosed within a tree, apparently a conifer, the trunk and branches of which are seen above and below the coffin.[5] The scene thus corresponds closely both to the myth and to the ceremony described by Firmicus Maternus. In another scene at Denderah a tree of the same sort is represented growing between the dead and the reviving Osiris, as if on purpose to indicate that the tree was the symbol of the divine resurrection.[6] A pine-cone often appears on the monuments as an offering presented to Osiris, and a manuscript of the Louvre speaks of the cedar as sprung from him.[7] The sycamore and the tamarisk were also his trees. In inscriptions he is spoken of as residing in them;[8] and in tombs his mother Nut is often portrayed standing in the midst of a sycamore-tree and pouring a libation for the benefit of the dead.[9] In one of the Pyramid Texts we read, "Hail to thee, Sycamore, which enclosest the god";[10] and in certain temples the statue of Osiris used to be placed for seven days upon branches of sycamores. The explanation appended in the sacred texts declares that the placing of the image on the tree was intended to recall the seven months passed by Osiris in the womb of his mother Nut, the goddess of the sycamore.[11] The rite recalls the story that Adonis was born after ten months' gestation from a myrrh-tree.[12] Further, in a sepulchre at How (Diospolis Parva) a tamarisk is depicted overshadowing the tomb of Osiris, while a bird is perched among the branches with the significant legend "the soul of Osiris,"[13] showing that the spirit of the dead god was believed to haunt his sacred tree. Again, in the series of sculptures which illustrate the mystic history of Osiris in the great temple of Isis at Philae, a tamarisk is figured with two men pouring water on it. The accompanying inscription leaves no doubt, says Brugsch, that the verdure of the earth was believed to be connected with the verdure of the tree, and that the sculpture refers to the grave of Osiris at Philae, of which Plutarch tells us that it was overshadowed by a *methide* plant, taller than any olive-tree. This sculpture, it may be observed, occurs in the same chamber in which the god is represented as a corpse with ears of corn springing from him.[14] In inscriptions he is referred to as "the one in the tree," "the solitary one in the acacia," and so forth.[15] On the monuments he sometimes appears as a mummy covered with a tree or with plants;[16] and trees are represented growing from his grave.[17]

It accords with the character of Osiris as a tree-spirit that his worshippers were forbidden to injure fruit-trees, and with his character as a god of vegetation in general that they were not allowed to stop up wells of water, which are so important for the irrigation of hot southern lands.[18] According to one legend, he taught men to train the vine to poles, to prune its superfluous foliage, and to extract the juice of the grape.[19] In the papyrus of Nebseni, written about 1550 B.C., Osiris is depicted sitting a shrine, from the roof of which hang clusters of grapes;[20] and in the papyrus of the royal scribe Nekht we see the god enthroned in front of a pool, from the banks of which a luxuriant vine, with many bunches of grapes, grows towards the green face of the seated deity.[21] The ivy was sacred to him, and was called his plant because it is always green.[22]

265. As a god of vegetation Osiris was naturally conceived as a god of creative energy in general, since men at a certain stage of evolution fail to distinguish between the reproductive powers of animals and of plants. Hence a striking feature in his worship was the coarse but expressive symbolism by which this aspect of his nature was presented to the eye not merely of the initiated but of the multitude. At his festival women used to go about the villages singing songs in his praise and carrying obscene images of him which they set in motion by means of strings.[1] The custom was probably a charm to ensure the growth of the crops. A similar image of him, decked with all the fruits of the earth, is said to have stood in a temple before a figure of Isis,[2] and in the chambers dedicated to him at Philae the dead god is portrayed lying on his bier in an attitude which indicates in the plainest way that even in death his generative virtue was not extinct but only suspended, ready to prove a source of life and fertility to the world when the opportunity should offer.[3] Hymns addressed to Osiris contain allusions to this important side of his nature. In one of them it is said that the world waxes green in triumph through him; and another declares, "Thou art the father and mother of mankind, they live on thy breath, they subsist on the flesh of thy body."[4] We may conjecture that in this paternal aspect he was supposed, like other gods of fertility, to bless men and women with offspring, and that the processions at his festival were intended to promote this object as well as to quicken the seed in the ground. It would be to misjudge ancient religion to denounce as lewd and profligate the emblems and the ceremonies which the Egyptians employed for the purpose of giving effect to this conception of the divine power. The ends which they proposed to themselves in these rites were natural and laudable; only the means they adopted to compass them were mistaken. A similar fallacy induced the Greeks to adopt a like symbolism in their Dionysiac festivals, and the superficial but striking resemblance thus produced between the two religions has perhaps more than anything else misled inquirers, both ancient and modern, into identifying worships which, though certainly akin in nature, are perfectly distinct and independent in origin.

266. We have seen that in one of his aspects Osiris was the ruler and judge of the dead.[1] To a people like the Egyptians, who not only believed in a life beyond the grave but actually spent much of their time, labour, and money in preparing for it, this office of the god must have appeared hardly, if at all, less important than his function of making the earth to bring forth its fruits in due season. We may assume that in the faith of his worshippers the two provinces of the god were intimately connected. In laying their dead in the grave they committed them to his keeping who could raise them from the dust to life eternal, even as he caused the seed to spring from the ground. Of that faith the corn-stuffed effigies of Osiris found in Egyptian tombs furnish an eloquent and unequivocal testimony.[2] They were at once an emblem and an instrument of resurrection. Thus from the sprouting of the grain the ancient Egyptians drew an augury of human immortality. They are not the only people who have built the same towering hopes on the same slender foundation. "Thou fool, that which thou sowest, thou sowest not that body that shall be, but bare grain, it may chance of wheat, or of some other grain: but God giveth it a body as it hath pleased him, and to every seed his own body. So also is the resurrection of the dead. It is sown in corruption; it is raised in incorruption: it is sown in weakness; it is raised in power: it is sown a natural body; it is raised a spiritual body."[3]

A god who thus fed his people with his own broken body in this life, and who held out to them a promise of a blissful eternity in a better world hereafter, naturally reigned supreme in their affections. We need not wonder, therefore, that in Egypt the worship of the other gods was overshadowed by that of Osiris, and that while they were revered each in his own district, he and his divine partner Isis were adored in all.[4]

267. Thus far we have discussed the character of Osiris as he is presented to us in the art and literature of Egypt and in the testimonies of Greek writers; and we have found that judged by these indications he was in the main a god of vegetation and of the dead. But we have still to ask, how did the conception of such a composite deity originate? Did it arise simply through observation of the great annual fluctuations of the seasons and a desire to explain them? Was it a result of brooding over the mystery of external nature? Was it the attempt of a rude philosophy to lift the veil and explore the hidden springs that set the vast machine in motion? That man at a very early stage of his long history meditated on these things and evolved certain crude theories which partially satisfied his craving after knowledge is certain; from such meditations of Babylonian and Phrygian sages appear to have sprung the pathetic figures of Adonis and Attis; and from such meditations of Egyptian sages may have sprung the tragic figure of Osiris.

Yet a broad distinction seems to sever the myth and worship of Osiris from the kindred myths and worships of Adonis and Attis. For while Adonis and Attis were minor divinities in the religion of Western Asia, completely overshadowed by the greater deities of their respective pantheons, the solemn figure of Osiris towered in solitary grandeur over all the welter of Egyptian gods, like a pyramid of his native land lit up by the last rays of the setting sun when all below it is in shadow. And whereas legend generally represented Adonis and Attis as simple swains, mere herdsmen or hunters whom the fatal love of a goddess had elevated above their homely sphere into a brief and melancholy pre-eminence, Osiris uniformly appears in tradition as a great and beneficent king. In life he ruled over his people, beloved and revered for the benefits he conferred on them and on the world; in death he reigned in their hearts and memories as lord of the dead, the awful judge at whose bar every man must one day stand to give an account of the deeds done in the body and to receive the final award.

In recent years the historical reality of Osiris as a king who once lived and reigned in Egypt has been maintained by more than one learned scholar; and without venturing to pronounce a decided opinion on so obscure and difficult a question, I think it worth while, following the example of Dr. Wallis Budge, to indicate certain modern African analogies which tend to confirm the view that beneath the mythical wrappings of Osiris there lay the mummy of a dead man. At all events the analogies which I shall cite suffice to prove that the custom of worshipping dead kings has not been confined to Egypt, but has been apparently widespread throughout Africa, though the evidence now at our disposal only enables us to detect the observance of the custom at a few points of that great continent.

268. In a former part of this work we saw that the Shilluks, a pastoral and partially agricultural people of the White Nile, worship the spirits of their dead kings.[1] The graves of the deceased monarchs form indeed the national or tribal temples; and as each king is interred at the village where he was born and where his afterbirth is buried, these grave-shrines are scattered over the country. Each of them usually comprises a small group of round huts, resembling the common houses of the people, the whole being enclosed by a fence; one of the huts is built over the grave, the others are occupied by the guardians of the shrine, who at first are generally the widows or old men-servants of the deceased king. When these women or retainers die, they are succeeded in office by their descendants, for the tombs are maintained in perpetuity, so that the number of temples and of gods is always on the increase. Cattle are dedicated to these royal shrines and animals sacrificed at them.

But of all the dead kings none is revered so deeply or occupies so large a place in the minds of the people as Nyakang, the traditional founder of the dynasty and the ancestor of all the kings who have reigned after him to the present day. It is said that Nyakang, like Romulus, disappeared in a great storm, which scattered all the people about him; in their absence the king took a cloth, tied it tightly round his neck, and strangled himself. According to one account, that is the death which all his successors on the throne have died; but while tradition appears to be unanimous as to the custom of regicide, it varies as to the precise mode in which the kings were relieved of their office and of life. But still the people are convinced that Nyakang did not really die but only vanished mysteriously away like the wind. When a missionary asked the Shilluks as to the manner of Nyakang's death, they were filled with amazement at his ignorance and stoutly maintained that he never died, for were he to die all the Shilluks would die also. The graves of this deified king are shown in various parts of the country. The transmission of the divine or semi-divine spirit of Nyakang to the reigning monarch appears to take place at the king's installation and to be effected by means of a rude wooden effigy of Nyakang, in which the spirit of that deified man is perhaps supposed to be immanent. But however the spiritual transmission may be carried out, "the fundamental idea of the cult of the Shilluk divine kings is the immanence in each of the spirit of Nyakang."[2] Thus the Shilluk kings are encircled with a certain halo of divinity because they are thought to be animated by the divine spirit of their ancestor, the founder of the dynasty. There seems, indeed, to be no doubt that in spite of the mythical elements which have gathered round his memory, Nyakang was a real man, who led the Shilluks to their present home on the Nile either from the west or south. Yet, he is now universally revered by the people as a demi-god; indeed, for all practical purposes his worship quite eclipses that of the supreme god Juok, the creator, who, having ordered the world, committed it to the care of ancestral spirits and demons, and now, dwelling aloft, concerns himself no further with human affairs.

The example of Nyakang seems to show that under favourable circumstances the worship of a dead king may develop into the dominant religion of a people. There is, therefore, no intrinsic improbability in the view that in ancient Egypt the religion of Osiris originated in that way. Certainly some curious resemblances can be traced between the dead Nyakang and the dead Osiris. Both died violent and mysterious deaths: the graves of both were pointed out in many parts of the country: both were deemed the great sources of fertility for the whole land: and both were associated with certain sacred trees and animals, particularly with bulls. And just as Egyptian kings identified themselves both in life and in death with their deified predecessor Osiris, so Shilluk kings are still believed to be animated by the spirit of their deified predecessor Nyakang and to share his divinity.

269. In Kiziba, a district of Central Africa on the western side of Lake Victoria Nyanza, the souls of dead kings become ruling spirits; temples are built in their honour, and priests appointed to serve them. The highest of them is a certain Wamara, who rules over the souls of the dead, and who would seem to have been a great king in his life. Temples are built for him; they are like the houses of men, but only half as large. A perpetual holy fire is kept up in each temple, and the priest passes the night in it. He receives white sheep or goats as victims, and generally acts also as a diviner or physician. When a man is very ill, he thinks that Wamara, the lord of the spirits of the dead, is summoning him to the far country; so he sends a sacrifice to Wamara's priest, who prays to the spirit to let the sick man live yet a while.[1] This great spirit of an ancient king, who now rules over the dead, resembles the Egyptian Osiris.

270. Among the Basutos, an important Bantu people of South Africa, "each family is supposed to be under the direct influence and protection of its ancestors; but the tribe, taken as a whole, acknowledges for its national gods the ancestors of the reigning sovereign. Thus, the Basutos address their prayers to Monaheng and Motlumi, from whom their chiefs are descended. The Baharutsis and the Barolongs invoke Tobege and his wife Mampa. Mampa makes known the will of her husband, announcing each of her revelations by these words, '*O re! O re!*' 'He has said! he has said!' "[1]

271. Another Bantu people that worships the spirits of its dead kings are the Barotse or Marotse of the Upper Zambesi. The Barotse believe in a supreme god, the creator of all things, whom they call Niambe.

Yet while they acknowledge the divine supremacy of Niambe, the Barotse address their prayers most frequently to the inferior deities, the *ditino,* who are the deified kings of the country. The tombs of the departed monarchs may be seen near the villages which they inhabited in life. Each tomb stands in a grove of beautiful trees and is encircled by a tall palisade of pointed stakes, covered with fine mats, like the palisade which surrounds the royal residence of a living king. Such an enclosure is sacred; the people are forbidden to enter it lest they should disturb the ghost of him who sleeps below. But the inhabitants of the nearest village are charged with the duty of keeping the tomb and the enclosure in good order, repairing the palisade, and replacing the mats when they are worn out. Once a month, at the new moon, the women sweep not only the grave and the enclosure but the whole village. The guardian of the tomb (called Ngomboti) is at the same time a priest; he acts as intermediary between the god and the people who come to pray to the deity. The spirits of dead kings are consulted on matters of public concern as well as by private individuals touching their own affairs. One of the most popular of the royal shrines is near Senanga at the southern end of the great plain of the Barotse. Voyagers who go down the Zambesi do not fail to pay their devotions at the shrine, that the god of the place may make their voyage to prosper and may guard the frail canoe from shipwreck in the rush and roar of the rapids; and when they return in safety they repair again to the sacred spot to deposit a thank-offering for the protection of the deity.[1]

272. These analogies lend some support to the theory that in ancient Egypt where the kings were worshipped by their people both in life and death, Osiris may have been originally nothing but one of these deified monarchs whose worship gradually eclipsed that of all the rest and ended by rivalling or even surpassing that of the great sun-god himself.

In support of this view we may quote the words in which the historian of European morals describes the necessity under which the popular imagination labours of embodying its cherished ideals in living persons. He is referring to the dawn of the age of chivalry, when in the morning twilight the heroic figure of Charlemagne rose like a bright star above the political horizon, to be thenceforth encircled by a halo of romance like the nimbus that shone round the head of Osiris. "In order that the tendencies I have described should acquire their full force, it was necessary that they should be represented or illustrated in some great personage, who, by the splendour and the beauty of his career, could fascinate the imaginations of men. It is much easier to govern great masses of men through their imagination than through their reason. Moral principles rarely act powerfully upon the world, except by way of example or ideals. When the course of events has been to glorify the ascetic or monarchical or military spirit, a great saint, or sovereign, or soldier will arise, who will concentrate in one dazzling focus the blind tendencies of his time, kindle the enthusiasm and fascinate the imagination of the people. But for the prevailing tendency, the great man would not have arisen, or would not have exercised his great influence. But for the great man, whose career appealed vividly to the imagination, the prevailing tendency would never have acquired its full intensity."[1]

Whether the parallel thus suggested between Charlemagne, the mediaeval ideal of a Christian knight, and Osiris, the ancient Egyptian ideal of a just and beneficent monarch, holds good or not, it is now impossible to determine. For while Charlemagne stands near enough to allow us clearly to discern his historical reality, Osiris is so remote that we can no longer discriminate with any certitude between the elements of history and fable which appear to have blended in his traditional character. I am content to indicate bare possibilities: dogmatism on such points would be in the highest degree rash and unbecoming. Whether Osiris and Isis were from first to last purely imaginary beings, the ideal creations of a primitive philosophy, or whether they were originally a real man and woman about whom after death the myth-making fancy wove its gossamer rainbow-tinted web, is a question to which I am not bold enough to give a decided answer.

DIONYSUS

273. The idea that the changes of the seasons, and particularly the annual growth and decay of vegetation, were episodes in the life of gods, whose mournful death and happy resurrection might be celebrated with dramatic rites of alternate lamentation and rejoicing, was by no means peculiar to the religious mysticism of the dreamy East, but was shared by the races of livelier fancy and more mercurial temperament who inhabited the shores and islands of the Aegean. The Greek had no need to journey into far countries to learn the vicissitudes of the seasons, to mark the fleeting beauty of the damask rose, the transient glory of the golden corn, the passing splendour of the purple grapes. Year by year in his own beautiful land he beheld, with natural regret, the bright pomp of summer fading into the gloom and stagnation of winter, and year by year he hailed with natural delight the outburst of fresh life in spring. Accustomed to personify the forces of nature, to tinge her cold abstractions with the warm hues of imagination, to clothe her naked realities with the gorgeous drapery of a mythic fancy, he fashioned for himself a train of gods and goddesses, of spirits and elves, out of the shifting panorama of the seasons, and followed the annual fluctuations of their fortunes with alternate emotions of cheerfulness and dejection, of gladness and sorrow, which found their natural expression in alternate rites of rejoicing and lamentation, of revelry and mourning. A consideration of some of the Greek divinities who thus died and rose again from the dead may furnish us with a series of companion pictures to set side by side with the sad figures of Adonis, Attis, and Osiris.

274. The god Dionysus or Bacchus is best known to us as a personification of the vine and of the exhilaration produced by the juice of the grape. His ecstatic worship, characterised by wild dances, thrilling music, and tipsy excess, appears to have originated among the rude tribes of Thrace, who were notoriously addicted to drunkenness.[1] Its mystic doctrines and extravagant rites were essentially foreign to the clear intelligence and sober temperament of the Greek race. Yet appealing as it did to that love of mystery and that proneness to revert to savagery which seem to be innate in most men, the religion spread like wildfire through Greece until the god whom Homer hardly deigned to notice had become the most popular figure of the pantheon. The resemblance which his story and his ceremonies present to those of Osiris have led some enquirers both in ancient and modern times to hold that Dionysus was merely a disguised Osiris, imported directly from Egypt into Greece.[2] But the great preponderance of evidence points to his Thracian origin, and the similarity of the two worships is sufficiently explained by the similarity of the ideas and customs on which they were founded.

275. While the vine with its clusters was the most characteristic manifestation of Dionysus, he was also a god of trees in general. Thus we are told that almost all the Greeks sacrificed to "Dionysus of the tree."[1] In Boeotia one of his titles was "Dionysus in the tree."[2] His image was often merely an upright post, without arms, but draped in a mantle, with a bearded mask to represent the head, and with leafy boughs projecting from the head or body to shew the nature of the deity.[3] On a vase his rude effigy is depicted appearing out of a low tree or bush.[4] At Magnesia on the Maeander an image of Dionysus is said to have been found in a plane-tree, which had been broken by the wind.[5] He was the patron of cultivated trees;[6] prayers were offered to him that he would make the trees grow;[7] and he was especially honoured by husbandmen, chiefly fruit-growers, who set up an image of

him, in the shape of a natural tree-stump, in their orchards.[8] He was said
to have discovered all tree-fruits, amongst which apples and figs are particularly mentioned;[9] and he was referred to as "well-fruited," "he of the
green fruit," and "making the fruit to grow."[10] One of his titles was "teem-
ing" or "bursting" (as of sap or blossoms);[11] and there was a Flowery
Dionysus in Attica and at Patrae in Achaia.[12] The Athenians sacrificed to
him for the prosperity of the fruits of the land.[13] Amongst the trees particularly sacred to him, in addition to the vine, was the pine-tree.[14] The
Delphic oracle commanded the Corinthians to worship a particular pine-tree
"equally with the god," so they made two images of Dionysus out of it, with
red faces and gilt bodies.[15] In art a wand, tipped with a pine-cone, is commonly carried by the god or his worshippers.[16] Again, the ivy and the fig-tree
were especially associated with him. In the Attic township of Acharnae
there was a Dionysus Ivy;[17] at Lacedaemon there was a Fig Dionysus; and
in Naxos, where figs were called *meilicha,* there was a Dionysus Meilichios,
the face of whose image was made of fig-wood.[18]

276. Further, there are indications, few but significant, that Dionysus was
conceived as a deity of agriculture and the corn. He is spoken of as himself
doing the work of a husbandman:[1] he is reported to have been the first to
yoke oxen to the plough, which before had been dragged by hand alone;
and some people found in this tradition the clue to the bovine shape in
which, as we shall see, the god was often supposed to present himself
to his worshippers. Thus guiding the ploughshare and scattering the seed
as he went, Dionysus is said to have eased the labour of the husbandman.[2]
Moreover, we are told that in the land of the Bisaltae, a Thracian tribe, there
was a great and fair sanctuary of Dionysus, where at his festival a bright
light shone forth at night as a token of an abundant harvest vouchsafed by
the deity; but if the crops were to fail that year, the mystic light was not
seen, darkness brooded over the sanctuary as at other times.[3]

277. Like the other gods of vegetation whom we have considered, Dionysus was believed to have died a violent death, but to have been brought to
life again; and his sufferings, death, and resurrection were enacted in his
sacred rites. His tragic story is thus told by the poet Nonnus. Zeus in the
form of a serpent visited Persephone, and she bore him Zagreus, that is,
Dionysus, a horned infant. Scarcely was he born, when the babe mounted
the throne of his father Zeus and mimicked the great god by brandishing
the lightning in his tiny hand. But he did not occupy the throne long; for
the treacherous Titans, their faces whitened with chalk, attacked him with
knives while he was looking at himself in a mirror. For a time he evaded
their assaults by turning himself into various shapes, assuming the likeness
successively of Zeus and Cronus, of a young man, of a lion, a horse, and
a serpent. Finally, in the form of a bull, he was cut to pieces by the
murderous knives of his enemies.[1] His Cretan myth, as related by Firmicus

Maternus, ran thus. He was said to have been the bastard son of Jupiter, a Cretan king. Going abroad, Jupiter transferred the throne and sceptre to the youthful Dionysus, but, knowing that his wife Juno cherished a jealous dislike of the child, he entrusted Dionysus to the care of guards upon whose fidelity he believed he could rely. Juno, however, bribed the guards, and amusing the child with rattles and a cunningly-wrought looking-glass lured him into an ambush, where her satellites, the Titans, rushed upon him, cut him limb from limb, boiled his body with various herbs, and ate it. But his sister Minerva, who had shared in the deed, kept his heart and gave it to Jupiter on his return, revealing to him the whole history of the crime. In his rage, Jupiter put the Titans to death by torture, and, to soothe his grief for the loss of his son, made an image in which he enclosed the child's heart, and then built a temple in his honour.[2] In this version a Euhemeristic turn has been given to the myth by representing Jupiter and Juno (Zeus and Hera) as a king and queen of Crete. The guards referred to are the mythical Curetes who danced a war-dance round the infant Dionysus, as they are said to have done round the infant Zeus.[3] Very noteworthy is the legend, recorded both by Nonnus and Firmicus, that in his infancy Dionysus occupied for a short time the throne of his father Zeus. So Proclus tells us that "Dionysus was the last king of the gods appointed by Zeus. For his father set him on the kingly throne, and placed in his hand the sceptre, and made him king of all the gods of the world."[4] Such traditions point to a custom of temporarily investing the king's son with the royal dignity as a preliminary to sacrificing him instead of his father. Pomegranates were supposed to have sprung from the blood of Dionysus, as anemones from the blood of Adonis and violets from the blood of Attis: hence women refrained from eating seeds of pomegranates at the festival of the Thesmophoria.[5] According to some, the severed limbs of Dionysus were pieced together, at the command of Zeus, by Apollo, who buried them on Parnassus.[6] The grave of Dionysus was shewn in the Delphic temple beside a golden statue of Apollo.[7] However, according to another account, the grave of Dionysus was at Thebes, where he is said to have been torn in pieces.[8] Thus far the resurrection of the slain god is not mentioned, but in other versions of the myth it is variously related. According to one version, which represented Dionysus as a son of Zeus and Demeter, his mother pieced together his mangled limbs and made him young again.[9] In others it is simply said that shortly after his burial he rose from the dead and ascended up to heaven;[10] or that Zeus raised him up as he lay mortally wounded;[11] or that Zeus swallowed the heart of Dionysus and then begat him afresh by Semele,[12] who in the common legend figures as mother of Dionysus. Or, again, the heart was pounded up and given in a portion to Semele, who thereby conceived him.[13]

278. Turning from the myth to the ritual, we find that the Cretans celebrated a biennial[1] festival at which the passion of Dionysus was represented in every detail. All that he had done or suffered in his last moments was enacted before the eyes of his worshippers, who tore a live bull to pieces with their teeth and roamed the woods with frantic shouts. In front of them was carried a casket supposed to contain the sacred heart of Dionysus, and to the wild music of flutes and cymbals they mimicked the rattles by which the infant god had been lured to his doom.[2] Where the resurrection formed part of the myth, it also was acted at the rites,[3] and it even appears that a general doctrine of resurrection, or at least of immortality, was inculcated on the worshippers; for Plutarch, writing to console his wife on the death of their infant daughter, comforts her with the thought of the immortality of the soul as taught by tradition and revealed in the mysteries of Dionysus.[4] A different form of the myth of the death and resurrection of Dionysus is that he descended into Hades to bring up his mother Semele from the dead.[5] The local Argive tradition was that he went down through the Alcyonian lake; and his return from the lower world, in other words his resurrection, was annually celebrated on the spot by the Argives, who summoned him from the water by trumpet blasts, while they threw a lamb into the lake as an offering to the warder of the dead.[6] Whether this was a spring festival does not appear, but the Lydians certainly celebrated the advent of Dionysus in spring; the god was supposed to bring the season with him.[7] Deities of vegetation, who are supposed to pass a certain portion of each year under ground, naturally come to be regarded as gods of the lower world or of the dead. Both Dionysus and Osiris were so conceived.

279. A feature in the mythical character of Dionysus, which at first sight appears inconsistent with his nature as a deity of vegetation, is that he was often conceived and represented in animal shape, especially in the form, or at least with the horns, of a bull. Thus he is spoken of as "cow-born," "bull," "bull-shaped," "bull-faced," "bull-browed," "bull-horned," "horn-bearing," "two-horned," "horned."[1] He was believed to appear, at least occasionally, as a bull.[2] His images were often, as at Cyzicus, made in bull shape,[3] or with bull horns;[4] and he was painted with horns.[5] On one statuette he appears clad in a bull's hide, the head, horns, and hoofs hanging down behind.[6] Again, he is represented as a child with clusters of grapes round his brow, and a calf's head, with sprouting horns, attached to the back of his head.[7] On a red-figured vase the god is portrayed as a calf-headed child seated on a woman's lap.[8] The people of Cynaetha in north-western Arcadia held a festival of Dionysus in winter, when men, who had greased their bodies with oil for the occasion, used to pick out a bull from the herd and carry it to the sanctuary of the god. Dionysus was supposed to inspire their choice of the particular bull,[9] which probably represented the deity himself; for at his festivals he was believed to appear in bull form. The women of Elis hailed him as a bull, and prayed him to come with his bull's foot. They

sang, "Come hither, Dionysus, to thy holy temple by the sea; come with the Graces to thy temple, rushing with thy bull's foot, O goodly bull, O goodly bull!"[10] The Bacchanals of Thrace wore horns in imitation of their god.[11] According to the myth, it was in the shape of a bull that he was torn to pieces by the Titans;[12] and the Cretans, when they acted the sufferings and death of Dionysus, tore a live bull to pieces with their teeth.[13] Indeed, the rending and devouring of live bulls and calves appear to have been a regular feature of the Dionysiac rites.[14]

280. Another animal whose form Dionysus assumed was the goat. One of his names was "Kid."[1] At Athens and at Hermion he was worshipped under the title of "the one of the Black Goatskin," and a legend ran that on a certain occasion he had appeared clad in the skin from which he took the title.[2] In the wine-growing district of Phlius, where in autumn the plain is still thickly mantled with the red and golden foliage of the fading vines, there stood of old a bronze image of a goat, which the husbandmen plastered with gold-leaf as a means of protecting their vines against blight.[3] The image probably represented the vine-god himself. To save him from the wrath of Hera, his father Zeus changed the youthful Dionysus into a kid;[4] and when the gods fled to Egypt to escape the fury of Typhon, Dionysus was turned into a goat.[5] Hence when his worshippers rent in pieces a live goat and devoured it raw,[6] they must have believed that they were eating the body and blood of the god.

281. The custom of killing a god in animal form, which we shall examine more in detail further on, belongs to a very early stage of human culture, and is apt in later times to be misunderstood. The advance of thought tends to strip the old animal and plant gods of their bestial and vegetable husk, and to leave their human attributes (which are always the kernel of the conception) as the final and sole residuum. In other words, animal and plant gods tend to become purely anthropomorphic. When they have become wholly or nearly so, the animals and plants which were at first the deities themselves, still retain a vague and ill-understood connexion with the anthropomorphic gods who have been developed out of them. The origin of the relationship between the deity and the animal or plant having been forgotten, various stories are invented to explain it. These explanations may follow one of two lines according as they are based on the habitual or on the exceptional treatment of the sacred animal or plant. The sacred animal was habitually spared, and only exceptionally slain; and accordingly the myth might be devised to explain either why it was spared or why it was killed. Devised for the former purpose, the myth would tell of some service rendered to the deity by the animal; devised for the latter purpose, the myth would tell of some injury inflicted by the animal on the god. The reason given for sacrificing goats to Dionysus exemplifies a myth of the latter sort. They were sacrificed to him, it was said, because they injured the vine.[1] Now the

goat, as we have seen, was originally an embodiment of the god himself. But when the god had divested himself of his animal character and had become essentially anthropomorphic, the killing of the goat in his worship came to be regarded no longer as a slaying of the deity himself, but as a sacrifice offered to him; and since some reason had to be assigned why the goat in particular should be sacrificed, it was alleged that this was a punishment inflicted on the goat for injuring the vine, the object of the god's especial care. Thus we have the strange spectacle of a god sacrificed to himself on the ground that he is his own enemy. And as the deity is supposed to partake of the victim offered to him, it follows that, when the victim is the god's old self, the god eats of his own flesh. Hence the goat-god Dionysus is represented as eating raw goat's blood;[2] and the bull-god Dionysus is called "eater of bulls."[3] On the analogy of these instances we may conjecture that wherever a deity is described as the eater of a particular animal, the animal in question was originally nothing but the deity himself.[4] Later on we shall find that some savages propitiate dead bears and whales by offering them portions of their own bodies.

282. All this, however, does not explain why a deity of vegetation should appear in animal form. But the consideration of that point had better be deferred till we have discussed the character and attributes of Demeter. Meantime it remains to mention that in some places, instead of an animal, a human being was torn in pieces at the rites of Dionysus. This was the practice in Chios and Tenedos,[1] and at Potniae in Boeotia the tradition ran that it had been formerly the custom to sacrifice to the goat-smiting Dionysus a child, for whom a goat was afterwards substituted.[2] At Orchomenus, as we have seen, the human victim was taken from the women of an old royal family.[3] As the slain bull or goat represented the slain god, so, we may suppose, the human victim also represented him.

DEMETER AND PERSEPHONE

283. Dionysus was not the only Greek deity whose tragic story and ritual appear to reflect the decay and revival of vegetation. In another form and with a different application the old tale reappears in the myth of Demeter and Persephone. Substantially their myth is identical with the Syrian one of Aphrodite (Astarte) and Adonis, the Phrygian one of Cybele and Attis, and the Egyptian one of Isis and Osiris. In the Greek fable, as in its Asiatic and Egyptian counterparts, a goddess mourns the loss of a loved one, who personifies the vegetation, more especially the corn, which dies in winter to revive in spring; only whereas the Oriental imagination figured the loved and lost one as a dead lover or a dead husband lamented by his leman or his wife, Greek fancy embodied the same idea in the tenderer and purer form of a dead daughter bewailed by her sorrowing mother.

284. The oldest literary document which narrates the myth of Demeter and

Persephone is the beautiful Homeric *Hymn to Demeter,* which critics assign
to the seventh century before our era.[1] The object of the poem is to explain
the origin of the Eleusinian mysteries, and the complete silence of the poet
as to Athens and the Athenians, who in after ages took a conspicuous part
in the festival, renders it probable that the hymn was composed in the
far off time when Eleusis was still a petty independent state, and before
the stately procession of the Mysteries had begun to defile, in bright September days, over the low chain of barren rocky hills which divides the flat
Eleusinian cornland from the more spacious olive-clad expanse of the
Athenian plain. Be that as it may, the hymn reveals to us the conception
which the writer entertained of the character and functions of the two
goddesses: their natural shapes stand out sharply enough under the thin
veil of poetical imagery. The youthful Persephone, so runs the tale, was
gathering roses and lilies, crocuses and violets, hyacinths and narcissuses in
a lush meadow, when the earth gaped and Pluto, lord of the Dead, issuing
from the abyss carried her off on his golden car to be his bride and queen
in the gloomy subterranean world. Her sorrowing mother Demeter, with
her yellow tresses veiled in a dark mourning mantle, sought her over land
and sea, and learning from the Sun her daughter's fate she withdrew in
high dudgeon from the gods and took up her abode at Eleusis, where she
presented herself to the king's daughters in the guise of an old woman,
sitting sadly under the shadow of an olive tree beside the Maiden's Well, to
which the damsels had come to draw water in bronze pitchers for their
father's house. In her wrath at her bereavement the goddess suffered not
the seed to grow in the earth but kept it hidden under ground, and she
vowed that never would she set foot on Olympus and never would she let
the corn sprout till her lost daughter should be restored to her. Vainly the
oxen dragged the ploughs to and fro in the fields; vainly the sower dropped
the barley seed in the brown furrows; nothing came up from the parched
and crumbling soil. Even the Rarian plain near Eleusis, which was wont to
wave with yellow harvests, lay bare and fallow.[2] Mankind would have
perished of hunger and the gods would have been robbed of the sacrifices
which were their due, if Zeus in alarm had not commanded Pluto to dis-
gorge his prey, to restore his bride Persephone to her mother Demeter. The
grim lord of the Dead smiled and obeyed, but before he sent back his queen
to the upper air on a golden car, he gave her the seed of a pomegranate to
eat, which ensured that she would return to him. But Zeus stipulated that
henceforth Persephone should spend two thirds of every year with her mother
and the gods in the upper world and one third of the year with her husband
in the nether world, from which she was to return year by year when the
earth was gay with spring flowers. Gladly the daughter then returned to
the sunshine, gladly her mother received her and fell upon her neck; and
in her joy at recovering the lost one Demeter made the corn to sprout

from the clods of the ploughed fields and all the broad earth to be heavy with leaves and blossoms. And straightway she went and shewed this happy sight to the princes of Eleusis, to Triptolemus, Eumolpus, Diocles, and to the king Celeus himself, and moreover she revealed to them her sacred rites and mysteries. Blessed, says the poet, is the mortal man who has seen these things, but he who has had no share of them in life will never be happy in death when he has descended into the darkness of the grave. So the two goddesses departed to dwell in bliss with the gods on Olympus; and the bard ends the hymn with a pious prayer to Demeter and Persephone that they would be pleased to grant him a livelihood in return for his song.[3]

285. It has been generally recognised, and indeed it seems scarcely open to doubt, that the main theme which the poet set before himself in composing this hymn was to describe the traditional foundation of the Eleusinian mysteries by the goddess Demeter. The whole poem leads up to the transformation scene in which the bare leafless expanse of the Eleusinian plain is suddenly turned, at the will of the goddess, into a vast sheet of ruddy corn; the beneficent deity takes the princes of Eleusis, shews them what she has done, teaches them her mystic rites, and vanishes with her daughter to heaven. The revelation of the mysteries is the triumphal close of the piece. This conclusion is confirmed by a more minute examination of the poem, which proves that the poet has given, not merely a general account of the foundation of the mysteries, but also in more or less veiled language mythical explanations of the origin of particular rites which we have good reason to believe formed essential features of the festival. Amongst the rites as to which the poet thus drops significant hints are the preliminary fast of the candidates for initation, the torchlight procession, the all-night vigil, the sitting of the candidates, veiled and in silence, on stools covered with sheepskins, the use of scurrilous language, the breaking of ribald jests, and the solemn communion with the divinity by participation in a draught of barley-water from a holy chalice.[1]

286. But there is yet another and a deeper secret of the mysteries which the author of the poem appears to have divulged under cover of his narrative. He tells us how, as soon as she had transformed the barren brown expanse of the Eleusinian plain into a field of golden grain, she gladdened the eyes of Triptolemus and the other Eleusinian princes by shewing them the growing or standing corn. When we compare this part of the story with the statement of a Christian writer of the second century. Hippolytus, that the very heart of the mysteries consisted in shewing to the initiated a reaped ear of corn,[1] we can hardly doubt that the poet of the hymn was well acquainted with this solemn rite, and that he deliberately intended to explain its origin in precisely the same way as he explained other rites of the mysteries, namely by representing Demeter as having set the example of performing the ceremony in her own person. Thus myth and ritual mutually explain and confirm each other. The poet of the seventh century before our era gives us the myth—he could not without sacrilege have revealed the ritual: the Christian father reveals the ritual, and his revelation accords perfectly with the veiled hint of the old poet. On the whole, then, we may, with many modern scholars, confidently accept the statement of the learned Christian father Clement of Alexandria, that the myth of Demeter and Persephone was acted as a sacred drama in the mysteries of Eleusis.[2]

287. But if the myth was acted as a part, perhaps as the principal part, of the most famous and solemn religious rites of ancient Greece, we have still to enquire, What was, after all, stripped of later accretions, the original kernel of the myth which appears to later ages surrounded and transfigured by an aureole of awe and mystery, lit up by some of the most brilliant rays of Grecian literature and art? If we follow the indications given by our oldest literary authority on the subject, the author of the Homeric hymn to Demeter, the riddle is not hard to read; the figures of the two goddesses, the mother and the daughter, resolve themselves into personifications of the corn.[1] At least this appears to be fairly certain for the daughter Persephone. The goddess who spends three or, according to another version of the myth, six months of every year with the dead under ground and the remainder of the year with the living above ground;[2] in whose absence the barley seed is hidden in the earth and the fields lie bare and fallow; on whose return in spring to the upper world the corn shoots up from the clods and the earth is heavy with leaves and blossoms—this goddess can surely be nothing else than a mythical embodiment of the vegetation, and particularly of the corn, which is buried under the soil for some months of every winter and comes to life again, as from the grave, in the sprouting cornstalks and the opening flowers and foliage of every spring. No other reasonable and probable explanation of Persephone seems possible. And if the daughter goddess was a personification of the young corn of the present year, may not the mother goddess be a personification of the old corn of last year, which has given birth to the new crops? The only alternative to this view of Demeter would seem to be to suppose that she is a personification of the earth, from whose broad bosom the corn and all other plants spring up, and of which accordingly they may appropriately enough be regarded as the daughters. This view of the original nature of Demeter has indeed been taken by some writers, both ancient and modern, and it is one which can be reasonably maintained. But it appears to have been rejected by the author of the Homeric hymn to Demeter, for he not only distinguishes Demeter from the personified Earth but places the two in the sharpest opposition to each other. He tells us that it was Earth who, in accordance with the will of Zeus and to please Pluto, lured Persephone to her doom by causing the narcissuses to grow which tempted the young goddess to stray far beyond the reach of help in the lush meadow.[3] Thus Demeter of the hymn, far from being identical with the Earth-goddess, must have regarded that divinity as her worst enemy, since it was to her insidious wiles that she owed the loss of her daughter. But if the Demeter of the hymn cannot have been a personification of the earth, the only alternative apparently is to conclude that she was a personification of the corn.

288. With this conclusion all the indications of the hymn-writer seem to harmonise. He certainly represents Demeter as the goddess by whose power and at whose pleasure the corn either grows or remains hidden in the ground; and to what deity can such powers be so fittingly ascribed as to the goddess of the corn? He calls Demeter yellow and tells how her yellow tresses flowed down on her shoulders;[1] could any colour be more appropriate with which to paint the divinity of the yellow grain? The same identification of Demeter with the ripe, the yellow corn is made even more clearly by a still older poet, Homer himself, or at all events the author of the fifth book of the *Iliad*. There we read: "And even as the wind carries the chaff about the sacred threshing-floors, when men are winnowing, what time yellow Demeter sifts the corn from the chaff on the hurrying blast, so that the heaps of chaff grow white below, so were the Achaeans whitened above by the cloud of dust which the hoofs of the horses spurned to the brazen heaven."[2] And just as the ripe or yellow corn was personified as the Yellow Demeter, so the unripe or green corn was personified as the Green Demeter. In that character the goddess has sanctuaries at Athens and other places; sacrifices were appropriately offered to Green Demeter in spring when the earth was growing green with the fresh vegetation, and the victims included sows big with young,[3] which no doubt were intended not merely to symbolise but magically to promote the abundance of the crops.

In Greek the various kinds of corn were called by the general name of "Demeter's fruits,"[4] just as in Latin they were called by the "fruits or gifts of Ceres,"[5] an expression which survives in the English word cereals. Tradition ran that before Demeter's time men neither cultivated corn nor tilled the ground, but roamed the mountains and woods in search of the wild fruits which the earth produced spontaneously from her womb for their subsistence. The tradition clearly implies not only that Demeter was the goddess of the corn, but that she was different from and younger than the goddess of the Earth, since it is expressly affirmed that before Demeter's time the earth existed and supplied mankind with nourishment in the shape of wild herbs, grasses, flowers, and fruits.[6]

In ancient art Demeter and Persephone are characterised as goddesses of the corn by the crowns of corn which they wear on their heads and by the stalks of corn which they hold in their hands.[7] Theocritus describes a smiling image of Demeter standing by a heap of yellow grain on a threshing-floor and grasping sheaves of barley and poppies in both her hands.[8] Indeed corn and poppies singly or together were a frequent symbol of the goddess, as we learn not only from the testimony of ancient writers[9] but from many existing monuments of classical art.[10] The naturalness of the symbol can be doubted by no one who has seen—and who has not seen?—a field of yellow corn bespangled thick with scarlet poppies; and we need not resort to the shifts of an ancient mythologist, who explained the symbolism of the poppy in Demeter's hand by comparing the globular shape of the poppy to the roundness of our globe, the unevenness of its edges to hills and valleys, and the hollow interior of the scarlet flower to the caves and dens of the earth.

289. As the goddess who first bestowed corn on mankind and taught them to sow and cultivate it, Demeter was naturally invoked and propitiated by farmers before they undertook the various operations of the agricultural year. In autumn, when he heard the sonorous trumpeting of the cranes, as they winged their way southward in vast flocks high overhead, the Greek husbandman knew that the rains were near and that the time of ploughing was at hand; but before he put his hand to the plough he prayed to Underground Zeus and to Holy Demeter for a heavy crop of Demeter's sacred corn. Then he guided the ox-drawn plough down the field, turning up the brown earth with the share, while a swain followed close behind with a hoe, who covered up the seed as fast as it fell to protect it from the voracious birds that fluttered and twittered at the plough-tail.[1] But while the ordinary Greek farmer took the signal for ploughing from the clangour of the cranes, Hesiod and other writers who aimed at greater exactness laid it down as a rule that the ploughing should begin with the autumnal setting of the Pleiades in the morning, which in Hesiod's time fell on the twenty-sixth of October.[2] The month in which the Pleiades set in the morning was generally recognised by the Greeks as the month of sowing; it corresponded apparently in part to our October, in part to our November. The Athenians called it Pyanepsion; the Boeotians named it significantly Damatrius, that is, Demeter's month, and they celebrated a feast of mourning because, says Plutarch, who as a Boeotian speaks with authority on such a matter, Demeter was then in mourning for the descent of Persephone.[3] It is possible to express more clearly the true original nature of Persephone as the corn-seed which has just been buried in the earth? The obvious, the almost inevitable conclusion did not escape Plutarch. He tells us that the mournful rites which were held at the time of the autumn sowing nominally commemorated the actions of deities, but that the real sadness was for the fruits of the earth, some of which at that season dropped of themselves and vanished from the trees, while others in the shape of seed were committed with anxious thoughts to the ground by men, who scraped the earth and then huddled it up over the seed, just as if they were burying and mourning for the dead.[4] Surely this interpretation of the custom and of the myth of Persephone is not only beautiful but true.

And just as the Greek husbandman prayed to the Corn Goddess when he committed the seed, with anxious forebodings, to the furrows, so after he had reaped the harvest and brought back the yellow sheaves with rejoicing to the threshing-floor, he paid the bountiful goddess her dues in the form of a thank-offering of golden grain. Theocritus has painted for us in glowing colours a picture of a rustic harvest-home, as it fell on a bright autumn day some two thousand years ago in the little Greek island of Cos.[5] The poet tells us how he went with two friends from the city to attend a festival given by farmers, who were offering first-fruits to Demeter from the store of barley with which she had filled their barns. The day was warm, indeed so hot that the very lizards, which love to bask and run about in the sun, were slumbering in the crevices of the stone-walls, and not a lark soared carolling into the blue vault of heaven. Yet despite the great heat there were everywhere signs of autumn. "All things," says the poet, "smelt of summer, but smelt of autumn too." Indeed the day was really autumnal; for a goat-herd who met the friends on their way to the rural merry-making, asked them whether they were bound for the treading of the grapes in the wine-presses. And when they had reached their destination and reclined at ease in the dappled shade of over-arching poplars and elms, with the babble of a neighbouring fountain, the buzz of the cicalas, the hum of bees, and the cooing of doves in their ears, the ripe apples and pears rolled in the grass at their feet and the branches of the wild-plum trees were bowed down to the earth with the weight of their purple fruit. So couched on soft beds of fragrant lentisk they passed the sultry hours singing ditties alternately, while a rustic image of Demeter, to whom the honours of the day were paid, stood smiling beside a heap of yellow grain on the threshing-floor, with corn-stalks and poppies in her hands.

290. In this description the time of year when the harvest-home was celebrated is clearly marked. Apart from the mention of the ripe apples, pears, and plums, the reference to the treading of the grapes is decisive. The Greeks gather and press the grapes in the first half of October,[1] and accordingly it is to this date that the harvest-festival described by Theocritus must be assigned. At the present day in Greece the maize-harvest immediately precedes the vintage, the grain being reaped and garnered at the end of September. Travelling in rural districts of Argolis and Arcadia at that time of the year you pass from time to time piles of the orange-coloured cobs laid up ready to be shelled, or again heaps of the yellow grain beside the pods. But maize was unknown to the ancient Greeks, who, like their modern descendants, reaped their wheat and barley crops much earlier in the summer, usually from the end of April till June. However, we may conclude that the day immortalized by Theocritus was one of those autumn days of great heat and effulgent beauty which in Greece may occur at any time up to the very verge of winter. I remember such a day at Panopeus on the borders of Phocis and

Boeotia. It was the first of November, yet the sun shone in cloudless splendour and the heat was so great, that when I had examined the magnificent remains of ancient Greek fortification-walls which crown the summit of the hill, it was delicious to repose on a grassy slope in the shade of some fine holly-oaks and to inhale the sweet scent of the wild thyme, which perfumed all the air. But it was summer's farewell. Next morning the weather had completely changed. A grey November sky lowered sadly overhead, and grey mists hung like winding-sheets on the lower slopes of the barren mountains which shut in the fatal plain of Chaeronea.

291. Other festivals held at Eleusis in honour of Demeter and Persephone were known as the Green Festival and the Festival of the Cornstalks.[1] Of the manner of their celebration we know nothing except that they comprised sacrifices, which were offered to Demeter and Persephone. But their names suffice to connect the two festivals with the green and the standing corn. We have seen that Demeter herself bore the title of Green, and that sacrifices were offered to her under that title which plainly aimed at promoting fertility.[2] Among the many epithets applied to Demeter which mark her relation to the corn may further be mentioned "Wheat-lover,"[3] "She of the Corn,"[4] "Sheaf-bearer,"[5] "She of the Threshing-floor,"[6] "She of the Winnowing-fan,"[7] "Nurse of the Corn-ears,"[8] "Crowned with Ears of Corn,"[9] "She of the Seed,"[10] "She of the Green Fruits,"[11] "Heavy with Summer Fruits,"[12] "Fruit-bearer,"[13] "She of the Great Loaf," and "She of the Great Barley Loaf."[14] Of these epithets it may be remarked that though all of them are quite appropriate to a Corn Goddess, some of them would scarcely be applicable to an Earth Goddess and therefore they add weight to the other arguments which turn the scale in favour of the corn as the fundamental attribute of Demeter.

292. How deeply implanted in the mind of the ancient Greeks was this faith in Demeter as goddess of the corn may be judged by the circumstance that the faith actually persisted among their Christian descendants at her old sanctuary of Eleusis down to the beginning of the nineteenth century. For when the English traveller Dodwell revisited Eleusis, the inhabitants lamented to him the loss of a colossal image of Demeter, which was carried off by Clarke in 1802 and presented to the University of Cambridge, where it still remains. "In my first journey to Greece," says Dodwell, "this protecting deity was in its full glory, situated in the centre of a threshing-floor, amongst the ruins of her temple. The villagers were impressed with a persuasion that their rich harvests were the effect of her bounty, and since her removal, their abundance, as they assured me, has disappeared."[1] Thus we see the Corn Goddess Demeter standing on the threshing-floor of Eleusis and dispensing corn to her worshippers in the nineteenth century of the Christian era, precisely as her image stood and dispensed corn to her worshippers on the threshing-floor of Cos in the days of Theocritus. And just as the people of Eleusis last century attributed the diminution of their harvests to the loss of

should not have stopped to weigh with too nice a hand the arguments that told for and against the prospect of human immortality. The reasoning that satisfied Saint Paul[2] and has brought comfort to untold thousands of sorrowing Christians, standing by the deathbed or the open grave of their loved ones, was good enough to pass muster with ancient pagans, when they too bowed their heads under the burden of grief, and, with the taper of life burning low in the socket, looked forward into the darkness of the unknown. Therefore we do no indignity to the myth of Demeter and Persephone—one of the few myths in which the sunshine and clarity of the Greek genius are crossed by the shadow and mystery of death—when we trace its origin to some of the most familiar, yet eternally affecting aspects of nature, to the melancholy gloom and decay of autumn and to the freshness, the brightness, and the verdure of spring.

296. If Demeter was indeed a personification of the corn, it is natural to ask, why did the Greeks personify the corn as a goddess rather than a god? why did they ascribe the origin of agriculture to a female rather than to a male power? They conceived the spirit of the vine as masculine; why did they conceive the spirit of the barley and wheat as feminine? To this it has been answered that the personification of the corn as feminine, or at all events the ascription of the discovery of agriculture to a goddess, was suggested by the prominent part which women take in primitive agriculture.[1] The theory illustrates a recent tendency of mythologists to explain many myths as reflections of primitive society rather than as personifications of nature. For that reason, apart from its intrinsic interest, the theory deserves to be briefly considered.

297. Before the invention of the plough, which can hardly be worked without resort to the labour of men, it was and still is customary in many parts of the world to break up the soil for cultivation with hoes, and among not a few savage peoples to this day the task of hoeing the ground and sowing the seed devolves mainly or entirely upon the women, while the men take little or no part in cultivation beyond clearing the land by felling the forest trees and burning the fallen timber and brushwood which encumber the soil. Thus, for example, among the Zulus, "when a piece of land has been selected for cultivation, the task of clearing it belongs to the men, but the women are the real laborers; for (except in particular cases) the entire business of digging, planting and weeding devolves upon them.[1] A special term of contempt is applied to any Zulu man who, deprived of the services of his wife and family, is compelled to handle the hoe himself.[2] Similarly among the Awemba, to the west of Lake Tanganyika, the bulk of the work in the plantations falls on the women; in particular the men refuse to hoe the ground. They have a saying, "Is not each male child born for the axe and each female child for the hoe?"[3]

The natives of the Tanganyika plateau "cultivate the banana, and have a curious custom connected with it. No man is permitted to sow; but when the hole is prepared a little girl is carried to the spot on a man's shoulders. She first throws into the hole a sherd of broken pottery, and then scatters the seed over it."⁴ Such acts, the natives say, must be performed by chaste and innocent hands, lest a contaminated touch should destroy the potency of the medicine or of the seedlings planted. Similarly among the people of the Lower Congo "women must remain chaste while planting pumpkin and calabash seeds, they are not allowed to touch any pig-meat, and they must wash their hands before touching the seeds. If a woman does not observe all these rules, she must not plant the seeds, or the crop will be bad; she may make the holes, and her baby girl, or another who has obeyed the restrictions, can drop in the seeds and cover them over."⁵ We can now perhaps understand why Attic matrons had to observe strict chastity when they celebrated the festival of the Thesmophoria. In Attica that festival was held in honour of Demeter in the month of Pyanepsion, corresponding to October,⁶ the season of the autumn sowing; and, as we shall see later, the rites included certain ceremonies which bore directly on the quickening of the seed.

Of the Caffres of South Africa in general we read that "agriculture is mainly the work of the women, for in olden days the men were occupied in hunting and fighting. The women do but scratch the land with hoes, sometimes using long-handled instruments, as in Zululand, and sometimes short-handled ones, as above the Zambesi. When the ground is thus prepared, the women scatter the seed, throwing it over the soil quite at random.⁷ So among the Wanyamwezi, who are an essentially agricultural people, to the south of Lake Victoria Nyanza, the men cut down the bush and hoe the hard ground, but leave the rest of the labour of weeding, sowing, and reaping to the women.⁸ The Baganda of Central Africa subsist chiefly on bananas, and among them "the garden and its cultivation have always been the woman's department. No woman would remain with a man who did not give her a garden and a hoe to dig it with.⁹ In Kiziba, a district immediately to the south of Uganda, the tilling of the soil is exclusively the work of the women. They turn up the soil with hoes, make holes in the ground with digging-sticks or their fingers, and drop a few seeds into each hole.¹⁰ Among the Niam-Niam of Central Africa "the men must studiously devote themselves to their hunting, and leave the culture of the soil to be carried on exclusively by the women";¹¹ and among the Monbuttoo of the same region in like manner, "whilst the women attend to the tillage of the soil and the gathering of the harvest, the men, unless they are absent either for war or hunting, spend the entire day in idleness."¹²

298. A similar division of labour between men and women prevails among many primitive agricultural tribes of Indians in South America.¹ Thus among the Caribs of the West Indies the men used to fell the trees and leave the fallen trunks to cumber the ground, burning off only the smaller boughs. Then the women came and planted manioc, potatoes, yams, and bananas wherever they found room. The men, we are told, would rather have died of hunger than undertake such agricultural labours.² Again, among the Tupinambas, a tribe of Brazilian Indians, an old superstition prevailed that if a sort of earth-almond, which the Portuguese call *amendoens,* was planted by the men, it would not grow.³ Similar accounts appear to apply to the Brazilian Indians in general: the men occupy themselves with hunting, war, and the manufacture of their weapons, while the women plant and reap the crops, and search for fruits in the forest;⁴ above all they cultivate the manioc, scraping the soil clear of weeds with pointed sticks and inserting the shoots in the earth.⁵

299. A similar distribution of labour between the sexes prevails among some savage tribes in other parts of the world. Thus among the Lhoosai of south-eastern India the men employ themselves chiefly in hunting or in making forays on their weaker neighbours, but they clear the ground and help to carry home the harvest. However, the main burden of the bodily labour by which life is supported falls on the women; they fetch water, hew wood, cultivate the ground, and help to reap the crops.¹ Among the Miris of Assam almost the whole of the field work is done by the women.² Among the Korwas, a savage hill tribe of Bengal, the men hunt with bows and arrows, while the women till the fields, dig for wild roots, or cull wild vegetables.³ Among the Papuans of Ayambori, near Doreh in Dutch New Guinea, it is the men who lay out the fields by felling and burning the trees and brushwood in the forest, and it is they who fence off the fields, but it is the women who sow and reap them and carry home the produce in sacks on their backs.⁴ So among the natives of Kaimani Bay in the same part of the world the men occupy themselves only with fishing and hunting, while all the field work falls on the women.⁵

300. Even among primitive peoples who have not yet learned to cultivate any plants the task of collecting edible seeds and digging up edible roots appears to devolve mainly on the women, while the men contribute their share to the common food supply by hunting and fishing, for which their superior strength, agility, and courage especially qualify them. For example, among the Indians of California, who were entirely ignorant of agriculture, the men killed the game and caught the salmon, while the women dug the roots and brought in most of the vegetable food, though the men helped them to gather acorns, nuts, and berries.¹ Among the Indians of San Juan Capistrano in California, while the men passed their time in fowling, fishing, dancing, and lounging, "the women were obliged to gather seeds in the fields, prepare them for cooking, and to perform all the meanest offices, as well as the most laborious.² Again, among the natives of Western Australia, "it is generally considered the province of women to dig roots";³ and so too among the aborigines of central Victoria.⁴

301. In these customs observed by savages who are totally ignorant of agriculture we may perhaps detect some of the steps by which mankind have advanced from the enjoyment of the wild fruits of the earth to the systematic cultivation of plants. For an effect of digging up the earth in the search for roots has probably been in many cases to enrich and fertilise the soil and so to increase the crop of roots or herbs; and such an increase would naturally attract the natives in larger numbers and enable them to subsist for longer periods on the spot without being compelled by the speedy exhaustion of the crop to shift their quarters and wander away in search of fresh supplies. Moreover, the winnowing of the seeds on ground which had thus been turned up by the digging-sticks of the women would naturally contribute to the same result. For though savages at the level of the Californian Indians and the aborigines of Australia have no idea of using seeds for any purpose but that of immediate consumption, and it has never occurred to them to incur a temporary loss for the sake of a future gain by sowing them in the ground, yet it is almost certain that in the process of winnowing the seeds as a preparation for eating them many of the grains must have escaped and, being wafted by the wind, have fallen on the upturned soil and borne fruit. Thus by the operations of turning up the ground and winnowing the seed, though neither operation aimed at anything beyond satisfying the immediate pangs of hunger, savage man or rather savage woman was unconsciously preparing for the whole community a future and more abundant store of food, which would enable them to multiply and to abandon the old migratory and wasteful manner of life for a more settled and economic mode of existence. So curiously sometimes does man, aiming his shafts at a near but petty mark, hit a greater and more distant target.

On the whole, then, it appears highly probable that as a consequence of a certain natural division of labour between the sexes women have contributed more than men towards the greatest advance in economic history, namely, the transition from a nomadic to a settled life, from a natural to an artificial basis of subsistence.

302. It remains only to add that of the two species of corn, namely barley and wheat, associated with Demeter in Greek religion, the former has perhaps the better claim to be her original element; for not only would it seem to have been the staple food of the Greeks in the Homeric age, but there are grounds for believing that it is one of the oldest, if not the very oldest, cereal cultivated by the Aryan race. Certainly the use of barley in the religious ritual of the ancient Hindus as well as of the ancient Greeks furnishes a strong argument in favour of the great antiquity of its cultivation, which is known to have been practised by the lake-dwellers of the Stone Age in Europe.[1]

NOTES

209 1. [For standard studies on Tammuz, see Additional Notes, ¶209.]
2. I.e., *Dumuzi-abzu*. [The precise meaning of the phrase is disputed; see: S. Langdon, *Tammuz and Ishtar* (Oxford 1914), 2; W. F. Albright, in *Journal of the American Oriental Society*, 40 (1920), 318.]

210 1. The lament for Adonis is mentioned by Sappho (fr. 94, Wharton), who flourished c. 600 B.C.
2. Ezekiel, 8 : 14.
3. Apollodorus, *Bibl.*, iii. 14, 4; Bion, *Id.*, i; Ovid, *Met.*, x. 503 ff.; W. W. Baudissin (*Adonis und Esmun* [Leipzig 1911], 142) inclines to think that the incident of the boar is a later importation into the myth of Adonis.

211 1. Philo Byblius, quoted by Eusebius, *Praep. ev.*, i. 10.
2. Strabo, xvi. 1, 18.
3. Lucian, *De dea Syria*, 6.
4. *Loc. cit.*
5. Strabo, *loc. cit.*
6. Lucian, *op. cit.*, 8; Pliny, *NH*, v. 78.
7. Lucian, *op. cit.*, 9.
8. Eusebius, *Vita Constant.*, iii. 55; Sozomen, *Hist. eccles.*, ii. 5; Socrates, *Hist. eccles.*, i. 18; Zosimus, i. 58.
9. *Etym. Magnum.* s.v. *Aphaka.*
10. Melito, "Oratio in Anton. Caesar.," in W. Cureton's *Specilegium Syriacum* (London 1855), 44.
11. Baudissin, *op. cit.*, plates i and ii. The monument is discussed, *ib.*, 78 ff.
12. *Sat.*, i. 21, 5.
13. Lucian, *op. cit.*, 8.

212 1. G. A. Cooke, *Text-Book of North-Semitic Inscriptions* (Oxford 1903), Nos. 12–25.
2. *Ib.*, No. 11.
3. Stephanus Byzantinus, s.v. *Amathous.*
4. D. G. Hogarth, *Devia Cypria* (London 1889), 1–2.

5. *Journal of Hellenic Studies*, 9 (1888), 193 ff.
6. C. Schuchhardt, *Schliemann's Ausgrabungen*[2] (Leipzig 1891), 231–33.
7. J. Selden, *De dis Syris* (Leipzig 1608), 274 f.
8. Herodotus i. 105; Pausanias, i. 14, 7.

213 1. Plutarch, *Alkibiades*, 18; id., *Nikias*, 13; Zenobius, *Centur.*, i. 49; Theocritus, *Id.*, xv. 132 ff.; Eustathius on *Odyssey*, xi. 590.
2. Lucian, *De dea Syria*, 8; Origen, *Selecta in Ezechielem* (in Migne, *PG* xiii. 80), Jerome, *Comm. in Ezech.*, 8. 13–14 (in Migne, *PL* xxv. 82 f.). Cyril of Alexandria, *In Isaiam*, lib. ii, tom. ii (in Migne, *PG* lxx. 441) describes the festival as still surviving in the fourth or even the fifth century.
3. Theocritus, *Id.*, xv. 132 f.
4. W. Mannhardt, *Antike Wald– und Feldkulte* (Berlin 1877), 277.
5. Lucian, *op. cit.*, 6.
6. Lucian, *op. cit.*, 8. The discoloration of the river was observed by Maundrell in the latter half of March, in 1696 and 1697. Renan observed it at the beginning of February: see his *Mission de Phénicie* (Paris 1864), 283. Milton, *Paradise Lost*, i. 446 f., erroneously transfers it to summer.
7. Ovid, *Met.*, x. 735; Servius on Vergil, *Aen.*, v. 72. Bion, however, represents the anemone as sprung from the tears of Aphrodite: *Id.*, i. 66.
8. Baudissin, *op. cit.*, 88 f.
9. Tzetzes, *Schol. in Lycophron*, 831; Geoponica, xi. 17; *Mythographi Graeci*, ed. A. Westermann (Brunswick 1843), 359. Cp. Bion, *loc. cit.*; Pausanias, vi. 24, 7.
10. Plutarch, *locc. citt.* Inscriptional evidence proves that processions in honor of Adonis were held in the Piraeus: Dittenberger, *Sylloge*[2], No. 726.
11. Ammianus Marcellinus, xxii. 9, 15.
12. See above, ¶207.
13. Apollodorus, *Bibl.*, iii. 14, 4; Schol. on Theocritus, i. 109; Antonius Liberalis, *Transform.*, 34; Ovid, *Met.* x. 489 ff.; Servius on Vergil, *Aen.* v. 72 and *Ecl.* x. 18; Hyginus, fab., 58, 164; Fulgentius, iii. 8.
14. Mannhardt, *op. cit.*, 383, n. 2.
15. See above, ¶209.
16. Jeremiah, 44 : 17–19.
17. Cornutus, *Theol. Graecae compendium*, 28, pp. 54 f. Lang; Schol. on Theocritus, iii. 48; Origen, in Migne, *PL* xiii. 800; Jerome, in Migne, *PL* xxv. 83; Clement of Alexandria, *Homilies* 6. 11; Sallustius philosophus, *De diis et mundo*, 4; Joannes Lydus, *De mensibus*, iv. 4.
18. D. Chwolsohn, *Die Ssabier und der Ssabismus* (St. Petersburg 1856), ii. 27; Baudissin, *op. cit.*, 111 ff.
19. M. J. Lagrange, *Études sur les religions sémitiques*[2] (Paris 1905), 307 ff.
20. Diodorus Siculus, i. 14, 2.

brother Adonijah (I Kings, 2 : 22–24). Similarly, when Abimelech became king of Shechem, he put his seventy brothers to death (Judges, 8 : 29–31; 9 : 5 ff., 18); and Jehoram, king of Judah, consigned all his brothers to the sword (II Chron. 21 : 4).

223 1. Hyginus, fab. 242.
2. Schol. and Eustathius on *Iliad*, xi. 20.
3. Anacreon, cited by Pliny, *NH*, vii. 154. Nonnus, *Dionys.*, xxxii. 212 f., also refers to the longevity of Cinyras.

224 1. Sophocles, *Trachiniae*, 1191 ff.; Apollodorus, *Bibl.*, ii. 7, 7; Diodorus Siculus, iv. 38; Hyginus, fab. 36.
2. [S. Clementis Romani], *Recognitiones*, x. 24 (in Migne, *PL*, i. 1434).
3. Josephus, *Ant.*, viii. 5, 3; *Contra Apionem*, i. 18.
4. Eudoxus of Cnidus, quoted by Athenaeus, ix. 47. See: M. J. Lagrange, *Études sur les religions sémitiques*[2] (Paris 1905), 308–11.
5. Zenobius, *Centur.*, v. 56 (in *Paroemiographi Graeci*, ed. Leutsch-Schneidewin, i. 143).
6. A. Newton, *Dictionary of Birds* (London 1893–96), 755.
7. H. B. Tristam, *The Fauna and Flora of Palestine* (London 1884), 124; [G. E. Post, in Hasting's Dictionary of the Bible, iv. 179].
8. The Tyrian Hercules was said to be a son of Zeus and Asteria (Eudoxus, as quoted in note 4); Cicero, *De natura decorum*, iii. 16, 42. Asteria may be a Greek approximation to Astarte: W. W. Baudissin, *Adonis und Esmun* (Leipzig 1911), 307. As to the transformation of her into a quail, see Apollodorus, *Bibl.*, i. 4, 1; Servius on Vergil, *Aen.*, iii. 73.

225 1. Strabo, iii. 5, 5; Seymus Chius, *Orbis Descriptio*, 159–161 (in *Geographi Graeci Minores*, ed. Müller, i. 200 f.).
2. Silus Italicus, iii. 14–32; Mela, iii. 46; Strabo, iii. 5, 3; 5, 7; Diodorus Siculus, v. 20, 2; Philostratus, *Vita Apollonii*, v. 4 f.; Appian, *Hispanica*, 65. The worship of Melqarth under the name of Hercules continued in the south of Spain down to the time of the Roman Empire: see J. Toutain, *Les cultes païens dans l'Empire Romain*, i (Paris 1907), 400 ff.
3. Livy, xxi. 21, 9; xxii. 5–9; Cicero, *De Divinatione*, i. 24, 49; Silus Italicus, iii. 1 ff., 158 ff.
4. Pausanias, x. 4, 5.
5. G. A. Cooke, *Text-Book of North-Semitic Inscriptions* (Oxford 1903), 351.

226 1. Justin, xviii. 6, 1–7; Vergil, *Aen.*, iv. 473 ff.; Ovid, *Fasti*, iii. 545 ff. [with Frazer's commentary *in loc.*]; Timaeus, in *FHG*, i. 197.
2. Justin, xviii. 6, 8.
3. Silus Italicus, i. 81 ff.
4. See above, ¶**224.**

227 1. Strabo, xiv. 5, 9; Arrian, *Anabasis*, ii. 5; Athenaeus, xii. 39. Cp. Stephanus Byzantinus, s. v. *Anchialê;* Georgius Syncellus, *Chronographia*, i. 312 Dindorf.

     2. According to Berosus and Abydenus, it was not Sardanapalus (Ashurbanipal) but Senacherib that built or rebuilt Tarsus after the model of Babylon, causing the river Cnidus to flow through it: *FHG*, ii. 504; iv. 282.

     3. Diodorus Siculus, ii. 27; Athenaeus, xii. 38; Justin, i. 3.

     4. G. Maspero, *Histoire ancienne des peuples de l'Orient classique*, iii (Paris 1899), 422.

     5. Abydenus, in *FHG*, iv. 282; Syncellus, *Chronographia*, i. 396 Dindorf. Compare the similar case of Zimri, king of Israel (I Kings, 16 : 18).

228 1. Herodotus, i. 86 f.

     2. D. Raoul-Rochette, in *Mémories de l'Académie des Inscriptions et Belles-Lettres*, 17, i (Paris 1848), 274.

     3. Zend-Avesta, Vendidâd, Fargard, v. 7, 39–44 (in *SBE*, iv. 60 f.).

     4. J. Damsteter trans., Zend-Avesta, i (*SBE*, iv), xc, 9, 110 f.

     5. Strabo, xv. 3, 14.

     6. Bacchylides, iii. 24–62.

     7. A. H. Smith, in *Journal of Hellenic Studies*, 18 (1898), 267–69.

     8. Herodotus, i. 7.

229 1. Raoul-Rochette, *op. cit.*, ii (Paris 1848), 247 f., 271 ff.

     2. As to Isis, cp. Plutarch, *De Iside et Osiride*, 16. As to DEMETER, cp. Homeric Hymn to Demeter, 231–62; Apollodorus, *Bibl.*, i. 5, 1; Ovid, *Fasti*, 547–50. As to THETIS, cp. Apollonius Rhodius, *Argonautica*, iv. 865, 879; Apollodorus, *Bibl.*, iii. 13, 6. On the custom of passing children over a fire as a means of purification, see J. G. Frazer, *Apollodorus* (Loeb Classics, 1921), ii. 311 ff.

     3. She is said to have thus restored the youth of her husband, Jason, her father-in-law, Aeson, the nurses of Dionysus, and all their husbands: Euripides, *Medea*, Argum.; Schol. on Aristophanes, *Knights*, 1321; cp. Plautus, *Pseudolus*, 879 ff. She likewise applied this process to an old man: Apollodorus, *Bibl.*, i. 9, 7; Pausanias, viii. 11, 2; Hyginus, fab. 24.

     4. Pindar, *Ol.*, i. 40 ff., with Scholiast *in loc.*

     5. Iamblichus, *De mysteriis*, v. 12.

     6. Lucian, *De morte Peregrini*, 27 f.

     7. Diogenes Laertius, viii. 2, 69 f.

     8. Lucian, *De morte Peregrini*, 25; Strabo, xv. 1, 64, 68; Arrian, *Anabasis*, vii. 3.

230 1. The ancient evidence concerning the myth and ritual of Attis is fully assembled in H. Hepding, *Attis: Seine Mythen und sein Kult* (Giessen 1903). It is therefore unnecessary to give detailed references to the original sources.

     2. So Hermesianax, an elegaic poet of the fourth century B.C., quoted by

pine tree (Helbig, *Führer*², i. 225 f.). Pliny, however, says that it was a *plane* tree (*NH*, xvi. 240).

4. Herodotus, vii. 26; Xenophon, *Anabasis*, i. 2, 8; Livy, xxxviii, 13, 6; Quintus Curtius, iii. 1, 1–5; Pliny, *NH*, v. 106.

5. Aelian, *Var. Hist.*, xiii. 21.

6. Catullus, lxiii. 22; Lucretius, ii. 620; Ovid, *Fastii*, iv. 181 ff., 341; Polyaenus, *Stratagem.*, viii. 53, 4. Flutes or pipes often appear on her monuments: see H. Dessau, *op. cit.*, Nos. 4100, 4143, 4145, 4152, 4153.

7. Hippolytus, *Refutat. omn. haeres.*, v. 9.

237 1. Adam of Bremen, *Descriptio insularum Aquilonis*, 27 (in Migne, *PL*, xxlvi. 643).

2. K. Simrock, *Die Edda*⁸ (Stuttgart 1882), 382. The old custom of hanging and disemboweling traitors was probably a survival of the sacrifice to Odin; see F. Liebrecht, *Zur Volkskunde* (Heilbronn 1879), 8 ff.; K. von Amira, in H. Paul's *Grundriss der germanischen Philigie²*, iii (Strasburg 1900), 197 f.; [R. Glanz, in *Jewish Social Studies*, 5 (1943), 3 ff.].

3. *Havamal*, 139 ff.

4. Cole Fay-Cooper, *The Wild Tribes of the Davao District, Mindanao* (Chicago 1913), 114 ff.

238 1. Pausanias, viii. 23, 6 f. The Arcadian worship of the Hanged Artemis was noticed by Callimachus; see Clem. Alex., *Protrept.*, ii. 38.

2. Eustathius on *Odyssey*, xii. 85; I. Bekker, *Anecdota Graeca* (Berlin 1814–21), i. 336 f., s.v. *Agalma Hekates*.

3. Antoninus Liberalis, *Transform.*, xiii.

4. Pausanias, iii. 19, 9 f.

5. H. von Fritze, in *Jahrb. d. kaiser. deutsch. Archäol. Inst.*, 18 (1903), 58 ff.

6. Lucian, *De dea Syria*, 49.

239 1. Diego Duran, *Historia de Las Indias de Nueva España* (Mexico 1867–80), ii. 179–84.

2. Herodotus, iv. 71 f.

3. Jean du Plan de Carpin, *Historia Monglorum*, ed. d'Avezac (Paris 1838), ch. iii, ¶3.

4. Ibn Batutah, ed. Défrémery-Sanguinetti (Paris 1853–58), iv. 300 f.

5. R. Fitz-Roy, *Narrative of the Surveying Voyages of His Majesty's Ships "Adventure" and "Beagle"* (London 1839), ii. 155 f.

6. Herodotus, iv. 103.

7. H. Low, *Sarawak* (London 1848), 206 f.

8. Spenser St. John, *Life in the Forests of the Far East²* (London 1863), i. 204; G. A. Wilken, in *BTLVNI*, 38 (1889), 89–129.

9. See below, ¶¶**368, 398–99.**

10. See below, ¶**397.**

240 1. [On Hyacinth, see M. Mellink, *Hyakinthos* (Utrecht 1943), where the ancient sources are assembled and discussed.]

2. Apollodorus, *Bibl.*, i. 3, 3; iii. 10, 3 [with Frazer's notes *in locc.*].

3. Theophrastus, *Hist. plant.*, vi. 8, 1 ff. See further J. Murr, *Die Pflanzenwelt in der griech. Mythologie* (Innsbruck 1890), 257 ff.

4. Xenophon, *Hellenica*, iv. 5, 7–17; Pausanias, iii. 1, 3; iii. 19, 1–5.

5. Pausanias, iii. 1, 3; iii. 19, 1–5.

6. Hesychius, s.v. *Hekatombeus;* G. G. Unger, in *Philologus*, 37 (1877), 13–33; [Mellink, *op. cit.*, 70 ff.].

7. Athenaeus, iv. 17; cf. Strabo vi. 3, 2.

8. Hesychius, s.v. *Polyboia.*

241 1. E. Rohde, *Psyche*[3] (Tübingen-Leipzig 1903, i. 137 ff.

2. Pausanias, iii. 19, 3. The Greek word here used for *"sacrifice"* (viz., *enagizein*) denotes sacrifices offered to the heroic dead; another word, viz., *thyein*, was used for those offered to gods. Sacrifices to the dead were often annual: Pausanias, iii. 1, 8; vii. 19, 10; viii. 41, 1; etc.

3. Pausanias, iii. 19, 14.

4. See above, ¶221.

242 1. Plutarch, *De Iside et Osiride*, 12–20; cp. E. A. W. Budge, *The Gods of the Egyptians* (London 1904), ii. 123 ff.

2. Diodorus Siculus, i. 21, 5–11; cp. id., iv. 6, 3; Strabo, xvii. 1, 23.

3. E. A. W. Budge, *Osiris and the Egyptian Resurrection* (London 1911), ii. 59 ff.

4. *Ib.*, ii. 59 ff.

5. *Ib.*, i. 70–75; 80–82; cp. Plutarch, *De Is. et Os.*, 79.

6. Budge, *op. cit.*, i. 305 ff.

243 1. G. Maspero, *Études de mythologie et d'archéologie égyptiennes* (Paris 1893–1912), i. 291 f.

244 1. J. H. Breasted, *History of the Ancient Egyptians* (London 1908), 149 f.

2. A. Moret, *Mystères Égyptiens* (Paris 1913), 40.

3. A. Erman, *Die ägyptische Religion*[2] (Berlin 1909), 111–13.

245 1. Plutarch, *De Is. et Os.*, 19, 55; Budge, *op. cit.*, i. 62 f., 64, 89 ff., 309 f.

246 1. Budge, *op. cit.*, i. 30 ff.

2. *Ib.*, i. 37, 67, 81, 210, 212, 214, 290; ii. 1, 2, 8–13, 82–85.

3. Plutarch, *op. cit.*, 20; Budge, *op. cit.*, i. 68 f.; ii. 3.

248 1. Pausanias, x. 32, 18.

249 1. Tibullus, i. 7, 21 f.; Aelian, *De nat. anim.*, x. 45; cp. L. Ideler, *Handbuch der mathematischen und technischen Chronologie* (Berlin 1825–

26), i. 124 ff. In later times, owing to the procession of the equinoxes, the rising of Sirius gradually diverged from the summer solstice, falling later and later in the solar year.

2. Plutarch, *De Is. et Os.*, 21, 22–38, 61; Diodorus Siculus, i. 27, 4; Porphyry, *De antro nympharum*, 24; Canopic Decree, lines 36 f. (in W. Dittenberger's *Orientis Graeci Inscriptiones Selectae* [Leipzig 1903–05], i. No. 58).

3. Porphyry and Canopic Decree, *locc. citt.*; Censorinus, *De die natali*, xviii. 10; xxi. 10.

4. *Eudoxi ars astronomica*, ed. F. Blass (Kiel 1887), 14. The annual festival in honor of Ptolemy and Berenice was fixed on the day of the rising of Sirius: see the Canopic Decree, *loc. cit.*

250   1. E. W. Lane, *Manners and Customs of the Modern Egyptians*, Chap. xxvi.

2. B. Gutmann, in *Zeitschrift für Ethnologie*, 45 (1913), 484 f.

3. K. R. Dundas, in *JAI*, 40 (1910), 54.

4. A. Colvin, *The Making of Modern Egypt* (London 1906), 278 f.

251   1. In antiquity, the Pleiades set about the end of October or early in November; see L. Ideler, *op. cit.*, i. 242.

2. Plutarch, *De Is. et Os.*, 69–71.

3. Psalm 126 : 5 f.

252   1. Diodorus Siculus, i. 14, 2.

2. Herodotus, ii. 79; Pausanias, ix. 29, 7; Julius Pollux, iv. 54; Athenaeus, xiv. 11 f.

253   1. J. Mooney, in *Nineteenth Ann. Report of the Am. Bureau of Ethnology* (1900), 423 f.

2. See below, ¶324.

3. A. C. Hollis, *The Nandi* (Oxford 1909), 46.

4. S. Powers, *Tribes of California* (Washington 1877), 25.

5. A. Jaussen, *Coutumes des Arabes au pays de Moab* (Paris 1908), 252 f.

254   1. H. Brugsch, *Die Aegytologie* (Leipzig 1891), 355.

255   1. Herodotus, ii. 170.

2. *Ib.*, ii. 129–32.

3. *Ib.*, ii. 41; Diodorus Siculus, i. 11, 4; Plutarch, *De Is. et Os.*, 19, 39; Aelian, *Nat. anim.*, x. 27.

4. She is thus depicted on a relief at Philae, pouring a libation for the soul of Osiris; see Budge, *op. cit.*, i. 8.

5. Plutarch, *De Is. et Os.*, 52.

6. Herodotus, ii. 62; cp. The Hibeh Papyri, ed. B. P. Grenfell and A. S. Hunt, i (London 1906), No. 27, lines 165–67.

256
1. In the period of the Middle Kingdom, the Egyptians of Siut used to light lamps for the dead on the last and first days of the year: A. Erman, in *Zeitschrift für aeg. Sprache u. Altert.*, 20 (1882), 164; id., *Aegypten und aegyptisches Leben im Altertum*, Tübingen n. d.), 434 ff.
2. E. W. Nelson, in *Eighteenth Ann. Report of the Am. Bureau of Ethnology* (1899), i. 363 ff.
3. H. H. Bancroft, *Native Races of the Pacific States* (London 1875–76), ii. 623.
4. "Lettre du curé de Santiago Tepehuacan à son evêque," in *Bull. soc. géogr. de Paris, IIéme ser.*, 2 (1854), 179.
5. E. N. Gordon, *Indian Folk Tales* (London 1908), 18.
6. F. Mason, in *Journal of the Asiatic Society of Bengal*, 1866, ii. 29 f.
7. E. Aymonier, *Notice sur le Cambodge* (Paris 1875), 59.
8. Mariny, *Relation nouvelle et curieux des royaumes de Tonquin et de Lao* (Paris 1666), 251–53.
9. E. Young, *The Kingdom of the Yellow Robe* (Westminster 1898), 135 ff.
10. C. von Hahn, in *Globus*, 76 (1899), 211 f.
11. M. Abeghian, *Der armenische Volksglaube* (Leipzig 1899), 23 f.
12. Albiruni, *The Chronology of Ancient Nations*, ed. E. Sachau (London 1879), 210.
13. L. F. Sauvé, *Le folk-lore des Hautes-Vosgues* (Paris 1889), 295 f.
14. O. Reinsberg-Düringsfeld, *Calendrier belge* (Brussels 1861–62), ii. 236–40; id., *Das festliche Jahr* (Leipzig 1863), 229 f.
15. K. von Leoprechting, *Aus dem Lechrain* (Munich 1855), 198 ff.
16. I. V. Zingerle, *Sitten, Bräuche und Meinungen des Tiroler Volkes*[2] (Innsbruck 1871), 176–78.
17. P. Einhorn, "Historia Lettica," in *Scriptores rerum Livonicarum*, ii (Riga-Leipzig 1848), 587, 598, 630 f., 645 f.
18. G. Finamore, *Usi e costumi abruzzesi* (Palermo 1890), 180–82.
19. J. Brand, *Popular Antiquities of Great Britain* (London 1882–83), i. 393.
20. J. Aubrey, *Remaines of Gentilisme and Judaisme* (London 1881), 23; C. S. Burne and G. F. Jackson, *Shropshire Folk-Lore* (London 1883), 381.

257
1. *De Is. et Os.*, 39.
2. See above, ¶255.
3. Plutarch, *op. cit.*, 39.
4. The rites are described also by Lactantius, *Divin. Instit.*, i. 21; *Epitome Div. Inst.*, 28, and by Minucius Felix, *Octavius*, xxii. 1.
5. Firmicus Maternus, *De errore prof. rel.*, 2.
6. See: Juvenal, viii. 29 f. [with Mayor's note *in loc.*]; Athenagoras, *Supplicatio pro Christianis*, 22; Tertullian, *Adversus Maricionem*, i. 13; Augustine, *De civitate Dei*, vi. 10.

258   1. V. Loret, in *Rec. Trav. relatifs à la philologie et à l'archéologie egypt. et assyr.*, 3 (1882), 43–57; 4 (1883), 21–33; 5 (1884), 85–103; Budge, *Osiris*, ii. 21 f.

2. [A. Moret, *La mise à mort du dieu en Égypte* (Paris 1927), 38 f.].

3. A. Wiedemann, *Herodotos zweites Buch* (Leipzig 1890), 262.

4. Budge, *Gods*, ii. 129.

5. H. Brugsch, in *Zeitschrift f. aeg. Sprache u. Altert.*, 1881, pp. 94, 99.

259   1. R. V. Lanzone, *Dizionario di mitologia egizia* (Turin 1881–84), 757 ff.; Budge, *Gods*, ii. 131–38; id., *Osiris*, ii. 31 ff.

2. Moret, *op. cit.*, 39.

3. Hippolytus, *Refutat. omn. haeres.*, v. 8.

260   1. A. Wiedemann, in *Le Muséon*, N. S. 4 (1903), 111; A. Moret, *Kings and Gods of Egypt* (New York-London 1912), 94, with plate xi; id., *Mystères égyptiens* (Paris 1913), 41.

2. B. P. Grenfell and A. S. Hunt, in *Egyptian Exploration Fund Annual Report*, 1902–03, p. 5.

3. Margaret A. Murray, *The Osireion at Abydos* (London 1904), 28 ff.

4. J. G. Wilkinson, *A Second Series of the Manners and Customs of the Ancient Egyptians* (London 1841), ii. 300.

5. *Die aegyptische Religion*[2] (Berlin 1909), 209 f.

261   1. See above, ¶253.

2. See above, ¶242.

3. See above, *ib.*

4. Servius on Vergil, *Georg.*, i. 166.

5. See above, ¶205.

6. See below, ¶¶344–48.

7. Plutarch, *De Iside et Osiride*, 73 (cf. *ib.*, 33).

8. Diodorus Siculus, i. 88, 5.

262   1. Scholia in *Caesaris Germanici Aratea*, in F. Eyseenhardt's edition of Martianus Capella (Leipzig 1866), 408.

2. Dion. Hal., ii. 56, 4; cf. Livy, i. 16, 1; Florus, i. 1, 16 f.; Plutarch, *Romulus*, 27; A. B. Cook, in *Folk-Lore*, 16 (1905), 324 f.

3. Cf. Varro, *De linguâ Latinâ*, 6. 18; Plutarch, *Romulus*, 29; Macrobius, *Sat.*, i. 11, 36–40; Theophrastus, *Hist. plantarum*, 2. 9; Columella, 11. 2, 56; Graf zu Sohns-Laubach, in *Abh. Königl. Ges. Wiss. zu Göttingen*, 28 (1882), 1–106.

4. Euripides, *Bacchae*, 43 ff., 1043 ff.; Theocritus, *Id.* xxvi; Pausanias, ii. 2, 7; Apollodorus, *Bibl.*, iii. 5, 1 f.; Hyginus, fab. 132, 184.

5. Nonnus, *Dionys.*, vi. 165–205; Clem. Alex., *Protrept.*, ii. 17; Justin Martyr, *Apology*, i. 54; Firmicus Maternus, *De errore prof. rel.*, 6; Arnobius, *Adv. nationes*, v. 19.

6. Porphyry, *De abstinentia*, ii. 55.

7. Lucian, *De saltatione*, 51; Plato, *Symposium*, 7, p. 179 D–E; Pausanias,

ix. 30, 5; Ovid, *Met.*, xi. 1–43. See E. Rohde, *Psyche*[3] (Tübingen-Leipzig 1903), ii. 118, n. 2; S. Reinach, *Cultes, mythes et religions,* ii (1906), 85 ff.

8. Apollodorus, *Bibl.*, iii. 5, 1.
9. R. M. Dawkins, in *Journal of Hellenic Studies*, 26 (1906), 191 ff.
10. Snorre Sturlason, *Heimskringlas Saga Halfardana Svarta*, Chap. 9.

263   1. See above, ¶261.
2. Plutarch, *De Is., et Os.*, 31; Herodotus, ii. 38.
3. Herrera, quoted by A. Bastian, *Die Culturlaender des alten Amerika* (Berlin 1878), ii. 639.
4. E. Lefébure, *Le mythe osirien* (Paris 1874–75), 188.
5. Firmicus Maternus, *De errore prof. rel.*, 2; Tertullian, *Adv. Marcionem*, i. 13; Plutarch, *De Is. et Os.*, 65; Eusebius, *Praep. ev.*, iii. 11, 31; Athenagoras, *Supplicatio pro Christianis*, 22.

264   1. *De errore prof. rel.*, 27.
2. See above, ¶231.
3. *De Is. et Os.*, 21.
4. See above, ¶242.
5. A. Mariette, *Dendérah*, iv (Paris 1880), plate 66.
6. *Ib.*, plate 72.
7. Lefébure, *op. cit.*, 194, 196.
8. S. Birch, in J. G. Wilkinson's *Manners and Customs of the Ancient Egyptians* (London 1878), iii. 84.
9. Wilkinson, *op. cit.*, iii. 62–64; Budge, *Gods*, ii. 106 f.
10. J. H. Breasted, *Development of Religion and Thought in Ancient Egypt* (London 1912), 28.
11. A. Moret, *Kings and Gods of Egypt* (New York-London 1912), 83.
12. See above, ¶213.
13. Wilkinson, *op. cit.*, iii. 349 f.
14. *Loc. cit.*
15. Lefébure, *op. cit.*, 188.
16. *Ib.*, 188.
17. Lanzone, *Dizionario*, pl. ccciv.
18. Plutarch, *De Is. et Os.*, 35.
19. Tibullus, i. 7, 33–36; Diodorus Siculus, i. 17, 1; i. 20, 4.
20. Budge, *Osiris*, i. 38 f.
21. *Ib.*, i. 19, 45, with frontispiece.
22. Diodorus Siculus, i. 17, 4 f.

265   1. Herodotus, ii. 48; Plutarch, *De Is. et Os.*, 12, 18, 36, 51; Diodorus Siculus, i. 21, 5; i. 22, 6 f.; iv. 6, 3.
2. Hippolytus, *Refutat. omn. haer.*, v. 7.
3. Mariette, *op. cit.*, plates 66–70; 88–90; cp. Budge, *Gods*, ii. 132, 136 f.
4. Margaret A. Murray, *op. cit.*, 270.

6. F. G. Welcker, *Alte Denkmaeler* (Göttingen 1849–64), v. pl. 2.

7. *Archäolog. Zeitung,* 9 (1851), pl. xxxiii, with Gerhard's remarks, 371–73.

8. *Gazette archéol.,* 5 (1879), pl. 3.

9. Pausanias, viii. 19, 2.

10. Plutarch, *Quaest. graec.,* 36; id., *De Is. et Os.,* 35.

11. Tzetzes, Schol. on Lycophron, 1236.

12. Nonnus, *Dionys.,* vi. 205.

13. Firmicus Maternus, *De errore prof. rel.,* 6.

14. Euripides, *Bacchae,* 735 ff.; Schol. on Aristophanes, *Frogs,* 357.

280 1. Hesychius, s. v. *Eriphos ho Dionysos;* Steph. Byz., s. v. *Akrôreia.*

2. Pausanias, ii. 35, 1; Schol. on Aristophanes, *Acharnians,* 146; *Etym. Magn.,* s. v. *Apatouria;* Suidas, s. vv. *Apatouria* and *melanaigida Dionyson;* Nonnus, *Dionys.,* xxvii. 302.

3. Pausanias, ii. 13, 6.

4. Apollodorus, *Bibl.,* iii. 4, 3.

5. Ovid, *Met.,* v. 329; Antonius Liberalis, *Transform.,* 28; *Mythogr. Vat.,* i. 86.

6. Arnobius, *Adv. nationes,* v. 19; Suidas, s.v. *aigizein.* Fawn-skins were worn both by the god and his worshippers: Cornutus, *Theol. gr. comp.,* 30. Similarly the female Bacchanals wore goat-skins.

281 1. Varro, *Re Rust.,* i. 2, 19; Vergil, *Georg.,* ii. 376–81, with Servius' comments *in loc.* and on *Aen.,* iii. 118; Ovid, *Fasti,* i. 353 ff. [with Frazer's note].

2. Euripides, *Bacchae,* 138 f.

3. Schol. on Aristophanes, *Frogs,* 357.

4. HERA *aigophagos:* Paus., iii. 15, 9; ZEUS *aigophagos:* Et. Magn., s. v.; ARTEMIS *kaprophagos:* Hesychius, s. v.; etc.

282 1. Porphyry, *De abstinentia,* ii. 55.

2. Pausanias, ix. 8, 2.

3. See above, On the Dying God, ¶163 ff.

284 1. [T. W. Allen, W. R. Halliday, and E. E. Sikes, *The Homeric Hymns*[2] (Oxford 1936), 111.]

2. Hymn to Demeter, 1 ff., 302 ff., 330 ff., 349 ff., 414 ff., 450 ff.

3. *Ib.,* 310 ff.; cp. Apollodorus, *Bibl.,* i. 5; Ovid, *Fasti,* iv. 425–618; id., *Met.,* v. 385 ff.

285 1. Hymn to Demeter, 47–50, 191–211, 292–95 [with Allen and Halliday's notes].

286 1. Hippolytus, *Refutat. omn. haeres.,* v. 8. The word which the poet uses to denote the demonstration (viz., *deixe,* Hymn to Demeter,

474) is a *terminus technicus* of the mysteries; cp. Lobeck, *Aglaophamus,* 51.

2. Clem. Alex., *Protrept.,* ii. 9. [See Allen-Halliday-Sikes, *op. cit.,* 117 ff.]

287   1. See L. Preller, *Demeter und Persephone* (Hamburg 1837), 315 ff.; W. Mannhardt, *Mythologische Forschungen* (Strasburg 1884), 202 ff.

     2. According to the Hymn to Demeter (398 ff., 445 ff.) and Apollodorus (*Bibl.,* i. 5, 3), Persephone had to spend a full year underground; according to Ovid (*Fasti,* iv. 613 f.; *Met.,* v. 564 f.) and Hyginus (fab. 146), only six months.

     3. Hymn to Demeter, 8 ff.

288   1. Hymn to Demeter, 279, 302.

     2. *Iliad,* v. 499–504.

     3. Pausanias, i. 22, 3, with Frazer's note; Dittenberger, *Sylloge*[2], No. 615; Farnell, *op. cit.,* iii. 312 f.

     4. Herodotus, i. 193; iv. 198; Xenophon, *Hellenica,* vi. 3, 6; Aelian, *Hist. an.,* xvii. 16; etc.

     5. *Cerealia* in Pliny, *NH,* xxiii. 1; *Cerealia munera* (and *dona*) in Ovid, *Met.,* xi. 121 f.

     6. Libanius, iv. 367 Reiske; cp. Diod. Sic., v. 68.

     7. Ovid, *Fasti,* iv. 616; Eusebius, *Praep. ev.,* iii. 11, 5; *Anth. Pal.,* vi. 104, 8; Mannhardt, *op. cit.,* 235; Farnell, *op. cit.,* iii. 217 ff.

     8. Theocritus, vii. 155 ff.; that the sheaves were of barley is proved by verses 31–34 of the same poem.

     9. Eusebius, *Praep. ev.,* iii. 11, 5; Cornutus, *Theol. graec. comp.,* 28; Vergil, *Georg.,* i. 212, with Servius' comment.

     10. Farnell, *op. cit.,* iii. 268, with plate xxviii.

289   1. Hesiod, *Works and Days,* 448–74; Epictetus, *Disc.,* iii. 21, 12.

     2. Hesiod, *ib.,* 383 f., 615–17; Aratus, *Phainomena,* 254–67. The popular practice seems to have been to commence sowing wheat, barley, and other cereals at the autumnal setting of the Pleiades: Vergil, *Georg.,* i. 219–26; Columella, *De re rust.,* ii. 18.

     3. Plutarch, *De Is. et Os.,* 69.

     4. *Ib.,* 70; Cornutus, 28.

     5. Theocritus, *Id.,* vii.

290   1. In ancient Greece the vintage seems to have fallen somewhat earlier, for Hesiod (*Works and Days,* 609 ff.) dates it to the time when Arcturus is a morning star, and in his age this was on September 18.

291   1. Dittenberger, *Sylloge*[2], No. 640.

     2. See above, ¶**16**.

     3. *Anth. Pal.,* vi. 36, 1 f.

     4. Polemo, cited by Athenaeus, iii. 6.

5. Nonnus, *Dionys.*, xvii. 153. The Athenians sacrificed to her under this title: Eustathius on *Iliad*, xviii. 553.
6. Theocritus, vii. 155; *Orphica*, 40. 5.
7. *Anth. Pal.*, vi. 98, 1.
8. *Orphica*, 40. 3.
9. *Anth. Pal.*, vi. 104, 8.
10. *Orphica*, 40. 5.
11. *Loc. cit.*
12. *Orphica*, 40. 18.
13. Pausanias, viii. 53, 7; Dittenberger, *Sylloge*², No. 655; Aristophanes, *Frogs*, 382. See Farnell, *op. cit.*, iii. 318, n. 39.
14. Polemo, cited by Athenaeus, iii. 73; x. 9.

292   1. E. Dodwell, *A Classical and Topographical Tour through Greece* (London 1819), i. 583. Cp. J. C. Lawson, *Modern Greek Folklore and Ancient Greek Religion* (Cambridge 1910), 80, who tells us that "the statue was regularly crowned with flowers in the avowed hope of obtaining good harvests."
2. Cicero, *In C. Verrem*, act. ii, lib. iv. 51.

293   1. *De civitate Dei*, vii. 20.

294   1. Farnell, *op. cit.*, iii. 27.
2. Pausanias, vi. 21, 11.
3. Farnell, *op. cit.*, iii. 256, with plate xxi *b*.
4. The distinction between Demeter (Ceres) and the Earth Goddess is clearly indicated by Ovid, *Fasti*, iv. 673 f.
5. Dittenberger, *Sylloge*², Nos. 20, 408, 411, 587, 646, 647, 652, 720, 789.

295   1. Homeric Hymn to Demeter, 480 ff.; Pindar, quoted by Clem. Alex., *Strom.*, iii. 3, 17; Sophocles, quoted by Plutarch, *De audiendis poetis*, 4; Isocrates, *Panegyricus*, 6; Cicero, *De legibus*, ii. 14, 36; Aristides, *Eleusin.*, i. 421 Dindorf.
2. I Corinthians, 15 : 35 ff.: "But some man will say, How are the dead raised up? and with what body do they come? Thou fool, that which thou sowest is not quickened, except it die. And that which thou sowest, thou sowest not that body that shall be, but bare grain, it may chance of wheat, or of some other grain."

296   1. F. B. Jevons, *Introduction to the History of Religion* (London 1896), 240; H. Hirt, *Die Indogermanen* (Strasburg 1905–07), i. 251 ff.

297   1. J. Shooter, *The Kafirs of Natal and the Zulu Country* (London 1857), 17 f.
2. A. Delegorgue, *Voyage dans l'Afrique australe* (Paris 1847), ii. 225.

3. G. Gouldsbury and H. Sheane, *The Great Plateau of Northern Rhodesia* (London 1911), 302.
4. L. Decle, *Three Years in Savage Africa* (London 1898), 295.
5. J. H. Weekes, in *Folk-Lore*, 20 (1909), 311.
6. Scholiast on Aristophanes, *Thesmophor.*, 80; Plutarch, *Demosthenes*, 30; A. Mommsen, *Feste der Stadt Athen im Altertum* (Leipzig 1898), 310 f.
7. D. Kidd, *The Essential Kafir* (London 1904), 323.
8. Fr. Stuhlmann, *Mit Emin Pascha ins Herz von Afrika* (Berlin 1894), 75.
9. J. Roscoe, *The Baganda* (London 1911), 426–27.
10. H. Rehse, *Kiziba, Land und Leute* (Stuttgart 1910), 53.
11. G. Schweinfurth, *The Heart of Africa*[3] (London 1878), i. 281.
12. *Ib.*, ii. 40.

298   1. A. D'Orbigny, *L'homme américain* [*de l'Amérique méridionale*] (Paris 1839), i. 198 f.
2. Le Sieur de la Borde, "Relations des origines, moeurs, coutumes, religion, guerres et voyages des Caraibes sauvages des Isles Antilles de l'Amérique," 21–23, in *Recueil des divers voyages faits en Afrique et en l'Amérique* (Paris 1684).
3. R. Southey, *History of Brazil*, i[2] (London 1822), 253.
4. J. B. von Spix and C. F. P. von Martins, *Reise in Brasilien* (Munich 1823–31), i. 381.
5. K. von den Steinen, *Unter den Naturvölkern Zentral-Brasiliens* (Berlin 1894), 214.

299   1. T. H. Lewin, *Wild Races of South-Eastern India* (London 1870), 255.
2. E. T. Dalton, *Descriptive Ethnology of Bengal* (Calcutta 1872), 33.
3. *Ib.*, 226 f.
4. *Nieuw Guinea, ethnographisch en naturkundig onderzocht en breschreven* (Amsterdam 1862), 159.
5. *Ib.*, 119; H. von Rosenberg, *Der Malayische Archipel* (Leipzig 1878), 433.

300   1. S. Powers, *Tribes of California* (Washington 1877), 23.
2. Father Geronimo Boscana, "Chinigchinich," in [A. Robinson's] *Life in California* (New York 1846), 267.
3. G. Grey, *Journals of Two Expeditions of Discovery in North-West and Western Australia* (London 1841), ii. 292 f.
4. W. Stanbridge, in *Trans. Ethnol. Soc. of London*, N. S., 1 (1861), 291.

302   1. A. de Candolle, *Origins of Cultivated Plants* (London 1884), 368 f. According to Pliny (*NH*, xviii. 72), barley was the oldest of foods. In the oldest Vedic ritual, barley and not rice is the chief cereal employed; see H. Oldenberg, *Die Religion des Vedas* (Berlin 1894), 353.

ADDITIONAL NOTES

Dying and Reviving Gods

There is probably no element of *The Golden Bough* that has become so familiar, or been so much exploited, as Frazer's theory of the Dying and Reviving God, or deposed and re-instated genius of fertility. Nevertheless, in the light of more recent research, this theory can be accepted only with considerable modification.

(*a*) It is no longer possible to see in Frazer's "dying and reviving gods" mere personifications of grain or fruit, or to regard their passion and resurrection as allegorizing harvest and growth. We now know that in many ancient and primitive cultures, increase and prosperity were thought to be dependent on the presence within a community or locality of its beneficent deity, and that failure of either or both was regarded as due to his temporary withdrawal. Now, that withdrawal could be the result either of umbrage or displeasure (as so frequently in the Old Testament) or, alternatively, of some discomfiture that he had suffered at hostile hands, e.g., in conflict with some other deity. Accordingly, the "passion" of the god cannot be interpreted uniformly and exclusively as representing the reaping of crops or fruits; as often as not, its purpose is simply to provide, in mythological terms, a reason for the god's absence: he has met with an "accident."

(*b*) Even admitting that these gods are not actual personifications of crops or fruits, it may be doubted whether they are genii of vegetation at all. Far more probably, they are genii of the community or locality as a whole. In other words, while the existence of specific spirits of grain, crops, fruits, increase, etc. cannot be questioned, there is room for doubt whether it is these, rather than some more comprehensive genii of corporate life as a whole, that undergo the annual or periodic passion and revival. For what is symbolized in such rites is not so much the particular fate of particular things as the temporary withdrawal of divine providence, or—to put it in seasonal terms—the rhythm of corporate life in *all* its manifestations.

(*c*) The modification here suggested will in turn obviate the formidable objections raised by Sir A. H. Gardiner against Frazer's identification of Osiris

390

with the grain. The distinguished Egyptologist points out that the myth and ritual of Osiris are concerned, in fact, with the succession to the kingship, not with the rhythms of nature. The setting is dynastic, not "vegetarian." In the first place, Osiris is always represented, alike on bas reliefs, in hieroglyphic script, and in the legends associated with him, as the exemplification of sovereignty, not of vegetation. Second, the subject of his myth is in fact the replacement of the defunct king Osiris by the new king, Horus; and nothing else. Third, what the *sed,* or so-called "jubilee-festival," really celebrated was not, as Frazer supposes, the seasonal rebirth of nature, but the periodic re-invigoration of the pharaoh. Fourthly, the vegetation-aspect of Osiris is not primitive, but developed only during the Middle Kingdom out of an assimilation of the character of Osiris as king of the netherworld to that of his father Geb, vivifying genius of the soil.

In a fair analysis, however, there is more to Frazer's interpretation of Osiris than the identification of him with grain. Once we abandon this and regard Osiris rather as a mythic representation of the kingship, there is nothing in the facts presented by Gardiner to militate against Frazer's basic contention. For in that case, the periodic passion and revival of Osiris (the latter, of course, in the person of his successor, Horus) will indeed epitomize the periodic eclipse and revival of communal life, the role of the king being, as Frazer has made abundantly plain, primarily to typify that life.

(*d*) With regard to the Mesopotamian myth of Tammuz, it is necessary only to observe that, since Frazer wrote, a good deal of earlier Sumerian material on the subject has come to light—and there is even more still unpublished. It now appears that the story of the disappearance or discomfiture of Tammuz was far more complicated than was previously suspected. The role of his sister Ishtar (Inanna), for example, is slowly emerging in another light. Apparently, she was at first his antagonist, who encompassed the disaster inflicted upon him. The myth may therefore have been told originally to account for the temporary withdrawal of that god's providence, rather than as an allegory of what actually happens to crops or fruits year by year.

Frazer's concept of the Dying and Reviving God has exercised a profound influence upon historians of literature; for attempts have been made to recognize in (or behind) certain established genres of composition the essential structure of a seasonal myth embodying the theme of the Dying and Reviving God. Gilbert Murray, for example, has sought to find in the standard structure of ancient Greek tragedy a survival of a more primitive ritual drama involving the combat between the old god (or "year-spirit") and the new, the death of the former and his eventual revival either in his own person or in that of his successor.[1] F. M. Cornford has extended the theory to Greek comedy, arguing that the basic pattern of an Aristophanic play can be traced directly to the primitive seasonal ritual of the Combat, the Sacred Marriage, and the Beanfeast or

---

[1] "Excursus on the Ritual Forms preserved in Greek Tragedy," in Jane Harrison's *Themis* (Cambridge 1912), 341 ff.

Banquet.[2] Others, such as R. J. Tiddy[3] and P. Toschi,[4] have detected further survivals of the rude drama in the European Mummers' Play, and even in the traditional form of the Punch-and-Judy puppet show! Bertha Philpotts has found the pattern of death and rebirth underlying the Scandinavian Elder Edda;[5] and Jessie L. Weston has traced it in the Grail legend.[6] An elaborate attempt to interpret certain ancient Egyption, Canaanite and Hittite myths on this basis has been made by T. H. Gaster;[7] while even the primary legend of Hamlet has been so explained![8]

Doubtless, in many of these attempts enthusiasm has outrun sobriety; but that is due mainly to the fact that the scholars who undertook them (and, be it added, all too many of their critics!) did not distinguish clearly enough between the history of particular compositions with which they were dealing and that of the literary genre to which those compositions belonged. It is the latter, not the former, that is really at issue. It may, for instance, be quite wrong to assume that a particular Hittite or Canaanite or Scandinavian myth, play, or epic actually goes back, in point of literary genealogy, to an earlier ritual libretto; but it may nevertheless be quite right to assume that this particular type of composition was inspired or conditioned in the first place by the standard pattern of seasonal rituals and that its structure and conventions were determined originally by those of the primitive performances. In other words, what is really at stake is not the dependence of a particular composition upon an actual performance, but rather the parallelism between a pattern of narrative and a pattern of ritual, or—to put it in broad terms—the ultimate relation of a genre of literature to a genre of ceremony.

Viewed in this light, Frazer's reconstruction of the primitive ritual patterns may in fact be epoch-making for literature as well as anthropology; for if that pattern can indeed be detected behind the conventions of certain literary genres, the way is open for an appreciation of literary forms not merely as the product of artistic creativity or individual inventiveness but also—at least, in certain aspects—as an expression of religion, running parallel to cult.

209. *Tammuz.* Basic sources for the myth and cult of Tammuz are: M. Witzel, *Tammuz-Liturgien und Verwandtes* (Rome 1935); C. Frank, *Kultlieder aus der Ishtar-Tammuz Kreis* (Leipzig 1939). Important monographs are: S. Langdon, *Tammuz and Ishtar* (Oxford 1914); L. Van den Berghe, "Reflexions critiques sur le culte de Tammuz," in *Neue Klio*, 6 (1954), 298–321; M. Witzel,

---

[2] *The Origin of Attic Comedy* (Cambridge 1914).

[3] *The Mummers' Play* (Oxford 1923).

[4] *Le origini del teatro italiano* (Turin 1955).

[5] *The Elder Edda and Ancient Scandinavian Drama* (Cambridge 1920).

[6] *From Ritual to Romance* (Cambridge 1920).

[7] *Thespis: Ritual, Myth and Drama in the Ancient Near East* (New York 1950).

[8] Gilbert Murray, *Hamlet and Orestes.* Annual Shakespeare Lecture before British Academy, London 1914.

In her *Epilegomena to the Study of Greek Religion* (Cambridge 1921), 26, n. 1, Jane Harrison records her "conviction . . . that the widespread legend, Don Juan, arose from a fertility ritual"! An attempt has also been made recently to interpret Homer along these lines: see E. Mireaux, *Les poèmes homériques et l'histoire grecque* (Paris 1948–49).

"Ishtar (Inanna) gegen Tammuz," in *Orientalia*, 21 (1952), 435–55. Most of what has been written on the subject will probably require radical modification when more of the earlier Sumerian sources are recovered and published. It may well turn out, in fact, that Tammuz was no "fertility-spirit" at all, but simply a hero who was put to death by the vengeance of an offended goddess, whose death caused infertility on earth and who was annually commemorated in rites of mourning. — The weeping for Tammuz (*taklimta kullumu*) is mentioned in several Mesopotamian texts: see W. von Soden, in *Zeitschrift für Assyriologie*, 42 (1935), 255 f. An Assyrian calendar prescribes it for the second day of the month named after him: R. Labat, in *Revue d'assyriologie*, 38 (1941), 28.

210. *Adonis.* See also: Ch. Velley, *Le culte et les fêtes d'Adonis. Thammouz dans l'Orient antique* (1904); R. de Vaux, "Sur quelques rapports entre Adonis et Osiris," in *Revue Biblique*, 42 (1933), 31–56; H. Stocks, "Adoniskult in Nord Afrika," in *Berytus*, 3 (1938), 51–75; P. Lambrechts, "De zog. Adonis-mysterieen," in *Med. Kon. Vlaanse Akad. Lett.*, 16 (1954), fasc. 1.

214. *"Adonis-gardens."* According to many scholars, Adonis-gardens are mentioned, under the name *"plantings of Na 'aman"* [Revised Standard Version: "pleasant plants"] in Isaiah 17 : 10. — On modern survivals, see W. Baumgartner, "Das Nachleben der Adonisgärten auf Sardinien und im übrigen Mittelmeergebiet," in *Archives suisses des traditions populaires*, 47 (1946), 122–48.

On the analogous Egyptian practice of making images of Osiris out of mould, sowing and watering them, and then regarding their subsequent germination as a symbol of the god's resurrection, see: G. Daressy, *Fouilles de la Vallée des Rois* (Cairo 1902), 25–26; A. Moret, *Rois et dieux d'Egypte* (Paris 1925), 102; N. de G. Davies and A. H. Gardiner, *The Tomb of Amenemhet* (London 1915), 115; H. Carter, *The Tomb of Tutankhamen* (London 1923), iii. 61, pl. LXIV.

218–21. *Sacred prostitution.* The whole question of sacred prostitution in the ancient Near East demands reconsideration, for there is now an impressive body of evidence to suggest (if not yet to demonstrate) that what were previously regarded as prostitutes in the strict sense of the term were really brides of the god, who may have mated ritually with the kings or priests who impersonated him in such ceremonies as the "sacred marriage" but who by no means bestowed their favors indiscriminately. To this category probably belongs the so-called "daughter of the god" (mârat ili) who is mentioned beside the *entu*, a kind of nun, in a Mesopotamian omen-text (Boissier, *Choix des textes religieux relatifs à la divination assyro-babylonienne* [Paris 1905–06], ii. 22) and in the Gilgamesh Epic. Comparable also is the female styled DUMU ᵈENZU in texts from Khafajah (1935, xxxiv. 4; lxxxi. 4; see R. Harris, in *Journal of Cuneiform Studies*, 9 [1955], 65). Of the same order, too, are, in all likelihood, the "daughters of God" (*bnt il*) mentioned on five statuette bases discovered at Hajar Koḥlan (ancient Timna) in S. Arabia: A. Jamme, in *Bull. Amer. Sch. Or. Res.*, 138 (1955), 39–46; A. F. L. Beeston, "The So-called Harlots of Hadramaut," in *Oriens* 52 (1952), 16–22. (It is significant that in the mythological texts from Ras Shamra-Ugarit, the brides of Baal are called *bnt*, "daughters," answering to the *bnt il* of the Qatabanian inscriptions and the *mârat ili* of the Mesopotamian texts.) — Similarly, again, the *qedeshoth*, or "hierodules" of the Old Testament (e.g., Gen. 38 : 21, 22; Deut. 23 : 18; Hos. 4 : 16) may have been simply the concubines of the god, exercising oracular functions like the protomantis at Patara, Lycia, who was locked in nightly (Herodotus, 1. 182). We hear of such a sacred concubine (*pallax*) in two inscriptions from Tralles (W. M. Ramsay, *Cities and Bishoprics of Phrygia* [Oxford 1895], i. No. 115; L. Robert, *Études anatoliennes* [1937], 407), and that they exercised mantic functions would seem to be indicated by the fact that in one of these texts, the woman in question is described as descended from "concubines and persons with unwashen feet," for the latter term only occurs elsewhere (*Iliad* 16. 235) in reference to the mantic priests of Dodona; see Kurt Latte, in *Harvard Theological Review*, 33 (1940), 9 ff., who suggests that the original Pythia may have been such a mantic concubine of the god.

219. It is now recognized that the name *anemone* has in reality nothing to do with Greek *anemos*, "wind," as was formerly supposed, but is simply a distortion of the Semitic *na 'aman*, "the handsome," an epithet of Adonis. In Arabic, the flower is indeed called "Naaman's wounds." The idea that plants are dyed by the blood of a slain god was taken over into Christian legend. In England, the flower bloodstained at the Crucifixion was identified as the *orchis mascula*, and in Cheshire is popularly known as Gethsemane. In Belgium, it is said to be *polygonum persicaris*, called Roodselken; and in Italy it is sorrel: *Notes and Queries*, V, i. (1874), 415.

224. *Melqarth.* The name would appear to mean "King of the city (*mlk qrt*)." W. F. Albright has suggested (*Archaeology and the Religion of Israel* [Baltimore 1942], 81) that "city" is here the conventional euphemism for the underworld, and that Melqarth is therefore simply an epithet for the god of that realm. For "city" = "underworld" in Sumerian and Semitic literature, see: K. Tallquist, *Namen der Totenwelt* (Helsingfors 1934), 15 f., 36; S. Langdon, *Semitic Mythology* (Boston 1931), 11; S. N. Kramer, *Sumerian Mythology* (Philadelphia 1944), 91; and cp. Dante, *Inferno*, iii. 1–2: *Per me si va nella città dolente, Per me si va nell'eterno dolore.*

227. *The fate of Saracus (Sinsharishkun), last king of Assyria.* Since Frazer wrote, a Babylonian chronicle describing the fall of Niniveh, in 612 B. C. has been identified among the cuneiform tablets in the British Museum: see C. J. Gadd, *The Newly-discovered Babylonian Chronicle No. 21,901 in the British Museum* (London 1923). Unfortunately, however, the passage describing the fate of Sinsharishkun, the Assyrian king, is imperfectly preserved; A. L. Oppenheim, in *ANET* 304b, restores it to read simply that he *fled*.

230. *The name Attis* was originally (like Adonis) a mere epithet, and is simply the familiar "baby-word" for "father," "daddy"; cp. Sumerian *adda*, Hittite *attas*, Ugaritic *addu*, Greek *atta*, Turkish *ata*, Hungarian *aty*, etc. Indeed, he was sometimes known alternatively as Papas! Similarly, the name of his mother, viz. Nana, was simply an epithet. Doubtless, the specific names varied from place to place.

235. *Human representatives of Attis.* It has been suggested that the Attis whose self-mutilation is commemorated in the famous poem of Catullus (No. 63) is not the god but his votary, who bore the same name and ritually sacrificed his manhood: see Grant Showerman, *The Mother of the Gods* (Madison 1901).

240. *Hyacinth.* See Machteld Mellink's exhaustive dissertation, *Hyakinthos* (Utrecht 1943). See also F. Hauser, in *Philologus,* 52 (1893), 209 ff.

242. *Osiris.* See, among recent studies: W. Helck, "Die Herkunft des abydenischen Osiris-Rituals," in *Archiv Orientání,* 1952. 72–85; H. Kees, "Das Eindringen des Osiris in die Pyramidentexte," in S. A. B. Mercer, *The Pyramid Texts* (London 1952), iv. 123–39; H. Werner, "Die Verstirnung von Motiven des Osiris-mythos," in *Internat. Achives of Ethnography,* 46 (1952), 147–62; B. H. Stricker, "Osiris en de obelisk," in *Oudheidkundige Medelelingen Rijkmuseums Oudheiden Leiden,* 33 (1953), 32–47; H. Frankfort, *Kingship and the Gods* (Chicago 1948). Among older studies reference may be made especially to: H. Gressmann, *Tod und Auferstehung des Osiris.* Der Alte Orient, 23/iii (Leipzig 1923); J. Frank-Kamenetski, "Ueber die Wasser– und Baumnatur des Osiris," in *Archiv fuer Religionswissenschaft,* 24 (1927), 234–43; A. Rusch, *Die Stellung des Osiris im theologischen System von Heliopolis.* Der Alte Orient, 24/i (Leipzig 1924); G. Van der Leeuw, "Zum Mythus und zur Gestalt des Osiris," in *Archiv fuer Orientforschung,* 3 (1926), 9–11. — On Plutarch's account of the Osiris-myth, see I. Lévy, "La légende d'Osiris et Isis chez Plutarque," in *Latomus,* 51 (1952), 147–62. — An interesting, though often highly fanciful, attempt to trace some of the essential motifs of the Osiris myth in other literature (including the Finnish *Kalevala!*) will be found in V. Vikentiev's article, "La légende d'Osiris à travers le monde," in *Fouad I University, Bulletin Fac. Arts,* 1953. 15–36.

In connection with the identification of Osiris with corn, it is of interest to observe that an early Egyptian text actually describes threshing as "hacking the god" (*ḥbꜣ, nṯr*); see K. Sethe, *Dramatische Texte zu altaegyptischen Mysterienspiele,* ii (Leipzig 1928), 136–37.

256. *Feasts of All Souls.* The celebrated Babylonian poem describing the Descent of Ishtar to the netherworld (IV R. 31; Dhorme, *Choix,* 341) concludes with some enigmatic lines referring, apparently, to an annual ascent of the dead. This has been taken to indicate that the Babylonians associated a Feast of All Souls with the annual wailing for Tammuz. Funerary offerings were indeed presented at the New Year (Akîtu) festival (S. Langdon, *Babylonian Menologies and the Semitic Calendars* [London 1935], 36, 99, 105); and at Erech, the dead were believed to ascend from the netherworld at the festival held in the month of Teshrit, at the beginning of the year (*KAVI,* 218, ii. 1–16). — Among the Mandaeans of Iraq, a feast of the dead is likewise held in Tishri (D. Chwolson, *Die Ssabier* [St. Petersburg 1856], ii. 31); and it is customary among Jews to visit graves in the same month. — In the Trobriand Islands, the dead are believed to return at the annual festival of *milmala;* B. Malinowski, *Myth in Primitive Psychology* (London 1926), 100 f. — Among the Tuareg, graves

inscription from Alistrati in W. Thrace: *Bull. corr. hell.*, 25 (1900), 327; O. Gruppe, *Griech. Mythologie* (Munich 1906), 1414, n. 1.

275. On Dionysus as a tree-spirit see O. Gruppe, *Griech. Mythologie* (Munich 1906), 1412; Panofka, in *Abh. Kgl. Akad. Wiss.*, 1852, pl. i, fig. 44; Kern, in *Arch. Jahrb.*, 11 (1896), 113–16.

284. On the *Homeric Hymn to Demeter* and its relation to the Eleusinian mysteries, see: G. E. Mylonas, *The Hymn to Demeter and her Sanctuary at Eleusis*. University of Washington [illegible] (St. Louis 1942); V. Magnien, *Les mystères d'Eleusis: Leurs origines, le rituel de leurs initiations* (1938). It should be observed, however, that the myth of the rape of Persephone was enacted also at the festivals of Thesmophoria, Skirophoria and (possibly) Haloa: Allen Sikes-Halliday, *The Homeric Hymns* (Oxford 1936), 120. —On Persephone, see also W. C. Greene, "The Return of Persephone," in *Classical Philology*, 41 (1946), 105–107, which discusses in detail the season of the year implied by the tale. See also E. Fraenkel, "Demeter und Proserpina," in *Lares*, 1948, 30–33.

285. On the role of women in agriculture, see: M. Eliade, *Traité d'histoire des religions* (Paris 1949), 236 ff.; A. V. Rantasalo, *Der Ackerbau im Volksaberglauben der Finnen und Esten* (1919–25), iii. 120 ff.; J. J. Meyer, *Trilogie altindischer Mächte und Feste der Vegetation* (Zurich-Leipzig 1937), i. 115, n. 1.

PART V

SPIRITS OF THE CORN

AND WILD

She is believed to be present in the handful of corn which is left standing last on the field; and with the cutting of this last handful she is caught, or driven away, or killed. In the first of these cases, the last sheaf is carried joyfully home and honoured as a divine being. It is placed in the barn, and at threshing the corn-spirit appears again.[1] In the Hanoverian district of Hadeln the reapers stand round the last sheaf and beat it with sticks in order to drive the Corn-mother out of it. They call to each other, "There she is! hit her! Take care she doesn't catch you!" The beating goes on till the grain is completely threshed out; then the Corn-mother is believed to be driven away.[2] In the neighbourhood of Danzig the person who cuts the last ears of corn makes them into a doll, which is called the Corn-mother or the Old Woman and is brought home on the last waggon.[3] In some parts of Holstein the last sheaf is dressed in woman's clothes and called the Corn-mother. It is carried home on the last waggon, and then thoroughly drenched with water. The drenching with water is doubtless a rain-charm.[4] In the district of Bruck in Styria the last sheaf, called the Corn-mother, is made up into the shape of a woman by the oldest married woman in the village, of an age from fifty to fifty-five years. The finest ears are plucked out of it and made into a wreath, which, twined with flowers, is carried on her head by the prettiest girl of the village to the farmer or squire, while the Corn-mother is laid down in the barn to keep off the mice.[5] In other villages of the same district the Corn-mother, at the close of harvest, is carried by two lads at the top of a pole. They march behind the girl who wears the wreath to the squire's house, and while he receives the wreath and hangs it up in the hall, the Corn-mother is placed on the top of a pile of wood, where she is the centre of the harvest supper and dance. Afterwards she is hung up in the barn and remains there till the threshing is over. The man who gives the last stroke at threshing is called the son of the Corn-mother; he is tied up in the Corn-mother, beaten, and carried through the village. The wreath is dedicated in church on the following Sunday; and on Easter Eve the grain is rubbed out of it by a seven-years-old girl and scattered amongst the young corn. At Christmas the straw of the wreath is placed in the manger to make the cattle thrive.[6] Here the fertilising power of the Corn-mother is plainly brought out by scattering the seed taken from her body (for the wreath is made out of the Corn-mother) among the new corn; and her influence over animal life is indicated by placing the straw in the manger. At Westerhüsen, in Saxony, the last corn cut is made in the shape of a woman decked with ribbons and cloth. It is fastened to a pole and brought home on the last waggon. One of the people in the waggon keeps waving the pole, so that the figure moves as if alive. It is placed on the threshing-floor, and stays there till the threshing is done.[7] Amongst the Slavs also the last sheaf is known as the Rye-mother, the Wheat-mother, the Oats-mother, the Barley-mother, and so on, according to the crop. In the district of Tarnow, Galicia, the wreath made out of the last stalks is called the Wheat-mother, Rye-mother, or Pea-mother. It is placed on a girl's head and kept till spring, when some of the grain is mixed with the seed-corn.[8] Here again the fertilising power of the Corn-mother is indicated. In France, also, in the neighbourhood of Auxerre, the last sheaf goes by the name of the Mother of the Wheat, Mother of the Barley, Mother of the Rye, or Mother of the Oats. They leave it standing in the field till the last waggon is about to wend homewards. Then they make a puppet out of it, dress it with clothes belonging to the farmer, and adorn it with a crown and a blue or white scarf. A branch of a tree is stuck in the breast of the puppet, which is now called the Ceres. At the dance in the evening the Ceres is set in the middle of the floor, and the reaper who reaped fastest dances round it with the prettiest girl for his partner. After the dance a pyre is made. All the girls, each wearing a wreath, strip the puppet, pull it to pieces, and place it on the pyre, along with the flowers with which it was adorned. Then the girl who was the first to finish reaping sets fire to the pile, and all pray that Ceres may give a fruitful year. Here, as Mannhardt observes, the old custom has remained intact, though the name Ceres is a bit of schoolmaster's learning.[9] In Upper Brittany the last sheaf is always made into human shape; but if the farmer is a married man, it is made double and consists of a little corn-puppet placed inside of a large one. This is called the Mother-sheaf. It is delivered to the farmer's wife, who unties it and gives drink-money in return.[10]

305. Sometimes the last sheaf is called, not the Corn-mother, but the Harvest-mother or the Great Mother. In the province of Osnabrück, Hanover, it is called the Harvest-mother; it is made up in female form, and then the reapers dance about with it. In some parts of Westphalia the last sheaf at the rye-harvest is made especially heavy by fastening stones in it. They bring it home on the last waggon and call it the Great Mother, though they do not fashion it into any special shape. In the district of Erfurt a very heavy sheaf, not necessarily the last, is called the Great Mother, and is carried on the last waggon to the barn, where all hands lift it down amid a fire of jokes.[1]

306. Sometimes again the last sheaf is called the Grandmother, and is adorned with flowers, ribbons, and a woman's apron. In East Prussia, at the rye or wheat harvest, the reapers call out to the woman who binds the last sheaf, "You are getting the Old Grandmother." In the neighbourhood of Magdeburg the men and women servants strive who shall get the last sheaf, called the Grandmother. Whoever gets it will be married in the next year, but his or her spouse will be old; if a girl gets it, she will marry a widower; if a man gets it, he will marry an old crone. In Silesia the Grandmother—a huge bundle made up of three or four sheaves by the person who tied the last sheaf —was formerly fashioned into a rude likeness of the human form.[1] In the neighbourhood of Belfast the last sheaf sometimes goes by the name of the Granny. It is not cut in the usual way, but all the reapers throw their sickles at

On that he took to his heels and made off as fast as he could run, and he was a lucky man if he escaped without being caught or cut by the flying sickles which the infuriated reapers hurled after him. In other cases the Hag was brought home to the farmhouse by one of the reapers. He did his best to bring it home dry and without being observed; but he was apt to be roughly handled by the people of the house, if they suspected his errand. Sometimes they stripped him of most of his clothes, sometimes they would drench him with water which had been carefully stored in buckets and pans for the purpose. If, however, he succeeded in bringing the Hag in dry and unobserved, the master of the house had to pay him a small fine; or sometimes a jug of beer "from the cask next to the wall," which seems to have commonly held the best beer, would be demanded by the bearer. The Hag was then carefully hung on a nail in the hall or elsewhere and kept there all the year. The custom of bringing in the Hag (*wrach*) into the house and hanging it up still exists in some farms of North Pembrokeshire, but the ancient ceremonies which have just been described are now discontinued.[1]

311. Similar customs are observed by Slavonic peoples. Thus in Poland the last sheaf is commonly called the Baba, that is, the Old Woman. "In the last sheaf," it is said, "sits the Baba." The sheaf itself is also called the Baba, and is sometimes composed of twelve smaller sheaves lashed together.[1] In some parts of Bohemia the Baba, made out of the last sheaf, has the figure of a woman with a great straw hat. It is carried home on the last harvest-waggon and delivered, along with a garland, to the farmer by two girls. In binding the sheaves the women strive not to be last, for she who binds the last sheaf will have a child next year.[2] The last sheaf is tied up with others into a large bundle, and a green branch is stuck on the top of it.[3] Sometimes the harvesters call out to the woman who binds the last sheaf, "She has the Baba," or "She is the Baba." She has then to make a puppet, sometimes in female, sometimes in male form, out of the corn; the puppet is occasionally dressed with clothes, often with flowers and ribbons only. The cutter of the last stalks, as well as the binder of the last sheaf, was also called Baba; and a doll, called the Harvest-woman, was made out of the last sheaf and adorned with ribbons. The oldest reaper had to dance, first with this doll, and then with the farmer's wife.[4]

In Lithuania the name for the last sheaf is Boba (Old Woman), answering to the Polish name Baba. The Boba is said to sit in the corn which is left standing last.[5] The person who binds the last sheaf or digs the last potato is the subject of much banter, and receives and long retains the name of the Old Rye-woman or the Old Potato-woman.[6] The last sheaf—the Boba—is made into the form of a woman, carried solemnly through the village on the last harvest-waggon, and drenched with water at the farmer's house; then every one dances with it.[7]

In Russia also the last sheaf is often shaped and dressed as a woman, and carried with dance and song to the farmhouse. Out of the last sheaf the Bulgarians make a doll which they call the Corn-queen or Corn-mother; it is dressed in a woman's shirt, carried round the village, and then thrown into the river in order to secure plenty of rain and dew for the next year's crop. Or it is burned and the ashes strewn on the fields, doubtless to fertilise them.[8] The name Queen, as applied to the last sheaf, has its analogies in central and northern Europe. Thus, in the Salzburg district of Austria, at the end of the harvest a great procession takes place, in which a Queen of the Corn-ears (*Āhrenkōnign*) is drawn along in a little carriage by young fellows.[9] The custom of the Harvest Queen appears to have been common in England. Brand quotes from Hutchinson's *History of Northumberland* the following: "I have seen, in some places, an image apparelled in great finery, crowned with flowers, a sheaf of corn placed under her arm, and a scycle in her hand, carried out of the village in the morning of the conclusive reaping day, with music and much clamour of the reapers, into the field, where it stands fixed on a pole all day, and when the reaping is done, is brought home in like manner. This they call the Harvest Queen, and it represents the Roman Ceres."[10]

312. Often customs of this sort are practised, not on the harvest-field but on the threshing-floor. The spirit of the corn, fleeing before the reapers as they cut down the ripe grain, quits the reaped corn and takes refuge in the barn, where it appears in the last sheaf threshed, either to perish under the blows of the flail or to flee thence to the still unthreshed corn of a neighbouring farm.[1] Thus the last corn to be threshed is called the Mother-Corn or the Old Woman. Sometimes the person who gives the last stroke with the flail is called the Old Woman, and is wrapt in the straw of the last sheaf, or has a bundle of straw fastened on his back. In some districts of Bavaria, Thüringen, and elsewhere, the man who threshes the last sheaf is said to have the Old Woman or the Old Corn-woman; he is tied up in straw, carried or carted about the village, and set down at last on the dunghill, or taken to the threshing-floor of a neighbouring farmer who has not finished his threshing.[2] In Poland the man who gives the last stroke at threshing is called Baba (Old Woman); he is wrapt in corn and wheeled through the village.[3] Sometimes in Lithuania the last sheaf is not threshed, but is fashioned into female shape and carried to the barn of a neighbour who has not finished his threshing.[4]

At Chorinchen, near Neustadt, the man who gives the last stroke at threshing is said to "get the Old Man."[5] In various parts of Austrian Silesia he is called the corn-fool, the oats-fool, and so forth according to the crop, and retains the name till the next kind of grain has been reaped.[6]

313. In these customs the spirit of the ripe corn is regarded as old, or at least as of mature age. But in other cases the corn-spirit is conceived as young. Thus at Saldern, near Wolfenbuttel, when the rye has been reaped, three

of Scotland in which both an Old Wife (*Cailleach*) and a Maiden are cut at harvest.[1]

The general rule seems to be that, where both a Maiden and an Old Wife (*Cailleach*) are fashioned out of the reaped corn at harvest, the Maiden is always made out of the last stalks left standing, and is kept by the farmer on whose land it was cut; while the Old Wife is made out of other stalks, sometimes out of the first stalks cut, and is regularly passed on to a laggard farmer who happens to be still reaping after his brisker neighbour has cut all his corn. Thus while each farmer keeps his own Maiden, as the embodiment of the young and fruitful spirit of the corn, he passes on the Old Wife as soon as he can to a neighbour, and so the old lady may make the round of all the farms in the district before she finds a place in which to lay her venerable head. The farmer with whom she finally takes up her abode is of course the one who has been the last of all the countryside to finish reaping his crops, and thus the distinction of entertaining her is rather an invidious one. Similarly we saw that in Pembrokeshire, where the last corn cut is called, not the Maiden, but the Hag, she is passed on hastily to a neighbour who is still at work in his fields and who receives his aged visitor with anything but a transport of joy. If the Old Wife represents the corn-spirit of the past year, as she probably does wherever she is contrasted with and opposed to a Maiden, it is natural enough that her faded charms should have less attractions for the husbandman than the buxom form of her daughter, who may be expected to become in her turn the mother of the golden grain when the revolving year has brought round another autumn. The same desire to get rid of the effete Mother of the Corn by palming her off on other people comes out clearly in some of the customs observed at the close of threshing, particularly in the practice of passing on a hideous straw puppet to a neighbour farmer who is still threshing his corn.

317. The harvest customs just described are strikingly analogous to the spring customs which we reviewed in the first part of this work. (1) As in the spring customs the tree-spirit is represented both by a tree and by a person, so in the harvest customs the corn-spirit is represented both by the last sheaf and by the person who cuts or binds or threshes it. The equivalence of the person to the sheaf is shewn by giving him or her the same name as the sheaf; by wrapping him or her in it; and by the rule observed in some places, that when the sheaf is called the Mother, it must be made up into human shape by the oldest married woman, but that when it is called the Maiden, it must be cut by the youngest girl. Here the age of the personal representative of the corn-spirit corresponds with that of the supposed age of the corn-spirit, just as the human victims offered by the Mexicans to promote the growth of the maize varied with the age of the maize. For in the Mexican, as in the European, custom the human beings were probably representatives of the corn-spirit rather than victims offered to it. (2) Again, the same fertilising influence which the tree-spirit is supposed to exert over vegetation, cattle, and even women is ascribed to the corn-spirit. Thus, its supposed influence on vegetation is shewn by the practice of taking some of the grain of the last sheaf (in which the corn-spirit is regularly supposed to be present), and scattering it among the young corn in spring or mixing it with the seed-corn. Its influence on animals is shewn by giving the last sheaf to a mare in foal, to a cow in calf, and to horses at the first ploughing. Lastly, its influence on women is indicated by the custom of delivering the Mother-sheaf, made into the likeness of a pregnant woman, to the farmer's wife; by the belief that the woman who binds the last sheaf will have a child next year; perhaps, too, by the idea that the person who gets it will soon be married.

318. Plainly, therefore, these spring and harvest customs are based on the same ancient modes of thought, and form parts of the same primitive heathendom, which was doubtless practised by our forefathers long before the dawn of history. Amongst the marks of a primitive ritual we may note the following:—

1. No special class of persons is set apart for the performance of the rites; in other words, there are no priests. The rites may be performed by any one, as occasion demands.

2. No special places are set apart for the performance of the rites; in other words, there are no temples. The rites may be performed anywhere, as occasion demands.

3. Spirits, not gods, are recognised. (*a*) As distinguished from gods, spirits are restricted in their operations to definite departments of nature. Their names are general, not proper. Their attributes are generic, rather than individual; in other words, there is an indefinite number of spirits of each class, and the individuals of a class are all much alike; they have no definitely marked individuality; no accepted traditions are current as to their origin, life, adventures, and character. (*b*) On the other hand gods, as distinguished from spirits, are not restricted to definite departments of nature. It is true that there is generally some one department over which they preside as their special province; but they are not rigorously confined to it; they can exert their power for good or evil in many other spheres of nature and life. Again, they bear individual or proper names, such as Demeter, Persephone, Dionysus; and their individual characters and histories are fixed by current myths and the representations of art.

4. The rites are magical rather than propitiatory. In other words, the desired objects are attained, not by propitiating the favour of divine beings through sacrifice, prayer, and praise, but by ceremonies which are believed to influence the course of nature directly through a physical sympathy or resemblance between the rite and the effect which it is the intention of the rite to produce.

the gods of the fields for an abundant crop the chamber was closed and covered over with earth. Immediately thereafter the sowing began. Finally, when the time of harvest drew near, the buried sheaf was solemnly disinterred by the priests, who distributed the grain to all who asked for it. The packets of grain so distributed were carefully preserved as talismans till the harvest.[1] In these ceremonies, which continued to be annually celebrated long after the Spanish conquest, the intention of keeping the finest sheaf buried in the maize field from seed-time to harvest was undoubtedly to quicken the growth of the maize.

321. The eastern Indians of North America, who subsisted to a large extent by the cultivation of maize, generally conceived the spirit of the maize as a woman, and supposed that the plant itself had sprung originally from the blood drops or the dead body of the Corn Woman. In the sacred formulas of the Cherokee the corn is sometimes invoked as "the Old Woman," and one of their myths relates how a hunter saw a fair woman issue from a single green stalk of corn.[1] The Iroquois believe the Spirit of the Corn, the Spirit of Beans, and the Spirit of Squashes to be three sisters clad in the leaves of their respective plants, very fond of each other, and delighting to dwell together. This divine trinity is known by the name of *De-o-ha'-ko,* which means "Our Life" or "Our Supporters." The three persons of the trinity have no individual names, and are never mentioned separately except by means of description. The Indians have a legend that of old the corn was easily cultivated, yielded abundantly, and had a grain exceedingly rich in oil, till the Evil One, envious of this good gift of the Great Spirit to man, went forth into the fields and blighted them. And still, when the wind rustles in the corn, the pious Indian fancies he hears the Spirit of the Corn bemoaning her blighted fruitfulness.[2] The Huichol Indians of Mexico imagine maize to be a little girl, who may sometimes be heard weeping in the fields; so afraid is she of the wild beasts that eat the corn.[3]

THE PUNJAB

322. In the Punjab, to the east of the Jumna, when the cotton boles begin to burst, it is usual to select the largest plant in the field, sprinkle it with buttermilk and rice-water, and then bind to it pieces of cotton taken from the other plants of the field. This selected plant is called Sirdar or *Bhogaldai,* that is "mother-cotton," from *bhogla,* a name sometimes given to a large cotton-pod, and *dai* (for *daiya*), "a mother," and after it has been saluted, prayers are offered that the other plants may resemble it in the richness of their produce.[1]

BERBERS

323. The conception of the corn-spirit as a bride seems to come out clearly in a ceremony still practised by the Berbers near Tangier, in Morocco. When the women assemble in the fields to weed the green barley or reap the crops, they take with them a straw figure dressed like a woman, and set it up among the corn. Suddenly a group of horsemen from a neighbouring village gallops up and carries off the straw puppet amid the screams and cries of the women. However, the ravished effigy is rescued by another band of mounted men, and after a struggle it remains, more or less dishevelled, in the hands of the women. That this pretended abduction is a mimic marriage appears from a Berber custom in accordance with which, at a real wedding, the bridegroom carries off his seemingly unwilling bride on horseback, while she screams and pretends to summon her friends to her rescue. No fixed date is appointed for the simulated abduction of the straw woman from the barley-field, the time depends upon the state of the crops, but the day and hour are made public before the event. Each village used to practise this mimic contest for possession of the straw woman, who probably represents the Barley Bride, but nowadays the custom is growing obsolete.[1]

East Indies, Burma, Sumatra, Malaya

324. If the reader still feels any doubts as to the meaning of the harvest customs which have been practised within living memory by European peasants, these doubts may perhaps be dispelled by comparing the customs observed at the rice-harvest by the Malays and Dyaks of the East Indies. For these Eastern peoples have not, like our peasantry, advanced beyond the intellectual stage at which the customs originated; their theory and their practice are still in unison; for them the quaint rites which in Europe have long dwindled into mere fossils, the pastime of clowns and the puzzle of the learned, are still living realities of which they can render an intelligible and truthful account. Hence a study of their beliefs and usages concerning the rice may throw some light on the true meaning of the ritual of the corn in ancient Greece and modern Europe.

Now the whole of the ritual which the Malays and Dyaks observe in connexion with the rice is founded on the simple conception of the rice as animated by a soul like that which these people attribute to mankind. They explain the phenomena of reproduction, growth, decay, and death in the rice on the same principles on which they explain the corresponding phenomena in human beings. They imagine that in the fibres of the plant, as in the body of a man, there is a certain vital element, which is so far independent of the plant that it may for a time be completely separated from it without fatal effects, though if its absence be prolonged beyond certain limits the plant will wither and die. This vital yet separable element is what, for the want of a better word, we must call the soul of a plant, just as a similar vital and separable element is commonly supposed to constitute the soul of man; and on this theory or myth of the plant-soul is built the whole worship of the cereals, just as on the theory or myth of the human soul is built

sonified as a young unmarried woman rather than as a mother. On the first day of reaping the crop only a few ears of rice are plucked and made up into a little sheaf. After that the reaping may begin, and while it is going forward offerings of rice and betel are presented in the middle of the field to the spirit of the rice, who is personified under the name of Miss Dajang. The offering is accompanied by a common meal shared by the reapers. When all the rice has been reaped, threshed and garnered, the little sheaf which was first cut is brought in and laid on the top of the heap in the granary, together with an egg or a stone, which is supposed to watch over the rice.[1]

329. Again, just as in Scotland the old and the young spirit of the corn are represented as an Old Wife (*Cailleach*) and a Maiden respectively, so in the Malay Peninsula we find both the Rice-mother and her child represented by different sheaves or bundles of ears on the harvest-field.[1] The ceremony of cutting and bringing home the Soul of the Rice was witnessed by Mr. W. W. Skeat at Chodoi in Selangor on the twenty-eighth of January 1897. The particular bunch or sheaf which was to serve as the Mother of the Rice-soul had previously been sought and identified by means of the markings or shape of the ears. From this sheaf an aged sorceress, with much solemnity, cut a little bundle of seven ears, anointed them with oil, tied them round with parti-coloured thread, fumigated them with incense, and having wrapt them in a white cloth deposited them in a little oval-shaped basket. These seven ears were the infant Soul of the Rice and the little basket was its cradle. It was carried home to the farmer's house by another woman, who held up an umbrella to screen the tender infant from the hot rays of the sun. Arrived at the house the Rice-child was welcomed by the women of the family, and laid, cradle and all, on a new sleeping-mat with pillows at the head. After that the farmer's wife was instructed to observe certain rules of taboo for three days, the rules being in many respects identical with those which have to be observed for three days after the birth of a real child. For example, perfect quiet must be observed, as in a house where a baby has just been born; a light was placed near the head of the Rice-child's bed and might not go out at night, while the fire on the hearth had to be kept up both day and night till the three days were over; hair might not be cut; and money, rice, salt, oil, and so forth were forbidden to go out of the house, though of course these valuable articles were quite free to come in. Something of the same tender care which is thus bestowed on the newly-born Rice-child is naturally extended also to its parent, the sheaf from whose body it was taken. This sheaf, which remains standing in the field after the Rice-soul has been carried home and put to bed, is treated as a newly-made mother; that is to say, young shoots of trees are pounded together and scattered broadcast every evening for three successive days, and when the three days are up you take the pulp of a coco-nut and what are called "goat-flowers," mix them up, eat them with a little sugar, and spit some of the mixture out among the rice. So after a real birth the young shoots of the jack-fruit, the rose-apple, certain kinds of banana, and the thin pulp of young coco-nuts are mixed with dried fish, salt, acid, prawn-condiment, and the like dainties to form a sort of salad, which is administered to mother and child for three successive days. The last sheaf is reaped by the farmer's wife, who carries it back to the house, where it is threshed and mixed with the Rice-soul. The farmer then takes the Rice-soul and its basket and deposits it, together with the product of the last sheaf, in the big circular rice-bin used by the Malays. Some grains from the Rice-soul are mixed with the seed which is to be sown in the following year.[2] In this Rice-mother and Rice-child of the Malay Peninsula we may see the counterpart and in a sense the prototype of the Demeter and Persephone of ancient Greece.

330. Once more, the European custom of representing the corn-spirit in the double form of bride and bridegroom[1] has its parallel in a ceremony observed at the rice-harvest in Java. Before the reapers begin to cut the rice, the priest or sorcerer picks out a number of ears of rice, which are tied together, smeared with ointment, and adorned with flowers. Thus decked out, the ears are called the *padi-pĕngantèn,* that is, the Rice-bride and the Rice-bridegroom; their wedding feast is celebrated, and the cutting of the rice begins immediately afterwards. Later on, when the rice is being got in, a bridal chamber is partitioned off in the barn, and furnished with a new mat, a lamp, and all kinds of toilet articles. Sheaves of rice, to represent the wedding guests, are placed beside the Rice-bride and the Rice-bridegroom. Not till this has been done may the whole harvest be housed in the barn. And for the first forty days after the rice has been housed, no one may enter the barn, for fear of disturbing the newly-wedded pair.[2]

331. The same notion of the propagation of the rice by a male and female power finds expression amongst the Szis of Upper Burma. When the paddy, that is, the rice with the husks still on it, has been dried and piled in a heap for threshing, all the friends of the household are invited to the threshing-floor, and food and drink are brought out. The heap of paddy is divided and one half spread out for threshing, while the other half is left piled up. On the pile food and spirits are set, and one of the elders, addressing "the father and mother of the paddy-plant," prays for plenteous harvest in future and begs that the seed may bear many fold. Then the whole party eat, drink, and make merry. This ceremony at the threshing-floor is the only occasion when these people invoke "the father and mother of the paddy."[1]

THE CORN-SPIRIT

IN HUMAN FORM

332. *The spirit of the corn manifests itself not merely in vegetable but also in human form.*

The Mandans and Minnetarees of North America used to hold a festival in spring which they called the Corn-medicine Festival of the Women. They thought that a certain Old Woman Who Never Dies made the crops grow and that, living somewhere in the south, she sent migratory waterfowl in spring as her tokens and representatives. Each sort of bird represented a special kind of crop cultivated by the Indians: the wild goose stood for the maize, the wild swan for the gourds, and the wild duck for the beans. So when the feathered messengers of the Old Woman began to arrive in spring the Indians celebrated the corn-medicine festival of the women. Scaffolds were set up, on which the people hung dried meat and other things by way of offerings to the Old Woman; and on a certain day the old women of the tribe, as representatives of the Old Woman Who Never Dies, assembled at the scaffolds each bearing in her hand an ear of maize fastened to a stick. They first planted these sticks in the ground, then danced around the scaffolds, and finally took up the sticks again in their arms. Meanwhile old men beat drums and shook rattles as a musical accompaniment to the performance of the old women. Further, young women came and put dried flesh into the mouths of the old women, for which they received in return a grain of the consecrated maize to eat. Three or four grains of the holy corn were also placed in the dishes of the young women, to be afterwards carefully mixed with the seed-corn, which they were supposed to fertilise. The dried flesh hung on the scaffold belonged to the old women, because they represented the Old Woman Who Never Dies. A similar corn-medicine festival was held in autumn for the purpose of attracting the herds of buffaloes and securing a supply of meat. At that time every woman carried in her arms an uprooted plant of maize. They gave the name of the Old Woman Who Never Dies both to the maize and to those birds which they regarded as symbols of the fruits of the earth, and they prayed to them in autumn saying, "Mother, have pity on us! send us not the bitter cold too soon, lest we have not meat enough! let not all the game depart, that we may have something for the winter!" In autumn, when the birds were flying south, the Indians thought that they were going home to the Old Woman and taking to her the offerings that had been hung up on the scaffolds, especially the dried meat, which she ate.[1] Here then we have the spirit or divinity of the corn conceived as an Old Woman and represented in bodily form by old women, who in their capacity of representatives receive some at least of the offerings which are intended for her.

333. The Miamis, another tribe of North American Indians, tell a tale in which the spirit of the corn figures as a broken-down old man. They say that corn, that is, maize, first grew in heaven, and that the Good Spirit commanded it to go down and dwell with men on earth. At first it was reluctant to do so, but the Good Spirit prevailed on it to go by promising that men would treat it well in return for the benefit they derived from it. "So corn came down from heaven to benefit the Indian, and this is the reason why they esteem it, and are bound to take good care if it, and to nurture it, and not raise more than they actually require, for their own consumption." But once a whole town of the Miamis was severely punished for failing in respect for the corn. They had raised a great crop and stored much of it under ground, and much of it they packed for immediate use in bags. But the corn was so plentiful that much of it still remained on the stalks, and the young men grew reckless and played with the shelled cobs, throwing them at each other, and at last they even broke the cobs from the growing stalks and pelted each other with them too. But a judgment soon followed on such wicked conduct. For when the hunters went out to hunt, though the deer seemed to abound, they could kill nothing. So the corn was gone and they could get no meat, and the people were hungry. Well, one of the hunters, roaming by himself in the woods to find something to eat for his aged father, came upon a small lodge in the wilderness where a decrepit old man was lying with his back to the fire. Now the old man was no other than the Spirit of the Corn. He said to the young hunter, "My grandson, the Indians have afflicted me much, and reduced me to the sad state in which you see me. In the side of the lodge you will find a small kettle. Take it and eat, and when you have satisfied your hunger, I will speak to you." But the kettle was full of such fine sweet corn as the hunter had never in his life seen before. When he had eaten his fill, the old man resumed the thread of his discourse, saying, "Your people have wantonly abused and reduced me to the state you now see me in: my back-bone is broken in many places; it was the foolish young men of your town who did me this evil, for I am Mondamin, or corn, that came down from heaven. In their play they threw corn-cobs and corn-ears at one another, treating me with contempt. I am the corn-spirit whom they have injured. That is why you experience bad luck and famine. I am the cause; you feel my just resentment, therefore your people are punished. Other Indians do not treat me so. They respect me, and so it is well with them. Had you no elders to check the youths at their wanton sport? You are an eye-witness of my sufferings. They are the effect of what you did to my body." With that he groaned and covered himself up. So the young hunter returned and reported what he had seen and heard; and since then the Indians have been very careful not to play with corn in the ear.[1]

334. In some parts of India the harvest-goddess Gauri is represented at once by an unmarried girl and by a bundle of wild balsam plants, which is made up into the figure of a woman and dressed as such with mask, garments, and ornaments. Both the human and the vegetable representative of the goddess are worshipped, and the intention of the whole ceremony appears to be to ensure a good crop of rice.[1]

335. The reader may have observed that in modern folk-customs the corn-spirit is generally represented either by a Corn-mother (Old Woman, etc.) or by a Maiden (Harvest-child, etc.), not both by a Corn-mother and by a Maiden. Why then did the Greeks represent the corn both as a mother and a daughter?

In the Breton custom the mother-sheaf—a large figure made out of the last sheaf with a small corn-doll inside of it—clearly represents both the Corn-mother and the Corn-daughter, the latter still unborn.[1] Again, in the Prussian custom cited earlier, the woman who plays the part of Corn-mother represents the ripe grain; the child appears to represent next year's corn, which may be regarded, naturally enough, as the child of this year's corn, since it is from the seed of this year's harvest that next year's crop will spring. Further, we have seen that among the Malays of the Peninsula and sometimes among the Highlanders of Scotland the spirit of the grain is represented in double female form, both as old and young, by means of ears taken alike from the ripe crop: in Scotland the old spirit of the corn appears as the Carline or *Cailleach,* the young spirit as the Maiden; while among the Malays of the Peninsula the two spirits of the rice are definitely related to each other as mother and child. Judged by these analogies Demeter would be the ripe crop of this year; Persephone would be the seed-corn taken from it and sown in autumn, to reappear in spring. The descent of Persephone into the lower world would thus be a mythical expression for the sowing of the seed; her reappearance in spring would signify the sprouting of the young corn. In this way the Persephone of one year becomes the Demeter of the next, and this may very well have been the original form of the myth. But when with the advance of religious thought the corn came to be personified, no longer as a being that went through the whole cycle of birth, growth, reproduction, and death within a year, but as an immortal goddess, consistency required that one of the two personifications, the mother or the daughter, should be sacrificed. However, the double conception of the corn as mother and daughter may have been too old and too deeply rooted in the popular mind to be eradicated by logic, and so room had to be found in the reformed myth both for mother and daughter. This was done by assigning to Persephone the character of the corn sown in autumn and sprouting in spring, while Demeter was left to play the somewhat vague part of the heavy mother of the corn, who laments its annual disappearance underground, and rejoices over its reappearance in spring. Thus instead of a regular succession of divine beings, each living a year and then giving birth to her successor, the reformed myth exhibits the conception of two divine and immortal beings, one of whom annually disappears into and reappears from the ground, while the other has little to do but to weep and rejoice at the appropriate seasons.

336. This theory of the double personification of the corn in Greek myth assumes that both personifications (Demeter and Persephone) are original. But if we suppose that the Greek myth started with a single personification, the after-growth of a second personification may perhaps be explained as follows. On looking over the harvest customs which have been passed under review, it may be noticed that they involve two distinct conceptions of the corn-spirit. For whereas in some of the customs the corn-spirit is treated as immanent in the corn, in others it is regarded as external to it. Thus when a particular sheaf is called by the name of the corn-spirit, and is dressed in clothes and handled with reverence,[1] the spirit is clearly regarded as immanent in the corn. But when the spirit is said to make the crops grow by passing through them, or to blight the grain of those against whom she has a grudge, she is apparently conceived as distinct from, though exercising power over, the corn. Conceived in the latter way the corn-spirit is in a fair way to become a deity of the corn, if she has not become so already. Of these two conceptions, that of the corn-spirit as immanent in the corn is doubtless the older, since the view of nature as animated by indwelling spirits appears to have generally preceded the view of it as controlled by external deities; to put it shortly, animism precedes deism. In the harvest customs of our European peasantry the corn-spirit seems to be conceived now as immanent in the corn and now as external to it. In Greek mythology, on the other hand, Demeter is viewed rather as the deity of the corn than as the spirit immanent in it.[2] The process of thought which leads to the change from the one mode of conception to the other is anthropomorphism, or the gradual investment of the immanent spirits with more and more of the attributes of humanity. As men emerge from savagery the tendency to humanise their divinities gains strength; and the more human these become the wider is the breach which severs them from the natural objects of which they were at first merely the animating spirits or souls. But in the progress upwards from savagery men of the same generation do not march abreast; and though the new anthropomorphic gods may satisfy the religious wants of the more developed intelligences, the backward members of the community will cling by preference to the old animistic notions. Now when the spirit of any natural object such as the corn has been invested with human

ears of rice are taken to represent either the Soul of the Rice or the Rice-child.[4] In parts of Russia the first sheaf is treated much in the same way that the last sheaf is treated elsewhere. It is reaped by the mistress herself, taken home and set in the place of honour near the holy pictures; afterwards it is threshed separately, and some of its grain is mixed with the next year's seed-corn.[5] In Aberdeenshire, while the last corn cut was generally used to make the *clyack* sheaf, it was sometimes, though rarely, the first corn cut that was dressed up as a woman and carried home with ceremony.[6]

339. In Phoenicia and Western Asia a plaintive song, like that chanted by the Egyptian corn-reapers, was sung at the vintage and probably (to judge by analogy) also at harvest. This Phoenician song was called by the Greeks Linus or Ailinus and explained, like Maneros, as a lament for the death of a youth named Linus.[1] According to one story Linus was brought up by a shepherd, but torn to pieces by his dogs.[2] But, like Maneros, the name Linus or Ailinus appears to have originated in a verbal misunderstanding, and to be nothing more than the cry *ai lanu,* that is "Woe to us," which the Phoenicians probably uttered in mourning for Adonis;[3] at least Sappho seems to have re-garded Adonis and Linus as equivalent.[4]

340. In Bithynia a like mournful ditty, called Bormos or Borimos, was chanted by Mariandynian reapers. Bormos was said to have been a handsome youth, the son of King Upias or of a wealthy and distinguished man. One summer day, watching the reapers at work in his fields, he went to fetch them a drink of water and was never heard of more. So the reapers sought for him, calling him in plaintive strains, which they continued to chant at harvest ever afterwards.[1]

341. In Phrygia the corresponding song, sung by harvesters both at reaping and at threshing, was called Lityerses. According to one story, Lityerses was a bastard son of Midas, King of Phrygia, and dwelt at Celaenae. He used to reap the corn, and had an enormous appetite. When a stranger happened to enter the corn-field or to pass by it, Lityerses gave him plenty to eat and drink, then took him to the corn-fields on the banks of the Maeander and compelled him to reap along with him. Lastly, it was his custom to wrap the stranger in a sheaf, cut off his head with a sickle, and carry away his body, swathed in the corn stalks. But at last Hercules undertook to reap with him, cut off his head with the sickle, and threw his body into the river.[1] As Hercules is reported to have slain Lityerses in the same way that Lityerses slew others (as Theseus treated Sinis and Sciron), we may infer that Lityerses used to throw the bodies of his victims into the river. According to another version of the story, Lity-erses, a son of Midas, was wont to challenge people to a reaping match with him, and if he vanquished them he used to thrash them; but one day he met with a stronger reaper, who slew him.[2]

342. There are some grounds for supposing that in these stories of Lity-erses we have the description of a Phrygian harvest custom in accordance with which certain persons, especially strangers passing the harvest field, were regularly regarded as embodiments of the corn-spirit, and as such were seized by the reapers, wrapt in sheaves, and beheaded, their bodies, bound up in the corn-stalks, being afterwards thrown into water as a rain-charm. The grounds for this supposition are, first, the resemblance of the Lityerses story to the harvest customs of European peasantry, and, second, the frequency of human sacrifices offered by savage races to promote the fertility of the fields.

In comparing the story with the harvest customs of Europe, three points deserve special attention, namely: I. the reaping match and the binding of persons in the sheaves; II. the killing of the corn-spirit or his representatives; III. the treatment of visitors to the harvest field or of strangers passing it.

I. In regard to the first head, we have seen that in modern Europe the person who cuts or binds or threshes the last sheaf is often exposed to rough treatment at the hands of his fellow-labourers. For example, he is bound up in the last sheaf, and, thus encased, is carried or carted about, beaten, drenched with water, thrown on a dunghill, and so forth. Or, if he is spared this horse-play, he is at least the subject of ridicule or is thought to be destined to suffer some misfortune in the course of the year. Hence the harvesters are naturally reluctant to give the last cut at reaping or the last stroke at threshing or to bind the last sheaf, and towards the close of the work this reluctance produces an emulation among the labourers, each striving to finish his task as fast as possible, in order that he may escape the invidious distinction of being last. For example, in the neighbourhood of Danzig, when the winter corn is cut and mostly bound up in sheaves, the portion which still remains to be bound is divided amongst the women binders, each of whom receives a swath of equal length to bind. A crowd of reapers, children, and idlers gather round to witness the contest, and at the word, "Seize the Old Man," the women fall to work, all binding their allotted swaths as hard as they can. The spectators watch them narrowly, and the woman who cannot keep pace with the rest and consequently binds the last sheaf has to carry the Old Man (that is, the last sheaf made up in the form of a man) to the farmhouse and deliver it to the farmer with the words, "Here I bring you the Old Man." At the supper which follows, the Old Man is placed at the table and receives an abundant portion of food, which, as he cannot eat it, falls to the share of the woman who carried him. Afterwards the Old Man is placed in the yard and all the people dance round him. Or the woman who bound the last sheaf dances for a good while with the Old Man, while the rest form a ring round them; afterwards they all, one after the other, dance a single round with him. Further, the woman who bound the last sheaf goes herself by the name of the Old Man till the next harvest, and is often mocked with the cry, "Here comes the Old Man."[1] At Aschbach in Bavaria, when the reaping is nearly finished, the reapers say, "Now, we will drive out the Old Man." Each of them sets himself to reap a patch of corn as fast as he can; he who cuts the last handful or the last stalk is

nosegay made of corn-ears and flowers, to his arm, and he is obliged to ransom himself by the payment of a fine.[18] In the canton of Putanges, in Normandy, a pretence of tying up the owner of the land in the last sheaf of wheat is still practised, or at least was still practised some quarter of a century ago. The task falls to the women alone. They throw themselves on the proprietor, seize him by the arms, the legs, and body, throw him to the ground, and stretch him on the last sheaf. Then a show is made of binding him, and the conditions to be observed at the harvest-supper are dictated to him. When he has accepted them, he is released and allowed to get up.[19] At Brie, Isle de France, when any one who does not belong to the farm passes by the harvest-field, the reapers give chase. If they catch him, they bind him in a sheaf and bite him, one after the other, in the forehead, crying, "You shall carry the key of the field."[20] "To have the key" is an expression used by harvesters elsewhere in the sense of to cut or bind or thresh the last sheaf;[21] hence, it is equivalent to the phrases "You have the Old Man," "You are the Old Man," which are addressed to the cutter, binder, or thresher of the last sheaf. Therefore, when a stranger, as at Brie, is tied up in a sheaf and told that he will "carry the key of the field," it is as much as to say that he is the Old Man, that is, an embodiment of the corn-spirit. In hop-picking, if a well-dressed stranger passes the hop-yard, he is seized by the women, tumbled into the bin, covered with leaves, and not released till he has paid a fine.[22] In some parts of Scotland, particularly in the counties of Fife and Kinross, down to recent times the reapers used to seize and dump, as it was called, any stranger who happened to visit or pass by the harvest-field. The custom was to lay hold of the stranger by his ankles and armpits, lift him up, and bring the lower part of his person into violent contact with the ground. Women as well as men were liable to be thus treated. The practice of interposing a sheaf between the sufferer and the ground is said to be a modern refinement.[23] Comparing this custom with the one practised at Putanges in Normandy, which has just been described, we may conjecture that in Scotland the "dumping" of strangers on the harvest-field was originally a preliminary to wrapping them up in sheaves of corn. Like the ancient Lityerses, modern European reapers have been wont to lay hold of a passing stranger and tie him up in a sheaf. It is not to be expected that they should complete the parallel by cutting off his head; but if they do not take such a strong step, their language and gestures are at least indicative of a desire to do so. For instance, in Mecklenburg on the first day of reaping, if the master or mistress or a stranger enters the field, or merely passes by it, all the mowers face towards him and sharpen their scythes, clashing their whet-stones against them in unison, as if they were making ready to mow. Then the woman who leads the mowers steps up to him and ties a band round his left arm. He must ransom himself by payment of a forfeit.[24] Near Ratzeburg, when the master or other person of mark enters the field or passes by it, all the harvesters stop work and march towards him in a body, the men with their scythes in front. On meeting him they form up in line, men and women. The men stick the poles of their scythes in the ground, as they do in whetting them; then they take off their caps and hang them on the scythes, while their leader stands forward and makes a speech. When he has done, they all whet their scythes in measured time very loudly, after which they put on their caps. Two of the women binders then come forward; one of them ties the master or stranger (as the case may be) with corn-ears or with a silken band; the other delivers a rhyming address. The following are specimens of the speeches made by the reaper on these occasions. In some parts of Pomerania every passer-by is stopped, his way being barred with a corn-rope. The reapers form a circle round him and sharpen their scythes, while their leader says:—

> "The men are ready,
> The scythes are bent,
> The corn is great and small,
> The gentleman must be mowed."

Then the process of whetting the scythes is repeated.[25] At Ramin, in the district of Stettin, the stranger, standing encircled by the reapers, is thus addressed:—

> "We'll stroke the gentleman
> With our naked sword,
> Wherewith we shear meadows and fields.
> We shear princes and lords.
> Labourers are often athirst;
> If the gentleman will stand beer and brandy
> The joke will soon be over.
> But, if our prayer he does not like,
> The sword has a right to strike."[26]

That in these customs the whetting of the scythes is really meant as a preliminary to mowing appears from the following variation of the preceding customs. In the district of Lüneburg, when any one enters the harvest-field, he is asked whether he will engage a good fellow. If he says yes, the harvesters mow some swaths, yelling and screaming, and then ask him for drink-money.[27]

343. On the threshing-floor strangers are also regarded as embodiments of the corn-spirit, and are treated accordingly. At Wiedingharde in Schleswig when a stranger comes to the threshing-floor he is asked, "Shall I teach you the flail-dance?" If he says yes, they put the arms of the threshing-flail round his neck as if he were a sheaf of corn, and press them together so tight that he is nearly choked.[1] In some parishes of Wermland (Sweden), when a stranger enters the threshing-floor where the threshers are at work, they say that "they will teach him the threshing-song." Then they put a flail round his neck and a

man victims to make fruits and crops plentiful, and at Ibadan numbers of men and women were immolated before the kola trees.[3b]

348. But the best known case of human sacrifices, systematically offered to ensure good crops, is supplied by the Khonds or Kandhs, another Dravidian race in Bengal. Our knowledge of them is derived from the accounts written by British officers who, about the middle of the nineteenth century, were engaged in putting them down.[1] The sacrifices were offered to the Earth Goddess, Tari Pennu or Bera Pennu, and were believed to ensure good crops and immunity from all disease and accidents. In particular, they were considered necessary in the cultivation of turmeric, the Khonds arguing that the turmeric could not have a deep red colour without the shedding of blood.[2] The victim or Meriah, as he was called, was acceptable to the goddess only if he had been purchased, or had been born a victim—that is, the son of a victim father, or had been devoted as a child by his father or guardian. Khonds in distress often sold their children for victims, "considering the beatification of their souls certain, and their death, for the benefit of mankind, the most honourable possible." A man of the Panua tribe was once seen to load a Khond with curses, and finally to spit in his face, because the Khond had sold for a victim his own child, whom the Panua had wished to marry. A party of Khonds, who saw this, immediately pressed forward to comfort the seller of his child, saying, "Your child has died that all the world may live, and the Earth Goddess herself will wipe that spittle from your face."[3] The victims were often kept for years before they were sacrificed. Being regarded as consecrated beings, they were treated with extreme affection, mingled with deference, and were welcomed wherever they went. A Meriah youth, on attaining maturity, was generally given a wife, who was herself usually a Meriah or victim; and with her he received a portion of land and farm-stock. Their offspring were also victims. Human sacrifices were offered to the Earth Goddess by tribes, branches of tribes, or villages, both at periodical festivals and on extraordinary occasions. The periodical sacrifices were generally so arranged by tribes and divisions of tribes that each head of a family was enabled, at least once a year, to procure a shred of flesh for his fields, generally about the time when his chief crop was laid down.[4]

349. One point in related savage customs deserves to be noted. The Pawnee chief devoured the heart of the captured Sioux girl, and the Marimos ate the victim's flesh. If, as we suppose, the victim was regarded as divine, it follows that in eating his flesh his worshippers believed themselves to be partaking of the body of their god.

HUMAN REPRESENTATIVES OF THE CORN-SPIRIT

350. The barbarous rites just described offer analogies to the harvest customs of Europe. Thus the fertilising virtue ascribed to the corn-spirit is shewn equally in the savage custom of mixing the victim's blood or ashes with the seed-corn and the European custom of mixing the grain from the last sheaf with the young corn in spring. Again, the identification of the person with the corn appears alike in the savage custom of adapting the age and stature of the victim to the age and stature, whether actual or expected, of the crop; in the Scotch and Styrian rules that when the corn-spirit is conceived as the Maiden the last corn shall be cut by a young maiden, but when it is conceived as the Corn-mother it shall be cut by an old woman; in the Lothringian warning given to old woman to save themselves when the Old Woman is being killed, that is, when the last corn is being threshed; and in the Tyrolese expectation that if the man who gives the last stroke at threshing is tall, the next year's corn will be tall also. Further, the same identification is implied in the savage custom of killing the representative of the corn-spirit with hoes or spades or by grinding him between stones, and in the European custom of pretending to kill him with the scythe or the flail. Finally, too, the Khond custom of pouring water on the buried flesh of the victim is parallel to the European customs of pouring water on the personal representative of the corn-spirit or plunging him into a stream. Both the Khond and the European customs are rain-charms.

351. To return now to the Lityerses story. It has been shewn that in rude society human beings have been commonly killed to promote the growth of the crops. There is therefore no improbability in the supposition that they may once have been killed for a like purpose in Phrygia and Europe; and when Phrygian legend and European folk-custom, closely agreeing with each other, point to the conclusion that men were so slain, we are bound, provisionally at least, to accept the conclusion. Further, both the Lityerses story and European harvest-customs agree in indicating that the victim was put to death as a representative of the corn-spirit, and this indication is in harmony with the view which some savages appear to take of the victim slain to make the crops flourish. On the whole, then, we may fairly suppose that both in Phrygia and in Europe the representative of the corn-spirit was annually killed upon the harvest-field. Grounds have been already shewn for believing that similarly in Europe the representative of the tree-spirit was annually slain. The proofs of these two remarkable and closely analogous customs are entirely independent of each other. Their coincidence seems to furnish fresh presumption in favour of both.

To the question, How was the representative of the corn-spirit chosen? one answer has been already given. Both the Lityerses story and European folk-custom shew that passing strangers were regarded as manifestations of the corn-spirit escaping from the cut or threshed corn, and as such were seized and slain. But this is not the only answer which the evidence suggests. According to the Phrygian legend the victims of Lityerses were not simply passing strangers, but persons whom he had vanquished in a reaping contest and afterwards wrapt up in corn-sheaves and beheaded. This suggests

that the representative of the corn-spirit may have been selected by means
of a competition on the harvest-field, in which the vanquished competitor
was compelled to accept the fatal honour. The supposition is countenanced
by European harvest-customs. We have seen that in Europe there is sometimes a contest amongst the reapers to avoid being last, and that the person
who is vanquished in this competition, that is, who cuts the last corn, is often
roughly handled. It is true we have not found that a pretence is made of killing him; but on the other hand we have found that a pretence is made of
killing the man who gives the last stroke at threshing, that is, who is vanquished in the threshing contest. Now, since it is in the character of representative of the corn-spirit that the thresher of the last corn is slain in
mimicry, and since the same representative character attaches (as we have
seen) to the cutter and binder as well as to the thresher of the last corn, and
since the same repugnance is evinced by harvesters to be last in any one of
these labours, we may conjecture that a pretence has been commonly made
of killing the reaper and binder as well as the thresher of the last corn, and
that in ancient times this killing was actually carried out. This conjecture
is corroborated by the common superstition that whoever cuts the last corn
must die soon.[1] Sometimes it is thought that the person who binds the last
sheaf on the field will die in the course of next year.[2] The reason for fixing
on the reaper, binder, or thresher of the last corn as the representative of
the corn-spirit may be this. The corn-spirit is supposed to lurk as long as he
can in the corn, retreating before the reapers, the binders, and the threshers
at their work. But when he is forcibly expelled from his refuge in the last
corn cut or the last sheaf bound or the last grain threshed, he necessarily
assumes some other form than that of the corn-stalks which had hitherto
been his garment or body. And what form can the expelled corn-spirit assume more naturally than that of the person who stands nearest to the corn
from which he (the corn-spirit) has just been expelled? But the person in
question is necessarily the reaper, binder, or thresher of the last corn. He
or she, therefore, is seized and treated as the corn-spirit himself.

Thus the person who was killed on the harvest-field as the representative
of the corn-spirit may have been either a passing stranger or the harvester
who was last at reaping, binding, or threshing. But there is a third possibility,
to which ancient legend and modern folk-custom alike point. Lityerses not
only put strangers to death; he was himself slain, and apparently in the same
way as he had slain others, namely, by being wrapt in a corn-sheaf, beheaded, and cast into the river; and it is implied that this happened to
Lityerses on his own land. Similarly in modern harvest-customs the pretence
of killing appears to be carried out quite as often on the person of the
master (farmer or squire) as on that of strangers. Now when we remember
that Lityerses was said to have been a son of the King of Phrygia, and that
in one account he is himself called a king, and when we combine with this

the tradition that he was put to death, apparently as a representative of the corn-spirit, we are led to conjecture that we have here another trace of the custom of annually slaying one of those divine or priestly kings who are known to have held ghostly sway in many parts of Western Asia and particularly in Phrygia. The custom appears, as we have seen,[3] to have been so far modified in places that the king's son was slain in the king's stead. Of the custom thus modified the story of Lityerses would be, in one version at least, a reminiscence.

352. Turning now to the relation of the Phrygian Lityerses to the Phrygian Attis, it may be remembered that at Pessinus—the seat of a priestly kingship —the high-priest appears to have been annually slain in the character of Attis, a god of vegetation, and that Attis was described by an ancient authority as "a reaped ear of corn." Thus Attis, as an embodiment of the corn-spirit, annually slain in the person of his representative, might be thought to be ultimately identical with Lityerses, the latter being simply the rustic prototype out of which the state religion of Attis was developed. It may have been so; but, on the other hand, the analogy of European folk-custom warns us that amongst the same people two distinct deities of vegetation may have their separate personal representatives, both of whom are slain in the character of gods at different times of the year. For in Europe, as we have seen, it appears that one man was commonly slain in the character of the tree-spirit in spring, and another in the character of the corn-spirit in autumn. It may have been so in Phrygia also. Attis was especially a tree-god, and his connexion with corn may have been only such an extension of the power of a tree-spirit as is indicated in customs like the Harvest-May. Again, the representative of Attis appears to have been slain in spring; whereas Lityerses must have been slain in summer or autumn, according to the time of the harvest in Phrygia. On the whole, then, while we are not justified in regarding Lityerses as the prototype of Attis, the two may be regarded as parallel products of the same religious idea, and may have stood to each other as in Europe the Old Man of harvest stands to the Wild Man, the Leaf Man, and so forth, of spring. Both were spirits or deities of vegetation, and the personal representatives of both were annually slain. But whereas the Attis worship became elevated into the dignity of a State religion and spread to Italy, the rites of Lityerses seem never to have passed the limits of their native Phrygia, and always retained their character of rustic ceremonies performed by peasants on the harvest-field. At most a few villages may have clubbed together, as amongst the Khonds, to procure a human victim to be slain as representative of the corn-spirit for their common benefit. Such victims may have been drawn from the families of priestly kings or kinglets, which would account for the legendary character of Lityerses as the son of a Phrygian king or as himself a king. When villages did not so club together, each village or farm may have procured its own representative of the corn-spirit by dooming to death either a passing stranger or the harvester who cut, bound, or threshed the last sheaf. Perhaps in the olden time the practice of head-hunting as a means of promoting the growth of the corn may have been as common among the rude inhabitants of Europe and Western Asia as it still is, or was till lately, among the primitive agricultural tribes of Assam, Burma, the Philippine Islands, and the Indian Archipelago. It is hardly necessary to add that in Phrygia, as in Europe, the old barbarous custom of killing a man on the harvest-field or the threshing-floor had doubt-less passed into a mere pretence long before the classical era, and was probably regarded by the reapers and threshers themselves as no more than a rough jest which the license of a harvest-home permitted them to play off on a passing stranger, a comrade, or even on their master himself.[1]

353. I have dwelt on the Lityerses song at length because it affords so many points of comparison with European and savage folk-custom. The other harvest songs of Western Asia and Egypt, to which attention has been called above, may now be dismissed much more briefly. The similarity of the Bithynian Bormos to the Phrygian Lityerses helps to bear out the interpreta-tion which has been given of the latter. Bormos, whose death or rather dis-appearance was annually mourned by the reapers in a plaintive song, was, like Lityerses, a king's son or at least the son of a wealthy and distinguished man. The reapers whom he watched were at work on his own fields, and he disappeared in going to fetch water for them; according to one version of the story he was carried off by the nymphs, doubtless the nymphs of the spring or pool or river whither he went to draw water.[1] Viewed in the light of the Lityerses story and of European folk-custom, this disappearance of Bormos may be a reminiscence of the custom of binding the farmer himself in a corn-sheaf and throwing him into the water. The mournful strain which the reapers sang was probably a lamentation over the death of the corn-spirit, slain either in the cut corn or in the person of a human representative; and the call which they addressed to him may have been a prayer that he might return in fresh vigour next year.

354. The Phoenician Linus song was sung at the vintage, at least in the west of Asia Minor, as we learn from Homer; and this, combined with the legend of Syleus, suggests that in ancient times passing strangers were handled by vintagers and vine-diggers in much the same way as they are said to have been handled by the reaper Lityerses. The Lydian Syleus, so ran the legend, compelled passers-by to dig for him in his vineyard, till Hercules came and killed him and dug up his vines by the roots.[1] This seems to be the outline of a legend like that of Lityerses; but neither ancient writers nor modern folk-custom enable us to fill in the details. But, further, the Linus song was probably sung also by Phoenician reapers, for Herodotus compares it to the Maneros song, which, as we have seen, was a lament raised by Egyptian reapers over the cut corn. Further, Linus was identified with Adonis, and Adonis has some claims to be regarded as especially a corn-deity. Thus the Linus lament, as sung at harvest, would be identical with the Adonis lament; each would be the lamentation raised by reapers over the dead spirit of the corn. But whereas Adonis, like Attis, grew into a stately figure of mythology, adored and mourned in splendid cities far beyond the limits of his Phoenician home, Linus appears to have remained a simple ditty sung by reapers and vintagers among the corn-sheaves and the vines. The analogy of Lityerses and of folk-custom, both European and savage, suggests that in Phoenicia the slain corn-spirit—the dead Adonis—may formerly have been represented by a human victim.

355. There is a good deal more evidence that in Egypt the slain corn-spirit —the dead Osiris—was represented by a human victim. For the legend of Busiris seems to preserve a reminiscence of human sacrifices once offered by the Egyptians in connexion with the worship of Osiris. Busiris was said to have been an Egyptian king who sacrificed all strangers on the altar of Zeus. The origin of the custom was traced to a dearth which afflicted the land of Egypt for nine years. A Cyprian seer informed Busiris that the dearth would cease if a man were annually sacrificed to Zeus. So Busiris instituted the sacrifice. But when Hercules came to Egypt, and was being dragged to the altar to be sacrificed, he burst his bonds and slew Busiris and his son.[1] Here then is a legend that in Egypt a human victim was annually sacrificed to prevent the failure of the crops, and a belief is implied that an omission of the sacrifice would have entailed a recurrence of that infertility which it was the object of the sacrifice to prevent. So the Pawnees, as we have seen, believed that an omission of the human sacrifice at planting would have been followed by a total failure of their crops. The name Busiris was in reality the name of a city, *pe-Asar*, "the house of Osiris,"[2] the city being so called because it contained the grave of Osiris. The human sacrifices were said to have been offered at his grave, and the victims were red-haired men, whose ashes were scattered abroad by means of winnowing-fans.[3] This tradition of human sacrifices offered at the tomb of Osiris is confirmed by the evidence of the monuments; for "we find in the temple of Dendereh a human figure with a hare's head and pierced with knives, tied to a stake before Osiris Khenti-Amentiu, and Horus is shown in a Ptolemaic sculpture at Karnak killing a bound hare-headed figure before the bier of Osiris, who is represented in the form of Harpocrates. That these figures are really human beings with the head of an animal fastened on is proved by another sculpture at Dendereh, where a kneeling man has the hawk's head and wings over his head and shoulders, and in another place a priest has the jackal's head on his shoulders, his own head appearing through the disguise. Besides, Diodorus tells us that the Egyptian kings in former times had worn on their

ceremony are thus described by an observer who wrote in the first half of the nineteenth century. "After the wheat is all cut, on most farms in the north of Devon, the harvest people have a custom of 'crying the neck.' I believe that this practice is seldom omitted on any large farm in that part of the country. It is done in this way. An old man, or some one else well acquainted with the ceremonies used on the occasion (when the labourers are reaping the last field of wheat), goes round to the shocks and sheaves, and picks out a little bundle of all the best ears he can find; this bundle he ties up very neat and trim, and plats and arranges the straws very tastefully. This is called 'the neck' of wheat, or wheaten-ears. After the field is cut out, and the pitcher once more circulated, the reapers, binders, and the women stand round in a circle. The person with 'the neck' stands in the centre, grasping it with both his hands. He first stoops and holds it near the ground, and all the men forming the ring take off their hats, stooping and holding them with both hands towards the ground. They then all begin at once in a very prolonged and harmonious tone to cry 'The neck!' at the same time slowly raising themselves upright, and elevating their arms and hats above their heads; the person with 'the neck' also raising it on high. This is done three times. They then change their cry to 'Wee yen!'—'Way yen!'—which they sound in the same prolonged and slow manner as before, with singular harmony and effect, three times. This last cry is accompanied by the same movements of the body and arms as in crying 'the neck.' . . . After having thus repeated 'the neck' three times, and 'wee yen,' or 'way yen' as often, they all burst out into a kind of loud and joyous laugh, flinging up their hats and caps into the air, capering about and perhaps kissing the girls. One of them then gets 'the neck' and runs as hard as he can down to the farmhouse, where the dairy-maid, or one of the young female domestics, stands at the door prepared with a pail of water. If he who holds 'the neck' can manage to get into the house, in any way unseen, or openly, by any other way than the door at which the girl stands with the pail of water, then he may lawfully kiss her; but, if otherwise, he is regularly soused with the contents of the bucket. On a fine still autumn evening the 'crying of the neck' has a wonderful effect at a distance, far finer than that of the Turkish muezzin, which Lord Byron eulogises so much, and which he says is preferable to all the bells in Christendom. I have once or twice heard upwards of twenty men cry it, and sometimes joined by an equal number of female voices. About three years back, on some high grounds, where our people were harvesting, I heard six or seven 'necks' cried in one night, although I know that some of them were four miles off. They are heard through the quiet evening air at a considerable distance sometimes."[1]

360. Similar customs appear to have been formerly observed in Pembrokeshire, as appears from the following account, in which, however, nothing is said of the sonorous cries raised by the reapers when their work was done: "At harvest-time, in South Pembrokeshire, the last ears of corn left standing in the field were tied together, and the harvesters then tried to cut this neck by throwing their hatchets at it. What happened afterwards appears to have varied somewhat. I have been told by one old man that the one who got possession of the neck would carry it over into some neighbouring field, leave it there, and take to his heels as fast as he could; for, if caught, he had a rough time of it. The men who caught him would shut him up in a barn without food, or belabour him soundly, or perhaps shoe him, as it was called, beating the soles of his feet with rods—a very severe and much-dreaded punishment. On my grandfather's farm the man used to make for the house as fast as possible, and try to carry in the neck. The maids were on the look-out for him, and did their best to drench him with water. If they succeeded, they got the present of half-a-crown, which my grandfather always gave, and which was considered a very liberal present indeed. If the man was successful in dodging the maids, and getting the neck into the house without receiving the wetting, the half-crown became his. The neck was then hung up, and kept until the following year, at any rate, like the bunches of flowers or boughs gathered at the St. Jean, in the south of France. Sometimes the necks of many successive years were to be found hanging up together. In these two ways of disposing of the neck one sees the embodiment, no doubt, of the two ways of looking at the corn-spirit, as good (to be kept) or as bad (to be passed on to the neighbour)."[1]

361. In the foregoing customs a particular bunch of ears, generally the last left standing,[1] is conceived as the neck of the corn-spirit, who is consequently beheaded when the bunch is cut down. Similarly in Shropshire the name "neck," or "the gander's neck," used to be commonly given to the last handful of ears left standing in the middle of the field when all the rest of the corn was cut. It was plaited together, and the reapers, standing ten or twenty paces off, threw their sickles at it. Whoever cut it through was said to have cut off the gander's neck. The "neck" was taken to the farmer's wife, who was supposed to keep it in the house for good luck till the next harvest came round.[2] Near Trèves, the man who reaps the last standing corn "cuts the goat's neck off."[3] At Aurich, in East Friesland, the man who reaps the last corn "cuts the hare's tail off."[4] In mowing down the last corner of a field French reapers sometime call out, "We have the cat by the tail."[5]

These examples leave no room to doubt the meaning of the Devonshire and Cornish expression "the neck," as applied to the last sheaf. The corn-spirit is conceived in human or animal form, and the last standing corn is part of its body—its neck, its head, or its tail. Lastly, the Devonshire custom of drenching with water the person who brings in "the neck" is a rain-charm, such as we have had many examples of. Its parallel in the mysteries of Osiris was the custom of pouring water on the image of Osiris or on the person who represented him.

362. In Germany cries of *Waul!* or *Wol!* or *Wôld!* are sometimes raised by

the reapers at cutting the last corn. Thus in some places the last patch of
standing rye was called the *Waul*-rye; a stick decked with flowers was inserted in it, and the ears were fastened to the stick. Then all the reapers took
off their hats and cried thrice, "*Waul! Waul! Waul!*" Sometimes they accompanied the cry by clashing with their whetstones on their scythes.[1]

THE CORN-SPIRIT

IN ANIMAL FORM

THERIOMORPHIC DEITIES OF FERTILITY

363. In peasant folk-lore the corn-spirit is very commonly conceived and represented in animal form. Generally each kind of crop is supposed to have its special animal, which is caught in the last sheaf, and called the Rye-wolf, the Barley-wolf, the Oats-wolf, the Pea-wolf, or the Potato-wolf, according to the crop; but sometimes the figure of the animal is only made up once for all at getting in the last crop of the whole harvest. Sometimes the creature is believed to be killed by the last stroke of the sickle or scythe. But oftener it is thought to live so long as there is corn still unthreshed, and to be caught in the last sheaf threshed. Hence the man who gives the last stroke with the flail is told that he has got the Corn-sow, the Threshing-dog, or the like. When the threshing is finished, a puppet is made in the form of the animal, and this is carried by the thresher of the last sheaf to a neighbouring farm, where the threshing is still going on. This again shews that the corn-spirit is believed to live wherever the corn is still being threshed. Sometimes the thresher of the last sheaf himself represents the animal; and if the people of the next farm, who are still threshing, catch him, they treat him like the animal he represents, by shutting him up in the pig-sty, calling him with the cries commonly addressed to pigs, and so forth.

364. There is a complete parallelism between the conceptions of the corn-spirit in human and in animal form. When the corn waves in the wind it is said either that the Corn-mother or that the Corn-wolf, etc., is passing through the corn. Children are warned against straying in corn-fields either because the Corn-mother or because the Corn-wolf, etc., is there. In the last corn cut or the last sheaf threshed either the Corn-mother or the Corn-wolf, etc., is supposed to be present. The last sheaf is itself called either the Corn-mother or the Corn-wolf, etc., and is made up in the shape either of a woman or of a wolf, etc. The person who cuts, binds, or threshes the last sheaf is called either the Old Woman or the Wolf, etc., according to the name bestowed on the sheaf itself. As in some places a sheaf made in human form and called the Maiden, the Mother of the Maize, etc., is kept from one harvest to the next in order to secure a continuance of the corn-spirit's blessing; so in some places the Harvest-cock and in others the flesh of the goat is kept for a similar purpose from one harvest to the next. As in some places the grain taken from the Corn-mother is mixed with the seed-corn in spring to make the crop abundant; so in some places the feathers of the cock, and in Sweden the Yule Boar, are kept till spring and mixed with the seed-corn for a like purpose. As part of the Corn-mother or Maiden is given to the cattle at Christmas or to the horses at the first ploughing, so part of the Yule Boar is given to the ploughing horses or oxen in spring. Lastly, the death of the corn-spirit is represented by killing or pretending to kill either his human or his animal representative; and the worshippers partake sacramentally either of the actual body and blood of the representative of the divinity, or of bread made in his likeness.

If it is asked why the corn-spirit should be thought to appear in the form of an animal and of so many different animals, we may reply that to primitive man the simple appearance of an animal or bird among the corn is probably enough to suggest a mysterious link between the creature and the corn; and when we remember that in the old days, before fields were fenced in, all kinds of animals must have been free to roam over them, we need not wonder that the corn-spirit should have been identified even with large animals like the horse and cow, which nowadays could not, except by a rare accident, be found straying in an English corn-field. This explanation applies with peculiar force to the very common case in which the animal embodiment of the corn-spirit is believed to lurk in the last standing corn. For at harvest a number of wild animals, such as hares, rabbits, and partridges, are commonly driven by the progress of the reaping into the last patch of standing corn, and make their escape from it as it is being cut down. So regularly does this happen that reapers and others often stand round the last patch of corn armed with sticks or guns, with which they kill the animals as they dart out of their last refuge among the stalks. Now, primitive man, to whom magical changes of shape seem perfectly credible, finds it most natural that the spirit of the corn, driven from his home in the ripe grain, should make his escape in the form of the animal which is seen to rush out of the last patch of corn as it falls under the scythe of the reaper. Thus the identification of the corn-spirit with an animal is analogous to the identification of him with a passing stranger. As the sudden appearance of a stranger near the harvest-field or threshing-floor is, to the primitive mind, enough to identify him as the spirit of the corn escaping from the cut or threshed corn, so the sudden appearance of an animal issuing from the cut corn is enough to identify it with the corn-spirit escaping from his ruined home. The two identifications are so analogous that they can hardly be dissociated in any attempt to explain them.

365. Among the many animals whose forms the corn-spirit is believed to take are: the wolf, dog,[1] hare,[2] fox,[3] cock,[4] quail,[5] cat,[6] goat,[7] cow (ox, bull),[8] pig,[9] horse, stag,[10] roe, sheep, bear, ass, mouse, stork, swan, and kite.[11] May not this fact explain the relation in which certain animals stood to the ancient deities of vegetation, Dionysus, Demeter, Adonis, Attis, and Osiris?

366. To begin with Dionysus. We have seen that he was represented sometimes as a goat and sometimes as a bull. As a goat he can hardly be separated from the minor divinities, the Pans, Satyrs, and Silenuses, all of whom are closely associated with him and are represented more or less completely in the form of goats. Further, the Fauns, the Italian counterpart of the Greek Pans and Satyrs, are described as being half goats, with goat-feet and goat-horns.[1] Again, all these minor goat-formed divinities partake more or less clearly of the character of woodland deities. Thus, Pan was called by the Arcadians the Lord of the Wood.[2] The Silenuses associated with the tree-nymphs.[3] The Fauns are expressly designated as woodland deities;[4] and their character as such is still further brought out by their association, or even identification, with Silvanus and the Silvanuses, who, as their name of itself indicates, are spirits of the woods.[5] Lastly, the association of the Satyrs with the Silenuses, Fauns, and Silvanuses,[6] proves that the Satyrs also were woodland deities.

367. These theriomorphic spirits of the woods have their counterparts in the folk-lore of Northern Europe. Thus, the Russian wood-spirits, called *Ljeschie* (from *ljes,* "wood") are believed to appear partly in human shape, but with the horns, ears, and legs of goats. The *Ljeschi* can alter his stature at pleasure; when he walks in the wood he is as tall as the trees; when he walks in the meadows he is no higher than the grass. Some of the *Ljeschie* are spirits of the corn as well as of the wood; before harvest they are as tall as the corn-stalks, but after it they shrink to the height of the stubble.[1] On the whole, then, as Mannhardt argues,[2] the Pans, Satyrs, and Fauns perhaps belong to a widey diffused class of wood-spirits conceived in goat-form. The fondness of goats for straying in woods and nibbling the bark of trees, to which indeed they are most destructive, is an obvious and perhaps sufficient reason why wood-spirits should so often be supposed to take the form of goats.* Accordingly, when we find, as we have done, that Dionysus—a tree-god—is sometimes represented in goat-form, we can hardly avoid concluding that this representation is simply a part of his proper character as a tree-god and is not to be explained by the fusion of two distinct and independent worships, in one of which he originally appeared as a tree-god and in the other as a goat.

368. Dionysus was also figured, as we have seen, in the shape of a bull. After what has gone before we are naturally led to expect that his bull form must

---

* The inconsistency of a god of vegetation subsisting upon the vegetation which he personifies is not one to strike the primitive mind. Such inconsistencies arise when the deity, ceasing to be immanent in the vegetation, comes to be regarded as its owner or lord; for the idea of owning the vegetation naturally leads to that of subsisting on it.

370. The Attic Thesmorphoria was an autumn festival, celebrated by women alone in October, and appears to have represented with mourning rites the descent of Persephone (or Demeter)[1] into the lower world, and with joy her return from the dead.[2] Hence the name Descent or Ascent variously applied to the first, and the name *Kalligeneia* (fair-born) applied to the third day of the festival. Now, it was customary at the Thesmophoria to throw pigs, cakes of dough, and branches of pine-trees into "the chasms of Demeter and Persephone," which appears to have been sacred caverns or vaults. Afterwards—apparently at the next annual festival[3]—the decayed remains of the pigs, the cakes, and the pine-branches were fetched by women called "drawers," who, after observing rules of ceremonial purity for three days, descended into the caverns, brought up the remains, and placed them on the altar. Whoever got a piece of the decayed flesh and cakes, and sowed it with the seed-corn in his field, was believed to be sure of a good crop.

To explain the rude and ancient ritual of the Thesmophoria the following legend was told. At the moment when Pluto carried off Persephone, a swineherd called Eubuleus chanced to be herding his swine on the spot, and his herd was engulfed in the chasm down which Pluto vanished with Persephone.[4] It follows from this that the casting of the pigs into the vaults at the Thesmophoria formed part of the dramatic representation of Persephone's descent into the lower world; and as no image of Persephone appears to have been thrown in, we may infer that the descent of the pigs was not so much an accompaniment of her descent as the descent itself, in short, that the pigs were Persephone. Afterwards when Persephone or Demeter (for the two are equivalent) took on human form, a reason had to be found for the custom of throwing pigs into caverns at her festival; and this was done by saying that when Pluto carried off Persephone, there happened to be some swine browsing near, which were swallowed up along with her. The story is obviously a forced and awkward attempt to bridge the gulf between the old conception of the corn-spirit as a pig and the new conception of her as an anthropomorphic goddess. A trace of the older conception survived in the legend that when the sad mother was searching for traces of the vanished Persephone, the footprints of the lost one were obliterated by the footprints of a pig;[5] originally, we may conjecture, the footprints of the pig were the footprints of Persephone and of Demeter herself. A consciousness of the intimate connexion of the pig with the corn lurks in the legend that the swineherd Eubuleus was a brother of Triptolemus, to whom Demeter first imparted the secret of the corn. Indeed, according to one version of the story, Eubuleus himself received, jointly with his brother Triptolemus, the gift of the corn from Demeter as a reward for revealing to her the fate of Persephone.[6] Further, it is to be noted that at the Thesmophoria the women appear to have eaten swine's flesh.[7] The meal, if I am right, must have been a solemn sacrament or communion, the worshippers partaking of the body of the god.

371. As thus explained, the Thesmophoria has its analogies in the folk-customs of Northern Europe which have been already described. In the neighbourhood of Grenoble, for instance, the goat killed on the harvest-field is partly eaten at the harvest-supper, partly pickled and kept till the next harvest;[1] so at Pouilly the ox killed on the harvest-field is partly eaten by the harvesters, partly pickled and kept till the first day of sowing in spring,[2] probably to be then mixed with the seed, or eaten by the ploughmen, or both; so at Udvarhely the feathers of the cock which is killed in the last sheaf at harvest are kept till spring, and then sown with the seed on the field;[3] so in Hesse and Meiningen the flesh of pigs is eaten on Ash Wednesday or Candlemas, and the bones are kept till sowing-time, when they are put into the field sown or mixed with the seed in the bag;[4] so, lastly, the corn from the last sheaf is kept till Christmas, made into the Yule Boar, and afterwards broken and mixed with the seed-corn at sowing in spring.[5]

372. Attis and Adonis had also their animal embodiments. The worshippers of Attis abstained from eating the flesh of swine.[1] This appears to indicate that the pig was regarded as an embodiment of him. And the legend that Attis was killed by a boar[2] points in the same direction. For after the examples of the goat Dionysus and the pig Demeter it may almost be laid down as a rule that an animal which is said to have injured a god was originally the god himself. Perhaps the cry of "Hyes Attes! Hyes Attes!"[3] which was raised by the worshippers of Attis, may be neither more nor less than "Pig Attis! Pig Attis!"—*hyes* being possibly a Phrygian form of the Greek *hȳs*, "a pig."

In regard to Adonis, his connexion with the boar was not always explained by the story that he had been killed by that animal.[4] According to another version, he perished at the hands of Hephaestus on Mount Lebanon while he was hunting wild boars.[5] These variations in the legend serve to shew that, while the connexion of the boar with Adonis was certain, the reason of the connexion was not understood. Certainly the pig ranked as a sacred animal among the Syrians. At the great religious metropolis of Hierapolis on the Euphrates pigs were neither sacrificed nor eaten, and if a man touched a pig he was unclean for the rest of the day. Some people said this was because the pigs were unclean; others said it was because the pigs were sacred.[6] This difference of opinion points to a hazy state of religious thought in which the ideas of sanctity and uncleanness are not yet sharply distinguished, both being blent in a sort of vaporous solution to which we give the name of taboo. It is quite consistent with this that the pig should have been held to be an embodiment of the divine Adonis, and the analogies of Dionysus and Demeter make it probable that the story of the hostility of the animal to the god was only a late misapprehension of the old view of the god as embodied in a pig. The rule that pigs were not sacrificed or eaten by worshippers of Attis and presumably of Adonis, does not exclude the possibility that in these rituals the pig was slain on solemn occasions as a representative of the god and consumed sacramentally by the worshippers.[7] Indeed, the sacramental killing and eating of an animal implies that the animal is sacred, and that, as a general rule, it is spared.

373. In ancient Egypt, within historical times, the pig occupied the same dubious position as in Syria and Palestine, though at first sight its uncleanness is more prominent than its sanctity. The Egyptians are generally said by Greek writers to have abhorred the pig as a foul and loathsome animal.[1] If a man so much as touched a pig in passing, he stepped into the river with all his clothes on, to wash off the taint.[2] To drink pig's milk was believed to cause leprosy to the drinker.[3] Swineherds, though natives of Egypt, were forbidden to enter any temple, and they were the only men who were thus excluded. No one would give his daughter in marriage to a swineherd, or marry a swineherd's daughter; the swineherds married among themselves.[4] Yet once a year the Egyptians sacrificed pigs to the moon and to Osiris, and not only sacrificed them, but ate of their flesh, though on any other day of the year they would neither sacrifice them nor taste of their flesh. Those who were too poor to offer a pig on this day baked cakes of dough, and offered them instead.[5] This can hardly be explained except by the supposition that the pig was a sacred animal which was eaten sacramentally by his worshippers once a year.

374. Again, the rule that, after touching a pig, a man had to wash himself and his clothes, also favours the view of the sanctity of the pig. For it is a common belief that the effect of contact with a sacred object must be removed, by washing or otherwise, before a man is free to mingle with his fellows. Thus, before coming forth from the tabernacle after the sin-offering, the Jewish high priest had to wash himself, and put off the garments which he had worn in the holy place.[1] It was a rule of Greek ritual that, in offering an expiatory sacrifice, the sacrificer should not touch the sacrifice, and that, after the offering was made, he must wash his body and his clothes in a river or spring before he could enter a city or his own house.[2] The Parjas, a small tribe of the Central Provinces in India, are divided into clans which have for their respective totems the tiger, the tortoise, the goat, a big lizard, a dove, and so on. If a man accidentally kills his totemic animal, "the earthen cooking-pots of his household are thrown away, the clothes are washed, and the house is purified with water in which the bark of the mango or *jamun* tree (*Eugenia jambolana*) has been steeped. This is in sign of mourning, as it is thought that such an act will bring misfortune."[3] If a Chadwar of the Central Provinces who has the pig for his totem should even see a pig killed by somebody else, he will throw away the household crockery and clean the house as if on the death of a member of his family.[4]

375. In the light of these parallels the beliefs and customs of the Egyptians touching the pig are probably to be explained as based upon an opinion of the extreme sanctity rather than of the extreme uncleanness of the animal;

or rather, to put it more correctly, they imply that the animal was looked on, not simply as a filthy and disgusting creature, but as a being endowed with high supernatural powers, and that as such it was regarded with that primitive sentiment of religious awe and fear in which feelings of reverence and abhorrence are almost equally blended. Now, when a being is thus the object of mixed and implicitly contradictory feelings, he may be said to occupy a position of unstable equilibrium. In course of time one of the contradictory feelings is likely to prevail over the other, and according as the feeling which finally predominates is that of reverence or abhorrence, the being who is the object of it will rise into a god or sink into a devil. The latter, on the whole, was the fate of the pig in Egypt. For in historical times the fear and horror of the pig seem certainly to have outweighed the reverence and worship of which he may once have been the object, and of which, even in his fallen state, he never quite lost trace. He came to be looked on as an embodiment of Set, the Egyptian devil and enemy of Osiris. For it was in the shape of a black pig that Set injured the eye of the god Horus, who burned him and instituted the sacrifice of the pig, the sun-god Ra having declared the beast abominable.[1] Again, the story that Set was hunting a boar when he discovered and mangled the body of Osiris, and that this was the reason why pigs were sacrificed once a year,[2] is clearly a modernised version of an older story that Osiris, like Adonis and Attis, was slain or mangled by a boar, or by Set in the form of a boar. Thus, the annual sacrifice of a pig to Osiris might naturally be interpreted as vengeance inflicted on the hostile animal that had slain or mangled the god. But, in the first place, when an animal is thus killed as a solemn sacrifice once and once only in the year, it generally or always means that the animal is divine, that he is spared and respected the rest of the year as a god and slain, when he is slain, also in the character of a god.[3] In the second place, the examples of Dionysus and Demeter, if not of Attis and Adonis, have taught us that the animal which is sacrificed to a god on the ground that he is the god's enemy may have been, and probably was, originally the god himself. Therefore, the annual sacrifice of a pig to Osiris, coupled with the alleged hostility of the animal to the god, tends to shew, first, that originally the pig was a god, and, second, that he was Osiris. At a later age, when Osiris became anthropomorphic and his original relation to the pig had been forgotten, the animal was first distinguished from him, and afterwards opposed as an enemy to him by mythologists who could think of no reason for killing a beast in connexion with the worship of a god except that the beast was the god's enemy; or, as Plutarch puts it, not that which is dear to the gods, but that which is the contrary, is fit to be sacrificed.[4] At this later stage the havoc which a wild boar notoriously makes amongst the corn would supply a plausible reason for regarding him as the foe of the corn-spirit, though originally, if I am right, the very freedom with which the boar ranged at will through the corn led people to identify him with the corn-spirit, to whom he was afterwards opposed as an enemy.

376. The view which identifies the pig with Osiris derives not a little support from the sacrifice of pigs to him on the very day on which, according to tradition, Osiris himself was killed;[1] for thus the killing of the pig was the annual representation of the killing of Osiris, just as the throwing of the pigs into the caverns at the Thesmophoria was an annual representation of the descent of Persephone into the lower world; and both customs are parallel to the European practice of killing a goat, cock, and so forth, at harvest as a representative of the corn-spirit.

ABSORBING THE

DIVINE ESSENCE

377. We have now seen that the corn-spirit is represented sometimes in human, sometimes in animal form, and that in both cases he is killed in the person of his representative and eaten sacramentally. To find examples of actually killing the human representative of the corn-spirit we had naturally to go to savage races; and the same sources as well as the harvest-suppers of European peasants have furnished unmistakeable examples of the sacramental eating of animals as representatives of the corn-spirit.

378. Twice a year, for example, an image of the great Mexican god Huitzilopochtli was made of dough, then broken in pieces, and solemnly eaten by his worshippers.[1] Similarly, the Brahmans taught that the rice-cakes offered in sacrifice were substitutes for human beings, and that they were actually converted into the real bodies of men by the manipulation of the priest. We read that "when it (the rice-cake) still consists of rice-meal, it is the hair. When he pours water on it, it becomes skin. When he mixes it, it becomes flesh: for then it becomes consistent; and consistent also is the flesh. When it is baked, it becomes bone: for then it becomes somewhat hard; and hard is the bone. And when he is about to take it off (the fire) and sprinkles it with butter, he changes it into marrow. This is the completeness which they call the fivefold animal sacrifice."[2]

379. At the festival of the winter solstice in December the Aztecs killed their god Huitzilopochtli in effigy first and ate him afterwards. As a preparation for this solemn ceremony an image of the deity in the likeness of a man was fashioned out of seeds of various sorts, which were kneaded into a dough with the blood of children. The bones of the god were represented by pieces of acacia wood. This image was placed on the chief altar of the temple, and on the day of the festival the king offered incense to it. Early next day it was taken down and set on its feet in a great hall. Then a priest, who bore the name and acted the part of the god Quetzalcoatl, took a flint-tipped dart and hurled it into the breast of the dough-image, piercing it through and through. This was called "killing the god Huitzilopochtli so that his body might be eaten." One of the priests cut out the heart of the image and gave it to the king to eat. The rest of the image was divided into minute pieces, of which every man great and small, down to the male children in the cradle, received one to eat. But no woman might taste a morsel. The ceremony was called *teoqualo,* that is, "god is eaten."[1]

380. The custom of entering into communion with a god by eating of his effigy survived till lately among the Huichol Indians of Mexico. In a narrow valley, at the foot of a beetling crag of red rock, they have a small thatched temple of the god of fire, and here down to recent years stood a small image of the deity in human form roughly carved out of solidified volcanic ash. The idol was very dirty and smeared with blood, and in his right side was a hole, which owed its existence to the piety and devotion of his worshippers. For they believed that the power of healing and a knowledge of mysteries could be acquired by eating a little of the god's holy body, and accordingly shamans, or medicine-men, who desired to lay in a stock of these accomplishments, so useful in the exercise of their profession, were wont to repair to the temple, where, having deposited an offering of food or a votive bowl, they scraped off with their finger-nails some particles of the god's body and swallowed them. After engaging in this form of communion with the deity they had to abstain from salt and from all carnal converse with their wives for five months.[1] Again, the Malas, a caste of pariahs in Southern India, communicate with the goddess Sunkalamma by eating her effigy. The communion takes place at marriage. An image of the goddess in the form of a truncated cone is made out of rice and green gram cooked together, and it is decorated with a nose jewel, garlands, and other religious symbols. Offerings of race, frankincense, camphor, and a coco-nut are then made to the image, and a ram or he-goat is sacrificed. After the sacrifice has been presented, all the persons assembled prostrate themselves in silence before the image, then they break it in pieces, and distributing the pieces among themselves they swallow them. In this way they are, no doubt, believed to absorb the divine essence of the goddess whose broken body has just passed into their stomachs.[2]

381. But further, as might have been anticipated, the new corn is itself eaten sacramentally, that is, as the body of the corn-spirit. In Wermland, Sweden, the farmer's wife uses the grain of the last sheaf to bake a loaf in the shape of a little girl; this loaf is divided amongst the whole household and eaten by them.[1] Here the loaf represents the corn-spirit conceived as a maiden; just as in Scotland the corn-spirit is similarly conceived and represented by the last sheaf made up in the form of a woman and bearing the name of the Maiden. As usual, the corn-spirit is believed to reside in the last sheaf; and to eat a loaf made from the last sheaf is, therefore, to eat the corn-spirit itself. Similarly at La Palisse, in France, a man made of dough is hung upon the fir-tree which is carried on the last harvest-waggon. The tree and the dough-man are taken to the mayor's house and kept there till the vintage is over. Then the close of the harvest is celebrated by a feast at which the mayor breaks the dough-man in pieces and gives the pieces to the people to eat.[2]

382. The Aino (or Ainu) of Japan are said to distinguish various kinds of millet as male and female respectively, and these kinds, taken together, are called "the divine husband and wife cereal" (*Umurek haru kamui*). "Therefore before millet is pounded and made into cakes for general eating, the old men have a few made for themselves first to worship. When they are ready they pray to them very earnestly and say:— 'O thou cereal deity, we worship thee. Thou hast grown very well this year, and thy flavour will be sweet. Thou art good. The goddess of fire will be glad, and we also shall rejoice greatly. O thou god, O thou divine cereal, do thou nourish the people. I now partake of thee. I worship thee and give thee thanks.' After having thus prayed, they, the worshippers, take a cake and eat it, and from this time the people may all partake of the new millet. And so with many gestures of homage and words of prayer this kind of food is dedicated to the well-being of the Ainu. No doubt the cereal offering is regarded as a tribute paid to god, but that god is no other than the seed itself; and it is only a god in so far as it is beneficial to the human body."[1]

383. At the close of the rice harvest in the East Indian island of Buru, each clan (*fenna*) meets at a common sacramental meal, to which every member of the clan is bound to contribute a little of the new rice. This meal is called "eating the soul of the rice," a name which clearly indicates the sacramental character of the repast.[1]

384. Even tribes which do not till the ground sometimes observe analogous ceremonies when they gather the first wild fruits or dig the first roots of the season. Thus among the Salish and Tinneh Indians of North-West America, "before the young people eat the first berries or roots of the season, they always addressed the fruit or plant, and begged for its favour and aid. In some tribes regular First-fruit ceremonies were annually held at the time of picking the wild fruit or gathering the roots, and also among the salmon-eating tribes when the run of the 'sockeye' salmon began. These ceremonies were not so much thanksgivings, as performances to ensure a plentiful crop or supply of the particular object desired, for if they were not properly and reverently carried out there was danger of giving offence to the 'spirits' of the objects, and being deprived of them." For example, these Indians are fond of the young shoots or suckers of the wild raspberry, and they observe the following ceremony at gathering the first of them in season. "When the shoots are ready to pick, that is, when they are about six or eight inches above the ground, the chief, or directing elder of the community, instructs his wife or his daughters to pluck a small bundle of these and prepare them for eating. This they do, using a new pot or kettle for cooking them in. In the meantime all the settlement comes together to take part in the ceremony. They stand in a great circle, the presiding chief, elder, or medicine-man as the case may be, and his assistants being in their midst. Whoever is conducting the ceremony now silently invokes the spirit of the plants, the tenor of his prayer being that it will be propitious to them and grant them a good supply of the suckers. While the invocation is being made all in the circle must keep their eyes reverently closed, this being an essential part in all such ceremonies, the non-observance of which would anger the spirits and cause them to withhold the favours sought. After this part of the ceremony is over the cooked suckers are handed to the presiding officer in a newly carved dish, and a small portion is given to each person present, who reverently and decorously eats it. This brings the ceremony to a close. Later, when the berries of this plant are ripe, a second and similar ceremony takes place."[1]

The Thompson Indians of British Columbia cook and eat the sunflower root (*Balsamorrhiza sagittata,* Nutt.), but they used to regard it as a mysterious being, and observed a number of taboos in connexion with it; for example, women who were engaged in digging or cooking the root must practise continence, and no man might come near the oven where the women were baking the root. When young people ate the first berries, roots, or other products of the season, they addressed a prayer to the Sunflower-Root as follows: "I inform thee that I intend to eat thee. Mayest thou always help me to ascend, so that I may always be able to reach the tops of mountains, and may I never be clumsy! I ask this from thee, Sunflower-Root. Thou art the greatest of all in mystery." To omit this prayer would make the eater lazy and cause him to sleep long in the morning.[2]

385. These customs of the Thompson and other Indian tribes of North-West America are instructive, because they clearly indicate the motive, or at least one of the motives, which underlies the ceremonies observed at eating the first fruits of the season. That motive is a belief that the plant itself is animated by a conscious and more or less powerful spirit, who must be propitiated before the people can safely partake of the fruits or roots which are supposed to be part of his body. Now if this is true of wild fruits and roots, we may infer with some probability that it is also true of cultivated fruits and roots, such as yams, and in particular that it holds good of the cereals, such as wheat, barley, oats, rice, and maize. In all cases it seems reasonable to infer that the scruples which savages manifest at eating the first fruits of any crop, and the ceremonies which they observe before they overcome their scruples, are due at least in large measure to a notion that the plant or tree is animated by a spirit or even a deity, whose leave must be obtained, or whose favour must be sought before it is possible to partake with safety of the new crop. This indeed is plainly affirmed of the Aino: they call the millet "the divine cereal," "the cereal deity," and they pray to and worship him before they will eat of the cakes made from the new millet. And even where the indwelling divinity of the first fruits is not expressly affirmed, it appears to be implied both by the solemn preparations made for eating them and by the danger supposed to be incurred by persons who venture to partake of them without observing the prescribed ritual. In all such cases, accordingly, we may not improperly describe the eating of the new fruits as a sacrament or communion with a deity, or at all events with a powerful spirit.

Among the usages which point to this conclusion are the custom of employing either new or specially reserved vessels to hold the new fruits, and the practice of purifying the persons of the communicants and even the houses and streets of the whole town, before it is lawful to engage in the solemn act of communion with the divinity.[1] Of all modes of purification adopted on these occasions none perhaps brings out the sacramental virtue of the rite so clearly as the practice of taking a purgative before swallowing the new corn. The intention is thereby to prevent the sacred food from being polluted by contact with common food in the stomach of the eater. For the same reason Catholics partake of the Eucharist fasting; and among the pastoral Masai of Eastern Africa the young warriors, who live on meat and milk exclusively, are obliged to eat nothing but milk for so many days and then nothing but meat for so many more, and before they pass from the one food to the other they must make sure that none of the old food remains in their stomachs; this they do by swallowing a very powerful purgative and emetic.[2] Similarly, among the Suk, a tribe of British East Africa, no one may partake of meat and milk on the same day, and if he has chewed raw millet he is forbidden to drink milk for seven days.[3] Among the Wataturu, another people of Eastern Africa akin to the Masai, a warrior who had eaten antelope's flesh might not drink of milk on the same day.[4] Before changing from one food to the other the Esquimaux must wash themselves.[5] In like manner the ancient Greeks, of whose intellectual kinship with savages like the Esquimaux and the Melanesians we have already met with many proofs, laid it down as a rule that a man who had partaken of the black ram offered to Pelops at Olympia might not enter into the temple of Zeus, and that persons who had sacrificed to Telephus at Pergamus might not go up to the temple of Aesculapius until they had washed themselves,[6] just as the Esquimaux who have eaten venison must wash before they may partake of seal or whale or walrus meat. Again, at Lindus in Rhodes there was a sanctuary of some god or hero unknown into which no one who had partaken of goat's flesh or peas-pudding might enter for three days, and no one who had eaten cheese might enter for one day.[7] The prescribed interval was probably calculated to allow the obnoxious food to pass out of the body of the eater before he entered into the presence of the deity, who for some reason or other cherished an antipathy to these particular viands. At Castabus in the Carian Chersonese there was a sanctuary of Hemithea, which no one might approach who had either eaten pork or touched a pig.[8]

386. In some of the festivals which we have examined, the sacrament of first-fruits is combined with a sacrifice or presentation of them to gods or spirits, and in course of time the sacrifice of first-fruits tends to throw the sacrament into the shade, if not to supersede it. The mere fact of offering the first-fruits to the gods or spirits comes now to be thought a sufficient preparation for eating the new corn; the higher powers having received their share, man is free to enjoy the rest. This mode of viewing the new fruits implies that they are regarded no longer as themselves instinct with divine life, but merely as a gift bestowed by the gods upon man, who is bound to express his gratitude and homage to his divine benefactors by returning to them a portion of their bounty.

THE CORN-SPIRIT EATEN IN A CAKE

387. We are now able to suggest an explanation of the ancient Roman proverb, "There are many Manii at Aricia." Certain loaves in the shape of men were called by the Romans *maniae,* and it appears that this kind of loaf was especially made at Aricia, beside Lake Nemi.[1] Now, Mania, the name of one of these loaves, was also the name of the Mother or Grandmother of the Ghosts,[2] to whom woollen effigies of men and women were dedicated at the festival of the Compitalia. These effigies were hung at the doors of all the houses in Rome; one effigy was hung up for every free person in the house, and one, of a different kind, for every slave. The reason was that on this day the ghosts of the dead were believed to be going about, and it was hoped that, either out of good nature or through simple inadvertence, they would carry off the effigies at the door instead of the living people in the house. According to tradition, these woollen figures were substitutes for a former custom of sacrificing human beings. Upon data so fragmentary and uncertain, it is impossible to build with confidence; but it seems worth suggesting that the loaves in human form, which appear to have been baked at Aricia, were sacramental bread, and that in the old days, when the divine King of the Wood was annually slain, loaves were made in his image, like the paste figures of the gods in Mexico, India, and Europe, and were eaten sacramentally by his worshippers. The tradition that the founder of the sacred grove at Aricia was a man named Manius, from whom many Manii were descended, would thus be an etymological myth invented to explain the technical name of the loaves.* Moreover, we are told explicitly by ancient writers that in cases where an animal could not be easily obtained for sacrifice, it was lawful to offer an image of it made of bread or wax.[3] This substitute was often adopted by poor people,[4] and bakers made a regular business of furnishing such theriomorphic cakes.[5] When Cyzicus was besieged by Mithridates and the people could not procure a black cow to sacrifice at the rites of Persephone, they made one of dough.[6] In a Boeotian sacrifice to Heracles, in place of the ram which was the proper victim, an apple was regularly substituted, four chips being stuck in it to represent legs and two to represent horns.[7] The Athenians are said to have once offered a similar substitute for an ox,[8] and the Locrians once presented an ox made out of figs and sticks.[9] At the Athenian festival of the Diasia cakes shaped like animals were sacrificed.[10] In the same way, too, the Cheremiss of Russia occasionally offer cakes in the shape of horses instead of the real animals;[11] while it is related of a North American Indian that he was permitted to sacrifice loaves in place of twenty elands prescribed to ensure the recovery of his sick daughter.[12]

The practice of putting up dummies to divert the attention of ghosts or demons from living people is, indeed, by no means uncommon. The Tibetans, for instance, stand in fear of innumerable earth-demons, all of whom are under the authority of Old Mother Khön-ma. This goddess, who may be compared to the Roman Mania, the Mother or Grandmother of Ghosts, is dressed in golden-yellow robes, holds a golden noose in her hand, and rides on a ram. In order to bar the dwelling-house against the foul fiends, of whom Old Mother Khön-ma is mistress, an elaborate structure somewhat resembling a chandelier is fixed above the door on the outside of the house. It contains a ram's skull, a variety of precious objects such as gold-leaf, silver, and turquoise, also some dry food, such as rice, wheat, and pulse, and finally images or pictures of a man, a woman, and a house. "The object of these figures of a man, wife, and house is to deceive the demons should they still come in spite of this offering, and to mislead them into the belief that the foregoing pictures are the inmates of the house, so that they may wreak their wrath on these bits of wood and so save the real human occupants." When all is ready, a priest prays to Old Mother Khön-ma that she would be pleased to accept these dainty offerings and to close the open doors of the earth, in order that the demons may not come forth to infest and injure the household.[13]

388. Further, it is often supposed that the spirits of persons who have re-

* Indeed, a similar custom is still observed annually at Frascati, in the Alban Hills, not very far from the Lake of Nemi. During Lent the local bakers sell gingerbread cakes in the shape of human figures with three long horns, peppercorns for eyes, and a red riband around the neck. They are said to represent the Devil, and are eaten as a symbolic renunciation of him and all his works. But the custom might well be pre-Christian, and the explanation a later addition.

cently departed this life are apt to carry off with them to the world of the dead the souls of their surviving relations. Hence the savage resorts to the device of making up of dummies or effigies which he puts in the way of the ghost, hoping that the dull-witted spirit will mistake them for real people and so leave the survivors in peace. In Tahiti the priest who performed the funeral rites used to lay some slips of plantain leaf-stalk on the breast and under the arms of the corpse, saying, "There are your family, there is your child, there is your wife, there is your father, and there is your mother. Be satisfied yonder (that is, in the world of spirits). Look not towards those who are left in the world." This ceremony, we are told, was designed "to impart contentment to the departed, and to prevent the spirit from repairing to the places of his former resort, and so distressing the survivors."[1] When the Galelareese bury a corpse, they bury with it the stem of a banana-tree for company, in order that the dead person may not seek a companion among the living. Just as the coffin is being lowered into the earth, one of the bystanders step up and throws a young banana-tree into the grave, saying, "Friend, you must miss your companions of this earth; here, take this as a comrade."[2] In the Pelew Islands, when a woman has died in childbed, her spirit comes and cries, "Give me the child!" So to beguile her they bury the stem of a young banana-tree with her body, cutting it short and laying it between her right arm and her breast.[3] The same device is adopted for the same purpose in the island of Timor.[4] Among the Yorubas of West Africa, when one of twins dies, the mother carries about, along with the surviving child, a small wooden figure roughly fashioned in human shape and of the sex of the dead twin. This figure is intended not merely to keep the live child from pining for its lost comrade, but also to give the spirit of the dead child something into which it can enter without disturbing its little brother or sister.[5]

At Onitsha, a town on the left bank of the Niger, a missionary once met a funeral procession which he describes as very singular. The real body had already been buried in the house, but a piece of wood in the form of a sofa and covered up was being borne by two persons on their heads, attended by a procession of six men and six women. The men carried cutlasses and the women clapped their hands as they passed along each street, crying, "This is the dead body of him that is dead, and is gone into the world of spirits." Meantime the rest of the villagers had to keep indoors.[6] The sham corpse was probably intended as a lure to draw away prowling demons from the real body.

389. Again, effigies are often employed as a means of preventing or curing sickness; the demons of disease either mistake the effigies for living people or are persuaded or compelled to enter them, leaving the real men and women well and whole. Thus the Alfoors of Minahassa, in Celebes, will some-times transport a sick man to another house, while they leave on his bed a dummy made up of a pillow and clothes. This dummy the demon is supposed to mistake for the sick man, who consequently recovers.[1] Among the Oloh Ngadju of Borneo, when a sick man is supposed to be suffering from the assaults of a ghost, puppets of dough or rice-meal are made and thrown under the house as substitutes for the patient, who thus rids himself of the ghost.[2]

Similarly in the island of Dama, between New Guinea and Celebes, where sickness is ascribed to the agency of demons, the doctor makes a doll of palm-leaf and lays it, together with some betel, rice, and half of an empty eggshell, on the patient's head. Lured by this bait the demon quits the sufferer's body and enters the palm-leaf doll, which the wily doctor thereupon promptly decapitates. This may reasonably be supposed to make an end of the demon and of the sickness together.[3] A Burmese mode of curing a sick man is to bury a small effigy of him in a tiny coffin, after which he ought certainly to recover.[4] In Siam, when a person is dangerously ill, the magician models a small image of him in clay and carrying it away to a solitary place recites charms over it which compel the malady to pass from the sick man into the image. The sorcerer then buries the image, and the sufferer is made whole.[5] So, too, in Cambodia the doctor fashions a rude effigy of his patient in clay and deposits it in some lonely spot, where the ghost or demon takes it instead of the man.[6]

390. With these examples before us we may fairly conclude that the woollen effigies, which at the festival of the Compitalia might be seen hanging at the doors of all the houses in ancient Rome, were not substitutes for human victims who had formerly been sacrificed at this season, but rather vicarious offerings presented to the Mother or Grandmother of Ghosts, in the hope that on her rounds through the city she would accept or mistake the effigies for the inmates of the house and so spare the living for another year.

EATING FLESH TO ABSORB QUALITIES

391. The savage commonly believes that by eating the flesh of an animal or man he acquires not only the physical, but even the moral and intellectual qualities which were characteristic of that animal or man; so when the creature is deemed divine, our simple savage naturally expects to absorb a portion of its divinity along with its material substance. It may be well to illustrate by instances this common faith in the acquisition of virtues or vices of many kinds through the medium of animal food, even when there is no pretence that the viands consist of the body or blood of a god. The doctrine forms part of the widely ramified system of sympathetic or homoeopathic magic.

392. Thus, for example, the Creeks, Cherokee, and kindred tribes of North American Indians "believe that nature is possest of such a property, as to transfuse into men and animals the qualities, either of the food they use, or of those objects that are presented to their senses; he who feeds on venison is, according to their physical system, swifter and more sagacious than the man who lives on the flesh of the clumsy bear, or helpless dunghill fowls, the slow-footed tame cattle, or the heavy wallowing swine."[1] The Zaparo Indians of Ecuador "will, unless from necessity, in most cases not eat any heavy meats, such as tapir and peccary, but confine themselves to birds, monkeys, deer, fish, etc., principally because they argue that the heavier meats make them unwieldy, like the animals who supply the flesh, impeding their agility, and unfitting them for the chase."[2] Similarly some of the Brazilian Indians would eat no beast, bird, or fish that ran, flew, or swam slowly, lest by partaking of its flesh they should lose their agility and be unable to escape from their enemies.[3] The Caribs abstained from the flesh of pigs lest it should cause them to have small eyes like pigs; and they refused to partake of tortoises from a fear that they might become heavy and stupid like the animal.[4] Similarly, the Thompson River Indians of British Columbia would not eat the heart of the fool-hen, nor would they allow their dogs to devour the bird, lest they should grow foolish like it.[5] The Bushmen will not give their children a jackal's heart to eat, lest it should make them timid like the jackal; but they give them a leopard's heart to make them correspondingly brave.[6] In British Central Africa aspirants after courage consume the flesh and especially the hearts of lions, while lecherous persons eat the testicles of goats.[7] Among the Suk of British East Africa the fat and heart of the lion are sometimes given to children to eat to make them strong; but they are not allowed to know what they are eating.[8] So to restore the aged Aeson to youth, the witch Medea infused into his veins a decoction of the liver of the long-lived deer and the head of a crow that had outlived nine human generations.[9] In Norse legend, Ingiald, son of King Aunund, was timid in his youth, but after eating the heart of a wolf he became very bold; Hialto gained courage by eating the heart of a bear and drinking its blood;[10] and when Sigurd killed the dragon Fafnir and tasted his heart's blood he thereby acquired a knowledge of the language of birds.[11]

A North American Indian thought that brandy must be a decoction of hearts and tongues, because, said he, "after drinking it I fear nothing and I talk wonderfully."[12]

393. Again, the flesh and blood of *dead men* are commonly eaten and drunk to inspire bravery, wisdom, or other qualities for which those men were remarkable, or which are supposed to have their special seat in the particular part consumed. Among the Yoruba-speaking Negroes of the Slave Coast the priests of Ogun, the war-god, usually take out the hearts of human victims, which are then dried, crumbled to powder, mixed with rum, and sold to aspirants after courage, who swallow the mixture in the belief that they thereby absorb the manly virtue of which the heart is supposed to be the seat.[1] Similarly, Indians of the Orinoco region used to toast the hearts of their enemies, grind them to powder, and then drink the powder in a liquid in order to be brave and valiant the next time they went forth to fight.[2] The Nauras Indians of New Granada ate the hearts of Spaniards when they had the opportunity, hoping thereby to make themselves as dauntless as the dreaded Castilian chivalry.[3] The Sioux Indians of North America used to reduce to powder the heart of a valiant enemy and swallow the powder, hoping thus to appropriate the dead man's valour.[4] Among the Esquimaux of Bering Strait, when young men had slain an enemy for the first time in war, they were wont to drink some of the blood and to eat a small piece of the heart of their victim in order to increase their bravery.[5]

On the same principle warriors of the Theddora and Ngarigo tribes in South-Eastern Australia used to eat the hands and feet of their slain enemies, believing that they thus acquired some of the qualities and courage of the dead.[6] In Tonquin also there is a popular superstition that the liver of a brave man emboldens any who partakes of it. Hence when a Catholic missionary was beheaded in Tonquin in 1837, the executioner cut out the liver of his victim and ate part of it, while a soldier attempted to devour another part.[7] With like intent the Chinese swallow the bile of notorious bandits who have been executed.[8] The Tolalaki, notorious head-hunters of the Central Celebes, drink the blood and eat the brains of their victims in order to become brave;[9] and the Efugaos, a tribe of the Philippines, suck the brains of their foes.[10]

In Tud, or Warrior Island, in the Torres Straits, men would drink the sweat of renowned warriors, and eat the scrapings form their finger-nails which had been coated and sodden with human blood, in order to make themselves "strong like stone, no afraid."[11]

394. Just as the savage thinks that he can swallow the moral and other virtues in the shape of food, so he fondly imagines that he can inoculate himself with them. So when the Barotsé wish to be swift of foot, to cripple the fleeing game, and to ensure an abundant catch, they scarify their arms and legs and rub into the wounds a powder made of the burnt bones of various beasts and birds.[1] Among some Caffre tribes the powdered charcoal with which the warriors are thus inoculated in various parts of their bodies is procured by burning the flesh of a live ox with a certain kind of wood or roots, to which magic virtue is attributed.[2] The Basutos think that they can render themselves invulnerable by inoculation,[3] and the Zulus imagine that they can protect themselves against snake-bite by similar means.[4]

395. It is not always deemed necessary either that the mystical substance should be swallowed by the communicant, or that he should receive it by the more painful process of scarification and inoculation. Sometimes it is thought enough merely to smear or anoint him with it. Among some of the Australian blacks it used to be a common practice to kill a man, cut out his caul-fat, and rub themselves with it, in the belief that all the qualities, both physical and mental, which had distinguished the original owner of the fat, were thus communicated by its means to the person who greased himself with it.[1] The Kamilaroi tribe of New South Wales sometimes deposited their dead on the forks of trees, and lighting fires underneath caught the fat as it dropped; for they hoped with the droppings to acquire the strength and courage of the deceased.[2] Again, the Negroes of Southern Guinea regard the brain as the seat of wisdom, and think it a pity that, when a wise man dies, his brain and his wisdom should go to waste together. So they sever his head from his body and hang it up over a mass of chalk, which, as the head decays, receives the drippings of brain and wisdom. Any one who applies the precious dripping to his forehead is supposed to absorb thereby the intelligence of the dead.[3] The Arabs of Eastern Africa believe that an unguent made out of lion's fat inspires a man with boldness and makes wild beasts flee in terror before him.[4]

In ancient Mexico the priests of the god Tezcatlipoca, before they engaged in religious rites which tried the nerve, used to smear their bodies with a magic ointment, which had the effect of banishing all fear, so that they would confront wild beasts in their dens or slaughter people in sacrifice with the utmost indifference. The ointment which had this marvellous property was compounded of the ashes of venomous reptiles and insects, such as spiders, scorpions, centipedes, and vipers, which were brayed up in a mortar along with living specimens of the same creatures, tobacco, soot, and the ashes of black caterpillars. This precious substance was then set before the god in little pots, because they said it was his victuals; therefore they called it a divine food. And when the priests had besmeared themselves with it, they were ready to discharge the duties of their holy office by butchering their fellow men in the human shambles without one qualm of fear or one visiting of compassion. Moreover, an unction of this ointment was deemed a sovereign remedy for sickness and disease; hence they named it "the divine physic"; and sick people came from all quarters to the priests, as to their saviours, to have their ailing parts anointed with the divine physic and to be made whole.[5]

396. It is now easy to understand why a savage should desire to partake of the flesh of an animal or man whom he regards as divine. By eating the body of the god he shares in the god's attributes and powers. And when the god is a corn-god, the corn is his proper body; when he is a vine-god, the juice of the grape is his blood; and so by eating the bread and drinking the wine the worshipper partakes of the real body and blood of his god. Thus the drinking of wine in the rites of a vine-god like Dionysus is not an act of revelry, it is a solemn sacrament.[1]

KILLING THE DIVINE ANIMAL

397. In the preceding chapters we saw that many communities which have progressed so far as to subsist mainly by agriculture have been in the habit of killing and eating their farinaceous deities either in their proper form of corn, rice, and so forth, or in the borrowed shapes of animals and men. It remains to shew that hunting and pastoral tribes, as well as agricultural peoples, have been in the habit of killing the beings whom they worship. Among the worshipful beings or gods, if indeed they deserve to be dignified by that name, whom hunters and shepherds adore and kill are animals pure and simple, not animals regarded as embodiments of other supernatural beings.

398. The Thebans and all other Egyptians who worshipped the Theban god Ammon held rams to be sacred, and would not sacrifice them. But once a year at the festival of Ammon they killed a ram, skinned it, and clothed the image of the god in the skin. Then they mourned over the ram and buried it in a sacred tomb. The custom was explained by a story that Zeus had once exhibited himself to Hercules clad in the fleece and wearing the head of a ram.[1] Of course the ram in this case was simply the beast-god of Thebes, as the wolf was the beast-god of Lycopolis, and the goat was the beast-god of Mendes. In other words, the ram was Ammon himself. It was killed therefore not as a sacrifice to Ammon, but as the god himself, whose identity with the beast is plainly shewn by the custom of clothing his image in the skin of the slain ram. The reason for thus killing the ram-god annually may have been that which I have assigned for the general custom of killing a god. As applied to Egypt, this explanation is supported by the analogy of the bull-god Apis, who was not suffered to outlive a certain term of years. The intention of thus putting a limit to the life of the human god was, as I have argued, to secure him from the weakness and frailty of age. The same reasoning would explain the custom—probably an older one—of putting the beast-god to death annually, as was done with the ram of Thebes.

399. One point in the Theban ritual—the application of the skin to the image of the god—deserves particular attention. If the god was at first the living ram, his representation by an image must have originated later. But how did it originate? One answer to this question is perhaps furnished by the practice of preserving the skin of the animal which is slain as divine. The skin in fact was kept as a token or memorial of the god, or rather as containing in it a part of the divine life, and it had only to be stuffed or stretched upon a frame to become a regular image of him. At first an image of this kind would be renewed annually, the new image being provided by the skin of the slain animal. But from annual images to permanent images the transition is easy. We have seen that the older custom of cutting a new May-tree every year was superseded by the practice of maintaining a permanent May-pole, which was, however, annually decked with fresh leaves and flowers, and even surmounted each year by a fresh young tree. Similarly when the stuffed skin, as a representative of the god, was replaced by a permanent image of him in wood, stone, or metal, the permanent image was annually clad in the fresh skin of the slain animal. When this stage had been

considerately placed beside it. Custom requires that the guests should eat up the whole animal before they depart: the use of salt and pepper at the meal is forbidden; and no morsel of the flesh may be given to the dogs. When the banquet is over, the head is carried away into the depth of the forest and deposited on a heap of bears' skulls, the bleached and mouldering relics of similar festivals in the past.[1]

403. The Gilyaks, a Tunguzian people of Eastern Siberia, hold a bear-festival of the same sort once a year in January. "The bear is the object of the most refined solicitude of an entire village and plays the chief part in their religious ceremonies."[1] An old she-bear is shot and her cub is reared, but not suckled, in the village. When the bear is big enough he is taken from his cage and dragged through the village. But first they lead him to the bank of the river, for this is believed to ensure abundance of fish to each family. He is then taken into every house in the village, where fish, brandy, and so forth are offered to him. Some people prostrate themselves before the beast. His entrance into a house is supposed to bring a blessing; and if he snuffs at the food offered to him, this also is a blessing. Nevertheless they tease and worry, poke and tickle the animal continually, so that he is surly and snappish. After being thus taken to every house, he is tied to a peg and shot dead with arrows. His head is then cut off, decked with shavings, and placed on the table where the feast is set out. Here they beg pardon of the beast and worship him. Then his flesh is roasted and eaten in special vessels of wood finely carved. They do not eat the flesh raw nor drink the blood, as the Aino do. The brain and entrails are eaten last; and the skull, still decked with shavings, is placed on a tree near the house. Then the people sing and both sexes dance in ranks, as bears.[2]

404. The Goldi, neighbours of the Gilyaks, treat the bear in much the same way. They hunt and kill it; but sometimes they capture a live bear and keep him in a cage, feeding him well and calling him their son and brother. Then at a great festival he is taken from his cage, paraded about with marked consideration, and afterwards killed and eaten. "The skull, jaw-bones, and ears are then suspended on a tree, as an antidote against evil spirits; but the flesh is eaten and much relished, for they believe that all who partake of it acquire a zest for the chase, and become courageous."[1]

405. The Orotchis, another Tunguzian people of the region of the Amoor, hold bear-festivals of the same general character. Any one who catches a bear cub considers it his bounden duty to rear it in a cage for about three years, in order at the end of that time to kill it publicly and eat the flesh with his friends. The feasts being public, though organised by individuals, the people try to have one in each Orotchi village every year in turn. When the bear is taken out of his cage, he is led about by means of ropes to all the huts, accompanied by people armed with lances, bows, and arrows. At each hut the bear and bear-leaders are treated to something good to eat and drink.

This goes on for several days until all the huts, not only in that village but also in the next, have been visited. The days are given up to sport and noisy jollity. Then the bear is tied to a tree or wooden pillar and shot to death by the arrows of the crowd, after which its flesh is roasted and eaten. Among the Orotchis of the Tundja River women take part in the bear-feasts, while among the Orotchis of the River Vi the women will not even touch bear's flesh.[1]

406. Thus the apparent contradiction in the practice of these tribes, who venerate and almost deify the animals which they habitually hunt, kill, and eat, is not so flagrant as at first sight it appears to us: the people have reasons, and some very practical reasons, for acting as they do. For the savage is by no means so illogical and unpractical as to superficial observers he is apt to seem; he has thought deeply on the questions which immediately concern him, he reasons about them, and though his conclusions often diverge very widely from ours, we ought not to deny him the credit of patient and prolonged meditation on some fundamental problems of human existence. In the present case, if he treats bears in general as creatures wholly subservient to human needs and yet singles out certain individuals of the species for homage which almost amounts to deification, we must not hastily set him down as irrational and inconsistent, but must endeavour to place ourselves at his point of view, to see things as he sees them, and to divest ourselves of the prepossessions which tinge so deeply our own views of the world. If we do so, we shall probably discover that, however absurd his conduct may appear to us, the savage nevertheless generally acts on a train of reasoning which seems to him in harmony with the facts of his limited experience.

The Propitiation of Animals by Huntsmen

407. The explanation of life by the theory of an indwelling and practically immortal soul is one which the savage does not confine to human beings but extends to the animate creation in general. In so doing he is more liberal and perhaps more logical than the civilised man, who commonly denies to animals that privilege of immortality which he claims for himself. The savage is not so proud; he commonly believes that animals are endowed with feelings and intelligence like those of men, and that, like men, they possess souls which survive the death of their bodies either to wander about as disembodied spirits or to be born again in animal form. Accordingly he makes it a rule to spare the life of those animals which he has no pressing motive for killing, at least such fierce and dangerous animals as are likely to exact a bloodly vengeance for the slaughter of one of their kind. For example, the Dyaks of Borneo will not kill a crocodile unless a crocodile has first killed a man;[1] and the same principle obtains also among the Alurs around the Albert Nyanza Lake,[2] and among various native tribes of Madagascar.[3]

408. Again, the *tiger* is another of those dangerous beasts whom the savage prefers to leave alone, lest by killing one of the species he should excite the hostility of the rest. No consideration will induce a Sumatran to catch or wound a tiger except in self-defence or immediately after a tiger has destroyed a friend or relation.[1] If it is necessary to kill a tiger which has wrought much harm in the village, the Minangkabauers of Sumatra try to catch him alive in order to beg for his forgiveness before despatching him, and in ordinary life they will not speak evil of him or do anything that might displease him.[2] The natives of Cochin China have a great respect for the tiger, whom they regard as a terrible divinity. Yet they set traps for him and leave no stone unturned to catch him. Once he is ensnared, they offer him their excuses and condolences for the painful position in which he finds himself.[3]

409. Again the Seminole Indians spared the *rattlesnake,* because they feared that the soul of the dead rattlesnake would incite its kinsfolk to take vengeance.[1] The Delaware Indians also paid great respect to the rattlesnake, whom they called their grandfather, and they would on no account destroy one of the reptiles. They said that the rattlesnake guarded them and gave them notice of impending danger by his rattle, and that if they were to kill a rattlesnake, the rest of the species would soon hear of it and bite the Indians in revenge.[2] Few Cherokee will venture to kill a rattlesnake, unless they cannot help it, and even then they must atone for the crime by craving pardon of the snake's ghost either in their own person or through the mediation of a priest, according to a set formula.[3]

410. When the Kwakiutl Indians of British Columbia have slain a *wolf* they lay the carcase on a blanket and take out the heart, of which every person who helped to kill the beast must eat four morsels. Then they wail over the body, saying, "Woe! our great friend!" After that they cover the carcase with a blanket and bury it. A bow or gun that killed a wolf is regarded as unlucky, and the owner gives it away.[1] When the Chuckchees of north-eastern Siberia have killed a wolf, they hold a festival, at which they cry, "Wolf, be not angry with us. It was not we who killed you, it was the Russians who destroyed you."[2] In ancient Athens any man who killed a wolf had to bury it by subscription.[3]

411. In Jebel-Nuba, a district of the eastern Sudan, it is forbidden to touch the nests or remove the young of a species of *black birds,* because the people believe that the parent birds would avenge the wrong by causing a stormy wind to blow, which would destroy the harvest.[1] Some of the Sudanese Negroes of Upper Egypt regard the great black raven (*Corvus umbrinus*) as their uncle and exact pecuniary compensation or blood-money from any one who has been so rash as to slay their sable relative. Having satisfied their scruples on that head, they give the bird a solemn burial, carrying the corpse to the graveyard on a bier with flags and shouts of *la il Allah,* just as if they were interring one of their kinsfolk.[2]

412. But the savage clearly cannot afford to spare all animals. He must either eat some of them or starve, and when the question thus comes to be whether he or the animal must perish, he is forced to overcome his superstitious scruples and take the life of the beast. At the same time he does all he can to appease his victims and their kinsfolk. Even in the act of killing them he testifies his respect for them, endeavours to excuse or even conceal his share in procuring their death, and promises that their remains will be honourably treated. By thus robbing death of its terrors he hopes to reconcile his victims to their fate and to induce their fellows to come and be killed also. For example, it was a principle with the Kamtchatkans never to kill a land or sea animal without first making excuses to it and begging that the animal would not take it ill. Also they offered it cedar-nuts and so forth, to make it think that it was not a victim but a guest at a feast.[1] When the Ostiaks have hunted and killed a bear, they cut off its head and hang it on a tree. Then they gather round in a circle and pay it divine honours. Next they run towards the carcase uttering lamentations and saying, "Who killed you? It was the Russians. Who cut off your head? It was a Russian axe. Who skinned you? It was a knife made my a Russian." They explain, too, that the feathers which sped the arrow on its flight came from the wing of a strange bird, and that they did nothing but let the arrow go.[2] When the Lapps had succeeded in killing a bear with impunity, they thanked him for not hunting them and for not breaking the clubs and spears which had given him his death wounds; and they prayed that he would not requite his death by sending storms or other adversities.[3]

413. The reverence of hunters for the *bear* whom they regularly kill and eat may thus be traced all along the northern region of the Old World, from the Bering Straits to Lappland. It reappears in similar forms in North America. When men of the Bear clan in the Otawa tribe killed a bear, they made him a feast of his own flesh, and addressed him thus: "Cherish us no grudge because we have killed you. You have sense; you see that our children are hungry. They love you and wish to take you into their bodies. Is it not glorious to be eaten by the children of a chief?"[1] Amongst the Nutka Indians of British Columbia, when a bear had been killed, it was brought in and seated before the head chief in an upright posture, with a chief's bonnet, wrought in figures, on its head, and its fur powdered over with white down. A tray of provisions was then set before it, and it was invited by words and gestures to eat. After that the animal was skinned, boiled, and eaten.[2] The Ojibways will not suffer dogs to eat the flesh or gnaw the bones of a bear, and they throw all the waste portions into the fire. They think that if the flesh were desecrated, they would have no luck in hunting bears thereafter.[3]

414. A like respect is testified for other dangerous creatures by the hunters who regularly trap and kill them. When Caffre hunters are in the act of showering spears on an *elephant,* they call out, "Don't kill us, great captain;

don't strike or tread upon us, mighty chief."[1] When he is dead they make their excuses to him, pretending that his death was a pure accident. As a mark of respect they bury his trunk with much solemn ceremony; for they say that "the elephant is a great lord; his trunk is his hand."[2] When the Baganda have killed an elephant, they extract the nerve from the tusk and bury it, taking care to mark the place of the burial. For they think that the ghost of the dead elephant attaches itself to the nerve, and that if a hunter were to step over the nerve, the elephant's ghost would cause him to be killed by an elephant the next time he went forth to hunt the beasts.[3] Among some tribes of Eastern Africa, when a lion is killed, the carcase is brought before the king, who does homage to it by prostrating himself on the ground and rubbing his face on the muzzle of the beast;[4] and in some parts of Western Africa if a Negro kills a *leopard* he is bound fast and brought before the chiefs for having killed one of their peers.[5]

415. The Baganda greatly fear the ghosts of *buffaloes* which they have killed, and they always appease these dangerous spirits. On no account will they bring the head of a slain buffalo into a village or into a garden of plantains: they always eat the flesh of the head in the open country. Afterwards they place the skull in a small hut built for the purpose, where they pour out beer as an offering and pray to the ghost to stay where he is and not harm them.[1]

416. Another formidable beast whose life the savage hunter takes with joy, yet with fear and trembling, is the *whale*.

When the inhabitants of the Isle of St. Mary, to the north of Madagascar, go a-whaling, they single out the young whales for attack and "humbly beg the mother's pardon, stating the necessity that drives them to kill her progeny, and requesting that she will be pleased to go below while the deed is doing, that her maternal feelings may not be outraged by witnessing what must cause her so much uneasiness."[1]

417. But it is not merely dangerous creatures with whom the savage desires to keep on good terms. It is true that the respect which he pays to wild beasts is in some measure proportioned to their strength and ferocity. Thus the savage Stiens of Cambodia, believing that *all* animals have souls which roam about after their death, beg an animal's pardon when they kill it, lest its soul should come and torment them.[1] Cherokee hunters ask pardon of the deer they kill. If they failed to do so, they think that the Little Deer, the chief of the deer tribe, who can never die or be wounded, would track the hunter to his home by the blood-drops on the ground and would put the spirit of rheumatism into him. Sometimes the hunter, on starting for home, lights a fire in the trail behind him to prevent the Little Deer from pursuing him.[2] Before they went out to hunt for deer, antelope, or elk the Apaches used to resort to sacred caves, where the medicine-men propitiated with prayer and sacrifice the animal gods whose progeny they intended to destroy.[3]

The Indians of Louisiana bewailed bitterly the death of the buffaloes which they were about to kill.[4] Some of the North American Indians believed that each sort of animal had its patron or genius who watched over and preserved it. An Indian girl having once picked up a dead mouse, her father snatched the little creature from her and tenderly caressed and fondled it. Being asked why he did so, he said that it was to appease the genius of mice, in order that he might not torment his daughter for eating the mouse. With that he handed the mouse to the girl and she ate it.[5] The Greenlanders are careful not to fracture the heads of seals or throw them into the sea, but pile them in a heap before the door, that the souls of the seals may not be enraged and scare their brethren from the coast.[6]

For like reasons, a tribe which depends for its subsistence, chiefly or in part, upon fishing is careful to treat the fish with every mark of honour and respect. The Kwakiutl Indians of British Columbia think that when a salmon is killed its soul returns to the salmon country. Hence they take care to throw the bones and offal into the sea, in order that the soul may reanimate them at the resurrection of the salmon. Whereas if they burned the bones the soul would be lost, and so it would be quite impossible for that salmon to rise from the dead.[7] In like manner the Otawa Indians of Canada, believing that the souls of dead fish passed into other bodies of fish, never burned fish bones, for fear of displeasing the souls of the fish, who would come no more to the nets.[8] The Hurons also refrained from throwing fish bones into the fire, lest the souls of the fish should go and warn the other fish not to let themselves be caught, since the Hurons would burn their bones.[9] The disappearance of herring from the sea about Heligoland in 1530 was attributed by the fishermen to the misconduct of two lads who had whipped a freshly-caught herring and then flung it back into the sea.[10]

418. With some savages a special reason for respecting the bones of game, and generally of the animals which they eat, is a belief that, if the bones are preserved, they will in course of time be reclothed with flesh, and thus the animal will come to life again. It is, therefore, clearly for the interest of the hunter to leave the bones intact, since to destroy them would be to diminish the future supply of game. Many of the Minnetaree Indians "believe that the bones of those bisons which they have slain and divested of flesh rise again clothed with renewed flesh, and quickened with life, and become fat, and fit for slaughter the succeeding June."[1] Hence on the western prairies of America, the skulls of buffaloes may be seen arranged in circles and symmetrical piles, awaiting the resurrection.[2] After feasting on a dog, the Dakotas carefully collect the bones, scrape, wash, and bury them, "partly, as it is said, to testify to the dog-species, that in feasting upon one of their number no disrespect was meant to the species itself, and partly also from a belief that the bones of the animal will rise and reproduce another.[3] The objection commonly entertained by primitive peoples against breaking the bones of animals which they have eaten or sacrificed[4] may be based either on a belief in the eventual resurrection of the animal or on a fear of intimidating other creatures of the same species and of offending the ghosts of the slain animals. The reluctance of North American Indians and Esquimaux to let dogs gnaw the bones of animals[5] may well belong to this sphere of ideas; it is perhaps only a precaution to prevent those bones from being broken.

419. Besides the animals which primitive man dreads for their strength and ferocity, and those which he reveres on account of the benefits which he expects from them, there is another class of creatures which he sometimes deems it necessary to conciliate by worship and sacrifice. These are the vermin that infest his crops and his cattle.

Thus Esthonian peasants, in the island of Oesel, stand in great awe of the weevil, an insect which is exceedingly destructive to the grain. They give it a fine name, and if a child is about to kill a weevil they say, "Don't do it; the more we hurt him, the more he hurts us." If they find a weevil they bury it in the earth instead of killing it. Some even put the weevil under a stone in the field and offer corn to it.[1] Among the Saxons of Transylvania, in order to keep sparrows from the corn, the sower begins by throwing the first handful of seed backwards over his head, saying, "That is for you, sparrows." To guard the corn against the attacks of leaf-flies (*Erdflöhe*) he shuts his eyes and scatters three handfuls of oats in different directions. Having made this offering to the leaf-flies he feels sure that they will spare the corn. A Transylvanian way of securing the crops against all birds, beasts, and insects, is this: after he has finished sowing, the sower goes once more from end to end of the field imitating the gesture of sowing, but with an empty hand. As he does so he says, "I sow this for the animals; I sow it for everything that flies and creeps, that walks and stands, that sings and springs, in the name of God the Father, etc."[2] The Huzuls of the Carpathians even celebrate a festival of weasels either on St. Matthew's day (9th August, old style, 21st August, new style), or on St. Catherine's day (24th November, old style, 6th December, new style), when no work may be done, lest the weasels should harm the herds.[3] The following is a German way of freeing a garden from caterpillars. After sunset or at midnight the mistress of the house, or another female member of the family, walks all round the garden dragging a broom after her. She must not look behind her, and must keep murmuring, "Good evening, Mother Caterpillar, you shall come with your husband to church." The garden gate is left open till the following morning.[4]

420. The attempts thus made by European peasants to mollify the rage and avert the ravages of vermin have their counterpart in the similar observances of savages. When the Matabele find caterpillars in their fields they put an ear of corn in a calabash, fill the vessel up with caterpillars, and set it down on a path leading to another village, hoping thus to induce the insects to migrate thither.[1] The Yabim of German New Guinea imagine that the caterpillars and worms which infest their fields of taro are animated by the souls of the human dead; hence in order to rid the crops of these vermin they politely request the insects to leave the fields and repair to the village. "Ye locusts, worms, and caterpillars," they say, "who have died or hanged yourselves, or have been killed by a falling log or devoured by a shark, go into the village."[2] There is a certain ant whose destructive ravages are dreaded by the people of Nias. Generally they wage war on it by means of traps and other devices; but at the time of the rice-harvest they cease to call the insect by its common name, and refer to it under the title of Sibaia, a good spirit who is supposed to protect the crop from harm.[3] In South Mirzapur, when locusts threaten to eat up the fruits of the earth, the people catch one, decorate his head with a spot of red lead, salaam to him, and let him go. After these civilities he immediately departs along with his fellows.[4]

421. Sometimes in dealing with vermin the farmer aims at hitting a happy mean between excessive rigour on the one hand and weak indulgence on the other; kind but firm, he tempers severity with mercy. An ancient Greek treatise on farming advises the husbandman who would rid his lands of mice to act thus: "Take a sheet of paper and write on it as follows: 'I adjure you, ye mice here present, that ye neither injure me nor suffer another mouse to do so. I give you yonder field' (here you specify the field); 'but if ever I catch you here again, by the Mother of the Gods I will rend you in seven pieces.' Write this, and stick the paper on an unhewn stone in the field before sunrise, taking care to keep the written side up."[1] In the Ardennes they say that to get rid of rats you should repeat the following words: "*Erat verbum, apud Deum vestrum.* Male rats and female rats, I conjure you, by the great God, to go out of my house, out of all my habitations, and to betake yourselves to such and such a place, there to end your days. *Decretis, reversis et desembarassis virgo potens, clemens, justitiae.*" Then write the same words on pieces of paper, fold them up, and place one of them under the door by which the rats are to go forth, and the other on the road which they are to take. This exorcism should be performed at sunrise.[2] Some years ago an American farmer was reported to have written a civil letter to the rats, telling them that his crops were short, that he could not afford to keep them through the winter, that he had been very kind to them, and that for their own good he thought they had better leave him and go to some of his neighbours who had more grain. This document he pinned to a post in his barn for the rats to read.[3]

422. Sometimes the desired object is supposed to be attained by treating with high distinction one or two chosen individuals of the obnoxious species, while the rest are pursued with relentless rigour. In the East Indian island of Bali, the mice which ravage the rice-fields are caught in great numbers, and burned in the same way that corpses are burned. But two of the captured mice are allowed to live, and receive a little packet of white linen. Then the people bow down before them, as before gods, and let them go.[1] In the Kangean archipelago, East Indies, when the mice prove very destructful to the rice-crop, the people rid themselves of the pest in the following manner. On a Friday, when the usual service in the mosque is over, four pairs of mice are solemnly united in marriage by the priest. Each pair is then shut up in a miniature canoe about a foot long. These canoes are filled with rice and other fruits of the earth, and the four pairs of mice are then escorted to the sea-shore just as if it were a real wedding. Wherever the procession passes the people beat with all their might on their rice-blocks. On reaching the shore, the canoes, with their little inmates, are launched and left to the mercy of the winds and waves.[2] In Albania, if the fields or vineyards are ravaged by locusts or beetles, some of the women will assemble with dishevelled hair, catch a few of the insects, and march with them in a funeral procession to a spring or stream, in which they drown the creatures. Then one of the women sings, "O locusts and beetles who have left us bereaved," and the dirge is taken up and repeated by all the women in chorus. Thus by celebrating the obsequies of a few locusts and beetles, they hope to bring about the death of them all.[3] When caterpillars invaded a vineyard or field in Syria, the virgins were gathered, and one of the caterpillars was taken and a girl made its mother. Then they bewailed and buried it. Thereafter they conducted the "mother" to the place where the caterpillars were, consoling her, in order that all the caterpillars might leave the garden.[4] On the first of September, Russian girls "make small coffins of turnips and other vegetables, enclose flies and other insects in them, and then bury them with a great show of mourning."[5] In South Africa a plague of caterpillars is removed by a number of small Caffre girls, who go singing through the fields. They wail as they pass through the languishing crops, and thus invoke the aid and pity of some ancestral spirits. The mournful rite ends with a dance on a plot of ground overlooking the fields.[6]

423. Another mode of getting rid of vermin and other noxious creatures without hurting their feelings or shewing them disrespect is to make images of them. Apollonius of Tyana is said to have cleared Antioch of scorpions by making a bronze image of a scorpion and burying it under a small pillar in the middle of the city.[1] Further, it is reported that he freed Constantinople from flies by means of a bronze fly, and from gnats by means of a bronze gnat.[2] In the Middle Ages Virgil passed for an enchanter and is said to have rid Naples of flies and grasshoppers by bronze or copper images of these insects; and when the waters of the city were infested by leeches, he made a golden leech, which put a stop to the plague.[3] It is reported that a mosque at Fez used to be protected against scorpions by an image of a bird holding a scorpion in its beak.[4] An Arab writer tells of a golden locust which guarded a certain town from a plague of locusts; and he also mentions two brazen oxen which checked a murrain among cattle.[5] So when a swarm of serpents afflicted the

Israelites in the desert, they made a serpent of brass and set it on a pole as a mode of staying the plague.[6]

TYPES OF ANIMAL SACRAMENTS

424. We are now perhaps in a position to understand the ambiguous behaviour of the Aino and Gilyaks towards the bear. It has been shewn that the sharp line of demarcation which we draw between mankind and the lower animals does not exist for the savage. To him many of the other animals appear as his equals or even his superiors, not merely in brute force but in intelligence; and if choice or necessity leads him to take their lives, he feels bound, out of regard to his own safety, to do it in a way which will be as inoffensive as possible not merely to the living animal, but to its departed spirit and to all the other animals of the same species, which would resent an affront put upon one of their kind much as a tribe of savages would revenge an injury or insult offered to a tribesman. We have seen that among the many devices by which the savage seeks to atone for the wrong done by him to his animal victims one is to shew marked deference to a few chosen individuals of the species, for such behaviour is apparently regarded as entitling him to exterminate with impunity all the rest of the species upon which he can lay hands. This principle perhaps explains the attitude, at first sight puzzling and contradictory, of the Aino towards the bear. The flesh and skin of the bear regularly afford them food and clothing; but since the bear is an intelligent and powerful animal, it is necessary to offer some satisfaction or atonement to the bear species for the loss which it sustains in the death of so many of its members. This satisfaction or atonement is made by rearing young bears, treating them, so long as they live, with respect, and killing them with extraordinary marks of sorrow and devotion. So the other bears are appeased, and do not resent the slaughter of their kind by attacking the slayers or deserting the country, which would deprive the Aino of one of their means of subsistence.

Thus the primitive worship of animals assumes two forms, which are in some respects the converse of each other. On the one hand, animals are worshipped, and are therefore neither killed nor eaten. On the other hand, animals are worshipped because they are habitually killed and eaten. In both forms of worship the animal is revered on account of some benefit, positive or negative, which the savage hopes to receive from it. In the former the benefit comes either in the positive form of protection, advice, and help which the animal affords the man, or in the negative one of abstinence from injuries which it is in the power of the animal to inflict. In the latter the benefit takes the material form of the animal's flesh and skin. The two forms are in some measure antithetical: in the one, the animal is not eaten because it is revered; in the other, it is revered because it is eaten. But both may be practised by the same people, as we see in the case of the North American Indians, who, while they apparently revere and spare their totem animals, also revere the animals

such as the return of a son home after a very prolonged absence."[3] The sorrow thus manifested by the people at the annual slaughter of the lamb clearly indicates that the lamb slain is a sacred or divine animal, whose death is mourned by his worshippers. The smearing each of the worshippers with the blood of the lamb is a form of communion with the divinity; the vehicle of the divine life is applied externally instead of being taken internally, as when the blood is drunk or the flesh eaten.

ABSORPTION BY OSMOSIS

427. The form of communion in which the sacred animal is taken from house to house, that all may enjoy a share of its divine influence, has been exemplified by the Gilyak custom of promenading the bear through the village before it is slain.[1] Ceremonies closely analogous have survived in Europe into recent times, and doubtless date from a very primitive paganism. The best-known example is the "hunting of the wren." By many European peoples— the ancient Greeks and Romans, the modern Italians, Spaniards, French, Danes, Germans, Dutch, Swedes, English, and Welsh—the wren has been designated the king, the little king, the king of birds, the hedge king, and so forth,[2] and has been reckoned amongst those birds which it is extremely unlucky to kill.

Nevertheless the custom of annually killing the wren has prevailed widely both in this country and in France. In the Isle of Man down to the eighteenth century it was observed on Christmas Eve or rather Christmas morning. On the twenty-fourth of December, towards evening, all the servants got a holiday; they did not go to bed all night, but rambled about till the bells rang in all the churches at midnight. When prayers were over, they went to hunt the wren, and having found one of these birds they killed it and fastened it to the top of a long pole with its wings extended. Thus they carried it in procession to every house chanting the following rhyme:—

> "We hunted the wren for Robin the Bobbin,
> We hunted the wren for Jack of the Can,
> We hunted the wren for Robin the Bobbin,
> We hunted the wren for every one."

When they had gone from house to house and collected all the money they could, they laid the wren on a bier and carried it in procession to the parish churchyard, where they made a grave and buried it "with the utmost solemnity, singing dirges over her in the Manks language, which they call her knell; after which Christmas begins." Even to the present time, in the twentieth century, the custom is generally observed, at least in name, on St. Stephen's Day (December 26), throughout the Isle of Man.[3]

A writer of the eighteenth century attests the same usage in Ireland;[4] while it is still observed sporadically in Leinster and Connaught.[5] In Essex a similar custom used to obtain at Christmas,[6] and in Pembrokeshire a wren, called the King, was formerly carried around on Twelfth Day in a box with glass windows surmounted by a wheel, from which hung variously coloured ribbons. The men and boys who carried it from house to house sang songs, in one of which they invoked joy, health, love, and peace upon the inhabitants.[7] At Entraigues men and boys used to hunt the wren on Christmas Eve. When they caught one alive they presented it to the priest, who, after the midnight mass, set the bird free in the church. At Mirabeau the priest blessed the bird. If the men failed to catch a wren and the women succeeded in doing so, the women had the right to mock and insult the men, and to blacken their faces with mud and soot, when they caught them.[8] At La Ciotat, near Marseilles, a large body of men armed with swords and pistols used to hunt the wren every year about the end of December. When a wren was caught it was hung on the middle of a pole, which two men carried, as if it were a heavy burden. Thus they paraded round the town; the bird was weighed in a great pair of scales; and then the company sat down to table and made merry.[9]

428. The parallelism between this custom of "hunting the wren" and some of those which we have considered, especially the annual procession with the bear among the Gilyaks of Siberia, seems too close to allow us to doubt that they all belong to the same circle of ideas. The worshipful animal is killed with special solemnity once a year; and before or immediately after death he is promenaded from door to door, that each of his worshippers may receive a portion of the divine virtues that are supposed to emanate from the dead or dying god.

429. In the "hunting of the wren," there is nothing to shew that the customs in question have any relation to agriculture. So far as appears, they may date from a time before the invention of husbandry when animals were revered as divine in themselves, not merely as divine because they embodied the corn-spirit; and the analogy of the Gilyak procession of the bear is in favour of assigning the corresponding European customs to this very early date. On the other hand, there are certain European processions of animals, or of men disguised as animals, which may perhaps be purely agricultural in their origin; in other words, the animals which figure in them may have been from the first nothing but representatives of the corn-spirit conceived in animal shape. Thus, for example, in country districts of Bohemia it is, or used to be, customary during the last days of the Carnival for young men to go about in procession from house to house collecting gratuities. Usually a man or boy is swathed from head to foot in pease-straw and wrapt round in straw-ropes: thus attired he goes by the name of the Shrovetide or Carnival Bear (*Fastnachtsbär*) and is led from house to house to the accompaniment of music and singing. In every house he dances with the girls, the maids, and the housewife herself, and drinks to the health of the good man, the good wife, and the girls. For this performance the mummer is regaled with food by the good wife, while the good man puts money in his box. In the Leitmeritz district the Shrovetide Bear, besides being wrapt in straw, sometimes wears a bear's mask to emphasise his resemblance to the animal.[1]

In England a custom like some of the preceding still prevails at Whittlesey in Cambridgeshire on the Tuesday after Plough Monday: a 'straw-bear'— that is, a man completely swathed in straw—is led by a string and made to dance in front of people's houses, in return for which money is expected.[2]

430. A comparison of this English custom with the similar Continental customs which have been described above, raises a presumption that the Straw-bear, who is thus led about from house to house, represents the corn-spirit bestowing his blessing on every homestead in the village. This interpretation is strongly confirmed by the date at which the ceremony takes place, for it can hardly be doubted that the old popular celebration of Plough Monday has a direct reference to agriculture. On that day it used to be the custom in various parts of England for a band of sturdy swains to drag a gaily decorated plough from house to house and village to village, collecting contributions which were afterwards spent in rustic revelry at a tavern. The men who drew the plough were called Plough Bullocks; they wore their shirts over their coats, and bunches of ribbons flaunted from their hats and persons. Among them there was always one who personated a much bedizened old woman called Bessy; under his gown he formerly had a bullock's tail fastened to him behind, but this appendage was afterwards discarded. He skipped, danced, and cut capers, and carried a money-box soliciting contributions from the on-lookers. Some of the band, in addition to their ribbons, "also wore small bunches of corn in their hats, from which the wheat was soon shaken out by the ungainly jumping which they called dancing. Occasionally, if the winter was severe, the procession was joined by threshers carrying their flails, reapers bearing their sickles, and carters with their long whips, which they were ever cracking to add to the noise, while even the smith and the miller were among the number, for the one sharpened the plough-shares and the other ground the corn; and Bessy rattled his box and danced so high that he shewed his worsted stockings and corduroy breeches; and very often, if there was a thaw, tucked up his gown skirts under his waistcoat, and shook the bonnet off his head, and disarranged the long ringlets that ought to have concealed his whiskers." Sometimes among the mummers there was a Fool, who wore the skin of a calf with the tail hanging down behind, and wielded a stick with an inflated bladder tied to it, which he applied with rude vigour to the heads and shoulders of the human team. Another mummer generally wore a fox's skin in the form of a hood with the tail dangling on his neck. If any churl refused to contribute to the money-box, the plough-bullocks put their shoulders to the plough and ploughed up the ground in front of his door.[1]

The clue to the meaning of these curious rites is probably furnished by the dances or rather jumps of the men who wore bunches of corn in their hats.

When we remember how often on the Continent about the same time of year the peasants dance and jump for the express purpose of making the crops grow tall, we may conjecture with some probability that the intention of the dancers on Plough Monday was similar; the original notion, we may suppose, was that the corn would grow that year just as high as the dancers leaped. If such was the real meaning of Plough Monday, we may the more confidently assume that the Straw-bear who makes his appearance at Whittlesey in Cambridgeshire on the day after Plough Monday represents indeed the corn-spirit. What could be more appropriate than for that beneficent being to manifest himself from house to house the very day after a magical ceremony had been performed to quicken the growth of the corn?

431. The foregoing interpretation of the rites observed in England on Plough Monday tallies well with the explanation which I have given of the very similar rites annually performed at the end of the Carnival in Thrace. The mock ploughing is probably practised for the same purpose in both cases, and what that purpose is may be safely inferred from the act of sowing and the offering of prayers for abundant crops which accompany and explain the Thracian ceremony. It deserves to be noted that ceremonies of the same sort and closely resembling those of Plough Monday are not confined to the Greek villages of Thrace but are observed also by the Bulgarians of that province and in Bulgaria itself. In that country the leading personage of the masquerade is the *Baba,* that is, the Old Woman or Mother. The part is played by a man in woman's clothes; she, or rather he, wears no mask, but in many villages she carries a spindle with which she spins. The *Kuker* and the *Kukerica* also figure in the performance, but they are subordinate to the Old Woman or Mother. Their costume varies in different villages. Usually they are clad in skins with a girdle of lime-tree bark and five or six bells fastened to it; on their back they wear a hump made up of rags. But the principal feature in their attire consists of their masks, which represent the heads of animals and men in fantastic combinations, such as the horned head of a man or a bird, the head of a ram, a bull, and so on. Much labour is spent on the manufacture of these masks. Early in the morning of Cheese Monday (the Monday of the last week in Carnival) the mummers go about the village levying contributions. Towards noon they form a procession and go from house to house. In every house they dance a round dance, while the Old Woman spins. It is believed that if any householder contrives to carry off the Old Woman and secrete her, a blessing and prosperity will enter into his dwelling; but the maskers defend the Old Woman stoutly against all such attempts of individuals to appropriate her beneficent presence. After the dance the mummers receive gifts of money, eggs, meal, and so on. Towards evening a round dance is danced in the village square, and there the Old Woman yokes the *Kuker* and *Kukerica* to a plough, ploughs with it a small piece of ground, and sows the ground with corn. Next day the performers reassemble, sell the presents they had collected, and with the produce hold a feast in the house of the Old Woman. It is supposed that if strange maskers make their way into a village, fertility will be drawn away to the village from which they have come; hence the villagers resist an inroad of strange maskers at any price. In general the people believe that the masquerade is performed for the purpose of increasing the luck and fertility of the village.[1]

In these Bulgarian rites, accordingly, we are not left to form conjectures as to the intention with which they are practised; that intention is plainly avowed. Perhaps we may go a step further and suggest that in the Bulgarian Old Woman or Mother, who guides the plough and sows the seed, and whose presence is believed to bring a blessing to any household that can contrive to appropriate her, we have the rustic prototype of Demeter, the Corn-Mother, who in the likeness of an Old Woman brought a blessing to the house of Celeus, king of Eleusis, and restored their lost fertility to the fallow Eleusinian fields. And in the pair of mummers, man and woman, who draw the plough, may we not discern the rude originals of Pluto and Persephone? If that is so, the gods of Greece are not wholly dead; they still hide their diminished heads in the cottages of the peasantry, to come forth on sunshine holidays and parade, with a simple but expressive pageantry, among a gazing crowd of rustics, at the very moment of the year when their help is most wanted by the husbandman.

NOTES

303   1. W. Mannhardt, *Mythologische Forschungen* (Strasburg 1884), 296.
2. *Ib.*, 297.
3. *Loc. cit.*
4. *Ib.*, 299.
5. *Ib.*, 300.
6. *Ib.*, 310 f.

304   1. *Ib.*, 316.
2. *Loc. cit.*
3. *Loc. cit.*
4. *Ib.*, 317.
5. *Loc. cit.*
6. *Loc. cit.*
7. *Ib.*, 318.
8. *Loc. cit.*
9. *Loc. cit.*
10. P. Sébillot, *Coutumes populaires de la Haute-Bretagne* (Paris 1886), 306.

305   1. Mannhardt, *op. cit.*, 319.

306   1. *Ib.*, 320.
2. *Ib.*, 321.

307   1. *Ib.*, 321, 323, 325 f.
2. *Ib.*, 323.
3. *Ib.*, 325.
4. *Ib.*, 323.
5. R. Krause, *Sitten, Gebräuche und Aberglauben in Westpreussen* (Berlin 1904), 51.
6. P. Drechsler, *Sitte, Brauch u. Volksglaube in Schlesien* (Leipzig 1903–06), ii. 65 f.
7. A. Kuhn, *Sagen, Gebräuche u. Märchen aus Westfalen* (Leipzig 1859), ii. 184, ¶¶512*b*, 514.

8. W. von Schulenburg, *Wendisches Volksthum* (Berlin 1882), 147.
9. A. Jaussen, *Coutumes des Arabes au pays de Moab* (Paris 1908), 252 f.

308   1. Mannhardt, *op. cit.*, 324.
2. *Ib.*, 320.
3. *Ib.*, 325.
4. See above, ¶111.

309   1. J. Jamieson, *Dictionary of the Scottish Language* (Paisley 1879–82), ii. 206, s. v. *Maiden;* Mannhardt, *op. cit.*, 326.
2. J. G. Campbell, *Superstitions of the Highlands and Islands of Scotland* (Glasgow 1900), 243 f.

310   1. D. J. Evans, in *Pembroke County Guardian,* December 7, 1895. The words mean: "I rose early, I pursued late on her neck" (E. S. Hartland).

311   1. Mannhardt, *op. cit.*, 328.
2. *Loc cit.*
3. *Ib.*, 329 ff.
4. *Loc. cit.*
5. *Loc. cit.*
6. *Ib.*, 331.
7. *Loc. cit.*
8. *Ib.*, 332.
9. T. Vernaleken, *Mythen u. Bräuche des Volkes in Oesterreich* (Vienna 1859), 310.
10. J. Brand, *Popular Antiquities of Great Britain* (London 1882–83), ii. 20.

312   1. Mannhardt, *op. cit.*, 333 f.
2. *Ib.*, 334.
3. *Loc. cit.*
4. *Ib.*, 336.
5. A. Kuhn and W. Schwartz, *Norddeutsche Sagen, Märchen und Gebräuche* (Leipzig 1848), 397.
6. A. Peter, *Volksthümliches aus Österreichisch-Schlesien* (Troppau 1856–67), ii. 270.

313   1. A. Kuhn, *Sagen, Gebräuche u. Märchen aus Westfalen* (Leipzig 1859), ii. 184 f., ¶515.
2. W. Mannhardt, *Die Korndämonen* (Berlin 1868), 28.
3. *Loc. cit.*
4. *Loc. cit.*
5. J. Wright, *English Dialect Dictionary*, i (London 1898), 605, s.v. *Churn;* iii (1902), 453, s.v. *Kirn;* iv (1903), 82 f. (It should be observed that "baby" in this context means simply "doll.")

6. Brand, *op. cit.*, iii. 21 f.
7. Jamieson, *op. cit.*, ii. 206, s. v. *Maiden.*

314 1. Mannhardt, *op. cit.*, 30.
2. W. Müller, *Beitraege zur Volkskunde der Deutschen in Mähren* (Vienna-Olmütz 1893), 327.
3. J. E. Waldfreund, in *Zeitschr. f. deutsche Mythologie und Sittenkunde,* 3 (1855), 340.
4. Vernaleken, *op. cit.*, 310.
5. R. Matheson, in *The Folk-lore Journal,* 7 (1889), 49 f.

315 1. Mannhardt, *op. cit.*, 30.
2. *Loc. cit.*
3. *Loc. cit.*

316 1. A. Nicholson, *A Collection of Gaelic Proverbs and Familiar Phrases, based on Macintosh's Collection* (Edinburgh-London 1881), 248.

319 1. J. de Acosta, *Natural and Moral History of the Indies,* Bk. V, Chap. 28 (London, Hakluyt Society, 1880), ii. 374.
2. W. Mannhardt, *Mythologische Forschungen,* 342 f. Mannhardt's account seems to be derived ultimately from De Arriaga's *Extirpacion de la idolatria del Piru* (Lima 1621), 16, where a full description of the "magic-mothers" may be found.

320 1. E. J. Payne, *History of the New World called America* (Oxford 1892), i. 419 f.

321 1. J. Mooney, in *Nineteenth Ann. Report of the Am. Bureau of Ethnology* (1900) i. 423, 432.
2. L. H. Morgan, *League of the Iroquois* (Rochester 1851), 161 f., 199.
3. C. Lumholtz, *Unknown Mexico* (London 1903), ii. 280.

322 1. H. M. Elliot, *Supplemental Glossary of Terms used in the N. W. Provinces,* ed. J. Beames (London 1869), i. 254.

323 1. W. B. Harris, in *JAI,* 27 (1898), 68.

324 1. R. J. Wilkinson, *Malay Beliefs* (London-Leyden 1906), 49–51.

325 1. A. W. Nieuwenhuis, *Quer durch Borneo* (Leyden 1904–07), i. 322–30.
2. *Ib.,* i. 317.

326 1. E. B. Cross, in *Journal of the American Oriental Society,* 4 (1854), 309.

327 1. J. L. van der Toorn, in *BTLVNI,* 39 (1890), 63–65.

328	1. M. Joustra, in *Med. Zendel.*, 46 (1902), 425 f.

329	1. W. W. Skeat, *Malay Magic* (London 1900), 225 f.
	2. *Ib.*, 235–49.

330	1. See above, ¶44.
	2. P. J. Veth, *Java* (Haarlem 1875–84), i. 524–26.

331	1. J. G. Scott and J. P. Hardiman, *Gazetteer of Upper Burma and the Shan States,* i (Rangoon 1900), 426.

332	1. Maximilian zu Wied, *Reise in das innere Nord-Amerika* (Coblenz 1839–41), ii. 182 f.

333	1. H. R. Schoolcraft, *Indian Tribes of the United States,* v (Philadelphia 1856), 193–95.

334	1. B. A. Gupta, in *Indian Antiquary,* 35 (1906), 61.

335	1. See above, ¶35.

336	1. W. Mannhardt, *Korndämonen,* 26; id., *Mythol. Forsch.,* 339. In some places it was customary to kneel down before the last sheaf, in others to kiss it. The custom of kneeling and bowing before the last corn has been observed sporadically in England: see *Folk-Lore Journal,* 7 (1888), 270. The Malayan sorceress who cut the seven ears of rice to fashion the Rice-child kissed the ears after she had cut them: W. W. Skeat, *op. cit.,* 241.
	2. So, for instance, in the Homeric Hymn to Demeter.
	3. W. G. Aston, *Shinto* (London 1905), 127.

338	1. Diodorus Siculus, i. 14.
	2. Herodotus, ii. 79; Julius Pollux, iv. 54; Pausanias, ix. 29, 7; Athenaeus, xiv. 11.
	3. H. Brugsch, *Die Adonisklage und das Linoslied* (Berlin 1852), 24; [E. A. W. Budge, *Osiris and the Egyptian Resurrection* (London 1911), ii. 59–66; Miriam Lichtheim, in *Journal of Near Eastern Studies,* 4 (1945), 180.]
	4. See above, ¶329.
	5. W. R. S. Ralston, *Songs of the Russian People*[2] (London 1872), 249 f.
	6. W. Gregor, in *Rev. des traditions populaires,* 3 (1888), 487.

339	1. Iliad xviii. 570; Herodotus, ii. 79; Pausanias, ix. 29, 6–9; Euripides, *Orestes,* 1395; Sophocles, *Ajax,* 627, etc.
	2. Conon, *Narrat.,* 19.
	3. F. C. Movers, *Die Phönizier* (Bonn 1841–56), i. 246; [Stummer, *De Lino* (Bonn 1855); O. Eissfeldt, in *Melanges syriens offerts à M. René*

Dussaud (Paris 1939), i. 161 ff.; T. H. Gaster, *Thespis* (New York 1950), 14].

4. Pausanias, ix. 29, 8.

340   1. Julius Pollux, iv. 54; Athenaeus, xiv. 11; Hesychius, s.vv. *Bormon* and *Mariandynos thrênos.*

341   1. Sositheus, *Daphnis,* as quoted by an anonymous writer *apud* A. Westermann, *Scriptores rerum mirabilium Graeci* (Brunswick 1839), 220 f. Cp. also: Athenaeus, x. 8; Schol. on Theocritus, x. 41; Photius, Suidas and Hesychius, s.v. *Lityerses.*
2. Julius Pollux, *Loc. cit.*

342   1. Mannhardt, *Mythologische Forschungen,* 19 f.
2. *Ib.,* 20.
3. *Ib.,* 31.
4. *Ib.,* 334.
5. *Ib.,* 330.
6. *Loc. cit.*
7. *Ib.,* 331.
8. *Ib.,* 335.
9. *Loc. cit.*
10. J. Nicholson, *Folk-lore of East Yorkhsire* (London 1890), 20 (supplemented by a private communication from E. S. Hartland).
11. Mannhardt, *Korndämonen,* 26.
12. Id., *Mythol. Forsch.,* 50.
13. *Loc. cit.*
14. *Ib.,* 32 f.
15. *Ib.,* 35 f.
16. *Ib.,* 36.
17. A. John, *Sitte, Brauch u. Volksglaube im deutschen Westböhmen* (Prague 1905), 194.
18. O. Hartung, in *Zeitschr. d. Vereins f. Volkskunde,* 7 (1897), 153.
19. J. Lecoeur, *Esquisses du Boscage Normand* (Condé-sur-Noireau 1883–87), ii. 240 f.
20. Mannhardt, *op. cit.,* 36.
21. *Ib.,* n. 2.
22. Private communication from Col. Henry Wilson, of Farnborough, Kent.
23. *Folk-Lore Journal,* 7 (1889), 52 f.
24. Mannhardt, *op. cit.,* 39.
25. *Loc. cit.*
26. *Ib.,* 40 f.; C. Lemke, *Volksthümliches in Ostpreussen* (Mohrungen 1884–87), i. 23 f.
27. Mannhardt, *op. cit.,* 41 f.

343   1. *Ib.*, 42.
2. *Loc. cit.*
3. *Ib.*, 47 f.

344   1. Cieza de Leon, *Travels*, tr. C. R. Markham (London, Hakluyt Society, 1864), 203.
2. Juan de Velasco, *Histoire du royaume de Quito*, i (Paris 1840), 121 f.
3. H. H. Bancroft, *Native Races of the Pacific States* (London 1875–76), ii. 340.
4. H. R. Schoolcraft, *Indian Tribes of the United States* (Philadelphia 1853–56), v. 77 ff.
5. J. B. Labat, *Relation historique de l'Ethiopie occidentale* (Paris 1732), i. 380.
6. J. Adams, *Sketches taken during Ten Voyages between the years 1786 and 1800* (London, n. d.), 25.
7. P. Bouche, *Le Côte des Esclaves* (Paris 1885), 132.

345   1. T. Arbousset and F. Damas, *Voyage d'exploration au Nord-est de la colonie du Cap de Bonne-Éspérance* (Paris 1842), 117 f.
2. Private communication from Rev. J. Roscoe, who resided for some time among the Wamegi and suppressed the sacrifice in 1886.

346   1. F. Blumentritt, in *Petermanns Mitteilungen*, 37 (1891), 110.
2. A. Schadenberg, in *Verh. d. Berliner Ges. f. Anthrop., Ethnol. und Urgeschichte*, 1878, p. 39 [bound with *Zeitschr. f. Ethnologie*, 20].
3. Id., *ib.*, 1889, p. 681 [bound with *Zeitscher. f. Ethnol.*, 21].

347   1. R. G. Woodthorpe, in *JAI*, 26 (1897), 24.
2. G. M. Godden, *ib.*, 27 (1898), 9 f., 38 f.
3. P. Dehon, in *Memoirs of the Asiatic Soc. of Bengal*, 1, No. 9 (1906), 141 f.
3a. P. A. Talbot, *Life in Southern Nigeria* (London 1923), 237.
3b. Id., *The Peoples of Southern Nigeria* (London 1926), iii. 859.

348   1. S. C. Macpherson, *Memorials of Service in India* (London 1865), 113–31.
2. J. Campbell, *Wild Tribes of Khondistan* (London 1864), 56.
3. Macpherson, *op. cit.*, 115 f.
4. *Ib.*, 117 f.; Campbell, *op. cit.*, 112.

351   1. Mannhardt, *Korndämonen*, 5.
2. H. Pfannenschmid, *Germanische Erntefeste* (Hanover 1878), 98.
3. See above, ¶**197**.

352   1. There are traces in Greek itself of an ancient custom of sacrificing human beings to promote the fertility of the crops; see above, ¶**197**.

353   1. Hesychius, s.v. *Bormon*.

354 1. Apollodorus, *Bibl.*, ii. 6, 3.

355 1. *Ib.*, ii. 5, 11; Schol. on Apollonius Rhodius, *Argon.*, iv. 1396; Plutarch, *Parall.*, 38. Herodotus (ii. 45) discredits the idea that the Egyptians ever offered human sacrifices, but his authority is outweighed by that of Manetho (*apud* Plutarch, *De Is. et Os.*, 73) who says they did. Cp. Budge, *Osiris*, 210 ff.
2. E. Meyer, *Geschichte des Altertums*, i (Stuttgart 1884), 68, ¶57.
3. Diodorus Siculus, i. 88; Plutarch, *op. cit.*, 73 (cp. *ib.*, 30, 33).
4. Margaret A. Murray, *The Osireion at Abydos* (London 1904), 30; cp. A. Mariette, *Dendérah*, iv (Paris 1880), plates xxxi, lvi, and lxxxi.

356 1. E. J. Payne, *History of the New World called America*, i (Oxford 1892), 422.
2. Brasseur de Bourbourg, *Histoire des nations civilisées du Mexique et de l'Amérique Centrale* (Paris 1857–59), iii. 535.
3. Festus, s.v. *catularia;* cp. id., s.v. *rutilae canes;* Columella, *De re rustica*, x. 342 f.; Ovid, *Fasti*, iv. 905 ff. [with Frazer's commentary]; Pliny, *NH*, xviii. 14.
4. D. Chwolsohn, *Die Ssabier und der Ssabismus* (St. Petersburg 1856), ii. 388 f.

357 1. See above, ¶**345**.
2. Plutarch, *op. cit.*, 18.
3. S. C. Macpherson, *Memorials of Service in India* (London 1865), 129; J. Campbell, *Wild Tribes of Khondistan* (London 1864), 55, 113, 121, 187.
4. See above, ¶**259**.

359 1. W. Hone, *Every-day Book* (London n. d.) ii. 1170 f.

360 1. F. Hoggan, in *Folk-Lore*, 4 (1893), 123.

361 1. J. Brand, *Popular Antiquities of Great Britain* (London 1882–83), ii. 20; C. S. Burne and G. F. Jackson, *Shropshire Folk-Lore* (London 1883), 371.
2. Burne and Jackson, *Loc. cit.*
3. Mannhardt, *Mythol. Forsch.*, 185.
4. *Loc. cit.*
5. *Loc. cit.*

362 1. E. Meier, in *Zeitschr. f. deutsche Mythologie u. Sittenkunde*, 1 (1853), 170–73; H. Pfannenschmid, *op. cit.*, 104 f.

365 1. W. Mannhardt, *Roggenwolf und Roggenhund*[2] (Danzig 1866), 6 ff.
2. *Ib.*, 1 ff., 29; *Folk-lore Journal*, 7 (1889), 47 f. [S. Ayrshire]; L. F. Sauvé, *Folk-lore des Hautes Vosges* (Paris 1889), 191; G. Georgakis and L. Pineau, *Folk-lore de Lesbos* (Paris 1894), 310.

3. Mannhardt, *Mythol. Forsch.*, 109 f.; L. Pineau, *Folk-lore du Poitou* (Paris 1892), 500 f.; Lafcadio Hearn, *Glimpses of Unfamiliar Japan* (London 1894), ii. 312 ff. (the rice-god Inari rides a fox).
4. Mannhardt, *Korndämonen*, 13 ff.; Pfannenschmid, *op. cit.*, 110
5. G. A. Heinrich, *Agrarische Sitten und Gebräuche unter den Sachsen Siebenbürgens* (Hermannstadt 1880), 21; A. Peter, *Volksthümliches aus Oesterreisch-Schlesien* (Troppau 1865–67), ii. 268; J. Lecoeur, *Esquisses du Boscage Normand* (Condé-sur-Noireau 1883–87), ii. 240; A. C. Kruijt, in *Med. Zendel.*, 44 (1900), 228 f. [Minahassa and Halmahera].
6. W. Mannhardt, *Antike Wald- und Feldkulte* (Berlin 1877), 172–74; id., *Mythol. Forsch.*, 30; *Sauvé, op. cit.*, 191; C. Beauquier, *Les mois en Franch-Comté* (Paris 1900), 102.
7. Mannhardt, *Antike Wald- und Feldkulte*, 155 f.; A. C. Kruijt, in *Med. Zendel.*, 44 (1900), 241 [Tomori of Central Celebes].
8. Mannhardt, *Mythol. Forsch.*, 58 f.; F. Panzer, *Beitrag zur deutschen Mythologie* (Munich 1848–55), ii. 233 f.
9. A. Witzchel, *Sagen, Sitten und Gebräuche aus Thüringen* (Vienna 1878), 213 f.; Mannhardt, *op. cit.*, 186 f.; Panzer, *op. cit.*, ii. 221 ff.; Mannhardt, *Antike Wald- und Feldkulte*, 197 f. [Scandinavian Yuleboar]; F. J. Widemann, *Aus dem inneren und äusseren Leben der Ehsten* (*St. Petersburg* 1876), 344, 485.
10. Mannhardt, *Mythol. Forsch.*, 62 f., 167; J. Brand, *op. cit.*, ii. 24; Laisnel de la Salle, *Croyances et légendes du centre de la France* (Paris 1875), ii. 133.
11. For these and other animal embodiments of the corn spirit, see Mannhardt, *Korndämonen*, 1 ff.

366 1. Ovid, *Fasti*, ii. 361; iii. 312; v. 101; id., *Heroides*, iv. 49.
2. Macrobius, *Sat.*, i. 22, 3.
3. Homeric Hymn to Aphrodite, 262 ff.
4. Pliny, *NH*, xii. 3; Ovid, *Met.*, vi. 392; id., *Fasti*, iii. 303, 309; cp. W. Mannhardt, *Antike Wald– und Feldkulte*, 43.
5. Pliny, *op. cit.*, xii. 3; Martianus Capella, ii. 167; Augustine, *De civitate Dei*, xv. 23; Aurelius Victor, *Origo gentis Romanae*, iv. 6.
6. Servius on Vergil, *Ecl.*, vi. 14; Ovid, *Met.*, vi. 392 f.; Martianus Capella, ii. 167.

367 1. Mannhardt, *Baumkultus*, 138 f.; id., *Antike Wald– und Feldkulte*, 145.
2. *Antike Wald- und Feldkulte*, 113–211. For a divergent view, cp. L. R. Farnell, *Cults of the Greek States*, v (Oxford 1909), 431 ff.

368 1. Pausanias, i. 24, 4; i. 28, 10; Porphyry, *De abstinentia*, ii. 29 f.; Aelian, *Var. hist.*, viii. 3; Scholiast on Aristophanes, *Peace*, 419, *Clouds*, 985; Hesychius, Suidas, and *Etym. Magn.*, s.v. *Bouphonia*.
2. On the import of the name, see W. Robertson Smith, *Religion of the Semites*[2] (London 1894), 304 ff.

3. *De re rustica*, ii. 5, 4; cp. Columella, vi, praef., ¶7.
4. Mannhardt, *Baumkultus*, 409.

369　1. See above, ¶365, n. 9.
2. Schol. on Aristophanes, *Acharnians*, 747.
3. J. Overbeck, *Griechische Kunstmythologie, Besonderer Theil*, ii (Leipzig 1873–76), 493.
4. Hyginus, fab. 277; Cornutus, *Theol. graec. comp.*, 28; Macrobius, *Sat.*, i. 12, 23; Schol. on Aristophanes, *Acharn.*, 747; Servius on Vergil, *Georg.*, ii. 380; Aelian, *Nat. anim.*, x. 16.
5. See above, ¶281.

370　1. [See T. W. Allen, W. R. Halliday, and E. E. Sikes, *The Homeric Hymns*[2] (Oxford 1936), 120 f.]; Photius, s.v. *stênia*.
2. Plutarch, *De Is. et Os.*, 59; Photius, *loc. cit.*
3. We deduce this from Pausanias, ix. 8, 1, although that passage is incomplete and apparently corrupt. However, at the spring and autumn festivals of Isis at Tithaera, geese and goats were indeed thrown into the *adyton* and left there until the following festival, when the remains were removed and buried: Pausanias, x. 32, 14. This would be a good analogy.
4. Scholia in Lucianum, 275 ff. Rabe.
5. Ovid, *Fasti*, iv. 461–66.
6. Pausanias, i. 14, 3.
7. Schol. on Aristophanes, *Frogs*, 338.

371　1. W. Mannhardt, *Antike Wald– und Feldkulte*, 166.
2. Id., *Mythologische Forschungen*, 60.
3. *Ib.*, 30.
4. *Ib.*, 187 f.
5. Id., *Antike Wald- und Feldkulte*, 197 f.

372　1. See above, ¶230.
2. *Loc. cit.*
3. Demosthenes, *De corona*, 313.
4. See above. ¶230. Cp. also: Athenaeus, ii. 80; Cornutus, 28; Plutarch, *Quaest. conviv.*, iv. 5, 3, ¶8; Aristides, *Apologia*, 11; Propertius, iii. 4 (5), 53 ff.; Joannes Lydus, *De mensibus*, iv. 44; Lactantius, *Div. Inst.*, i. 17; Firmicus Maternus, *De errore prof. rel.*, 9; Macrobius, *Sat.*, i. 21, 4; W. W. Baudissin, *Adonis und Esmun* (Leipzig 1911), 142 ff.
5. W. Cureton, *Spicilegium Syriacum* (London 1855), 44.
6. Lucian, *De dea Syria*, 54.
7. [On the connection of the boar with Adonis, see W. W. Baudissin, *Adonis und Esmun* (Leipzig 1911), 142 ff.]

373　1. Herodotus, ii. 47; Plutarch, *De Is. et Os.*, 8; Aelian, *Nat. anim.*, x. 16.
2. Herodotus, *loc. cit.*

3. Plutarch and Aelian, *locc. citt.*
4. Herodotus, *loc. cit.* At Castabus in Chersonese there was a sacred precinct forbidden to any who had touched or tasted of a pig: Diod. Sic., v. 62, 5.
5. Herodotus, Plutarch, and Aelian, *locc. citt.*

374
1. Leviticus, 16 : 23 f.
2. Porphyry, *De abstinentia*, ii. 44.
3. *Central Provinces Ethnographic Survey*, VII (Allahabad 1911), 97.
4. *Ib.*, I (1907), 32.

375
1. E. Lefébure, *Le Mythe osirien*, i (Paris 1874), 44; Budge, *Osiris*, i. 62 f.
2. Plutarch, *De Is. et Os.*, 8.
3. This important principle was first recognized by W. Robertson Smith; see his *Religion of the Semites*[2] (London 1894), 373, 410 f.
4. *De Is. et Os.*, 31.

376
1. Lefébure, *op. cit.*, 43 f.

378
1. J. de Acosta, *Natural and Moral History of the Indies* (London, Hakluyt Society, 1880), ii. 356–60.
2. Satapatha Brahmana, tr. Eggeling (*SBE*, xii), 51.

379
1. H. H. Bancroft, *Native Races of the Pacific States* (London 1875–76), iii. 297 ff.

380
1. C. Lumholtz, *Unknown Mexico* (London 1903), ii. 166–71.
2. E. Thurston, *Castes and Tribes of S. India* (Madras 1909), iv. 357 f.

381
1. Mannhardt, *Mythol. Forsch.*, 179.
2. Id., *Baumkultus*, 205.

382
1. J. Batchelor, *The Ainu and their Folk-lore* (London 1901), 204, 206.

383
1. G. A. Wilken, in *Verh. v. het Batav. Gen. v. Kunsten en Wetenschappen*, 38 (Batavia 1875), 26.

384
1. C. Hill-Tout, *The Far West, The Home of the Salish and Déné* (London 1907), 168 f.
2. J. Teit, *The Thompson Indians of British Columbia* (1900), 349.

385
1. See above, ¶382.
2. J. Thompson, *Through Masai Land* (London 1885), 430.
3. W. H. Beech, *The Suk, Their Language and Folklore* (Oxford 1911), 9.
4. O. Baumann, *Durch Masailand zur Nilquelle* (Berlin 1894), 171.
5. F. Boas, in *Sixth Ann. Report of the Am. Bureau of Ethnology* (1888), 595; id., in *Bull. Am. Museum of Nat. History*, 15, i (1901), 122–24.

6. Pausanias, v. 13, 3.
7. Dittenberger, *Sylloge*², No. 576.
8. Diodorus Siculus, v. 62, 5.

387 1. Festus, 128, 129, 145 Müller.
2. Varro, *De lingua Latina,* ix. 61; Arnobius, *Adv. nationes,* iii. 41; Macrobius, *Sat.,* i. 7, 35; Festus, 128 Müller.
3. Servius on Vergil, *Aen.,* iii. 116; Pausanias, x. 18, 5.
4. Suidas, s.v. *bous hebdomos;* Hesychius, s.v. *hebdomos bous.*
5. Proclus, quoted and emended by C. A. Lobeck, *Aglaophamus* (Königsberg 1829), 1079.
6. Plutarch, *Lucullus,* 10.
7. Julius Pollux, i. 30 f.
8. Zenobius, *Cent.,* v. 22.
9. *Ib.,* v. 5.
10. Schol. on Thucydides, i. 126.
11. P. von Stenin, in *Globus,* 58 (1890), 203 f.
12. *Relations des Jésuites,* 1636, p. 11.
13. L. A. Waddell, *The Buddhism of Tibet* (London 1895), 484–86.

388 1. W. Ellis, *Polynesian Researches*² (London 1832–36), i. 402.
2. M. J. van Baarda, in *BTLVNI,* 45 (1895), 539.
3. J. Kubary, in A. Bastian's *Allerlei aus Volks– und Menschenkunde* (Berlin 1888), i. 9.
4. W. M. Donselaar, in *Med. Zendel.,* 1 (1857), 290.
5. A. B. Ellis, *The Yoruba-speaking Peoples of the Slave Coast* (London 1894), 80.
6. S. Crowther and J. C. Taylor, *The Gospel on the Banks of the Niger* (London 1859), 250 f.

389 1. N. Graafland, *De Minahassa* (Rotterdam 1869), i. 326.
2. F. Grabowsky, in *Internat. Archiv für Ethnographie,* 1 (1888), 132 f.
3. J. G. F. Riedel, *De sluik- en kroesharige rassen tusschen Selebes en Papua* (The Hague 1886), 465.
4. Shway Yoe, *The Burman* (London 1882), ii. 138.
5. Pellegoix, *Description du royaume Thai ou Siam* (Paris 1854), ii. 48 f.; E. Young, *The Kingdom of the Yellow Robe* (Westminster 1898), 121.
6. J. Moura, *Le royaume de Cambodge* (Paris 1883), i. 176.

392 1. J. Adair, *History of the American Indians* (London 1775), 133.
2. A. Simson, *Travels in the Wilds of Ecuador* (London 1857), 168.
3. A. Thevet, *Les singularitez de la France antarctique, autrement nommée Amerique* (Antwerp 1558), 55.
4. Rochefort, *Histoire naturelle et morale des Iles Antilles*² (Rotterdam 1665), 465.
5. J. Teit, *The Thompson Indians of British Columbia* (1900), 348.

6. W. H. Bleek and L. C. Lloyd, *Specimens of Bushman Folklore* (London 1911), 373.
7. H. H. Johnston, *British Central Africa* (London 1897), 438.
8. M. W. H. Beech, *The Suk, their Language and Folklore* (Oxford 1911), 11.
9. Ovid, *Met.*, vii. 271 ff. On the supposed longevity of deer and crows, see Frazer on Pausanias, viii. 10, 10.
10. P. E. Müller on Saxo Grammaticus, *Historia Danica* (Copenhagen 1839–58), ii. 60.
11. *Die Edda,* tr. K. Simrock[8] (Stuttgart 1882), 180, 309.
12. Charlevoix, *Histoire de la Nouvelle France* (Paris 1744), vi. 8.

393
1. A. B. Ellis, *op. cit.,* 69.
2. A. Caulin, *Historia Coro-graphica natural y evangelica dela Nueva Andalucia* (1779), 98.
3. A. de Herrera, *General History of the vast Continent and Islands of America,* tr. J. Stevens (London 1725–26), vi. 187.
4. F. de Castelnau, *Expédition dans les parties centrales de l'Amérique du Sud* (Paris 1850–51), iv. 382.
5. E. W. Nelson, in *Eighteenth Ann. Report of the Am. Bureau of Ethnology* (1899), 328.
6. A. W. Howitt, *The Native Tribes of S. E. Australia* (London 1904), 752.
7. *Annales de la Propagation de la Foi,* 11 (Lyons 1838–39), 258.
8. J. Henderson, in *Journal of the N. China Branch of the Royal Asiatic Society,* N. S. 1 (1865), 35 f.
9. N. Adriani and A. C. Kruijt, in *Med. Zendel.,* 44 (1900), 162.
10. F. Blumentritt, in *Mitt. Wiener Geogr. Ges.,* 1882, p. 154.
11. A. C. Haddon, in *JAI,* 19 (1890), 414; cp. *ib.,* 312.

394
1. E. Holub, *Sieben Jahre in Süd Afrika* (Vienna 1881), ii. 361.
2. Col. Maclean, *Compendium of Kafir Laws and Customs* (Cape Town 1886), 82.
3. Porte, in *Missions Catholiques,* 28 (1896), 149.
4. D. Kidd, *Savage Childhood* (London 1906), 70.

395
1. Howitt, *op. cit.,* 367 ff.
2. W. Ridley, *Kamilaroi* (Sidney 1875), 160.
3. J. L. Wilson, *Western Africa* (London 1856), 394.
4. J. Becker, *La vie en Afrique* (Paris-Brussels 1887), ii. 366.
5. J. de Acosta, *op. cit.,* ii. 364–67.

396
1. On the custom of eating a god, see also F. Liebrecht, *Zur Volkskunde* (Heilbronn 1879), 436–39, and W. Robertson Smith's classic article, "Sacrifice," in the ninth edition of the Encyclopaedia Britannica.

398
1. Herodotus, ii. 42.

Spirits of the Corn and Wild 499

400 1. T. J. Hutchinson, *Impressions of Western Africa* (London 1858), 196 ff. The writer does not state expressly that a serpent is killed *annually*, but his remarks imply it.
     2. Tautain, in *Revue d'Ethnographie*, 3 (1885), 397.
     3. Varro, in *Priscian*, x. 32; Pliny, *NH*, viii. 14. (Pliny's statement is to be corrected by Varro's.)

401 1. "Ieso-Ki, ou description de l'ile de Iesso, avec une notice sur la révolte de Samsay-in, composée par l'interprète Kannemon," printed in Malte-Brun's *Annales des Voyages* (Paris 1814), 154.

402 1. P. Labbé, *Un bagne russe, l'Isle de Sakhaline* (Paris 1903), 227, 232–58.

403 1. *Journal of the Royal Geographical Society*, 28 (1858), 396.
     2. W. Joest, in B. Scheube, *Die Ainos* (Yokohama), 17. Other accounts in: *Revue d'Ethnographie*, 2 (1883), 307 f.; *Internat. Archiv f. Ethnographie*, 1 (1889), 102; *Archiv für Anthropologie*, 26 (1900), 796. [See also J. Batchelor, in the Encyclopaedia of Religion and Ethics, i. 249–51.]

404 1. E. G. Ravenstein, *The Russians on the Amur* (London 1861), 379 ff.; T. W. Atkinson, *Travels in the Regions of the Upper and Lower Amoor* (London 1860), 482 ff.

405 1. E. H. Fraser, in *Journal of the China Branch of the Royal Asiatic Society*, N. S. 26 (1891092), 36–39.

407 1. J. Perham, in *Journal of the Straits Branch of the Royal Asiatic Society*, No. 10 (1883), 221. Cp. M. T. H. Perelaer, *Ethnographische Beschrijving der Dayaks* (Zalt-Bommel 1870), 7.
     2. Fr. Stuhlmann, *Mit Emin Pascha ins Herz von Afrika* (Berlin 1894), 510 f.
     3. J. Sibree, *The Great African Island* (London 1880), 269.

408 1. W. Marsden, *History of Sumatra* (London 1811), 292.
     2. J. L. van der Toorn, in *BTLVNI*, 39 (1891), 74 ff.
     3. *Ann. de la Prop. de la Foi*, 5 (1831), 353 ff.

409 1. W. Bartram, *Travels through North and South Carolina, Georgia, East and West Florida, etc.* (London 1792), 258–61.
     2. J. Heckewelder, in *Trans. of the Historical and Literary Committee of the American Philosophical Society*, 1 (1819), 245.
     3. J. Mooney, in *Nineteenth Ann. Report of the Am. Bureau of Ethnology*, i (1900), 294–96.

410 1. F. Boas, in *Eleventh Ann. Report on the N. W. Tribes of Canada* (1896), 9 f.

2. T. de Pauly, *Description ethnographique des peuples de la Russie* (St. Petersburg 1862): Peuples de la Sibérie orientale, 7.

3. Scholiast on Apollonius Rhodius, *Argonautica*, ii. 124.

411   1. *Missions Catholiques*, 14 (1882), 458.

    2. C. B. Klunzinger, *Upper Egypt* (London 1878), 402 f.

412   1. G. W. Steller, *Beschreibung von dem Lande Kamtschatha* (Frankfort-Leipzig 1774), 85, 280, 331.

    2. *Recueil de Voyages au Nord* (Amsterdam 1727), viii. 41, 416; J. G. Georgi, *Beschreibung aller Nationen des russischen Reichs* (St. Petersburg 1776), 83.

    3. J. Scheffer, *Lapponia* (Frankfort 1673), 233 f. Cp. E. Roe, *The White Sea Peninsula* (London 1881), 276.

413   1. *Lettres édifiantes et curieuses*, vi (Paris 1781), 171.

    2. *A Narrative of the Adventures and Sufferings of John R. Jewitt* (Middletown 1826), 117.

    3. A. P. Reid, in *JAI*, 3 (1874), 111.

414   1. S. Kay, *Travels and Researches in Caffraria* (London 1833), 138.

    2. L. Alberti, *De Kaffers aan de Zuidkust van Afrika* (Amsterdam 1810), 95; C. Rose, *Four Years in Southern Africa* (London 1829), 155.

    3. J. Roscoe, *The Baganda* (London 1911), 447.

    4. J. Becker, *La vie en Afrique* (Paris-Brussels 1887), ii. 298 f., 305.

    5. A. Bastian, *Loango-Küste*, ii. 243.

415   1. Roscoe, *op. cit.*, 289, 448.

416   1. W. F. W. Owen, *Narrative of Voyages to the Shores of Africa, Arabia, and Madagascar* (London 1833), ii. 170.

417   1. H. Mouhot, *Travels in the Central Parts of Indo-China* (London 1864), i. 252.

    2. J. Mooney, in *Amer. Journal of Folklore*, 3 (1890), 45 f.

    3. J. G. Bourke, in *Folk-Lore*, 2 (1891), 438.

    4. L. Hennepin, *Description de la Lousiane* (Paris 1683), 82 f.

    5. Charlevoix, *Histoire de la Nouvelle France* (Paris 1744), v. 443.

    6. D. Crantz, *History of Greenland* (London 1767), i. 216.

    7. F. Boas, in *Sixth Ann. Report on the N. W. Tribes of Canada* (1890), 61 f.

    8. *Relations des Jésuites*, 1667, p. 12.

    9. F. G. Sagard, *Le grand voyage du pays de Hurons* (Paris 1865), 178 ff.

    10. M. J. Schleiden, *Das Salz* (Leipzig 1875), 47.

418   1. E. James, *Expedition from Pittsburgh to the Rocky Mounatins* (London 1823), i. 257.

    2. D. G. Brinton, *Myths of the New World*[2] (New York 1876), 278.

3. W. H. Keating, *Expedition to the Source of St. Peter's River* (London 1825), i. 452.
4. E.g. at the sacrifice of the White Dog among the IROQUOIS (L. H. Morgan, *League of the Iroquois* [Rochester 1851], 210); among the TARTARS (Carpini, *Historia Mongolorum* [Paris 1838], cap. iii, ¶1, 2, p. 620); amng the AMERICAN INDIANS (Charlevoix, *op. cit.*, vi. 72); among the ESQUIMAUX (F. Boas, in *Sixth Ann. Report of the Am. Bureau of Ethnology* [1888], 595 f.; in modern SYRIA (S. I. Curtiss, *Primitive Semitic Religion Today* [Chicago 1902], 178). For WEST AFRICAN examples, see J. Spieth, *Die Ewe-Stämme* (Berlin 1906), 458, 466, 480, 527, 712, 796, 824.
5. *Relations des Jésuites*, 1634, p. 25; A. Mackenzie, *Voyage through the Continent of America* (London 1801), p. civ; A. P. Reid, in *JAI*, 3 (1874), 111 [Ojibway]; F. Boas, in *Sixth Ann. Report of the Am. Bureau of Ethnology* (1888), 596 [Central Esquimaux]; W. M. Gabb, "On the Indian Tribes and Languages of Costa Rica," in *Trans. Amer. Philos. Soc.*, 1875, p. 520.

419   1. J. B. Holzmayer, in *Verh. d. gelehrten Estnischen Ges. zu Dorpat*, 7, ii (1872), 105, n.
2. G. A. Heinrich, *Agrarische Sitten und Gebräuche unter den Sachsen Siebenbürgens* (Hermannstadt 1880), 15 f.
3. R. F. Kaindl, *Die Huzulen* (Vienna 1894), 79, 103.
4. E. Krause, in *Zeitschr. f. Ethnologie*, 15 (1883), 93.

420   1. L. Decle, *Three Years in Savage Africa* (London 1898), 160.
2. Veter, in *Mitt. d. Geogr. Ges. zu Jena*, 12 (1893), 95 f.
3. E. Modigliani, *Un viaggio a Nias* (Milan 1890), 626.
4. W. Crooke, *Popular Religion and Folklore of Northern India* (Westminster 1896), ii. 303.

421   1. *Geoponica*, xiii. 5. The charm is said to have been employed formerly in the neighborhood of Paris: A. de Nore, *Coutumes, mythes et traditions des provinces de France* (Paris-Lyons 1846), 383.
2. A. Meyrac, *Traditions, coutumes, légendes et contes des Ardennes* (Charleville 1890), 176.
3. *Amer. Journal of Folklore*, 11 (1898), 161.

422   1. R. van Eck, in *Tijdschrift voor Nederlandsch–Indië*, N. S. 8 (1879), 215.
2. J. L. van Gennep, in *BTLVNI*, 46 (1896), 101.
3. J. G. von Hahn, *Albanesische Studien* (Jena 1854), i, 157.
4. P. de Lagarde, *Reliquiae juris ecclesiastici antiquissimae* (Leipzig 1857), 135.
5. W. R. S. Ralston, *Songs of the Russian People²* (Lindon 1872), 255.
6. D. Kidd, *Savage Childhood* (London 1906), 292.

423   1. Joh. Malalas, *Chronographia,* 264 Dindorf.
2. D. Comparetti, *Vergil in the Middle Ages* (London 1895), 265.
3. *Ib.,* 259, 293, 341.
4. E. Doutté, *Magie et religion dans l'Afrique du nord* (Algiers 1908), 144.
5. *Encyclopaedia Biblica,* iv. col. 4395.
6. Numbers 21 : 6–9.

424   1. G. Catlin, *O-Kee-Pas: A Religious Ceremony and other Customs of the Mandans* (London 1867); Lewis and Clarke, *Travels to the Source of the Missouri River* (London 1814), i. 205 f.

425   1. A. Bastian, in *Verh. d. Berliner Ges. f. Anthropologie, Ethnologie und Urgeschichte,* 1870–71, p. 59.

426   1. W. E. Marshall, *Travels among the Todas* (London 1873), 129 f.
2. *Ib.,* 80 f., 130.
3. R. W. Felkin, in *Proc. Royal Soc. Edinburgh,* 12 (1882–84), 336 f.

427   1. See above, ¶403.
2. See: Ch. Vallancey, *Collectanea de rebus Hibernicis,* iv (Dublin 1786), 97; J. Brand, *Popular Antiquities of Great Britain* (London 1882–83), iii. 195 f.; E. Rolland, *Faune populaire de la France* (Paris 1877–83). ii. 288 ff.; N. W. Thomas, in *Folk-Lore,* 17 (1908), 270 ff., 280; L. Eckstein, *Comparative Studies in Nursery Rhymes* (London 1906), 172 ff.
3. J. Train, *Account of the Isle of Man* (Douglas 1845), ii. 124 ff., 141.
4. Vallancey, *loc. cit.*
5. C. Swainson, *Folk-lore of British Birds* (London 1886), 35 f.
6. W. Henderson, *Folk-Lore of the Northern Counties* (London 1879), 125.
7. Swainson, *op. cit.,* 40 f.
8. Rolland, *op. cit.,* ii. 296 f.
9. C. S. Sonnini, *Travels in Upper and Lower Egypt, translated from the French* (London 1800), 11 f.; Brand, *op. cit.,* iii. 198.

429   1. O. von Reinsberg-Düringsfeld, *Fest-Kalender aus Böhmen* (Prague 1861), 49–52; E. Cortet, *Essai sur les fêtes religieuses* (Paris 1867), 83.
2. G. C. Moore Smith in *Folk-Lore,* 20 (1909), 202.

430   1. R. Chambers, *The Book of Days* (London-Edinburgh 1886, i. 94 ff.; Brand, *op. cit.,* i. 506 ff.; T. C. Thistleton Dyer, *British Popular Customs* (London 1876), 37 ff.; O. von Reinsberg-Düringsfeld, *Das festliche Jahr* (Leipzig 1863), 27 f.; W. Mannhardt, *Baumkultus* (Berlin 1875), 557 f.; E. K. Chambers, *The Mediaeval Stage* (Oxford 1903), i. 208–10.

431   1. G. Kazarow, in *Archiv für Religionswissenschaft,* 11 (1908), 408 f.

ADDITIONAL NOTES

TREE-SPIRITS AND CORN-SPIRITS

Frazer's notion of a central spirit of fertility embodied in a tree is derived from the earlier work of Willhelm Mannhardt, *Antike Wald– und Feldkulte* (Berlin 1877). It is now increasingly recognized, however, that such a general spirit is a mere schematic concoction, the fact being that trees are regarded by primitive peoples as the habitats of several different spirits, each representing a different aspect of them or a different impression or impact created by them upon human beings. For a detailed critique of Frazer's position, see: W. Liungman, *Traditionswanderung, I* (Helsinki 1937), 336 ff.; M. Eliade, *Traité d'histoire des religions* (Paris 1949), 309 ff.

Nor is it methodologically correct to assert that trees are considered by the primitive to be animate; for this ignores the crucial distinction between a power which controls a thing and may temporarily lodge within it, and the personification of the thing itself as a sensate, self-determinate being. The primitive may well believe in the former concept, but the latter involves recognition of organic natures and structures, and of these he is unaware. In a word, E. B. Tylor's famous theory of "primitive animism" (under the influence of which Frazer wrote) is an anthropological anachronism.

The same objections may be raised also against Frazer's concept of a general Corn-spirit. This, too, is an artificial, schematic unification of what are really several distinct spirits representing the different "effects" or "impacts" of corn in different circumstances or situations.

Moreover, a sharper distinction needs to be drawn between mere personifications of the corn (e.g., the Sumerian Nisaba) and spirits which inhabit and "condition" it, though the distinction is, to be sure, often hard to draw because of the factor of verbal metonomy.

Finally, Frazer's theory (in the wake of Mannhardt) that theriomorphic corn-demons represent animals seen by reapers fails to account for the representation of such a demon as, e.g., a horse, for horses are not found in corn-fields! The factor of transference from the current characterizations of other "bogies" must be considered. Furthermore, Eliade's view that the sacrifice of animals at sowing or reaping was really a rite of renewal, designed to convey

503

the animal's strength (or other properties) to the community at the beginning of a new lease of life, is at least worthy of careful attention.

337. *Laments.* It has been suggested that Lityerses is simply a personification of the *litê ersês,* or "prayer for rain": R. H. Klausen, *Aeneas und die Penaten* (Hamburg-Gotha 1839–40), i. 121, endorsed by O. Gruppe, *Gr. Myth.,* 966, n. 6. Exactly comparable would be the Egyptian Maneros from *mââ-n per.k,* "come to thy house," the first words of the ritual dirge (see below, ¶338); the Greek corn-goddess Ioulô from *iouloi,* the seasonal ululations for the slain corn-spirit (Semus, quoted by Athenaeus 618E); Iacchos, a by-name of Dionysus, from the ritual cry *iacchos* (Pausanias, iv. 31, 4); Ailinus from the Phoenician *ai lanu,* "woe unto us" (see below, ¶339); Hylas from the *hylagmos,* or "howling" (P. Kretschmer, in *Glotta,* 14 [1923], 13); and the Basque popular hero Lelo, from a word which itself means "dirge" (F. G. Welcker, *Schriften* [Bonn 1844–47], i. 27 ff.; K. Schwenk, *Die Mythologie der Slawen* [Frankfurt 1853], 227–29).

338. *Maneros.* For the Egyptian dirge beginning *mââ-n per.k,* "come to thy house," see: R. O. Faulkner, in *Journal of Egyptian Archaeology,* 22 (1936), 121 ff.; J. de Horrack, *Les lamentations d'Isis et Nephthys* (Paris 1866); E. A. W. Budge, *Osiris and the Egyptian Resurrection* (London 1911), ii. 59–66; H. Kees, *Totenglauben und Jenseitsvorstellungen der alten Aegypter* (Leipzig 1926), 451; id., in *Zs. Aeg. Spr.,* 62 (1927), 77. — The subject of Egyptian harvest dirges has now been fully treated by Miriam Lichtheim in *Journal of Near Eastern Studies,* 4 (1943), 180 f.

339. *Ailinus.* See now O. Eissfeldt, in *Mélanges Syriens offers à René Dussaud* (Paris 1939), i. 161 ff. — On Linus, see also Stammer, *De Lino* (Bonn 1855).

354. *Laments at harvest.* See A. Moret, "Rituels agraires de l'ancien Orient à la lumière des nouveaux textes de Ras Shamra," in *Annuaire de l'Institut de Philologie et d'Histoire orientales,* 3 (1935), 311 ff. — On the *eloolê* cry at vintage, see R. Eisler, *Orphisch-Dionysische Mysterien-gedanken, etc.* (Leipzig 1925), 274, n. 6. Plutarch mentions the *eleleu*-cry intoned at the festival of Oschophoria (*Theseus,* 22), — Not impossibly, this is the real meaning of the Hebrew term *hillulîm,* mentioned in Judges 9 : 27 as a seasonal celebration; while in Micah 7 : 1, the words *alelai lî* [E. V. "Woe is me"], for I am as the gatherings of summer-fruit, as the gleanings of the vintage," may be a play upon the traditional laments. — At Oldenburg, Germany, weeping is customary also at the *sowing* of crops: L. Strackerjan, *Aberglaube und Sagen aus der Herzogtum Oldenburg*[2] (Oldenburg 1887), i. 47.

391. *Eating and drinking the god.* It has been suggested by Emil Forrer (in *Actes du XXème Congrés internat. des Orientalistes* [Louvain 1940], 124–28) that the ancient Hittite practise of drinking, in certain rites, out of a theriomorphic vessel (called *bibru*) is a survival or attenuation of an original drinking of the divine blood or essence, comparable with the Christian communion. — Cp. also Chrysostom, *Hom. in Joann.:* "He [Christ] hath given those who desire Him . . .

to fix their teeth in His flesh"; see S. A. Cook, in W. R. Smith, *Religion of the Semites*[3] (London 1927), 599.

401–05. *Bear-cult in Siberia, etc.* See A. P. Oklandicow, in *Archaeologia Sovietica,* 14 (1850), 7–19 (summarized in Italian by Maria Gibellino in *Studi e Materiali di Storia delle Religioni,* 23 [1952], 129–33). On the Tunguzian ceremony, see B. A. Vassiliev, in *Etnografia Sovietica,* 4 (1948), 76–104. On the Gilyak ceremony, see: A. Slawik, "Zum Problem des Bärenfestes bei den Ainu und Gilyaken," in *Kultur und Sprache. Wiener Beiträge zur Kulturgeschichte und Linguistik,* 52 (1952), 189–203; Kaiser Wilhelm II, *Studien zur Gorgo* (Berlin 1936), 69 ff. (with photographs).

PART VI

THE RIDDANCE OF EVIL

THE TRANSFERENCE

OF EVIL

432. Because it is possible to shift a load of wood, stones, or what not from our own back to the back of another, the primitive fancies that it is equally possible to shift the burden of his pains and sorrows to another, who will suffer them in his stead. Upon this idea he acts, and the result is an endless number of very unamiable devices for palming off on someone else the trouble which a man shrinks from bearing himself.

Transference to an Inanimate Object

433. At the outset it is to be observed that the evil of which a man seeks to rid himself need not be transferred to a person; it may equally well be transferred to an animal or a thing, though in the last case the thing is often only a vehicle to convey the trouble to the first person who touches it. In some of the East Indian islands they think that epilepsy can be cured by striking the patient on the face with the leaves of certain trees and then throwing them away. The disease is believed to have passed into the leaves, and to have been thrown away with them.[1] In the Warramunga and Tjingilli tribes of Central Australia men who suffered from headache have often been seen wearing women's head-rings. "This was connected with the belief that the pain in the head would pass into the rings, and that then it could be thrown away with them into the bush, and so got rid of effectually."[2]

Among the Sihanaka of Madagascar, when a man is very sick, his relatives are sometimes bidden by the diviner to cast out the evil by means of a variety of things, such as a stick of a particular sort of tree, a rag, a pinch of earth from an ant's nest, a little money, or what not. Whatever they may be, they are brought to the patient's house and held by a man near the door, while an exorcist stands in the house and pronounces the formula necessary for casting out the disease. When he has done, the things are thrown away in a southward direction, and all the people in the house, including the sick man, if he has strength enough, shake their loose robes and spit towards the door in order to expedite the departure of the malady.[3] In Vedic times a younger brother who married before his elder brother was thought to have sinned in so doing, but there was a ceremony by which he could purge himself of his sin. Fetters of reed-grass were laid on him in token of his guilt, and when they had been washed and sprinkled they were flung into a foaming torrent, which swept them away, while the evil was bidden to vanish with the foam of the stream.[4] The Matse Negroes of Togoland think that the river Awo has power to carry away the sorrows of mankind. So when one of their friends has died, and their hearts are heavy, they go to the river with leaves of the raphia palm tied round their necks and drums in their hands. Standing on the bank they beat the drums and cast the leaves into the stream. As the leaves float away out of sight to the sound of the rippling water and the roll of the drums, they fancy that their sorrow too is lifted from them.[5] Similarly, the ancient Greeks imagined that the pangs of love might be healed by bathing in the river Selemnus.[6] The Indians of Peru sought to purify themselves from their sins by plunging their heads in a river; they said that the river washed their sins away.[7]

An Arab cure for melancholy or madness caused by love is to put a dish of water on the sufferer's head, drop melted lead into it, and then bury the lead in an open field; thus the mischief that was in the man goes away.[8] Amongst the Miotse of China, when the eldest son of the house attains the age of seven years, a ceremony called "driving away the devil" takes place. The father makes a kite of straw and lets it fly away in the desert, bearing away all evil with it.[9]

Dyak priestesses expel ill-luck from a house by hewing and slashing the air in every corner of it with wooden swords, which they afterwards wash in the river, to let the ill-luck float away down stream. Sometimes they sweep misfortune out of the house with brooms made of the leaves of certain plants and sprinkled with rice-water and blood. Having swept it clean out of every room and into a toy-house made of bamboo, they set the little house with its load of bad luck adrift on the river. The current carries it away out to sea, where it shifts its baleful cargo to a certain kettle-shaped ship, which floats in midocean and receives in its capacious hold all the ills that flesh is heir to.[10]

434. Often, however, the transference of evil to a material object is only a step towards foisting it upon a living person. To cure toothache some of the Australian blacks apply a heated spear-thrower to the cheek. The spear-thrower is then cast away, and the toothache goes with it in the shape of a black stone called *karriitch*. Stones of this kind are found in old mounds and sandhills. They are carefully collected and thrown in the direction of enemies in order to give them toothache.[1] In Mirzapur a mode of transferring disease is to fill a pot with flowers and rice and bury it in a pathway covered up with a flat stone. Whoever touches this is supposed to contract the disease. The practice is called *chalauwa,* or "passing on" the malady. This sort of thing goes on daily in Upper India. Often while walking of a morning in the bazaar you will see a little pile of earth adorned with flowers in the middle of the road. Such a pile usually contains some scabs or scales from the body of a smallpox patient, which are placed there in the hope that some one may touch them, and by catching the disease may relieve the sufferer.[2] The Bahima, a pastoral people of the Uganda Protectorate, often suffer from deep-seated abscesses: "their cure for this is to transfer the disease to some other person by obtaining herbs from the medicine-man, rubbing them over the place where the swelling is, and burying them in the road where people continually pass; the first person who steps over these buried herbs contracts the disease, and the original patient recovers."[3]

435. Sometimes in case of sickness the malady is transferred to an effigy as a preliminary to passing it on to a human being. Thus among the Baganda the medicine-man would sometimes make a model of his patient in clay; then a relative of the sick man would rub the image over the sufferer's body and either bury it in the road or hide it in the grass by the wayside. The first person who stepped over the image or passed by it would catch the disease. Sometimes the effigy was made out of a plantain-flower tied up so as to look like a person; it was used in the same way as the clay figure.[1] Among the Sena-speaking people to the north of the Zambesi, when any one is ill, the doctor makes a little pig of straw to which he transfers the sickness. The little pig is then set on the ground where two paths meet, and any passer-by who chances to kick it over is sure to absorb the illness and to draw it away from the patient.[2]

To Sticks and Stones

436. In the western district of the island of Timor, when men or women are making long and tiring journeys, they fan themselves with leafy branches, which they afterwards throw away on particular spots where their forefathers did the same before them. The fatigue which they felt is thus supposed to have passed into the leaves and to be left behind. Others use stones instead of leaves.[1] Similarly in the Babar Archipelago tired people will strike themselves with stones, believing that they thus transfer to the stones the weariness which they felt in their own bodies. They then throw away the stones in places which are specially set apart for the purpose.[2]

Among the Toradyas of Central Celebes, when a person is suffering from a certain inflammation of the skin he will sometimes take a stout stick, and press it against the affected part of his body, saying, "Go over into this." He believes that he thus transfers the inflammation to the stick, leaving his body whole.[2a]

But it is not mere bodily fatigue which the savage fancies he can rid himself of by the simple expedient of throwing a stick or a stone. Unable clearly to distinguish the immaterial from the material, the abstract from the concrete, he is assailed by vague terrors, he feels himself exposed to some ill-defined danger on the scene of any great crime or great misfortune. The place to him seems haunted ground. The thronging memories that crowd upon his mind, if they are not mistaken by him for goblins and phantoms, oppress his fancy with a leaden weight. His impulse is to flee from the dreadful spot, to shake off the burden that seems to cling to him like a nightmare. This, in his simple sensuous way, he thinks he can do by casting something at the horrid place and hurrying by. For will not the contagion of misfortune, the horror that clutched at his heart-strings, be diverted from himself into the thing? will it not gather up in itself all the evil influences that threatened him, and so leave him to pursue his journey in safety and peace? Some such train of thought, if these gropings and fumblings of a mind in darkness deserve the name of thought, seems to explain the custom, observed by wayfarers in many lands, of throwing sticks or stones on places where something horrible has happened or evil deeds have been done. In the Norwegian district of Tellemarken a cairn is piled up wherever anything fearful has happened, and every passer-by must throw another stone on it, or some evil will befall him.[3] In Sweden and the Esthonian island of Oesel the same custom is practised on scenes of clandestine or illicit love, with the strange addition in Oesel that when a man has lost his cattle he will go to such a spot, and, while he flings a stick or stone on it, will say, "I bring thee wood. Let me soon find my lost cattle."[4] Far from these northern lands, the Dyaks of Batang Lupar keep up an observance of the same sort in the forests of Borneo. Beside their paths may be seen heaps of sticks or stones which are called "lying heaps." Each heap is in memory of some man who told a stupendous lie or disgracefully failed in carrying out an engagement, and everybody who passes adds a stick or stone to the pile, saying as he does so, "For So-and-so's lying heap."[5] The Dyaks think it a sacred duty to add to every such "liar's mound" (*tugong bula*) which they pass; they imagine that the omission of the duty would draw down on them a supernatural punishment.[6]

But it is on scenes of murder and sudden death that this rude method of overting evil is most commonly practised. The custom that every passer-by must cast a stone or stick on the spot where some one has come to a violent end, whether by murder or otherwise, has been observed in practically the same form in such many and diverse parts of the world as Ireland, France, Spain, Sweden, Germany, Bohemia, Lesbos, Morocco, Armenia, Palestine, India, North America, and New Zealand.[7]

Sometimes the scene of the murder or death may also be the grave of the victim, but it need not always be so, and in Europe, where the dead are buried in consecrated ground, the two places would seldom coincide. However, the custom of throwing stones or sticks on a grave has undoubtedly been observed by passers-by in many parts of the world, and that, too, even when the graves are not those of persons who have come to a violent end. Thus we are told that the people of Unalashka, one of the Aleutian Islands, bury their dead on the summits of hills and raise a little hillock over the grave. "In a walk into the country, one of the natives, who attended me, pointed out several of these receptacles of the dead. There was one of them, by the side of the road leading from the harbour to the village, over which was raised a heap of stones. It was observed, that every one who passed it, added one to it."[8] The Hottentot god or hero Heitsi-eibib died several times and came to life again. When the Hottentots pass one of his numerous graves they throw a stone, a bush, or a fresh branch on it for good luck.[9] Near the former mission-station of Bly-deuitzigt in Cape Colony there was a spot called Devil's Neck where, in the opinion of the Bushmen, the devil was interred. To hinder his resurrection stones were piled in heaps about the place. When a Bushman, travelling in the company of a missionary, came in sight of the spot he seized a stone and hurled it at the grave, remarking that if he did not do so his neck would be twisted round so that he would have to look backwards for the term of his natural life.[10]

437. When we survey the many different cases in which passing travellers are accustomed to add stones or sticks to existing piles, it seems difficult, if not impossible, to explain them all on one principle; different and even opposite motives appear, at least at first sight, to have operated in different cases to produce customs superficially alike. Sometimes the motive for throwing the stone is to ward off a dangerous spirit; sometimes it is to cast away an evil; sometimes it is to acquire a good. Yet, perhaps, if we could trace them back to their origin in the mind of primitive man, we might find that they all resolve themselves more or less exactly into the principle of the transference of evil. For to rid ourselves of an evil and to acquire a good are often merely opposite sides of one and the same operation; for example, a convalescent regains health in exactly the same proportion as he shakes off his malady. And though the practice of throwing stones at dangerous spirits, especially at mischievous and malignant ghosts of the dead, appears to spring from a different motive, yet it may be questioned whether the difference is really as great to the savage as it seems to us. To primitive man the idea of spiritual and ghostly powers is still more indefinite than it is to his civilized brother: it fills him with a vague uneasiness and alarm; and this sentiment of dread and horror he, in accordance with his habitual modes of thought, conceives in a concrete form as something material which either surrounds and oppresses him like a fog, or has entered into and taken temporary possession of his body. In either case he imagines that he can rid himself of the uncanny thing by stripping it from his skin or wrenching it out of his body and transferring it to some material substance, whether a stick, a stone, or what not, which he can cast from him, and so, being eased of his burden, can hasten away from the dreadful spot with a lighter heart. Thus the throwing of the sticks or stones would be a form of ceremonial purification, which among primitive peoples is com-

monly conceived as a sort of physical rather than moral purgation, a mode of sweeping or scouring away the morbid matter by which the polluted person is supposed to be infected.

The theory that the throwing of stones is practised in certain circumstances as a mode of purification tallies very well with the tradition as to the origin of those cairns which were to be seen by wayside images of Hermes in ancient Greece, and to which every passer-by added a stone. It was said that when Hermes was tried by the gods for the murder of Argus all the gods flung stones at him as a means of freeing themselves from the pollution contracted by bloodshed; the stones thus thrown made a great heap, and the custom of rearing such heaps at wayside images of Hermes continued ever afterwards.[1] Similarly Plato recommended that if any man had murdered his father or mother, his brother or sister, his son or daughter, he should be put to death, and that his body should be cast forth naked at a cross-road outside of the city. There the magistrates should assemble on behalf of the city, each carrying in his hand a stone, which he was to cast at the head of the corpse by way of purifying the city from the pollution it had contracted by the crime. After that the corpse was to be carried away and flung outside the boundaries.[2] In these cases it would seem that the pollution incurred by the vicinity of a murderer is thought to be gathered up in the stones as a material vehicle and to be thrown away with them.

To Animals

438. Animals are often employed as a vehicle for carrying away or transferring the evil. A Guinea Negro who happens to be unwell will sometimes tie a live chicken round his neck, so that it lies on his breast. When the bird flaps its wings or cheeps the man thinks it a good sign, supposing the chicken to be afflicted with the very pain from which he hopes soon to be released, or which he would otherwise have to endure.[1] In some parts of Algeria people think that typhoid fever can be cured by taking a tortoise, putting it on its back in the road, and covering it over with a pot. The patient recovers, but whoever upsets the pot catches the fever. In Tlemcen a pregnant woman is protected against jinn by means of a black fowl which is kept in the house from the seventh month of her pregnancy till her delivery. Finally, the oldest woman in the house releases the fowl in the Jews' quarter; the bird is supposed to carry the jinn away with it.[2] After an illness a Bechuana king seated himself upon an ox which lay stretched on the ground. The native doctor next poured water on the king's head till it ran down over his body. Then the head of the ox was held in a vessel of water until the animal expired; whereupon the doctor declared, and the people believed, that the ox had died of the king's disease which had been transferred from him to it.[3]

In antiquity Greek women seem to have done the following with swallows which they caught in the house: they poured oil on them and let them fly away, apparently for the purpose of removing ill-luck from the household.[4]

At the cleansing of a leper and of a house suspected of being tainted with leprosy among the Hebrews the priest used to let a living bird fly away into the open field,[5] no doubt in order to carry away the leprosy with it. Similarly among the ancient Arabs a widow was expected to live secluded in a small tent for a year after her husband's death; then a bird or a sheep was brought to her, she made the creature touch her person, and let it go. It was believed that the bird or the sheep would not live long thereafter; doubtless it was supposed to suffer from the uncleanness or taint of death which the widow has transferred to it.[6] Among the Badagas of the Neilgherry Hills at a funeral witnessed by the Rev. A. C. Clayton the buffalo calf was led thrice round the bier, and the dead man's hand was laid on its head. "By this act, the calf was supposed to receive all the sins of the deceased. It was then driven away to a great distance, that it might contaminate no one, and it was said that it would never be sold, but looked on as a dedicated sacred animal."[7] "The idea of this ceremony is, that the sins of the deceased enter the calf, or that the task of his absolution is laid on it. They say that the calf very soon disappears, and that it is never after heard of."[8]

To Human Beings

439. Again, men sometimes play the part of a scapegoat by diverting to themselves the evils that threaten others. An ancient Hindu ritual describes how the pangs of thirst may be transferred from a sick man to another. The operator seats the pair on branches, back to back, the sufferer with his face to the east, and the whole man with his face to the west. Then he stirs some gruel in a vessel placed on the patient's head and hands the stir-about to the other man to drink.[1] There is a painful Telugu remedy for a fever: it is to embrace a bald-headed Brahman widow at the earliest streak of dawn. By doing so you get rid of the fever, and no doubt (though this is not expressly affirmed) you at the same time transfer it to the bald-headed widow.[2] When a Cingalese is dangerously ill, and the physicians can do nothing, a devil-dancer is called in, who by making offerings to the devils, and dancing in the masks appropriate to them, conjures these demons of disease, one after the other, out of the sick man's body and into his own. Having thus successfully extracted the cause of the malady, the artful dancer lies down on a bier, and shamming death, is carried to an open place outside the village. Here, being left to himself, he soon comes to life again, and hastens back to claim his reward.[3] In 1590 a Scottish witch of the name of Agnes Sampson was convicted of curing a certain Robert Kers of a disease "laid upon him by a westland warlock when he was at Dumfries, whilk sickness she took upon herself, and kept the same with great groaning and torment till the morn, at whilk time there was a great din heard in the house." The noise was made by the witch in her efforts to shift the disease, by means of clothes, from herself to a cat or dog. Unfortunately the attempt partly miscarried. The disease missed the animal and hit Alexander Douglas of Dalkeith, who dwined and died of it, while the original patient, Robert Kers, was made whole.[4] The Dyaks believe that certain men possess in themselves the power of neutralizing bad omens. So, when evil omens have alarmed a farmer for the safety of his crops, he takes a small portion of his farm produce to one of these wise men, who eats it raw for a small consideration, "and thereby appropriates to himself the evil omen, which in him becomes innocuous, and thus delivers the other from the ban of the *pemali* or taboo."[5]

"In one part of New Zealand an expiation for sin was felt to be necessary; a service was performed over an individual, by which all the sins of the tribe were supposed to be transferred to him, a fern stalk was previously tied to his person, with which he jumped into the river, and there unbinding, allowed it to float away to the sea, bearing their sins with it."[6] In great emergencies the sins of the Rajah of Manipur used to be transferred to somebody else, usually to a criminal, who earned his pardon by his vicarious sufferings. To effect the transference the Rajah and his wife, clad in fine robes, bathed on a scaffold erected in the bazaar, while the criminal crouched beneath it. With the water which dripped from them on him their sins also were washed away and fell on the human scapegoat. To complete the transference the Rajah and his wife made over their fines robes to their substitute, while they themselves, clad in new raiment, mixed with the people till evening. But at the close of the day they entered into retreat and remained in seclusion for about a week, during which they were esteemed sacred or tabooed.[7]

In Travancore, when a rajah is near his end, they seek out a holy Brahman, who consents to take upon himself the sins of the dying man in consideration of the sum of ten thousand rupees. Thus prepared to immolate himself on the altar of duty as a vicarious sacrifice for sin, the saint is introduced into the chamber of death, and closely embraces the dying rajah, saying to him, "O King, I undertake to bear all your sins and diseases. May your Highness live long and reign happily." Having thus, with a noble devotion, taken to himself the sins of the sufferer, and likewise the rupees, he is sent away from the country and never more allowed to return.[8] Closely akin to this is the old Welsh custom known as "sin-eating." Says a letter dated February 1, 1714–15, "within the memory of our fathers, in Shropshire, in those villages adjoyning to Wales, when a person dyed, there was notice given to an old sire (for so they called him), who presently repaired to the place where the deceased lay, and stood before the door of the house, when some of the family came out and furnished him with a cricket, on which he sat down facing the door. Then they gave him a groat, which he put in his pocket; a crust of bread, which he eat; and a full bowle of ale, which he drank off at a draught. After this he got up from the cricket and pronounced, with a

composed gesture, the ease and rest of the soul departed for which he would
pawn his own soul."[9]

IN EUROPEAN FOLK-LORE

440. Similar attempts to shift the burden of disease, misfortune, and sin
from one's self to another person, or to an animal or thing, have been common also among the civilized nations of Europe, both in ancient and modern
times. A Roman cure for fever was to pare the patient's nails, and stick
the parings with wax on a neighbour's door before sunrise; the fever then
passed from the sick man to his neighbour.[1]

In the fourth century of our era Marcellus of Bordeaux prescribed a cure
for warts, which still enjoys a certain vogue among superstitious folk in
various parts of Europe. You are to touch your warts with as many little
stones as you have warts; then wrap the stones in an ivy leaf, and cast them
out upon the road. Whoever picks them up will get the warts, and you will
be rid of them. A similar cure, with trifling variations, has been prescribed
in modern times in Italy, France, Austria, England and Scotland.[2] In Oldenburg they say that when a person lies sweating with fever, he should take a
piece of money to himself in bed. The money is afterwards thrown away
on the street, and whoever picks it up will catch the fever, but the original
patient will be rid of it.[3]

441. Often in Europe, as among savages, an attempt is made to transfer a
pain or malady from a man to an animal. Grave writers of antiquity recommended that, if a man be stung by a scorpion, he should sit upon an ass
with his face to the tail, or whisper in the animal's ear, "A scorpion has stung
me"; in either case, they thought, the pain would be transferred from the man
to the ass.[1] A Northamptonshire, Devonshire, and Welsh cure for a cough
is to put a hair of the patient's head between two slices of buttered bread and
give the sandwich to a dog. The animal will thereupon catch the cough and
the patient will lose it.[2] Sometimes an ailment is transferred to an animal by
sharing food with it. A peasant woman in Abbèhausen told her pastor that
she suffered from fever for a whole year and found no relief. At last somebody advised her to give some of her food to a dog and a cat. She did so
and the fever passed from her into the animals. But when she saw the poor
sick beasts always before her, she wished it undone. Then the fever left
the cat and the dog and returned to her.[3]

A Saxon remedy for rupture in a child is to take a snail, thrust it at sunset
into a hollow tree, and stop up the hole with clay. Then as the snail perishes
the child recovers.[4]

442. Often the sufferer seeks to shift his burden of sickness to some inanimate object. In Athens there is a little chapel of St. John the Baptist built
against an ancient column. Fever patients resort thither and, by attaching
a waxed thread to the inner side of the column, believe that they transfer

the fever from themselves to the pillar.[1] In the Mark of Brandenburg they say that if you suffer from giddiness you should strip naked and run thrice round a flax-field after sunset; in that way the flax will get the giddiness, and you will be rid of it.[2]

443. But perhaps the thing most commonly employed in Europe as a receptacle for sickness and trouble of all sorts is a tree or bush.

In Sicily it is believed that all kinds of marvellous cures can be effected on the night which precedes Ascension Day. For example, people who suffer from goitre bite the bark of a peach-tree just when the clocks are striking midnight. The malady is thus transferred to the sap of the tree, and the leaves wither away in exact proportion as the patient recovers.[1] A Bulgarian cure for fever is to run thrice round a willow-tree at sunrise, crying, "The fever shall shake thee, and the sun shall warm me."[2] In the Greek island of Karpathos the priest ties a red thread round the neck of a sick person. Next morning the friends of the patient remove the thread and go out to the hillside, where they tie the thread to a tree, thinking that they thus transfer the sickness to the tree.[3] In Bohemia the friends of a fever patient will sometimes carry him head foremost, by means of straw ropes, to a bush, on which they dump him down. Then he must jump up and run home. The friends who carried him also flee, leaving the straw ropes and likewise the fever behind them on the bush.[4]

THE PUBLIC

EXPULSION OF EVIL

OCCASIONAL EXPULSION

444. Public attempts to expel the accumulated ills of a whole community may be divided into two classes, according as those ills are immaterial and invisible or are embodied in a material vehicle or scapegoat. The former may be called the direct or immediate expulsion of evils; the latter the indirect or mediate expulsion, or the expulsion by scapegoat. We begin with examples of the former.

In the island of Rook, between New Guinea and New Britain, when any misfortune has happened, all the people run together, scream, curse, howl, and beat the air with sticks to drive away the devil (*Marsába*), who is supposed to be the author of the mishap. From the spot where the mishap took place they drive him step by step to the sea, and on reaching the shore they redouble their shouts and blows in order to expel him from the island. He generally retires to the sea or to the island of Lottin.[1] The natives of New Britain ascribe sickness, drought, the failure of crops, and in short all misfortunes, to the influence of wicked spirits. So at times when many people sicken and die, as at the beginning of the rainy season, all the inhabitants of a district, armed with branches and clubs, go out by moonlight to the fields, where they beat and stamp on the ground with wild howls till morning, believing that this drives away the devils; and for the same purpose they rush through the village with burning torches.[2] The natives of New Caledonia are said to believe that all evils are caused by a powerful and malignant spirit; hence in order to rid themselves of him they will from time to time dig a great pit, round which the whole tribe gathers. After cursing the demon, they fill up the pit with earth, and trample on the top with loud shouts. This they call burying the evil spirit.[3] Among the Dieri tribe of Central Australia, when a serious illness occurs, the medicine-men expel Cootchie or the devil by beating the ground in and outside of the camp with the stuffed tail of

519

a kangaroo, until they have chased the demon away to some distance from the camp.[4] The Alfurs of Halmahera attribute epidemics to the devil who comes from other villages to carry them off. So, in order to rid the village of the disease, the sorcerer drives away the devil. From all the villagers he receives a costly garment and places it on four vessels, which he takes to the forest and leaves at the spot where the devil is supposed to be. Then with mocking words he bids the demon abandon the place.[5]

The Solomon Islanders of Bougainville Straits believe that epidemics are always, or nearly always, caused by evil spirits; and accordingly when the people of a village have been suffering generally from colds, they have been known to blow conch-shells, beat tins, shout, and knock on the houses for the purpose of expelling the demons and so curing their colds.[6] The Shans of Kengtung, a province of Upper Burma, imagine that epidemics are brought about by the prowling ghosts of wicked men, such as thieves and murderers, who cannot rest but go about doing all the harm they can to the living. Hence when sickness is rife, the people take steps to expel these dangerous spirits. The Buddhist priests exert themselves actively in the beneficent enterprise. They assemble in a body at the Town Court and read the scriptures. Guns are fired and processions march to the city gates, by which the fiends are supposed to take their departure. There small trays of food are left for them, but the larger offerings are deposited in the middle of the town.[7] When smallpox first appeared amongst the Kumis of South-Eastern India, they thought it was a devil come from Aracan. The villages were placed in a state of siege, no one being allowed to leave or enter them. A monkey was killed by being dashed on the ground, and its body was hung at the village gate. Its blood, mixed with small river pebbles, was sprinkled on the houses, the threshold of every house was swept with the monkey's tail, and the fiend was adjured to depart.[8] At Great Bassam, in Guinea, the French traveller Hecquard witnessed the exorcism of the evil spirit who was believed to make women barren. The women who wished to become mothers offered to the fetish wine-vessels or statuettes representing women suckling children. Then being assembled in the fetish hut, they were sprinkled with rum by the priest, while young men fired guns and brandished swords to drive away the demon.[9] When sickness was prevalent in a Huron village, and all other remedies had been tried in vain, the Indians had recourse to the ceremony called *Lonouyroya*, "which is the principal invention and most proper means, so they say, to expel from the town or village the devils and evil spirits which cause, induce, and import all the maladies and infirmities which they suffer in body and mind." Accordingly, one evening the men would begin to rush like madmen about the village, breaking and upsetting whatever they came across in the wigwams. They threw fire and burning brands about the streets, and all night long they ran howling and singing without cessation. Then they all dreamed of something, a knife, dog, skin, or whatever it might be, and when morning came they went from wigwam to wigwam asking for presents. These they received silently, till the particular thing was given them which they had dreamed about. On receiving it they uttered a cry of joy and rushed from the hut, amid the congratulations of all present. The health of those who received what they had dreamed of was believed to be assured; whereas those who did not get what they had set their hearts upon regarded their fate as sealed.[10]

445. Sometimes, instead of chasing the demon of disease from their homes, savages prefer to leave him in peaceable possession, while they themselves take to flight and attempt to prevent him from following in their tracks. Thus when the Patagonians were attacked by smallpox, which they attributed to the machinations of an evil spirit, they used to abandon their sick and flee, slashing the air with their weapons and throwing water about in order to keep off the dreadful pursuer; and when after several days' march they reached a place where they hoped to be beyond his reach, they used by way of precaution to plant all their cutting weapons with the sharp edges turned towards the quarter from which they had come, as if they were re-pelling a charge of cavalry.[1] Similarly, when the Lules or Tonocotes Indians of the Gran Chaco were attacked by an epidemic, they regularly sought to evade it by flight, but in so doing they always followed a sinuous, not a straight, course; because they said that when the disease made after them he would be so exhausted by the turnings and windings of the route that he would never be able to come up with them.[2] When the Indians of New Mexico were decimated by smallpox or other infectious disease, they used to shift their quarters every day, retreating into the most sequestered parts of the mountains and choosing the thorniest thickets they could find, in the hope that the smallpox would be too afraid of scratching himself on the thorns to follow them.[3] When some Chins on a visit to Rangoon were attacked by cholera, they went about with drawn swords to scare away the demon, and they spent the day hiding under bushes so that he might not be able to find them.[4]

SEASONAL AND PERIODIC EXPULSION

446. Certain seasons of the year mark themselves out naturally as appropriate moments for a general expulsion of evils.

The Koryaks of the Taigonos Peninsula, in north-eastern Asia, celebrate annually a festival after the winter solstice. Rich men invite all their neighbours to the festival, offer a sacrifice to "The-One-on-High," and slaughter many reindeer for their guests. If there is a shaman present he goes all round the interior of the house, beating the drum and driving away the demons (*kalau*). He searches all the people in the house, and if he finds a demon's arrow sticking in the body of one of them, he pulls it out, though naturally the arrow is invisible to common eyes. In this way he protects them against disease and death. If there is no shaman present, the demons may be expelled by a woman skilled in incantations.[1] The chief festival of the Cherokee Indians was the Propitiation, "Cementation," or Purification festival. "It was celebrated shortly after the first new moon of autumn, and consisted of a multiplicity of rigorous rites, fastings, ablutions, and purifications. Among the most important functionaries on the occasion were seven exorcisers or cleansers, whose duty it was, at a certain stage of the proceedings, to drive away evil and purify the town. Each one bore in his hand a white rod of sycamore. 'The leader, followed by the others, walked around the national heptagon, and coming to the treasurer or store-house to the west of it, they lashed the eaves of the roofs with their rods. The leader then went to another house, followed by the others, singing, and repeated the same ceremony until every house was purified.' This ceremony was repeated daily during the continuance of the festival. In performing their ablutions they went into the water, and allowed their old clothes to be carried away by the stream, by which means they supposed their impurities removed."[2]

In September the Incas of Peru celebrated a festival called Situa, the object of which was to banish from the capital and its vicinity all disease and trouble.[3]

At Onitsha, on the Niger, Mr. J. C. Taylor witnessed in 1858 the celebration of New Year's Day by the Negroes. Every family brought a firebrand out into the street, threw it away, and exclaimed as they returned, "The gods of the new year! New Year has come round again." Mr. Taylor adds, "The meaning of the custom seems to be that the fire is to drive away the old year with its sorrows and evils, and to embrace the new year with hearty reception."[4]

Down to recent years the State of Perak, in the Malay Peninsula, "used to be 'cleansed' periodically by the propitiation of friendly spirits and the expulsion of malignant influences. . . . The royal State shaman, his royal assistant, and the chief magicians from the river parishes assembled at a village at the foot of the rapids below which the habitations of the Perak Malays began. *Séances* occupied seven days. A pink buffalo was killed and a feast was held. The head and other pieces of the victim were piled on one of the rafts, which was then set out down-stream. The four leading rafts were prepared for the four leading classes of spirits and were manned by their appropriate magicians. The foremost raft carried a branching tree, erect and supported by stays, and was for the shaman's familiars. The fifth raft bore Muslim elders. Next came the royal band with its sacred drums and trumpets, and then the Raja Kechil Muda (the title of the assistant State shaman) and his followers. As they floated down the river, the magicians waved white cloths and invoked the spirits of the districts passed to come aboard and consume the offerings. Whenever they reached a mosque, they halted for one night while a *séance* was held and the villagers slaughtered a buffalo, placing its head on one of the spirit rafts and eating the rest of the carcase. At the mouth of the river the rafts were abandoned and allowed to drift to sea. The State shaman did not accompany the procession downstream, leaving the escort of the spirit rafts with their grisly freight to his assistant. So, too, the magicians of the different parishes of the river-banks stayed behind in turn, each of them supplying a substitute to go downstream with the assistant State shaman. . . . The 'cleansing' of the States of Perak and Kelantan is said to have been triennial. One account indeed states that Perak was cleansed once in seven years or once in a Sultan's reign, but this is probably a native explanation of the gradual lapse of the custom."[4a]

447. Sometimes the date of the annual expulsion of devils is fixed with reference to the agricultural seasons. Thus at Kiriwina, in South-Eastern New Guinea, when the new yams had been harvested, the people feasted and danced for many days, and a great deal of property, such as armlets, native money, and so forth, was displayed conspicuously on a platform erected for the purpose. When the festivities were over, all the people gathered together and expelled the spirits from the village by shouting, beating the posts of the houses, and overturning everything under which a wily spirit might be supposed to lurk.[1]

Among some of the Hindu Kush tribes, the expulsion of devils takes place after harvest. When the last crop of autumn has been got in, it is thought necessary to drive away evil spirits from the granaries. A kind of porridge called *mool* is eaten, and the head of the family takes his matchlock and fires it into the floor. Then, going outside, he sets to work loading and firing till his powder-horn is exhausted, while all his neighbours are simply employed. The next day is spent in rejoicings. In Chitral this festival is called "devil-driving."[2]

448. The people of Bali, an island to the east of Java, have periodical expulsions of devils upon a great scale. Generally the time chosen is the day of the "dark moon" in the ninth month. When the demons have been long unmolested the country is said to be "warm," and the priest issues orders to expel them by force, lest the whole of Bali should be rendered uninhabitable. On the day appointed the people of the village or district assemble at the principal temple. Here at a cross-road offerings are set out for the devils. After prayers have been recited by the priests, the blast of a horn summons the devils to partake of the meal which has been prepared for them. At the same time a number of men step forward and light their torches at the holy lamp which burns before the chief priest. Immediately afterwards, followed by the bystanders, they spread in all directions and march through the streets and lanes crying, "Depart! go away!" Wherever they pass, the people who have stayed at home hasten, by a deafening clatter on doors, beams, rice-blocks, and so forth, to take their share in the expulsion of devils. Thus chased from the houses, the fiends flee to the banquet which has been set out for them; but

uorvi, esciti fora tentaziuni, esca u malu ed entri u bene." At the same time they knock on doors and windows, on chests and other articles of furniture.[2] Again, in Albania on Easter Eve the young people light torches of resinous wood and march in procession, swinging them, through the village. At last they throw the torches into the river, crying, "Ha, Kore! we throw you into the river, like these torches, that you may never return."[3] Silesian peasants believe that on Good Friday the witches go their rounds and have great power for mischief. Hence about Oels, near Strehlitz, the people on that day arm themselves with old brooms and drive the witches from house and home, from farmyard and cattle-stall, making a great uproar and clatter as they do so.[4]

In Central Europe it was apparently on Walpurgis Night, the Eve of May Day, above all other times that the baleful powers of the witches were exerted to the fullest extent; nothing therefore could be more natural than that men should be on their guard against them at that season, and that, not content with merely standing on their defence, they should boldly have sought to carry the war into the enemy's quarters by attacking and forcibly expelling the uncanny crew. Amongst the weapons with which they fought their invisible adversaries in these grim encounters were holy water, the fumes of incense or other combustibles, and loud noises of all kinds, particularly the clashing of metal instruments, amongst which the ringing of church bells was perhaps the most effectual.[5] Thus in the Böhmerwald Mountains, which divide Bavaria from Bohemia, all the young fellows of the village assemble after sunset on some height, especially at a cross-road, and crack whips for a while in unison with all their strength. This drives away the witches; for so far as the sound of the whips is heard, these maleficent beings can do no harm. In other places, again, the youth blow upon so-called shawms made of peeled willow-wood in front of every house, especially in front of such houses as are suspected of harbouring a witch.[6]

In Bohemia many are the precautions taken by the peasantry, both German and Czech, to guard themselves and their cattle against the witches on Walpurgis Night. Thus in Absrot the village youth go out to cross-roads and there beat the ground with boards, no doubt for the purpose of thrashing the witches who are commonly supposed to assemble at such spots. In Deslawen, after the evening bells have rung, people go through the houses beating the walls or floors with boards; then they issue forth into the roads, headed by a boy who carries the effigy of a witch made up of rags. Thereupon grown-up folk crack whips and fire shots. In Schönwert the young people go in bands through the village and the meadows, making a great noise with bells, flutes, and whips, for the more noise they make the more effectual is the ceremony supposed to be. Meantime the older men are busy firing shots over the fields and the dungheaps. In Hochofen troops of children go from house to house on Walpurgis Evening, making a great clatter with tin cans and kettles, while they scream, "Witch, go out, your house is burning." This is called "Driving out the Witches."[7]

At Penzance in Cornwall boys run about blowing horns on the thirtieth of April (Walpurgis Day), and when questioned why they do so they say that they are "scaring away the devil." The horns used for this purpose are made of tin and shaped like a herald's trumpet; they vary in length from a foot to a yard and can give forth a very loud blast.[8] The custom is probably a relic of a general expulsion of witches and demons on that day.

452. Another witching time is the period of twelve days between Christmas (the twenty-fifth of December) and Epiphany (the sixth of January). A thousand quaint superstitions cluster round that mystic season. It is then that the Wild Huntsman sweeps through the air, the powers of evil are let loose, werewolves are prowling round, and the witches work their wicked will. Hence in some parts of Silesia the people burn pine-resin all night long between Christmas and the New Year in order that the pungent smoke may drive witches and evil spirits far away from house and homestead; and on Christmas Eve and New Year's Eve they fire shots over fields and meadows, into shrubs and trees, and wrap straw round the fruit-trees, to prevent the spirits from doing them harm.[1] On New Year's Eve, which is Saint Sylvester's Day, Bohemian lads, armed with guns, form themselves into circles and fire thrice into the air. This is called "Shooting the Witches" and is supposed to frighten the witches away. While the young fellows are rendering this service to the community, the housewives go about their houses sprinkling holy water in all the rooms and chalking three crosses on every door,[2] no doubt to accelerate the departure of the witches, and to prevent their return.

The last of the mystic twelve days is Epiphany or Twelfth Night, and it too has been selected as a proper season for the expulsion of the powers of evil in various parts of Europe. Thus at Brunnen on the Lake of Lucerne the boys go about in procession on Twelfth Night, carrying torches and lanterns, and making a great noise with horns, cowbells, whips, and so forth. This is said to frighten away the two female spirits of the wood, Strudeli and Strätteli. Of these two names Strudeli seems to mean "witch" and Strätteli "nightmare." The people believe that if they do not make enough noise, there will be little fruit that year.[3] In Labruguière, also, a canton of Southern France, the evil spirits are expelled at the same season. On the eve of Twelfth Day the inhabitants rush through the streets jangling bells, clattering kettles, and doing everything to make a discordant noise. Then by the light of torches and blazing faggots they set up a prodigious hue and cry, an ear-splitting uproar, hoping thereby to chase all the wandering ghosts and devils from the town.[4]

With this noisy ceremony we may compare a similar custom which used to be observed year by year at the same season in the long and spacious Piazza Navona at Rome. There on the night before Epiphany a dense crowd assembles and diverts itself by raising a hideous uproar. Soon after supper

the furrow which has thus been traced. In the village of Dubrowitschi a puppet is carried before the plough with the cry, "Out of the village with the unclean spirit!" and at the end of the ceremony it is torn in pieces and the fragments scattered about.[3] Sometimes in an Esthonian village a rumour will get about that the Evil One himself has been seen in the place. Instantly the entire population, armed with sticks, flails, and scythes, turns out to give him chase. They generally expel him in the shape of a wolf or a cat, occasionally they brag that they have beaten the devil to death.[4] At Carmona, in Andalusia, on one day of the year, boys are stripped naked and smeared with glue in which feathers are stuck. Thus disguised, they run from house to house, the people trying to avoid them and to bar their houses against them.[5] The ceremony is probably a relic of an annual expulsion of devils.

454. More often, however, the expelled demons are not represented at all, but are understood to be present invisibly in the material and visible vehicle which conveys them away. Here, again, it will be convenient to distinguish between occasional and periodical expulsions. We begin with the former.

The vehicle which conveys away the demons may be of various kinds. A common one is a little ship or boat. Thus, in the southern district of the island of Ceram, when a whole village suffers from sickness, a small ship is made and filled with rice, tobacco, eggs, and so forth, which have been contributed by all the people. A little sail is hoisted on the ship. When all is ready, a man calls out in a very loud voice, "O all ye sicknesses, ye smallpoxes, agues, measles, etc., who have visited us so long and wasted us so sorely, but who now cease to plague us, we have made ready this ship for you and we have furnished you with provender sufficient for the voyage. Ye shall have no lack of food nor of betel-leaves nor of areca nuts nor of tobacco. Depart, and sail away from us directly; never come near us again; but go to a land which is far from here. Let all the tides and winds waft you speedily thither, and so convey you thither that for the time to come we may live sound and well, and that we may never see the sun rise on you again." Then ten or twelve men carry the vessel to the shore, and let it drift away with the land-breeze, feeling convinced that they are free from sickness for ever, or at least till the next time.[1]

Similar ceremonies are commonly resorted to in other East Indian islands. Thus in Timor-laut, to mislead the demons who are causing sickness, a small proa, containing the image of a man and provisioned for a long voyage, is allowed to drift away with wind and tide. As it is being launched, the people cry, "O sickness, go from here; turn back! What do you here in this poor land?"[2]

The plan of putting puppets in the boat to represent sick persons, in order to lure the demons after them, is not uncommon.[3] For example, most of the pagan tribes on the coast of Borneo seek to drive away epidemic disease as follows. They carve one or more rough human images from the pith of the sago palm and place them on a small raft or boat or full-rigged Malay ship together with rice and other food. The boat is decked with blossoms of the areca palm and with ribbons made from its leaves, and thus adorned the little craft is allowed to float out to sea with the ebb-tide, bearing, as the people fondly think or hope, the sickness away with it.[4]

In Selangor, one of the native states in the Malay Peninsula, the ship employed in the export of disease is, or used to be, a model of a special kind of Malay craft called a *lanchang*. This was a two-masted vessel with galleries fore and aft, armed with cannon, and used by Malay rajahs on the coast of Sumatra. So gallant a ship would be highly acceptable to the spirits, and to make it still more beautiful in their eyes it was not uncommonly stained yellow with tumeric or saffron, for among the Malays yellow is the royal colour. Some years ago a very fine model of a *lanchang*, with its cargo of sickness, was towed down the river to the sea by the Government steam launch. A common spell uttered at the launching of one of these ships runs as follows:—

"Ho, elders of the upper reaches,
Elders of the lower reaches,
Elders of the dry land,
Elders of the river-flats,
Assemble ye, O people, lords of hill and hill-foot,
Lords of cavern and hill-locked basin,
Lords of the deep primeval forest,
Lords of the river-bends,
Come on board this *lanchang*, assembling in your multitudes.
So may ye depart with the ebbing stream,
Depart on the passing breeze,
Depart in the yawning earth,
Depart in the red-dyed earth.
Go ye to the ocean which has no wave,
And the plain where no green herb grows,
And never return hither.
But if ye return hither,
Ye shall be consumed by the curse.
At sea ye shall get no drink,
Ashore ye shall get no food,
But gape in vain about the world."[5]

When the Tagbanuas and other tribes of the Philippines suffered from epidemics, they used to make little models of ships, supply them with rice and fresh drinking water, and launch them on the sea, in order that the evil spirits might sail away in them.[6] When the people of Tikopia, a small island in the Pacific, to the north of the New Hebrides, were attacked by an epidemic cough, they made a little canoe and adorned it with flowers. Four sons of the principal chiefs carried it on their shoulders all round the island, accompanied by the whole population, some of whom beat the bushes, while others uttered

On the Day of Atonement, which was the tenth day of the seventh month, the Jewish high-priest laid both his hands on the head of a live goat, confessed over it all the iniquities of the Children of Israel, and, having thereby transferred the sins of the people to the beast, sent it away into the wilderness.[2]

459. The periodic scapegoat may also be a human being. At Onitsha, on the Niger, two human beings used to be annually sacrificed to take away the sins of the land. The victims were purchased by public subscription. All persons who, during the past year, had fallen into gross sins, such as incendiarism, theft, adultery, witchcraft, and so forth, were expected to contribute 28 *ngugas,* or a little over £2. The money thus collected was taken into the interior of the country and expended in the purchase of two sickly persons "to be offered as a sacrifice for all these abominable crimes—one for the land and one for the river." A man from a neighbouring town was hired to put them to death.[1]

In Siam it used to be the custom on one day of the year to single out a woman broken down by debauchery, and carry her on a litter through all the streets to the music of drums and hautboys. The mob insulted her and pelted her with dirt; and after having carried her through the whole city, they threw her on a dunghill or a hedge of thorns outside the ramparts, forbidding her ever to enter the walls again. They believed that the woman thus drew upon herself all the malign influences of the air and of evil spirits.[2] There was formerly a practice at Asakusa in Tokio on the last day of the year for a man got up as a devil to be chased round the pagoda there by another wearing a mask. After this 3,000 tickets were scrambled for by the spectators. These were carried away and pasted up over the doors as a charm against pestilence."[3]

460. Human scapegoats, as we shall see presently, were well known in classical antiquity, and even in mediaeval Europe the custom seems not to have been wholly extinct. In the town of Halberstadt, in Thüringen, there was a church said to have been founded by Charlemagne. In this church every year they chose a man, who was believed to be stained with heinous sins. On the first day of Lent he was brought to the church, dressed in mourning garb, with his head muffled up. At the close of the service he was turned out of the church. During the forty days of Lent he perambulated the city barefoot, neither entering the churches nor speaking to any one. The canons took it in turn to feed him. After midnight he was allowed to sleep in the streets. On the day before Good Friday, after the consecration of the holy oil, he was re-admitted to the church and absolved from his sins. The people gave him money. He was called Adam, and was now believed to be in a state of innocence.[1] At Entlebuch, in Switzerland, down to the close of the eighteenth century, the custom of annually expelling a scapegoat was preserved in the ceremony of driving "Posterli" from the village into the lands of the neighbouring village. "Posterli" was represented by a lad disguised as an old witch or as a goat or an ass. Amid a deafening noise of horns, clarionets, bells, whips, and so forth, he was driven out. Sometimes "Posterli" was represented by a puppet, which was drawn on a sledge and left in a corner of the neighbouring village. The ceremony took place on the Thursday evening of the last week but one before Christmas.[2]

In Munich down to about a hundred years ago the expulsion of the devil from the city used to be annually enacted on Ascension Day. On the Eve of Ascension Day a man disguised as a devil was chased through the streets, which were then narrow and dirty in contrast to the broad, well-kept thoroughfares, lined with imposing buildings, which now distinguish the capital of Bavaria. His pursuers were dressed as witches and wizards and provided with the indispensable crutches, brooms, and pitchforks which make up the outfit of these uncanny beings. While the devil fled before them, the troop of maskers made after him with wild whoops and halloos, and when they overtook him they ducked him in puddles or rolled him on dunghills. In this way the demon at last succeeded in reaching the palace, where he put off his hideous and now filthy disguise and was rewarded for his vicarious sufferings by a copious meal. The devilish costume which he had thrown off was then stuffed with hay and straw and conveyed to a particular church (the Frauenkirche), where it was kept over night, being hung by a rope from a window in the tower. On the afternoon of Ascension Day, before the Vesper service began, an image of the Saviour was drawn up to the roof of the church, no doubt to symbolize the event which the day commemorates. Then burning tow and wafers were thrown on the people. Meantime the effigy of the devil, painted black, with a pair of horns and a lolling red tongue, had been dangling from the church tower, to the delight of a gaping crowd of spectators gathered before the church. It was now flung down into their midst, and a fierce struggle for possession of it took place among the rabble. Finally, it was carried out of the town by the Isar gate and burned on a neighbouring height, "in order that the foul fiend might do no harm to the city." The custom died out at Munich towards the end of the eighteenth century; but it is said that similar ceremonies are observed to this day in some villages of Upper Bavaria.[3]

This quaint ceremony suggests that the pardoned criminal who used to play the principal part in a solemn religious procession on Ascension Day at Rouen may in like manner have originally served, if not as a representative of the devil, at least as a public scapegoat, who relieved the whole people of their sins and sorrows for a year by taking them upon himself. This would explain why the gaol had to be raked in order to furnish one who would parade with the highest ecclesiastical dignitaries in their gorgeous vestments through the streets of Rouen, while the church bells pealed out, the clergy chanted, banners waved, and every circumstance combined to enchance the pomp and splendour of the pageant. It would add a pathetic significance to the crowning act of the ceremony, when on a lofty platform in the public square, with the eyes of a great and silent multitude turned upon him, the

the gods to prevent sickness and other evils among the people, "and, as a peace-offering, sacrifice one man. The man is not killed purposely, but the ceremony he undergoes often proves fatal. Grain is thrown against his head, and his face is painted half white, half black." Thus grotesquely disguised, and carrying a coat of skin on his arm, he is called the King of the Years, and sits daily in the market-place, where he helps himself to whatever he likes and goes about shaking a black yak's tail over the people, who thus transfer their bad luck to him. On the tenth day, all the troops in Lhasa march to the great temple and form in line before it. The King of the Years is brought forth from the temple and receives small donations from the assembled multitude. He then ridicules the Jalno, saying to him, "What we perceive through the five senses is no illusion. All you teach is untrue," and the like. The Jalno, who represents the Grand Lama for the time being, contests these heretical opinions; the dispute waxes warm, and at last both agree to decide the questions at issue by a cast of the dice, the Jalno offering to change places with the scapegoat should the throw be against him. If the King of the Years wins, much evil is prognosticated; but if the Jalno wins, there is great rejoicing, for it proves that his adversary has been accepted by the gods as a victim to bear all the sins of the people of Lhasa. Fortune, however, always favours the Jalno, who throws sixes with unvarying success, while his opponent turns up only ones. Nor is this so extraordinary as at first sight it might appear; for the Jalno's dice are marked with nothing but sixes and his adversary's with nothing but ones. When he sees the finger of Providence thus plainly pointed against him, the King of the Years is terrified and flees away upon a white horse, with a white dog, a white bird, salt, and so forth, which have all been provided for him by the government. His face is still painted half white and half black, and he still wears his leathern coat. The whole populace pursues him, hooting, yelling, and firing blank shots in volleys after him. Thus driven out of the city, he is detained for seven days in the great chamber of horrors at the Samyas monastery, surrounded by monstrous and terrific images of devils and skins of huge serpents and wild beasts. Thence he goes away into the mountains of Chetang, where he has to remain an outcast for several months or a year in a narrow den. If he dies before the time is out, the people say it is an auspicious omen; but if he survives, he may return to Lhasa and play the part of scapegoat over again the following year.[3]

This quaint ceremonial, still annually observed in the secluded capital of Buddhism—the Rome of Asia—is interesting because it exhibits, in a clearly marked religious stratification, a series of divine redeemers themselves redeemed, of vicarious sacrifices vicariously atoned for, of gods undergoing a process of fossilization, who, while they retain the privileges, have disburdened themselves of the pains and penalties of divinity. In the Jalno we may without undue straining discern a successor of those temporary kings, those mortal gods, who purchase a short lease of power and glory at the price of their lives. That he is the temporary substitute of the Grand Lama is certain; that he is, or was once, liable to act as scapegoat for the people is made nearly certain by his offer to change places with the real scapegoat—the King of the Years—if the arbitrament of the dice should go against him. It is true that the conditions under which the question is now put to the hazard have reduced the offer to an idle form. But such forms are no mere mushroom growths, springing up of themselves in a night. If they are now lifeless formalities, empty husks devoid of significance, we may be sure that they once had a life and a meaning; if at the present day they are blind alleys leading nowhere, we may be certain that in former days they were paths that led somewhere, if only to death. That death was the goal to which of old the Tibetan scapegoat passed after his brief period of licence in the market-place, is a conjecture that has much to commend it. Analogy suggests it; the blank shots fired after him, the statement that the ceremony often proves fatal, the belief that his death is a happy omen, all confirm it. We need not wonder then that the Jalno, after paying so dear to act as deputy-deity for a few weeks, should have preferred to die by deputy rather than in his own person when his time was up. The painful but necessary duty was accordingly laid on some poor devil, some social outcast, some wretch with whom the world had gone hard, who readily agreed to throw away his life at the end of a few days if only he might have his fling in the meantime. For observe that while the time allowed to the original deputy—the Jalno—was measured by weeks, the time allowed to the deputy's deputy was cut down to days, ten days according to one authority, seven days according to another. So short a rope was doubtless thought a long enough tether for so black or sickly a sheep; so few sands in the hour-glass, slipping so fast away, sufficed for one who had wasted so many precious years. Hence in the jack-pudding who now masquerades with motley countenance in the market-place of Lhasa, sweeping up misfortune with a black yak's tail, we may fairly see the substitute of a substitute, the vicar of a vicar, the proxy on whose back the heavy burden was laid when it had been lifted from nobler shoulders. But the clue, if we have followed it aright, does not stop at the Jalno; it leads straight back to the pope of Lhasa himself, the Grand Lama, of whom the Jalno is merely the temporary vicar. The analogy of many customs in many lands points to the conclusion that, if this human divinty stoops to resign his ghostly power for a time into the hands of a substitute, it is, or rather was once, for no other reason than that the substitute might die in his stead. Thus through the mist of ages unillumined by the lamp of history, the tragic figure of the pope of Buddhism—God's vicar on earth for Asia—looms dim and sad as the man-god who bore his people's sorrows, the Good Shepherd who laid down his life for the sheep.

HUMAN SCAPEGOATS IN CLASSICAL ANTIQUITY

463. We are now prepared to notice the use of the human scapegoat in classical antiquity. Every year on the fourteenth of March a man clad in skins was led in procession through the streets of Rome, beaten with long white rods, and driven out of the city. He was called Mamurius Veturius,[1] that is, "the old Mars,"[2] and as the ceremony took place on the day preceding the first full moon of the old Roman year (which began on the first of March), the skin-clad man must have represented the Mars of the past year, who was driven out at the beginning of a new one. Now Mars was originally not a god of war but of vegetation. For it was to Mars that the Roman husbandman prayed for the prosperity of his corn and his vines, his fruit-trees and his copses,[3] it was to Mars that the priestly college of the Arval Brothers, whose business it was to sacrifice for the growth of the crops,[4] addressed their petitions almost exclusively;[5] and it was to Mars that a horse was sacrificed in October to secure an abundant harvest. Moreover, it was to Mars, under his title of "Mars of the woods" (*Mars Silvanus*), that farmers offered sacrifice for the welfare of their cattle.[6] Thus the Roman custom of expelling the old Mars at the beginning of the new year in spring is identical with the Slavonic custom of "carrying out Death," if the view here taken of the latter custom is correct. The similarity of the Roman and Slavonic customs has been already remarked by scholars.[7] In both, the representative of the god appears to have been treated not only as a deity of vegetation but also as a scapegoat.

464. The ancient Greeks were also familiar with the use of a human scapegoat. In Plutarch's native town of Chaeronea a ceremony of this kind was performed by the chief magistrate at the Town Hall, and by each householder at his own home. It was called the "expulsion of hunger." A slave was beaten with rods of the *agnus castus,* and turned out of doors with the words, "Out with hunger, and in with wealth and health." When Plutarch held the office of chief magistrate of his native town he performed this ceremony at the Town Hall, and he has recorded the discussion to which the custom afterwards gave rise.[1]

465. But in civilized Greece the custom of the scapegoat took darker forms than the innocent rite over which the amiable and pious Plutarch presided. Whenever Marseilles, one of the busiest and most brilliant of Greek colonies, was ravaged by a plague, a man of the poorer classes used to offer himself as a scapegoat. For a whole year he was maintained at the public expense, being fed on choice and pure food. At the expiry of the year he was dressed in sacred garments, decked with holy branches, and led through the whole city, while prayers were uttered that all the evils of the people might fall on his head. He was then cast out of the city or stoned to death by the people outside of the walls.[1] The Athenians regularly maintained a number of degraded and useless beings at the public expense; and when any calamity, such as plague, drought, or famine, befell the city, they sacrificed two of these outcasts as scapegoats. One of the victims was sacrificed for the men and the other for the women. The former wore round his neck a string of black, the latter a string of white figs. Sometimes, it seems, the victim slain on behalf of the women was a woman. They were led about the city and then sacrificed, apparently by being stoned to death outside the city.[2] But such sacrifices were not confined to extraordinary occasions of public calamity; it appears that every year, at the festival of the Thargelia in May, two victims, one for the men and one for the women, were led out of Athens and stoned to death.[3] The city of Abdera in Thrace was publicly purified once a year, and one of the burghers, set apart for the purpose, was stoned to death as a scapegoat or vicarious sacrifice for the life of all the others; six days before his execution he was excommunicated, "in order that he alone might bear the sins of all the people."[4]

466. As practised by the Greeks of Asia Minor in the sixth century before our era, the custom of the scapegoat was as follows. When a city suffered from plague, famine, or other public calamity, an ugly or deformed person was chosen to take upon himself all the evils which afflicted the community. He was brought to a suitable place, where dried figs, a barley loaf, and cheese were put into his hand. These he ate. Then he was beaten seven times upon his genital organs with squills and branches of the wild fig and other wild trees, while the flutes played a particular tune. Afterwards he was burned on a pyre built of the wood of forest trees; and his ashes were cast into the sea.[1]

BEATING WITH SQUILLS, "EASTER SMACKS"

467. In the ritual just described the scourging of the victim with squills, branches of the wild fig, and so forth, cannot have been intended to aggravate his sufferings, otherwise any stick would have been good enough to beat him with. The true meaning of this part of the ceremony has been explained by Mannhardt.[1] He points out that the ancients attributed to squills a magical power of averting evil influences, and that accordingly they hung them up at the doors of their houses and made use of them in purificatory rites.[2] Hence the Arcadian custom of whipping the image of Pan with squills at a festival, or whenever the hunters returned empty-handed,[3] must have been meant, not to punish the god, but to purify him from the harmful influences which were impeding him in the exercise of his divine functions as a god who should supply the hunter with game. Similarly the object of beating the human scapegoat on the genital organs with squills and so on, must have been to release his reproductive energies from any restraint or spell under which they might be laid by demoniacal or other malignant agency; and as the Thargelia at which he was annually sacrificed was an early harvest festival celebrated in May,[4] we must recognize in him a representative of the creative and fertilizing god of vegetation. The representative of the god was annually slain for the purpose I have indicated, that of maintaining the divine life in perpetual vigour, untainted by the weakness of age; and before he was put to death it was not unnatural to stimulate his reproductive powers in order that these might be transmitted in full activity to his successor, the new god or new embodiment of the old god, who was doubtless supposed immediately to take the place of the one slain. Similar reasoning would lead to a similar treatment of the scapegoat on special occasions, such as drought or famine. If the crops did not answer to the expectation of the husbandman, this would be attributed to some failure in the generative powers of the god whose function it was to produce the fruits of the earth. It might be thought that he was under a spell or was growing old and feeble. Accordingly he was slain in the person of his representative, with all the ceremonies already described, in order that, born young again, he might infuse his own youthful vigour into the stagnant energies of nature. On the same principle we can understand why Mamurius Veturius was beaten with rods, why the slave at the Chaeronean ceremony was beaten with the *agnus castus* (a tree to which magical properties were ascribed),[5] why the effigy of Death in some parts of Europe is assailed with sticks and stones,[6] and why at Babylon the criminal who played the god was scourged.[7]

468. In some parts of Eastern and Central Europe a similar custom is very commonly observed in spring. On the first of March the Albanians strike men and beast with cornel branches, believing that this is very good for their health.[1] In March the Greek peasants of Cos switch their cattle, saying, "It is March, and up with your tail!" They think that the ceremony benefits the animals, and brings good luck. It is never observed at any other time of the year.[2] In some parts of Mecklenburg it is customary to beat the cattle before sunrise on the morning of Good Friday with rods of buckthorn, which are afterwards concealed in some secret place where neither sun nor moon can shine on them. The belief is that though the blows light upon the animals, the pain of them is felt by the witches who are riding the beasts.[3] In the neighbourhood of Iserlohn, in Westphalia, the herdsman rises at peep of dawn on May morning, climbs a hill, and cuts down the young rowan-tree which is the first to catch the beams of the rising sun. With this he returns to the farm-yard. The heifer which the farmer desires to "quicken" is then led to the dunghill, and the herdsman strikes it over the hind-quarters, the haunches, and the udders with a branch of the rowan-tree, saying,

> "Quick, quick, quick!
> Bring milk into the dugs.
> The sap is in the birches.
> The heifer receives a name.

> "Quick, quick, quick!
> Bring milk into the dugs.
> The sap comes in the beeches,
> The leaf comes on the oak.
>
> "Quick, quick, quick!
> Bring milk into the dugs.
> In the name of the sainted Greta,
> Gold-flower shall be thy name,"

and so on.[4] The intention of the ceremony appears to be to make sure that the heifer shall in due time yield a plentiful supply of milk; and this is perhaps supposed to be brought about by driving away the witches, who are particularly apt to rob the cows of their milk on the morning of May Day. Certainly in the northeast of Scotland pieces of rowan-tree and woodbine used to be placed over the doors of the byres on May Day to keep the witches from the cows; sometimes a single rod of rowan, covered with notches, was found to answer the purpose. An even more effectual guard against witchcraft was to tie a small cross of rowan-wood by a scarlet thread to each beast's tail; hence people said,

> "Rawn-tree in red-threed
> Pits the witches t' their speed."[5]

In Germany also the rowan-tree is a protection against witchcraft;[6] and Norwegian sailors and fishermen carry a piece of it in their boats for good luck.[7] Thus the benefit to young cows of beating them with rowan appears to be not so much the positive one of pouring milk into their udders, as merely the negative one of averting evil influence; and the same may perhaps be said of most of the beatings with which we are here concerned.

469. On Good Friday and the two previous days people in Croatia and Slavonia take rods with them to church, and when the service is over they beat each other "fresh and healthy."[1] In some parts of Russia people returning from the church on Palm Sunday beat the children and servants who have stayed at home with palm branches, saying, "Sickness into the forest, health into the bones."[2] A similar custom is widely known under the name of *Schmeckostern* or "Easter Smacks" in some parts of Germany and Austria. The regions in which the practice prevails are for the most part districts in which the people either are or once were predominantly of Slavonic blood, such as East and West Prussia, Voigtland, Silesia, Bohemia, and Moravia. While the German population call the custom *Schmeckostern,* the Slavonic inhabitants give it, according to their particular language or dialect, a variety of names which signify to beat or scourge. It is usually observed on Easter Monday, less frequently on Easter Saturday or Easter Sunday.

470. In some parts of Germany and Austria a custom like that of "Easter Smacks" is observed at the Christmas holidays, especially on Holy Innocents'

Day, the twenty-eighth of December. Young men and women beat each other mutually, but on different days, with branches of fresh green, whether birch, willow, or fir. Thus, for example, among the Germans of western Bohemia it is customary on St. Barbara's Day (the fourth of December) to cut twigs or branches of birch and to steep them in water in order that they may put out leaves or buds. They are afterwards used by each sex to beat the other on subsequent days of the Christmas holidays. In some villages branches of willow or cherry-trees or rosemary are employed for the same purpose. With these green boughs, sometimes tied in bundles with red or green ribbons, the young men go about beating the young women on the morning of St. Stephen's Day (the twenty-sixth of December) and also on Holy Innocents' Day (the twenty-eighth of December). The beating is inflicted on the hands, feet, and face; and in Neugramatin it is said that she who is not thus beaten with fresh green will not herself be fresh and green. As the blows descend, the young men recite verses importing that the beating is administered as a compliment and in order to benefit the health of the victim. For the service which they thus render the damsels they are rewarded by them with cakes, brandy, or money. Early in the morning of New Year's Day the lasses pay off the lads in the same kind.[1] A similar custom is also observed in central and south-west Germany, especially in Voigtland. Thus in Voigtland and the whole of the Saxon Erz-gebirge the lads beat the lasses and women on the second day of the Christmas holidays with something green, such as rosemary or juniper; and if possible the beating is inflicted on the women as they lie in bed. As they beat them, the lads say

> "Fresh and green! Pretty and fine!
> Gingerbread and brandy-wine!"

The last words refer to the present of gingerbread and brandy which the lads expect to receive from the lasses for the trouble of thrashing them. Next day the lasses and women retaliate on the lads and men.[2] In Thüringen on Holy Innocents' Day (the twenty-eighth of December) children armed with rods and green boughs go about the streets beating passers-by and demanding a present in return; they even make their way into the houses and beat the maid-servants. In Orlagau the custom is called "whipping with fresh green." On the second day of the Christmas holidays the girls go to their parents, godparents, relations, and friends, and beat them with fresh green branches of fir; next day the boys and lads do the same. The words spoken while the beating is being administered are "Good morning! fresh green! Long life! You must give us a bright thaler," and so on.[3]

In these European customs the intention of beating persons, especially of the other sex, with fresh green leaves appears unquestionably to be the beneficent one of renewing their life and vigour, whether the purpose is supposed to be accomplished directly and positively by imparting the vital energy of the fresh green to the persons, or negatively and indirectly by dispelling any injurious influences, such as the machinations of witches and demons, by which the persons may be supposed to be beset. The application of the blows by the one sex to the other, especially by young men to young women, suggests that the beating is or was originally intended above all to stimulate the reproductive powers of the men or women who received it; and the pains taken to ensure that the branches with which the strokes are given should have budded or blossomed out just before their services are wanted speak strongly in favour of the view that in these customs we have a deliberate attempt to transfuse a store of vital energy from the vegetable to the animal world.

NOTES

433   1. J. G. F. Riedel, *De sluik- en kroesharige rassen tusschen Selebes en Papua* (The Hague 1886), 266 ff., 305, 357.
  2. B. Spencer and F. J. Gillen, *The Northern Tribes of Central Australia* (London 1904), 474.
  3. J. Pearse, in *The Antanarivo Annual and Madagascar Magazine*, 2 (Reprinted 1896), 146 f.
  4. H. Oldenberg, *Die Religion des Veda* (Berlin 1894), 322.
  5. J. Spieth, *Die Ewe-Stämme* (Berlin 1906), 800.
  6. Pausanias, vii. 23, 3.
  7. P. J. de Arriaga, *Extirpacion de la idolatria del Piru* (Lima 1621), 29.
  8. David of Antioch, Tazyin, in the story "Orwa."
  9. R. Andree, *Ethnographische Parallelen und Vergleiche* (Stuttgart 1878), 39 f.
  10. C. Hupe, in *Tijdschrift Voor Neerlands Indië*, 1846, dl. iii. 149 f.

434   1. J. Dawson, *Australian Aborigines* (Melbourne 1881), 59.
  2. W. Crooke, *Popular Religion and Folklore of Northern India* (Westminster 1896), i. 164 f.
  3. J. Roscoe in *JAI*, 37 (1907), 103.

435   1. J. Roscoe, *The Baganda* (London 1911), 343 f.
  2. D. Kidd, *The Essential Kafir* (London 1904), 146.

436   1. J. G. F. Riedel, in *Deutsche geographische Blaetter*, 10. 231.
  2. Id., *De sluik- en kroesharige rassen*, 340.
  2a. N. Adriani and A. C. Kruijt, *De Bare'e–sprekende Toradja's van Midden-Celebes* (Batavia 1913–14), i. 267.
  3. F. Liebrecht, *Zur Volkskunde* (Heilbronn 1879), 274 f.
  4. *Loc. cit.*
  5. Spenser St. John, *Life in the Forests of the Far East*[2] (London 1863), i. 88.
  6. E. H. Gomes, *Seventeen Years among the Sea Dyaks of Borneo* (London 1911), 66 f.

546

7. A. C. Haddon, "A Batch of Irish Folk-lore," in *Folk-Lore*, 4 (1893), 357 f.; J. Brand, *Popular Antiquities of Great Britain* (London 1882–83), ii. 309; F. Liebrecht, *op. cit.*, 274; A. Treichel, in *Am Urquell*, 6 (1896), 220; G. Georgakis and L. Pineau, *Le Folk-lore de Lesbos* (Paris 1894), 323; E. Doutté, *Magie et religion dans l'Afrique du nord* (Algiers 1908), 424 f.; A. von Haxthausen, *Transkaukasia* (Leipzig 1856), i. 222; C. T. Wilson, *Peasant Life in the Holy Land* (London 1906), 285; W. Crooke, *op. cit.*, i. 267 f.; J. Adair, *History of the North American Indians* (London 1775), 184; G. C. Musters, "Notes on Bolivia," in *Journal of the Royal Geogr. Soc.*, 47 (1877), 211; R. A. Cruise, *Journal of a Ten Months' Residence in New Zealand* (London 1823), 186.

8. J. Cook, *Voyages* (London 1809), vi. 479.

9. H. Lichtenstein, *Reisen im Südlichen Africa* (Berlin 1811–12), i. 349 f.

10. T. Hahn, in *Globus*, 18 (1866), 141.

437 1. Et. Magn., s.v. *Hermaion;* Eustathius on *Odyssey,* xvi. 471. Concerning the heap of stones, see Cornutus, *Theol. Graec. compend.*, 16; Babrius, fab. xlviii. 1 f.; Scholiast on Nicander, *Ther.*, 150; M. P. Nilsson, *Griechische Feste* (Liepzig 1906), 388 ff.

2. Plato, *Laws,* ix. 12.

438 1. J. Smith, *Trade and Travels in the Gulph of Guinea* (London 1851), 77.

2. E. Doutté, *op. cit.*, 454 f.

3. J. Campbell, *Travels in South Africa* (London 1822), ii. 207 f.

4. Dio Chrysostom, *Orat.*, 52 = ii. 164 f. Dindorf; cp. Plato, *Republic*, iii. 9.

5. Leviticus, 14 : 7, 53.

6. J. Wellhausen, *Reste arabischen Heidentums* (Berlin 1887), 156.

7. E. Thurston, *Castes and Tribes of Southern India* (Madras 1909), i. 113–17.

8. H. Harkness, *Description of a Singular Aboriginal Race inhabiting the Summit of the Neilgherry Hills* (London 1832), 133.

439 1. Hymns of the Atharva-Veda, tr. Bloomfield (*SBE*, xlii), 308 f.

2. M. N. Venketswami, in *Indian Antiquary*, 24 (1895), 359.

3. A. Grünwedel, in *Intern. Archiv f. Ethnogr.*, 6 (1893), 85 f.

4. J. G. Dalyell, *The Darker Superstitions of Scotland* (Edinburgh 1834), 104 f.

5. J. Perham, in *Journal of the Straits Branch of the Royal Asiatic Society*, No. 10 (December 1882), 232.

6. R. Taylor, *Te Ika A Maui, or New Zealand and its Inhabitants*[2] (London 1870), 101.

7. T. C. Hodson, *The Meitheis* (London 1908), 106 f.

8. S. Mateer, *Native Life in Travancore* (London 1883), 136.

9. Bagford's letter in Leland's *Collectanea*, i. 76, quoted by Brand, *op. cit.*, ii. 246 f. (Bagford's authority is John Aubrey.)

440 1. Pliny, *NH*, xxviii. 86.
  2. Marcellus, *De medicamentis*, xxiv. 102; cp. Pliny, *op. cit.*, xxii. 49. See also J. Hardy, in *Folk-lore Record*, 1 (1878), 216–28.
  3. L. Strackerjan, *Aberglaube und Sagen aus dem Herzogthum Oldenburg* (Oldenburg 1887), i. 71, ¶85.

441 1. *Geoponica*, xiii. 9; xv. 1; Pliny, *NH*, xxviii. 155.
  2. W. G. Black, *Folk Medicine* (London 1883), 35.
  3. Strackerjan, *op. cit.*, i. 72, ¶86.
  4. R. Wuttke, *Sächsische Volkskunde*[2] (Dresden 1901), 372.

442 1. B. Schmidt, *Das Volksleben der Neugriechen* (Leipzig 1871), 82.
  2. A. Kuhn, *Märkische Sagen und Märchen* (Berlin 1843), 386.

443 1. *Le Tour du Monde*, 67 (1894), 308; ib., N. S., 5 (1899), 521.
  2. A. Strausz, *Die Bulgaren* (Leipzig 1898), 400 f.
  3. *Blackwood's Magazine*, February 1886, p. 239.
  4. J. V. Grohmann, *Aberglaube und Gebräuche aus Böhmen und Mähren* (Prague-Leipzig 1864), 167, ¶1178.

444 1. P. Reina, in *Zeitschrift fuer allgemeine Erdkunde*, N. F. 4 (1858), 356.
  2. R. Parkinson, *Im Bismarck-Archipel* (Leipzig 1887), 142.
  3. O. Opigez, in *Bull. soc. géogr. de Paris*, VIIme sér., 7 (1886), 443.
  4. S. Gason, in *JAI*, 24 (1895), 170.
  5. J. G. F. Riedel, in *Zeitschrift fuer Ethnologie*, 17 (1885), 82.
  6. G. C. Wheeler, in *Archiv für Religionswissenschaft*, 15 (1910), 49, 51 f.
  7. J. G. Scott and J. P. Hardiman, *Gazetteer of Upper Burma and the Shan States*, I. ii (Rangoon 1901), 440.
  8. T. H. Lewin, *Wild Tribes of South-Eastern India* (London 1870), 226.
  9. H. Hecquard, *Reise an die Küste und in das Innere von West-Afrika* (Leipzig 1854), 43.
  10. P. G. Sagard, *Le grande voyage au pays des Hurons* (Paris 1865), 195 f.

445 1. A. d'Orbigny, *Voyage dans l'Amérique méridionale*, ii (Paris-Strasburg 1839–43), 40.
  2. P. Lozano, *Descripcion Chorographica del terreno, rios, arboles, y animales de las dilatadissmas Provincias del Gran Chaco, Gualamba*, etc. (Cordova 1733), 100.
  3. H. H. Bancroft, *Native Races of the Pacific States* (London 1875–76), ii. 589, n. 259 (quoting Arlegui, *Chron. de Zacatecas*, 152–53, 182).
  4. B. S. Carey and H. N. Tuck, *The Chin Hills*, i (Rangoon 1896), 198.

446 1. W. Jochelson, *The Koryak* (Leyden-New York 1908), 88.

2. E. G. Squire, in *Trans. Amer. Ethnol. Soc.*, 3. i (1853), 78 (quoting J. H. Payne).

3. C. Gay, in *Bull. soc. géogr. de Paris, IIme sér*, 19 (1843), 29 f.

4. S. Crowther and J. C. Taylor, *The Gospel on the Banks of the Niger* (London 1859), 320.

4a. R. O. Winstedt, *Shaman, Saiva, and Sufi* (London 1925), 113 ff.

447 1. G. Brown, *Melanesians and Polynesians* (London 1910), 413 f.

2. J. Biddulph, *Tribes of the Hindoo Koosh* (Calcutta 1880), 103.

448 1. R. von Eck, in *Tijdschrift voor Nederl. Indië*, N. S. 8 (1879), 58–60.

2. A. Humbert, *Le Japon illustré* (Paris 1870), ii. 326.

3. J. J. M. de Groot, *The Religion of China* (New York 1910), 38 f.

4. W. W. Rockhill, in *The American Anthropologist*, 4 (1891), 185.

449 1. Hesychius, s.v. *miarai hemerai;* Photius, s.v. *thyraze Kares;* Pollux, viii. 141. See fully: E. Rohde, *Psyche*[3] (Tübingen-Leipzig 1903), i. 236 ff.; Jane Harrison, *Prolegomena to the Study of Greek Religion*[2] (Cambridge 1908), 32 ff.

2. Scholiast on Aristophanes, *Frogs*, 218.

3. Ovid, *Fasti*, v. 419–86; Varro, quoted by Nonius Marcellus, 135 (p. 142 Quicherat), s.v. *Lemures;* W. W. Fowler, *The Roman Festivals of the Period of the Republic* (London 1899), 106 ff.

450 1. M. Buch, *Die Wotjäken* (Stuttgart 1882), 153 f.

2. P. v. Stenin, in *Globus*, 57 (1890), 204.

451 1. V. Dorsa, *La tradizione greco-latina negli usi e nelle credenze popolari della Calabria Citeriore* (Cosenza 1884), 42 f.

2. *Ib.*, 48.

3. J. G. von Hahn, *Albanesische Studien* (Jena 1854), i. 160.

4. P. Drechsler, *Sitte, Brauch u. Volksglaube in Schlesien* (Leipzig 1903–06), i. 86.

5. G. Bilfinger, *Das germanische Julfest* (Stuttgart 1901), 76.

6. O. von Reinsberg-Düringsfeld, *Das festliche Jahr* (Leipzig 1863), 137.

7. A. John, *Sitte, Brauch u. Volksglaube im deutschen Westböhmen* (Prague 1905), 71.

8. Lady Agnes Macdonell in *The Times* (London), May 3, 1913, p. 6.

452 1. P. Drechsler, *Sitte, Brauch und Volksglaube in Schlesien* (Leipzig 1903–06), i. 15–18; A. Wuttke, *Der deutsche Volksaberglaube*,[2] (Berlin 1869), 61 ff.

2. O. von Reinsberg-Düringsfeld, *Fest-Kalender aus Böhmen* (Prague 1861), 602.

3. E. Hoffmann-Krayer, *Feste und Bräuche d. Schweizervolkes* (Zurich 1913), 101; H. Usener, *Kleine Schriften* (Leipzig-Berlin 1913), 109.

4. A. de Nore, *Coutumes, mythes et traditions des provinces de France* (Paris-Lyons 1846), 81, 85.

5. As to Befana, see J. Grimm, *Deutsche Mythologie*[4] (Berlin 1875–78), i. 234. She is known also in Sicily: G. Pitrè, *Spettacoli e feste popolari Sciliani* (Palermo 1881), 167. [The celebration in the Piazza Navona at Rome, though still colorful, has degenerated into a mere fair, featuring especially the sale of toys.]

453
1. G. Catlin, *North American Indians*[4] (London 1844), i. 66 f.

2. Diego de Landa, *Relation des choses de Yucatan* (Paris 1864), 203–05, 211–15. Cp. C. Thomas, *The Mayan Year* (Washington 1894), 19 ff.

3. A. C. Winter, in *Globus*, 69 (1901), 302; W. R. S. Ralston, *Songs of the Russian People*[2] (London 1872), 396 ff.

4. J. G. Kohl, *Die deutsch-russischen Ostseeprovinzen* (Dresden-Leipzig 1841), ii. 278.

5. *Folk-lore Journal*, 7 (1889), 174.

454
1. F. Valentyn, *Oud en niuew Ost-Indien* (Dordrecht-Amsterdam 1724–26), iii. 14.

2. J. G. F. Riedel, *De sluik- en kroesharigen rassen*, 304 f.

3. *Ib.*, 266, 304 f., 327, 257; H. Ling Roth, *Natives of Sarawak and British North Borneo* (London 1896), i. 284.

4. C. Hose and W. McDougall, *The Pagan Tribes of Borneo* (London 1912), ii. 122 f.

5. W. W. Skeat, *Malay Magic* (London 1900), 433–35.

6. F. Blumentritt, in *Globus*, 59 (1891), 183.

7. J. Dumont D'Urville, *Voyage autour du monde à la recherche de la Pérouse sur la corvette* Astrolabe (Paris 1832–35), v. 311.

455
1. *Punjab Notes and Queries*, 9 (1886), 81, ¶373.

2. W. Crooke, *op. cit.*, i. 142.

3. F. Fawcett, in *Journal of the Anthropological Soc. of Bombay*, 1. 213, n.

4. Y. V. Athalye, *ib.*, 1. 37.

5. Crooke, *op. cit.*, i. 169 f.

6. D. Forbes, in *Journal of the Ethnological Soc. of London*, 2 (1870), 237.

456
1. J. H. Gray, *China* (London 1875), ii. 306.

2. F. Hahn, in *Journal of the Asiatic Soc. of Bengal*, 72, iii (1904), 17.

457
1. A. Bastian, *Der Mensch in der Geschichte* (Leipzig 1860), ii. 91.

2. V. Solomon, in *JAI*, 32 (1902), 228 f.

3. W. W. Rockhill, in *The American Anthropologist*, 4 (1891), 185.

458
1. E. T. Atkinson, *The Himalayan Districts of the N. W. Provinces of India*, ii (Allahabad 1884), 871.

1a. C. E. Fox, *The Threshold of the Pacific* (London 1924), 239n.
2. Leviticus 16.

459 1. S. Crowther and J. C. Taylor, *The Gospel on the Banks of The Niger,* 344–45. Cp. J. F. Schön and S. Crowther, *Journals* (London 1848), 48 f.
2. Turpin, "History of Siam," in *Pinkerton's Voyages and Travels,* ix. 579.
3. W. G. Aston, *Shinto* (London 1905), 308 ff.

460 1. Aeneas Sylvius, *Opera* (Basle 1571), 423 f.
2. H. Usener, *Kleine Schriften* (Leipzig-Berlin 1913), iv. 109 f.; Cp. H. Herzog, *Schweizerische Volksfeste, Sitten und Gebräuche* (Aarau 1884), 293 f.
3. L. Curtius, in *Archiv für Religionswissenschaft,* 14 (1911), 307 (quoting the *Münchener Neuste Nachrichten* of May 21, 1909).
4. For a somewhat analogous custom, at Manipur, of appointing a man as responsible for all mishaps each year, see T. C. Hudson, *The Meitheis* (London 1908), 104–06.

461 1. J. T. Phillips, *Account of the Religion, Manners, and Learning of the People of Malabar* (London 1717), 6, 12 f.
2. Herodotus, ii. 39.
3. See above, ¶426.

462 1. *Punjab Notes and Queries,* 2 (1884), 54, ¶335.
2. Strabo, xi. 4, 7. For the custom of standing on a sacrificial victim, cp. Demosthenes, *Or.,* xxiii. 68, p. 642; Pausanias, iii. 20, 9.
3. *Journal of the Royal Geographical Society,* 38 (1868), 167, 170 f.; *Proc. Royal Geogr. Soc.,* N. S. 7 (1885), 67 f.; L. A. Waddell, *The Buddhism of Tibet* (London 1895), 504 ff., 512 f.

463 1. Joannes Lydus, *De mensibus,* iii. 29; iv. 36. Lydus places the ceremony on the Ides, i.e., March 15. Cp. Varro, *De lingua latina,* vi. 45; Festus, 131 Müller; Plutarch, *Numa,* 13.
2. Usener, *op. cit.,* iv. 125 f.; W. H. Roscher, *Apollon und Mars* (Leipzig 1873), 27; L. Preller, *Römische Mythologie³* (Berlin 1881–82), i. 360.
3. Cato, *De agri cultura,* 141.
4. Varro, *De lingua latina,* v. 85.
5. See the song of the Arval Brotherhood in F. D. Allen, *Remnants of Early Latin* (Boston 1880), 65, No. 149; [A. C. Bouquet, *Sacred Books of the World* (London, Penguin Books, 1954), 32 f.].
6. Cato, *De agri cultura,* 83.
7. Preller, *op. cit.,* 1. 360; Roscher, *op. cit.,* 49; Usener, *loc. cit.*

464 1. Plutarch, *Quaest. conviv.,* vi. 8.

465 1. Servius on Vergil, *Aen.*, iii. 57; Lactantius Placidius, *Commentar. in Statii Theb.*, x. 793, p. 452 Jahnke.
2. Helladius, in Photius, *Bibl.*, 534 A, Bekker; Schol. on Aristophanes, *Frogs*, 734, and *Knights*, 1136; Hesychius, s.v. *pharmakos;* Lysias, *Orat.*, vi. 53. [The evidence is assembled and discussed by Gilbert Murray in his *Rise of the Greek Epic* (Oxford 1907), Appendix A, pp. 253–58.]
3. Harpocration, s.v. *pharmakos*. See also Murry, *loc. cit.;* W. Mannhardt, *Mythologische Forschungen*, (Strasburg 1884), 124 ff.; J. Töpffer, *Beitraege zur griech. Altertumswissenschaft* (Berlin 1897), 130 ff.; Jane Harrison, *op. cit.*, 95 ff.; M. P. Nilsson, *Griechische Feste* (Leipzig 1906), 105 ff.
4. Ovid, *Ibis*, 467 f.

466 1. Tzetzes, *Chiliades*, v. 726–61 (based on Helladius).

467 1. *Op. cit.*, 113 ff.
2. Pliny, *NH*, xx. 101; Dioscorides, *De materia medica*, ii. 202; Lucian, *Nekyom.*, 7; id., *Alexander*, 47; Theophrastus, *Superstitious Man*.
3. Theocritus, vii. 106 ff., with Scholiast *in loc.*
4. Cp. A. Mommsen, *Heortologie* (Leipzig 1864), 414 ff.; Nilsson, *op. cit.*, 105, 111 ff.; W. Mannhardt, *Antike Wald- u. Feldkulte* (Berlin 1877), 215.
5. Aelian, *Nat. animalium*, ix. 26.
6. See above, ¶203.
7. See above, ¶194.

468 1. J. G. von Hahn, *Albanesische Studien*, i. 155.
2. W. H. D. Rouse, in *Folk-Lore*, 10 (1899), 179.
3. K. Bartsch, *Sagen, Märchen u. Gebräuche aus Mecklenburg* (Vienna 1879–80), ii. 258, ¶1348.
4. J. F. L. Woeste, *Volksüberlieferungen in der Grafschaft Mark* (Iserlohn 1848), 25 f. The ceremony takes its name of "quickening" from *Quicke*, a German name for the rowan-tree. Quicken is also one of its English names.
5. W. Gregor, *Notes on the Folk-lore of the North-East of Scotland* (Londan 1881), 188.
6. A. Wuttke, *Der deutsche Volksaberglaube*[2] (Berlin 1869), 106, ¶145.
7. Woeste, *op. cit.*, 26.

469 1. F. S. Krauss, *Kroatien und Slavonien* (Vienna 1889), 108.
2. Mannhardt, *Baumkultus*, 257.

470 1. A. John, *Sitte, Bräuche u. Volksglaube im deutschen Westböhmen* (Prague 1905), 5, 23 ff.; cp. T. Vernaleken, *Mythen und Bräuche des Volkes in Oesterreich* (Vienna 1859), 301 f.

2. J. A. E. Köhler, *Volksbrauch . . . im Voigtlande* (Leipzig 1867), 174; Mannhardt, *op. cit.*, 264 ff.

3. Mannhardt, *op. cit.*, 265; A. Witzschel, *Sage, Sitten u. Gebräuche aus Thüringen* (Vienna 1878), 265; G. Bilfinger, *Das germanische Julfest* Stuttgart 1901), 85 f.

ADDITIONAL NOTES

SCAPEGOATS

Frazer lumps together *scapegoats* and *surrogates*, but they should be distinguished and designated by separate names.

A surrogate is any substitute for the person (or persons) performing a rite or for whose benefit it is performed. Such surrogates are designed to disencumber him (or them) of unpleasant ritual or legal obligations. They figure, for instance, in rites designed to remove sickness, and do not necessarily involve the factor of *sin.*

A scapegoat, on the other hand, is an animal or human being used in public ceremonies to remove the taint or impairment consequent upon sin which, for one reason or other, cannot be saddled upon a particular individual. Such a scapegoat is a means of "cleansing" a community of a collective stain which cannot be wiped out by the normal procedure of individual penitence, restitution, and reform. *The execution or despatch of it is always and necessarily accompanied by a blanket public confession.* Its purpose is not, as in the case of surrogates, to transfer punishment or discomfort, but to remove from the body politic any pollution or disaster responsibility for which cannot be precised: see T. H. Gaster, *Festivals of the Jewish Year* (New York 1953), 141 ff.

438. *Animal scapegoats in antiquity.* On the animal scapegoat among the BABYLONIANS, see S. Langdon in *The Expository Times,* 24. 9–15; E. Dhorme, in *Revue d'assyriologie,* 8. 41 ff. On the institution among the HITTITES, see V. Gebhart, in *Archiv für Religionswissenschaft,* 29 (1931), 243; O. Gurney, *The Hittites* (Penguin Books, 1952), 162.

On the HEBREW scapegoat on the Day of Purgation (Atonement), see I. Schur, *Versöhnungstag und Sündenbock* (Helsingfors 1934); G. B. Gray, *Sacrifice in the Old Testament* (Cambridge 1937), 315–18. For a later Jewish survival, see: I. Scheftelowitz, *Der stellvertretende Huhnopfer* (Giessen 1914); T. H. Gaster, *Festivals of the Jewish Year* (New York 1953), 134.

452. *The Twelve Days.* See: J. Loth, "Les douze jours supplémentaires (jourdeziou) des Bretons et les douze jours Germains et Indous," in *Revue celtique,* 24 (1903), 311 ff.; J. G. Frazer, *The Fasti of Ovid* (London 1925), vol. ii, pp.

46 ff.; J. H. Moulton, *Two Lectures on the Science of Languages* (Cambridge 1903), 47 ff. According to A. Weber, in *Sitz. Berl. Akad. Wiss.*, 37 (1898), Phil. –hist. Kl., 2 ff., the twelve days were a sacred period in Brahmaṇa literature; this, however, is denied by O. Schrader, in *ERE*, ii. 47b.

454. *Expulsion of evil by boat.* A ceremony exactly comparable with that common in Indonesia was performed by the Babylonians at the dedication or renovation of a house or temple: the celebrant or foreman prepared a model ship, duly equipped with sails, provisioned it, and set it adrift with accompanying incantations; text and translation in P. Jensen, *Keilschriftliches Bibliothek*, vi/2 (Berlin 1915). — Furthermore, in Mesopotamian amulets against the child-stealing witch Lamashtu, she is often depicted being carried off in a boat: C. Frank, *Bab. Beschwörungsreliefs* (Leipzig 1900); and we are told by Festus that in a formula used by the Romans against the analogous *strix,* she was banished to "the swift-faring ships"; see T. H. Gaster, in *Studi e Materiali di Storia delle Religioni,* 25 (1951–52), 154–57.

456. *Human scapegoat in Babylon.* On the sixth day of the Babylonian New Year (Akîtu) festival, a condemned felon (*bêl ḫiṭṭi*) was paraded through the streets and scourged: *VAT* 9555, rev. 10–11.

462. *Human scapegoats.* See now Igor Caruso, "Le surmoi et le bouc émissaire," in *Psyche,* 7 (1953), 272–76.

463. *Mamurius Veturius.* Ovid, *Fasti,* iii. 541–42, says that in the procession of Anna Perenna, on the Ides of March, a drunken old woman, known as the Petreia, was dragged along the streets by a drunken old man. E. H. Alton suggests (in *Hermathena,* 43 [1920], 100–04) that they personified Anna Perenna and Mamurius Veturius (Old Mars) on whom she had been palmed off.

464. *The Human scapegoat (Pharmakos) in ancient Greece.* The evidence for this practice is collected and discussed by Gilbert Murray in *The Rise of the Greek Epic* (Oxford 1907), 253–58; see also Jane Harrison, *Prolegomena to the Study of Greek Religion*[3] (Cambridge 1922), 95 ff.; F. Schwenn, *Menschenopfer bei den Griech. u. Röm.* (Giessen 1915), 36 ff. — According to Havers, *Indogerm. Forsch.,* 25 (1909), 388 f., the name *pharmakos* has, in this connection, nothing to do with *pharmakos,* "drug, sorcerer," as usually supposed, but represents an earlier **pharmak-vos,* meaning "beaten, crippled." — Not impossibly, the famous fifty-third chapter of Isaiah, with its allusions to one who "has no form nor comeliness," but who "has borne our sins, carried our diseases," who was "taken without due process," and "by whose trouncing we are healed," is based on an analogous ceremony.

466–70. *Scourging with squills, etc.* See on this: C. Clemen, in *Archiv für Religionswiss.,* 18 (1915), 147; M. Nilsson, *ib.,* 19 (1916), 111 ff.; I. Scheftelowitz, *Altpal. Bauernglaube* (Hanover 1925), 90 ff.; E. Fehrle, *Die kultische Keuschheit im Altertum* (Giessen 1910), 159 ff.; M. H. Friedlaender, "Der Abschlagen der Bachweiden," in *Neuzeit* (Vienna), 10 (1870), 489. On the seventh day of the autumnal festival of Ingathering (or Booths) Jews used to perform a similar rite: see H. Graetz, "Der Ritus mit dem Weidenzwingen ᴋm Hüttenfeste, seine Alter und seine Bedeutung," in *Monatsschrift f. Ges. Wiss. Judentums*, 36 (1887), 509–21.

On the "Easter Smacks" in Germany, see further: *Handwörterbuch d. deutsch. Aberglaubens*, s.v. *Schmekostern;* C. Clemen, *Religionsgeschichte Europas*, I (Heidelberg 1926), 213 f.; M. H. Friedländer, in *Neuzeit*, 10 (1870), 489; E. Stübiger, "Peitschschlagen," in *Mitteldeutsch. Blätter f. Volkskunde*, 10 (1935), 58 f.

PART VII

BETWEEN OLD AND NEW

PERIODS OF LICENSE

SATURNALIA

471. We have seen that many peoples have been used to observe an annual period of license, when the customary restraints of law and morality are thrown aside, when the whole population give themselves up to extravagant mirth and jollity, and when the darker passions find a vent which would never be allowed them in the more staid and sober course of ordinary life.

Of such periods of license the one which is best known and which in modern languages has given its name to the rest, is the Saturnalia. This famous festival fell in December, the last month of the Roman year, and was popularly supposed to commemorate the merry reign of Saturn, god of sowing and husbandry, who lived on earth long ago as a righteous and beneficent king of Italy, drew the rude and scattered dwellers on the mountains together, taught them to till the ground, gave them laws, and ruled in peace. His reign was the fabled Golden Age. At last the good god, the kindly king, vanished suddenly; but his memory was cherished to distant ages, shrines were reared in his honour, and many hills and high places in Italy bore his name.[1] Yet the bright tradition of his reign was crossed by a dark shadow: his altars are said to have been stained with the blood of human victims, for whom a more merciful age afterwards substituted effigies.[2] Of this gloomy side of the god's religion there is little or no trace in the descriptions which ancient writers have left us of the Saturnalia. Feasting and revelry and all the mad pursuit of pleasure are the features that seem to have especially marked this carnival of antiquity, as it went on for seven days in the streets and public squares and houses of Ancient Rome from the seventeenth to the twenty-third of December.[3]

But no feature of the festival is more remarkable, nothing in it seems to have struck the ancients themselves more than the license granted to slaves at this time. The slave might rail at his master, intoxicate himself like his

559

betters, sit down at table with them, and not even a word of reproof would be administered to him.[4] Nay, more, masters actually changed places with their slaves and waited on them at table.[5] So far was this inversion of ranks carried, that each household became for a time a mimic republic in which the high offices of state were discharged by the slaves, who gave their orders and laid down the law as if they were indeed invested with all the dignity of the consulship, the praetorship, and the bench.[6] Like the pale reflection of power thus accorded to bondsmen at the Saturnalia was the mock kingship for which freemen cast lots at the same season. The person on whom the lot fell enjoyed the title of king, and issued commands of a playful and ludicrous nature to his temporary subjects.[7]

Now, when we remember that the liberty allowed to slaves at this festive season was supposed to be an imitation of the state of society in Saturn's time, and that in general the Saturnalia passed for nothing more or less than a temporary revival or restoration of the reign of that merry monarch, we are tempted to surmise that the mock king who presided over the revels may have originally represented Saturn himself.

472. The conjecture is strongly confirmed, if not established, by a very curious and interesting account of the way in which the Saturnalia was celebrated by the Roman soldiers stationed on the Danube in the reign of Maximian and Diocletian. The account is preserved in a narrative of the martyrdom of St. Dasius, which was unearthed from a Greek manuscript in the Paris library, and published by Franz Cumont. Two briefer descriptions of the event and of the custom are contained in manuscripts at Milan and Berlin; one of them had already seen the light in an obscure volume printed at Urbino in 1727, but its importance for the history of the Roman religion, both ancient and modern, appears to have been overlooked until Professor Cumont drew the attention of scholars to all three narratives by publishing them together some years ago.[1] According to these narratives, which have all the appearance of being authentic, and of which the longest is probably based on official documents, the Roman soldiers at Durostorum in Lower Moesia celebrated the Saturnalia year by year in the following manner. Thirty days before the festival they chose by lot from amongst themselves a young and handsome man, who was then clothed in royal attire to resemble Saturn. Thus arrayed and attended by a multitude of soldiers he went about in public with full license to indulge his passions and to taste of every pleasure, however base and shameful. But if his reign was merry, it was short and ended tragically; for when the thirty days were up and the festival of Saturn had come, he cut his own throat on the altar of the god whom he personated. In the year 303 A.D. the lot fell upon the Christian soldier Dasius, but he refused to play the part of the heathen god and soil his last days by debauchery. The threats and arguments of his commanding officer Bassus failed to shake his constancy, and accordingly he was beheaded, as the Christian martyrologist records with minute accuracy, at Durostorum by the soldier John on Friday the twentieth day of November, being the twenty-fourth day of the moon, at the fourth hour.

473. This account sets in a new and lurid light the office of the King of the Saturnalia, the ancient Lord of Misrule, who presided over the winter revels at Rome in the time of Horace and of Tacitus. It seems to prove that his business had not always been that of a mere harlequin or merry-andrew whose only care was that the revelry should run high and the fun grow fast and furious, while the fire blazed and crackled on the hearth, while the streets swarmed with festive crowds, and through the clear frosty air, far away to the north, Soracte shewed his coronal of snow. When we compare this comic monarch of the gay, the civilized metropolis with his grim counterpart of the rude camp on the Danube, and when we remember the long array of similar figures, ludicrous yet tragic, who in other ages and in other lands, wearing mock crowns and wrapped in sceptred palls, have played their little pranks for a few brief hours or days, then passed before their time to a violent death, we can hardly doubt that in the King of the Saturnalia at Rome, as he is depicted by classical writers, we see only a feeble emasculated copy of that original, whose strong features have been fortunately preserved for us by the obscure author of the *Martyrdom of St. Dasius*. In other words, the martyrologist's account of the Saturnalia agrees so closely with the accounts of similar rites elsewhere, which could not possibly have been known to him, that the substantial accuracy of his description may be regarded as established; and further, since the custom of putting a mock king to death as a representative of a god cannot have grown out of a practice of appointing him to preside over a holiday revel, whereas the reverse may very well have happened, we are justified in assuming that in an earlier and more barbarous age it was the universal practice in ancient Italy, wherever the worship of Saturn prevailed, to choose a man who played the part and enjoyed all the traditionary privileges of Saturn for a season, and then died, whether by his own or another's hand, whether by the knife or the fire or on the gallows-tree, in the character of the good god who gave his life for the world. In Rome itself and other great towns the growth of civilization had probably mitigated this cruel custom long before the Augustan age, and transformed it into the innocent shape it wears in the writings of the few classical writers who bestow a passing notice on the holiday King of the Saturnalia. But in remoter districts the older and sterner practice may long have survived; and even if after the unification of Italy the barbarous usage was suppressed by the Roman government, the memory of it would be handed down by the peasants and would tend from time to time, as still happens with the lowest forms of superstition among ourselves, to lead to a recrudescence of the practice, especially among the rude soldiery on the outskirts of the empire over whom the once iron hand of Rome was beginning to relax its grasp.[1]

The resemblance between the Saturnalia of ancient and the Carnival of

modern Italy has often been remarked; but in the light of all the facts that
have come before us, we may well ask whether the resemblance does not
amount to identity. We have seen that in Italy, Spain, and France, that is, in
the countries where the influence of Rome has been deepest and most lasting,
a conspicuous feature of the Carnival is a burlesque figure personifying the
festive season, which after a short career of glory and dissipation is publicly
shot, burnt, or otherwise destroyed, to the feigned grief or genuine delight of
the populace. If the view here suggested of the Carnival is correct, this grotesque personage is no other than a direct successor of the old King of the
Saturnalia, the master of the revels, the real man who personated Saturn and,
when the revels were over, suffered a real death in his assumed character.

THE FEAST OF FOOLS

474. The King of the Bean on Twelfth Night and the medieval Bishop of
Fools, Abbot of Unreason, or Lord of Misrule are figures of the same sort
and may perhaps have had a similar origin. For it seems on the whole difficult
to suppose that the curious superstitions and quaint ceremonies, the outbursts
of profanity and the inversions of rank, which characterize the popular celebration of the twelve days from Christmas to Epiphany, have any connexion
with the episodes of Christian history believed to be commemorated by these
two festivals. More probably they are relics of an old heathen festival celebrated during the twelve intercalary days which our forefathers annually inserted in their calendar at midwinter in order to equalize the short lunar year
of twelve months with the longer solar year of three hundred and sixty-five or
sixty-six days. We need not assume that the license and buffooneries of the
festive season were borrowed from the Roman Saturnalia; both celebrations
may well have been parallel and independent deductions from a like primitive
philosophy of nature. There is not indeed, so far as I am aware, any direct
evidence that the Saturnalia at Rome was an intercalary festival; but the
license which characterized it, and the temporary reign of a mock king, who
personated Saturn, suggest that it may have been so. If we were better
acquainted with the intercalary periods of peoples at a comparatively low
level of culture, we might find that they are commonly marked by similar out-
breaks of lawlessness and similar reigns of more or less nominal and farcical
rulers. But unfortunately we know too little about the observances of such
periods among primitive peoples to be warranted in making any positive
affirmation on the subject.

However, there are grounds for thinking that intercalary periods have commonly been esteemed unlucky. The Aztecs certainly regarded as very unlucky
the five supplementary days which they added at the end of every year in
order to make up a total of three hundred and sixty-five days. These five supplementary days, corresponding to the last four of January and the first of
February, were called *nemontemi,* which means "vacant," "superfluous," or

"useless." Being dedicated to no god, they were deemed inauspicious, equally unfit for the services of religion and the transaction of civil business. During their continuance no sacrifices were offered by the priests and no worshippers frequented the temples. No cases were tried in the courts of justice. The houses were not swept. People abstained from all actions of importance and confined themselves to performing such as could not be avoided, or spent the time in paying visits to each other. In particular they were careful during these fatal days not to fall asleep in the daytime, not to quarrel, and not to stumble; because they thought that if they did such things at that time they would continue to do so for ever. Persons born on any of these days were deemed unfortunate, destined to fail in their undertakings and to live in wretchedness and poverty all their time on earth.[1] The Mayas of Yucatan employed a calendar like that of the Aztecs, and they too looked upon the five supplementary days at the end of the year as unlucky and of evil omen; hence they gave no names to these days, and while they lasted the people stayed for the most part at home; they neither washed themselves, nor combed their hair, nor loused each other; and they did no servile or fatiguing work lest some evil should befall them.[2]

The ancient Egyptians like the Aztecs considered a year to consist of three hundred and sixty ordinary days divided into months and eked out with five supplementary days so as to bring the total number of days in the year up to three hundred and sixty-five; but whereas the Aztecs divided the three hundred and sixty ordinary days into eighteen arbitrary divisions or months of twenty days each, the Egyptians, keeping much closer to the natural periods marked by the phases of the moon, divided these days into twelve months of thirty days each.[3] This mode of regulating the calendar appears to be exceedingly ancient in Egypt and may even date from the prehistoric period; for the five days over and above the year are expressly mentioned in the texts of the pyramids.[4] The myth told to explain their origin was as follows. Once on a time the earth-god Keb lay secretly with the sky-goddess Nut, and the sun-god Ra in his anger cursed the goddess, saying that she should give birth to her offspring neither in any month nor in any year. He thought, no doubt, by this imprecation to prevent her from bringing forth the fruit of her womb. But he was outwitted by the wily Thoth, who engaged the goddess of the moon in a game of draughts and having won the game took as a forfeit from her the seventieth part of every day in the year, and out of the fractions thus abstracted he made up five new days, which he added to the old year of three hundred and sixty days. As these days formed no part either of a month or of a year, the goddess Nut might be delivered in them without rendering the sun-god's curse void and of no effect. Accordingly she bore Osiris on the first of the days, Horus on the second, Set or Typhon on the third, Isis on the fourth, and Nephthys on the fifth. Of these five supplementary or intercalary days the third, as the birthday of the evil deity Set or Typhon, was deemed unlucky, and the Egyptian kings neither transacted business on it nor attended to their persons till nightfall.[5] Thus it appears that the ancient Egyptians regarded the five supplementary or intercalary days as belonging neither to a month nor to a year, but as standing outside of both and forming an extraordinary period quite apart and distinct from the ordinary course of time. It is probable, though we cannot prove it, that in all countries intercalary days or months have been so considered by the primitive astronomers who first observed the discrepancy between solar and lunar time and attempted to reconcile it by the expedient of intercalation.

Thus we infer with some probability that the sacred Twelve Days or Nights at midwinter derive their peculiar character in popular custom and super-stition from the circumstance that they were originally an intercalary period inserted annually at the end of a lunar year of three hundred and fifty-four days for the purpose of equating it to a solar year reckoned at three hundred and sixty-six days.

475. The custom of electing by lot a King and often also a Queen of the Bean on Twelfth Night (Epiphany, the sixth of January) or on the eve of that festival used to prevail in France, Belgium, Germany, and England, and it is still kept up in some parts of France. It may be traced back to the first half of the sixteenth century at least, and no doubt dates from a very much more re-mote antiquity.

Immediately on his election the King of the Bean was enthroned, saluted by all, and thrice lifted up, while he made crosses with chalk on the beams and rafters of the ceiling. Great virtue was attributed to these white crosses. They were supposed to protect the house for the whole year against

"all injuryes and harmes
Of cursed devils, sprites, and bugges, of conjurings and charmes."

Then feasting and revelry began and were kept up merrily without respect of persons. Every time the King or Queen drank, the whole company was ex-pected to cry, "The King drinks!" or "The Queen drinks!" Any person who failed to join in the cry was punished by having his face blackened with soot or a burned cork or smeared with the lees of wine.[1] Every family as a rule elected its own King. On the eve of the festival a great cake was baked with a bean in it; the cake was divided in portions, one for each member of the family, together with one for God, one for the Virgin, and sometimes one also for the poor. The person who obtained the portion containing the bean was proclaimed King of the Bean. Where a Queen of the Bean was elected as well as a King, a second bean was sometimes baked in the cake for the Queen. Thus at Blankenheim, near Neuerburg, in the Eifel, a black and a white bean were baked in the cake; he who drew the piece with the black bean was King, and she who drew the white bean was Queen. In Franche-Comté, at the be-ginning of the nineteenth century, they used to put as many white haricot beans in a hat as there were persons present, and two coloured beans were added; the beans were drawn at haphazard from the hat by a child, and they who got the coloured beans were King and Queen. In England and perhaps elsewhere the practice was to put a bean in the cake for the King and a pea for the Queen. But in some places only the King was elected by lot, and after his election he chose his Queen for himself.

476. Thus far, apart from the crosses chalked up to ban hobgoblins, witches, and bugs, the King and Queen of the Bean might seem to be merely playful personages appointed at a season of festivity to lead the revels. However, a more serious significance was sometimes attached to the office and to the ceremonies of Twelfth Day in general. Thus in Lorraine the height of the hemp crop in the coming year was prognosticated from the height of the King and Queen; if the King was the taller of the two, it was supposed that the male hemp would be higher than the female, but that the contrary would happen if the Queen were taller than the King.[1] Again, in the Vosges Mountains, on the borders of Franche-Comté, it is customary on Twelfth Day for people to dance on the roofs in order to make the hemp grow tall.[2] Further, in many places the beans used in the cake were carried to the church to be blessed by the clergy, and people drew omens from the cake as to the good or ill that would befall them throughout the year. Moreover, certain forms of divination were resorted to on Twelfth Night for the purpose of ascertaining in which month of the year wheat would be dearest.[3]

In Franche-Comté, particularly in the Montagne du Doubs, it is still the custom on the Eve of Twelfth Night (the fifth of January) to light a bonfire, which appears to have, in the popular mind, some reference to the crops. While it blazes, the people dance round it, crying, "Good year, come back! Bread and wine, come back!"[4]

A similar custom is commonly observed on the same day (the Eve of Twelfth Night, the fifth of January) in the Bocage of Normandy, except that it is the fruit-trees rather than the sowed fields to which the fire is applied.[5] Customs of the same sort used to be observed on the same day (the Eve of Epiphany, the fifth of January) in the Ardennes. People ran about with burning torches, commanding the moles and field-mice to go forth. Then they threw the torches on the ground, and believed that by this proceeding they purified the earth and made it fruitful.[6]

This ceremony appears to be intended to ensure a good crop of fruit by burning out the animals and insects that harm the fruit-trees. In some parts of England it used to be customary to light fires at the same season for the purpose, apparently, of procuring a plentiful crop of wheat in the ensuing autumn. Thus, "in the parish of Pauntley, a village on the borders of the county of Gloucester, next Worcestershire, and in the neighbourhood, a custom revails, which is intended to prevent the smut in wheat. On the Eve of

Twelfth-day, all the servants of every farmer assemble together in one of the fields that has been sown with wheat. At the end of twelve lands, they make twelve fires in a row with straw, around one of which, much larger than the rest, they drink a cheerful glass of cider to their master's health, and success to the future harvest; then, returning home, they feast on cakes soaked in cider, which they claim as a reward for their past labours in sowing the grain."[7] The custom was known as Wassailing.

477. In Great Britain a popular figure during the Christmas holidays was the Lord of Misrule, or (as he was called in Scotland) the Abbot of Unreason, who led the revels at that merry season in the halls of colleges, the Inns of Court, the royal palace, and the mansions of the nobles.[1]

The Lords of Misrule often or even generally reigned for more than three months in winter, namely from Allhallow Even (the thirty-first of October, the Eve of All Saints' Day) till Candlemas (the second of February). Sometimes, however, their reign seems to have been restricted to the Twelve Nights. Thus we are told that George Ferrers of Lincoln's Inn was Lord of Misrule for twelve days one year when King Edward VI kept his Christmas with open house at Greenwich.[2] At Trinity College, Cambridge, a Master of Arts used to be appointed to this honourable office, which he held for the twelve days from Christmas to Twelfth Day, and he resumed office on Candlemas Day. His duty was to regulate the games and diversions of the students, particularly the plays which were acted in the college hall. Similar masters of the revels were commonly instituted in the colleges at Oxford; for example, at Merton College the fellows annually elected about St. Edmund's Day, in November a Lord of Misrule or, as he was called in the registers, a King of the Bean (*Rex Fabarum*), who held office till Candlemas and sometimes assumed a number of ridiculous titles. In the Inner Temple a Lord of Misrule used to be appointed on St. Stephen's Day (the twenty-sixth of December); surrounded by his courtiers, who were dubbed by various derogatory or ribald names, he presided at the dancing, feasting, and minstrelsy in the hall.[3]

478. In France the counterparts of these English Lords of Misrule masqueraded in clerical attire as mock Bishops, Archbishops, Popes, or Abbots. The festival at which they disported themselves was known as the Festival of Fools (*Fête des Fous*), which fell in different places at different dates, sometimes on Christmas Day, sometimes on St. Stephen's Day (the twenty-sixth of December), sometimes on New Year's Day, and sometimes on Twelfth Day. According to one account "on the first day, which was the festival of Christmas, the lower orders of clergy and monks cried in unison *Noël* (Christmas) and gave themselves up to jollity. On the morrow, St. Stephen's Day, the deacons held a council to elect a Pope or Patriarch of Fools, a Bishop or Archbishop of Innocents, an Abbot of Ninnies; next day, the festival of St. John, the subdeacons began the dance in his honour; afterwards, on the fourth day, the festival of the Holy Innocents, the choristers and minor clergy claimed the

Pope or Bishop or Abbot elect, who made his triumphal entry into the church on Circumcision Day (the first of January) and sat enthroned pontifically till the evening of Epiphany. It was then the joyous reign of this Pope or this Bishop or this Abbot of Folly which constituted the Festival of Fools and dominated its whimsical phases, the grotesque and sometimes impious masquerades, the merry and often disgusting scenes, the furious orgies, the dances, the games, the profane songs, the impudent parodies of the catholic liturgy."[1] At these parodies of the most solemn rites of the church the priests, wearing grotesque masks and sometimes dressed as women, danced in the choir and sang obscene chants: laymen disguised as monks and nuns mingled with the clergy: the altar was transformed into a tavern, where the deacons and subdeacons ate sausages and black-puddings or played at dice and cards under the nose of the celebrant; and the censers smoked with bits of old shoes instead of incense, filling the church with a foul stench. After playing these pranks and running, leaping, and cutting capers through the whole church, they rode about the town in mean carts, exchanging scurrilities with the crowds of laughing and jeering spectators.[2]

479. Among the buffooneries of the Festival of Fools one of the most remarkable was the introduction of an ass into the church, where various pranks were played with the animal. At Autun the ass was led with great ceremony to the church under a cloth of gold, the corners of which were held by four canons; and on entering the sacred edifice the animal was wrapt in a rich cope, while a parody of the mass was performed. A regular Latin liturgy in glorification of the ass was chanted on these occasions, and the celebrant priest imitated the braying of an ass. At Beauvais the ceremony was performed every year on the fourteenth of January. A young girl with a child in her arms rode on the back of the ass in imitation of the Flight into Egypt. Escorted by the clergy and the people she was led in triumph from the cathedral to the parish church of St. Stephen. There she and her ass were introduced into the chancel and stationed on the left side of the altar; and a long mass was performed which consisted of scraps borrowed indiscriminately from the services of many church festivals throughout the year. In the intervals the singers quenched their thirst: the congregation imitated their example; and the ass was fed and watered. The services over, the animal was brought from the chancel into the nave, where the whole congregation, clergy and laity mixed up together, danced round the animal and brayed like asses. Finally, after vespers and compline, the merry procession, led by the precentor and preceded by a huge lantern, defiled through the streets to wind up the day with indecent farces in a great theatre erected opposite the church.[1]

480. A pale reflection or diminutive copy of the Festival of Fools was the Festival of the Innocents, which was celebrated on Childermas or Holy Innocents' Day, the twenty-eighth of December. The custom was widely observed both in France and England. In France on Childermas or the eve of the

The opinion that the Saturnalia originally fell in February or the beginning of March receives some support from the circumstance that the festival of the Matronalia, at which mistresses feasted their slaves just as masters did theirs at the Saturnalia, always continued to be held on the first of March, even when the Roman year began with January.[2] It is further not a little recommended by the consideration that this date would be eminently appropriate for the festival of Saturn, the old Italian god of sowing and planting. It has always been a puzzle to explain why such a festival should have been held at midwinter; but on the present hypothesis the mystery vanishes. With the Italian farmer February and March were the great season of the spring sowing and planting;[3] nothing could be more natural than that the husbandman should inaugurate the season with the worship of the deity to whom he ascribed the function of quickening the seed. It is no small confirmation of this theory that the last day of the Carnival, namely Shrove Tuesday, is still, or was down to recent times, the customary season in Central Europe for promoting the growth of the crops by means of leaps and dances. The custom fits in very well with the view which derives the Carnival from an old festival of sowing such as the Saturnalia probably was in its origin. Further, the orgiastic character of the festival is readily explained by the help of facts which met us in a former part of our investigation. We have seen that between the sower and the seed there is commonly supposed to exist a sympathetic connexion of such a nature that his conduct directly affects and can promote or retard the growth of the crops. What wonder then if the simple husbandman imagined that by cramming his belly, by swilling and guzzling just before he proceeded to sow his fields, he thereby imparted additional vigour to the seed?

But while his crude philosophy may thus have painted gluttony and intoxication in the agreeable colours of duties which he owed to himself, to his family, and to the commonwealth, it is possible that the zest with which he acquitted himself of his obligations may have been whetted by a less comfortable reflection. In modern times the indulgence of the Carnival is followed immediately by the abstinence of Lent; and if the Carnival is the direct descendant of the Saturnalia, may not Lent in like manner be merely the continuation, under a thin disguise, of a period of temperence which was annually observed, from superstitious motives, by Italian farmers long before the Christian era? Direct evidence of this, so far as I am aware, is not forthcoming; but we have seen that a practice of abstinence from fleshly lusts has been observed by various peoples as a sympathetic charm to foster the growth of the seed; and such an observance would be an appropriate sequel to the Saturnalia, if that festival was indeed, as I conjecture it to have been, originally held in spring as a religious or magical preparation for sowing and planting. When we consider how widely diffused is the belief in the sympathetic influence which human conduct, and especially the intercourse of the sexes, exerts on the fruits of the earth, we may be allowed to conjecture that the

Lenten fast, with the rule of continence which is recommended, if not strictly enjoined, by the Catholic and Coptic churches during that season, was in its origin intended, not so much to commemorate the sufferings of a dying god, as to foster the growth of the seed, which in the bleak days of early spring the husbandman commits with anxious care and misgiving to the bosom of the naked earth. Ecclesiastical historians have been puzzled to say why after much hesitation and great diversity of usage in different places the Christian church finally adopted forty days as the proper period for the mournful celebration of Lent.[4] Perhaps in coming to this decision the authorities were guided, as so often, by a regard for an existing pagan celebration of similar character and duration which they hoped by a change of name to convert into a Christian solemnity. Such a heathen Lent they may have found to hand in the rites of Persephone, the Greek goddess of the corn, whose image, carved out of a tree, was annually brought into the cities and mourned for forty nights, after which it was burned.[5] The time of year when these lamentations took place is not mentioned by the old Christian writer who records them; but they would fall most appropriately at the season when the seed was sown or, in mythical language, when the corn-goddess was buried, which in ancient Italy, as we saw, was done above all in the months of February and March. We know that at the time of the autumnal sowing Greek women held a sad and serious festival because the Corn-goddess Persephone or the Maiden, as they called her, then went down into the earth with the sown grain, and Demeter fondly mourned her daughter's absence; hence in sympathy with the sorrowful mother the women likewise mourned and observed a solemn fast and abstained from the marriage bed.[6] It is reasonable, therefore, to suppose that they practised similar rules of mourning and abstinence for a like reason at the time of the spring sowing, and that the ancient ritual survives in the modern Lent, which preserves the memory of the *Mater Dolorosa,* though it has substituted a dead Son for a dead Daughter.

Be that as it may, it is worthy of note that in Burma a similar fast, which English writers call the Buddhist Lent, is observed for three months every year while the ploughing and sowing of the fields go forward; and the custom is believed to be far older than Buddhism, which has merely given it a superficial tinge like the veneer of Christianity which, if I am right, has overlaid an old heathen observance in Lent. This Burmese Lent, we are told, covers the rainy season from the full moon of July to the full moon of October. "This is the time to plough, this is the time to sow; on a villagers' exertions in these months depends all their maintenance for the rest of the year. Every man, every woman, every child, has hard work of some kind or another. And so, what with the difficulties of travelling, what with the work there is to do, and what with the custom of Lent, every one stays at home. It is the time for prayer, for fasting, for improving the soul. Many men during these months will live even as the monks live, will eat but before midday, will abstain from tobacco. There are no plays during Lent, and there are no marriages. It is the time for preparing the land for the crop; it is the time for preparing the soul for eternity. The congregations on the Sundays will be far greater at this time than at any other; there will be more thought of the serious things of life."[7]

NOTES

471 1. Vergil, *Georg.*, ii. 538–40; *Aen.*, viii. 319–27; Tibullus, i. 3, 35–48; Ovid, *Fasti*, i. 233 ff.; Lucian, *Saturnalia*, 7; Macrobius, *Sat.*, i. 7, 21–26; Justin, xliii. 1, 3–5; Dio. Hal., i. 34.

    2. Dio Hal., i. 38; Macrobius, *Sat.*, i. 7, 31; Lactantius, *Div. Inst.*, i. 21; Arnobius, *Adv. nationes*, ii. 68.

    3. See Seneca, *Epist.*, ii. 7, 4 f. For the seven days, cp. Martial, xiv. 72, 2; Macrobius, *Sat.*, i. 10, 2; Lucian, *Saturnalia*, 21.

    4. Horace, *Sat.*, ii. 7, 4 f.; Macrobius, *Sat.*, i. 7, 26; Plutarch, *Sulla*, 18; Porphyry, *De antro nympharum*, 23.

    5. Solinus, i. 35; Joannes Lydus, *De mensibus*, iii. 15; Athenaeus, xiv. 44; Dio Cassius, ix. 9.

    6. Seneca, *Epist.*, xlvii. 14; cp. Porphyry, *De abstinentia*, ii. 23.

    7. Tacitus, *Ann.*, xiii. 15; Arrian, *Epicteti Dissert.*, i. 25. 8; Lucian, *Saturnalia*, 4.

472 1. "Les Actes de S. Dasius," in *Analecta Bollandiana*, xvi (1897), 5–16. The bearing of this document on the Saturnalia has been further discussed by Parmentier and Cumont, "Le roi des Saturnales," in *Revue de Philologie*, 21 (1897), 142–53.

473 1. See Tertullian, *Apol.*, 9; *Contra Scorp.*, 7; Minucius Felix, *Octavius*, 22, 30; Lactantius, *Div. Inst.*, i. 21; Porphyry, *De abstinentia*, ii. 56.

474 1. B. de Sahagun, *Histoire générale des choses de la Nouvelle Espagne*, tr. Jourdanet-Simeon (Paris 1880), 77, 283.

    2. Diego de Landa, *Relation des choses de Yucatan* (Paris 1864), 204 f., 276 f.

    3. Geminus, *Elementa Astronomiae*, viii. 18, p. 106 Manitius.

    4. G. Foucart, in *ERE*, iii. 93.

    5. Plutarch, *De Iside et Osiride*, 12.

475 1. J. Boemus, *Moses: Leges et Ritus omnium Gentium* (Lyons 1541), 122; J. Brand, *Popular Antiquities of Great Britain* (London 1882–

83), i. 21 ff.; R. Chambers, *Book of Days* (Edinburgh-London 1886), i. 61 ff.; E. Cortet, *Essai sur les fetes religieuses* (Paris 1867), 29–30; P. Sébillot, in *Revue des traditions populaires*, 3 (1888), 7–12.

476 1. L. Beaulieu, *Archéologie de la Lorraine* (Paris 1840–43), i. 256, n. 1.

2. L. F. Sauvé, *Le Folk-lore des Hautes Vosges* (Paris 1889), 17 f.

3. Anatole France, "Le roi boit," in *Annales politiques et littéraires*, Jan. 5, 1902, p. 5. Cp. Sébillot, *Le Folk-lore de France*, iii (Paris 1906), 510 f.

4. C. Beauquier, *Les mois en Franche-Comté* (Paris 1900), 12.

5. J. Lecoueur, *Esquisees du Boscage Normande* (Condé-sur-Noireau 1883–87), ii. 126–29.

6. A. Meyrac, *Traditions, coutumes, légendes et contes des Ardennes* (Charleville 1890), 75 f.

7. Brand, *op. cit.*, i. 33.

477 1. Brand, *op. cit.*, i. 497 ff.; E. K. Chambers, *The Mediaeval Stage* (Oxford 1903), i. 403.

2. Brand, *op. cit.*, i. 499.

3. *Ib.*, i. 497; Chambers, *op. cit.*, i. 407 ff.

478 1. L. J. B. Bérenger-Féraud, *Superstitions et survivances* (Paris 1896), 4 f.

2. *Ib.*, iv. 9; Chambers, *op. cit.*, i. 293 f.; A. de Nore, *Coutumes, mythes et traditions des provinces de France* (Paris-Lyons 1846), 293–95.

479 1. Bérenger-Féraud, *op. cit.*, iv. 28–41; Chambers, *op. cit.*, i. 330–34.

480 1. Cortet, *op. cit.*, 58; Bérenger-Féraud, *op. cit.*, iv. 25–28; Chambers, *op. cit.*, i. 317 f., 336 ff.

2. Brand, *op. cit.*, i. 421–31; Chambers, *op. cit.*, i. 352 ff.

3. Brand, *op. cit.*, i. 426.

481 1. Cp. Livy, xxii. 1, 19 f.

2. Macrobius, *Sat.*, i. 12, 7; Solinus, i. 35; J. Lydus, *De mens.*, iii. 15.

3. Palladius, *De re rustica*, books iii–iv, *passim*.

4. L. Duschene, *Origines du culte chrétien* (Paris 1903), 241–43.

5. Firmicus Maternus, *De errore prof. rel.*, 27.

6. Plutarch, *De Is. et Os.*, 69.

7. H. Fielding, *The Soul of a People* (London 1898), 172 ff.

ADDITIONAL NOTES

472. *The Saturnalia at Durostorum.* See: Weber, in *Archiv für Relig.*, 19 (1916–19), 315 f.; O. S. Rankin, *The Origin of the Festival of Hanukkah* (Edinburgh 1930), 206 ff.

476. *Fire rites.* The widespread custom of kindling fires at major seasonal festivals or at New Year is scarcely to be explained, with Frazer, as a magical means of reluming the sun. In many cases, the fire simply symbolizes domestic activity, as in the English popular expression, "to keep the home fires burning." In the Old Testament, for example (II Sam. 21 : 17; Prov. 13 : 9, 20 : 20, 24 : 20, 31 : 18; Job 18 : 5–6, 21 : 17), "to quench the fire" is a poetic expression for domestic disaster; and the same idiom appears in Arabic: A. Schultens, *Liber Iobi* (Leyden 1737), 440 f.; while the Sumerian word for "heir," viz., *ibila*, has been interpreted as meaning literally "fire-lighter." Accordingly, the periodic extinction and rekindling of a communal fire betokens simply the periodic or seasonal eclipse and regeneration of communal life. Thus, among the Tonga, Sotho and Venda—Bantu tribes of S. E. Africa—as also among the Zulus, it is the practise to extinguish the main communal fire at the death of a chieftain, and to light a new one as soon as his successor is appointed: O. Petersson, *Chiefs and Gods* (Lund 1953), 214 f.; E. J. and J. D. Krige, *The Realm of a Rain Queen* (London 1947), 168; A. T. Bryant, *The Zulu People* (Pietermaritzburg 1949), 469. Similarly, among the Hungwe, a Shona tribe, a new chief's first act is to light fires; while in Bechuanaland, a new fire is kindled by the chief at the establishment of a village, and the fires of all the constituent kraals are lit from it: L. Frobenius, *Erythräen* (Berlin-Zurich 1934), 117; W. C. Willoughny, in *Africa*, 1 (1928), 296. Conversely, among the Cwana, fires are put out at moments of public calamity, as when an epidemic occurs: Petersson, *op. cit.*, 339. Now, since seasonal festivals mark the rhythmic eclipse and renewal of corporate life, it is only natural that fires should be extinguished and relumed on such occasions. Among the Zulus, for instance, this is common practise at the feast of firstfruits: H. Brincker, "Pyrolatrie in Südafrika," in *Globus*, 67 (1895), 69 f.; Petersson, *op. cit.*, 333 ff.

Then, too, it must be remembered that fire has purificatory properties and serves to burn up evil and noxious influences. Fields, for example, are lustrated by means of burning torches: see Kirby Smith on Tibullus, i. 2, 61; while in Morocco and Tunis children and unmarried men leap over fires on the feast of 'Ashura (the Moslem New Year), crying, "We shake out upon thee, O bonfire, fleas and lice and sicknesses of heart and bones": E. Westermarck, *Pagan Survivals in Mohammedan Civilisation* (London 1933), 146 f., 169 ff.

On fire-rites in general see: Winifred S. Blackman, "The Magical and Ceremonial Uses of Fire," in *Folk-Lore*, 27 (1916), 352–77; O. C. de C. Ellis, *A History of Fire and Flame* (London 1932); P. E. Froment, *Essai sur le rôle du feu en religion* (Montauban 1900); C. E. Edsman, *Ignis Divinus* (Leipzig-Uppsala 1940); J. Hertel, *Die arische Feuerlehre*, i–ii (Leipzig 1925–31); E. W. Hopkins, "The Cult of Fire in Christianity," in *Oriental Studies in honor of C. E. Parry* (London 1933), 142–50; T. F. Dexter, *Fire Worship in Britain* (London 1931); F. Corjon, "Les rites du feu et de l'eau chez les Berbéres du Maroc," in *Bull. Publ. Maroc.*, 39 (1953), 199–208.

PART VIII

THE GOLDEN BOUGH

'TWIXT HEAVEN

AND EARTH

TABOO ON TOUCHING THE EARTH

482. We have travelled far since we turned our backs on Nemi and set forth in quest of the secret of the Golden Bough. We now enter on the last stage of our long journey. The reader who has had the patience to follow the enquiry thus far may remember that at the outset two questions were proposed for answer: Why had the priest of Aricia to slay his predecessor? And why, before doing so, had he to pluck the Golden Bough? Of these two questions the first has now been answered. The priest of Aricia, if I am right, was one of those sacred kings or human divinities on whose life the welfare of the community and even the course of nature in general are believed to be intimately dependent.

But we have still to ask, What was the Golden Bough? and why had each candidate for the Arician priesthood to pluck it before he could slay the incumbent priest?

483. Now, the first thing to notice about the Golden Bough is that, being a bough, it is poised, as it were, between heaven and earth. Since, then, it is a prerequisite for the acquisition of kingship, and hence, in all likelihood, believed to be endowed with some special quality characteristic of kings, this immediately suggests a connection with the widespread taboo that the divine king or priest may not touch the ground with his foot. Thus, among the Zapotecs of Mexico, the supreme pontiff was deemed to have profaned his sanctity if he so much as stepped on the ground.[1] Montezuma, emperor of Mexico, never set foot on the ground; he was always carried on the shoulders of noblemen, and if he lighted anywhere they laid rich tapestry for him to walk upon.[2] For the Mikado of Japan to touch the ground with his foot was a shameful degradation; indeed, in the sixteenth century, it was enough to deprive him of his office. Outside his palace he was carried on men's shoulders; within it he walked on exquisitely wrought mats.[3] The king and queen of

Tahiti might not touch the ground anywhere but within their hereditary do-mains; for the ground on which they trod became sacred. In travelling from place to place they were carried on the shoulders of sacred men. They were always accompanied by several pairs of these sanctified attendants; and when it became necessary to change their bearers, the king and queen vaulted on to the shoulders of their new bearers without letting their feet touch the ground.[4] Within his palace the king of Persia walked on carpets on which no one else might tread; outside of it he was never seen on foot but only in a chariot or on horseback.[5] In old days the king of Siam never set foot upon the earth, but was carried on a throne of gold from place to place.[6] Formerly neither the kings of Uganda, nor their mothers, nor their queens might walk on foot out-side of the spacious enclosures in which they lived. Whenever they went forth they were carried on the shoulders of men of the Buffalo clan, several of whom accompanied any of these royal personages on a journey and took it in turn to bear the burden.[7] Among the Bakuba or rather Bushongo, a nation in the southern region of the Congo, down to a few years ago persons of the royal blood were forbidden to touch the ground; they must sit on a hide, a chair, or the back of a slave, who crouched on hands and feet; their feet rested on the feet of others. When they travelled they were carried on the backs of men; but the king journeyed in a litter supported on shafts.[8] Among the Ibo people about Awka, in Southern Nigeria, the priest of the Earth may not sit on the bare ground, nor eat things that have fallen on the ground, nor may earth be thrown at him.[9] According to ancient Brahmanic ritual a king at his inauguration trod on a tiger's skin and a golden plate; he was shod with shoes of boar's skin, and so long as he lived thereafter he might not stand on the earth with his fare feet.[10]

484. But besides persons who are permanently sacred or tabooed and are therefore permanently forbidden to touch the ground with their feet, there are others who enjoy the character of sanctity or taboo only on certain occa-sions, and to whom accordingly the prohibition in question only applies at the definite seasons during which they exhale the odour of sanctity. Thus among the Kayans or Bahaus of Central Borneo, while the priestesses are engaged in the performance of certain rites they may not step on the ground, and boards are laid for them to tread on.[1] With the Dyaks of Landak and Tajan, two districts of Dutch Borneo, it is a custom that for a certain time after marriage neither bride nor bridegroom may tread on the earth.[2] Warriors, again, on the war-path are surrounded, so to say, by an atmosphere of taboo; hence some Indians of North America might not sit on the bare ground the whole time they were out on a warlike expedition.[3] In Laos the hunting of elephants gives rise to many taboos; one of them is that the chief hunter may not touch the earth with his foot. Accordingly, when he alights from his elephant, the others spread a carpet of leaves for him to step upon.[4] German wiseacres recom-mended that when witches were led to the block or the stake, they should not be allowed to touch the bare earth, and a reason suggested for the rule was that if they did so they might make themselves invisible and so escape.[5]

485. Apparently holiness, magical virtue, taboo, or whatever we may call that mysterious quality which is supposed to pervade sacred or tabooed persons, is conceived by the primitive as a physical substance or fluid which can be drained away by contact with the earth. Hence, to preserve the charge from running to waste, the sacred or tabooed personage must be carefully prevented from touching the ground; in electrical language he must be *insulated*. And in many cases, apparently, the insulation is recommended as a precaution not only for the sake of the tabooed person but also for the sake of others, for since the virtue of holiness or taboo is, so to say, a powerful explosive which the smallest touch may detonate, it is necessary in the interest of the general safety to keep it within narrow bounds, lest breaking out it should blast, blight, and destroy whatever it comes into contact with.

486. But things as well as persons are often charged with the mysterious quality of holiness or taboo; hence it frequently becomes necessary for similar reasons to guard them also from coming into contact with the ground. Thus, among the Carrier Indians of North-West America, who burned their dead, the ashes of a chief used to be placed in a box and set on the top of a pole beside his hut; the box was never allowed to touch the ground.[1] In the Omaha tribe of North American Indians the sacred clam shell of the Elk clan was wrapt up from sight in a mat, placed on a stand, and never suffered to come in contact with the earth.[2] The Cherokees and kindred Indian tribes of the United States used to have certain sacred boxes or arks, which they took with them to war, but special precautions were taken to keep the holy object off the ground.[3] Again, in Scotland, when water was carried from sacred wells to sick people, the water-vessel might not touch the earth.[4] In some parts of Aberdeenshire the last bunch of standing corn, which is commonly viewed as very sacred, being the last refuge of the corn-spirit retreating before the reapers, is not suffered to touch the ground; the master or "gueedman" sits down and receives each handful of corn as it is cut on his lap.[5]

Similarly, too, sacred food may not under certain circumstances be brought into contact with the earth. Some of the aborigines of Victoria used to regard the fat of the emu as sacred, believing that it had once been the fat of the black man. In taking it from the bird or giving it to another they handled it reverently and took special care not to let it fall on the ground.[6] So, too, at certain festivals in south-eastern Borneo, foot-bridges made of thin poles are constructed from the private dwellings to the common hall lest any of the food then to be consumed fall accidentally upon the bare earth.[7]

487. Sometimes magical implements and remedies are believed to lose their virtue by contact with the ground. Thus in the Boulia district of Queensland the magical bone which the native sorcerer points at his victim as a means of killing him is never allowed to touch the earth.[1] And among the peasantry of the north-east of Scotland the prehistoric weapons called celts went by the name of "thunderbolts" and were coveted as the sure bringers of success, provided always that they were not allowed to fall to the ground.[2]

Pliny mentions several medicinal plants, which, if they were to retain their healing virtue, ought not to be allowed to touch the earth.[3] The curious medical treatise of Marcellus, a native of Bordeaux in the fourth century of our era, abounds with prescriptions of this sort; and we can well believe the writer when he assures us that he borrowed many of his quaint remedies from the lips of common folk and peasants rather than from the books of the learned.[4] Thus he tells us that certain white stones found in the stomachs of young swallows assuage the most persistent headache, always provided that their virtue be not impaired by contact with the ground.[5] Another of his cures for the same malady is a wreath of fleabane placed on the head, but it must not touch the earth.[6] On the same condition a decoction of the root of elecampane in wine kills worms; a fern, found growing on a tree, relieves the stomach-ache; and the pastern-bone of a hare is an infallible remedy for colic, provided, first, it be found in the dung of a wolf, second, that it does not touch the ground, and, third, that it is not touched by a woman.[7] Another cure for colic is effected by certain hocus-pocus with a scrap of wool from the forehead of a first-born lamb, if only the lamb, instead of being allowed to fall to the ground, has been caught by hand as it dropped from its dam.[8] In Andjra, a district of Morocco, the people attribute many magical virtues to rain-water which has fallen on the twenty-seventh day of April, Old Style; accordingly they collect it and use it for a variety of purposes. Mixed with tar and sprinkled on the door-posts it prevents snakes and scorpions from entering the house: sprinkled on heaps of threshed corn it protects them from the evil eye: mixed with an egg, henna, and seeds of cress it is an invaluable medicine for sick cows: poured over a plate, on which a passage of the Koran has been written, it strengthens the memory of schoolboys who drink it; and if you mix it with cowdung and red earth and paint rings with the mixture round the trunks of your fig-trees at sunset on Midsummer Day, you may depend on it that the trees will bear an excellent crop and will not shed their fruit untimely on the ground. But in order to preserve these remarkable properties it is absolutely essential that the water should on no account be allowed to touch the ground; some say too that it should not be exposed to the sun nor breathed upon by anybody.[9] Again, the Moors ascribe great magical efficacy to what they call "the sultan of the oleander," which is a stalk of oleander with a cluster of four pairs of leaves springing from it. They think that the magical virtue is greatest if the stalk has been cut immediately before midsummer. But when the plant is brought into the house, the branches may not touch the ground, lest they should lose their marvellous qualities.[10] In the olden days, before a Lithuanian or Prussian farmer went forth to plough for the first time in spring, he called in a wizard to perform a certain ceremony for the good of the crops. The sage seized a mug of beer with his teeth, quaffed the liquor, and then tossed the mug over his head. This signified that the corn in that year should grow taller than a man. But the mug might not fall to the ground; it had to be caught by somebody stationed at the wizard's back, for if it fell to the ground the consequence naturally would be that the corn also would be laid low on the earth.[11]

TABOO ON SEEING THE SUN

488. The second rule to be here noted is that the sun may not shine upon the divine person. The Japanese would not allow that the Mikado should expose his sacred person to the open air, and the sun was not thought worthy to shine on his head.[1] The Indians of Granada, in South America, "kept those who were to be rulers or commanders, whether men or women, locked up for several years when they were children, some of them seven years, and this so close that they were not to see the sun, for if they should happen to see it they forfeited their lordship.[2] So, too, the heir to the kingdom of Sogamoso, before succeeding to the crown, had to fast for seven years in the temple, being shut up in the dark and not allowed to see the sun or light.[3] The prince who was to become Inca of Peru had to fast for a month without seeing light.[4] On the day when a Brahman student of the Veda took a bath, to signify that the time of his studentship was at an end, he entered a cow-shed before sunrise, hung over the door a skin with the hair inside, and sat there; on that day the sun should not shine upon him.[5]

Again, women after childbirth and their offspring are more or less tabooed all the world over; hence in Corea the rays of the sun are rigidly excluded from both mother and child for a period of twenty-one or a hundred days, according to their rank, after the birth has taken place.[6] Among some of the tribes on the north-west coast of New Guinea a woman may not leave the house for months after childbirth. When she does go out, she must cover her head with a hood or mat; for if the sun were to shine upon her, it is thought that one of her male relations would die.[7] Again, mourners are everywhere taboo; accordingly in mourning the Ainos of Japan wear peculiar caps in order that the sun may not shine upon their heads.[8] During a solemn fast of three days the Indians of Costa Rica eat no salt, speak as little as possible, light no fires, and stay strictly indoors, or if they go out during the day they carefully cover themselves from the light of the sun, believing that exposure to the sun's rays would turn them black.[9] On Yule Night it has been customary in parts of Sweden from time immemorial to go on pilgrimage, whereby people learn many secret things and know what is to happen in the coming year. As a preparation for this pilgrimage, "some secrete themselves for three days previously in a dark cellar, so as to be shut out altogether from the light of heaven. Others retire at an early hour of the preceding morning to some out-of-the-way place, such as a hay-loft, where they bury themselves in the hay, that they may neither see nor hear any living creature; and here they remain, in silence and fasting, until after sundown; whilst there are those who think it sufficient if they rigidly abstain from food on the day before commencing their wanderings. During this period of probation a man ought not to see fire, but should this have happened, he must strike a light with flint and steel, whereby the evil that would otherwise have ensued will be obviated."[10] During the sixteen days that a Pima Indian is undergoing purification for killing an Apache he may not see a blazing fire.[11]

Acarnanian peasants tell of a handsome prince called Sunless, who would die if he saw the sun. So he lived in an underground palace on the site of the ancient Oeniadae, but at night he came forth and crossed the river to visit a famous enchantress who dwelt in a castle on the further bank. She was loth to part with him every night long before the sun was up, and as he turned a deaf ear to all her entreaties to linger, she hit upon the device of cutting the throats of all the cocks in the neighbourhood. So the prince, whose ear had learned to expect the shrill clarion of the birds as the signal of the growing light, tarried too long, and hardly had he reached the ford when the sun rose over the Aetolian mountains, and its fatal beams fell on him before he could regain his dark abode.[12]

The Taboos Imposed on Girls at Puberty

489. Now, it is remarkable that the foregoing two rules—not to touch the ground and not to see the sun—are observed either separately or conjointly by girls at puberty in many parts of the world. Thus amongst the Negroes of Loango girls at puberty are confined in separate huts, and they may not touch the ground with any part of their bare body.[1] Among the Zulus and kindred tribes of South Africa, when the first signs of puberty shew themselves "while a girl is walking, gathering wood, or working in the field, she runs to the river and hides herself among the reeds for the day, so as not to be seen by men. She covers her head carefully with her blanket that the sun may not shine on it and shrivel her up into a withered skeleton. After dark she returns to her home and is secluded" in a hut for some time.[2] During her seclusion, which lasts for about a fortnight, neither she nor the girls who wait upon her may drink any milk, lest the cattle should die. And should she be overtaken by the first flow while she is in the fields, she must, after hiding in the bush, scrupulously avoid all pathways in returning home.[3] A reason for this avoidance is assigned by the A-Kamba of British East Africa, whose girls under similar circumstances observe the same rule. "If," they say, "a stranger accidentally trod on a spot of blood and then cohabited with a member of the opposite sex before the girl was better again, it is believed that she would never bear a child." She remains at home until the symptoms have ceased, and during that time she may be fed by none but her mother. When the flux is over, her father and mother are bound to cohabit with each other, else the girl will be barren for life.[4] In New Ireland girls are confined for four or five years in small cages, being kept in the dark and not allowed to set foot on the ground.[5] Among the Uiyumkwi tribe in Red Island the girl lies at full length in a shallow trench dug in the foreshore, and sand is thrown lightly over her legs and body up to the breasts, which appear not to be covered. A rough shelter of boughs is then built over her, and thus she remains lying for a few hours. Then she and her attendant go into the bush and look for food, which they cook at a fire close to the shelter.[6]

Among the Hareskin Tinneh a girl at puberty was secluded for five days in a hut made specially for the purpose; she might only drink out of a tube made from a swan's bone, and for a month she might not break a hare's bones, nor taste blood, nor eat the heart or fat of animals, nor birds' eggs.[7] Among the Tinneh Indians of the middle Yukon valley, in Alaska, the period of the girl's seclusion lasts exactly a lunar month; for the day of the moon on which the symptoms first occur is noted, and she is sequestered until the same day of the next moon.[8] "When a Delaware Indian girl has her first monthly period, she must withdraw into a hut at some distance from the village. Her head is wrapped up for twelve days, so that she can see nobody, and she must submit to frequent vomits and fasting, and abstain from all labor. After this she is washed and new clothed, but confined to a solitary life for two months, at the close of which she is declared marriageable."[9] Again, among the Cheyennes, an Indian tribe of the Missouri valley, a girl at her first menstruation is painted red all over her body and secluded in a special little lodge for four days.[10]

When symptoms of puberty appeared on a girl for the first time, the Guaranis of Southern Brazil, on the borders of Paraguay, used to sew her up in her hammock, leaving only a small opening in it to allow her to breathe. In this condition, wrapt up and shrouded like a corpse, she was kept for two or three days or so long as the symptoms lasted, and during this time she had to observe a most rigorous fast.[11]

Among the Yuracares, an Indian tribe of Bolivia, at the eastern foot of the Andes, when a girl perceives the signs of puberty, her father constructs a little hut of palm leaves near the house. In this cabin he shuts up his daughter so that she cannot see the light, and there she remains fasting rigorously for four days.[12]

Among the Matacos or Mataguayos, an Indian tribe of the Gran Chaco, a girl at puberty has to remain in seclusion for some time. She lies covered up with branches or other things in a corner of the hut, seeing no one and speaking to no one, and during this time she may eat neither flesh nor fish. Meantime a man beats a drum in front of the house.[13]

When a Hindu maiden reaches maturity she is kept in a dark room for four days, and is forbidden to see the sun. She is regarded as unclean; no one may touch her. The Rarhi Brahmans of Bengal compel a girl at puberty to live alone, and do not allow her to see the face of any male. For three days she remains shut up in a dark room, and has to undergo certain penances. Fish, flesh, and sweetmeats are forbidden her; she must live upon rice and ghee.[14] Similarly among the Parivarams of Madura, when a girl attains to puberty she is kept for sixteen days in a hut, which is guarded at night by her relations; and when her sequestration is over the hut is burnt down and the pots she used are broken into very small pieces, because they think that if rain-water gathered in any of them, the girl would be childless.[15]

In Cambodia a girl at puberty is put to bed under a mosquito curtain, where she should stay a hundred days. Usually, however, four, five, ten, or twenty days are thought enough; and even this, in a hot climate and under the close meshes of the curtain, is sufficiently trying.[16]

490. The idea that women may be impregnated by the sun is not uncommon in legends. Thus, for example, among the Indians of Guacheta in Colombia, it is said, a report once ran that the sun would impregnate one of their maidens, who should bear a child and yet remain a virgin. The chief had two daughters, and was very desirous that one of them should conceive in this miraculous manner. So every day he made them climb a hill to the east of his house in order to be touched by the first beams of the rising sun. His wished were fulfilled, for one of the damsels conceived and after nine months gave birth to an emerald. So she wrapped it in cotton and placed it in her bosom, and in a few days it turned into a child, who received the name of Garanchacha and was universally recognized as a son of the sun.[1] Again, the Samoans tell of a woman named Mangamangai, who became pregnant by looking at the rising sun. Her son grew up and was named "Child of the Sun." At his marriage he applied to his mother for a dowry, but she bade him apply to his father, the sun, and told him how to go to him. So one morning he took a long vine and made a noose in it; then climbing up a tree he threw the noose over the sun and caught him fast. Thus arrested in his progress, the luminary asked him what he wanted, and being told by the young man that he wanted a present for his bride, the sun obligingly packed up a store of blessings in a basket, with which the youth descended to the earth.[2]

The old Greek story of Danae who was confined by her father in a subterranean chamber or a brazen tower but impregnated by Zeus, who reached her in the shape of a shower of gold,[3] perhaps belongs to the same class of tales. It has its counterpart in the legend which the Kirghiz of Siberia tell of their ancestry. A certain Khan had a fair daughter, whom he kept in a dark iron house, that no man might see her. An old woman tended her; and when the girl was grown to maidenhood she asked the old woman, "Where do you go so often?" "My child," said the old dame, "there is a bright world. In that bright world your father and mother live, and all sorts of people live there. That is where I go." The maiden said, "Good mother, I will tell nobody, but shew me that bright world." So the old woman took the girl out of the iron house. But when she saw the bright world, the girl tottered and fainted; and the eye of God fell upon her, and she conceived. Her angry father put her in a golden chest and sent her floating away (fairy gold can float in fairyland) over the wide sea.[4] The shower of gold in the Greek story, and the eye of God in the Kirghiz legend, probably stand for sunlight and the sun.

491. Even in the marriage customs of various races we may perhaps detect traces of this belief that women can be impregnated by the sun. Thus amongst the Chaco Indians of South America a newly married couple used to sleep the first night on a mare's or bullock's skin with their heads towards the west, "for the marriage is not considered ratified till the rising sun shines on their feet the succeeding morning."[1] At old Hindu marriages the first ceremony was the "Impregnation-rite" (*Garbhādhāna*); during the previous day the bride was made to look towards the sun or to be in some way exposed to its rays.[2] Amongst the Turks of Siberia it was formerly the custom on the morning after the marriage to lead the young couple out of the hut to greet the rising sun. The same custom is said to be still practised in Iran and Central Asia under a belief that the beams of the rising sun are the surest means of impregnating the new bride.[3]

THE TABOOS IMPOSED ON KINGS AND PRIESTS

492. The same explanation applies to the observance of the same rules by divine kings and priests; for the uncleanness, as it is called, of girls at puberty and the sanctity of holy men do not, to the primitive mind, differ materially from each other, being only different manifestations of the same mysterious energy which, like energy in general, is in itself neither good nor bad, but becomes beneficent or maleficent according to its application. *Accordingly the reason why divine personages may neither touch the ground nor see the sun, is, on the one hand, a fear lest their divinity might, at contact with earth or heaven, discharge itself with fatal violence on either; and, on the other, an apprehension that the divine being, thus drained of his ethereal virtue, might thereby be incapacitated for the future performance of those magical functions, upon the proper discharge of which the safety of the people and even of the world is believed to hang. Thus the rules in question fall under the head of the taboos which we have previously examined; they are intended to preserve the life of the divine person and with it the life of his subjects and worshippers. Nowhere, it is thought, can his precious yet dangerous life be at once so safe and so harmless as when it is neither in heaven nor in earth, but, as far as possible, suspended between the two.*

In legends and folk-tales, which reflect the ideas of earlier ages, we find this suspension between heaven and earth attributed to beings who have been endowed with the coveted yet burdensome gift of immortality. The wizened remains of the deathless Sibyl are said to have been preserved in a jar or urn which hung in a temple of Apollo at Cumae; and when a group of merry children, tired, perhaps, of playing in the sunny streets, sought the shade of the temple and amused themselves by gathering underneath the familiar jar and calling out, "Sibyl, what do you wish?" a hollow voice, like an echo, used to answer from the urn, "I wish to die."[1] A story, taken down from the lips of a German peasant at Thomsdorf, relates that once upon a time there was a girl in London who wished to live for ever, so they say:

> "London, London is a fine town.
> A maiden prayed to live for ever."

And still she lives and hangs in a basket in a church, and every St. John's Day, about the hour of noon, she eats a roll of bread.[2] Another German story tells of a lady who resided at Danzig and was so rich and so blest with all that life can give that she wished to live always. So when she came to her latter end, she did not really die but only looked like dead, and very soon they found her in a hollow of a pillar in the church, half standing and half sitting, motionless. She stirred never a limb, but they saw quite plainly that she was alive, and she sits there down to this blessed day. Every New Year's Day the sacristan comes and puts a morsel of the holy bread in her mouth, and that is all she has to live on. Long, long has she rued her fatal wish who set this transient life above the eternal joys of heaven.[3] A third German story tells of a noble damsel who cherished the same foolish wish for immortality. So they put her in a basket and hung her up in a church, and there she hangs and never dies, though many a year has come and gone since they put her there. But every year on a certain day they give her a roll, and she eats it and cries out, "For ever! for ever! for ever!" And when she has so cried she falls silent again till the same time next year, and so it will go on for ever and for ever.[4] A fourth story, taken down near Oldenburg in Holstein, tells of a jolly dame that ate and drank and lived right merrily and had all that heart could desire, and she wished to live always. For the first hundred years all went well, but after that she began to shrink and shrivel up, till at last she could neither walk nor stand nor eat nor drink. But die she could not. At first they fed her as if she were a little child, but when she grew smaller and smaller they put her in a glass bottle and hung her up in the church. And there she still hangs, in the church of St. Mary, at Lübeck. She is as small as a mouse, but once a year she stirs.[5]

Nor is it only in popular custom and folk-tale that this idea finds expression. It may be found also, as we shall now see, on a somewhat more exalted level.

THE MISTLETOE

THE MYTH OF BALDER

493. A deity whose life might in a sense be said to be neither in heaven nor on earth but between the two, was the Norse Balder, the good and beautiful god, the son of the great god Odin, and himself the wisest, mildest, best beloved of all the immortals. The story of his death, as it is told in the younger or prose *Edda,* runs thus.[1] Once on a time Balder dreamed heavy dreams which seemed to forebode his death. Thereupon the gods held a council and resolved to make him secure against every danger. So the goddess Frigg took an oath from fire and water, iron and all metals, stones and earth, from trees, sicknesses and poisons, and from all four-footed beasts, birds, and creeping things, that they would not hurt Balder. When this was done Balder was deemed invulnerable; so the gods amused themselves by setting him in their midst, while some shot at him, others hewed at him, and others threw stones at him. But whatever they did, nothing could hurt him; and at this they were all glad. Only Loki, the mischief-maker, was displeased, and he went in the guise of an old woman to Frigg, who told him that the weapons of the gods could not wound Balder, since she had made them all swear not to hurt him. Then Loki asked, "Have all things sworn to spare Balder?" She answered, "East of Walhalla grows a plant called mistletoe; it seemed to me too young to swear." So Loki went and pulled the mistletoe and took it to the assembly of the gods. There he found the blind god Hother standing at the outside of the circle. Loki asked him, "Why do you not shoot at Balder?" Hother answered, "Because I do not see where he stands; besides I have no weapon." Then said Loki, "Do like the rest and shew Balder honour, as they all do. I will shew you where he stands, and do you shoot at him with this twig." Hother took the mistletoe and threw it at Balder, as Loki directed him. The mistletoe struck Balder and pierced him through and through, and he fell down dead. And that was the greatest misfortune that ever befell gods and men. For a while the gods stood speechless, then they lifted up their voices and wept bitterly. They took Balder's body and brought it to the sea-shore. There stood Balder's ship; it was called Ringhorn, and was the hugest of all ships. The gods wished to launch the ship and to burn Balder's body on it, but the ship would not stir. So they sent for a giantess called Hyrrockin. She came riding on a wolf and gave the ship such a push that fire flashed from the rollers and all the earth shook. Then Balder's body was taken and placed on the funeral pile upon his ship. When his wife Nanna saw that, her heart burst for sorrow and she died. So she was laid on the funeral pile with her husband, and fire was put to it. Balder's horse, too, with all its trappings, was burned on the pile.

Whatever historical kernel may underlie this story is, for our present purpose, quite irrelevant. We are concerned only with the mythical husk. The details of the tale, in the form in which it has come down to us, suggest that it belongs to that class of myths that have been dramatized in ritual, or, to put it otherwise, that have been performed as magical ceremonies for the sake of producing those natural effects which they describe in figurative language. This probability will be enhanced if we can prove that ceremonies resembling the several incidents in the tale have indeed been performed by Norsemen and other European peoples. Now, the main incidents are two: first, the pulling of the mistletoe, and second, the death and burning of the god; and both of them may perhaps be found to have had their counterparts in yearly rites observed, whether separately or conjointly, by peoples in various parts of Europe.

The Folk-lore of the Mistletoe

494. From time immemorial the mistletoe has been an object of superstitious veneration in Europe. Pliny tells us in a famous passage[1] that it was worshipped by the Druids; and elsewhere he relates that in medicine the variety of it which grows on the oak was esteemed the most efficacious. Its efficacy, he adds, was popularly supposed to be enhanced if it were gathered on the first day of the moon without the use of iron, and if when gathered it were not allowed to touch the earth.[2]

If in the latter passages the Roman writer is referring, as is apparently the case, to beliefs held by his contemporaries in Italy, it will follow that the Druids and the Italians were to some extent agreed as to the valuable properties possessed by mistletoe which grows on an oak.

With these beliefs of the ancient Gauls and Italians we may compare similar notions entertained by the modern Ainos of Japan. They too, we are told, hold the mistletoe in peculiar veneration, regarding it as a panacea and esteeming that which grows on the willow (a sacred tree) as the most efficacious.[3]

Again, the Druidical idea that the mistletoe was an "all-healer" may be compared with a popular belief of the Walos of Senegambia. These people "have much veneration for a sort of mistletoe which they call *tob;* they carry leaves of it on their persons when they go to war as a preservative against wounds, just as if the leaves were real talismans (*gris-gris*)." The French writer who records this practice adds: "Is it not very curious that the mistletoe should be in this part of Africa what it was in the superstitions of the Gauls? This prejudice, common to the two countries, may have the same origin; blacks and whites will doubtless have seen, each of them for themselves, something supernatural in a plant which grows and flourishes without having roots in the earth. May they not have believed, in fact, that it was a plant fallen from the sky, a gift of the divinity?"[4]

This suggestion as to the origin of the superstition is strongly confirmed by the Druidical belief, reported by Pliny, that whatever grew on an oak was sent from heaven and was a sign that the tree had been chosen by the god himself. Such a belief explains why the Druids cut the mistletoe, not with a common knife, but with a golden sickle, and why, when cut, it was not suffered to touch the earth; probably they thought that the celestial plant would have been profaned and its marvellous virtue lost by contact with the ground. With the ritual observed by the Druids in cutting the mistletoe we may compare that which in Cambodia is prescribed in a similar case. They say that when you see an orchid growing as a parasite on a tamarind tree, you should dress in white, take a new earthenware pot, then climb the tree at noon, break off the plant, put it in the pot, and let the pot fall to the ground. We may conjecture that in both places the notion of invulnerability is suggested by the position of the plant, which, occupying a place of comparative security above the ground, appears to promise to its fortunate possessor a similar security from some of the ills that beset the life of man upon earth. Indeed, the Gallas of Africa say that the mistletoe is grafted on a tree as the soul is grafted on the body; and they show their veneration for it by gathering it at a special ceremony and placing it in their houses to bring good luck.[4a]

495. Whatever may be the origin of these beliefs and practices concerning the mistletoe, certain it is that some of them have their analogies in the folk-lore of modern European peasants. For example, it is laid down as a rule in various parts of the continent that mistletoe may not be cut in the ordinary way but must be shot or knocked down with stones from the tree on which it happens to be growing. Thus, in the Swiss canton of Aargau "all parasitic plants are esteemed in a certain sense holy by the country folk, but most particularly so the mistletoe growing on an oak. They ascribe great powers to it, but shrink from cutting it off in the usual manner. Instead of that they procure it in the following manner. When the sun is in Sagittarius and the moon is on the wane, on the first, third, or fourth day before the new moon, one ought to shoot down with an arrow the mistletoe of an oak and to catch it with the left hand as it falls. Such mistletoe is a remedy for every ailment of children."¹ Here among the Swiss peasants, as among the Druids of old, special virtue is ascribed to mistletoe which grows on an oak: it may not be cut in the usual way: it must be caught as it falls to the ground; and it is esteemed a panacea for all diseases, at least of children. In Sweden, also, it is a popular superstition that if mistletoe is to possess its peculiar virtue, it must either be shot down out of the oak or knocked down with stones.² Similarly, "so late as the early part of the nineteenth century, people in Wales believed that for the mistletoe to have any power, it must be shot or struck down with stones off the tree where it grew."³

496. Again, in respect of the healing virtues of mistletoe the opinion of modern peasants, and even of the learned, has to some extent agreed with that of the ancients. The Druids appear to have called the plant, or perhaps the oak on which it grew, the "all-healer"¹ and "all-healer" is said to be still a name of the mistletoe in the modern Celtic speech of Brittany, Wales, Ireland, and Scotland.²

497. Again, mistletoe acts as a master-key as well as a lightning-conductor. It is believed to open all locks.¹ However, in the Tyrol it can only exert this power "under certain circumstances," which are not specified.² But perhaps the most precious of all the virtues of mistletoe is that it affords efficient protection against sorcery and witchcraft.³ That, no doubt, is the reason why in Austria a twig of mistletoe is laid on the threshold as a preventive of nightmare;⁴ and it may be the reason why in the north of England they say that if you wish your dairy to thrive you should give your bunch of mistletoe to the first cow that calves after New Year's Day,⁵ for it is well known that nothing is so fatal to milk and butter as witchcraft. In Sweden mistletoe is diligently sought after on St. John's Eve, the people "believing it to be, in a high degree, possessed of mystic qualities; and that if a sprig of it be attached to the ceiling of the dwelling-house, the horse's stall, or the cow's crib, the Troll will then be powerless to injure either man or beast."⁶

498. With regard to the time when the mistletoe should be gathered opinions have varied. The Druids gathered it above all on the sixth day of the moon, the ancient Italians apparently on the first day of the moon. In modern times some have preferred the full moon of March and others the waning moon of winter when the sun is in Sagittarius. But the favourite time would seem to be Midsummer Eve or Midsummer Day. We have seen that both in France and Sweden special virtues are ascribed to mistletoe gathered at Midsummer. The rule in Sweden is that "mistletoe must be cut on the night of Midsummer Eve when sun and moon stand in the sign of their might."¹ Again, in Wales it was believed that a sprig of mistletoe gathered on St. John's Eve (Midsummer Eve), or at any time before the berries appeared, would induce dreams of omen, both good and bad, if it were placed under the pillow of the sleeper.² Thus mistletoe is one of the many plants whose magical or medicinal virtues are believed to culminate with the culmination of the sun on the longest day of the year.

Certain it is that the mistletoe, the instrument of Balder's death, has been regularly gathered for the sake of its mystic qualities on Midsummer Eve in Scandinavia, Balder's home. The plant is found commonly growing on pear-trees, oaks, and other trees in thick damp woods throughout the more temperate parts of Sweden.[3] Thus one of the two main incidents of Balder's myth is reproduced in the great midsummer festival of Scandinavia. But the other main incident of the myth, the burning of Balder's body on a pyre, has also its counterpart in the bonfires which still blaze, or blazed till lately, in Denmark, Norway, and Sweden on Midsummer Eve. It does not appear, indeed, that any effigy is burned in these bonfires; but the burning of an effigy is a feature which might easily drop out after its meaning was forgotten. And the name of Balder's balefires (*Balder's Bålar*), by which these midsummer fires were formerly known in Sweden,[4] puts their connexion with Balder beyond the reach of doubt, and makes it probable that in former times either a living representative or an effigy of Balder was annually burned in them. Midsummer was the season sacred to Balder, and the Swedish poet Tegner, in placing the burning of Balder at midsummer,[5] may very well have followed an old tradition that the summer solstice was the time when the good god came to his untimely end.

BALDER AND THE MISTLETOE

499. Thus it has been shewn that the leading incidents of the Balder myth have their counterparts in those fire-festivals of our European peasantry which undoubtedly date from a time long prior to the introduction of Christianity. From all this we may reasonably infer that in the Balder myth on the one hand, and the fire-festivals and custom of gathering mistletoe on the other hand, we have, as it were, the two broken and dissevered halves of an original whole. In other words, we may assume with some degree of probability that the myth of Balder's death was not merely a myth, that is, a description of physical phenomena in imagery borrowed from human life, but that it was at the same time the story which people told to explain why they annually burned a human representative of the god and cut the mistletoe with solemn ceremony. The story of Balder's tragic end formed, so to say, the text of the sacred drama which was acted year by year as a magical rite to cause the sun to shine, trees to grow, crops to thrive, and to guard man and beast from the baleful arts of fairies and trolls, of witches and warlocks.

But if the victims—the human Balders—who died by fire, whether in spring or at midsummer, were put to death as living embodiments of tree-spirits or deities of vegetation, it would seem that Balder himself must have been a tree-spirit or deity of vegetation.

In the first place, the story of the external soul is told, in various forms, by all Aryan peoples from Hindustan to the Hebrides. A very common form of it is this: A warlock, giant, or other fairyland being is invulnerable and immortal because he keeps his soul hidden far away in some secret place; but a fair princess, whom he holds enthralled in his enchanted castle, wiles his secret from him and reveals it to the hero, who seeks out the warlock's soul, heart, life, or death (as it is variously called), and, by destroying it, simultaneously kills the warlock. Thus a Hindu story tells how a magician called Punchkin held a queen captive for twelve years, and would fain marry her, but she would not have him. At last the queen's son came to rescue her, and the two plotted together to kill Punchkin. So the queen spoke the magician fair, and pretended that she had at last made up her mind to marry him. "And do tell me," she said, "are you quite immortal? Can death never touch you? And are you too great an enchanter ever to feel human suffering?" "It is true," he said, "that I am not as others. Far, far away, hundreds of thousands of miles from this, there lies a desolate country covered with thick jungle. In the midst of the jungle grows a circle of palm trees, and in the centre of the circle stand six chattees full of water, piled one above another: below the sixth chattee is a small cage, which contains a little green parrot;— on the life of the parrot depends my life;—and if the parrot is killed I must die. It is, however," he added, "impossible that the parrot should sustain any injury, both on account of the inaccessibility of the country, and because, by my appointment, many thousand genii surround the palm trees, and kill all who approach the place." But the queen's young son overcame all difficulties, and got possession of the parrot. He brought it to the door of the magician's palace, and began playing with it. Punchkin, the magician, saw him, and, coming out, tried to persuade the boy to give him the parrot. "Give me my parrot!" cried Punchkin. Then the boy took hold of the parrot and tore off one of his wings; and as he did so the magician's right arm fell off. Punchkin then stretched out his left arm, crying, "Give me my parrot!" The prince pulled off the parrot's second wing, and the magician's left arm tumbled off. "Give me my parrot!" cried he, and fell on his knees. The prince pulled off the parrot's right leg, the magician's right leg fell off; the prince pulled off the parrot's left leg, down fell the magician's left. Nothing remained of him except the trunk and the head; but still he rolled his eyes, and cried, "Give me my parrot!" "Take your parrot, then," cried the boy; and with that he wrung the bird's neck, and threw it at the magician; and, as he did so, Punchkin's head twisted round, and, with a fearful groan, he died![1]

Now, if we suppose that Balder was the oak, the origin of the myth becomes intelligible. The mistletoe was viewed as the seat of life of the oak, and so long as it was uninjured nothing could kill or even wound the oak. The conception of the mistletoe as the seat of life of the oak would naturally be suggested to primitive people by the observation that while the oak is deciduous, the mistletoe which grows on it is evergreen. In winter the sight of its fresh foliage among the bare branches must have been hailed by the worshippers of the tree as a sign that the divine life which had ceased to animate the branches yet survived in the mistletoe, as the heart of a sleeper still beats when his body is motionless. Hence when the god had to be killed—when the sacred tree had to be burnt—it was necessary to begin by breaking off the mistletoe. For so long as the mistletoe remained intact, the oak (so people might think) was invulnerable; all the blows of their knives and axes would glance harmless from its surface. But once tear from the oak its sacred heart—the mistletoe—and the tree nodded to its fall. And when in later times the spirit of the oak came to be represented by a living man, it was logically necessary to suppose that, like the tree he personated, he could neither be killed nor wounded so long as the mistletoe remained uninjured. The pulling of the mistletoe was thus at once the signal and the cause of his death.

The Concept of the External Soul

500. The foregoing explanation of Balder's relation to the mistletoe is based on a principle which is deeply engraved on the mind of primitive man. Since, however, the idea of a being whose life is, in a sense, outside of himself, must be strange to many readers, it will be worth while to illustrate it by examples drawn both from story and from custom.

501. In a Siamese or Cambodian story, probably derived from India, we are told that Thossakan or Ravana, the King of Ceylon, was able by magic art to take his soul out of his body and leave it in a box at home, while he went to the wars. Thus he was invulnerable in battle.[1] In the legend of the origin of Gilgit there figures a fairy king whose soul is in the snows and who can only perish by fire.[2]

502. In Greek tales, ancient and modern, the idea of an external soul is not uncommon. When Meleager was seven days old, the Fates appeared to his mother and told her that Meleager would die when the brand which was blazing on the hearth had burnt down. So his mother snatched the brand from the fire and kept it in a box. But in after-years, being enraged at her son for slaying her brothers, she burnt the brand in the fire and Meleager expired in agonies, as if flames were preying on his vitals.[1] Again, Nisus, King of Megara, had a purple or golden hair on the middle of his head, and it was fated that whenever the hair was pulled out the king should die. When Megara was besieged by the Cretans, the king's daughter Scylla fell in love with Minos, their king, and pulled out the fatal hair from her father's head. So he died.[2] Similarly Poseidon made Pterelaus immortal by giving him a golden hair on his head. But when Taphos, the home of Pterelaus, was besieged by Amphitryo, the daughter of Pterelaus fell in love with Amphitryo and killed her father by plucking out the golden hair with which his life was bound up.³ In a modern Greek folk-tale a man's strength lies in three golden hairs on his head. When his mother pulls them out, he grows weak and timid and is slain by his enemies.⁴

503. Ancient Italian legend furnishes a close parallel to the Greek story of Meleager. Silvia, the young wife of Septimius Marcellus, had a child by the god Mars. The god gave her a spear, with which he said that the fate of the child would be bound up. When the boy grew up he quarrelled with his maternal uncles and slew them. So in revenge his mother burned the spear on which his life depended.¹ In one of the stories of the *Pentamerone* a certain queen has a twin brother, a dragon. The astrologers declared at her birth that she would live just as long as the dragon and no longer, the death of the one involving the death of the other. If the dragon were killed, the only way to restore the queen to life would be to smear her temples, breast, pulses, and nostrils with the blood of the dragon.² In a modern Roman version of "Aladdin and the Wonderful Lamp," the magician tells the princess, whom he holds captive in a floating rock in mid-ocean, that he will never die. The princess reports this to the prince her husband, who has come to rescue her. The prince replies, "It is impossible but that there should be some one thing or other that is fatal to him; ask him what that one fatal thing is." So the princess asked the magician, and he told her that in the wood was a hydra with seven heads; in the middle head of the hydra was a leveret, in the head of the leveret was a bird, in the bird's head was a precious stone, and if this stone were put under his pillow he would die. The prince procured the stone, and the princess laid it under the magician's pillow. No sooner did the enchanter lay his head on the pillow than he gave three terrible yells, turned himself round and round three times, and died.³ Similarly in a story from the western Riviera a sorcerer called Body-without-Soul can only be killed by means of an egg which is in an eagle, which is in a dog, which is in a lion; and the egg must be broken on the sorcerer's forehead. The hero, who achieves the adventure, has received the power of changing himself into a lion, a dog, an eagle, and an ant from four creatures of these sorts among whom he had fairly divided the carcase of a dead ass.⁴

504. Stories of the same sort are current among Slavonic peoples. In some of them, as in the biblical story of Samson and Delilah, the warlock is questioned by a treacherous woman as to the place where his strength resides or his life or death is stowed away; and his suspicions being roused by her curiosity, he at first puts her off with false answers, but is at last beguiled into telling her the truth, thereby incurring his doom through her treachery.¹

505. Amongst peoples of the Teutonic stock stories of the external soul are not wanting. In a tale told by the Saxons of Transylvania it is said that a young man shot at a witch again and again. The bullets went clean through her but did her no harm, and she only laughed and mocked at him. "Silly earthworm," she cried, "shoot as much as you like. It does me no harm. For know that my life resides not in me but far, far away. In a mountain is a pond, on the pond swims a duck, in the duck is an egg, in the egg burns a light, that light is my life. If you could put out that light, my life would be at an end. But that can never, never be." However, the young man got hold of the egg, smashed it, and put out the light, and with it the witch's life went out also.[1]

506. In a Celtic tale, a sea beast has carried off a king's daughter, and an old smith declares that there is no way of killing the beast but one. "In the island that is in the midst of the loch is Eillid Chaisfhion—the white-footed hind, of the slenderest legs, and the swiftest step, and though she should be caught, there would spring a hoodie out of her, and though the hoodie should be caught, there would spring a trout out of her, but there is an egg in the mouth of the trout, and the soul of the beast is in the egg, and if the egg breaks, the beast is dead." As usual the egg is broken and the beast dies.[1]

507. The notion of an external or separable soul appears also in the folk-tales of non-Aryan peoples. A few representative examples must suffice.

In the ancient Egyptian story of the Two Brothers, inscribed on a papyrus of the fourteenth century B.C.,[1] the younger of the pair commits his heart to a flower atop of an acacia tree. "If they cut the tree," he tells the elder, "and my heart fall to the ground, come thou and seek it, and when thou hast found it place it in a vessel of fresh water. Then I shall come to live again. Moreover, if the pot of beer in thy hand begin to bubble, it will be a sign that ill-hap has befallen me." The subsequent narrative turns, of course, very largely on the occurrence of these signs.

In the same vein, we read in the *Arabian Nights* how Seif-el-Muluk after wandering for four months over mountains and hills and deserts, came to a lofty palace in which he found the lovely daughter of the King of India sitting alone on a golden couch in a hall spread with silken carpets. She tells him that she is held captive by a jinnee, who had swooped down on her and carried her off while she was disporting her with her female slaves in a tank in the great garden of her father the king. Seif-el-Muluk then offers to smite the jinnee with the sword and slay him. "But," she replied, "thou canst not slay him unless thou kill his soul." "And in what place," said he, "is his soul?" She answered, "I asked him respecting it many times; but he would not confess to me its place. It happened, however, that I urged him, one day, and he was enraged against me, and said to me, 'How often wilt thou ask me respecting my soul? What is the reason of thy question respecting my soul?' So I answered him, 'O Hátim, there remaineth to me no one but thee, excepting God; and I, as long as I live, would not cease to hold thy soul in my embrace; and if I do not take care of thy soul, and put it in the midst of my eye, how can I live after thee? If I knew thy soul, I would take care of it as of my right eye.' And thereupon he said to me, 'When I was born, the astrologers declared that the destruction of my soul would be effected by the hand of one of the sons of the human kings. I therefore took my soul, and put it into the crop of a sparrow, and I imprisoned the sparrow in a little box, and put this into another small box, and this I put within seven other small boxes, and I put these within seven chests, and the chests I put into a coffer of marble within the verge of this circumambient ocean; for this part is remote from the countries of mankind, and none of mankind can gain access to it.' " But Seif-el-Muluk got possession of the sparrow and strangled it, and the jinnee fell upon the ground a heap of black ashes.[2]

508. A West African story from Southern Nigeria relates how a king kept his soul in a little brown bird, which perched on a tall tree beside the gate of the palace. The king's life was so bound up with that of the bird that whoever should kill the bird would simultaneously kill the king and succeed to the kingdom. The secret was betrayed by the queen to her lover, who shot the bird with an arrow and thereby slew the king and ascended the vacant throne.[1]

Another story of an external soul comes from Nias, an island to the west of Sumatra. Once on a time a chief was captured by his enemies, who tried to put him to death but failed. Water would not drown him nor fire burn him nor steel pierce him. At last his wife revealed the secret. On his head he had a hair as hard as a copper wire; and with this wire his life was bound up. So the hair was plucked out, and with it his spirit fled.[2]

509. Ideas of the same sort meet us in stories told by the North American Indians. Thus the Navajos tell of a certain mythical being called "the Maiden that becomes a Bear," who learned the art of turning herself into a bear from the prairie wolf. She was a great warrior and quite invulnerable; for when she went to war she took out her vital organs and hid them, so that no one could kill her; and when the battle was over she put the organs back in their places again.[1] The Kwakiutl Indians of British Columbia tell of an ogress, who could not be killed because her life was in a hemlock branch. A brave boy met her in the woods, smashed her head with a stone, scattered her brains, broke her bones, and threw them into the water. Then, thinking he had disposed of the ogress, he went into her house. There he saw a woman rooted to the floor, who warned him, saying, "Now do not stay long. I know that you have tried to kill the ogress. It is the fourth time that somebody has tried to kill her. She never dies; she has nearly come to life. There in that covered hemlock branch is her life. Go there, and as soon as you see her enter, shoot her life. Then she will be dead." Hardly had she finished speaking when sure enough in came the ogress, singing as she walked:—

> "I have the magical treasure,
> I have the supernatural power,
> I can return to life."

Such was her song. But the boy shot at her life, and she fell dead to the floor.[2]

The External Soul in Plants and Animals

510. Thus the idea that the soul may be deposited for a longer or shorter time in some place of security outside the body, or at all events in the hair, is found in the popular tales of many races. It remains to shew that the idea is not a mere figment devised to adorn a tale, but is a real article of primitive faith, which has given rise to a corresponding set of customs.

We have seen that in the tales the hero, as a preparation for battle, sometimes removes his soul from his body, in order that his body may be invulnerable and immortal in the combat. With a like intention the savage removes his soul from his body on various occasions of real or imaginary peril. Thus among the people of Minahassa in Celebes, when a family moves into a new house, a priest collects the souls of the whole family in a bag, and afterwards restores them to their owners, because the moment of entering a new house is supposed to be fraught with supernatural danger.

Among the Dyaks of Pinoeh, a district of south-eastern Borneo, when a child is born, a medicine-man is sent for, who conjures the soul of the infant into half a coco-nut which he thereupon covers with a cloth and places on a square platter or charger suspended by cords from the roof. This ceremony he repeats at every new moon for a year.[1] Similarly among the Esquimaux of Alaska, when a child is sick, the medicine-man will sometimes extract its soul from its body and place it for safe-keeping in an amulet, which for further security he deposits in his own medicine-bag.[2]

The belief that human souls can be deposited in external objects was discovered by Mrs. Talbot in the Banana tribe of the Logone river, in French Central Africa. There she found that for every female child born a long plaited bag was woven by her mother or grandmother, and with it the thread of the girl's life was thought to be mysteriously linked. "No bribe would induce a living woman to part with one, since with its departure her soul must leave her, but we were fortunate enough to purchase several which had belonged to dead members of the tribe."[2a]

511. Again, in folk-tales a man's soul or strength is sometimes represented as bound up with his hair, and thus when his hair is cut off he dies or grows weak. So the natives of Amboyna used to think that their strength was in their hair and would desert them if it were shorn. A criminal under torture in a Dutch Court of that island persisted in denying his guilt till his hair was cut off, when he immediately confessed. One man, who was tried for murder, endured without flinching the utmost ingenuity of his torturers till he saw the surgeon standing with a pair of shears. On asking what this was for, and being told that it was to cut his hair, he begged they would not do it, and made a clean breast. In subsequent cases, when torture failed to wring a confession from a prisoner, the Dutch authorities made a practice of cutting off his hair.[1] In Ceram it is still believed that if young people have their hair cut they will be weakened and enervated thereby.[2]

512. In folk-tales the life of a person is sometimes so bound up with that of a plant that the withering of the plant will immediately follow or be followed by the death of the person. This idea is equally attested in folk-custom. A few instances only need be quoted. Among the Wajagga of German East Africa, when a child is born, it is usual to plant a cultivated plant of some sort behind the house. The plant is thenceforth carefully tended, for they believe that were it to wither away the child would die. When the navel-string drops from the infant, it is buried under the plant. The species of birth-plant varies with the clan; members of one clan, for example, plant a particular sort of banana, members of another clan plant a sugar-cane, and so on.[1] In the Cameroons, also, the life of a person is believed to be sympathetically bound up with that of a tree.[2] The chief of Old Town in Calabar kept his soul in a sacred grove near a spring of water. When some Europeans, in frolic or ignorance, cut down part of the grove, the spirit was most indignant and threatened the perpetrators of the deed, according to the king, with all manner of evil.[3] Among the Fons of the French Congo, when a chief's son is born, the remains of the navel-string are buried under a sacred fig-tree, and "thenceforth great importance is attached to the growth of the tree; it is strictly forbidden to touch it. Any attempt on the tree would be considered as an attack on the human being himself."[4]

In the Chatham Islands, when the child of a leading man received its name, it was customary to plant a tree, "the growth of which was to be as the growth of the child," and during the planting priests chanted a spell.[5]

It is said that there are still families in Russia, Germany, England, France, and Italy who are accustomed to plant a tree at the birth of a child. The tree, it is hoped, will grow with the child, and it is tended with special care.[6] The custom is still pretty general in the canton of Aargau in Switzerland; an apple-tree is planted for a boy and a pear-tree for a girl, and the people think that the child will flourish or dwindle with the tree.[7]

Near the Castle of Dalhousie, not far from Edinburgh, there grows an oak-tree, called the Edgewell Tree, which is popularly believed to be linked to the fate of the family by a mysterious tie; for they say that when one of the family dies, or is about to die, a branch falls from the Edgewell Tree.[8]

513. But in practice, as in folk-tales, it is not merely with inanimate objects and plants that a person is occasionally believed to be united by a bond of physical sympathy. The same bond, it is supposed, may exist between a man and an animal, so that the welfare of the one depends on the welfare of the other, and when the animal dies the man dies also. The analogy between the custom and the tales is all the closer because in both of them the power of thus removing the soul from the body and stowing it away in an animal is often a special privilege of wizards and witches. Thus the Yakuts of Siberia

believe that every shaman or wizard keeps his soul, or one of his souls, incarnate in an animal which is carefully concealed from all the world. "Nobody
can find my external soul," said one famous wizard, "it lies hidden far away
in the stony mountains of Edzhigansk."[1]

In Melanesia a native doctor was once attending to a sick man. Just then
"a large eagle-hawk came soaring past the house, and Kaplen, my hunter,
was going to shoot it; but the doctor jumped up in evident alarm, and said,
'Oh, don't shoot; that is my spirit' (*niog,* literally, my shadow); 'if you shoot
that, I will die.' He then told the old man, 'if you see a rat to-night, don't
drive it away, 'tis my spirit (*niog*), or a snake which will come to-night, that
also is my spirit.' "[2] A family in Nauru, one of the Marshall Islands, apparently imagine that their lives are bound up with a species of large fish, which
has a huge mouth and devours human beings; for when one of these fish was
killed, the members of the family cried, "Our guardian spirit is killed, now
we must all die!"[3]

The Balong of the Cameroons think that every man has several souls, of
which one is in his body and another in an animal, such as an elephant, a
wild pig, a leopard, and so forth. When a man comes home, feeling ill, and
says, "I shall soon die," and dies accordingly, the people aver that one of
his souls has been killed in a wild pig or a leopard, and that the death of the
external soul has caused the death of the soul in his body. Hence the corpse
is cut open, and a diviner determines, from an inspection of the inwards,
whether the popular surmise is correct or not.[4]

A similar belief in the external souls of living people is entertained by the
Ibos, an important tribe of the Niger delta, who inhabit a country west of
the Cross River. They think that a man's spirit can quit his body for a time
during life and take up its abode in an animal. This is called *ishi anu,* "to
turn animal."[5] A like belief is reported to prevail among the tribes of the
Obubura Hill district on the Cross River in Southern Nigeria. Once when
Mr. Partridge's canoe-men wished to catch fish near a town of the Assiga
tribe, the people objected, saying, "Our souls live in those fish, and if you
kill them we shall die."[6]

Many primitive peoples believe that their lives are so sympathetically bound
up with those of animals that when the animal dies the man dies, and that
conversely when the man expires the animal dies simultaneously. This belief
is especially prevalent among the tribes of Western Africa, where the conception of a man's soul permanently or temporarily lodged in an animal is
conveniently spoken of as a "bush-soul." Thus for example among the
Nounoumas of the Western Sudan people do not sacrifice to crocodiles, because they say that crocodiles are not gods, but only their own human souls
in animal form. The soul of every human being is at once in the man and in
the crocodile. When the crocodile dies, the man dies the day after. If the
crocodile loses an eye, the man loses an eye, and *vice versa.* If the crocodile

loses a paw, the man becomes lame. The human crocodiles are of a small species, and each man knows the crocodile that corresponds to himself. When a crocodile is about to die, it comes into the village of the person whose soul is lodged in it. When it dies they wrap the carcase in white clothing and bury it, and sacrifice fowls to it. Then the man whose soul was in the crocodile dies in turn. The people of Leo believe that when one kills a crocodile in the river, one also kills a man in the village. This is because the soul of each inhabitant of the village is connected with that of a crocodile, and when the soul of the crocodile dies or leaves its material body, the same thing happens to the inhabitant of the village who corresponds to it.[6a]

Similarly among the Kassounas-Fras, another tribe of the Western Sudan, most people believe that crocodiles are their souls, and that if they kill a crocodile the man who corresponds to it dies immediately. Thus they pay great respect to the reptiles, but do not offer them sacrifices. But at Pou it is not the crocodiles but the iguanas which are thus venerated and respected. Each iguana, it appears, possesses the soul of some person in the village. Hence if somebody kills an iguana, a man simultaneously dies in the village.[6b]

Similar beliefs as to human souls in animal bodies are current among the natives in the interior of the Gold Coast of West Africa. We are told that among them "everyone has some animal which is a species of *alter ego*— not to be slain or eaten, an animal which is recognized as one's friend, one's brother. Most noteworthy of these animals is the crocodile, which is called by the Paga people their soul. The life of a man or woman is identical with that of his crocodile, *alter ego*. When he is born the crocodile is born; they are ill at the same time; and it is said that when a man is at the point of death one can hear at night the groaning of his crocodile.[6c]

Beliefs of the same sort as to human souls in animal bodies are often held by the peoples of Southern Nigeria, and have been fully described by Mr. and Mrs. Talbot.[6d] To quote a single example: "Not long ago a man of Usun Inyan town asserted that his wife, Esiet Idung by name, had told him that her soul sometimes left her and went to dwell in the body of a fish in the Kwa Ibo River. One day she came to her husband, crying: 'I am caught! I am caught and must die! for a fisherman has snared my soul in his trap by the waterside. Go therefore to the place of which I shall tell you and release me before it is too late; for should the man come and kill my affinity, I must die also.' On this, in all haste, the husband took a canoe and went with his friends to the trap which his wife had described. They opened the door and let all the fish swim out into the river. Among the others they noticed one of great size, which plunged early out into the current. On their return they found that the woman had recovered; but all believe that, had the fish been killed, she must have perished also."[6e]

At Bia, in the island of San Cristoval, it is believed that the soul (*aunga*) of a living person may take the form of one of several species of animals, such as the shark, the hawk, the bonito, the skate, the green lizard, the yellow-breast bird, red and black snakes, the rat, the prawn, the hermit crab, and the millipede. Hence children at Bia are warned not to kill any of these animals, because the soul of a living man may take any one of these forms. If the green lizard is seen in a tree, the soul of a man may be in it, and if the lizard is killed, the man would die; the souls of living men are supposed often to go about in the form of green lizards. A man may also send his soul into the yellow-breast, and the bird will fly off and tell the man's friends that he wants them to come to him.[6f] Elsewhere in San Cristoval persons are supposed to have their souls in sharks. Such relations to sharks are hereditary, the descent being from father to son. When a shark-man has a son born to him he is initiated soon after birth into the mystery by his father, either in the house or at the shark-rock, Mr. Fox is not sure which. His father, the shark-man, takes the child in his arms and hugs him to his breast, and then crooks his left arm to represent a shark's fin, and puts the infant under his arm. Then at the shark-rock the child and his future familiar shark receive the same name. The child's soul (*aunga*) goes into the shark, and Mr. Fox thinks that the shark's soul is supposed to go into the child, or else the two become one so completely that they share the same soul. From that time the shark-child has his familiar at the shark-rock. If the child dies the shark will die, if the shark is injured the child will fall sick. The connection between the two is exceedingly close. Shark-boys have gone to Norfolk Island and their familiars have followed them and been seen on the fishing grounds. The shark-boy goes regularly to the shark-rock, and sacrifices yams, nuts, money, and betel to his shark-brother.[6g]

Amongst the Zapotecs of Central America, when a woman was about to be confined, her relations assembled in the hut, and began to draw on the floor figures of different animals, rubbing each one out as soon as it was completed. This went on till the moment of birth, and the figure that then remained sketched upon the ground was called the child's *tona* or second self. "When the child grew old enough, he procured the animal that represented him and took care of it, as it was believed that health and existence were bound up with that of the animal's, in fact that the death of both would occur simultaneously," or rather that when the animal died the man would die too.[7] Among the Indians of Guatemala and Honduras the *nagual* or *naual* is "that animate or inanimate object, generally an animal, which stands in a parallel relation to a particular man, so that the weal and woe of the man depend on the fate of the *nagual*."[8] Similarly, the Wotjobaluk tribe of South-Eastern Austrialia held that the life of Ngunungnunut (the Bat) is the life of a man, and that of Yartatgurk (the Nightjar) the life of a women, and that when either of these creatures is killed the life of some man or woman is curtailed.[9] So too among the Kurnai all emu-wrens were "brothers" of the men, and all the men were emu-wrens; all superb warblers were "sisters" of the women, and all the women were superb warblers.[10]

THE GOLDEN BOUGH AND THE EXTERNAL SOUL

514. Thus the view that Balder's life was in the mistletoe is entirely in harmony with primitive modes of thought. It may indeed sound like a contradiction that, if his life was in the mistletoe, he should nevertheless have been killed by a blow from the plant. But when a person's life is conceived as embodied in a particular object, with the existence of which his own existence is inseparably bound up, and the destruction of which involves his own, the object in question may be regarded and spoken of indifferently as his life or his death, as happens in the fairy-tales. Hence if a man's death is in an object, it is perfectly natural that he should be killed by a blow from it. In the Russian fairy-tale of Koschei the Deathless, he is killed by a blow from the egg or the stone in which his life or death is secreted.[1] In a Norse tale, ogres burst when a certain grain of sand—evidently containing their life or death—is carried over their heads.[2] In a modern Roman version of the Aladdin story, the magician dies when the stone in which his life or death is contained is put under his pillow.[3] And in a Tartar poem, the hero is warned that he may be killed by the golden arrow or golden sword in which his soul has been stowed away.[4]

515. The idea that the life of the oak was in the mistletoe was probably suggested, as I have said, by the observation that in winter the mistletoe growing on the oak remains green while the oak itself is leafless. But the position of the plant—growing not from the ground but from the trunk or branches of the tree—might confirm this idea. Primitive man might think that, like himself, the oak-spirit had sought to deposit his life in some safe place, and for this purpose had pitched on the mistletoe, which, being in a sense neither on earth nor in heaven, might be supposed to be fairly out of harm's way.

In an Indian legend, which offers a parallel to the Balder myth, Indra swore to the demon Namuci that he would slay him neither by day nor by night, neither with staff nor with bow, neither with the palm of the hand nor with the fist, neither with the wet nor with the dry. But he killed him in the morning twilight by sprinkling over him the foam of the sea.[1] The foam of the sea is just such an object as a savage might choose to put his life in, because it occupies that sort of intermediate or nondescript position between earth and sky or sea and sky in which primitive man sees safety. It is therefore not surprising that the foam of the river should be the totem of a clan in India.[2]

516. Again, the view that the mistletoe owes its mystic character partly to its not growing on the ground is confirmed by a parallel superstition about the mountain-ash or rowan-tree. In Jutland a rowan that is found growing out of the top of another tree is esteemed "exceedingly effective against witchcraft: since it does not grow on the ground witches have no power over it; if it is to have its full effect it must be cut on Ascension Day."[1] Hence it is placed over doors to prevent the ingress of witches.[2] In Sweden and Norway, also, magical properties are ascribed to a "flying-rowan" (*flögrönn*), that is to a rowan which is found growing not in the ordinary fashion on the ground but on another tree, or on a roof, or in a cleft of the rock, where it has sprouted from seed scattered by birds. They say that a man who is out in the dark should have a bit of "flying-rowan" with him to chew; else he runs a risk of being bewitched and of being unable to stir from the spot.[3]

517. It is not a new opinion that the Golden Bough was the mistletoe.[1] True, Virgil does not identify but only compares it with mistletoe. But this may be only a poetical device to cast a mystic glamour over the humble plant. Or, more probably, his description was based on a popular superstition that at certain times the mistletoe blazed out into a supernatural golden glory. The poet tells how two doves, guiding Aeneas to the gloomy vale in whose depth grew the Golden Bough, alighted upon a tree, "whence shone a flickering gleam of gold. As in the woods in winter cold the mistletoe—a plant not native to its tree—is green with fresh leaves and twines its yellow berries about the boles; such seemed upon the shady holm-oak the leafy gold, so rustled in the gentle breeze the golden leaf."[2] Here Virgil definitely describes the Golden Bough as growing on a holm-oak, and compares it with the mistletoe. The inference is almost inevitable that the Golden Bough was nothing but the mistletoe seen through the haze of poetry or of popular superstition.

Now, grounds have been shewn for believing that the priest of the Arician grove—the King of the Wood—personified the tree on which grew the Golden Bough. Hence if that tree was the oak, the King of the Wood must have been a personification of the oak-spirit. It is, therefore, easy to understand why, before he could be slain, it was necessary to break the Golden Bough. As an oak-spirit, his life or death was in the mistletoe on the oak, and so long as the mistletoe remained intact, he, like Balder, could not die. To slay him, therefore, it was necessary to break the mistletoe, and probably, as in the case of Balder, to throw it at him. And to complete the parallel, it is only necessary to suppose that the King of the Wood was formerly burned, dead or alive, at the midsummer fire festival which, as we have seen, was annually celebrated in the Arician grove. The perpetual fire which burned in the grove, like the perpetual fire which burned in the temple of Vesta at Rome and under the oak at Romove, was probably fed with the sacred oak-wood; and thus it would be in a great fire of oak that the King of the Wood formerly met his end. At a later time, as I have suggested, his annual tenure of office was lengthened or shortened, as the case might be, by the rule which allowed him to live so long as he could prove his divine right by the strong hand. But he only escaped the fire to fall by the sword.

Thus it seems that at a remote age in the heart of Italy, beside the sweet Lake of Nemi, the same fiery tragedy was annually enacted which Italian merchants and soldiers were afterwards to witness among their rude kindred, the Celts of Gaul, and which, if the Roman eagles had ever swooped on Norway, might have been found repeated with little difference among the barbarous Aryans of the North. The rite was probably an essential feature in the ancient Aryan worship of the oak.

518. It remains only to ask, Why was the mistletoe called the Golden Bough? The whitish-yellow of the mistletoe berries is hardly enough to account for the name, for Virgil says that the bough was altogether golden, stem as well as leaves.[1] Perhaps the name may be derived from the rich golden yellow which a bough of mistletoe assumes when it has been cut and kept for some months; the bright tint is not confined to the leaves, but spreads to the stalks as well, so that the whole branch appears to be indeed a Golden Bough. Breton peasants hang up great bunches of mistletoe in front of their cottages, and in the month of June these bunches are conspicuous for the bright golden tinge of their foliage.

519. Mistletoe is gathered either at Midsummer or Christmas[1]—that is, at the summer and winter solstices—and it is supposed to possess the power of revealing treasures in the earth. On Midsummer Eve people in Sweden make divining-rods of mistletoe, or of four different kinds of wood one of which must be mistletoe. The treasure-seeker places the rod on the ground after sundown, and when it rests directly over the treasure, the rod begins to move as if it were alive.[2] Now, if the mistletoe discovers gold, it must be in its character of the Golden Bough; and if it is gathered at the solstices, must not the Golden Bough be an emanation of the sun's fire? The question cannot be answered with a simple affirmative. The old Aryans perhaps kindled the solstitial and other ceremonial fires in part as sun-charms, that is, with the intention of supplying the sun with fresh fire; and as these fires were usually made by the friction or combustion of oak-wood, it may have appeared to them that the sun was periodically recruited from the fire which resided in the sacred oak. In other words, the oak may have seemed to him the original storehouse or reservoir of the fire which was from time to time drawn out to feed the sun. But if the life of the oak was conceived to be in the mistletoe, the mistletoe must on that view have contained the seed or germ of the fire which was elicited by friction from the wood of the oak. Thus, instead of saying that the mistletoe was an emanation of the sun's fire, it might be more correct to say that the sun's fire was regarded as an emanation of the mistletoe. No wonder, then, that the mistletoe shone with a golden splendour, and was called the Golden Bough. Further, we can perhaps see why in antiquity it was believed to possess the remarkable property of extinguishing fire,[3] and why in Sweden it is still kept in houses as a safeguard against conflagration.[4] Its fiery nature marks it out, on homoeopathic principles, as the best possible cure or preventive of injury by fire. Probably, however, it was thought to assume its golden aspect only at those stated times, especially midsummer, when fire was drawn from the oak to light up the sun. At Pulverbatch, in Shropshire, it was believed within living memory that the oak-tree blooms on Midsummer Eve and the blossom withers before daylight.[5]

THE GOLDEN BOUGH AS MISTLETOE

520. A tree which has been struck by lightning is naturally regarded by the savage as charged with a double or triple portion of fire; for has he not seen the mighty flash enter into the trunk with his own eyes? It is therefore a plausible theory that the reverence which the ancient peoples of Europe paid to the oak was derived from the much greater frequency with which the oak appears to be struck by lightning than any other tree of our European forests. Some remarkable statistics have been adduced in support of this view by W. Warde Fowler.[1] Observations, annually made in the forests of Lippe-Detmold for seventeen years, yielded the result that while the woods were mainly stocked with beech and only to a small extent with oak and Scotch pine, yet far more oaks and Scotch pines were struck by lightning than beeches, the number of stricken Scotch pines exceeding the number of stricken beeches in the proportion of thirty-seven to one, and the number of stricken oaks exceeding the number of stricken beeches in the proportion of no less than sixty to one. Similar results have been obtained from observations made in French and Bavarian forests.[2] In short, it would seem from statistics compiled by scientific observers, who have no mythological theories to maintain, that the oak suffers from the stroke of lightning far oftener than any other forest tree in Europe. However we may explain it, the fact itself may well have attracted the notice of our rude forefathers, who dwelt in the vast forests which then covered a large part of Europe; and they might naturally account for it in their simple religious way by supposing that the great sky-god, whom they worshipped and whose awful voice they heard in the roll of thunder, loved the oak above all the trees of the wood and often descended into it from the murky cloud in a flash of lightning, leaving a token of his presence or of his passage in the riven and blackened trunk and the blasted foliage. Such trees would thenceforth be encircled by a nimbus of glory as the visible seats of the thundering sky-god.[3]

521. This explanation of the Aryan reverence for the oak and of the association of the tree with the great god of the thunder and the sky was suggested or implied long ago by Jakob Grimm[1] and later powerfully reinforced by W. Warde Fowler.[2] Perhaps it has the further advantage of throwing light on the special sanctity ascribed to mistletoe which grows on an oak. The mere rarity of such a growth on an oak hardly suffices to explain the extent and the persistence of the superstition. A hint of its real origin is possibly furnished by the statement of Pliny that the Druids worshipped the plant because they be-

THE FIRE-FESTIVALS

OF EUROPE

523. So much, then, for the mistletoe. We now come to our second problem: Why did the myth of Balder relate that he had been burned? Here, too, the answer may come from a consideration of seasonal rites. All over Europe the peasants have been accustomed from time immemorial to kindle bonfires on certain days of the year, and to dance round or leap over them. Customs of this kind can be traced back to the Middle Ages,[1] and their analogy to similar customs observed in antiquity goes with strong internal evidence to prove that their origin must be sought in a period long prior to the spread of Christianity. Indeed the earliest proof of their observance in Northern Europe is furnished by the attempts made by Christian synods in the eighth century to put them down as heathenish rites.[2] Not uncommonly effigies are burned in these fires, or a pretence is made of burning a living person in them; and there are grounds for believing that anciently human beings were actually burned on these occasions.

The seasons of the year when these bonfires are most commonly lit are spring and midsummer; but in some places they are kindled also at the end of autumn or during the course of the winter, particularly on Halloween, Christmas Day, and the Eve of Twelfth Day. We shall begin with the fire-festivals of spring, which usually fall on the first Sunday in Lent (*Quadragesima*), Easter Eve, and May Day.

Lenten Fires

524. The custom of kindling bonfires on the first Sunday in Lent has prevailed in Belgium, the north of France, and many parts of Germany. At Pâturages, in the province of Hainaut, down to about 1840 the custom was observed under the name of *Escouvion* or *Scouvion*. Every year on the first Sunday of Lent, which was called the Day of the Little Scouvion, young folks

610

and children used to run with lighted torches through the gardens and orchards. As they ran they cried at the pitch of their voices,

> "Bear apples, bear pears
> And cherries all black
> To Scouvion!"

At these words the torch-bearer whirled his blazing brand and hurled it among the branches of the apple-trees, the pear-trees, and the cherry-trees. The next Sunday was called the Day of the Great Scouvion, and the same race with lighted torches among the trees of the orchards was repeated in the afternoon till darkness fell. The same custom was observed on the same two days at Wasmes.[1] In the neighbourhood of Liège, where the Lenten fires were put down by the police about the middle of the nineteenth century, girls thought that by leaping over the fires without being smirched they made sure of a happy marriage. Elsewhere in order to get a good husband it was necessary to see seven of the bonfires from one spot. In Famenne, a district of Namur, men and cattle who traversed the Lenten fires were thought to be safe from sickness and witchcraft. Anybody who saw seven such fires at once had nothing to fear from sorcerers. An old saying ran, that if you do not light "the great fire," God will light it for you; which seems to imply that the kindling of the bonfires was deemed a protection against conflagrations throughout the year.[2] At Epinal in the Vosges, on the first Sunday in Lent, bonfires used to be kindled at various places both in the town and on the banks of the Moselle. They consisted of pyramids of sticks and faggots, which had been collected some days earlier by young folks going from door to door. When the flames blazed up, the names of various couples, whether young or old, handsome or ugly, rich or poor, were called out, and the persons thus linked in mock marriage were forced, whether they liked it or not, to march arm in arm round the fire amid the laughter and jests of the crowd. The festivity lasted till the fire died out, and then the spectators dispersed through the streets, stopping under the windows of the houses and proclaiming the names of the *féchenots* and *féchenottes* or Valentines whom the popular voice had assigned to each other. These couples had to exchange presents; the mock bridegroom gave his mock bride something for her toilet, while she in turn presented him with a cockade of coloured ribbon. Next Sunday, if the weather allowed it, all the couples, arrayed in their best attire and attended by their relations, repaired to the wood of Saint Antony, where they mounted a famous stone called the *danserosse* or *danseresse*. Here they found cakes and refreshments of all sorts, and danced to the music of a couple of fiddlers. The evening bell, ringing the Angelus, gave the signal to depart. As soon as its solemn chime was heard, every one quitted the forest and returned home. The exchange of presents between the Valentines went by the name of ransom or redemption (*rachat*), because it was supposed to redeem the couple from the flames of the bonfire.

Any pair who failed thus to ransom themselves were not suffered to share the merrymaking at the great stone in the forest; and a pretence was made of burning them in small fires kindled before their own doors.[3]

In the French province of Franche-Comté, to the west of the Jura Mountains, the first Sunday of Lent is known as the Sunday of the Firebrands (*Brandons*), on account of the fires which it is customary to kindle on that day. On the Saturday or the Sunday the village lads harness themselves to a cart and drag it about the streets, stopping at the doors of the houses where there are girls and begging for a faggot. When they have got enough, they cart the fuel to a spot at some little distance from the village, pile it up, and set it on fire. All the people of the parish come out to see the bonfire. In some villages, when the bells have rung the Angelus, the signal for the observance is given by cries of, "To the fire! to the fire!" Lads, lasses, and children dance round the blaze, and when the flames have died down they vie with each other in leaping over the red embers. He or she who does so without singeing his or her garments will be married within the year. Young folk also carry lighted torches about the streets or the fields, and when they pass an orchard they cry out, "More fruit than leaves!" Down to recent years at Laviron, in the department of Doubs, it was the young married couples of the year who had charge of the bonfires. In the midst of the bonfire a pole was planted with a wooden figure of a cock fastened to the top. Then there were races, and the winner received the cock as a prize.[4]

In Auvergne fires are everywhere kindled on the evening of the first Sunday in Lent. Every village, every hamlet, even every ward, every isolated farm has its bonfire or *figo,* as it is called, which blazes up as the shades of night are falling. The fires may be seen flaring on the heights and in the plains; the people dance and sing round about them and leap through the flames. Then they proceed to the ceremony of the *Grannas-mias.* A *granno-mio* is a torch of straw fastened to the top of a pole. When the pyre is half consumed, the bystanders kindle the torches at the expiring flames and carry them into the neighbouring orchards, fields, and gardens, wherever there are fruit-trees. As they march they sing at the top of their voices,

> "Granno, mo mio,
> Granno, mon pouère,
> Granno, mo mouère!"

that is, "Grannus my friend, Grannus my father, Grannus my mother." Then they pass the burning torches under the branches of every tree, singing,

> "Brando, brandounci
> Tsaque brantso, in plan panei!"

that is, "Firebrand burn; every branch a basketful!" In some villages the people also run across the sown fields and shake the ashes of the torches on the ground; also they put some of the ashes in the fowls' nests, in order that the hens may lay plenty of eggs throughout the year. When all these ceremonies have been performed, everybody goes home and feasts; the special dishes of the evening are fritters and pancakes.⁵ Here the application of the fire to the fruit-trees, to the sown fields, and to the nests of the poultry is clearly a charm intended to ensure fertility; and the Granno to whom the invocations are addressed, and who gives his name to the torches, may possibly be no other than the ancient Celtic god Grannus, whom the Romans identified with Apollo, and whose worship is attested by inscriptions found not only in France but in Scotland and on the Danube.⁶

525. The custom of carrying lighted torches of straw (*brandons*) about the orchards and fields to fertilize them on the first Sunday of Lent seems to have been common in France, whether it was accompanied with the practice of kindling bonfires or not. In some parts of the country, while the people scoured the country with burning brands on the first Sunday in Lent, they warned the fruit-trees that if they did not take heed and bear fruit they would surely be cut down and cast into the fire.¹ On the same day peasants in the department of Loiret used to run about the sowed fields with burning torches in their hands, while they adjured the field-mice to quit the wheat on pain of having their whiskers burned.² In the department of Ain the great fires of straw and faggots which are kindled in the fields at this time are or were supposed to destroy the nests of the caterpillars.³ In the peninsula of La Manche the Norman peasants used to spend almost the whole night of the first Sunday in Lent rushing about the country with lighted torches for the purpose, as they supposed, of driving away the moles and field-mice; fires were also kindled on some of the dolmens.⁴

526. In Germany, Austria, and Switzerland at the same season similar customs have prevailed. Thus in the Eifel Mountains, Rhenish Prussia, on the first Sunday in Lent young people used to collect straw and brushwood from house to house. These they carried to an eminence and piled up round a tall, slim beech-tree, to which a piece of wood was fastened at right angles to form a cross. The structure was known as the "hut" or "castle." Fire was set to it and the young people marched round the blazing "castle" bareheaded, each carrying a lighted torch and praying aloud. Sometimes a straw-man was burned in the "hut." People observed the direction in which the smoke blew from the fire. If it blew towards the corn-fields, it was a sign that the harvest would be abundant. On the same day, in some parts of the Eifel, a great wheel was made of straw and dragged by three horses to the top of a hill. Thither the village boys marched at nightfall, set fire to the wheel, and sent it rolling down the slope. At Oberstattfeld the wheel had to be provided by the young man who was last married.¹ About Echternach in Luxemburg the same ceremony is called "burning the witch"; while it is going on, the older men ascend the heights and observe what wind is blowing, for that is the wind which will prevail the whole year.² At Voralberg in the Tyrol, on the first Sunday in Lent, a slender young fir-tree is surrounded with a pile of straw and firewood. To the top of the tree is fastened a human figure called the "witch," made of old clothes and stuffed with gunpowder. At night the whole is set on fire and boys and girls dance round it, swinging torches and singing rhymes in which the words "corn in the winnowing-basket, the plough in the earth" may be distinguished.[3] In Swabia on the first Sunday in Lent a figure called the "witch" or the "old wife" or "winter's grandmother" is made up of clothes and fastened to a pole. This is stuck in the middle of a pile of wood, to which fire is applied. While the "witch" is burning, the young people throw blazing discs into the air. The discs are thin round pieces of wood, a few inches in diameter, with notched edges to imitate the rays of the sun or stars. They have a hole in the middle, by which they are attached to the end of a wand. Before the disc is thrown it is set on fire, the wand is swung to and fro, and the impetus thus communicated to the disc is augmented by dashing the rod sharply against a sloping board. The burning disc is thus thrown off, and mounting high into the air, describes a long fiery curve before it reaches the ground. A single lad may fling up forty or fifty of these discs, one after the other. The object is to throw them as high as possible. The wand by which they are hurled must, at least in some parts of Swabia, be of hazel. Sometimes the lads also leap over the fire brandishing lighted torches of pine-wood. The charred embers of the burned "witch" and discs are taken home and planted in the flax-fields the same night, in the belief that they will keep vermin from the fields.[4] At Wangen, near Molsheim in Baden, a like custom is observed on the first Sunday in Lent. The young people kindle a bonfire on the crest of the mountain above the village; and the burning discs which they hurl into the air are said to present in the darkness the aspect of a continual shower of falling stars. When the supply of discs is exhausted and the bonfire begins to burn low, the boys light torches and run with them at full speed down one or other of the three steep and winding paths that descend the mountain-side to the village.[5] At Konz, on the Moselle, on the Thursday before the first Sunday in Lent, the two guilds of the butchers and the weavers used to repair to the Marxberg and there set up an oak-tree with a wheel fastened to it. On the following Sunday the people ascended the hill, cut down the oak, set fire to the wheel, and sent both oak and wheel rolling down hillside.[6] The same custom of rolling lighted wheels down hill is attested by old authorities for the cantons of Aargau and Basle in Switzerland. The more bonfires could be seen sparkling and flaring in the darkness, the more fruitful was the year expected to be; and the higher the dancers leaped beside or over the fire, the higher, it was thought, would grow the flax. In Prättigau the words uttered in launching the fiery discs referred to the abundance which was apparently expected to follow the performance of the ceremony. Among them were, "Grease in the pan, corn in the fan, and the plough in the earth!"[7]

In the islands of North Friesland there was formerly an old heathen festival on the evening of February 21, when sacrificial fires (*Biiken*) were kindled, and men and youths danced hand-in-hand with women and marriageable girls round the flames and invoked Woden in the words of a prayer which was still in use in the seventeenth century. In Christian times this festival was brought into connection with St. Peter's Day, February 22, on which St. Peter was supposed to come and throw a warm stone into the water. In Föhr the sacred fires (*Biiken*) are kindled on February 21, "to light St. Peter to bed, to singe off his beard." In Sylt the feast of St. Peter has sunk into a children's festival. For days and weeks before the festival boys go from house to house collecting fuel for the bonfire (*Biiken*). They receive bundles of straw and twigs, which they carry to "the holy hill." There they heap the fuel about a petroleum or tar barrel. At nightfall the bonfire is kindled and kept up as long as possible by means of bundles of straw cast into the flames. The children dance singing round the hill to the light of the bonfires, while some of the boys run up and down the slope with burning wisps of straw.[7a]

In Savoy on the first day of Lent "the young men in many villages go round to every house, carrying an enormous straw figure, which they afterwards burn in the market-place. On the first Sunday in Lent, bonfires are lit, round which the young people dance and sing old songs. The children, in one very popular song, demand fritters, and the quaint refrain runs thus: 'If my mother does not give me fritters, I shall set fire to her petticoats.' "[7b] In Savoy too "*the Calavrais,*" the old fires of joy, are still lit by the children on the night of Easter Sunday. As they dance round, they brandish torches and sing, and then they all throw their torches into the fire.[7c]

In some districts of the Caucasus the Mountain Jews celebrate the beginning of spring as follows: Thus in the district of Kuba all the girls assemble and go out into the wood. Here they seek to forecast the future in all sorts of ways, and weave crowns of snowdrops, violets, and other flowers. Then they collect a quantity of brushwood and drag it with songs to the town, helped by the young men, who come at evening to the wood. In the evening the brushwood is piled up and kindled, and the young men leap through the fire. The same thing is done on the night before the Russian Easter. For the Jews believe that Jesus Christ hovers over the earth, threatening them with misery and misfortune. So they kindle the fires to keep him from their dwellings. That is why on that night in all the villages you may see bonfires flaring. The Jews settled in towns do not observe this last custom.[7d]

In Mingrelia, on the evening of the day when the orthodox cult celebrates the Assumption (August 15), the people, throughout the country, light great fires near the churches on public places, through which everyone, great and small, leaps. They believe that in this way they frighten the devils, of which the most powerful resides at Tabakhela, a mountain situated near Martvili. In Georgia the same custom is observed on the Thursday evening of the last week of the great Lent: the date alone differs.[7e]

EASTER FIRES

527. On Easter Eve, it has been customary in Catholic countries to extinguish all the lights in the churches, and then to make a new fire, sometimes with flint and steel, sometimes with a burning-glass. At this fire is lit the great Paschal or Easter candle, which is then used to rekindle all the extinguished lights in the church. In many parts of Germany a bonfire is also kindled, by means of the new fire, on some open space near the church. It is consecrated, and the people bring sticks of oak, walnut, and beech, which they char in the fire, and then take home with them. Some of these charred sticks are thereupon burned at home in a newly-kindled fire, with a prayer that God will preserve the homestead from fire, lightning, and hail. Thus every house receives "new fire." Some of the sticks are kept throughout the year and laid on the hearth-fire during heavy thunder-storms to prevent the house from being struck by lightning, or they are inserted in the roof with the like intention. Others are placed in the fields, gardens, and meadows, with a prayer that God will keep them from blight and hail. Such fields and gardens are thought to thrive more than others; the corn and the plants that grow in them are not beaten down by hail, nor devoured by mice, vermin, and beetles; no witch harms them, and the ears of corn stand close and full. The charred sticks are also applied to the plough.[1]

PAGAN ANALOGIES TO EASTER FIRES

528. In spite of the thin cloak of Christianity thrown over these customs we can hardly doubt that they are really of pagan origin; for while, on the one hand, they lack the authority of Christ or of his disciples, they possess, on the other, abundant analogies in popular custom and superstition.

The Incas of Peru celebrated a festival called Raymi, a word which their native historian Garcilasso de la Vega tells us was equivalent to our Easter. It was held in honour of the sun at the solstice in June. For three days before the festival the people fasted, men did not sleep with their wives, and no fires were lighted in Cuzco, the capital. The sacred new fire was obtained direct from the sun by concentrating his beams on a highly polished concave plate and reflecting them on a little cotton wool. With this holy fire the sheep and lambs offered to the sun were consumed, and the flesh of such as were to be eaten at the festival was roasted. Portions of the new fire were also conveyed to the temple of the sun and to the convent of the sacred virgins, where they were kept burning all the year, and it was an ill omen if the holy flame went out.[1] At a festival held in the last month of the old

Mexican year all the fires both in the temples and in the houses were extinguished, and the priest kindled a new fire by rubbing two sticks against each other before the image of the fire-god.² Once a year the Iroquois priesthood supplied the people with a new fire. By way of preparation for this annual rite the fires in all the huts were extinguished and the ashes scattered about. Then the priest, wearing the insignia of his office, went from hut to hut relighting the fires by means of a flint.³ Among the Esquimaux of Iglulik, when the sun first rises above the horizon after the long night of the Arctic winter, the children who have watched for his reappearance run into the houses and blow out the lamps. Then they receive from their mothers presents of pieces of wick.⁴

In the Sudanese kingdom of Wadai all the fires in the villages are put out and the ashes removed from the houses on the day which precedes the New Year festival. At the beginning of the new year a new fire is lit by the friction of wood in the great straw hut where the village elders lounge away the sultry hours together; and every man takes thence a burning brand with which he rekindles the fire on his domestic hearth.⁵

Some tribes of British Central Africa carefully extinguish the fires on the hearths at the beginning of the hoeing season and at harvest; the fires are afterwards rekindled by friction, and the people indulge in dances of various kinds.⁶ The Todas of the Neilgherry Hills, in southern India, annually kindle a sacred fire by the friction of wood in the month which begins with the October moon.⁷

In China, at the beginning of April, certain officials, call *Sz'hüen,* used of old to go about the country armed with wooden clappers. Their business was to summon the people and command them to put out every fire. This was the beginning of a season called *Han-shih-tsieh,* or "eating cold food." For three days all household fires remained extinct as a preparation for the solemn renewal of the fire, which took place on the fifth or sixth day of April, being the hundred and fifth day after the winter solstice.⁸

In classical antiquity the Greek island of Lemnos was devoted to the worship of the smith-god Hephaestus, who was said to have fallen on it when Zeus hurled him from heaven.⁹ Once a year every fire in the island was extinguished and remained extinct for nine days, during which sacrifices were offered to the dead and to the infernal powers. New fire was brought in a ship from the sacred isle of Delos, and with it the fires in the houses and the workshops were relit. The people said that with the new fire they made a new beginning of life.¹⁰ At Rome the sacred fire in the temple of Vesta was kindled anew every year on the first of March, which used to be the beginning of the Roman year.¹¹

Among the Celts of Ireland a new fire was annually kindled on Hallowe'en or the Eve of Samhain, as they called it, the last day of October, from which the Irish new year began; and all the hearths throughout the country are said to have been relighted from the fresh fire.[12]

In villages near Moscow the peasants put out all their fires on the eve of the first of September, and next morning at sunrise a wise man or a wise woman rekindled them with the help of muttered incantations and spells.[13]

BELTANE FIRES

529. In the central Highlands of Scotland bonfires, known as the Beltane fires, were formerly kindled with great ceremony on the first of May, and the traces of human sacrifices at them were particularly clear and unequivocal. The custom lasted in various places far into the eighteenth century. The fullest description, so far as I know, is the one bequeathed to us by John Ramsay, laird of Ochtertyre, near Crieff, the patron of Robert Burns and friend of Sir Walter Scott. "Like the other public worship of the Druids," says Ramsay, "the Beltane feast seems to have been performed on hills or eminences. . . . But since the decline of superstition, it has been celebrated by the people of each hamlet on some hill or rising ground around which their cattle was pasturing. Thither the young folks repaired in the morning and cut a trench, on the summit of which a seat of turf was formed for the company. And in the middle a pile of wood or other fuel was placed, which of old they kindled with *tein-eigin—i.e.,* forced fire or *need-fire.* . . .

"The night before, all the fires in the country were carefully extinguished, and next morning the materials for exciting this sacred fire were prepared. The most primitive method seems to be that which was used in the islands of Skye, Mull, and Tiree. A well-seasoned plank of oak was procured, in the midst of which a hole was bored. A wimble of the same timber was then applied, the end of which they fitted to the hole. But in some parts of the mainland the machinery was different. They used a frame of green wood, of a square form, in the centre of which was an axle-tree. In some places three times three persons, in others three times nine, were required for turning round by turns the axle-tree or wimble. If any of them had been guilty of murder, adultery, theft, or other atrocious crime, it was imagined either that the fire would not kindle, or that it would be devoid of its usual virtue. So soon as any sparks were emitted by means of the violent friction, they applied a species of agaric which grows on old birch-trees, and is very combustible. This fire had the appearance of being immediately derived from heaven, and manifold were the virtues ascribed to it. They esteemed it a preservative against witchcraft, and a sovereign remedy against malignant diseases, both in the human species and in cattle; and by it the strongest poisons were supposed to have their nature changed.

"After kindling the bonfire with the *tein-eigin* the company prepared their victuals. And as soon as they had finished their meal, they amused themselves a while in singing and dancing round the fire. Towards the close of the entertainment, the person who officiated as master of the feast produced a large cake baked with eggs and scalloped round the edge, called *am bonnach beal-tine*—i.e., the Beltane cake. It was divided into a number of pieces, and distributed in great form to the company. There was one particular piece which whoever got was called *cailleach beal-tine*—i.e., the Beltane *carline,* a term of great reproach. Upon his being known, part of the company laid hold of him and made a show of putting him into the fire; but the majority interposing, he was rescued. And in some places they laid him flat on the ground, making as if they would quarter him. Afterwards, he was pelted with egg-shells, and retained the odious appellation during the whole year. And while the feast was fresh in people's memory, they affected to speak of the *cailleach beal-tine* as dead. . . .

"It is probable that at the original Beltane festival there were two fires kindled near one another. When any person is in a critical dilemma, pressed on each side by unsurmountable difficulties, the Highlanders have a proverb, *The e' eada anda theine bealtuin*—i.e., he is between the two Beltane fires. There are in several parts small round hills, which, it is like, owe their present names to such solemn uses. One of the highest and most central in Icolmkil is called *Cnoch-nan-ainneal*—i.e., the hill of the fires. There is another of the same name near the kirk of Balquhidder; and at Killin there is a round green eminence which seems to have been raised by art. It is called *Tom-nan-ainneal*—i.e., the eminence of the fires. Around it there are the remains of a circular wall about two feet high. On the top a stone stands upon end. According to the tradition of the inhabitants, it was a place of Druidical worship; and it was afterwards pitched on as the most venerable spot for holding courts of justice for the country of Breadalbane. The earth of this eminence is still thought to be possessed of some healing virtue, for when cattle are observed to be diseased some of it is sent for, which is rubbed on the part affected."[1]

In the north-east of Scotland the Beltane fires were still kindled in the latter half of the eighteenth century; the herdsmen of several farms used to gather dry wood, kindle it, and dance three times "southways" about the burning pile.[2] But in this region, according to a later authority, the Beltane fires were lit not on the first but on the second of May, Old Style. They were called bone-fires. The people believed that on that evening and night the witches were abroad and busy casting spells on cattle and stealing cows' milk. To counteract their machinations, pieces of rowan-tree and woodbine, but especially of rowan-tree, were placed over the doors of the cow-houses, and fires were kindled by every farmer and cottar. Old thatch, straw, furze, or broom was piled in a heap and set on fire a little after sunset. While some of the bystanders kept tossing the blazing mass, others hoisted portions of it on pitchforks or poles and ran hither and thither, holding them as high as they could. Meantime the young people danced round the fire or ran through the smoke shouting, "Fire! blaze and burn the witches; fire! fire! burn the witches." In some districts a large round cake of oat or barley meal was rolled through the ashes. When all the fuel was consumed, the people scattered the ashes far and wide, and till the night grew quite dark they continued to run through them, crying, "Fire! burn the witches."[3]

530. In Wales also the custom of lighting Beltane fires at the beginning of May used to be observed, but the day on which they were kindled varied from the Eve of May Day to the third of May. The flame was sometimes elicited by the friction of two pieces of oak, as appears from the following description. "The fire was done in this way. Nine men would turn their pockets inside out, and see that every piece of money and all metals were off their persons. Then the men went into the nearest woods, and collected sticks of nine different kinds of trees. These were carried to the spot where the fire had to be built. There a circle was cut in the sod, and the sticks were set crosswise. All around the circle the people stood and watched the proceedings. One of the men would then take two bits of oak, and rub them together until a flame was kindled. This was applied to the sticks, and soon a large fire was made. Sometimes two fires were set up side by side. These fires, whether one or two, were called *coelcerth* or bonfire. Round cakes of oatmeal and brown meal were split in four, and placed in a small flour-bag, and everybody present had to pick out a portion. The last bit in the bag fell to the lot of the bag-holder. Each person who chanced to pick up a piece of brown-meal cake was compelled to leap three times over the flames, or to run thrice between the two fires, by which means the people thought they were sure of a plentiful harvest. Shouts and screams of those who had to face the ordeal could be heard ever so far, and those who chanced to pick the oatmeal portions sang and danced and clapped their hands in approval, as the holders of the brown bits leaped three times over the flames, or ran three times between the two fires. As a rule, no danger attended these curious celebrations, but occasionally somebody's clothes caught fire, which was quickly put out. The greatest fire of the year was the eve of May, or May first, second, or third. The Midsummer Eve fire was more for the harvest. Very often a fire was built on the eve of November. The high ground near the Castle Ditches at Llantwit Major, in the Vale of Glamorgan, was a familiar spot for the Beltane on May third and on Midsummer Eve. . . . Sometimes the Beltane fire was lighted by the flames produced by stone instead of wood friction. Charred logs and faggots used in the May Beltane were carefully preserved, and from them the next fire was lighted. May fires were always started with old faggots of the previous year, and midsummer from those of the last summer. It was unlucky to build a midsummer fire from May faggots. People carried the ashes left after these fires to their homes, and a charred brand was not only effectual against pestilence, but magical in its use. A few of the ashes placed in a person's shoes protected the wearer from any great sorrow or woe."[1]

531. "The Druidical anniversary of Beil or Baal is still celebrated in the Isle of Man. On the first of May, 1837, the Baal fires were, as usual on that day, so numerous as to give the island the appearance of a general conflagration."[1] By May Day in Manx folk-lore is meant May Day Old Style, or *Shenn Laa Boaldyn,* as it is called in Manx. The day was one on which the power of elves and witches was particularly dreaded, and the people resorted to many precautions in order to protect themselves against these mischievous beings. Hence at daybreak they set fire to the ling or gorse, for the purpose of burning out the witches, who are wont to lurk in the form of hares.[2] On the Hemlock Stone, a natural pillar of sandstone standing on Stapleford Hill in Nottinghamshire, a fire used to be solemnly kindled every year on Beltane Eve. The custom seems to have survived down to the beginning of the nineteenth century; old people could remember and describe the ceremony long after it had fallen into desuetude.

532. The Beltane fires appear to have been kindled also in Ireland, for Cormac, "or somebody in his name, says that *belltaine,* May-day, was so called from the 'lucky fires,' or the 'two fires,' which the druids of Erin used to make on that day with great incantations; and cattle, he adds, used to be brought to those fires, or to be driven between them, as a safeguard against the diseases of the year." Again, a very ancient Irish poem, enumerating the May Day celebrations, mentions among them a bonfire on a hill (*tendal ar cnuc*); and another old authority says that these fires were kindled in the name of the idol-god Bel.[1]

May Fires

533. The first of May is a great popular festival in the more midland and southern parts of Sweden. On the eve of the festival, huge bonfires, which should be lighted by striking two flints together, blaze on all the hills and knolls. Every large hamlet has its own fire, round which the young people dance in a ring.[1] Similarly, in Bohemia, on the eve of May Day, young people kindle fires on hills and eminences, at crossways, and in pastures, and dance round them. They leap over the glowing embers or even through the flames. The ceremony is called "burning the witches." In some places an effigy representing a witch used to be burnt in the bonfire.[2] We have to remember that the eve of May Day is the notorious Walpurgis Night, when the witches are everywhere speeding unseen through the air on their hellish errands. On this witching night children in Voigtland also light bonfires on the heights and leap over them. Moreover, they wave burning brooms or toss them into the air. So far as the light of the bonfire reaches, so far will a blessing rest on the fields. The kindling of the fires on Walpurgis Night is called "driving away the witches."[3] The custom of kindling fires on the eve of May

Day (Walpurgis Night) for the purpose of burning the witches is, or used
to be, widespread in the Tyrol, Moravia, Saxony, and Silesia.

MIDSUMMER FIRES

534. But the season at which these fire-festivals have been mostly generally held all over Europe is the summer solstice, that is Midsummer Eve (the
twenty-third of June) or Midsummer Day (the twenty-fourth of June). A
faint tinge of Christianity has been given to them by naming Midsummer Day
after St. John the Baptist, but we cannot doubt that the celebration dates
from a time long before the beginning of our era. The summer solstice, or
Midsummer Day, is the great turning-point in the sun's career, when, after
climbing higher and higher day by day in the sky, the luminary stops and
thenceforth retraces his steps down the heavenly road. Such a moment could
not but be regarded with anxiety by primitive man so soon as he began to
observe and ponder the courses of the great lights across the celestial vault;
and having still to learn his own powerlessness in face of the vast cyclic
changes of nature, he may have fancied that he could help the sun in his
seeming decline—could prop his failing steps and rekindle the sinking flame
of the red lamp in his feeble hand. In some such thoughts as these the midsummer festivals of our European peasantry may perhaps have taken their
rise. Whatever their origin, they have prevailed all over this quarter of the
globe, from Ireland in the west to Russia in the east, and from Norway and
Sweden in the north to Spain and Greece in the south.[1]

535. A good general account of the midsummer customs, together with
some of the reasons popularly alleged for observing them, is given by Thomas
Kirchmeyer, a writer of the sixteenth century, in his poem *The Popish Kingdome:*—

> "Then doth the joyfull feast of John the Baptist take his turne,
> When bonfiers great with loftie flame, in every towne doe burne;
> And yong men round about with maides, doe daunce in every streete,
> With garlands wrought of Motherwort, or else with Vervain sweete,
> And many other flowres faire, with Violets in their handes,
> Whereas they all do fondly thinke, that whosoever standes,
> And thorow the flowres beholds the flame, his eyes shall feele no paine.
> When thus till night they daunced have, they through the fire amaine
> With striving mindes doe runne, and all their hearbes they cast therein,
> And then with wordes devout and prayers, they solemnely begin,
> Desiring God that all their illes may there consumed bee,
> Whereby they thinke through all that yeare from Agues to be free.
> Some others get a rotten wheele, all worne and cast aside,
> Which covered round about with strawe, and tow, they closely hide:
> And caryed to some mountaines top, being all with fire light,
> They hurle it downe with violence, when darke appears the night:

Resembling much the Sunne, that from the heavens downe should fal,
A straunge and monstrous sight it seemes, and fearfull to them all:
But they suppose their mischiefes all are likewise throwne to hell,
And that from harmes and daungers now, in safetie here they dwell."[1]

From these general descriptions, which to some extent still hold good, or did so till lately, we see that the main features of the midsummer fire-festival resemble those which we have found to characterize the vernal festivals of fire. The similarity of the two sets of ceremonies will plainly appear from the following examples.

536. A writer of the first half of the sixteenth century informs us that in almost every village and town of Germany public bonfires were kindled on the Eve of St. John, and young and old, of both sexes, gathered about them and passed the time in dancing and singing. People on this occasion wore chaplets of mugwort and vervain, and they looked at the fire through bunches of larkspur which they held in their hands, believing that this would preserve their eyes in a healthy state throughout the year. As each departed, he threw the mugwort and vervain into the fire, saying, "May all my ill-luck depart and be burnt up with these."[1] According to one account, German tradition required that the midsummer fire be lighted, not from a common hearth, but by the friction of two sorts of wood, namely oak and fir.

In Silesia, from the south-eastern part of the Sudeten range and northwestward as far as Lausitz, the mountains are ablaze with bonfires on Midsummer Eve; and from the valleys and the plains round about Leobschütz, Neustadt, Zülz, Oels, and other places answering fires twinkle through the deepening gloom. While they are smouldering and sending forth volumes of smoke across the fields, young men kindle broom-stumps, soaked in pitch, at the bonfires and then, brandishing the stumps, which emit showers of sparks, they chase one another or dance with the girls round the burning pile. Shots, too, are fired, and shouts raised. The fire, the smoke, the shots, and the shouts are all intended to scare away the witches, who are let loose on this witching day, and who would certainly work harm to the crops and the cattle, if they were not deterred by these salutary measures. Mere contact with the fire brings all sorts of blessings. Hence when the bonfire is burning low, the lads leap over it, and the higher they bound, the better is the luck in store for them. He who surpasses his fellows is the hero of the day and is much admired by the village girls. It is also thought to be very good for the eyes to stare steadily at the bonfire without blinking; moreover he who does so will not drowse and fall asleep betimes in the long winter evenings.[3]

537. In Denmark and Norway also Midsummer fires were kindled on St. John's Eve on roads, open spaces, and hills. In Norway people thought that such fires banished sickness from among the cattle.[1] The custom persists to the present day, and popular lore asserts that the fires keep away the witches who are flying to their coven on the Blocksberg. In Sweden the Eve of St. John (St. Hans) is the most joyous night of the whole year. Throughout some parts of the country, especially in the provinces of Bolus and Scania and in districts bordering on Norway, it is celebrated by the frequent discharge of firearms and by huge bonfires, called "Balder's balefires," which are kindled at dusk on hills and high places and throw a glare of light over the surrounding landscape.[2]

538. In Switzerland on Midsummer Eve fires are, or used to be, kindled on high places in the cantons of Bern, Neuchatel, Valais, and Geneva.[1] In Austria the midsummer customs and superstitions resemble those of Germany. Thus in some parts of the Tyrol bonfires are kindled and burning discs hurled into the air.[2] In the lower valley of the Inn a tatterdemalion effigy is carted about the village on Midsummer Day and then burned. He is called the *Lotter,* which has been corrupted to Luther.[3] Similarly at Gratz, on St. John's Eve the people used to make a puppet called the *Taterman,* which they dragged to the bleaching-ground and pelted with burning besoms until it took fire.[4]

539. All over Bohemia bonfires still burn on Midsummer Eve. In the afternoon boys go about with handcarts from house to house collecting fuel, such as sticks, brushwood, old besoms, and so forth. They make their request at each house in rhyming verses, threatening with evil consequences the curmudgeons who refuse them a dole. Sometimes the young men fell a tall straight fir in the woods and set it up on a height, where the girls deck it with nosegays, wreaths of leaves, and red ribbons. Then brushwood is piled about it, and at nightfall the whole is set on fire. While the flames break out, the young men climb the tree and fetch down the wreaths which the girls had placed on it. After that, lads and lasses stand on opposite sides of the fire and look at one another through the wreaths to see whether they will be true to each other and marry within the year. Also the girls throw the wreaths across the flames to the men, and woe to the awkward swain who fails to catch the wreath thrown him by his sweetheart. When the blaze has died down, each couple takes hands, and leaps thrice across the fire. He or she who does so will be free from ague throughout the year, and the flax will grow as high as the young folks leap. A girl who sees nine bonfires on Midsummer Eve will marry before the year is out. The singed wreaths are carried home and carefully preserved throughout the year. During thunderstorms a bit of the wreath is burned on the hearth with a prayer; some of it is given to kine that are sick or calving, and some of it serves to fumigate house and cattle-stall, that man and beast may keep hale and well. Sometimes an old cart-wheel is smeared with resin, ignited, and sent rolling down the hill. Often the boys collect all the worn-out besoms they can get hold of, dip them in pitch, and having set them on fire wave them about or throw them high into the air. Or they rush down the hillside in troops, brandishing the flaming brooms and shouting, only however to return to the bonfire on the summit when the brooms have burnt out. The stumps of the brooms and embers from the fire are preserved and stuck in cabbage gardens to protect the cabbages from caterpillars and gnats. Some people insert charred sticks and ashes from the bonfire in their sown fields and meadows, in their gardens and the roofs of their houses, as a talisman against lightning and foul weather; or they fancy that the ashes placed in the roof will prevent any fire from breaking out in the house. In some districts they crown or gird themselves with mugwort while the midsummer fire is burning, for this is supposed to be a protection against ghosts, witches, and sickness; in particular, a wreath of mugwort is a sure preventive of sore eyes. Sometimes the girls look at the bonfires through garlands of wild flowers, praying the fire to strengthen their eyes and eyelids. She who does this thrice will have no sore eyes all that year. In some parts of Bohemia they used to drive the cows through the midsummer fire to guard them against witchcraft.[1]

540. The Germans of Moravia in like manner still light bonfires on open grounds and high places on Midsummer Eve; and they kindle besoms in the flames and then stick the charred stumps in the cabbage-fields as a powerful protection against caterpillars.[1] In Austrian Silesia the custom also prevails of lighting great bonfires on hilltops on Midsummer Eve, and here too the boys swing blazing besoms or hurl them high in the air, while they shout and leap and dance wildly. Next morning every door is decked with flowers and birchen saplings.[2] In the district of Cracow, especially towards the Carpathian Mountains, great fires are kindled by the peasants in the fields or on the heights at nightfall on Midsummer Eve, which among them goes by the name of Kupalo's Night. The fire must be kindled by the friction of two sticks. The young people dance around or leap over it; and a band of sturdy fellows run a race with lighted torches, the winner being rewarded with a peacock's feather, which he keeps throughout the year as a distinction. Cattle also are driven round the fire in the belief that this is a charm against pestilence and disease of every sort.[3]

541. The name of Kupalo's Night, applied in this part of Galicia to Midsummer Eve, reminds us that we have now passed from German to Slavonic ground; even in Bohemia the midsummer celebration is common to Slavs and Germans. We have already seen that in Russia the summer solstice or Eve of St. John is celebrated by young men and maidens, who jump over a bonfire in couples carrying a straw effigy of Kupalo in their arms. In some parts of Russia an image of Kupalo is burnt or thrown into a stream on St. John's Night.[1] Again, in some districts of Russia the young folk wear garlands of flowers and girdles of holy herbs when they spring through the smoke or flames; and sometimes they drive the cattle also through the fire in order to protect the animals against wizards and witches, who are then ravenous after milk. In Little Russia a stake is driven into the ground on St. John's

Night, wrapt in straw, and set on fire. As the flames rise the peasant women throw birchen boughs into them, saying, "May my flax be as tall as this bough!" In Ruthenia the bonfires are lighted by a flame procured by the friction of wood. While the elders of the party are engaged in thus "churning" the fire, the rest maintain a respectful silence; but when the flame bursts from the wood, they break forth into joyous songs. As soon as the bonfires are kindled, the young people take hands and leap in pairs through the smoke, if not through the flames; and after that the cattle in their turn are driven through the fire.[2]

542. In many parts of Prussia and Lithuania great fires are kindled on Midsummer Eve;[1] thus, in Masuren, a district of East Prussia inhabited by a branch of the Polish family, it used formerly to be the custom on the evening of Midsummer Day to put out all the fires in the village. Then an oaken stake was driven into the ground, and a wheel was fixed on it as on an axle. This wheel the villagers, working by relays, caused to revolve with great rapidity till fire was produced by friction. Everyone took home a lighted brand from the new fire and with it rekindled the fire on the domestic hearth.[2]

543. Among the Letts bonfires gleam on all the hills at twilight on Midsummer Day, and wild shouts of "Ligho! Ligho!" echo from the woods and fields.[1]

544. Bonfires are commonly kindled by the South Slavonian peasantry on Midsummer Eve, and lads and lasses dance and shout round them in the usual way.[1] And in Serbia, on the same occasion, herdsmen light torches of birch bark and march round the sheepfolds and cattle stalls; then they climb the hills and there allow the torches to burn out.[2]

545. In Hungary the midsummer fire-festival is marked by the same features that meet us in so many parts of Europe. On Midsummer Eve in many places it is customary to kindle bonfires and to leap over them; and similar usages prevail also among the Esthonians and the Finns.[1]

546. When we pass from the east to the west of Europe we still find the summer solstice celebrated with rites of the same general character. Down to about the middle of the nineteenth century the custom of lighting bonfires at midsummer prevailed so commonly in France that there was hardly a town or a village, we are told, where they were not kindled.[1] Though the pagan origin of the custom may be regarded as certain, the Catholic Church threw a Christian cloak over it by boldly declaring that the bonfires were lit in token of the general rejoicing at the birth of the Baptist, who opportunely came into the world at the solstice of summer, just as his greater successor did at the solstice of winter.

547. In Belgium the Eve of St. Peter's Day (June 29) is celebrated by bonfires and dances exactly like those which commemorate St. John's Eve. According to some people, the fires of St. Peter were likewise lighted to drive away dragons.[1] In French Flanders down to 1789 a straw figure representing a man was always burned in the midsummer fire and the figure of a woman on St. Peter's Day.[2]

548. The custom of lighting bonfires at midsummer has been observed in many parts of the British Isles. In the streets of London they were kindled in the time of Queen Elizabeth down to the end of the sixteenth century;[1] while nearly one hundred years later, the antiquary John Aubrey tells us that they were still lighted in many places, but that the civil wars had thrown many of these old customs out of fashion. Wars, he adds, extinguish superstition as well as religion and laws, and there is nothing like gunpowder for putting phantoms to flight![2]

In Wales, three or nine different kinds of wood and charred faggots carefully preserved from the last midsummer were deemed necessary to build the bonfire, which was generally done on rising ground. In the Vale of Glamorgan a cart-wheel swathed in straw used to be ignited and sent rolling down the hill. It it kept alight all the way down and blazed for a long time, an abundant harvest was expected.[3] On Midsummer Eve people in the Isle of Man were wont to light fires to the windward of every field, so that the smoke might pass over the corn; and they folded their cattle and carried blazing furze or gorse round them several times.[4] In Ireland cattle, especially barren cattle, were driven through the midsummer fires, and the ashes were thrown on the fields to fertilise them, or live coals were carried into them to prevent blight.[5] In Scotland the traces of midsummer fires are few; but at that season in the highlands of Perthshire cowherds used to go round their folds thrice, in the direction of the sun, with lighted torches. This they did to purify the flocks and herds and to keep them from falling sick.[6]

The practice of lighting bonfires on Midsummer Eve and dancing or leaping over them is, or was till recently, common in some parts of Italy and Sicily.[7] In Malta great fires are kindled in the streets and squares of the towns and villages on the Eve of St. John (Midsummer Eve); formerly the Grand Master of the Order of St. John used on that evening to set fire to a heap of pitch barrels placed in front of the sacred Hospital.[8] In Greece, too, the custom of kindling fires on St. John's Eve and jumping over them is said to be still universal. One reason assigned for it is a wish to escape from the fleas.[9] According to another account, the women cry out, as they leap over the fire, "I leave my sins behind me."[10] In Lesbos the fires on St. John's Eve are usually lighted by threes, and the people spring thrice over them, each with a stone on his head, saying, "I jump the hare's fire, my head a stone!"[11] In Calymnos the midsummer fire is supposed to ensure abundance in the coming year as well as deliverance from fleas. The people dance round the fires singing, with stones on their heads, and then jump over the blaze or the glowing embers. When the fire is burning low, they throw the stones into it; and when it is nearly out, they make crosses on their legs and then go straightway and bathe in the sea.[12]

The principal fire-festivals of the Celts, which have survived, though in a restricted area and with diminished pomp, to modern times and even to our own day, were seemingly timed without any reference to the position of the sun in the heaven. They were two in number, and fell at an interval of six months, one being celebrated on the eve of May Day and the other on Allhallow Even or Hallowe'en, as it is now commonly called, that is, on the thirty-first of October, the day preceding All Saints' or Allhallows' Day. These dates coincide with none of the four great hinges on which the solar year revolves, to wit, the solstices and the equinoxes. Nor do they agree with the principal seasons of the agricultural year, the sowing in spring and the reaping in autumn. Yet the first of May and the first of November mark turning-points of the year in Europe; the one ushers in the genial heat and the rich vegetation of summer, the other heralds, if it does not share, the cold and barrenness of winter. Now these particular points of the year, while they are of comparatively little moment to the European husbandman, do deeply concern the European herdsman; for it is on the approach of summer that he drives his cattle out into the open to crop the fresh grass, and it is on the approach of winter that he leads them back to the safety and shelter of the stall. Accordingly it seems not improbable that the Celtic bisection of the year into two halves at the beginning of May and the beginning of November dates from a time when the Celts were mainly a pastoral people, dependent for their subsistence on their herds, and when accordingly the great epochs of the year for them were the days on which the cattle went forth from the homestead in early summer and returned to it again in early winter. Even in Central Europe, remote from the region now occupied by the Celts, a similar bisection of the year may be clearly traced in the great popularity, on the one hand, of May Day and its Eve (Walpurgis Night), and, on the other hand, of the Feast of All Souls at the beginning of November, which under a thin Christian cloak conceals an ancient pagan festival of the dead. Hence we may conjecture that everywhere throughout Europe the celestial division of the year according to the solstices was preceded by what we may call a terrestrial division of the year according to the beginning of summer and the beginning of winter.

Be that as it may, the two great Celtic festivals of May Day and the first of November or, to be more accurate, the Eves of these two days, closely resemble each other in the manner of their celebration and in the superstitions associated with them, and alike, by the antique character impressed upon both, betray a remote and purely pagan origin. The festival of May Day or Beltane, as the Celts called it, which ushered in summer, has already been described; it remains to give some account of the corresponding festival of Hallowe'en, which announced the arrival of winter.

552. Of the two feasts Hallowe'en was perhaps of old the more important, since the Celts would seem to have dated the beginning of the year from it rather than from Beltane. In the Isle of Man, one of the fortresses in which the Celtic language and lore longest held out against the siege of the Saxon invaders, the first of November, Old Style, has been regarded as New Year's Day down to recent times. Thus Manx mummers used to go round on Hallowe'en (Old Style), singing, in the Manx language, a sort of Hogmanay song which began "To-night is New Year's Night, *Hogunnaa!*"[1] In ancient Ireland, a new fire used to be kindled every year on Hallowe'en or the Eve of Samhain, and from this sacred flame all the fires in Ireland were re-kindled.[2] Such a custom points strongly to Samhain or All Saints' Day (the first of November) as New Year's Day, since the annual kindling of a new fire takes place most naturally at the beginning of the year, in order that the blessed influence of the fresh fire may last throughout the whole period of twelve months. Another confirmation of the view that the Celts dated their year from the first of November is furnished by the manifold modes of divination which, as we shall see presently, were commonly resorted to by Celtic peoples on Hallowe'en for the purpose of ascertaining their destiny, especially their fortune in the coming year; for when could these devices for prying into the future be more reasonably put in practice than at the beginning of the year? As a season of omens and auguries Hallowe'en seems to have far surpassed Beltane in the imagination of the Celts; from which we may with some probability infer that they reckoned their year from Hallowe'en rather than Beltane. Another circumstance of great moment which points to the same conclusion is the association of the dead with Hallowe'en. Not only among the Celts but throughout Europe, Hallowe'en, the night which marks the transition from autumn to winter, seems to have been of old the time of year when the souls of the departed were supposed to revisit their old homes in order to warm themselves by the fire and to comfort themselves with the good cheer provided for them in the kitchen or the parlour by their affectionate kinsfolk.[3] It was, perhaps, a natural thought that the approach of winter should drive the poor shivering hungry ghosts from the bare fields and the leafless woodlands to the shelter of the cottage with its familiar fireside. Did not the lowing kine then troop back from the summer pastures in the forests and on the hills to be fed and cared for in the stalls, while the bleak winds whistled among the swaying boughs and the snow drifts deepened in the hollows? and could the good-man and the good-wife deny to the spirits of their dead the welcome which they gave to the cows?

But it is not only the souls of the departed who are supposed to be hovering unseen on the day "when autumn to winter resigns the pale year." Witches then speed on their errands of mischief, some sweeping through the air on besoms, others galloping along the roads on tabby-cats, which for that evening are turned into coal-black steeds.[4] The fairies, too, are all let loose, and hobgoblins of every sort roam freely about. In South Uist and Eriskay there is a saying:—

"Hallowe'en will come, will come,
Witchcraft [or divination] will be set agoing,
Fairies will be at full speed,
Running in every pass.
Avoid the road, children, children."[5]

In Cardiganshire on November Eve a bogie sits on every stile.[6] On that night in Ireland all the fairy hills are thrown wide open and the fairies swarm forth; any man who is bold enough may then peep into the open green hills and see the treasures hidden in them.

553. But while a glamour of mystery and awe has always clung to Hallowe'en in the minds of the Celtic peasantry, the popular celebration of the festival has been, at least, in modern times, by no means of a prevailingly gloomy cast; on the contrary it has been attended by picturesque features and merry pastimes, which rendered it the gayest night of all the year. Among the things which in the Highlands of Scotland contributed to invest the festival with a romantic beauty were the bonfires which used to blaze at frequent intervals on the heights.[1]

In the northern part of Wales it used to be customary for every family to make a great bonfire called *Coel Coeth* on Hallowe'en. The fire was kindled on the most conspicuous spot near the house; and when it had nearly gone out everyone threw into the ashes a white stone, which he had first marked. Then having said their prayers round the fire, they went to bed. Next morning, as soon as they were up, they came to search out the stones, and if any one of them was found to be missing, they had a notion that the person who threw it would die before he saw another Hallowe'en.[2]

554. The equivalent of Hallowe'en bonfires is reported also from France. We are told that in the department of Deux-Sèvres, which forms part of the old province of Poitou, young people used to assemble in the fields on All Saints' Day (the first of November) and kindle great fires of ferns, thorns, leaves, and stubble, at which they roasted chestnuts. They also danced round the fires and indulged in noisy pastimes.[1]

MIDWINTER FIRES

555. If the heathen of ancient Europe celebrated, as we have good reason to believe, the season of Midsummer with a great festival of fire, of which the traces have survived in many places down to our own time, it is natural to suppose that they should have observed with similar rites the corresponding season of Midwinter; for Midsummer and Midwinter, or, in more technical language, the summer solstice and the winter solstice, are the two great turning-points in the sun's apparent course through the sky, and from the standpoint of primitive man nothing might seem more appropriate than to kindle fires on earth at the two moments when the fire and heat of the great luminary in heaven begin to wane or to wax. In this way the savage philos-

opher, to whose meditations on the nature of things we owe many ancient customs and ceremonies, might easily imagine that he helped the labouring sun to relight his dying lamp, or at all events to blow up the flame into a brighter blaze. Certain it is that the winter solstice, which the ancients erroneously assigned to the twenty-fifth of December, was celebrated in antiquity as the Birthday of the Sun, and that festal lights or fires were kindled on this joyful occasion. Our Christmas festival is nothing but a continuation under a Christian name of this old solar festivity; for the ecclesiastical authorities saw fit, about the end of the third or the beginning of the fourth century, arbitrarily to transfer the nativity of Christ from the sixth of January to the twenty-fifth of December, for the purpose of diverting to their Lord the worship which the heathen had hitherto paid on that day to the sun.

556. In modern Christendom the ancient fire-festival of the winter solstice appears to survive, or to have survived down to recent years, in the old custom of the Yule log, clog, or block, as it was variously called in England. The custom was widespread in Europe, but seems to have flourished especially in England, France, and among the South Slavs; at least the fullest accounts of the custom come from these quarters. That the Yule log was only the winter counterpart of the Midsummer bonfire, kindled within doors instead of in the open air on account of the cold and inclement weather of the season, was pointed out long ago by our English antiquary John Brand;[1] and the view is supported by the many quaint superstitions attaching to the Yule log, superstitions which have no apparent connexion with Christianity but carry their heathen origin plainly stamped upon them. But while the two solstitial celebrations were both festivals of fire, the necessity or desirability of holding the winter celebration within doors lent it the character of a private or domestic festivity, which contrasts strongly with the publicity of the summer celebration, at which the people gathered on some open space or conspicuous height, kindled a huge bonfire in common, and danced and made merry round it together.

557. Among the Germans the custom of the Yule log is known to have been observed as early as the eleventh century; for in 1184 the parish priest of Ahlen, in Münsterland, spoke of "bringing a tree to kindle the festal fire at the Lord's Nativity."[1] In some parts of the Eifel Mountains, to the west of Coblenz, a log of wood called the *Christbrand* used to be placed on the hearth on Christmas Eve; and the charred remains of it on Twelfth Night were put in the corn-bin to keep the mice from devouring the corn.[8] At Weidenhausen and Girkshausen, in Westphalia, the practice was to withdraw the Yule log (*Christbrand*) from the fire so soon as it was slightly charred; it was then kept carefully to be replaced on the fire whenever a thunderstorm broke, because the people believed that lightning would not strike a house in which the Yule log was smouldering.[3] In some villages near Berleburg in Westphalia the old custom was to tie up the Yule log in the last sheaf cut at harvest.[4] On Christmas Eve the peasantry of the Oberland, in Meiningen, a province of Central Germany, used to put a great block of wood called the *Christklotz* on the fire before they went to bed; it should burn all night, and the charred remains were believed to guard the house for the whole year against the risk of fire, burglary, and other misfortunes.[5]

558. The Yule log seems to be known only in the French-speaking parts of Switzerland, where it goes by the usual French name of *Bûche de Noël.* In the Jura mountains of the canton of Bern, while the log is burning on the hearth the people sing a blessing over it as follows:—

> "May the log burn!
> May all good come in!
> May the women have children
> And the sheep lambs!
> White bread for every one
> And the vat full of wine!"

The embers of the Yule log were kept carefully, for they were believed to be a protection against lightning.[1]

559. "The Christmas fires, which were formerly lit everywhere in the Low Countries, have fallen into disuse. But in Flanders a great log of wood, called the *kersavondblok* and usually cut from the roots of a fir or a beech, is still put on the fire; all the lights in the house are extinguished, and the whole family gathers round the log to spend part of the night in singing, in telling stories, especially about ghosts, were-wolves, and so on, and also in drinking gin. At Grammont and in the neighbourhood of that town, where the Yule log is called *Kersmismot,* it is customary to set fire to the remainder of the gin at the moment when the log is reduced to ashes. Elsewhere a piece of the log is kept and put under the bed to protect the house against thunder and lightning. The charcoal of the log which burned during Christmas Night, if pounded up and mixed with water, is a cure for consumption. In the country of Limburg the log burns several nights, and the pounded charcoal is kept as a preventive (so they say), of toothache."[1]

560. In several provinces of France, and particularly in Provence, the custom of the Yule log or *tréfoir,* as it was called in many places, was long observed. A French writer of the seventeenth century tells us that on Christmas Eve the log was prepared, and when the whole family had assembled in the kitchen or parlour of the house, they went and brought it in, walking in procession and singing Provençal verses to the following effect:—

> "Let the log rejoice,
> To-morrow is the day of bread;
> Let all good enter here;
> Let the women bear children;
> Let the she-goats bring forth kids;

> Let the ewes drop lambs;
> Let there be much wheat and flour,
> And the vat full of wine."

Then the log was blessed by the smallest and youngest child of the house, who poured a glass of wine over it saying, *In nomine patris,* etc.; after which the log was set on the fire. The charcoal of the burnt wood was kept the whole year, and used as an ingredient in several remedies.[1]

561. In England the customs and beliefs concerning the Yule log, clog, or block, as it was variously called, used to be similar. On the night of Christmas Eve, says the antiquary John Brand, "our ancestors were wont to light up candles of an uncommon size, called Christmas Candles, and lay a log of wood upon the fire, called a Yule-clog or Christmas-block, to illuminate the house, and, as it were, to turn night into day. This custom is, in some measure, still kept up in the North of England. In the buttery of St. John's College, Oxford, an ancient candle-socket of stone still remains ornamented with the figure of the Holy Lamb. It was formerly used to burn the Christmas Candle in, on the high table at supper, during the twelve nights of that festival."[1] "A tall mould candle, called a Yule candle, is lighted and set on the table; these candles are presented by the chandlers and grocers to their customers. The Yule-log is bought of the carpenters' lads. It would be unlucky to light either of them before the time, or to stir the fire or candle during the supper; the candle must not be snuffed, neither must any one stir from the table till supper is ended. In these suppers it is considered unlucky to have an odd number at table. A fragment of the log is occasionally saved, and put under a bed, to remain till next Christmas: it secures the house from fire; a small piece of it thrown into a fire occurring at the house of a neighbour, will quell the raging flame. A piece of the candle should likewise be kept to ensure good luck."[2] In the seventeenth century, as we learn from some verses of Herrick, the English custom was to light the Yule log with a fragment of its predecessor, which had been kept throughout the year for the purpose; where it was so kept, the fiend could do no mischief.[3]

562. Among the Serbs of Dalmatia, Herzegovina, and Montenegro it is customary on Christmas Eve (*Badnyi Dan*) to fetch a great Yule log (*badnyak*), which serves as a symbol of family luck. It is generally cut from an evergreen oak, but sometimes from an olive-tree or a beech. At nightfall the master of the house himself brings in the log and lays it on the fire. Then he and all present bare their heads, sprinkle the log with wine, and make a cross on it. After that the master of the house says, "Welcome, O log! May God keep you from mishap!" So saying he strews peas, maize, raisins, and wheat on the log, praying for God's blessing on all members of the family living and dead, for heaven's blessing on their undertakings, and for domestic prosperity. In Montenegro they meet the log with a loaf of bread and a jug of wine, drink to it, and pour wine on it, whereupon the whole family drinks

on the fields to protect the crops against vermin; sometimes they were taken home to be employed as remedies in sickness, being sprinkled on the ailing part or mixed in water and drunk by the patient. Special virtue was attributed to the smoke of the bonfire; in Sweden fruit-trees and nets were fumigated with it, in order that the trees might bear fruit and the nets catch fish.[9] In the Highlands of Scotland the need-fire was accounted a sovereign remedy for witchcraft. In the island of Mull, when the fire was kindled as a cure for the murrain, we hear of the rite being accompanied by the sacrifice of a sick heifer, which was cut in pieces and burnt.[10] Slavonian and Bulgarian peasants conceive cattle-plague as a foul fiend or vampire which can be kept at bay by interposing a barrier of fire between it and the herds.[11] A similar conception may perhaps have originally everywhere underlain the use of the need-fire as a remedy for the murrain. It appears that in some parts of Germany the people did not wait for an outbreak of cattle-plague, but, taking time by the forelock, kindled a need-fire annually to prevent the calamity. Similarly in Poland the peasants are said to kindle fires in the village streets every year on St. Rochus's day and to drive the cattle thrice through them in order to protect the beasts against the murrain.[12] We are told that in the Hebrides the cattle were in like manner driven annually round the Beltane fires for the same purpose. In some cantons of Switzerland children still kindle a need-fire by the friction of wood for the sake of dispelling a mist.[13]

The Origin of Fire-Festivals

565. The foregoing survey of the popular fire-festivals of Europe suggests some general observations. In the first place we can hardly help being struck by the resemblance which the ceremonies bear to each other, at whatever time of the year and in whatever part of Europe they are celebrated. The custom of kindling great bonfires, leaping over them, and driving cattle through or round them would seem to have been practically universal throughout Europe, and the same may be said of the processions or races with blazing torches round fields, orchards, pastures, or cattle-stalls. Less widespread are the customs of hurling lighted discs into the air and trundling a burning wheel down hill; for to judge by the evidence which I have collected these modes of distributing the beneficial influence of the fire have been confined in the main to Central Europe. The ceremonial of the Yule log is distinguished from that of the other fire-festivals by the privacy and domesticity which characterize it; but, as we have already seen, this distinction may well be due simply to the rough weather of midwinter, which is apt not only to render a public assembly in the open air disagreeable, but also at any moment to defeat the object of the assembly by extinguishing the all-important fire under a downpour of rain or a fall of snow. Apart from these local or seasonal differences, the general resemblance between the fire-festivals at all times of the year and in all places is tolerably close. And as the ceremonies themselves resemble each other, so do the benefits which the people expect to reap from them. Whether applied in the form of bonfires blazing at fixed points, or of torches carried about from place to place, or of embers and ashes taken from the smouldering heap of fuel, the fire is believed to promote the growth of the crops and the welfare of man and beast, either positively by stimulating them, or negatively by averting the dangers and calamities which threaten them from such causes as thunder and lightning, conflagration, blight, mildew, vermin, sterility, disease, and not least of all witchcraft.

But we naturally ask, How did it come about that benefits so great and manifold were supposed to be attained by means so simple? In what way did people imagine that they could procure so many goods or avoid so many ills by the application of fire and smoke, of embers and ashes? In short, what theory underlay and prompted the practice of these customs? For that the institution of the festivals was the outcome of a definite train of reasoning may be taken for granted; the view that primitive man acted first and invented his reasons to suit his actions afterwards, is not borne out by what we know of his nearest living representatives, the savage and the peasant.

566. The conception of fire as a destructive agent, which can be turned to account for the consumption of evil things, is so simple and obvious that it could hardly escape the minds even of the rude peasantry with whom these festivals originated. In the case of the fire-festivals and the destructive aspect of fire is one upon which the people dwell again and again; and it is highly significant that the great evil against which the fire is directed appears to be witchcraft. Again and again we are told that the fires are intended to burn or repel the witches; and the intention is sometimes graphically expressed by burning an effigy of a witch in the fire. Hence, when we remember the great hold which the dread of witchcraft has had on the popular European mind in all ages, we may suspect that the primary intention of all these fire-festivals was simply to destroy or at all events get rid of the witches, who were regarded as the causes of nearly all the misfortunes and calamities that befall men, their cattle, and their crops.

567. This suspicion is confirmed when we examine the evils for which the bonfires and torches were supposed to provide a remedy. Foremost, perhaps, among these evils we may reckon the diseases of cattle; and of all the ills that witches are believed to work there is probably none which is so constantly insisted on as the harm they do to the herds, particularly by stealing the milk from the cows.[1] Now it is significant that the need-fire, which may perhaps be regarded as the parent of the periodic fire-festivals, is kindled above all as a remedy for a murrain or other disease of cattle; and the circumstance suggests, what on general grounds seems probable, that the custom of kindling the need-fire goes back to a time when the ancestors of the European peoples subsisted chiefly on the products of their herds, and when

of corruption, the spells of magicians, or any other evil influences that might impair or impede his divine energies. The same theory would explain the custom of obliging the priest ceremonially to pass through the fire; the custom need not be a mitigation of an older practice of burning him in the flames, it may only be a purification designed to enable him the better to discharge his sacred duties as representative of the deity in the coming year. Similarly, when the rite is obligatory, not on the people as a whole, but only on certain persons chosen for the purpose, we may suppose that these persons act as representatives of the entire community, which thus passes through the fire by deputy and consequently participates in all the benefits which are believed to accrue from the purificatory character of the rite. In both cases, therefore, if my interpretation of them is correct, the passage over or through a fire is not a substitute for human sacrifice; it is nothing but a stringent form of purification.

573. Yet, in the popular customs connected with the fire-festivals of Europe there are certain features which appear to point to a former practice of human sacrifice. We have seen reasons for believing that in Europe living persons have often acted as representatives of the tree-spirit and corn-spirit and have suffered death as such. There is no reason, therefore, why they should not have been burned, if any special advantages were likely to be attained by putting them to death in that way. The consideration of human suffering is not one which enters into the calculations of primitive man. Now, in the fire-festivals which we are discussing, the pretence of burning people is sometimes carried so far that it seems reasonable to regard it as a mitigated survival of an older custom of actually burning them. Thus in Aachen, for example, the man clad in peas-straw acts so cleverly that the children really believe he is being burned. At Jumièges in Normandy the man clad all in green, who bore the title of the Green Wolf, was pursued by his comrades, and when they caught him they feigned to fling him upon the midsummer bonfire. Similarly at the Beltane fires in Scotland the pretended victim was seized, and a show made of throwing him into the flames, and for some time afterwards people affected to speak of him as dead. Again, in the Hallowe'en bonfires of north-eastern Scotland we may perhaps detect a similar pretence in the custom observed by a lad of lying down as close to the fire as possible and allowing the other lads to leap over him. The titular king at Aix, who reigned for a year and danced the first dance round the midsummer bonfire, may perhaps in days of old have discharged the less agreeable duty of serving as fuel for that fire which in later times he only kindled. In the following customs Mannhardt is probably right in recognizing traces of an old custom of burning a leaf-clad representative of the spirit of vegetation. At Wolfeck, in Austria, on Midsummer Day, a boy completely clad in green fir branches goes from house to house, accompanied by a noisy crew, collecting wood for the bonfire. As he gets the wood he sings—

"Forest trees I want,
No sour milk for me,
But beer and wine,
So can the wood-man be jolly and gay."[1]

In some parts of Bavaria, also, the boys who go from house to house collecting fuel for the midsummer bonfire envelop one of their number from
head to foot in green branches of firs, and lead him by a rope through the
whole village.[2] At Moosheim, in Wurtemberg, the festival of St. John's Fire
usually lasted for fourteen days, ending on the second Sunday after Midsummer Day. On this last day the bonfire was left in charge of the children,
while the older people retired to a wood. Here they encased a young fellow
in leaves and twigs, who, thus disguised, went to the fire, scattered it, and
trod it out. All the people present fled at the sight of him.[3]

574. But it seems possible to go farther than this. Of human sacrifices offered on these occasions the most unequivocal traces, as we have seen, are
those which, about a hundred years ago, still lingered at the Beltane fires in
the Highlands of Scotland, that is, among a Celtic people who, situated in a
remote corner of Europe and almost completely isolated from foreign influence, had till then conserved their old heathenism better perhaps than any
other people in the West of Europe. It is significant, therefore, that human
sacrifices by fire are known, on unquestionable evidence, to have been systematically practised by the Celts. The earliest description of these sacrifices
has been bequeathed to us by Julius Caesar. As conqueror of the hitherto
independent Celts of Gaul, Caesar had ample opportunity of observing the
national Celtic religion and manners, while these were still fresh and crisp
from the native mint and had not yet been fused in the melting-pot of Roman
civilization. With his own notes Caesar appears to have incorporated the observations of a Greek explorer, by name Posidonius, who travelled in Gaul
about fifty years before Caesar carried the Roman arms to the English Channel. The Greek geographer Strabo and the historian Diodorus seem also to
have derived their descriptions of the Celtic sacrifices from the work of Posidonius, but independently of each other, and of Caesar, for each of the three
derivative accounts contains some details which are not to be found in either
of the others. By combining them, therefore, we can restore the original account of Posidonius with some probability, and thus obtain a picture of the
sacrifices offered by the Celts of Gaul at the close of the second century before our era.[1] The following seem to have been the main outlines of the
custom. Condemned criminals were reserved by the Celts in order to be sacrificed to the gods at a great festival which took place once in every five years.
The more there were of such victims, the greater was believed to be the
fertility of the land.[2] If there were not enough criminals to furnish victims,
captives taken in war were immolated to supply the deficiency. When the
time came the victims were sacrificed by the Druids or priests. Some they

shot down with arrows, some they impaled, and some they burned alive in the following manner. Colossal images of wicker-work or of wood and grass were constructed; these were filled with live men, cattle, and animals of other kinds; fire was then applied to the images, and they were burned with their living contents.

575. Such were the great festivals held once every five years. But besides these quinquennial festivals, celebrated on so grand a scale, and with, apparently, so large an expenditure of human life, it seems reasonable to suppose that festivals of the same sort, only on a lesser scale, were held annually, and that from these annual festivals are lineally descended some at least of the fire-festivals which, with their traces of human sacrifices, are still celebrated year by year in many parts of Europe. The gigantic images constructed of osiers or covered with grass in which the Druids enclosed their victims remind us of the leafy framework in which the human representative of the tree-spirit is still so often encased. Hence, seeing that the fertility of the land was apparently supposed to depend upon the due performance of these sacrifices, Mannhardt interpreted the Celtic victims, cased in osiers and grass, as representatives of the tree-spirit or spirit of vegetation.

576. These wicker giants of the Druids seem to have had till lately their representatives at the spring and midsummer festivals of modern Europe. At Douai, down to the early part of the nineteenth century, a procession took place annually on the Sunday nearest to the seventh of July. The great feature of the procession was a colossal figure, some twenty or thirty feet high, made of osiers, and called "the giant," which was moved through the streets by means of rollers and ropes worked by men who were enclosed within the effigy.[1] At Dunkirk the procession of the giants took place on Midsummer Day. The giant was a huge figure of wicker-work, occasionally as much as 45 feet high, dressed in a long blue robe with golden stripes, which reached to his feet, concealing the dozen or more men who made it dance and bob its head to the spectators. It went by the name of Papa Reuss, and carried in its pocket a bouncing infant of Brobdingnagian proportions, who kept bawling "Papa! papa!" in a voice of thunder, only pausing from time to time to devour the victuals which were handed out to him from the windows.[2]

577. Most towns and even villages of Brabant and Flanders have, or used to have, similar wicker giants which were annually led about to the delight of the populace, who loved these grotesque figures, spoke of them with patriotic enthusiasm, and never wearied of gazing at them. The name by which the giants went was Reuzes, and a special song called the Reuze song was sung in the Flemish dialect while they were making their triumphal progress through the streets. The most celebrated of these monstrous effigies were those of Antwerp and Wetteren. At Ypres a whole family of giants contributed to the public hilarity at the Carnival. At Cassel and Hazebrouch, in the French department of Nord, the giants made their annual appearance on

Shrove Tuesday.¹ At Antwerp the giant was so big that no gate in the city
was large enough to let him go through; hence he could not visit his brother
giants in neighbouring towns, as the other Belgian giants used to do on solemn
occasions. At Ath, in the Belgian province of Hainaut, the popular procession of the giants took place annually in August down to the year 1869 at
least. For three days the colossal effigies of Goliath and his wife, of Samson
and an Archer (*Tirant*), together with a two-headed eagle, were led about
the streets on the shoulders of twenty bearers concealed under the flowing
drapery of the giants, to the great delight of the townspeople and a crowd of
strangers who assembled to witness the pageant. The custom can be traced
back by documentary evidence to the middle of the fifteenth century.²

578. In England artificial giants seem to have been a standing feature of
the midsummer festival. A writer of the sixteenth century speaks of "Mid-
sommer pageants in London, where to make the people wonder, are set
forth great and uglie gyants marching as if they were alive, and armed at all
points, but within they are stuffed full of browne paper and tow, which the
shrewd boyes, underpeering, do guilefully discover, and turne to a greate
derision."¹ At Chester the annual pageant on Midsummer Eve included the
effigies of four giants, with animals, hobby-horses, and other figures.² At
Burford, in Oxfordshire, Midsummer Eve used to be celebrated with great
jollity by the carrying of a giant and a dragon up and down the town. The
last survivor of these perambulating English giants dragged out a miserable
existence at Salisbury, where an antiquary found him mouldering to decay in
the neglected hall of the Tailors' Company about the year 1844. His bodily
framework was of lath and hoop like the one which used to be worn by
Jack-in-the-Green on May Day. The learned called him St. Christopher, the
vulgar simply the giant.³

579. In these cases the giants only figure in the processions. But sometimes they were burned in the summer bonfires. Thus the people of the Rue
aux Ours in Paris used annually to make a great wicker-work figure, dressed
as a soldier, which they promenaded up and down the streets for several
days, and solemnly burned on the third of July, the crowd of spectators singing *Salve Regina*. A personage who bore the title of king presided over the
ceremony with a lighted torch in his hand. The burning fragments of the
image were scattered among the people, who eagerly scrambled for them.
The custom was abolished in 1743.¹ In Brie, Isle de France, a wicker-work
giant, eighteen feet high, was annually burned on Midsummer Eve.²

580. Again, the Druidical custom of burning live animals, enclosed in
wicker-work, has its counterpart at the spring and midsummer festivals. At
Luchon in the Pyrenees on Midsummer Eve "a hollow column, composed
of strong wicker-work, is raised to the height of about sixty feet in the centre
of the principal suburb, and interlaced with green foliage up to the very top;
while the most beautiful flowers and shrubs procurable are artistically ar-

ranged in groups below, so as to form a sort of background to the scene. The column is then filled with combustible materials, ready for ignition. At an appointed hour—about 8 P.M.—a grand procession, composed of the clergy, followed by young men and maidens in holiday attire, pour forth from the town chanting hymns, and take up their position round the column. Meanwhile, bonfires are lit, with beautiful effect, in the surrounding hills. As many living serpents as can be collected are then thrown into the column, which is set on fire at the base by means of torches.[1] At Metz midsummer fires were lighted with great pomp on the esplanade, and a dozen cats, enclosed in wicker-cages, were burned alive in them, to the amusement of the people.[2] Similarly at Gap, in the department of the High Alps, cats used to be roasted over the midsummer bonfire.[3] In Russia a white cock was sometimes burned in the midsummer bonfire;[4] in Meissen or Thuringia a horse's head used to be thrown into it.[5] Sometimes animals are burned in the spring bonfires. In the Vosges cats were burned on Shrove Tuesday; in Alsace they were thrown into the Easter bonfire.[6] In the department of the Ardennes cats were flung into the bonfires kindled on the first Sunday in Lent.[7]

581. Thus it appears that the sacrificial rites of the Celts of ancient Gaul can be traced in the popular festivals of modern Europe. Naturally it is in France, or rather in the wider area comprised within the limits of ancient Gaul, that these rites have left the clearest traces in the customs of burning giants of wicker-work and animals enclosed in wicker-work or baskets. These customs, it will have been remarked, are generally observed at or about midsummer. From this we may infer that the original rites of which these are the degenerate successors were solemnized at midsummer. This inference harmonizes with the conclusion suggested by a general survey of European folk-custom, that the midsummer festival must on the whole have been the most widely diffused and the most solemn of all the yearly festivals celebrated by the primitive Aryans in Europe. At the same time we must bear in mind that among the British Celts the chief fire-festivals of the year appear certainly to have been those of Beltane (May Day) and Halloween (the last day of October); and this suggests a doubt whether the Celts of Gaul also may not have celebrated their principal rites of fire, including their burnt sacrifices of men and animals, at the beginning of May or the beginning of November rather than at Midsummer.

582. We have still to ask, What is the meaning of such sacrifices? If we are right in interpreting the modern European fire-festivals as attempts to break the power of witchcraft by burning or banning the witches and warlocks, it seems to follow that we must explain the human sacrifices of the Celts in the same manner; that is, we must suppose that the men whom the Druids burnt in wicker-work images were condemned to death on the ground that they were witches or wizards, and that the mode of execution by the fire was chosen because, as we have seen, burning alive is deemed the surest mode of getting rid of these noxious and dangerous beings. The same explanation would apply to the cattle and wild animals of many kinds which the Celts burned along with the men.[1] They, too, we may conjecture, were supposed to be either under the spell of witchcraft or actually to be the witches and wizards, who had transformed themselves into animals for the purpose of prosecuting their infernal plots against the welfare of their fellow creatures. This conjecture is confirmed by the observation that the victims most commonly burned in bonfires have been cats, and that cats are precisely the animals into which, with the possible exception of hares, witches were most usually supposed to transform themselves. Again, we have seen that serpents and foxes used sometimes to be burnt in the midsummer fires; and Welsh and German witches are reported to have assumed the form both of foxes and serpents.[2] In short, when we remember the great variety of animals whose forms witches can assume at pleasure, it seems easy on this hypothesis to account for the variety of living creatures that have been burnt at festivals both in ancient Gaul and modern Europe; all these victims, we may surmise, were doomed to the flames, not because they were animals, but because they were believed to be witches who had taken the shape of animals for their nefarious purposes.

FAREWELL TO NEMI

583. We are at the end of our enquiry, but as often happens in the search after truth, if we have answered one question, we have raised many more; if we have followed one track home, we have had to pass by others that opened off it and led, or seemed to lead, to far other goals than the sacred grove at Nemi. Some of these paths we have followed a little way; others, if fortune should be kind, the writer and the reader may one day pursue together. For the present we have journeyed far enough together, and it is time to part. Yet before we do so, we may well ask ourselves whether there is not some more general conclusion, some lesson, if possible, of hope and encouragement, to be drawn from the melancholy record of human error and folly which has engaged our attention in these volumes.

If then we consider, on the one hand, the essential similarity of man's chief wants everywhere and at all times, and on the other hand, the wide difference between the means he has adopted to satisfy them in different ages, we shall perhaps be disposed to conclude that the movement of the higher thought, so far as we can trace it, has on the whole been from magic through religion to science. In magic man depends on his own strength to meet the difficulties and dangers that beset him on every side. He believes in a certain established order of nature on which he can surely count, and which he can manipulate for his own ends. When he discovers his mistake, when he recognizes sadly that both the order of nature which he had assumed and the control which he had believed himself to exercise over it were purely imaginary, he ceases to rely on his own intelligence and his own unaided efforts, and throws himself humbly on the mercy of certain great invisible beings behind the veil of nature, to whom he now ascribes all those far-reaching powers which he once arrogated to himself. Thus in the acuter minds magic is gradually superseded by religion, which explains the succession of natural phenomena as regulated by the will, the passion, or the caprice of spiritual beings like man in kind, though vastly superior to him in power.

But as time goes on this explanation in its turn proves to be unsatisfactory. For it assumes that the succession of natural events is not determined by immutable laws, but is to some extent variable and irregular, and this assumption is not borne out by closer observation. On the contrary, the more we scrutinize that succession the more we are struck by the rigid uniformity, the punctual precision with which, wherever we can follow them, the operations of nature are carried on. Every great advance in knowledge has extended the sphere of order and correspondingly restricted the sphere of apparent disorder in the world, till now we are ready to anticipate that even in regions where chance and confusion appear still to reign, a fuller knowledge would everywhere reduce the seeming chaos to cosmos. Thus the keener minds, still pressing forward to a deeper solution of the mysteries of the universe, come to reject the religious theory of nature as inadequate, and to revert in a measure to the older standpoint of magic by postulating explicitly, what in magic had only been implicitly assumed, to wit, an inflexible regularity in the order of natural events, which, if carefully observed, enables us to foresee their course with certainty and to act accordingly. In short, religion, regarded as an explanation of nature, is displaced by science.

584. But while science has this much in common with magic that both rest on a faith in order as the underlying principle of all things, readers of this work will hardly need to be reminded that the order presupposed by magic differs widely from that which forms the basis of science. The difference flows naturally from the different modes in which the two orders have been reached. For whereas the order on which magic reckons is merely an extension, by false analogy, of the order in which ideas present themselves to our minds, the order laid down by science is derived from patient and exact observation of the phenomena themselves. The abundance, the solidity, and the splendour of the results already achieved by science are well fitted to inspire us with a cheerful confidence in the soundness of its method. Here at last, after groping about in the dark for countless ages, man has hit upon a clue to the labyrinth, a golden key that opens many locks in the treasury of nature. It is probably not too much to say that the hope of progress—moral and intellectual as well as material—in the future is bound up with the fortunes of science, and that every obstacle placed in the way of scientific discovery is a wrong to humanity.

Yet the history of thought should warn us against concluding that because the scientific theory of the world is the best that has yet been formulated, it is necessarily complete and final. We must remember that at bottom the generalizations of science or, in common parlance, the laws of nature are merely hypotheses devised to explain that ever-shifting phantasmagoria of thought which we dignify with the high-sounding names of the world and the universe. In the last analysis magic, religion, and science are nothing but theories of thought; and as science has supplanted its predecessors, so it may hereafter be itself superseded by some more perfect hypothesis, perhaps by some totally different way of looking at the phenomena—of registering the shadows on the screen—of which we in this generation can form no idea. The advance of knowledge is an infinite progression towards a goal that for ever recedes. We need not murmur at the endless pursuit:—

> "Fatti non foste a viver come bruti
> Ma per seguir virtute e conoscenza."

Great things will come of that pursuit, though we may not enjoy them. Brighter stars will rise on some voyager of the future—some great Ulysses of the realms of thought—than shine on us. The dreams of magic may one day be the waking realities of science. But a dark shadow lies athwart the far end of this fair prospect. For however vast the increase of knowledge and of power which the future may have in store for man, he can scarcely hope to stay the sweep of those great forces which seem to be making silently but relentlessly for the destruction of all this starry universe in which our earth swims as a speck or mote. In the ages to come man may be able to predict, perhaps even to control, the wayward courses of the winds and clouds, but hardly will his puny hands have strength to speed afresh our slackening planet in its orbit or rekindle the dying fire of the sun. Yet the philosopher who trembles at the idea of such distant catastrophes may console himself by reflecting that these gloomy apprehensions, like the earth and the sun themselves, are only parts of that unsubstantial world which thought has conjured up out of the void, and that the phantoms which the subtle enchantress has evoked to-day she may ban to-morrow. They too, like so much that to common eyes seems solid, may melt into air, into thin air.

Without dipping so far into the future, we may illustrate the course which thought has hitherto run by likening it to a web woven of three different threads—the black thread of magic, the red thread of religion, and the white thread of science, if under science we may include those simple truths drawn from observation of nature, of which men in all ages have possessed a store. Could we then survey the web of thought from the beginning, we should probably perceive it to be at first a chequer of black and white, a patchwork of true and false notions, hardly tinged as yet by the red thread of religion. But carry your eye further along the fabric and you will remark that, while the black and white chequer still runs through it, there rests on the middle portion of the web, where religion has entered most deeply into its texture, a dark crimson stain, which shades off insensibly into a lighter tint as the white thread of science is woven more and more into the tissue. To a web thus chequered and stained, thus shot with threads of diverse hues, but gradually changing colour the farther it is unrolled, the state of modern thought, with all its divergent aims and conflicting tendencies, may be compared. Will the great movement which for centuries has been slowly altering the complexion of thought be continued in the near future? or will a reaction set in which may arrest progress and even undo much that has been done? To keep up our parable, what will be the colour of the web which the Fates are now weaving on the humming loom of time? will it be white or red? We cannot tell. A faint glimmering light illumines the backward portion of the web. Clouds and thick darkness hide the other end.

585. Our long voyage of discovery is over and our bark has drooped her weary sails in port at last. Once more we take the road to Nemi. It is evening, and as we climb the long slope of the Appian Way up to the Alban Hills, we look back and see the sky aflame with sunset, its golden glory resting like the aureole of a dying saint over Rome and touching with a crest of fire the dome of St. Peter's. The sight once seen can never be forgotten, but we turn from it and pursue our way darkling along the mountain side, till we come to Nemi and look down on the lake in its deep hollow, now fast disappearing in the evening shadows. The place has changed but little since Diana received the homage of her worshippers in the sacred grove. The temple of the sylvan goddess, indeed, has vanished and the King of the Wood no longer stands sentinel over the Golden Bough. But Nemi's woods are still green, and as the sunset fades above them in the west, there comes to us, borne on the swell of the wind, the sound of the church bells of Rome ringing the Angelus. *Ave Maria!* Sweet and solemn they chime out from the distant city and die lingeringly away across the wide Campagnan marshes. *Le roi est mort, vive le roi! Ave Maria!*

NOTES

483
1. H. H. Bancroft, *Native Races of the Pacific States* (London 1875–76), ii. 142.
2. J. de Acosta, *The Natural and Moral History of the Indies,* tr. E. Grinston (London, Hakluyt Society, 1880), ii. 505.
3. T. Rundall, ed., *Memorials of the Empire of Japan in the XVIth and XVIIth Centuries* (London, Hakluyt Society, 1850), 14, 141.
4. W. Ellis, *Polynesian Researches*[2] (London 1832–36), iii. 102 f.
5. Athenaeus, xii. 8.
6. *The Voyages of John Struys* (London 1684), 30.
7. J. Roscoe, *The Baganda* (London 1911), 154 f.
8. E. Torday and T. A. Joyce, *Les Bushongo* (Brussels 1910), 61.
9. N. W. Thomas, *Anthropol. Report on the Ibo-speaking Peoples of Nigeria* (London 1913), i. 57 f.
10. Satapatha Brahmana, tr. Eggeling (*SBE,* xii), pt. iii, pp. 81, 91, 92, 102, 108 f.

484
1. A. W. Niuwenhuis, *Quer durch Borneo* (Leyden 1904–07), i. 172.
2. M. C. Schadee, in *BTLVNI,* 63 (1910), 433.
3. J. Adair, *History of the North American Indians* (London 1775), 382.
4. E. Aymonier, *Notes sur les Laos* (Saigon 1885), 26.
5. *Die gestriegelte Rockenphilosophie*[5] (Chemnitz 1759), 586 ff.

486
1. J. K. Lord, *The Naturalist in Vancouver Island and British Columbia* (London 1868), ii. 237.
2. J. O. Dorsey, in *Third Annual Report of the Bureau of Ethnology* (Washington 1884), 226.
3. J. Adair, *op. cit.,* 161–63.
4. Miss C. F. Gordon Cumming, *In the Hebrides* (London 1883), 211.
5. W. Gregor, in *Revue des traditions populaires,* 3 (1888), 485 B.
6. R. Brough Smyth, *Aborigines of Victoria* (Melbourne-London 1878), i. 450.
7. F. Grabowsky, in *Das Ausland,* 1884, No. 24, p. 470.

487   1. W. E. Roth, *Ethnol. Studies among the N. W.-Central Queensland Aborigines* (Brisbane-London 1897), 156.

2. W. Gregor, *Notes on the Folk-lore of the N. E. of Scotland* (London 1881), 184.

3. *NH*, xxiv. 12, 68; xxv. 171.

4. *De medicamentis,* ed. Helmreich (Leipzig 1889), Preface, p. i.

5. *Ib., i.* 68.

6. *Ib.,* i. 76.

7. *Ib.,* xxviii. 28, 71; xxix. 35.

8. *Ib.,* xxix. 51.

9. E. Westermarck, in *Folk-lore,* 16 (1905), 32 f.

10. *Ib.,* 35.

11. M. Prätorius, *Deliciae Prussicae,* ed. W. Pierson (Berlin 1871), 54.

488   1. Kaempfer, "History of Japan," in Pinkerton's *Voyages and Travels,* vii. 717; Caron, *ib.,* vii. 113.

2. A. de Herrera, *General History of the vast Continent and Islands of America,* tr. J. Stevens (London 1725–26), v. 88.

3. A. Bastian, *Die Culturländer des alten Amerika* (Berlin 1878), ii. 204.

4. Cieza de Leon, *Second Part of the Chronicle of Peru* (London, Hakluyt Society, 1883), 18.

5. The Grihya Sutras, tr. H. Oldenburg, ii (*SBE* xxx), 165, 275.

6. Mrs. Bishop, *Korea and her Neighbours* (London 1898), ii. 248.

7. J. L. van Hasselt, in *TILV,* 31 (1886), 587.

8. A. Bastian, *Die Völker des östlichen Asien,* v (Jena 1869), 366.

9. W. M. Gabb, in *Proc. Am. Philos. Soc.,* 14 (1876), 510.

10. L. Lloyd, *Peasant Life in Sweden* (London 1870), 194.

11. H. H. Bancroft, *op. cit.,* i. 553.

12. L. Heuzey, *Le Mont Olympe et l'Acarnanie* (Paris 1860), 458 f.

489   1. Pechuel-Loesche, in *Zeitschr. f. Ethnol.,* 10 (1878), 23.

2. J. Macdonald, in *JAI,* 20 (1891), 118.

3. D. Kidd, *The Essential Kafir* (London 1904), 209.

4. C. W. Hobley, *Ethnology of A-Kamba and other E. African Tribes* (Cambridge 1910), 65.

5. B. Danks, *Melanesians and Polynesians* (London 1910), 105–07; W. Powell, *Wanderings in a Wild Country* (London 1883), 249.

6. C. G. Seligman, in *Reports of the Cambridge Anthropol. Expedition to Torres Straits,* v (Cambridge 1904), 205.

7. E. Petitot, *Traditions indiennes du Canada Nord-ouest* (Paris 1886), 257 f.

8. J. Teit, *The Lilooet Indians* (Leyden-New York 1906), 263–65. Cp. C. H. Tout, in *JAI,* 35 (1905), 136.

9. G. H. Loskiel, *History of the Mission of the United Brethren among the Indians of N. America* (London 1794), i, 56 f.

10. G. B. Grinnell, in *The American Anthropologist,* N. S. 4 (1902), 13 f.

11. J. F. Lafitau, *Moeurs des sauvages Ameriquains* (Paris 1724), i. 262 f.

12. A. d'Orbigny, *Voyage dans l'Amérique méridionale* (Paris-Strasburg 1844), 205 f.

13. A. Thouar, *Explorations dans l'Amérique du Sud* (Paris 1891), 56 f.; Father Cardus, quoted in J. Pelleschi, *Los Indios Matacos* (Buenos Aires 1897), 47 f.

14. H. H. Risley, *Tribes and Castes of Bengal, Ethnographic Glossary* (Calcutta 1891–92), i. 152.

15. E. Thurston, *Castes and Tribes of Southern India* (Madras 1909), vi. 157.

16. J. Moura, *Le royaume du Cambodge* (Paris 1883), i. 377.

490 1. H. Ternaux-Compans, *Essai sur l'ancien Cundimarca* (Paris n. d.), 18.

2. G. Turner, *Samoa* (London 1884), 200. For other examples of such tales, see A. Bastian, *Die Völker des östlichen Asien*, i. 416, vi. 25; *Punjab Notes and Queries*, 2 (1885), 148, ¶797.

3. Sophocles, *Antigone*, 944 ff.; Apollodorus, *Bibl.*, ii. 4, 1 [with Frazer's note].

4. W. Radloff, *Proben der Volkslitteratur der türkischen Stämme Süd-Siberiens* (St. Petersburg 1870), 82 f.

491 1. T. J. Hutchinson, in *Trans. Ethnol. Soc. London*, N. S. 3 (1865), 327.

2. Monier Williams, *Religious Thought and Life in India* (London 1883), 354.

3. H. Vambery, *Das Türkenvolk* (Leipzig 1885), 112.

492 1. Petronius, *Sat.*, 48; Pausanias, x. 12, 8; Justin Martyr, *Cohort. ad Graecos*, 37, p. 34 C.

2. A. Kuhn and W. Schwartz, *Nord-deutsche Sagen, Märchen und Gebräuche* (Leipzig 1848), 70, No. 72, 1; cf. M. R. James, in *Classical Review*, 6 (1892), 74.

3. Kuhn and Schwartz, *op. cit.*, No. 72, 2.

4. *Ib.*, No. 72, 3.

5. K. Müllenhoff, *Sagen, Märchen und Lieder der Herzogthümer Holstein und Lauenburg* (Kiel 1845), 158 ff., No. 217.

493 1. The story is related in English in J. Rhys, *Celtic Heathendom* (London 1888), 529 ff. In the older, or poetic, Edda, the story is hinted at rather than told at length, e.g., in the Voluspa; cp. G. Vigfusson and F. York Powell, *Corpus Poeticum Boreale*, i (Oxford 1883), 197.

494 1. *NH*, xvi. 249–51.

2. *Ib.*, xxiv. 11 f.

3. J. Batchelor, *The Ainu and their Folk-lore* (London 1911), 222.

4. Baron Roger, in *Bull. de la soc. géogr. de Paris*, 8 (1827), 357 f.

4a. R. Chambard, in *Revue d'ethnogr. et des traditions populaires,* γ (1926), 122.

495 1. E. Meier, in *Zeitschr. f. Deutsche Mythol. u. Sittenkunde,* 1 (1853), 443 f. The sun enters Sagittarius around November 22.
   2. Grimm, *Deutsche Mythologie*⁴ (Berlin 1875–78), iii. 533.
   3. Marie Trevelyan, *Folk-lore and Folk-stories of Wales* (London 1909) 87.

496 1. Pliny, *NH,* xvi. 250: *omnia sanantem appellantes suo vocabulo.*
   2. Grimm, *op. cit.,* ii. 1009. In Gaelic it is called *an t' uil,* which means "all-healer."

497 1. A. Kuhn, *Die Herabkunft des Feuers und des Göttertranks*² (Gütersloh 1886), 206; P. J. Veth, in *Internat. Archiv f. Ethnogr.,* 7 (1894), 111.
   2. J. N. von Alpenburg, *Mythen und Sagen Tirols* (Zurich 1857), 398.
   3. Wuttke, *Der deutsche Volksaberglaube*² (Berlin 1869), 97, ¶128; Veth, *loc. cit.*
   4. Wuttke, *op. cit.,* 267, ¶419.
   5. W. Henderson, *Notes on the Folklore of the Northern Counties of England and the Borders* (London 1879), 114.
   6. Lloyd, *op. cit.,* 269.

498 1. Grimm, *op. cit.,* iii. 353.
   2. Trevelyan, *op. cit.,* 88.
   3. G. Wahlenberg, *Flora Suecica* (Uppsala 1824–26), ii. 649 f., No. 1143.
   4. Lloyd, *op. cit.,* 259.
   5. Grimm, *op. cit.,* iii. 78, who adds, "Do the Midsummer fires have reference to the funeral pyre of Balder?" This pregnant hint perhaps contains in germ the solution of the whole myth!

499 1. Mary Frere, *Old Deccan Days*³ (London 1881), 12–16.

501 1. A. Bastian, *Die Völker des östlichen Asien,* iv (Jena 1868), 304 f.
   2. G. W. Leitner, *The Languages and Races of Dardistan*³ (Lahore 1878), 9.

502 1. Apollodorus, *Bibl.,* i. 8 with Frazer's note *in loc.;* see G. Knaack, in *Rheinisches Museum,* N. F. 49 (1894), 310–13.
   2. Apollodorus, *Bibl.,* iii. 15.
   3. Id., ii. 4, 5, 7.
   4. J. G. von Hahn, *Griechische und Albanesische Märchen* (Leipzig 1864), i. 217; ii. 262.

503 1. Plutarch, *Parallela*, 26.
2. G. Basile, *Pentamerone*, tr. R. Burton (New York 1927), 318 ff.
3. R. H. Busk, *Folk-lore of Rome* (London 1874), 164 ff.
4. J. B. Andrews, *Contes Ligures* (Paris 1892), 213 ff.

504 1. A. Dietrich, *Russian Popular Tales* (London 1857), 21–24; J. Curtin, *Myths and Folk-tales of the Russians, Western Slavs, and Magyars* (London 1891), 119–22.

505 1. J. Haltrich, *Deutsche Volksmärchen aus dem Sachsenlande in Sieben-bürgen*[4] (Vienna 1885), 149 f.

506 1. J. F. Campbell, *Popular Tales of the West Highlands*[2] (Paisley-London 1890), i. 80 ff.

507 1. [This story is contained in the famous Papyrus D'Orbiney (c. 1225 B.C.) in the British Museum. The most recent English translation is that by John Wilson in *Ancient Near Eastern Texts relating to the Old Testament*, ed. J. B. Pritchard (Princeton 1950), 23 f.]
2. *The Thousand and One Nights*, tr. E. W. Lane (London 1839–41), iii. 339 ff.

508 1. A. G. Leonard, *The Lower Niger and its Tribes* (London 1906), 319–21.
2. J. T. Nieuwenhuisen and H. C. B. von Rosenberg, in *Verh. d. Bataviaasch Gen. v. Kunsten en Wetenschappen*, 30 (1863), 111.

509 1. W. Matthews, in *Fifth Ann. Report of the Bureau of Ethnology* (Washington 1887), 406 f.
2. F. Boas, in *Report of the U. S. National Museum for 1895* (Washington 1897), 373.

510 1. A. H. B. Agerbeek, in *TILV*, 51 (1909), 447 f.
2. J. A. Jacobsen, *Reisen in die Inselwelt des Banda-Meeres* (Berlin 1896), 199.
2a. P. A. Talbot, *Women's Mysteries of a Primitive People* (London 1915), 172.

511 1. F. Valentyn, *Oud en Nieuw Oost-Indien* (Dordrecht-Amsterdam 1724–26), ii. 143 f.
2. J. G. F. Riedel, *De sluik- en kroesharige rassen tusschen Selebes en Papua* (The Hague 1886), 137.

512 1. B. Gutmann, in *Zeitschr. f. Ethnologie*, 45 (1913), 496.
2. A. Bastian, *Die Loango-Expedition* (Jena 1874–75), i. 165.
3. J. Macdonald, *Religion and Myth* (London 1893), 178.
4. H. Trilles, *Le totémisme chez les Fan* (Munster i. W. 1912), 570.

5. W. T. L. Travers, in *Trans. and Proc. New Zealand,* 9 (1876), 22.
6. A. de Gubernatis, *Mythologie des Plantes* (Paris 1878–82), i, pp. xxviii f.
7. W. Mannhardt, *Der Baumkultus der Germanen und ihren Nachbarstämmen* (Berlin 1875), 50; H. Ploss, *Das Kind*[2] (Leipzig 1884), i. 79.
8. Sir Walter Scott's *Journal* (First ed., Edinburgh 1890), ii. 282, with the editor's note.

513 1. V. M. Mikailoviskij, in *JAI,* 24 (1895), 133 f.
2. G. Brown, *Melanesians and Polynesians* (London 1910), 177.
3. *Anthropos,* 8 (1913), 251.
4. J. Keller, in *Deutsches Kolonialblatt,* Oct. 1, 1895, p. 484; H. Seidel, in *Globus,* 69 (1896), 277.
5. J. Parkinson, in *JAI,* 36 (1906), 314 f.
6. C. Partridge, *Cross River Natives* (London 1905), 225 f.
6a. L. Tauxier, *Le Noir du Soudan* (Paris 1912), 192 f.
6b. *Ib.,* 238 f.
6c. A. W. Cardinall, *The Natives of the Northern Territories of the Gold Coast* (London 1920), 39.
6d. P. A. Talbot, *Life in Southern Nigeria* (London 1923), 81 ff.
6e. *Ib.,* 91.
6f. C. E. Fox, *The Threshold of the Pacific* (London 1924), 271.
6g. *Ib.,* 231.
7. H. H. Bancroft, *The Native Races of the Pacific States* (London 1875–76), i. 661.
8. O. Stoll, *Die Ethnologie der Indianerstämme von Guatemala* (Leyden 1889), 57.
9. A. W. Howitt, in *JAI,* 18 (1889), 57 f.
10. Id., *The Native Tribes of S. E. Australia* (London 1904), 148–51.

514 1. W. R. S. Ralston, *Russian Folk-tales* (London 1873), 100–05, 109.
2. G. W. Dasent, *Tales from the Fjeld* (London 1874), 229–39.
3. See above, ¶503.
4. W. Radloff, *Proben der Volksliteratur der türkischen Stämme Südsibiriens* (St. Petersburg 1866), 345 f.

515 1. Satapatha Brahmana, tr. Eggeling (*SBE* xliv), 22 f.
2. E. T. Dalton, in *Trans. Ethnol. Soc.,* N. S. 6 (1868), 36.

516 1. J. Kamp, *Danske Folkeminder* (Odense 1877), 172, 65 f.
2. E. T. Kristensen, *Iydske Folkeminder,* vi. 380, n. 262.
3. A. Kuhn, *op. cit.,* 175 f.

517 1. See J. Sowerby, *English Botany,* xxi (London 1805), 1470. The matter is discussed at length by E. Norden in his *P. Vergilius Maro, Aeneis Buch VI* (Leipzig 1903), 161–71.
2. *Aen.,* vi. 203 ff.

518   1. *Aen.*, vi. 137 f.

519   1. At York, in the eighteenth century, mistletoe was carried to the high altar of the Cathedral and a public amnesty and "universal liberty" was proclaimed: J. Brand, *Popular Antiquities of Great Britain*, i. 525. The traditional privilege accorded to men of kissing any woman found under mistletoe is a relic of the same thing.
2. Grimm, *op. cit.*, iii. 289; L. Lloyd, *op. cit.*, 266 f.; C. Lemke, *Volksthümliches in Ostpreussen* (Mohrungen 1884–87), ii. 283.
3. Pliny, *NH*, xxxiii. 94.
4. A. Kuhn, *Die Herabkunft des Feuers und des Göttergehanks*[2] (Gütersloh 1886), 205.
5. C. S. Burne and G. F. Jackson, *Shropshire Folk-lore* (London 1883), 242.

520   1. *Archiv für Religionswissenschaft*, 16 (1913), 318 f.
2. W. R. Fischer, *Forest Protection*, vol. iv of W. Schlich's *Manual of Forestry*[2] (London 1907), 662 f.
3. For Greek belief and custom pertaining to this, see H. Usener, *Kleine Schriften*, iv (Leipzig-Berlin 1913), 471 ff. For Roman ideas, see Festus, s. vv. *fulgaritum, provorsum fulgur*, and G. Wissowa, *Religion und Kultus der Römer*[2] (Munich 1912), 121 f.

521   1. *Op. cit.*, iii. 64.
2. *Archiv für Religionswissenschaft*, 16 (1913), 317–20.
3. Grimm, *op. cit.*, i. 153.

522   1. This interpretation of Balder's death was anticipated by W. Schwartz, *Der Ursprung d. Mythologie* (Berlin 1860), 176. That work suffers, however, from exaggeration.

523   1. J. Grimm, *op. cit.*, i. 502, 510, 516.
2. W. Mannhardt, *Baumkultus*, 518 f.

524   1. E. Hublard, *Fêtes du temps jadis, les feux du Carême* (Mons 1899), 25.
2. *Ib.*, 27 f.
3. E. Cortet, *Essai sur les fêtes religieuses* (Paris 1867), 101 f.
4. Ch. Beauquier, *Les mois en Franche-Comté* (Paris 1900), 33 f.
5. Pommerol, in *Bull. et Mém. Soc. d'Anthropol. de Paris*, 5/ii (1901), 427–29.
6. Cf. H. Dessau, *Inscriptiones Latinae Selectae*, ii, pt. i (Paris 1902), Nos. 4646–52.

525   1. E. Cortet, *op. cit.*, 99 f.
2. A. de Nore, *Coutumes, mythes et traditions des provinces de France* (Paris-Lyons 1846), 283 f.

3. *Ib.*, 302.

4. J. Lecoeur, *Esquisses du Bocage Normand* (Condé-sur-Noireau 1887), ii. 131 f.

526 1. Mannhardt, *op. cit.*, 501.

2. *Loc. cit.*

3. *Loc. cit.*; F. J. Vonbun, *Beitraege zur deutschen Mythologie* (Chut 1862), 20.

4. Mannhardt, *ib.;* E. Meier, *Deutsche Sagen, Sitten u. Gebräuche aus Schwaben* (Stuttgart 1852), 380 ff.; F. Panzer, *Beitrag zur Deutschen Mythologie* (Munich 1848–55), i. 211, ¶232.

5. H. Gaidoz, in *Rev. archéol.*, 3/iv (1884), 139 f.

6. A. Kuhn, *Die Herabkunft des Feuers*,[2] 86; Mannhardt, *op. cit.*, 501.

7. H. Herzog, *Schweizerische Volksfeste, Sitten u. Gebräuche* (Aarau 1884), 214–16; E. Hoffmann-Krayer, *Feste u. Bräuche des Schweizervolkes* (Zurich 1913), 135 f.

7a. C. Jensen, *Die nordfriesischen Inseln* (Hamburg 1899), 354 ff.

7b. E. Canziani, *Costumes, Traditions and Songs of Savoy* (London 1911), 136.

7c. *Ib.*, 137 f.

7d. C. Hahn, *Aus dem Kaukasus* (Leipzig 1892), 196 f.

7e. J. Mourier, in *RHR,* 16 (1887), 85 f.

527 1. Mannhardt, *op. cit.*, 502–05; K. von Leoprechting, *Aus dem Lechrain* (Munich 1855), 172 f.; F. Panzer, *op. cit.*, ii. 241 ff.; E. Meier, *op. cit.*, 139 f.; I. v. Zingerle, *Sitten, Bräuche u. Meinungen des Tiroler Volkes*[2] (Innsbruck 1871), 149, ¶¶1286–89; W. Kolbe, *Hessische Volks-Sitten u. Gebräuche*[2] (Marburg 1888), 49 ff.; C. J. Billson, *Country Folklore: Leicestershire and Rutland* (London 1895), 75 f.; A. Tiraboschi, in *Archivio per lo studio delle tradizione popolari*, 1 (1892), 492 f.; J. Brand, *Popular Antiquities of Great Britain* (London 1882–83), i. 157 ff.

528 1. Garcilasso de la Vega, *Royal Commentaries of the Yncas*, tr. C. R. Markham (London, Hakluyt Society, 1869–71), ii. 155–63.

2. B. de Sahagun, *Histoire générale des choses de la Nouvelle Espagne,* tr. Jourdanet-Simeon (Paris 1880), Book ii. Chaps. 18, 37.

3. H. R. Schoolcraft, *Notes on the Iroquois* (Albany 1847), 137.

4. F. Boas, in *Bull. Am. Mus. Nat. History*, 15/i (1901), 151.

5. C. Nachtigal, *Sahara und Sudan*, iii (Leipzig 1889), 251.

6. H. H. Johnson, *British Central Africa* (London 1897), 426, 439.

7. W. H. R. Rivers, *The Todas* (London 1906), 290–92.

8. G. Schlegel, *Uranographie Chinoise* (Hague-Leyden 1875), 139–43; J. J. M. de Groot, *Les fêtes annuellement célebrées à Émoui* (Paris 1886), i. 208 ff.

9. Ovid, *Fasti*, iii. 82; *Iliad*, i. 590 ff.

10. Philostratus, *Heroica*, xx. 24.

11. Ovid, *op. cit.*, iii. 143 f.; Macrobius, *Sat.*, i. 12, 6.
12. J. Rhys, *Celtic Heathendom* (London 1888), 514 f.
13. W. R. S. Ralston, *Songs of the Russian People*[2] (London 1872), 254 f.

529   1. A. Allardyce, ed., *Scotland and Scotsmen in the Eighteenth Century, from the MSS. of John Ramsay, of Ochtertyre* (Edinburgh-London 1888), ii. 439–45.
2. Shaw, in Pennant's "Tour in Scotland," printed in Pinkerton's *Voyages and Travels*, iii. 136.
3. W. Gregor, *Notes on the Folk-lore of the N.E. of Scotland* (London 1881), 167.

530   1. Marie Trevelyan, *Folk-lore and Folk-stories of Wales* (London 1909), 20–24.

531   1. J. Train, *An Historical and Statistical Account of the Isle of Man* (Douglas 1845), i. 314 f.
2. J. Rhys, *Celtic Folk-lore, Welsh and Manx* (Oxford 1901), i. 309.

532   1. P. W. Joyce, *A Social History of Ancient Ireland* (London 1903), i. 290 (referring to Kuno Meyer, *Hibernia Minora*, 49).

533   1. L. Lloyd, *Peasant Life in Sweden* (London 1870), 233 f.
2. F. Reinsberg-Düringsfeld, *Fest-Kalender aus Böhmen* (Prague n. d.), 211 f.
3. J. A. E. Kohler, *Volksbrauch, Aberglauben, Sagen und andre alte Ueberlieferungen im Voigtland* (Leipzig 1867), 373.

534   1. As to the midsummer festivals of Europe in general, see the evidence assembled in the "Specimen Calendarii Gentilis" appended to the *Edda Rhythmica seu Antiquior*, pt. iii (Copenhagen 1828), 1086–97.

535   1. R. C. Hope, ed., *The Popish Kingdome or Reigne of Antichrist*, written in Latin verse by Thomas Naogeorgus and Englished by Barnaby Goodge, 1570 (London 1880), 54 *verso*.

536   1. J. Boemus, *Mores, leges et ritus omnium gentium* (Lyons 1541), 225 f.
2. Montanus, *Die deutschen Volksfeste, Volksbräuche u. Deutscher Volksglaube* (Iserlohn n. d.), 33 f.
3. P. Drechsler, *Sitte, Brauch und Volksglaube in Schlesien* (Leipzig 1903–06), i. 136 f.

537   1. J. Grimm, *Deutsche Mythologie*[4], i. 517 f.
2. L. Lloyd, *op. cit.*, 259, 265.

538   1. E. Hoffmann-Krayer, *Feste und Bräuche des Schweizervolkes* (Zurich 1913), 164.

2. I. V. Zingerle, *Sitten, Bräuche u. Meinungen des Tiroler Volkes*[2] (Innsbruck 1871), ii. 159), ii. 159, ¶1354.

3. *Ib.*, ¶¶1353, 1355–56; Mannhardt, *Baumkultus*, 513.

4. Mannhardt, *loc. cit.*

539 1. Grimm, *op. cit.*, i. 519; T. Vernaleken *Mythen und Bräuche des Volkes in Oesterreich* (Vienna 1859), 308; Reinsberg-Düringsfeld, *op. cit.*, 306–11; A. John, *Sitte, Brauch und Volkslaube im deutschen Westböhmen* (Prague 1905), 84–86.

540 1. W. Müller, *Beiträge zur Volkskunde der Deutschen in Mähren* (Vienna-Olmutz 1893), 263–65.

2. A. Peter, *Volkstümliches aus Österreichisch-Schlesien* (Troppau 1865–67), ii. 287.

3. Vernaleken, *loc. cit.*

541 1. W. R. S. Ralston, *Songs of the Russian People*[2] (London 1872), 240.

2. *Ib.*, 240, 391.

542 1. W. J. A. von Tettau and J. D. H. Temme, *Die Volkssagen Ostpreussens, Lithauens und Westpreussens* (Berlin 1837), 277.

2. M. Töppen, *Aberglauben aus Masuren*[2] (Danzig 1867), 71.

543 1. J. G. Kohl, *Die deutsch-russischen Ostseeprovinzen* (Dresden-Leipzig 1841), i. 178–80; ii, 24 f. (Ligho was an ancient heathen deity whose festival fell in spring.)

544 1. F. S. Krauss, *Sitte u. Brauch der Südslaven* (Vienna 1885), 176 f.

2. Grimm, *op. cit.*, i. 519.

545 1. H. von Wislocki, *Volksglaube und religiöser Brauch der Magyar* (Münster i. W. 1893), 40–44; A. von Ipolyi, in *Zeitschr. f. deutsch. Mythol. u. Sittenkunde*, 1 (1853), 270 f.; F. J. Wiedemann, *Aus dem inneren u. äusseren Leben der Ehsten* (St. Petersburg 1876), 362; F. Kreutzwald and H. Neus, *Mythische und Magische Lieder der Ehsten* (St. Petersburg 1854), 62; J. G. Kohl, *op. cit.*, ii. 447 f.

546 1. A. de Nore, *Coutumes, mythes et traditions des provinces de France* (Paris 1846), 19.

547 1. F. Reinsberg-Düringsfeld, *Calendrier Belge* (Brussels 1861–62), i. 439–42.

2. Madame Clément, *Histoire des fêtes religieuses, etc. du Département du Nord* (Cambrai 1836), 364.

548 1. John Stow, *A Survey of London*, ed. H. Morley (London, n. d.), 126 f. (Stow's work was written in 1598.)

2. John Aubrey, *Remaines of Gentilisme and Judaisme* (London 1881), 26.

3. Marie Trevelyan, *Folk-lore and Folk-stories of Wales* (London 1909), 27 f.

4. J. Train, *op. cit.*, ii. 120.

5. Lady Wilde, *Ancient Legends, Mystic Charms and Superstitions of Ireland* (London 1887), i. 214 f.; G. H. Kinahan, in *Folk-lore Record*, 4 (1881), 57.

6. A. Allardyce, ed., *op. cit.*, ii. 436.

7. G. Finamore, *Credenze, usi e costumi abruzzesi* (Palermo 1890), 154, 158–60; G. Pitrè, *Usi e costumi, credenze e pregiudizi del popolo siciliano* (Palermo 1889), 146 f.

8: V. Busuttil, *Holiday Customs in Malta, and Sports, Usages, Ceremonies, Omens and Superstitions of the Maltese People* (Malta 1894), 56 ff.

9. W. R. Paton, in *Folk-lore*, 2 (1891), 128.

10. Grimm, *op. cit.*, i. 519.

11. G. Georgeakis and L. Pineau, *Le Folk-lore de Lesbos* (Paris 1894), 308 f.

12. W. R. Paton, in *Folk-lore*, 6 (1895), 94.

549   1. K. von den Stein, *Unter den Natur-Völkern Zentral-Brasiliens* (Berlin 1894), 561.

2. A. d'Orbigny, *Voyage dans l'Amérique Méridionale* (Paris-Strasburg 1839–43), ii. 420; D. Forbes, in *Journal Ethnol. Soc. of London*, 2 (1870), 235.

550   1. E. Doutté, *Magie et religion dans l'Afrique du nord* (Algiers 1908), 566 f.

2. *Ib.*, 496, 509, 532, 543, 569.

3. E. Westermarck, in *Folk-lore*, 16 (1905), 40–42.

552   1. J. Rhys, *op. cit.*, i. 316 f.

2. See above, ¶502.

3. See above, ¶235.

4. E. J. Guthrie, *Old Scottish Customs* (London-Glasgow 1883), 68.

5. A. Goodrich-Freer, in *Folk-lore*, 13 (1902), 53.

6. J. Rhys, *Celtic Heathendom* (London-Edinburgh 1888), 516.

553   1. See A. Goodrich-Freer, *op. cit.*, 55.

2. Pennant's MS., quoted by J. Brand, *Popular Antiquities of Great Britain* (London 1882–83), i. 389 f.

554   1. Baron Dupin, in *Mémoires publiées par la Société Royale des Antiquaires de France*, 4 (1823), 108.

556   1. *Op. cit.*, i. 471.

557 1. Quoted by Grimm, *op. cit.*, i. 522.
2. J. H. Schmitz, *Sitten und Sagen, Lieder, Sprüchwörter und Räthsel des Eifler Volkes* (Treves 1856–58), i. 4.
3. A. Kuhn, *Sagen, Gebräuche und Märchen aus Westfalen* (Leipzig 1859), ii. 103 f., ¶319.
4. *Ib.*, ii. 187, ¶523.
5. A. Witzschel, *Sagen, Sitten u. Gebräuche aus Thüringen* (Vienna 1878), 172.

558 1. E. Hoffmann-Krayer, *op. cit.*, 108 f.

559 1. F. Reinsberg-Düringsfeld, *Calendrier Belge* (Brussels 1861–62), ii. 326 f.

560 1. J. B. Thiers, *Traité des Superstitions*[5] (Paris 1741), i. 302 f.; E. Cortet, *Essai sur les fêtes religieuses* (Paris 1867), 266 f.

561 1. Brand, *op, cit.*. i. 467.
2. *Ib.*, i. 455.
3. Robert Herrick, *Hesperides*, "Ceremonies for Christmasse": "Come, bring with a noise/My merrie merrie boyes,/The Christmas log to the firing . . ./With the last yeares brand/Light the new block."

562 1. Baron Rajaesich, *Das Leben, die Sitten u. Gebräuche der im Kaiserthume Oesterreich lebenden Südslaven* (Vienna 1873), 129–31.
2. M. E. Durham, *High Albania* (London 1909), 129.
3. R. F. Kaindl, *Die Huzulen* (Vienna 1894), 71.

564 1. On the need-fire, see: Grimm, *op. cit.*, i. 501 ff.; J. W. Wolf, *Beiträge zur deutschen Mythologie* (Göttingen-Leipzig 1852–57), i. 116 f., ii. 378 ff.; A. Kuhn, *Die Herabkunft des Feuers* 41 ff.; Mannhardt, *Baumkultus*, 518 ff.; U. Jahn, *Die deutschen Opfergebräuche bei Ackerbau und Viehzucht* (Breslau 1884), 26 ff.; J. Reiskius, *Untersuchung des Notfeuers* (Frankfurt-Leipzig 1696).
2. E.g., by a synod of prelates and nobles held under the presidency of Boniface, Archbishop of Mainz (see R. Andree, *Braunschweiger Volkskunde* [Brunswick 1896], 312), and in Article XV of the *Indiculus Superstitionum et Paganiarum* (ed. H. A. Saupe, [Leipzig 1891]), usually dated 743, though some scholars assign it to the reign of Charlemagne.
3. Grimm, *loc. cit.*; K. Bartsch, *Sagen, Märchen u. Gebräuche aus Mecklenburg* (Vienna 1879–80), ii. 149–51; H. Prohle, *Harzbilder* (Leipzig 1855), 74 f.; P. Drechsler, *Sitte, Brauch u. Volksglaube in Schlesien* (Leipzig 1903–06), ii. 204; C. L. Rochholz, *Deutscher Glaube und Brauch* (Berlin 1867), iii. 149; [P. Sartori, *Sitte und Brauch* (Leipzig 1910–14), iii. 109].
4. *Country Folklore, ii: North Riding of Yorkshire, etc.*, ed. Gutch (Lon-

don 1901), 181; H. Speight, *The Craven and N. W. Yorkshire High-lands* (London 1892), 206 f.; W. Henderson, *Notes on the Folklore of the Northern Counties of England and the Borders* (London 1879), 167 f.; [T. F. Dexter, *Fire-Worship in Britain* (London 1931)].

5. See: W. Grant Stewart, *The Popular Superstitions and Festive Amusements of the Highlanders of Scotland* (Edinburgh 1823), 214–16; R. C. Maclagan, in *Folk-lore*, 9 (1898), 280 f.; W. Gregor, *Notes on the Folk-lore of the North-East of Scotland* (London 1881), 186.

6. L. L. Duncan, in *Folk-lore*, 7 (1896), 181 f.

7. See F. S. Krauss, in *Globus*, 59 (1891), 140.

8. V. Titelbach, in *Internat. Archiv für Ethnographie*, 13 (1900), 3.

9. Grimm, *op. cit.*, i. 505.

10. *Ib.*, i. 506.

11. A. Strauss, *Die Bulgaren* (Leipzig 1898), 194–99.

12. F. S. Krauss, in *Globus*, 59 (1891), 318 (quoting O. Kolberg, in Mazowesse, *ib.*, 138).

13. E. Hoffmann-Krayer, in *Schweizerisches Archiv für Volkskunde*, ii (1907), 244–46.

567   1. See, for example, A. Wuttke *Der deutsche Volksaberglaube*[2] (Berlin 1869), 149, ¶216; W. G. Stewart, *op. cit.*, 201 f.

568   1. Wuttke, *op. cit.*, 351, ¶395.
      2. *Ib.*; L. Strackerjan, *Aberglaube und Sagen aus dem Herzogthum Oldenburg* (Oldenburg 1867), i. 298, ¶209.

569   1. F. S. Krauss, *Volksglaube u. religiöser Brauch der Südslaven* (Münster i. W. 1890), 118 f.

570   1. In German such spells are called *Nestelknüpfen;* see Grimm, *op. cit.*, ii. 897, 983; Wuttke, *op. cit.*, 252, ¶396. In French, the practice is known as *nouer l'aiguilette;* see E. Doutté, *Magie et religion dans l'Afrique du nord* (Algiers 1908), 87 f., 294 ff; J. L. M. Noguès, *Les moeurs d'autrefois en Saintonge et en Aunis* (Saintes 1891), 171 f.

573   1. Mannhardt, *Baumkultus*, 524.
      2. *Loc. cit.*
      3. *Ib.*, 524 f.; A. Birlinger, *Volksthümliches aus Schwaben* (Freiburg i. Br. 1861–62), ii. 121 f., ¶146.

574   1. Caesar, *Bell. Gall.*, vi. 15; Strabo, iv. 4, 5; Diodorus Siculus, v. 32; see Mannhardt, *Baumkultus*, 525 f.
      2. Strabo, iv. 4, 4; Mannhardt, *op. cit.*, 529 ff.

576   1. A. de Nore, *Coutumes, mythes et traditions des provinces de France* (Paris-Lyons 1846), 323 f.; F. W. Fairholt, *Gog and Magog* (London 1859), 78–87.

2. A. de Nore, *op. cit.*, 332; J. Brand, *Popular Antiquities of Great Britain* (London 1882–83), i. 325 f.; *The Gentleman's Magazine*, 29 (1759), 263–65.

577 1. Madame Clément, *Histoire des fêtes civiles et religieuses etc. de la Belgique méridionale* (Avesnes 1846), 252; F. von Reinsberg-Düringsfeld, *Calendrier Belge* (Brussels 1861–62), i. 123–26. (We may conjecture that the Flemish *Reuze*, like the *Reuss* of Dunkirk, is simply another form of the German *Riese*, "giant."

2. Fairholt, *op. cit.*, 64–78.

578 1. George Puttenham, *The Arte of English Poesie* (London 1589, reprinted 1811), 128.

2. J. Strutt, *The Sports and Pastimes of the People of England*, ed. W. Hone (London 1834), pp. xliii-xlv; Fairholt, *op. cit.*, 52–59.

3. Fairholt, *op. cit.*, 61–63.

579 1. F. Liebrecht, ed., *Des Gervasius von Tilbury Otia Imperialia* (Hanover 1856), 212 f.; de Nore, *op. cit.*, 354 f.; Mannhardt, *Baumkultus*, 514.

2. Mannhardt, *op. cit.*, 523.

580 1. *The Athenaeum*, July 24, 1869, p. 115; Mannhardt, *op. cit.*, 515; *Folklore*, 12 (1901), 315–17.

2. Tessier, in *Mémoires et dissertations publiées par la Société des Antiquaires de France*, 5 (1823), 388; Mannhardt, *op. cit.*, 515.

3. A. Bertrand, *La religion des Gaulois* (Paris 1897), 407.

4. Grimm, *op. cit.*, i. 519; Mannhardt, *loc. cit.*

5. Montanus, *Die deutschen Volksfeste, Volksbräuche und deutscher Volksglaube* (Iserlohn n. d.), 34; Mannhardt, *Loc. cit.*

6. Mannhardt, *loc. cit.*

7. A. Meyrac, *Traditions, coutumes, légendes et contes des Ardennes* (Charleville 1890), 68.

582 1. Strabo, iv 4, 5.

2. Marie Trevelyan, *Folk-lore and Folk-stories of Wales* (London 1909), 214, 310 f.; U. Jahn, *Hexenwesen und Zauberei in Pommern* (Breslau 1886), 7.

ADDITIONAL NOTES

483. *Taboo on touching the ground.* See S. Eitrem, *Papyri Osloenses I* (Oslo 1925), 114 ff., where many instances are cited.

490. *Conception by sunlight.* See Stith Thompson, *Motif-Index*, T 521. In the ancient Hittite myth of Appu, a lean cow is impregnated by the sun and gives birth to a wondrous human child: see T. H. Gaster, *The Oldest Stories in the World* (New York 1952), 164, 169.

496. *Balder.* See: O. Höfler, "Balders Bestattung und die nordischen Felszeichnungen," in *Oesterreichische Anzeiger*, 51 (1953), 343–72; G. Neckel, *Die Ueberlieferungen vom Gotte Balder* (1920); F. Kauffmann, *Balder* (1902).

550. *Tarasque.* On the French giant Tarasque see now L. Dumont, *Le Tarasque* (Paris 1951). The legend is related in Countess Martinengo-Cesaresco's *Essays in the Study of Folk-Songs* (London, Everyman Library), 152.

575. *Tree as life-token.* On the concept that the life of a human being is bound up with that of a tree see in general: H. Ploss, *Das Kind*[2] (Leipzig 1884), i. 71 ff.; A. de Gubernatis, *Mythologie des plantes* (Paris 1878–82), i. pp. xxviii ff.; I. Scheftelowitz, *Altpal. Bauernglaube* (Hanover 1925), 25 ff.; R. Andree, *Ethnographische Parallelen und Vergleiche*, N. F. (Leipzig 1889), 21 ff.; R. Köhler, *Kleinere Schriften* (Weimar 1898), i. 179; A. Porteous, *Forest Folklore, Mythology and Romance* (New York 1928), 155–60; E. S. McCartney, in *Papers of the Michigan Academy of Science, Arts and Letters*, 16 (1931), 115 ff.

The concept is attested in many parts of the world, e.g.: SOLOMON ISLANDS: *Archiv für Religionswissenschaft*, 1913. 475. — MALĀKA PENINSULA: H. V. Stevens and A. Grundwedel, *Materialen z. Kenntniss d. wilden Stämme auf d. Halbinsel Malāka* (1894), ii. 113, 117. — MADAGASCAR: J. Sibree, in *Folk-lore Journal*, 2 (1884), 52, 130. — KALMUK: W. A. Clouston, *Popular Tales and Fictions* (London 1897), 222 f. — CHINA: *Die Woche*, 31 August 1901, p. 3. — SCOTLAND: M. Cox, *Introduction to Folklore* (London 1897), 222 f. — POLYNESIA: R. B. Dixon, *Oceanic Mythology* (Boston 1916), 234, n. 46. — KAFFIR: D. Kidd, *Savage Childhood* (London 1906), 225 — BELGIUM: Cox, *op. cit.*, 79. — GERMANY: P. Sartori, *Sitte und Brauch* (Leipzig 1910–14), i. 26 f., ii. 118. — INDIA: R. Norton, "Life-Index," in *Studies in honor of M.*

Bloomfield (New Haven 1920). — GUINEA: *Zeitschrift f. Volkskunde,* 5. 297.
— ANGOLA: H. Chatelain, *Folk-tales of Angola* (Boston-New York 1894), 87,
No. 5. — GREEK AND ROMAN: E. Ries, in *Rhein. Mus.,* 12 (1894), 186. —
SCANDINAVIAN: In the Poetic Edda, Gudrunarquitha, ii. 40, Atli is warned that
his child has been slain by seeing in a dream that the tree which he had planted
has been felled. (Similarly, in a legendary paraphrase of Genesis, discovered
among the celebrated "Dead Sea Scrolls," Abraham is forewarned of Pharaoh's
plot on his life by dreaming that a cedar has been cut down: T. H. Gaster, *The
Scriptures of the Dead Sea Sect* [London 1957], 332, 341.) — JEWISH: It is a
Jewish custom to plant a cedar at the birth of a boy and a pine at that of a girl.
When they marry, the trees are cut down to provide wood for the "wedding
bower" (*ḥuppah*): Bab. Talmud, *Giṭṭin,* 57a; Josephus, *Contra Apionem,* ii. ¶25.
(In Switzerland, an apple tree is planted for a boy, and a nut tree for a girl:
McCartney, *op. cit.,* 115–17). For this concept in folk-tales see Stith Thompson,
Motif-Index, T 589. 3.

THE GOLDEN BOUGH

Frazer's interpretation of the Golden Bough is open to the gravest question,
and has been generally rejected by Classical scholars. Most probably, the bough
which the fugitive slave had to pluck before he could challenge the King of the
Wood was simply the "suppliant's branch" (*hiketêrion*) often mentioned in
Greek literature and specified also in legal inscriptions from Elis and Cyrene
as a necessary perquisite of anyone approaching a shrine; see: Aeschylus, *Suppl.,*
192; Sophocles, *Oedipus Rex,* 3; Euripides, *Iph. in Aulis,* 1216; Herodotus, 5.
51, 7. 141; Demosthenes, 262. 16; Aeschines, 14. 41; Andocides, 15. 2; Dittenberger, *Sylloge*[3], ii. 550; Suppl. *Epigraph. Graec.,* ix. 72, ¶¶18–20. On such
branches, see: M. Delcourt, in *L'antiquité classique,* 6 (1937), 63 f.; E. Balogh,
Political Refugees in Ancient Greece (Johannesburg 1943), 2, 88, n. 6.

In the poetic and popular conception of this ancient practice, the plucking
of the bough seems to have been fused with the well-known "Excalibur motif"
in which the plucking of a branch, or the extraction of a sword from a stone,
is regarded as a test of prowess entitling him who performs the feat to a special
privilege, e.g., sovereignty.

The sanctuary at Nemi was probably no more than an asylum for runaway
slaves. Among ancient and primitive peoples, sanctuaries and sacred groves
frequently serve this purpose. By repairing to them, a man becomes the guest
of the resident deity and stands under his protection against assault. Thus, in
I Kings, 1 : 50, Adonijah, fleeing the wrath of Solomon, "goes and grasps the
horns of the altars," and *ib.,* 2 : 28, his ally Joab does likewise; while in Exodus
21 : 14 the principle is so far recognized as to be expressly banned to deliberate
murderers. Similarly, in Islamic usage, one who seeks shelter beside the *ka'aba,*
or Black Stone, at Mecca is styled a "guest of the God" (*jar Allah*), and in a
Canaanite myth from Ras Shamra-Ugarit, of the fourteenth century B.C., the
curse is invoked upon an unknown assassin that he may be forever "a client at
sanctuaries"; see T. H. Gaster, *Thespis* (New York 1950), 303 f.

An even clearer parallel to the procedure at Aricia is afforded by the statement of Herodotus (ii. 113) that if a fugitive slave reached the temple of
"Heracles" at the Canobic mouth of the Nile, and there submitted to branding
with the mark of the god, he could not be reclaimed by his master, having thereby
declared himself of the household of the deity. Analogous, too, is the ancient
practice in Upolu, a Samoan island, where a god called Vave had his residence
in an old tree which served as an asylum for homicides and other major offend-
ers: G. Turner, *Samoa* (London 1884), 16 f. Similarly, in the Caucasus, sacred
groves offer refuge to criminals and hunted beasts: Hahn, *Kaukasische Reisen*
(1890), 122.

The golden bough at Aricia has nothing whatsoever to do with that borne by
Aeneas on his journey to the netherworld (Vergil, *Aeneid*, vi. 133 f.). On the
latter, see below, concerning ¶580. Frazer has misunderstood the comment of
Servius, the third-century commentator on Vergil, who says only that the bough
of Aeneas was of the same color as that at Aricia; see O. Gruppe, *Berl. Phil.
Wochenschrift*, 32 (1912), 745.

580. *The Golden Bough.* See: J. Hermann, "L'arbre aux rameaux d'or,"
in *Mel. Smets.* (1952), 400–06; Gladys Martin, "Golden Apples and Golden
Boughs," in *Studies presented to David Moore Robinson* (St. Louis 1953), ii.
1191–97. — As an alternative to Frazer's theory that the sacred tree at Nemi
was an *oak*, the late A. B. Cook suggested (*Zeus*, ii [Cambridge 1925], 420, n. 1)
that it may have been an *apple-tree*, since apple-trees are still to be found there,
and mistletoe grows on them; or else a *beech*, since the district is in fact known
as La Faiola (=*faggiuola*, "beech"), and Diana was recognized nearby as a beech-
goddess.

On *mistletoe* in folklore, see: K. Tubeuf, *Monographie der Mistel* (München-
Berlin 1923); R. Folkard, *Plant-lore, Legends and Lyrics* (London 1884), 440;
W. Schwartz, *Indogermanischer Volksglaube* (Berlin 1885), 100; E. Norden,
Aeneis VI (Leipzig 1916), 161 ff. — Interesting statistics concerning the frequency of mistletoe on different types of trees are given by J. Buckman in *Notes
and Queries*, I, iii (1851), 226: the apple comes first, but the black poplar runs
a close second. A further note by R. Cooke, *ib.*, vii (1853), 264 f., lists the
following trees as "hosts" to mistletoe: horse chestnut, maple, poplar, acacia,
laburnum, pear, large-leaved sallow, locust, larch, Scottish fir, spruce, service
(*pyrus domestica*), olive, vine, walnut, plum, common laurel, medlar, and grey
poplar. See further *ib.*, I. iii (1851), 163, 214; iv (1851), 110; IV. vi (1870),
279, 399, 427. Sir Thomas Browne, *Vulgar Errors*, iii. 6, ¶3, says that mistletoe
is found on sallow and hazel as well as on oak. Others have observed it on ash,
lime, rowan, crab, and white thorn. In Spain and in many parts of the Pyrenees, it
is found on spruce and silver fir: *Notes and Queries*, I. vi (1852), 219; and on
the Swiss side of the Simplon Pass, on pine fir: *ib.*, 589.

INDEX

INDEX

A NOTE ON THE USE OF THIS INDEX

This Index includes, so far as possible, topics, places, and persons mentioned in text, Notes, or Additional Notes. For articles or books cited in the Notes, only authors or editors are shown—not the titles. Continental and national cross-references are confined to those shown in the text and are listed in accordance with Frazer's original identifications and spellings. Thus, the page containing a reference to a village that Frazer describes only as Silesian will be included under "Silesia" (as well as under the village name), but it will not be cross-referenced under any of the several nations to which Silesia has belonged over the years. Accordingly, the reader is cautioned to refer to regional and local place names, to topics, and to names of peoples or tribes, as well as to the necessarily incomplete national or continental listings.

Dalzell, A., 197, 272
Dama (island, South Pacific), 463
Damas, F., 492
Damsteter, J., 375
Dana, R. H., 113
Danae, 586–87
Dancing
  for absent husbands, 21, 22
  as fertility charm, 22–23, 130
  rain-making, 38–39
  before oracles, 63–64
  at festivals, 249 ff., 293–294, 295, 311–
    12, 401 ff., 570, 610 ff.
Danger Island, 156
Danicourt, 117
Danks, B., 653
Dante, 394
Danube Valley, 560, 613
Danzig district, 427, 588
Daphnis, 185
Dapper, O., 116, 197
Daremberg, 384
Daressy, G., 393
Darfur (Africa), 164
Darling River, 31
Dasahra (Indian festival), 296
Dasent, G. W., 657
Dasius, St., 560
"Daughters of the gods," 393
Davao (district, Philippines), 63–64
David of Antioch, 546
Davies, N. deG., 393
Dawkins, R. M., 383
Dawn, 11, 136
Dawson, G. M., 113
Dawson, J., 546
Day of Atonement, 534, 554
Day of Blood, 311, 312, 315
Day of the Old Wives, 261
Days of the Cross, 51
de Acosta, J., 496, 498
Dead, the
  homoeopathy, 23–24, 130–31
  and rain-making, 44–45
  souls animating trees, 75–77
  name avoidance, 191–92
  Dead, book of the, 216, 425
  contact with, taboos, 307
  festivals, 334–37, 395–96
  "soul-cakes," 335–37, 396
  Osiris as Lord of, 345–46
  eating flesh and blood of, to absorb
    qualities, 464–65
  sticks and stones, 511–12
  banishment of ghosts, 524–25
  See also Burial; Mourning; Sacrifices;
    etc.

"Dead One, The" (Corn-spirit), 265
Dead Sea Scrolls, 667
Dead Sunday, 252, 260
de Arriaga, P. J., 101, 102, 105, 110, 122,
  123, 197, 546
Death
  at ebb-tide, 28–29, 132
  and immortality, primitive beliefs,
    150 ff., 223–24, 278
  and resurrection of vegetation gods,
    283–84, 285 ff., 390–92
  See also Burial; Mourning; Souls; etc.
"Death" (effigies or personifications), 83,
  542
  "carrying out" or "driving out" of, 251–
    52, 275–65
  resurrection of, 262–63
  as fertility or tree-spirit, 263–65, 341
Debang monastery (Tibet), 537
Debden, England, 81
Decle, L., 120, 389, 501
Deer, 474, 498
de Fabrega, H. Pittier, 203
Defrénery, C., 202, 272, 378
de Groot, J. J. M., 101, 107, 118, 200,
  206, 212, 549, 659
de Herrera, A., 498, 653
Dehon, P., 492
Deir el Bahari (Egypt), 93
Deism, vs. animism, 423–24
Deities. See Gods
de Landa, Diego, 550, 573
Delaware Indians, 472, 585
Delegoa Bay (Southeast Africa), 26, 40
Delcourt, Marie, 140, 667
Delegorgue, A., 102, 388
de Leon, Cieza, 492, 653
Delilah, 596
Delos (island), "new fire," 617
De los Reyes y Florentino, 199
Delphi, 233, 243, 278, 352
  graves of gods, 224, 353
Deluge, myths of, 136
Demeter, 308, 375
  Thesmophoria, 314, 331, 367, 397
  and Cybele, 315, 356
  and Poseidon, 315
  and Aphrodite, 315, 356
  and Eleusis, 339–40, 356–60, 363–64,
    365, 397
  as Sorrowful One, 331
  as mother of Dionysus, 353
  and Persephone, 356–66
  as corn-goddess, 359–66, 388
  mother role, as old corn, 359, 364–65
  "Demeter's fruits," 360
  rites and festivals, 361–64, 561

Eleusinian mysteries, 5, 339, 357–65, 417, 448, 486
  explained by Hymn to Demeter, 358–59
  re-enactments as sacred drama, 359, 397
Eleusis, 193, 308. *See also* Eleusinian mysteries
Éliade, M., 135, 218, 397, 503
Elijah, 39, 133
Elis, Greece, 48, 101, 354–55, 667
Elissa, Queen, 305
Elizabeth I, Queen, 59, 69, 627
Elk clan (Omahas), 581
Ellgoth, Silesia, 85
Elliot, H. M., 489
Ellis, A. B., 109, 119, 123, 199, 202, 206, 208, 273, 497, 498
Ellis, O. C. de C., 576
Ellis, W., 101, 115, 202, 204, 207, 208, 212, 274, 497, 652
El Obeid, Africa, 20
Elton, O., 106, 109, 117
Elworthy, F. T., 218
Emin Pasha, 271
Empedocles, 66, 309
Emu, 581
Emu-wrens, 604
Encounter Bay (Australia), 191, 192
Ende, L. von, 205
Engel, W. H., 373
England, 394, 575
  charms and taboos, 20, 31, 131, 133, 218, 219, 220, 517
  tide superstitions, 28–29
  agents of wounds, 34–35
  healing by royal touch, 59–60, 137
  the Crown, 69, 126
  forests, 72
  May Day, 80–82, 86–87, 90
  Jack-in-the-Green, 85
  "beating of the bounds," 136
  bush-burning, 139
  idea of soul as bird, 215
  mock kings, 241
  Lenten effigies, 256
  boy bishops, 279
  mummers' play, 279
  All Souls, 337
  Easter rites analogous to Adonis rites, 372
  harvest customs, 407, 408, 490
  wren, 482–83
  Straw-bear, 484–85
  King of the Bean, 564, 565
  fire-rites, 565–66

Christmas festivals, 566, 567, 568–69, 633, 635
  Feast of Innocents, 567–69
  birth-trees, 600
  mistletoe, 607
  Yule log, 633, 635
  Christmas candles, 635
  need-fire, 636
  giants at Midsummer festival, 645
Engnell, I., 117, 279
E-ninu (Babylonian god), 136
Entlebuch, Switzerland, 534–35
Entraigues, France, 483
Ephesus (Asia Minor), 311, 318
Epic of Creation (Babylonia), 135
Epictetus, 387
Epidemics, 258, 520–21, 529, 530–45 *passim*
Epilepsy, 509
Epinal, France, 611
Epiphany, 527, 562, 565
Equinoxes, 630
Erdland, P. A., 108
Erdweg, M. J., 108
Eresh-Kigal (Babylonian goddess), 285
Erfurt, Germany, 403
Ergamenes (king of Ethiopia), 228
Erica-tree, 324, 344
Eridu, Babylonia, 136
Eriskay, Ireland, 631
Erlangen, Germany, 257–58
Erman, A., 117, 340, 379, 381
Ertingen, Germany, 85
Erzgebirge (mountains), 250
Esagila (Babylonia), 235
Escouvion (Lenten fires), 610–11
Esne (calendar), 334
Esquimaux, 20, 268, 465, 501
  human fertility rites, 10
  fish and animal magic, 18, 26, 475–76
  sun-rites, 49
  ideas of soul, 151–52, 216, 599
  childbed taboos, 167
  mourning practices, 176
  name magic, 192
  festival of the dead, 334–35
  ritual purity, 459
  "new fires," 617
Essex, England, 34–35, 81, 482–83
Esthonia(n), 257, 512, 530, 626
  wind superstitions, 51–52, 53
  wood-spirit, 264–65
  vermin, 476
Etana, 126
Eteocles, 76
Ethiopia, kings, 137, 164, 225, 228, 236
Etna, Mount, 309

Hercules—*Continued*
and Lityerses, 426
and Syleus, 438
and Busiris, 439
Hercynian forest, 72
Hereford(shire), England, 139, 568
Herero (of Southwest Africa), 171
Hermann, J., 668
Hermann, P., 123
Hermes (god), 224, 514
Hermion, Dionysus worship, 355
Hermisianax, 375
Hermopolis, 224
Hermotimos of Clazomenae, 154
Hermsdorf, Silesia, 404
Herod, 568
Hero(n)das, 198, 214
Herodias, 376, 640
Herodotus, 53, 101, 112, 114, 122, 137,
    198, 206, 210, 272, 274, 289, 307,
    371–87 *passim*, 394, 438, 490–98
    passim, 551, 667–68
Herois, Greece, 278
Herrera, 383
Herrick, Robert, 635, 663
Hersilia, 124
Hertel, J., 576
Herve, G., 111
Herzegovina, Yule log, 635
Herzog, H., 551, 659
Hesiod, 106, 136, 387
Hess, P. F., 109
Hesse, Germany, 35, 84–85, 451
Hesychius of Alexandria, 122, 204, 373,
    379, 384, 386, 491, 492, 494, 497,
    549, 552
Henzy, L., 653
Hialto, 464
Hibeh Papyri, 380
Hidatsa Indians, 74
Hicks, 278
Hickson, S. J., 113
Hierapolis (Asia Minor), 136, 311–12,
    318, 451
Higgling, blind cats as charm in, 26
High History of the Holy Grail, 237, 240
Hilaria (festival of joy), 313, 376
Hildesheim, Germany, 86
Hill, Goddess of the, 124
Hill-Tout, C., 496
Hillebrandt, A., 102
Hillebrandt, J. M., 211
Hillner, J., 208
Himalayas, 294–95, 533
Himerius, 385

Hindu(s)
charms and taboos, 8, 11, 12, 25, 40,
    151, 175, 180, 189, 218, 585–86
Laws of Manu, 59, 67
human deities, 67
tree-marriage, 75
sun-chariot, 136
gardens of Adonis, 294–95
barley in religious rituals, 369, 389
transference of illness, 515
sacred cows, 536
marriage rites, 587
external soul myths, 594
See also India
Hindu Kush, 22, 63, 64, 523
Hindustan, 594
Hippasus, 245
Hippolytus, 358, 377, 378, 382, 383, 386
Hirt, H., 388
History of Northumberland (Hutchin-
    son), 407
Hittites, 128, 129, 136, 141, 392, 394,
    504, 554, 666
Hixon, S. J., 52, 113
Hobgoblins, 631–32
Hobley, C. W., 206, 653
Hochofen, Bohemia, 526–27
Hodson, T. C., 204, 210, 547
Hoffmann-Krayer, E., 105, 121, 122, 277,
    549, 659, 660, 663, 664
Hoffmayr, P. W., 271
Höfler, D., 396, 666
Hogarth, D. G., 370
Hoggan, F., 493
Hogmanay, song, 631
Holland, cauls, 33. *See also* Dutch
Holley, 275
Hollis, A. C., 199, 204, 210, 211, 380
Holmberg, U., 134
Holstein, 131, 402, 588
Holsti, 130
Holub, E., 498
Holy Innocents' Day, 543–44, 566–67,
    569–70
Holyrood, 59
Holzmayer, J. B, 114, 501
Homoeopathy, 7–31, 128–32
    malevolent uses, 7–10, 128–29
    benevolent uses, 10–14, 128–29
    cure performed on doctor, 13
    food-gathering, 14–17
    taboos, 17–21, 129–30
    plants, 22–24, 130
    burglars, 24–25
    the dead, 24–25, 131
    animals, 25–26, 131
    inanimate objects, 26–28, 131–32

Rome—*Continued*
 transference of illness, 517
 banishment of ghosts, 524–25
 Befana ceremonies, 527–28, 550
 scapegoat, 540, 551, 555
 evil expelled in boats, 555
 Saturnalia, 559–62, 575
 calendar, 569
 perpetual fire, 605
 Temple of Vesta, "new fire," 617
Romove, oak at, 605
Romsdal, Norway, threshing, 428
Romulus, 73, 99, 341, 347
Ronga (of Africa), 139
Rook Island, 519
Roscher, W. H., 273, 278, 551
Roscoe, Rev. J., 116, 122, 200–7 *passim*,
 212, 272, 389, 492, 500, 546, 652
Rose, C., 500
Rose, H. A., 198
Rose, H. J., 198, 205
Rosenberg, H. C. B. von, 274, 389, 656
Roslin, Scotland, Corn-bride, 409
Ross, L., 373
Roth, H. Ling, 103, 104, 113, 119, 198,
 199, 202, 550
Roth, W. E., 653
Rotti (island, East Indies), 77
Rotuma (Fiji), 32
Rouen, France, scapegoats, 535-36
Roumania, 42, 84, 134, 159, 176
Rouse, W. H. D., 552
Rowan-tree, 542–43, 552, 604–5, 619
Roy, S. C., 111, 372
Ruanda (Africa), king as god, 126
Ruhla, Thüringen, Little Leaf Man, 84
Ruler of the Dead (Osiris), 326
Rundall, 652
Rurikwi River, 148
Rusch, A., 395
Russell, R. V., 116
Russia, 396
 magic, 32, 38, 43–45
 sacred groves, 77–78
 Whitsunday, 81
 rolling of priests, 90
 theogamy, 94
 fear of silhouettes, 160
 Armament of Igor, 215
 mock funerals, 269–70
 suicide by fire, 309
 harvest customs, 407, 426
 wood-spirits, 447
 sacramental cakes, 461
 insects, 478
 expelling evil, 525, 529–30
 "Easter Smacks," 543

birth-trees, 600
fairy-tales, 604
Midsummer festivals, 622, 626, 646
Ruthenia, 25, 626
Rutilius Benincasa, 132
Rye-bride, 409
Rye-mother, 401, 402, 403. *See also*
 Corn-mother
Rye-woman, 401
Rye-wolf, 445
Rzach (editor), 136

Sabine priests, 174
Sacaea (Babylonian festival), 235, 279
Sachau, E., 381
Sacramental meals. *See* Eating; Communion
Sacrifice, animal, 30–31, 49, 66, 71, 78,
 162, 174, 448–54
 role of kings, 5, 125–27, 347, 355–56
 for inspiration of priest, 63–64
 to trees, 73–74, 76, 77, 78
 after adultery, 90
 warrior purification, 171
 ram with golden fleece, 243
 bull, to Attis, 313–14, 376–77
 hanging and stabbing, 318
 stuffing of hides, 319–20
 to ditches and canals, 330
 in Dionysiac rites, 355–56
 to Demeter, 360
 absorbing the divine essence, 445–86
 "murder of the ox," 448
 as rite of renewal, 503–4
 for illness, 514
 in expelling evil, 520, 521, 522, 532, 534,
 536
 to sun, 616
 for murrain, 638
 burning in wicker-work, 645–47
 as witches, 647
Sacrifice, human, 65, 94, 164, 173, 234,
 317–19
 role of kings, 5, 125–27
 to waters, 96–97, 140–41, 329–31
 kings and their proxies, 229–33, 238–46,
 244–46
 by fire, 305, 307, 593, 610 ff., 641–46
 by hanging and disembowelling, 317–
 19, 378
 to heroic dead, 321, 379
 to promote fertility, 341–43, 432–34,
 439, 440
 Dionysiac rites, 356
 mock ceremonies, 435–38
 as corn-spirit, 435–39, 455